An Introduction to
Indonesian Historiography

An Introduction to Indonesian Historiography

Edited by

SOEDJATMOKO

and

MOHAMMAD ALI, G. J. RESINK,

and G. McT. KAHIN

*Prepared under the auspices of
the Modern Indonesia Project
Southeast Asia Program
Cornell University*

Cornell University Press

ITHACA AND LONDON

Published in the United Kingdom by Cornell University Press Ltd., 2-4 Brook Street, London W1Y 1AA.

First published 1965
Second printing 1968
Third printing 1975

International Standard Book Number 0-8014-0403-7
Library of Congress Catalog Card Number 64-25273
Printed in the United States of America

PREFACE

THIS collection of studies on Indonesian history and historiography was initiated by Indonesian scholars to meet the growing demand in their country for a more vigorous and enlightened study of Indonesia's history. Originally only an Indonesian edition was planned, but the editors, aware of the potential interest in such a book, were receptive to the proposal that an English-language version also be produced so that wider availability might be assured. Because of Cornell University's long-standing interest in Indonesia, I am particularly pleased to have had the opportunity of participating in the preparation of this edition. For social scientists generally, as well as for historians, the book will, I believe, become a valuable introduction to and reference work on the field of Indonesian history. Although directed primarily to the serious scholar, it also has much to offer the general student of Indonesia.

The list of contributors to our symposium is a distinguished one; that their combined knowledge and broad range of views on matters pertaining to Indonesian historiography should be made available in one volume is in itself a considerable accomplishment. The articles incorporated in it help fill many of those gaps which have most seriously impeded the English-speaking scholar who endeavors to enter the field of Indonesian history. Those chapters dealing with sources provide the most substantial guide yet to appear in English on primary materials in Indonesian history (including Indonesia's relations with Portugal, Britain, and the Netherlands and with other Asian states). Here are brought together the annotated selected compilations of outstanding scholars in the field; collectively they provide the reader access to a broad area of history which thus far has been little traversed and wherein no one scholar has ever been at home in more than a small sector.

The chapters dealing with historiography describe a wide variety of approaches to the study of Indonesian history—a range of methodological confrontation which we hope will serve to stimulate others to explore some of these potentially rewarding but as yet little traveled paths. It is hoped that in addition to serving as a helpful introduction to the content of and issues surrounding Indonesian historiography these chapters may also prove useful to those whose interest in historiography transcends Indonesia. Clearly a number of the contributions should be pertinent for those concerned with the historiography of India, China, and Indonesia's Southeast Asian neighbors. Moreover, from the articles by the Indonesian contributors much insight may be gained into the preoccupations and problems of contemporary Indonesian historians. The several chapters taken together should serve to acquaint the reader with some of the major lacunae in our substantive knowledge of Indonesian history and with a number of its salient unsolved questions, thus providing him with an assessment of the work which has been done and an indication of what can and should be done.

In his Introduction, Mr. Soedjatmoko, editor in chief of the volume, says a little about each of the contributors, including his two Indonesian coeditors, and gives a brief description of the nature of each of the articles. Thus an introduction to Mr. Soedjatmoko should be in order here. As a long-time editor of *Siasat*—during its lifetime one of the most influential Indonesian weeklies—and still president of one of his country's major publishing houses, he has worked consistently to stimulate research in Indonesian history, his own recent writings being particularly concerned with problems of historiography. Several of these, including his important essay *An Approach to Indonesian History: Towards an Open Future* (Cornell Modern Indonesia Project, Translation Series; Ithaca, N.Y., 1960), have already been translated into English and published in the United States. In 1961 Mr. Soedjatmoko accepted the joint invitation of the Department of History and the Southeast Asia Program of Cornell University to serve as Visiting Lecturer in History.

A few words are necessary concerning the policies followed in editing this book. English is the second or third language of many of the contributors and, in cases where translations have been made, for some of the translators as well. Although we have undertaken to correct obvious errors in grammar, we have not felt justified in making structural changes except in the few cases where clarity was involved. The editors have tried to follow a consistent pattern of spelling, and at the very least to ensure that any one word is spelled the same way throughout the book. The problem faced by the editors may be indicated by the fact that among the manuscripts as first submitted there were eleven variant spellings of the word Nagarakertagama. Insofar as it has been possible for us to achieve uniformity, the following rules of pronunciation apply: *j* as in *jay; y* as in *you; w* approximately as a *v; c* as the *ch* in *chair*. Diacritical marks can be disregarded except for the *ñ* (i.e., *bañak*), pronounced as in *onion*. We have abbreviated the titles of the most frequently cited journals, and an explanation of the abbreviations will be found just preceding the main text. We refer the reader to the text and footnotes of individual articles for the extensive bibliographical information available in this book.

The difficulties in producing this symposium have been considerable, the effort requiring much more time than was originally envisaged. The editors are grateful for the patience and understanding shown them by the contributors, and especially for their restraint in incorporating new data developed subsequent to the submission of their manuscripts; a few of the manuscripts reached the editors as early as September 1958, and most of the remainder were received by mid-1960.

The completion of a publishing venture of this kind would have been impossible without the active assistance of a great number of people and the continuous interest and encouragement of many more. The editors are particularly grateful to Mrs. Laura L. Smail, who provided invaluable assistance throughout the process of preparing the English-language edition of this symposium. The editors also wish to express their gratitude to Ruth T. McVey, Mr. and Mrs. A. Milono, and Messrs. H. Bachtiar, Kismadi, and A. B. Loebis for their help in translating the papers not originally written in English; to Mrs. Bernard Kalb and Messrs. Daniel Lev, Alfred Hudson, and Akira Nagazumi for checking these translations and suggesting improvements; and to my colleague Professor John M. Echols for suggestions which helped guide us in matters of spelling and pronunciation. To all of them we are very much beholden. The editors also wish to thank Mrs. Susan Finch for help in many stages of the editorial process and especially for maintenance of liaison between often widely scattered editors and Cornell University Press, where as usual the Cornell Modern Indonesia Project is very much indebted to Miss Evelyn Boyce for her editorial perceptiveness and understanding patience. Finally, the editors wish to acknowledge their gratitude to Miss D. Wiradikarta, whose diligence, devotion, and unfailing readiness as editorial assistant in Indonesia throughout the preparation of the manuscript have been of invaluable help in the organizational and editorial aspects of this project. Needless to say, the editors remain fully responsible for any shortcomings the book may still have.

We wish also to express our appreciation for the permission given us to use copyrighted material as follows: by C. C. Berg for translations we made from three of his papers appearing in the periodicals *Indonesië* and *MKAWAL* and in *Geschiedenis van Nederlandsch Indië* edited by F. W. Stapel; by W. M. Hawley, Publishers, for a quotation from Han Yu-Shan's *Elements of Chinese Historiography;* and by Oxford University Press for quotations from R. G. Collingwood's *An Autobiography* and D. G. E. Hall's *Historians of South East Asia.*

In addition, the editors gratefully acknowledge their indebtedness to the Royal Netherlands Geographical Society for its generosity in extending permission for the utilization of its *Atlas of the Tropical Netherlands* (The Hague, 1938) in the drafting of maps for this book. The first three maps given here are adaptations, and the fourth largely a reproduction, of maps appearing on page 10 of the *Atlas.*

GEORGE McT. KAHIN

Ithaca, New York
August 25, 1964

CONTENTS

MAPS

INTRODUCTION

I

IT is not surprising that Indonesia's attainment of independence has sharpened the general interest of Indonesians in their own history. The awakened sense of their own individuality as a nation has led many, searching for a clearer definition of that identity and for a deeper understanding of its development in time, to turn to the mirror of history. The developments of the last few years and the problems besetting us in our national life have further stimulated such interest. Apart from this, history instruction is an important means of training good citizens and of developing love and loyalty for one's country; it is essential to a young country like Indonesia for the "nation building" in which its people are all engaged. Writing new textbooks for use in primary and secondary schools is therefore a very practical and important need. In response to all this, a National Historical Committee was set up by the Indonesian Government in 1951, consisting of both Indonesian and Dutch historians connected with the University of Indonesia and the Archaeological Service. For various reasons, however, this committee was unable to make any progress. A second attempt was of a more pronounced national character. In 1957 a National History Seminar was organized jointly by the University of Gadjah Mada and the University of Indonesia under the auspices of the Ministry of Education. Although the Seminar did not —and could not be expected to—reach any definite conclusions, many of its participants clearly felt that renewed research and a reevaluation of existing materials should precede any serious attempt at writing a new history of Indonesia.

Reflecting the haphazard development of Indonesian historiography, Indonesian history that has been written so far is notoriously full of gaps, and our knowledge of its periods is quite uneven. There is no continuous historical narrative nor is there any central point of vision, and the reconstruction of several periods is often based on extremely limited evidence. Although for some periods there is a more or less continuous historical narrative, the material is organized according to a viewpoint that was not, and in all fairness could not have been, an Indonesia-centric viewpoint—e.g., the Hindu-Javanese, East India Company, and Netherlands Indies Government periods. Finally, historical interest in the different areas of Indonesia has not always been equally strong. There has been a definite preference for Java, understandable when one considers the prevalence of Javanese sources and monuments. This is one of the reasons why the historical picture of Indonesia has been developed rather irregularly and in some cases has even become somewhat distorted.

Still, one cannot but be impressed by the important changes which have taken place in Indonesian historical studies during the last two decades. They have been the result mainly of the availability of new material and the application of new methods of study. There is, in the first place, the discovery of Buginese-Macassarese historiography as an important indigenous historical source. Secondly, several new countries, among which are the Soviet Union and Japan, have embarked upon studies in Indonesian history. In addition, the application of social science methods to Indonesian history has led to the development of interdisciplinary approaches that have proved to be very fruitful. Even though we have barely scratched the surface in this respect, approaches through the fields of cultural anthropology and, more recently, of sociology and international law have already led to significant changes in several existing historical images. Finally, mention should be made of the very significant recent trend toward consideration of the theoretical problems involved in modern Indonesian historiography. In view of all this, it would seem unnecessary to explain the need for a general but comprehensive survey of the field of Indonesian history, as it presents itself to those who want to explore it further.

This book is a first attempt to bring together in one volume the existing strands of Indonesian historical studies. It should be seen as a provisional stocktaking of available sources, of the present state of critical examination, of research methods and approaches which have proved, or might prove, useful in studying the material, and of the theoretical problems connected with writing a modern Indonesian history. The editors have not been entirely successful in their attempt to encompass the whole range of Indonesia's history in this symposium. Of those invited to join in this project, nine historians—four Indonesians, two Dutch, one British, one American, and one Indian —either were unable to accept or, after acceptance, had to withdraw, and a very few failed to respond altogether. Fortunately it was possible to enlist the cooperation of other outstanding scholars, so that only two of the chapters planned had to be abandoned—those on prehistory and on Indian sources. (The editors have made no systematic attempt to incorporate a discussion of sources and problems concerning Indonesia's most recent history.) Despite this setback, the editors have felt adequately justified in going ahead with the project and in presenting the available material to the reader. In setting up the symposium the editors have been guided by their conviction that only on the basis of such a provisional survey can the groundwork be laid for a rational plan of attack on the problem of further research. The editors have little doubt that once research is begun systematically, new materials will be found and more adequate methods and approaches will be developed.

In continuation of the international character of past efforts to arrive at a history of the Indonesian archipelago and in contrast with F. W. Stapel's massive, five-volume *Geschiedenis van Nederlandsch Indië,* written exclusively by Dutchmen, this symposium consists of contributions by Western Europeans, Asians, and an American, each with his own cultural background and scientific tradition. The international background has resulted unavoidably in a wide variety of approaches and presentations among the papers brought together here. However, although a more tightly organized book might have been more desirable, especially for those readers not yet familiar with the background and present state of Indonesian historical studies, no attempt has been made to force its contributors into an editorial straitjacket; uniformity has been imposed as little as is consistent with the minimum requirements of readability. Moreover, the geographical distance between the contributors, scattered over four continents, and the editors would have in itself made impracticable any attempt to do more. In the present stage of the development of Indonesian historical studies, it would also be presumptuous on the part of the editors to impose their own ideas of order and consistency in presentation upon their collaborators. The direction or directions which historical research on Indonesia should take will, we hope, emerge naturally from this general review.

Many of the contributors to this volume have already left their mark on the study of Indonesian history and need little introduction to the reader. A few words should be said, however, about some of the Indonesian participants. They belong to the younger generation of Indonesian historians and are engaged mostly in teaching and research at Indonesian universities and scientific institutes. The editors hope that publication of this book will be of some help to them in facing their difficult task.

The book was first conceived with the needs of the Indonesian historian and the Indonesian student of history in mind. But the wide geographical dispersion of source material on Indonesia's history makes it evident that without international cooperation little progress can be made in bringing together the materials from which the Indonesian historical narrative will be woven. To this end the editors decided to bring out both an English edition and an Indonesian edition of the symposium. In addition, the editors believe that an English-language edition can reach a wider audience, since many of the problems confronting the development of the study of history in Indonesia may well be similar to those which other new countries in Asia must face. Undoubtedly a regional comparative approach to the history of these new nations will result in considerable clarification of many of their problems. This would, for instance, be the case in connection with the search for an indigenous vantage point from which to view the unfolding of the history of each of these nations—and of the region as a whole—as opposed to the Europe-centric view of the former colonial powers. A second problem would be the critical evaluation of indigenous source material; a third would be the definition and analysis of traditional views and attitudes toward history. Moreover, new findings in one country may be of importance for the understanding of particular events or processes in other countries. An understanding of trends which cover a larger area than one country, and which are not always discernible within the limited purview of one nation's history, may enable us to place particular events in their proper perspective. The editors feel that the availability of this book in English might also be helpful in increasing the reader's familiarity with and understanding of the problems and challenges facing the historians of Southeast Asia as well as other historians who have made that area their main scholarly concern.

The editors hope this book will show how closely Indonesian history is linked with the history of Southeast, South, and Eastern Asia (and the world) and how a "Copernican" approach based on such lines can contribute to a deeper understanding of Indonesian history and society. They also hope that the subject will be of interest to the general reader who is not a professional historian but who is sufficiently interested in Indonesia's problems to want to know a little more about its history, its cultural background, and the problems with which it is wrestling in an attempt to orient itself in the world of the twentieth century.

It should be clearly stated that this is not a history book. It is a book about the study of Indonesian history. It is a book of sources and problems, but also, it is hoped, of pointers on how to use these sources and where to find possible answers to the problems. It was conceived and written in the hope of stimulating the study of Indonesian history by showing the directions in which this study might be most fruitfully pursued. Therefore, the bibliographies at the end of those chapters which do not give their bibliographical information in the text of the article constitute an essential element in this symposium. Study of the papers collected here will undoubtedly leave the reader, as it has the editors, with a deepened awareness of the overwhelming richness of the material and of the immensity of the work to be done. If at the same time he feels stimulated, not discouraged, and is inspired to contribute his share—which in the light of the formidable quantity and the refractory nature of the material can at best be only a very modest share—to the gradual construction of the edifice of Indonesia's history, the editors will consider themselves greatly rewarded.

II

The comparatively unorganized state of Indonesian historical studies makes it impossible to present the subject matter in a completely systematic fashion. The following chapters fall generally into three categories—sources, methods of study or approaches, and theoretical questions—but in several cases it has been impossible to discuss source material apart from its method of study. This has added to the difficulties of systematic presentation. Therefore we present the following paragraphs in the hope that they will give the reader some idea of what he will find in this symposium.

The first two chapters are of a general nature. In Chapter I, Mohammad Ali reviews the present state of historical studies in Indonesia and introduces some general problems resulting from Indonesia's emergence as an independent nation: the question of defining the concept of an Indonesian national history, its subject matter as well as its territorial delimitation, and the place of history instruction in a national education policy. He deals also with certain theoretical problems that the Indonesian historian must inevitably confront in the course of his work. They mainly concern the process of integrating and synthesizing data into historical narrative. These problems are connected with the search for an Indonesia-centric vantage point, from which the whole panorama of Indonesian history might be encompassed and comprehended. This search turns primarily on the question of a new Indonesia-centric system of periodization and the choice of a theme or themes around which the Indonesian historical narrative might fruitfully be organized. Mohammad Ali's article reflects the laborious and sometimes agonizing efforts which Indonesian historians are making in wrestling with these problems. No final answers are given, and none can be expected until, with the resumption of research, a great deal more historical data become available. It would be wrong to expect to find the answer to such problems by abstract reasoning alone. It is only when one actually works with the material that data emerge from which theoretical implications can be drawn and from which the appropriate tools of analysis can be developed. It is therefore to the historical material itself that we constantly have to turn.

In Chapter II, Louis Damais surveys the historical material and the use made of it for preseventeenth-century Indonesian history. He discusses the original sources, both internal and external, the transcriptions and translations now available in modern languages, reference works (word lists, etc.) useful for study of the original sources, and theories which have been advanced on the basis of the sources. In a final section he outlines the steps he considers necessary before a new history of Indonesia can be written. These can be said to fall into two categories: efforts toward making source materials available to a wider public and more intensive study and review of their content from various disciplinary viewpoints. He suggests a reevaluation of Western sources on the period from the seventeenth to the twentieth century for what they reveal of specifically Indonesian history and society.

The chapters that follow reveal some of the work which is being done on the problems raised by Ali and Damais.

In Chapter III, Soekmono deals with the significance of archaeology for Indonesian history. For the period from the fifth century, when the prehistoric period is generally supposed to end, to the fifteenth, archaeology provides the primary indigenous data from which the historical reconstruction of parts of that period becomes possible. Several of these reconstructions are, however, still of a very hypothetical nature, based on flimsy evidence. Despite some monumental scholarly achievements, so far only a small dent has been made in our general ignorance of the period. For the later periods, archaeology provides valuable checking points on what little documentary material is available, while for Indonesia's many nonliterate cultures it constitutes the only source and method for historical study. In the field of epigraphy (Chapter IV), Buchari tells us why, of the three thousand inscriptions of which estampages have been made, only a fraction have been transcribed and an even smaller fraction translated and studied. We get a glimpse of one of the difficulties involved in his statement that only one epigraphical expert is available in Indonesia to work this veritable gold mine of historical and sociological information. It is in these two fields of archaeology and epigraphy that we should make an intensive effort. This is bound to be a costly affair, and considerable government support will be necessary. Although there is no certainty that the results will be commensurate with the energy and money expended, without such an attempt knowledge of our ancient history will remain even more tentative and provisional than is necessary.

The considerable store of local historical traditions constitutes an often rather scornfully rejected source of historical data. Here too, so it seems, we stand only at the beginning of the systematic work which needs to be done. Hoesein Djajadiningrat, in what has turned out to be his last finished article,[1] discusses the significance of some of the written local historical traditions (Chapter V). He deals with the nature of these traditions and gives his evaluation of them as historical source material. Pointing to the need for checking data found in these traditions against information from nonindigenous

[1] Professor Hoesein Djajadiningrat died on November 12, 1960.

sources, he also gives instances in which local historical traditions have proved useful for the verification of foreign accounts. For this, as he points out, an adequate knowledge of Islam in Indonesia is often necessary. Sometimes these traditions are also helpful in putting otherwise isolated pieces of information in their proper context. Djajadiningrat thus assigns a greater importance to local traditions as a source of historical material than several Western authorities have been inclined to do. He concludes his chapter with a brief discussion of the value to be attached to the exactness of the chronological data mentioned in some of the local traditions, and he points to the possibility of their having a symbolic value.

We now come to one of the most controversial problems of Indonesian historiography—the evaluation of Javanese historiography as a historical source. The problem is that many of the existing classical Javanese documentary sources, apart from the considerable philological difficulties, do not seem to yield to the conventional methods of historical examination. The most ambitious attempt at solving this riddle has been made by C. C. Berg, who raised the question of the function of the historiography of a particular culture and tried to understand it in terms of the cultural pattern of the society at that time. This approach, which Berg calls the "syntypical" method, led him to see Javanese historiography as part of the priestly activities that served to enhance the magic powers (*sekti*) of the ruler. Berg explains some of his views in Chapter VI.

That several contributors to this symposium have felt obliged to devote parts of their papers to an evaluation of this theory, which Berg has constantly developed, adjusted, and readjusted since its first presentation, certainly bears witness to the special place occupied by him in the study of Javanese historiography. In the other papers, however, it is also made clear why several of the contributors find it difficult to accept all the implications of Berg's reasoning. The most fundamental of these reservations seems to be the methodological one posed by J. P. Zoetmulder. In Chapter XVII, Zoetmulder points out the almost insurmountable difficulties of having to acquire an understanding of a past culture as the key to understanding the meaning of certain sources when it is the very same sources for which the key is sought. Buchari in his paper on epigraphy (Chapter IV) wonders what would be left of his own particular discipline if inscriptions should no longer be taken at their face value. In distinct contrast to Berg, H. J. de Graaf in Chapter VII attributes to the Javanese a much greater historical sense. In his view, Javanese historiography, especially after the middle of the seventeenth century, does yield to conventional critical examination and does, with the necessary checks against non-Javanese sources, constitute a treasure house of historical information. It is clear that much more philological spadework and careful evaluation of the results are necessary before any final characterization can be made regarding Javanese historiography and before it can be definitely established to what extent recourse should be made to nonconventional methods of interpretation and reconstruction. Nevertheless for the present Berg's basic assumption cannot be ignored, and his provocative theory stands as a challenge to those historians who, on the basis of Javanese historical writings, are working toward the "reenactment of past thoughts"—to borrow R. G. Collingwood's phrase.

C. C. Berg's views also throw into sharper relief the question of the origins of other types of historiography to be found in the Indonesian archipelago. In Chapter VIII, J. Noorduyn discusses the intriguing phenomenon of South Celebes historiography, which makes its quite sudden appearance in the seventeenth century and which in its lack of prophecies, scarcity of mythological elements, exactness, and terseness differs strikingly from Javanese historiography. Noorduyn explores several possibilities concerning its origins and the factors contributing to its development. Another indigenous source is Malay historical writings, and J. C. Bottoms in Chapter IX discusses the historical texts written in Malay about Malaysia, i.e., the Malay Peninsula, Sumatra, the Riau Archipelago, and Borneo. In addition, he refers to four other categories of material of historical interest: autobiographical work, descriptive poems, codes of law, and diaries, personal letters, and memoranda. Some works of old Malay literature are mentioned that might also prove to yield valuable historical material. In his paper, which should be read in conjunction with Hoesein Djajadiningrat's article (Chapter V), Bottoms gives some general characteristics of these writings and discusses their meaning to the people concerned. He also evaluates their significance for the modern historian.

Next come the Chinese sources. The main problem here, as Tjan Tjoe Som states in his paper (Chapter X), is their abundance and the difficulty of determining where in this mass of material to look for the widely scattered information pertinent to Indonesia's history. Tjan Tjoe Som discusses the sources which have a bearing on the relations between China and other countries, with particular reference, of course, to Indonesia. Reference is also made to the collection of Chinese accounts concerning various people "throughout history," which since 1958 has been in process of publication by the Central Academy of Minorities in Peking.

He also discusses the matter of language. The problem here is one not only of translation from the Chinese but also of transliteration, in particular of references to place names in Indonesia and other countries. A list of the works on the early-fifteenth-century courtier and ambassador Chêng Ho is added to this article.

The article on Japanese sources (Chapter XI), by Koichi Kishi, is in two sections. The first lists and describes the following sources pertaining to the Japanese occupation of Indonesia from 1942 to 1945: key government and military documents; Japanese newspapers and periodicals published in Indonesia during that period; and notes and memoirs published by participants in the events. In the second section, Kishi lists and describes some of the principal articles produced by Japanese scholars of Indonesian history in the postwar period. The range of interests extends from the invasion of Java by the Mongols and the early history of Islam in Java, for which Chinese sources were used, up to scholarly studies of the Japanese occupation. Because of the presence of large numbers of Japanese in Southeast Asia, primarily as traders, around the turn of the seventeenth century, a good deal of research has been done on this period based on information from Dutch East India Company documents.

The Western European documentary sources discussed in this book consist mainly of accounts and reports by travelers, missionaries, merchants, employees of the great trading companies, civil servants, jurists, archaeologists, and so forth and of official documents, to be found in the archives in England, the Netherlands, the Iberian Peninsula, India, Indonesia, and Malaya. These have already yielded large amounts of data. Nevertheless the papers of John Bastin, Graham Irwin, and C. R. Boxer, which deal with these sources, clearly indicate that in comparison with their impressive quantity very little has been done so far.

Although the bulk of the material that has been used for certain periods of Indonesian history has been drawn predominantly from Dutch sources, there has been an increasing awareness of the significance of Portuguese sources. In Chapter XII, C. R. Boxer surveys these sources in the three categories into which they can be divided:

early official chronicles, other secular narrative and eyewitness accounts, and missionary literature. He discusses the work which has
been done and is being done on this material and also gives us an
idea of what still needs to be done. Reference is also made to the
principal modern works in this field and to some Spanish sources.
Boxer concludes by giving some pointers regarding possible research
in Indonesian history in the libraries and archives of Lisbon and
Madrid.

The continued importance of Dutch sources, however, despite the
changed perspectives of today, is amply demonstrated in some of
the postwar work which has been done. Using documents of the
Dutch East India Company and English sources, the Danish historian
F. K. Glamann showed in his recently published *The Dutch Asiatic
Trade, 1620–1740* the very limited effectiveness of the so-called monopoly of the Dutch East India Company in Indonesia, contrary to
formerly held views.

In his paper on the significance of Dutch sources in this book
(Chapter XIII), Graham Irwin gives a selective list of manuscripts
and published materials on the periods of the Dutch East India
Company and the Netherlands East Indies Government. He too holds
the view that the exclusion of Dutch sources, for whatever reasons,
can only be detrimental to the study of Indonesian history and that
even from an Indonesia-centric point of view much of this material
can and should be used.

Equally deserving of a fresh look by anyone who wants to study
the period from Indonesia's first contacts with the West onward are
the English sources. In Chapter XIV, John Bastin deals with the vast
body of English documentary materials. They constitute a necessary
complement to the Dutch sources, partly because British scholarly
interest in some parts of Indonesia was aroused earlier than that of
the Dutch and also because their interest, depending on the main
area of their commercial and political concern, was often directed to
sections in which the Dutch were not then particularly interested.
There is a great deal of neglected material here, as Bastin points out,
especially on the nineteenth century. He also mentions some American sources and work done by American scholars.

Of much more recent date is the interest of Soviet scholars. Ruth
T. McVey gives a survey of Soviet historical writings on Indonesia
(Chapter XV), of interest not only as a source of facts but in particu-
lar for their interpretation of available data.

The next chapters deal with methods of study or approaches to the source material. The existence of various types of historiography in the Indonesian archipelago clearly indicates the necessity of intimate collaboration among philologists, anthropologists, religious phenomenologists, and historians for the study of indigenous written sources. The use of the anthropological approach in the study of Indonesian history is actually not a new phenomenon. In Chapter XVI, Koentjaraningrat indicates some of the contributions which anthropology has already made in this respect. He discusses the anthropological methods which should be considered in any systematic use of this discipline for the study of Indonesian history, with reference both to its prehistoric period and to the later periods. A chart of these methods is added to the article.

The cross-fertilization of history and the social sciences has been one of the most rewarding among recent developments in the study of history. As Richard Hofstadter points out, the value of participation of the social scientist lies in the specific intellectual concerns and professional perspectives that he brings to the historical material before him and to the questions derived from them. It might also be said that as far as Indonesia is concerned, there is little doubt that the social scientist will profit from a more historical approach.

In the study of Indonesian history the interdisciplinary approach has also borne significant fruits in the use of sociological methods. This approach has helped to deepen our understanding of particular periods in history by bringing to bear sociological data needed for the reconstruction of the social background against which historical events took place. In this way the sociological approach has often been able to make us feel closer to the historical reality of some particular time. W. F. Wertheim illustrates this point in Chapter XVIII. He points to the new analytical tools which sociology can bring to the study of Indonesian history and mentions a few conceptual refinements. Such developments might be important in eventually liberating us from the historical categories and terminology which derive from the analysis of Western European society and history and which, if uncritically applied to other cultures and societies, are bound to distort our understanding of them.

The late J. M. Romein,[2] who enjoyed the distinction of being the first foreign historian to be invited to teach as a guest professor at an Indonesian university, stresses in Chapter XX the importance of

[2] Professor Romein died on July 12, 1962.

the comparative method and demonstrates the significance of what he calls the "time factor" in using the comparative method.

Compared with the sociological approach, the economic approach has made far less progress. The field of economic history is, at least in Indonesia, still almost virgin territory. The student of Indonesian economic history is confronted primarily by questions and problems, rather than with answers or clearly established facts. F. J. E. Tan in Chapter XXI poses some of these problems and tries to give some tentative answers to them. He raises, for example, the question of defining the subject matter to be dealt with by the economic historian of Indonesia. He also points to the need to get away from the Java-centric examination of available data and the need to view them in a more general Indonesian setting. There is little doubt that the concept of a dualistic economy derives mainly from a generalization of data concerning Java, where modern economy coexists with village economy. The inadequacy of this concept for understanding economic history in Borneo, East Indonesia, and that part of Sumatra which lies outside the economic enclaves of the big estates and the oil concessions is now more generally realized. It is also clear that the difficulties faced by economic history are the same as those faced by descriptive economics itself. Both have to be able to encompass within their scope the pluralistic character of Indonesia's economic structure, ranging as it does from capitalist to closed economic systems. The variety of historical experience in the different parts of Indonesia has also brought about a difference in the economic history of each part. The study of the history of the autochthonous economic structures in Indonesia clearly calls also for the use of economic anthropology and of *adat* law, as has already been done for Borneo, for example (J. Mallinckrodt, *Het adatrecht van Borneo,* 1928). The significance of the economic approach has of course been proved amply by van Leur's study of Indonesian trade, and continued research along these lines will no doubt prove to be very important. In his paper, F. J. E. Tan raises some other questions which might stimulate the examination of particular fields of economic history.

One of the most important recent developments in the study of Indonesian history is the unexpected significance of Indonesia's international legal history. It has been mainly G. J. Resink who has drawn our attention to it for the period of the last four centuries and who has broken the surface in this promising field. His findings have already helped to destroy the once current picture of the extent of

Dutch colonial rule in the nineteenth century; instead he has given a picture of a limited Netherlands East Indies as one among many other states in the archipelago, with several of which it maintained complex and varied relationships. In his paper (Chapter XIX) Resink discusses the history of international law in Indonesia, the scholarly interest in this subject, and the significance of studies in this field for the general political, economic, and theoretical history of Indonesia.

One last problem remains. The success of our attempts to further the study of history as a scholarly discipline in Indonesia and to set it on a firm and permanent footing will be determined by more than the proper transference of skills and techniques. The modern study of history is still the rather new product of a long cultural and scientific development in a particular environment. For it to strike firm roots in a young country with an old and distinct cultural tradition of its own requires a grasp of the wider cultural implications of historical studies, as well as an awareness on the part of its disciples of the connections between the study of history and the nature of its cultural environment. The closing chapter of this symposium (Chapter XXII) offers some reflections by one of the editors on the problem this creates for the modern Indonesian historian.

Several general observations can be made from the discussion of sources, methods of study, and approaches presented in the chapters of this book. We will mention here only a few that concern the most fruitful course the study of history might take in Indonesia.

It seems feasible to draw up a rational plan for the systematic development of Indonesian history. Such a plan should cover a deliberate search for new materials and data and the training of historians, a more vigorous examination of the already available but still unstudied material for the different periods of Indonesian history, and the reexamination of the known data and the materials from which they derive. In such a plan the examination of Western European sources continues to be important, especially since only a small part of the available material has already been studied. But at the same time a deliberate effort should be made to look for new indigenous and general Asian material. Greater attention should be paid to the local historical traditions, while extensive archaeological exploration and study should be high in priority. It is only in this way that we can hope to fill the considerable gaps in our knowledge of certain periods of Indonesian history.

A few words might also be said about the search for an Indonesia-centric viewpoint.[3] It should be realized that this search is not an isolated phenomenon. It takes place in the wider setting of the search for an Asia-centric viewpoint for Asia's history, as distinct from the Europe-centricity which has so long dominated modern historiography. This search entails a reevaluation of the past relationship between Europe and Asia, which as K. M. Pannikar's bold but not entirely successful attempt (*Asia and Western Dominance*) shows, is attainable in any degree of definitiveness only on the basis of a great deal more research. Apart from the need to follow developments in this wider setting, it will be necessary for Indonesian historians to find out much more about the relationships between Indonesia and the rest of Asia, as well as about their common historical experiences. What is important, then, is the general orientation of the Indonesian historian. Only when he focuses his mind on the area of Southeast Asia will he be able to overcome the hold which the great mass of Western European sources inevitably has on him. The matter of orientation therefore arises not only in relation to the synthesizing of the data and the writing of the historical narrative but much earlier —in relation to the sources. With such a general Southeast Asian orientation it will be easier for him to look to the histories of the neighboring countries for material that must throw additional light on his own problems. It is likely that such a search will coincide with attempts in those countries to find new data in order to write their own history anew. Furthermore, a comparative study of the histories of the neighboring countries might reveal some useful insights into the social and political structure and the historical development of what is now called, for lack of a better term, traditional society in Southeast Asia. International cooperation for the development of Indonesian historiography is therefore a must. This cooperation should cover not only Southeast Asia but also China, India, Japan, the Middle East, and Europe. It should take the form of exchange of scholars, exchange of microfilmed historical material, and joint international research projects.

Another conclusion that emerges is that closer and more systematic interdisciplinary cooperation and coordination are needed. The uni-

[3] See also John Smail's thoughtful and provocative essay on this subject, published after the final organization of this book had been decided upon: "On the Possibility of an Autonomous History of Modern Southeast Asia," *Journal of Southeast Asian History*, II, no. 2 (July, 1961), 72–102.

versities should encourage students in history to familiarize themselves with anthropology, sociology, and economics. Conversely, it should be made possible for students with training in the social sciences to have—if they want it—an additional exposure to history. The training of historians in the university should aim early at giving them a solid grounding in the techniques of the critical method and a thorough familiarity with its use. Early specialization in the periods of Indonesian history seems also to be called for—each period of Indonesian history requires its own particular combination of disciplines and languages, and during the training period of Indonesian historians the foundations for this should be laid. Of course there should be a recruitment program designed to draw a sufficiently large number of students into the field of Indonesian history. We will also have to reconcile ourselves to the fact that before we can write our history on a sound scholarly foundation, a great deal more research needs to be done with a firmly held Indonesia-centric orientation. The studies which will have to be made at this stage are mainly monographical. It might not be too much to hope, however, that with a vigorously pursued policy based on the principles outlined above we will be able successfully to approach the actual writing of the history of Indonesia.

SOEDJATMOKO

Ithaca and Jakarta, 1962

ABBREVIATIONS

BEFEO   *Bulletin de l'Ecole Française d'Extrême Orient* (Bulletin of the French School of the Far East).

BKI   *Bijdragen tot de Taal-, Land- en Volkenkunde (van Nederlandsch-Indië), uitgegeven door het Koninklijk Instituut voor Taal-, Land- en Volkenkunde (van Nederlandsch-Indië)* (Contributions to the Philology, Geography, and Ethnology [of the Netherlands East Indies]. Published by the Royal Institute for Philology, Geography, and Ethnology [of the Netherlands East Indies]).

HJG   N. J. Krom, *Hindoe-Javaansche geschiedenis* (2d rev. ed.; The Hague, 1931).

JIAEA   *Journal of the Indian Archipelago and Eastern Asia.*

JRAS   *Journal of the Royal Asiatic Society.*

JRASMB   *Journal of the Royal Asiatic Society, Malayan Branch.*

JRASSB   *Journal of the Royal Asiatic Society, Singapore Branch.*

MKAWAL   *Mededeelingen der Koninklijke Akademie van Wetenschappen, Afdeeling Letterkunde* (Communications of the [Dutch] Royal Academy of Sciences, Literary Section).

Nag.   *Nāgarakĕrtāgama.* For English translation see Theo-
dore Pigeaud, *Java in the Fourteenth Century,* vol. III,
Translations (The Hague, 1960).

OJO   N. J. Krom, ed., "Oud-Javaansche oorkonden: Nagelaten
transcripties van wijlen Dr. J. L. A. Brandes" (Old
Javanese Inscriptions: Transcripts Left Behind by the
late Dr. J. L. A. Brandes), *VBG,* LX (1913), 1–267.

OV   *Oudheidkundig Verslag uitgegeven door het (Koninklijk) Bataviaasch Genootschap van Kunsten en Wetenschappen* (Archaeological Report Published by the
[Royal] Batavian Society of Arts and Sciences).

ROD *Rapport van den Oudheidkundigen Dienst in Nederlandsch-Indië* (Report of the Archaeological Survey of
the Netherlands East Indies).

TBG   *Tijdschrift voor Indische Taal-, Land- en Volken-
kunde uitgegeven door het (Koninklijk) Bataviaasch
Genootschap van Kunsten en Wetenschappen* (Journal
of Indonesian Philology, Geography, and Ethnology
Published by the [Royal] Batavian Society of Arts and
Sciences).

VBG   *Verhandelingen van het (Koninklijk) Bataviaasch Genootschap van Kunsten en Wetenschappen* (Proceedings of the [Royal] Batavian Society of Arts and
Sciences).

VKI   *Verhandelingen van het Koninklijk Instituut voor de
Taal-, Land- en Volkenkunde (van Nederlandsch-
Indië)* (Publications of the Royal Institute for Phi-
lology, Geography, and Ethnology [of the Netherlands
East Indies]).

An Introduction to
Indonesian Historiography

I

Historiographical Problems

BY MOHAMMAD ALI

*Chief, National Archives, Jakarta, and Lecturer
in History, University of Padjadjaran, Bandung*

I

IF one day the Ministry of Education of the Republic of Indonesia decides to bring "uniformity" into the teaching of Indonesian history, such a decision will undoubtedly be the result of the obvious confusion about Indonesian history at present. Only since 1942 has Indonesian history been officially included in the curriculum of Indonesian schools. Prior to 1942 there were the "Geschiedenis van Nederlands Indië" (History of the Netherlands Indies) and the "Indische geschiedenis" or "Hikayat Tanah Hindia" (History of the Indies).[1]

Between 1942 and 1945, under the strict supervision and censorship of the propaganda and cultural agencies established by the Japanese Military Government, "The History of the Indies" was transformed into "Indonesian History." Along with the change from "the Netherlands Indies" to "Indonesia" came an exaggerated adulation of the Indonesian people and its culture, while simultaneously the Dutch were pictured as colonialists, enemies, and the cause of all misery and suffering in Indonesia.[2]

---

[1] Well-known textbooks are: for primary schools (HIS), A. Brand, *Aangeklede jaartallen* (5th ed., 1939); for junior secondary schools (MULO), A. J. Eykman and F. W. Stapel, *Beknopt leerboek der geschiedenis van Nederlands Indië* (16th ed., 1939); for senior secondary schools (AMS), A. J. Eykman and F. W. Stapel, *Leerboek der geschiedenis van Nederlands Indië* (9th ed., 1939); for teacher training schools (Normaalschool), L. van Rijckevorsel, *Kitab Riwajat Kepoelauan Hindia Timor* (1929).

[2] Prijono, *Sedikit tentang Sedjarah Asia Timoer Raja dan Sedjarah Tanah Djawa* (Jakarta, 2605 [1945]), pp. 36–37; Sanusi Pane, *Sedjarah Indonesia* (Jakarta, 2605 [1945]), IV, 175 ff.

1

tion arose whether there was any fundamental identity between the history of Indonesia and the history of the Netherlands Indies—whether Indonesian history was merely the antithesis of the history of the Netherlands Indies.

It is obvious that this chaotic situation was not conducive to the cultivation of a national spirit in the field of education. In view of these problems, the Minister of Education and Culture of the Republic of Indonesia, "considering also that the different methods of history instruction should be studied in order to meet scientific requirements, decided to hold a history seminar and to entrust its organization to the universities of Gadjah Mada and Indonesia." [6]

These considerations clearly show the dilemma faced by the Education Ministry. In the first place, there is the *political* problem of trying, in the national interest, to define and develop the national character. Secondly, there is the problem posed by the *scientific* requirements for the study of history, which might be in conflict with political needs. This basic dilemma becomes even more apparent from the wording of the topics selected for discussion at the History Seminar. These topics were:

I   The Philosophical Concept of National History
II   Periodization of Indonesian History
III   Requirements for the Writing of Textbooks on Indonesian National History
IV   Teaching Indonesian National History in the Schools
V   The Training of Historians
VI   The Preservation and Use of Historical Materials [7]

Topics I–IV reflect the desire to achieve absolute uniformity in the

---

cultuurgeschiedenis (3 vols.; Groningen, 1932–1935). B. M. Vlekke, *Geschiedenis van de Indische Archipel* (Roermond, 1947), and H. J. de Graaf, *Geschiedenis van Indonesië* (The Hague, 1949), became available *after* 1950 and have therefore not been made use of. Other books of a general nature, such as the following, are not well known: H. T. Colenbrander, *Koloniale geschiedenis* (3 vols.; The Hague, 1925–1926); M. L. van Deventer, *Geschiedenis der Nederlanders op Java* (2 vols.; Haarlem, 1886); J. S. Furnival, *Netherlands-India* (Cambridge, Eng., 1944); E. S. de Klerck, *History of the Netherlands East Indies* (2 vols.; Rotterdam, 1938); J. J. Meinsma, *Geschiedenis van de Nederlandsch Oost Indische bezittingen* (2 vols.; Delft and The Hague, 1872–1875); J. M. Somer, *Vestiging, doorvoering en consolidatie van het Nederlandsche gezag in Nederlandsch Indië* (Breda, 1935). Cf. *Catalogus der Bibliotheek Koninklijk Bataviaasch Genootschap voor Kunst en Wetenschappen* (Jakarta, 1940), pp. 259–262.

[6] *Laporan Seminar Sedjarah*, Gadjah Mada University, I (1958), 82. All translations in this article are mine.

[7] *Ibid.*, p. 88.

presentation of national history. Such a uniformity would, in this view, become an important factor in molding the national character. Thus national history would have an important function in the national education system.

Behind the phrasing of topics I–IV stands the opinion that since history allows for many interpretations and can be looked at from many viewpoints, it should be possible to use the outlook on life of a whole people, its *Weltanschauung*, as the basis from which to view its own history. The topic "The Philosophical Concept of National History"— it was hoped—might be the telescope through which Indonesia's historical narrative could be viewed and interpreted, in order to make possible its presentation as a national history.[8] A philosophy of national history might then provide a system of periodization,[9] which in turn could constitute a framework for the organization of the historical material according to both the teaching requirements and the function of history in the national education system. Once such a national historical narrative was formulated, it would be necessary to determine the way it should be taught in the schools. Thus uniformity would be achieved.[10]

The problems as posed by the Seminar, as well as their discussion, were not, however, conducive to creation of a system of history instruction which could meet scientific requirements. On the contrary, the Seminar gave rise to a new problem—the question whether it would be possible at all to arrive at the formulation of a philosophy of national history. Put in different words, it posed the question whether a philosophy of history in general would be of any use in trying to present the history of a specific nation or of a specific area.[11] In short, the crux of

[8] The Indonesian term "filsafat sedjarah nasional" can be read to mean (1) philosophy of national history or (2) national philosophy of history. What is meant is the philosophical foundation of Indonesian history.

[9] J. H. J. van der Pot, *De periodisering der geschiedenis* (The Hague, 1951), pp. 9–13, 17; Muhammad Yamin, *6000 Tahun Sang Merah Putih* (Jakarta, 1954), ch. iii, pp. 113–170.

[10] Cf. Richard E. Thursfield, *The Study and Teaching of American History* (17th yearbook of the National Council for Social Studies; Washington, D.C., 1946), secs. ii, iv, v, vii.

[11] Please note the use of such terms as (1) "challenge and response," in connection with the Brantas River, to provide an explanation of the rise of the kingdom and culture of Kĕḍiri (see Sutjipto Wirjosuparto, "Apa Sebabnja Daerah Kediri dan Sekitarnja Muntjul dalam Sedjarah," *Indonesian Abstracts*, I, no. 3 [April 1959], 91); (2) "introvert," for an explanation of the mental change in Mataram, as the result of the isolation caused by the blockade of the northern coast of Java by the East India Company (see R. Moh. Ali, *Perdjoangan Feodal* [Bandung, 1954]); (3) "caesarism, saecularisation, porfyrism," the modern categories used by J. M. van der Kroef in *Indonesia in the Modern World*, I (Bandung, 1954), 112, 208, 178.

the problems entrusted to the History Seminar for an *integrated* solution turned out to be a philosophical matter and not merely a historical one.

Because the topics of the Seminar were not dealt with as parts of a whole, the discussion on the writing of history did not bring any clarification either. It merely produced several varying and conflicting opinions regarding the writing and teaching of Indonesian history as national history, which were the more confusing since in the course of the discussion the demands arising from the scientific discipline of history were not sufficiently observed.[12]

Although it was not the purpose of the Seminar to come up with a "system" of national history, complete with its method of instruction, it could at least have led to a clarification of the problem. Unfortunately this did not happen either. A similar fate befell papers V and VI, which dealt with the disciplinary subjects of the training of historians and the preservation of historical sources. These two topics, which should have been discussed together, were dealt with separately and consequently only on a purely technical level.

In general, the History Seminar did not succeed in becoming more than a forum for the presentation of various opinions regarding history and the concepts of nationalism and national character, and these were not based on historical facts and were not illuminated by a sense of history. The way in which the historiographical problems were treated at this History Seminar actually only served to emphasize the importance of Resink's dictum:

If the writing of national history is not to lead to too lofty a flight of the imagination, if it is not only to develop into a nationally recognized science, but also to become internationally accepted, then the grand design should be

---

[12] History as a science has not yet been given much attention in Indonesia. The training in history at the departments of literature of our universities has not yet developed sufficiently to create a "historical atmosphere." Nor has it yet been possible firmly to establish and develop historical scholarship. The "B. I" and "B. II" history courses train teachers for secondary schools. These courses emphasize proficiency in accepted history rather than history as a science. However, there is a great general interest in history mainly of a "speculative" character and less of a "critical analytical" nature. This may be caused by the present stage of our social and political development, the youth of our scholarship in general, and the limited availability of history books of a scholarly character. The complete report of the Jogjakarta History Seminar will indicate that views on history in Indonesia are still magico-historical in character, or, in Yamin's terms, are still dominated by "agama shakti" (mysticism), or, as expressed by O. Notohamidjojo in his paper at the History Seminar, are imbued with a magic-mystical sense of participation. Cf. G. W. Locher, "Myth in a Changing World," *BKI*, CXII (1956), 168–192.

accompanied by the minute examination of facts, the beautiful idea joined with lowly workmanship, the vision supported by verification.[13]

In the light of this statement it is easy to understand that the History Seminar could not fulfill the task entrusted to it, mainly because it did not sufficiently realize the nature of the proper task of history—the utilization of historical sources, the careful and patient application of scientific discipline to those sources, with a view to uncovering and establishing historical facts.

In general, the shortage of historians devoting themselves to scientific research might be the reason why the significance of facts as the basis on which any historical interpretation rests, with the subsequent organization of these facts into the historical narrative, does not get the attention it should. The insufficient number of historians trained in historical theory and familiar with the idea of a philosophy of history might similarly be the reason for the superficial treatment, both in a critical analytical and in a speculative sense, of the subject of the philosophy of history.

The Indonesian Government's awareness of this situation is evident from the preparations it is making for the establishment of a Historical Institute, to be entrusted with the task of coordinating the training of historians and of conducting research, as well as of strengthening the agencies charged with the preservation of historical material, such as the National Archives and the Archaeological Service.

Once we have become aware of the present state of the science of history in Indonesia, it becomes necessary to realize the basic problems confronting it. This may give us a better understanding of the efforts of the Indonesian people to write their own history, especially since they have now proved to be able to make their own history! [14]

II

The writing of Indonesian history to all intents and purposes revolves around the interpretation of the term "Indonesia." Content, scope, and depth of the writing of that history determine the shape and character of the Indonesian historical narrative. In this connection the term "reconstruction" is often used in the sense of improving upon a construction which already exists—the reconstruction of Indonesian

---

[13] G. J. Resink, "Tussen de mythen," *De Nieuwe Stem*, VI (June, 1952), 352.
[14] G. J. Resink, "Passe-partout om geschiedschrijvers," *Indonesië*, VI (1952–1953), 374.

history.[15] Sometimes the term "rewriting" is used, indicating that existing writings are out of date and must be rewritten.[16] What should subsequently be discussed is whether the object of the historical narrative remains unchanged throughout the ages, and therefore does not need to be corrected, or whether the object does change in the course of time and necessitates a corresponding correction of the narrative. We should therefore stress the importance of the object of the historical narrative of Indonesia. In this way we will be able to place the term "writing" in its proper perspective. If what is meant by Indonesian history is the history of the Indonesian people inhabiting the territory of the Republic of Indonesia, then the object of our historical narrative is that political organization, and it must be discussed. When did it come into being?

The Republic of Indonesia became a reality on August 17, 1945, and as of that date it became a political body. What existed before 1945? According to a commentary on Article 2 of the provisional constitution (1950), "What is defined as the territory of Indonesia comprises the former Netherlands Indies." [17] The delimitation of the territory of the Republic of Indonesia as the continuation of the territory of the Netherlands Indies requires a statement as to the period during which the term "Netherlands Indies" had any significance; when did the Netherlands control the whole of the East Indies (Indonesia) so that the whole of the East Indies became the Dutch colony called the Netherlands Indies? According to the findings of Resink, the time of establishment of the Netherlands Indies, in the sense of the political unit comprising the *whole* of Indonesia, should be placed at about 1910.[18] If these Netherlands Indies became a fact about 1910, what was their political organization before that? Prior to 1910 there existed in the

[15] A rather disturbing use of the term "reconstruction" can be found in Warsito Sastroprajitno, *Rekonstruksi Sedjarah Indonesia Zaman Hindu* (Jogjakarta, 1958). This book ends as follows: "In fact, it would be more accurate to call the Hindu period the period of Indian colonization, because these Indians were colonists, people who migrated from their land of origin for political, religious, and economic reasons. There is no difference between them and the British who migrated to America and Australia" (p. 224). This view is a weak echo of the theory regarding the advent of the Hindus or of the theory regarding the rise of Hindu culture in Java, propounded by G. H. von Faber in his book *Er werd een stad geboren* (Surabaya, 1953), pp. 29 ff.

[16] Cf. J. M. van der Kroef, "On the Writing of Indonesian History," *Pacific Affairs*, XXXI, no. 4 (Dec., 1958), 352.

[17] R. Soepomo, *Undang² Dasar Sementara R.I.* (Jakarta, 1950), p. 20.

[18] G. J. Resink, "Onafhankelijke vorsten, rijken en landen in Indonesië tussen 1850 en 1910," *Indonesië*, IX (1956), 265.

Indonesian Archipelago (occupying the same territory as the former Netherlands Indies) three forms of political organization, viz., (1) the independent Indonesian kingdoms and their vassals, which did not yet accept Dutch sovereignty, (2) the Netherlands Indies, comprising all areas already under direct Dutch administration along with the native kingdoms recognizing Dutch suzerainty, and (3) areas under Portuguese and British control. The oldest area to be administered by the Dutch was a fortification in Ambon, which was not seized from Indonesian rule but from the Portuguese (1605).[19] The period between 1605 and 1910 saw the growth of Dutch power from one fortress in Ambon to the Netherlands Indies, after the Dutch succeeded in forcing the native kingdoms, not yet under their suzerainty, to sign the "Short Declaration," by which they recognized Dutch overlordship over their territories. Before the East India Company (VOC) could establish its power in Southeast Asia, the Portuguese succeeded in establishing their suzerainty in various territories there, through war in Malacca from 1511 and through diplomacy in Ternate from 1521. In 1575 Baabullah succeeded in destroying Portuguese power in Ternate, and from then on the Portuguese could maintain themselves only in Ambon, Tidore, Malacca, and several places in Timor. It may therefore be concluded that from 1511 the Indonesian Archipelago saw a great deal of political activity, diplomacy, war, trade, alliances, controversies, intimidations, etc., between native Indonesian states, the Portuguese, the Dutch, and the British.[20] After the East India Company eliminated them as trade competitors from the Indonesian kingdoms (their last vestige was Bantam, from which they were driven out in 1684),[21] the Portuguese completely disappeared from the scene of Indonesian history. After a brief eclipse as a result of defeat in Ambon in 1623, England again became a decisive factor, when during the coalition wars its supremacy of the seas was established—until ultimately English diplomacy determined the shape of the Netherlands Indies.[22]

This brief historical survey shows how difficult it is to limit the object of Indonesian history between 1511 and 1910 to the present

[19] *Corpus Diplomaticum Neerlando Indicum I* (1907), Treaty XIV and XV, pp. 31–34.

[20] Resink, "Onafhankelijke vorsten."

[21] *Corpus Diplomaticum Neerlando Indicum III* (1934), Treaty CDLXXXIII, pp. 336 ff.

[22] See the entry "Grondgebied" in *Encyclopaedie van Nederlandsch Indië*, vol. I (1917). See also, regarding the role of the British in the formation of the Netherlands Indies, Nicholas Tarling, "The Relation between British Policies and the Extent of Dutch Power in the Malay Archipelago, 1784–1871," *Australian Journal of Politics and History*, IV, no. 2 (Nov., 1958), 179 ff.

territory of the Republic of Indonesia, or to the territory controlled by the Netherlands Indies only, especially since the extent of authority of the Netherlands Indies was a result of international political pressures in the nineteenth and twentieth centuries.

The period before 1511 presents an even more complicated problem. For example, Shrīwijaya could, because of the geographical extension of its influence and power, be regarded as a Southeast Asian kingdom with its power centered in Indonesia. The same could be said of the kingdoms of Majapahit, Malayu, and Malacca and later of Acheh, Ternate, and Riau. The sphere of influence and the extension of the areas controlled by the great Indonesian kingdoms such as Shrīwijaya and Majapahit are not essentially identical with the present territory of the Republic of Indonesia.[23] The territory covered by Indonesian history prior to 1511 was much larger than the present Indonesian Archipelago, and in that territory the Indonesian kingdoms carried on their politics, trade, wars, and all interkingdom relations in an atmosphere and on a level of international relations very similar to the situation between 1511 and 1910.[24]

If indigenous written sources determine the beginning of history, the inscriptions of Kutai (fourth century) form the border line between history and prehistory-protohistory. The period of prehistory-protohistory covers a geographical area much larger than Indonesia. The conclusion may therefore be drawn that the object of Indonesian history, even in its territorial aspects, is not definitely established. We should rather look at this object as a process of concentration, from Southeast Asia to the Netherlands Indies/the Republic of Indonesia. If territorial extension were to be made the object, there would be several areas of history:

1) native Indonesian kingdoms, which one after the other vanish, including those which lost their sovereignty about 1910
2) territories under Portuguese rule, 1511– , gradually coming under Dutch control
3) territories under British rule, up to 1824

[23] The history books on Southeast Asian history are clearer on this point. On Shrīwijaya, see G. Nye Steiger, H. Otley Beyer, and Conrado Benitez, *History of the Orient* (Boston, 1929), ch. ix, "Indian Civilization in Malaysia," pp. 106 ff.; Brian Harrison, *South East Asia: A Short History* (London, 1954), ch. iii, "Early Indianized States," pp. 21 ff., and ch. v, "Indianized States of Sumatra and Java," p. 41; D. G. E. Hall, *A History of South-east Asia* (New York and London, 1955), ch. ii, "The Island Empires," pp. 37 ff.

[24] G. J. Resink, "Eeuwen volkenrecht in Indonesië," *Indonesië*, X (1957), 441–471.

4) the Netherlands Indies, 1605–1910–1945–(1949)
5) the Republic of Indonesia since 1945

By concentrating on their history alone, one might establish the existence of a "History of the Indonesian People(s)," i.e., a history of the Indonesian people from prehistory-protohistory to the present. Such a history would consist of:

1) the history of the Indonesian people in regions and kingdoms which managed to maintain their sovereignty until approximately 1910
2) the history of the Indonesian people in regions and kingdoms which recognized the suzerainty of the British, until 1824, or the Portuguese or the Dutch, until approximately 1910
3) the history of the Indonesia people as a whole in the period of the Netherlands Indies
4) the history of the Indonesian people after 1945

In addition, it would be quite impossible to ignore the existence of territories and kingdoms under Portuguese (from 1511), British (until 1824), and Dutch power until the present. Colonial history is the history of foreign nations in Indonesia, viewed and presented according to the understanding and the interests of those foreign nations. The history of the Dutch has been written up thoroughly, and efforts at improvement are constantly being made. Although English and Portuguese sources have not been investigated and studied as thoroughly as they should have been, the history of the Portuguese in Indonesia and that of the British in our archipelago can be learned from works by various historians.

Meanwhile, for our present purpose, it is sufficient to establish the existence of a history of the Indonesian people and of a colonial history. We can also draw the conclusion that besides the "History of the Indonesian People" there exists a "History of Indonesia" which is a synthesis of the former and of colonial history.[25]

Colonial history is generally regarded with pride by those peoples

[25] W. Ph. Coolhaas, "Van koloniale geschiedenis en geschiedenis van Indonesië van historici en taalambtenaren," *Jubileum Koninklijk Instituut, 1851–1951* ('s Gravenhage, 1951), p. 155. This discusses in a rather cursory fashion the possibility of a synthesis between colonial history and history of Indonesia. See also C. C. Berg, "De evolutie der Javaanse geschiedschrijving," *MKAWAL*, new ser., XIV, no. 2 (1951), 121–146, and "Javaansche geschiedschrijving," in F. W. Stapel, ed., *Geschiedenis van Nederlandsch-Indië* (Amsterdam, 1938–1940), II, 5–148; H. J. de Graaf, "Nederlandsch-Indische historiographie," *Koloniaal Tijdschrift*, XXIX (1940), 548 ff.; G. W. J. Drewes, "Over werkelijke en vermeende geschiedschrijving in de Nieuw Javaansche literatuur," *Djawa*, XIX (1939), 244–256.

who at one time or another have been colonizers. Information about it is available in a great variety of forms, and it is therefore open to study. Is that also the case with the history of the Indonesian people? Basically there does not yet exist a fixed structure of the history of the Indonesian people. What is usually called the written history of the Indonesian people is in reality a number of ethnic-regional narratives which are already known or which still have to be studied: *babads, sĕjarahs, kisahs, salsilahs, riwayats,* etc. Colonial history can be an invaluable complement to these regional histories, as it gives a picture of inter-regional political relations, diplomacy, trade, etc., and also a picture of relations between the Indonesian kingdoms and foreign nations.[26] It is these international relations which often reflect the role and prestige of a particular region in history. In addition, the history of areas under colonial rule can be found in the colonial histories.

A comparison between the history of the Indonesian people and colonial history shows this difference between the two, viz., that neither in form nor in content does the history of the Indonesian people constitute a unity; moreover, it is incomplete. On the other hand, Portuguese, English, and Dutch colonial history are all the histories of nations in a particular time period. If there were a complete history of the Indonesian people and also a colonial history, how could these two histories be used to achieve the synthesis which we have termed Indonesian history?

The fundamental historiographical problem is, then, to find the meeting point between the many local histories of the Indonesian people and colonial history and so determine how to unite the two. What criteria are to be used in order to write one single narrative out of so many histories? Is it possible to blend a history of Indonesia which is Indonesian in character (Indonesia-centric) out of local histories which are regio-centric or ethnocentric and out of colonial histories which are to us essentially xenocentric [27] in character? The synthesis of these

[26] That scientific research into the sources can produce new facts and insights, opening up an entirely new historical world for us, is demonstrated by the studies of J. C. van Leur, *Indonesian Trade and Society* (The Hague, 1955); B. J. O. Schrieke, *Indonesian Sociological Studies*, pt. I, *Selected Writings* (The Hague, 1955), pt. II, *Ruler and Realm in Early Java* (The Hague, 1957); J. Bastin, *Raffles' Ideas on the Land Rent System in Java* (The Hague, 1954), and *The Native Policies of Sir Stamford Raffles in Java and Sumatra* (Oxford, 1957). In a more popular vein, see also Sapija, *Sedjarah Perdjuangan Pattimura* (Jakarta, 1957); Katoppo, *Nuku: Riwajat Hidup seorang Sultan Tidore* (Bandung, 1957).

[27] Regarding the use of this term see G. J. Resink, "Iets over Europacentrische, regiocentrische en indocentrische geschiedschrijving," *Orientatie*, XXXVII (Oct., 1950), 22.

strands into a general "Indonesian History," meeting rigid scientific standards, will be the test by which the quality of historical writing in Indonesia will be judged. Such a general history will have to strike a delicate balance between historical imagination and factual historical data. It will have to do justice to the ethnic-regional elements, as well as to the foreign components, in its exposition of the different possibilities of historical vision for the Indonesian people.[28] The task of the study of history therefore is, among others, to formulate the possibilities of synthesis, based on the precepts of theory and on a philosophy of history, as well as on as many data as possible both assembled from the numerous but still unstudied sources and derived from the reevaluation of already available data.[29]

III

A basic condition for the writing of Indonesian history is an Indonesian outlook and also the availability of facts resulting from scientific research. At the same time it should be said that these very facts tend

[28] G. J. Resink, "Over ons gemeenschappelijk verleden in het recht van vrede," *Gedenkboek rechtswetenschappelijk hoger onderwijs in Indonesië, 1924–1949* (Groningen and Jakarta, 1949), p. 256; G. W. Locher, "Inleidende beschouwingen over de ontmoeting van Oost en West in Indonesië," *Indonesië*, II (1948–1949), 411. It is important to note in this connection Resink's statement in "Iets over Europacentrische," p. 30, which deals with the essential conditions for the development of Indonesian historiography; see also his "Tussen de mythen." No less important are some ideas regarding the value of regional history and the relationship between regional history and Indonesian history in van der Kroef, "On the Writing of Indonesian History," p. 371; Boejoeng Saleh, "De mythe als opium en zelfkennis als zweep," *Indonesië*, IX (1956), 449–452.

[29] The Archaeological Service, the Indonesian Cultural Institute (Lembaga Kebudajaan Indonesia), and some museums abroad are the "custodians" of an exceptionally large number of ancient Indonesian historical sources, the largest part of which has never been studied; the National Archives and the archives of several ministries in Indonesia, as well as archives in some European countries and in America, hold a large number of Indonesian historical sources, dating from the period after 1600, which for the greater part have not yet been sorted out or studied. As has already been stated (see note 12), responsible research, both in terms of theory as well as in terms of methodology, has not been given enough attention, with the result that to a large extent history has been "studied" only as something to be learned by rote, as a chain of extraordinary events, as prophesies, or as fantasies. A representative example of this type of "history" is R. Tanojo, *Sedjarah Pangeran Dipanagara* (History of Dipanagara; Surabaya, year of publication unknown but most likely around the beginning of 1959). This book elaborates on Dipanagara's alleged ancestry which he connects up with Bra Wijaya-Majapahit; he also reports that Dipanagara (± 1820) received a message from Sunan Kalijaga (± 1500) and that Dipanagara was visited by Nyai Ratu Lara Kidul, the mythical Queen of the South Sea.

to dissuade people from writing on history or from expressing their views about history. What about the facts of the history of the Indonesian people and of colonial history? [30]

As is already known, the main effort of historical research should be in the regional-ethnical histories and in colonial history, two very different fields of scientific endeavor. This difference, as was clearly stated by van Leur among others, led to two kinds of historical vision.[31]

De Casparis, in his study of twenty years of historical research,[32] pointed to the works of various scholars of different nationalities and in different fields. It may well be that because of this great variety the necessary scientific discipline was not always applied to the methods of research, a requirement stated in somewhat exaggerated form by van Leur.[33]

In the light of these opinions as expressed by de Casparis and van Leur, it becomes necessary to consider the question of scientific discipline in the specific field of research into the history of the Indonesian people. This history has been approached from a great variety of disciplines—prehistory, archaeology, Islamology, philology, theology—but rarely do we encounter studies by historians. With no attempt to do injustice to the significance of their work, it might be said that, generally speaking, the study of the history of the Indonesian people is dominated by people who are not professional historians, and therefore from the historian's point of view this field has not yet been studied and investigated in such a way as to make all the required facts available.[34]

For this reason students of history in Indonesia have a wide scope for cooperation with experts from many other disciplines in the field of Indonesian history. Each type of cooperation will have to evolve the methods peculiar to its own problems. In the training of Indonesian historians, the necessity of interdisciplinary cooperation will have to be taken into consideration.

It may be something of an exaggeration to say that with regard to

[30] Colenbrander, *Koloniale geschiedenis*, vols. II and III, differentiates colonial history and local or regional history. The latter, however, is generally also part of colonial history. The history books of the Netherlands Indies mostly contain colonial history and the history of the Indonesians, viewed from a Dutch angle.

[31] Van Leur, *Indonesian Trade and Society*, p. 261.

[32] J. G. de Casparis, "Twintig jaar studie van de oudere geschiedenis van Indonesië," *Orientatie*, XLVI (Jan., 1954), 626–665.

[33] Van Leur, *Indonesian Trade and Society*, p. 153; de Casparis, "Twintig jaar studie," p. 661, bibliography of ancient historiography.

[34] Van Leur, *Indonesian Trade and Society*, p. 153.

these problems Berg has been one of the important pioneers in *establishing* an interdisciplinary approach. Although he is not entirely free of a philologist's bias, it must be noted that his studies are based on the clear recognition that a nation's culture forms one single totality—that historiography cannot be separated from the culture which gave birth to it.[35] Because of its inclusiveness and especially because of its incomparable use of literary evidence, the Berg method stands out sharply. About his method Berg says: "There is comparatively little scientific need for knowledge of Javanese *history;* however, a study of the process and of the results of Javanese historiography opens insights which may be also useful outside of Java: it helps determine the yardstick without which the value of our own culture would not be definable." [36] This statement becomes clearer if compared with a previous statement:

To the question of whether the following observations are also valid for the historiography of other Indonesian peoples, I dare not reply in the affirmative. It is not *a priori* inconceivable . . . so that the possibility of a common basis and of a parallel development does not seem to be out of the question. Nor does it seem to be out of the question, however, that historiography outside Java has its own characteristics. [Further] . . . in order to deal with the historiography of any other Indonesian people, we should look for the man who has made a special effort to familiarize himself with the culture of that people.[37]

Essentially Berg succeeded in finding an approach, or rather a method of research, regarding the use of historical sources—regional-ethnical chronicles—which had previously been regarded as mere tales. Archaeology, which had originally monopolized the study of ancient historical sources, got stiff competition after Berg, with his method, discovered the key to Javanese histories. This method proved to be useful also for other regions, as was demonstrated by Proposition I of Noorduyn's thesis: "For a description of the history of Southwest

---

[35] C. C. Berg, "De Saḍeng-oorlog en de mythe van Groot-Majapahit," *Indonesië,* V (1951–1952), 422. Important as a comparison are the following results of the use of specific research methods: J. G. de Casparis, *Prasasti Indonesia I: Inscripties uit de Çailendratijd* (Bandung, 1950), regarding the Borobudur and its role in history; J. L. Moens, "Hindoe-Javaansche portretbeelden: Çaiwapratista en Boddhapratista," *TBG,* LVIII (1919), 493–527; J. L. Moens, "Tjandi Mendoet," *TBG,* LIX (1921), 529–600; J. L. Moens, "Wisnuwarddhana," *TBG,* LXXXV (1955), 365–436. See also P. H. Pott, *Yoga en Yantra* (Leyden, 1946). This book opens new perspectives for our understanding of ancient Indonesian history.
[36] Berg, "De evolutie der Javaanse geschiedschrijving," p. 22.
[37] Berg, "Javaansche geschiedschrijving," p. 10.

Celebes, a philological and critical historical study of the products of
Macassarese and Buginese historiography is indispensable." [38]

Berg's conclusions created a revolution in the views on ancient
history. If Indonesian historiography is influenced by them, it may
liberate the Indonesian people from the domination of "facts" established by other than historical methods in the modern sense.[39] With his
theory new methods can be developed to study regional-ethnical historical sources. By employing certain methods of investigation and
by comparing them with colonial sources, these regional-ethnical
chronicles can be used for Indonesian historiography.[40] The studies by
Poerbatjaraka and de Casparis, using archaeological materials, and
by de Graaf, using *babads,* colonial sources, etc., demonstrate that the
possibilities of improving old concepts always exist.[41]

The above exposition is meant only to open some possibilities in the
field of the "History of the Indonesian People." The conclusion can be

[38] J. Noorduyn, *Een achttiende-eeuwse kroniek van Wadjo'* (The Hague, 1955),
Stellingen (Proposition) I, p. 6. Notable as an attempt toward the development of
a specific method is the work of H. J. H. Alers in *Dilemma in Zuid-Oost Azië*
(Leyden, 1955), pp. 167 ff. It portrays an "impressionistic history" from an Asia-
centric viewpoint. In *Om een rode of groene merdeka* (Eindhoven, 1956), he offers
a "congenial method" in the following words: "There are attempts to describe
problems concerning man as a group on a congenial basis. On this basis social,
cultural, and religious systems are described from the inside. The investigator tries
to put himself in the place of a member of the group system to be described" (p.
8, my translation).

[39] Regarding this revolution, cf. G. J. Resink, "Uit het stof van een beeldenstorm,"
Indonesië, IX (1956), 433–448; van der Kroef, "On the Writing," p. 353; de
Casparis, "Twintig jaar studie," pp. 637–641.

[40] H. Djajadiningrat, *Critische beschouwingen over de Sĕjarah Bantĕn* (Haarlem,
1913).

[41] R. Ng. Poerbatjaraka, *Riwajat Indonesia,* vol. I (Jakarta, 1952); de Casparis,
Prasasti Indonesia, vol. I; H. J. de Graaf, *De regering van Panembahan Senapati
Ingalaga* (The Hague, 1954), and *De regering van Sultan Agung, vorst van Mataram
1613–1645 en die van zijn voorganger Panembahan Seda-Ing-Krapjak 1601–1613*
(The Hague, 1958). R. Soekmono's study regarding the location of Shrīwijaya opens
the prospect that geography will become an important factor in the establishment of
historical facts: "Tentang lokalisasi Çriwijaya," *Indonesian Abstracts,* I, no. 3
(April, 1959), 90. Cf. J. L. Moens, "Çrivijaya, Yava en Kataha," *TBG,* LXXVII
(1937), 317–487.

Another possibility is envisaged by Slametmuljana, who attempts to prove that
Prapanca is not a court poet, in *Bahasa dan Budaja,* vol. II (Dec., 1952); it was
followed by a translation of the *Nāgarakĕrtāgama* by Slametmuljana in Indonesian
(Jakarta, 1953). Since this article was written, Th. Pigeaud's translation into English of the *Nāgarakĕrtāgama* and other contemporary writings has been published
as *Java in the Fourteenth Century* (The Hague, 1960).

drawn that the accepted views in the field of ancient history, as propounded by Krom and others, have now been shaken by the work of experts such as Poerbatjaraka, Berg, and de Casparis and also that, by using specific methods of investigation, regional-ethnical histories now become accessible.

The history of the Indonesian people in the colonies and during colonial rule over the whole of Indonesia has not yet been written in its entirety and must be compiled from the sources of colonial history. An attempt has been made to do so by de Graaf, who arranged the history of Indonesia and colonial history as follows:

I. The Indonesians and Southeast Asia
   (to 1650)

II. The Westerners in Indonesia
   (1511–1800)

III. The Indonesians during the East India Company
   (1600–1800)

IV. The East India Company outside Indonesia

V. The Indonesians in the Netherlands East Indies
   (from 1800) [42]

De Graaf described the History of the Indonesian People under the administration of the East India Company as though the whole of Indonesia were already under its rule—in spite of the fact that van Leur's thesis had proved that the power of the East India Company did not extend over such a wide area. However, as van Leur's thesis challenged some fundamental assumptions of colonial historians, it was largely ignored.[43] Therefore in studying the History of the Indonesian People in colonial territories, one should fully realize which territories were involved and what was the nature of that foreign control.

Resink's findings,[44] coupled with van Leur's theories, do serve to change the scope of the History of the Indonesian People as well as of colonial history until 1910. This change is significant in connection with the evaluation of the Dutch colonial period, as well as of regional

[42] De Graaf, *Geschiedenis van Indonesië.*   [43] See note 39.
[44] Resink, "Uit het stof van een beeldenstorm," p. 441.

history, both separately and as elements of Indonesian history, but it has completely been neglected by de Graaf and by most writers of Indonesian history.

However, more important than these changes as such, is the way in which they came about. Both van Leur and Resink used specific methods based on specific standards in their research and study of colonial history. In this way a broader and deeper understanding was achieved of both colonization and the colonized. It is clear that the way they treated regional-ethnical histories is quite different from the way in which colonial history has been investigated. Considering that van Leur, Resink, and some others made use only of a small part of all the available sources, one can imagine how great the result would be if more experts were to study the other sources with the use of methods derived from particular social sciences.[45] The History of the Indonesian People would then show a great variety of ways of life in the small and large kingdoms, side by side with the "trading state" of the East India Company, and later the state of the Netherlands Indies.

When finally these kingdoms are incorporated into the Netherlands Indies by way of the "Short Declaration," the History of the Indonesian People turns into the history of a colonized people suffering from the same fate and misery. This stage differs from the previous period, because it is in the later period of the Netherlands Indies' colonization that are found the seeds of a nation state.[46] The History of the Indonesian People in this phase is awaiting further study, as most sources have been studied only in the interest of colonial history. That methodical research is bound to bring out valuable historical material is demonstrated by the works of foreign experts like Pluvier, Kahin, and Wertheim.[47]

Meanwhile colonial history does not give rise to any special difficulties. The materials are readily available, although with a colonial bias, resulting from a xenocentric outlook. Would it be possible for us

[45] Cf. note 16. Van Leur utilizes the sociological categories of Max Weber; Resink is an international jurist; W. F. Wertheim wrote *Herrijzend Azië* (Arnhem, 1950) and *Indonesian Society in Transition* (The Hague, 1956) as an expert in Indonesian sociology.

[46] The political transition from "Contract" to "Korte verklaring" to "the Netherlands Indies" was dealt with by J. M. Somer in his doctoral dissertation, "De korte verklaring" (Utrecht, 1934). Regarding the formation of the nation-state (*état-nation*), see Resink, "Over ons gemeenschappelijk verleden," pp. 256 ff.

[47] J. M. Pluvier, *Overzicht van de ontwikkeling der nationalistische beweging in Indonesië* (The Hague, 1953); George McT. Kahin, *Nationalism and Revolution in Indonesia* (Ithaca, N.Y., 1952); Wertheim, *Indonesian Society in Transition*.

to write this history anew with an Indonesian perspective? [48] To do so would require completing the collection of source material of colonial history already published, as well as the publication of other important sources. In this case it would be good for us to get over our reluctance to publish the Dutch, English, or Portuguese sources in their original languages, since through such publication we would open up larger opportunities for research both at home and abroad.[49]

This review of the historical field in Indonesia points out that the History of the Indonesian People with its varied wealth is very incompletely known. This is not the case with colonial history, which has already been written and which, usually but not always, is presented with pride by the colonialists. The conclusion might then be drawn that the task of the historian in Indonesia is to develop methods of research appropriate to the type of historical sources and to improve the collection, preservation, and, wherever possible, the publication of such sources. At the same time, it is important that a bibliography as complete as possible of the History of the Indonesian People be compiled.[50]

---

[48] Attempts toward a Marxist historiography are, among others, S. J. Rutgers and A. Guber, *Indonesië*, vols. I (Amsterdam, 1937) and II (Amsterdam, 1947); D. N. Aidit, *Indonesian Society and the Indonesian Revolution* (Jakarta, 1958). Both are rather too free in using facts to suit their purpose. Outside Indonesia, Indians especially have attempted a new look at colonial history: K. M. Panikkar, *Asia and Western Dominance* (London, 1955); Ramkrishna Mukherjee, *The Rise and Fall of the East India Company* (Berlin, 1958). Tan Malaka presented his rather original views on Indonesian history in *Massa-actie* (Singapore, 1927; reissued, Jakarta, 1947), pp. 7–13; *Pandangan Hidup* (Jakarta, 1952), pp. 83–91; *Madilog* (Jakarta, 1951), pp. 403–404.

[49] The most important Dutch sources already published are J. K. J. de Jonge and M. L. van Deventer, eds., *De opkomst van het Nederlandsch gezag in Oost-Indië: Verzameling van onuitgegeven stukken uit het Oud-Koloniaal Archief* in 13 vols. plus 2 vols. of supplement and 1 vol. of index (Amsterdam and The Hague, 1862–1909), and J. E. Heeres and F. W. Stapel, eds., *Corpus Diplomaticum Neerlando-Indicum* in 6 vols. appearing in series of the *BKI* from 1907 to 1955. Portuguese sources are not available in Indonesia; the well-known English translation of Tomé Pires' *Suma Oriental* is very important for the period around 1500 (A. Cortesão, ed. and trans., *The Suma Oriental of Tomé Pires* [2 vols.; London, 1944]). The English sources stored in the National Archives cover especially the period of 1811–1818 and have not been published; see J. A. van der Chijs, *Inventaris van 's Landsarchief te Batavia* (1882), pp. 96–99. That a study of English sources outside is bound to produce new facts and new insights into the British colonization of Indonesia is shown by Bastin in *Raffles' Ideas on the Land Rent System* and *The Native Policies of Sir Stamford Raffles*.

[50] There is as yet no bibliography dealing specifically with Indonesian history. Important in this connection are, among others, *Koninklijk Bataviaasch Genootschap van Kunsten en Wetenschappen. Catalogus der bibliotheek* (F. Geschiedenis),

IV

It would seem that by breaking it down into its component parts—historical vision, research, and its method—historiography itself ceases to be a problem. However, this is not the case. On the contrary, the problem is now even more acute, at least if one looks a little further. In 1913, after comparing Javanese historiography with medieval European historiography, Djajadiningrat concluded his doctoral thesis by stating: "Their Javanese colleagues completely lacked the critical faculty. The meaning of historical research was alien to them."

He said further that one's attitude toward Javanese historiography should be "none other than what one has to take when observing any phenomenon which is foreign to one's own spiritual and emotional life and which is indicated by the words: non ridere, non lugere, neque detestari, sed intelligere." [51] It is no coincidence that in 1955 Berg writes:

The historiographical pattern is a thought structure imposed upon primary reality. The very deviation from primary reality, which we outsiders observe when studying, for instance, Javanese historiography, makes it possible that historiography is not rooted in a felt need to describe that reality. This need is surely not a characteristic of Homo sapiens, and should rather be regarded as a recent local product of an evolution which was characterized in its earlier stages by its lack of capacity for objectivity; just as in the evolution of language nonsense is indispensable for the production of sense, it seems that in historiography the myth is a necessary preliminary stage to the objective description of the real events.[52]

Essentially both opinions state that the fundamental difference between Indonesian [53] and European historiography lies in the *purpose and function* of historiography. If our historians are not familiar with historical research, it is because they do not feel the need for it, because to them the historical vision, the outlook on historical development, is more important than the mere facts. Now we can understand the significance of the condition put forward by O. Notohamidjojo—that an aspiring historian should abandon the magical way of thinking and its mythology and place himself firmly within historical reality. This

comp. by A. J. Bernet Kempers (1940), pp. 253–332. De Casparis, "Twintig jaar studie," pp. 658–664, gives a short bibliography (see note 33).

[51] Djajadiningrat, *Critische beschouwingen,* pp. 310–311.

[52] Berg, "De evolutie der Javaanse geschiedschrijving," pp. 21–22.

[53] In this case no difference is made between Javanese historiography and the historiography of other regions (see notes 36, 37, 38).

philosophical problem does not mean only the shift of one's attention from the world of magic to the world of history; it means a complete psychological change. Historical research, historiography which attempts "objective description of reality as it occurs," is possible only when one needs and respects objective description as an essential condition for his way of life. Resink's warning that the vision should not dominate the facts seems to indicate that in his opinion this change has already completely taken place. This can also be inferred from his statement:

A language of one's own, a cultural environment of one's own, an indocentric perspective of the future and a corresponding vision of the past, the reinterpretation of old facts—*but not yet the discovery of new facts*—are some of the phenomena accompanying, and sometimes pushing too far, the transformation from an outlandish colonial history into an inlandish national one.[54]

Locher expresses his concern that the

heavier struggle the East has to face in order to break through to a world perspective, and *not to fall* back to a limited ethnocentric way of thinking in which all events revolve around one's own people, confers on Western Europe, preeminently trained in historical thinking, the very special task to be the bearer of the world historical view.[55]

He is referring to a way of thinking which has not yet abandoned its *cosmocentric* character and which is not prepared to accept the realities of the world around it.[56]

Therefore the problem to be considered is the problem of the experience of time in general and especially of the experience of historical time.[57] The root of the difference between Indonesian historiography

[54] Resink, "Passe-partout," p. 374 (our italics); cf. note 14. For these reasons the term *re*-construction is not entirely correct, nor is the term *re*-writing.

[55] Locher, "Inleidende beschouwingen," p. 555.

[56] Nicolas Berdyaev, *The Beginning and the End* (New York, 1952), p. 198: "No philosophy of history could arise among the Greeks on account of their cosmocentric way of looking at the world." Mircea Eliade, in *The Myth of the Eternal Return* (New York, 1955), describes the conflict between the historical outlook on life and the ahistorical, from the viewpoint of those who are caught in between these two outlooks.

[57] The problem of history is essentially a problem of time consciousness. History is possible only in an outlook on life which links human life to the absoluteness of historical time. This time problem *(Zeitlichkeit)* has been impressively stated by M. Heidegger in *Sein und Zeit* (Halle, 1949), I, 372–404. Although possibly difficult to accept at first reading, it constitutes an important basis for our (i.e., for the Indonesians') sense of time in our efforts to leave the ahistorical world, because Heidegger's vision gives the impression of being in accord with the ahis-

and Western historiography is not unlike the issue stated in the following quotation:

The Greeks and the Hebrews lived in different times, not *at* a different time, but in a different kind of time. The view which sees the world as a cosmos is cosmocentric. That which regards the world as history is anthropocentric. The point at issue is this: must man be interpreted in terms of the cosmos or the cosmos in terms of man? Is human history a subordinate part of the cosmic process or is the cosmic process a subordinate part of human history? [58]

Against this background it becomes clear that the problem of history is the problem of man. It concerns the collective concept of the Indonesian people in reply to the question: "What is man?" At one time Tan Malaka gave his reply in a revolutionary vein:

You, 55,000,000 people of Indonesia, you will not possibly become independent, as long as you have not thrown all the "dirt" of magic out of your heads, as long as you still hold to the ancient culture which is full of fallacies, resignation, and fossilized notions, and as long as you still have a slave mentality. You must unite all economic and social forces available to fight Western imperialism, which is well organized, but which is now in trouble; use as your weapon the revolutionary proletarian spirit, viz., *dialectical materialism*. You should not accept second place from the Westerners in the field of analytical thinking. Admit in all honesty that you will and must learn from the Westerners. . . . Only when your society has produced men who are better than a Darwin, a Newton, Marx, or Lenin, only then can you be proud.[59]

It was because he wanted to put his imprint on the process of mental change in his people that Tan Malaka wrote *Madilog* as the basic ex-

torical view; e.g., "Das eigentliche Sein zum Tode, d.h. die Endlichkeit der Zeitlichkeit, ist der verborgene Grund der Geschichtlichkeit des Daseins" (p. 386). Heidegger's "Problematik" as discussed by K. H. Roessingh in his dissertation "De godsdienstwijsgerige problematiek in het denken van Martin Heidegger" (Assen, 1956) is valuable for our attempts to comprehend the ahistorical world view. An attempt to deal with the problems connected with the synthesis between both systems of thought in Asia is to be found in L. Abegg, *The Mind of East Asia* (London and New York, 1952), pp. 329 ff. Sir Mohammad Iqbal gives a personalistic interpretation of Islam, in which, starting from serial Time, he transcends it, thus entering Absolute or Divine Time: *Asrar-i-khudi* (Lahore, 1950), pp. 80 ff., and *The Reconstruction of Religious Thought in Islam* (London, 1930), pp. 110 ff. Regarding this time problem cf. M. Meyer, "Tijd en werkelijkheid" in *Aspecten van de tijd* (Assen, 1950), pp. 95 ff.

[58] Berdyaev, *The Beginning*, p. 197.   [59] Tan Malaka, *Massa-actie*, pp. 69–70.

position of his philosophy, which he also formulated in a booklet *Pandangan Hidup* (Way of Life). What Tan Malaka offered was *Materialism-Dialectics-Logic* or dialectic materialism as an outlook on life, so that Indonesian man could free himself from a cosmocentric world. The process of mental revolution from a cosmocentric world to the world of *Madilog* is taking vast strides in the People's Republic of China, North Korea, North Vietnam, Eastern Europe, etc., and it moves, voluntarily as well as forcibly, those peoples from the natural world into the world of man.[60]

This process is important for a nation as it completely changes its way of life and its culture. This problem emerges clearly from Tjan Tjoe Som's statement about Chinese historiography that "history of this kind is different from the history which is demanded by the modern Western world. Such a history cannot now be written, because the pattern on which it always relied has been radically destroyed. It is not only the pattern of history that has been destroyed, it is the whole pattern of life." So if historiography develops from the main body of a culture, then can a pattern of life which has already broken up produce a historiography? That is why it is emphasized that "one facet of the problem of the meeting of East and West is how to furnish a new pattern of life for the one that has been destroyed." [61]

In principle the writing of Indonesian history cannot be regarded as a work of reediting old stories. In order to become a scientific discipline,

---

[60] Tan Malaka's purpose is clear from his introduction to *Madilog*: "They [i.e., the industrial and rural proletariat in Indonesia] lack a Weltanschauung. They lack a philosophy. They are still swathed in doctrines for the hereafter and confused superstitions. However, there already is a philosophy for the proletariat, in the West. But we will not have any satisfactory result merely by translating all the books on dialectical materialism and showing them to the Indonesian proletarian. I do not think that the brains of the industrial proletariat of Indonesia could absorb this concept which is rooted and developed in Western society which differs from the Indonesian in climate, history, psychology, and ideals. At least in the beginning the Indonesian proletarian should have at his disposal literature which still has some relationship to his present ideas. This type of literature could then later on *become the bridge to Western proletarian philosophy*" (*Madilog*, p. 13). "With Madilog I mean in the first place a *way of thinking*. Not a Weltanschauung, not an outlook on the world, although way of thinking and outlook on the world or philosophy stand close together, like the ladder and the house. From the way he thinks we can get an idea of his philosophy, and from his philosophy we can find out how, by which method he came to that philosophy" (*Madilog*, p. 22). Cf. B. M. Schuurman, *Mystik und Glaube in Zusammenhang mit der Mission auf Java* (The Hague, 1933), pp. 122, 125.

[61] Tjan Tjoe Som, "The Meeting of East and West: The Oriental View," in *Eastern and Western World: Selected Readings* (The Hague, 1953), p. 21.

historiography has to develop from the living body of a living society. Therefore the writing of Indonesian history cannot be separated from the efforts to achieve a new culture suitable to life in the modern world. The history to be written is the history which attempts to describe the life of our people in accordance with the criteria of scientific truth.

The science of history with its standards is an essential part of the world of man which produced it. Does therefore the problem of historiography become a vicious circle? To break this circle is to break with the inevitability of fate.

It means we should choose from among the offers of the outside world those which are suitable to our individuality, but it also means that, once we have chosen, we should not lose ourselves in that which we have chosen.[62] This, in my opinion, is the road the scientific centers, universities, institutes, etc., of Indonesia should take for the preparation of scholars with an adequate command of the techniques of science as their tool and with a strong consciousness of the meaning of history and of man's significance in it.[63]

[62] Resink, "Iets over Europacentrische," p. 30; cf. note 13.
[63] D. P. Mukerji's *On Indian History* (Bombay, 1945) attempts to solve the problem of rewriting Indian history. "Our historians must have a *philosophy*. If that word stinks, they should have a *method*, a *critique*. Otherwise they had better remain professors of History" (p. 102). Essentially he looks at historiography as a technique, a tool of history as a science. In doing so he places history outside of men's life, and maintains the cosmocentric character of his outlook. For other discussions of the problem of history see Heidegger in *Sein und Zeit*, pp. 392–393, and R. F. Beerling, "Essentials of History," *Weerklank op het werk van Jan Romein* (Amsterdam, 1953), p. 33.

II

Preseventeenth-Century
Indonesian History: *Sources and Directions*

By L. CH. DAMAIS

*Professor, Ecole Pratique des Hautes Etudes, Paris,
and Ecole Française d'Extrême-Orient, Jakarta*

I would like to give, in the following pages, a brief outline of what I think would be the best approach, in our time, to further the study of Indonesian history.

To this end, I shall try to point out in which direction the few of us who are dedicated to this part of world history could or should concentrate our efforts in order to extend and deepen, on a firm basis, our still very imperfect knowledge of the Indonesian past. I must, in fact, add here that what I have in mind concerns, first of all, the period which forms the main object of my research work, i.e., before the arrival of the first Europeans—this means, practically, before the sixteenth century of the Christian Era. It comprises the whole of the Indianized period and the beginning of Moslem influence.

I shall not speak here about prehistory or about the history of art (architecture, iconography, or evolution of decorative elements) which are outside my field of study.

I

What are the original sources for such a study of the history of what is now Indonesia and how can they best be used? Although most of them are already known, it may be useful to recall them here briefly, in order to clarify the argumentation.

We have, first of all, the inscriptions, most of them charters, in

Sanskrit, Old Malay, Old Javanese, Old Balinese, and a few in Old Sundanese. In Sumatra we have also some documents in Indian languages (other than Sanskrit), but they have not yet been studied. These inscriptions are the real basis of our knowledge of the chronological setting and are for the greater part original documents in which we can have absolute confidence. A certain number of these charters are, however, later copies. Most of these copies were written in the Majapahit period, a few centuries after the date of the originals which are lost, save for a few exceptions. Depending on the state of the original at the moment of the copy, the latter merits more or less confidence from a historical point of view. Only a few of such copies seem practically devoid of any value. To put it more cautiously, we have no means of ascertaining the degree of confidence we should give to information found in them because it is not verifiable from other sources.

Next to the documents on stone or copper we have, in Java, Bali, and Sunda, a few texts on palm leaves (*lontar*) which do have a historical, or at least a semihistorical, value, although they are literary in character. First among this class of texts is the well-known *Nāgarakĕrtāgama* that came to us in a unique manuscript and the *Pararaton,* the value of which, historically speaking, is less but which is, nevertheless, an extremely interesting work.

These are the most important internal sources for the period under consideration.

We have, further, the external sources, which consist in the first place of Chinese texts and also of some Indian and Moslem documents.

In the Chinese *Dynastic Histories,* there is a section called the *Imperial Annals (Pen chi),* and in most of these we find a mention of numerous "embassies" sent by foreign countries to the Chinese Court, with a more or less detailed account of the gifts presented, which were considered by the Chinese officials as a "tribute" to the Chinese emperor and recorded as such. They give sometimes also the name of the foreign king at the time of the embassy, or of his son, and, in a few cases, even of the envoys themselves.

Next to the *Imperial Annals,* we find, in nearly all the *Dynastic Histories,* various *Notices (chuan),* dedicated to each country known to the Chinese historiographers. Some of those are rather elaborate and give particulars not always recorded in the *Imperial Annals,* and vice versa.

When the information is dated—this is always the case in the *Pen chi* and sometimes in the *Notices*—one finds often even the day itself of the event, a precision that is in some cases of great value. In other cases, one finds only the reign period *(nien-hao)*, which duration can be anything from a few months to some dozens of years, the majority of them being of course in between.

Encyclopaedias have also chapters on the "South Seas," and a few works are even dedicated to them.

To point out the importance to Indonesia of the Chinese documents, it will be enough to remind the reader that for the period prior to the eighth century the dated information is in the case of Java mostly and in the case of Bali exclusively of Chinese origin.

Moslem works, mainly in Arabic and Persian, are of a nature differing considerably from that of the Chinese texts. They are written by geographers and travelers, who are very often more interested in stories of a marvelous nature than in dry facts, although the latter are not altogether missing. In any case, we have here documents written from an angle quite different from that of the Chinese texts which do add to our knowledge of the countries described.

From India, the most important documents for our point of view are a few inscriptions on copper, respectively from the ninth and the eleventh centuries, which mention Java and Sumatra. We have, on the other hand, a few literary works (in Sanskrit and in Pāli), some of them dating from the beginning of the Christian Era, which show us that a few localities of the archipelago were well known in India at the time.

Scanty but valuable information can be also gained from a few Cambodian, Cham, and Vietnamese documents.

Lastly, we have some Greek sources, the most important of which being the geographer Claudios Ptolemaios, who mentions a few toponyms situated in Indonesia.

II

Now to what degree have the existing sources, briefly described above, been used in the reconstruction of Indonesian history?

There are two collections of Old Javanese charters. One by Cohen Stuart was published with a volume of facsimiles some eighty years ago. The second, much richer, is a posthumous work, published after Brandes' death, without any change by Krom. Although still extremely useful, both are now antiquated, and it is a pity that Brandes' transcriptions, many of which were not ready for the press when he died, are incomplete (even if the fact is not always mentioned), so that a new transcription of a good number of them is—next to that of documents unknown at the time—a prerequisite. Another difficulty is that both volumes give only the original text, without commentary of any kind, index, or translations. Consequently, even by specialists, they can be used only as a preliminary basis to work on, many details having to be carefully verified.

Scattered through various periodicals, we have further the epigraphical studies by Hendrik Kern (later reprinted in his *Verzamelde geschriften*) and, for documents discovered or studied after 1913, various articles, some of them of outstanding importance, chiefly by Vogel, Krom, Stutterheim, Crucq, B. Ch. Chhabra, F. D. K. Bosch, R. Ng. Poerbatjaraka, R. Goris, and J. G. de Casparis. Most of the inscriptions so published have a Dutch (exceptionally an English) translation, with a more or less extensive commentary and notes.

After World War II, a new start was made by Dr. de Casparis with his series *Prasasti Indonesia,* in which we find a transcription, a translation with numerous notes, and philological, historical, and religious commentaries of charters and other epigraphic material unknown or unpublished heretofore.

The *Nāgarakĕrtāgama,* first published in Balinese characters by Brandes in 1902, was translated by Kern in various issues of a Dutch scientific periodical. Late in 1960 there appeared the first three volumes of a five-volume work by Dr. Pigeaud which includes translation and commentaries in English not only of this important text but also of various contemporaneous documents. Thus Kern's first Dutch rendering of the *Nāgarakĕrtāgama* is now completely superseded.

The first edition of the *Pararaton* was published by Brandes in 1896 with a Dutch translation and numerous notes in which he tried to collect all the information known at the time. A second edition was published in 1920 with additional notes by Krom, Jonker, Poerbatjaraka, and G. Ferrand. Both publications are of outstanding quality, but even the second edition should be brought up to date.

An important work in Old Sundanese, the *Carita Parahiyangan,* which unique manuscript is unluckily in rather bad shape (many palm leaves are missing and the order of the existing ones is not easy to determine), was published by Professor Poerbatjaraka some forty years ago, without any translation, however. It still has to be studied.

Some Javanese and Balinese semihistorical texts have been published but, with a few exceptions, without any translation.

Concerning Balinese inscriptions, we had till World War II only two articles, by van der Tuuk and Brandes, dating from the last century. The charters were edited without translation, but the introduction by Brandes to the first Old Balinese texts published was an excellent piece of work for the time. By van Stein Callenfels we have a recueil of newly discovered charters in Old Balinese and Old Javanese, rather poorly edited and without translation or notes. By the same author, there are three lists of Balinese kings, made up in the early twenties from data taken from epigraphic material known to him. Stutterheim's work, *Oudheden van Bali*, has also a few inscriptions of great interest, and further, there are a few studies by Dr. Goris which are of very great value.

Since the war, Dr. Goris has published the first two volumes of his *Prasasti Bali*, which is to be a complete inventory of Balinese inscriptions. For the oldest period we already have in this publication, along with the inventory, a transcription of the oldest documents (up to the middle of the tenth century) with Dutch and English translations, notes, and different indexes.

For the Sumatran epigraphs, there are only a few scattered articles. In fact, no serious attempt has as yet been made to survey the whole field, a certain amount of inscriptions being still unpublished. But we are fortunate in having two luminous papers by Professor Coedès, which are the best studies to date on the first known documents relating to Shrīwijaya. By the same author, there are various historical papers on Indonesia and continental Southeast Asia.

Other historical studies covering part of the field or giving a general view of the problems involved have been published by the scholars already mentioned and also by B. R. Chatterji, Hirananda Shastri, R. C. Majumdar, K. A. Nilakanta Sastri, Hoesein Djajadiningrat, H. G. Quaritch Wales, K. V. Subrahmanya Ayer, Himansu Bhusan Sarkar, etc.

Very few scholars have shown an interest in Sundanese epigraphs. Among those not mentioned above, Pleyte deserves special notice.

Studies of the oldest Moslem tombs in Java have been made by van Ronkel, Ravaisse, Moquette, Verbeek, Krom, and the present writer. For northern Sumatra, where the material is much richer, we have only studies by Moquette. Much remains to be done, as numerous estampages are still undeciphered. A unique Persian inscription, on the tomb of a descendant of the Abbasid caliphs, has been published by Cowan.

Substantial numbers of Chinese texts dealing with the Indonesian Archipelago and the Malay Peninsula were published in English translation by Groeneveldt as early as 1880. This work, however, is marred by a few important errors and unwarranted identifications. Furthermore, the author made no use of the *Imperial Annals,* all the data translated having been taken from the *Notices* and some *Encyclopaedias.*

Somewhat later, we have a French translation of the ethnographical chapters of the *Wen hsien t'ung k'ao* by D'Hervey de Saint-Denis. While not always reliable, it is the only one in existence.

Much better studies were published by Ed. Chavannes and J. Takakusu, including translations (respectively in French and in English) of I Ching's two celebrated works, in which so many important details on Indonesia are to be found.

In 1904, P. Pelliot published his epoch-making contribution *Deux Itinéraires de la Chine en Inde au VIIIᵉ siècle;* in this many identifications made earlier by Groeneveldt, Gerini, and Schlegel were corrected. A few years later appeared an English translation by Hirth and Rockhill of the *Chu fan chih.* Since then, a few contributions on the relations of various countries with the Chinese Court have been published by Pelliot, Duyvendak, etc. Recently, a study on the *Nan-hai* trade by Wang Gungwu, a Chinese scholar, was published in English.

However, several hitherto unpublished Chinese works which have come out in recent years are still awaiting study as far as the "South Seas" are concerned. A case in point is the *Sung hui yao ti kao,* which contains a certain amount of information on Indonesia not available elsewhere. Other works, among them the *Ts'ê fu yuan kui,* are still in manuscript although a detailed index of the chapters on foreign countries has been published in Japan.

Some Arabic texts mentioning Indonesia were published in France more than a hundred years ago. Other data are scattered throughout various Moslem works published in England, the Netherlands, etc. A French translation of all the texts available at the time describing Eastern countries was published by Ferrand in 1913, with some critical notes. The same author wrote a few studies in which he tried to coordinate various materials existing on a given subject. They are very valuable, but many details should be studied in a new light.

A masterpiece is the new edition of the *Akhbār us-Sind wa'l-Hind,* with French translation and extremely valuable commentary by the late Sauvaget, a model of impartial and scholarly treatment of a very important text. Sauvaget's translation of the *Marvels of India,* another work of the same kind, was published posthumously, without notes, so that the old edition (text, French translation, and numerous notes) by van der Lith and M. Devic is still useful. A Russian translation by R. L. Ehrlich (who died in 1930), based on van der Lith's edition of the text, was published in Moscow in 1959, but the notes are insufficient and completely antiquated.

There have also been published several new original texts in Arabic and Persian, some with a translation and excellent notes such as those by Professor Minorsky, some without (e.g., a *Jahān Nāme* of Muh. Ibn Najīb Bakrān by Borshchewsky which appeared in 1960). They should be studied for the information they contain on Indonesia.

From what has been said above, it can easily be seen that much source material is as yet unused, or insufficiently studied, especially from an Indonesian point of view, so that we can expect that a fresh approach to these documents would yield valuable results.

III

Now, what are the reference works with the help of which scholars can study original sources? For texts in Chinese, Arabic, or Persian, there are adequate dictionaries, even if they are not perfect. But for Old Javanese, we have only a lexicon (*Oudjavaansch-Nederlandsch woordenlijst*) compiled by H. H. Juynboll from translations published before 1923. Although very useful, it is inadequate in many respects and should be completely rewritten and brought up to date. This could be done by taking into account not only the editions of various Old Javanese literary texts published during the last decades which have lists of new words, but especially the material furnished by the inscriptions, very poorly represented in Juynboll's work.

The monumental *Kawi-Balineesch-Nederlandsch woordenboek* by van der Tuuk (published after his death) is more a collection of citations than a dictionary and, although of first-rank importance, is not very useful for epigraphic studies.

For Old Balinese, we luckily have now the word list added by Goris to the second volume of his *Prasasti Bali*. It is the only one in existence of its kind but somewhat too concise.

IV

On the historical perspective with which documents have been studied and from which conclusions have been drawn so far, it can be said that too often theories have been proposed which are not warranted by the existing documents. They sometimes cannot be disproved, but neither can they be proved. Consequently, they cannot be considered of great value from a strictly historical point of view. It has, it seems, been too tempting for some scholars to fill in with their imagination the numerous lacunae still existing in the documentation. Or, starting from a preestablished theory, such scholars have taken into account, among the facts known to them, only those which seem to support their theory and have not given serious enough attention to evidence pointing to the contrary, if they have not simply dismissed it.

Cases in point are the theory of the "colonization" of the Indonesian islands (or Southeast Asia as a whole) from India or by Indians, which led to such misleading denominations as "Greater India" in English, "Hindoe-Javaansche kunst" in Dutch, or "Inde Extérieure" in French; or the many suppositions as to the factors causing the shift of political power from central to eastern Java in the tenth century; or those concerning the relationship between Java and Sumatra in the so-called Shailendra period. There are, of course, minor problems as well, such as the reputation attributed without reason to Java as a center of "magical" knowledge and the like.

In certain cases, there is even a tendency, when the sources are rather clear, to prefer without any grounds a tortuous solution to a simple one. Examples of this strange way of reasoning are the localization of the toponym "Jawa" from the Chinese texts (in modern pronunciation Shê-p'o) and the origin of the Javanese era which bears the name of Sanjaya.

There are even more adventurous theories, such as those set forth by Moens in his "Çrīvijaya, Yāva en Kaṭāha" and various other papers, not only on the localization of various toponyms but also on historical events, and also those by Wellan concerning the peoples of South Sumatra. Given the lack of direct access to original sources, one can scarcely reach a well-founded personal opinion on the many debated questions. How, then, is it possible to offer these more or less astounding theories without at least assembling what material is available and checking carefully the various pieces of information it contains?

Professor Berg, in a series of papers, most of them written since the last war, has presented a vision of Javanese history which, although on a much higher level, suffers equally from a much too theoretical approach, the sources used being accepted only if they seem in accordance with his theories but systematically rejected—declared apocryphal and the like—when they are in flagrant contradiction to them. Even if part of his reasoning can apply to the semicolonial and colonial periods, it is a fact that the results he arrives at do come in direct conflict with original documents of the period under consideration, inscriptions as well as the *Nāgarakĕrtāgama*. They have for this reason to be discarded for, if we deny our confidence to original documents and change at will what they tell us, how are we to work without falling into the most arbitrary explanations? Purely subjective speculations have not much in common with historical facts.

I am afraid that the important publications by de Casparis, already mentioned above, although based on a serious and detailed study of original inscriptions, are also subject to this criticism. Along with a great number of hasty generalizations, they show too much of a tendency to try to reconstruct such particulars as the family relations of the royal persons known to us and, more generally, to fill all the gaps so as to explain everything from a given point of view, instead of letting the documents speak for themselves and trying, only after that, to give a more or less probable explanation of the lacunae as well as of the way in which the known facts are interrelated.

This being so, one could ask (as has been done more than once of this writer): Why don't you write a new history of Indonesia? The answer is: The time has not yet come. Krom did the best possible thirty years ago when he published the second edition of his *Hindoe-Javaansch geschiedenis* in 1931. In a broader perspective, George Coedès also did the maximum in his *Les Etats hindouisés d'Indochine et d'Indonésie* published in 1948. Both works are still extremely useful —the first giving more details on Indonesia than the second, which includes other Indianized countries of Southeast Asia.[1] But there remain many original inscriptions still unpublished or insufficiently studied—charters of mpu Sinḍok or Erlangga and of the so-called Dynasty of Kĕḍiri, to cite only a few examples. And at the same time, new documents are being added, as, for instance, the discovery in 1960 by the Archaeological Service of Indonesia of an extremely important inscription of the eighth century. There can be no progress in our knowledge until all the available data have been collected and made available to scholars.

V

The conclusion is, then, that preliminary studies which furnish the basic material, still lacking in practically every field, have to be under-

---

[1] I shall not mention here Professor Hall's *History of South-east Asia* because, as far as I can see, for the period of Indonesian history in which we are interested here it is not the result of direct reference to original sources.

taken, along with the publication of new documents. I would cite among the most important:

1) Publication of photographs of the original documents or of estampages in order to make the inscriptions and some manuscripts available to a larger public than is the case now. This would be in the line of the *Inscriptions du Cambodge* and the *Inscriptions of Burma*.

2) Study of the paleography of the old documents, taking into account the related Indian scripts, to bring up to date Holle's *Tables*, now antiquated and insufficient. Next to the value of such a study in itself, a systematic review of all the paleographic material would make it possible to estimate within narrower limits, i.e., with a greater accuracy than is feasible now, the dates of undated inscriptions, especially the oldest ones of Kalimantan and West Java.

3) Transcriptions, translations, notes, and commentaries in preparation for a corpus of Indonesian inscriptions such as was planned many years ago but was never really started. De Casparis' and Goris' publications after the war are in that line.

4) All kinds of lists, word indexes (toponyms, personal names, titles and personal determinatives, names of animals, of plants, of professions, etc.), and grammatical studies of the language of the inscriptions as contrasted with that of the literary texts, especially for Old Javanese, where the material is much richer.

5) A special study, for the Sanskrit inscriptions, of the words or forms which are not used in Indian (or, to put it more precisely, in "grammatical") Sanskrit or which are used in a sense differing from their usual meaning in India.

6) A similar study of Sanskrit words which have become an integral part of the Javanese, Malay, or Balinese languages. There is already a basis of such studies in Professor Gonda's *Sanskrit in Indonesia*, but someone should dig deeper into the subject.

7) Technical studies on the calendar, the metrology, the administration, and the sociology of Old Javanese and Old Balinese societies, as they are (partly) revealed to us by the inscriptions.

8) For the more modern period, up to World War II, a new study of the Portuguese, English, and Dutch sources (and a few Spanish and French ones) to find out what they have to tell us of Indonesia rather than of the actions of travelers, missionaries, trading companies, and European countries in Indonesia as has been too often the case in the past.

We shall not speak here about the contemporary period for which the problems are quite different and the source material less frag-

mentary. Good studies have already been published by various Indonesian, Dutch, and American scholars.

9) The final task in such a preliminary collecting of the historical
material should be the coordination of all the data from different
origins and in different languages. Only then can we see every detail
in its proper perspective and bring into focus the true implication of
facts perhaps already known to us for a long time but never properly
evaluated.

These are examples of what ought to be done before a History of
Indonesia, pretending to be more than a bare outline of the subject, can
be written, although it will always be possible, in the meantime, to
study a well-defined problem, providing all the precautions are taken
to make sure that, as far as the evidence goes, all aspects are impartially
treated. And if the difficulty is resolved—this need not always be the
case—the result can later be used in a broader context.

It is a fact that the gathering of basic material as described above
demands considerable patience and sometimes rather tedious work, but
it is only on this condition that a less incomplete view of the Old
Javanese or Old Balinese milieus can be obtained. When all this preliminary work, or at least a considerable part of it, is done, there will
remain the essential and in a way the most difficult task—that of a
careful and impartial appraisal, as far as humanly possible, of all the
evidence available, especially in cases where data are insufficient, so
that all facts of a given question may be brought to light; in addition,
it must not be forgotten that a serious and detailed study of all aspects
of a problem, even if the result is not conclusive, can be of greater
importance to the advance of our knowledge of history than a conclusion based on insufficient evidence or on evidence utilized with a
bias.

Then a really new history of Indonesia can be written, giving, it is to
be hoped, a new insight into the forces which have been at work in the
past of one of the most important regions of Southeast Asia.

Before this small *profession de foi* is concluded, it may be added that
this writer has published since 1954, especially in the *Bulletin de
l'Ecole Française d'Extrême-Orient,* various papers on Indonesian
epigraphy and history which are, if he is not too much mistaken, in
accordance with the program outlined above. These studies are of
course only a small fraction of what has to be done, and they will need
numerous additions and corrections. If they are mentioned here, it is
because they may be considered as examples of what this writer has
in mind.

It goes without saying that what could to some readers be considered as criticism of the work done so far is by no means meant in that spirit, as the present writer is the first to recognize and appreciate what has been done by his predecessors. But this contribution, being tuned to the future and not to the past, had naturally to stress the task still lying before us, credit for what has already been achieved being considered as a matter of course.

It is impossible to give here a complete account of all the books and articles that have been published since the above contribution was written. Attention should, however, be drawn to the various publications by authors whose names were not mentioned above, such as Buchari, C. Hooykaas, Mrs. J. H. Hooykaas-van Leeuwen Boomkamp, R. Soekmono, Paul Wheatley, and O. W. Wolters. Dr. J. Noorduyn has undertaken an important study of the Old Sundanese *Carita Parahiyangan* and begun a translation of this remarkable text. A new edition, wholly revised by the author, has appeared of Professor G. Coedès' *Les Etats hindouisés d'Indochine et d'Indonesie,* which incorporates the results of recent research.

III

Archaeology and Indonesian History

By R. SOEKMONO

Head, Archaeological Service, Jakarta, and Lecturer
in Archaeology, Gadjah Mada University, Jogjakarta

ARCHAEOLOGY in Indonesia is in the very first place concerned with ancient history. Although the field of prehistory is not neglected either—in fact, it has from its early beginnings in the 1920's been a separate branch of archaeological investigations—nevertheless it very definitely takes second place. If, therefore, O. G. S. Crawford says of archaeology that "in practice it is concerned more, but not exclusively, with early and prehistoric phases than those illustrated by written documents," [1] for Indonesia this sentence must be amended in the sense that it is more, but not exclusively, concerned with early historic phases.

We observe that in Europe, its birthplace, archaeology has in the course of its development shifted its field of operation from classical archaeology to prehistoric archaeology.[2] Furthermore, in America "Americanist archaeology" has since its inception been a part of cultural anthropology and hence has especially operated in the field of non-literate cultures; consequently it is also more of a prehistoric archaeology.[3]

---

[1] O. G. S. Crawford, *Archaeology in the Field* (London, 1953), p. 15.

[2] Cf. Mortimer Wheeler: "Classical archaeology is here [in England] largely under an eclipse whilst prehistory flourishes as never before" (*Archaeology from the Earth* [London, 1954], p. 206). Regarding the history of archaeology in several European countries, see, e.g., Walter W. Taylor, *A Study of Archaeology* (Memoir of the AAA, no. 69; Menasha, Wis., 1948), especially ch. i, "The Development of Archaeology," with its footnotes on pp. 203–204.

[3] Cf. Taylor, *A Study of Archaeology*, p. 24. Cf. also ch. iii, "An Analysis of Americanist Archaeology in the United States."

The object of archaeology is the remains of past cultures, other than written documents. Now prehistory is distinguished from history in that it does not yield written information. It would therefore be only natural if archaeology were to limit itself to prehistory.

Nevertheless, the period of ancient history also yields a very large number of remains, other than written documents, which are important evidence of the glory of a culture (its architecture), and it is these remains which provide inexhaustible material for archaeology. Therefore, although the recent statement that "archaeology besides archaeology in general means: classical archaeology" [4] is not valid any longer and needs to be revised in the light of this development, the last part of that statement cannot yet merely be replaced by "prehistoric archaeology." [5]

Actually the shift in field which has taken place in several countries in Europe cannot be interpreted as the complete abandonment of the field of ancient or classical history. It is mainly a shift in emphasis, and even this is not a very decided one. Taylor is therefore quite correct in stating that "within the ranks of those who call themselves archaeologists there has been a separation: on the one hand a drift toward cultural anthropology, on the other a persistence in history" [6]: those who incline toward cultural anthropology will favor prehistory, while those who stick to history will mainly concern themselves with ancient or classical history.

In view of the existence of these two schools of thought, there must be valid and decisive reasons for the "persistence in history" in Indonesia. Indonesia's ancient history seems to be a well-ordered structure, but in fact it is still very fragmentary. It still has many blank areas as well as many parts which can be written only with the help of hypotheses. These—being hypotheses—are constantly exposed to the necessity of revision every time a new finding is made contradicting them. At first glance it might be said that Indonesian ancient history has left us with a not inconsiderable number of written documents in

[4] A. J. Bernet Kempers, "Archaeology," *India Antiqua* (Leyden, 1947), p. 17.

[5] We often find that treatises on archaeology concern themselves only with "prehistoric archaeology"; cf., e.g., V. Gordon Childe, *Piecing Together the Past* (London, 1955) and *A Short Introduction to Archaeology* (London, 1956). Grahame Clark, in his book *Archaeology and Society* (London, 1960), p. 22, considers it necessary to give the following explanation: "Although in discussing the nature of archaeological evidence and the methods used to salvage this, I shall not hesitate to draw examples from the archaeology of literate societies, my main theme in this book will be prehistoric archaeology."

[6] Taylor, *A Study of Archaeology*, p. 24.

the form of inscriptions and literary works, but actually these have proved to be inadequate when it comes to writing that history consecutively and completely. The gaps are still too great and too many.[7] On the other hand, ancient Indonesian history has left us a great many buildings, statues, and household and religious utensils which are all unwritten documents. It is the glory and magnificence of these architectural products which testify to Indonesia's greatness during that period.

In the light of this contradictory situation it was therefore not only justifiable, but indeed necessary, that in Indonesia archaeology—as the supplier of the historical materials—more and more concerned itself with the field of ancient history. To borrow Grahame Clark's words: "It is the gaps even more in many cases than the imperfections in the surviving written record that enhance the value of archaeological evidence." [8]

I

As stated before, the written information from Indonesia's ancient history is primarily contained in inscriptions. These documents, being state charters, generally do not relate an occurrence but merely commemorate a particular event.[9] We therefore cannot obtain very much from them in the way of information regarding the historical course of events. The oldest kingdoms in East Borneo and West Java, for instance, have each contributed seven inscriptions—which is a considerable number—but none of them has produced historiographical material. In the absence of additional archaeological material the entire history of these two kingdoms therefore remains shrouded in darkness.

There are one or two inscriptions which do relate a sequence of events, such as the inscription of Erlangga, known as the Calcutta stone (A.D. 1041), and the history of this period is consequently comparatively complete. However, this is an exception; in general, inscriptions alone prove to be not enough.

In our attempts to write ancient Indonesian history despite the insufficiency of material, written information from outside Indonesia has proved very helpful, particularly that obtained from Chinese sources. It was by collating all the written material (inscriptions and Chinese reports) that George Coedès was able to draw the conclusion—and

[7] How great these gaps are can be seen from Buchari's article in Chapter IV of this book.

[8] Clark, *Archaeology*, p. 21.   [9] Krom, *HJG*, pp. 1-3.

subsequently to defend his proposition—that Shrīwijaya was a great kingdom with Palembang as its center.[10]

Regarding the existence of the kingdom of Shrīwijaya [11] and its greatness Coedès has been able to dominate scholarly opinion, but regarding its location many experts have held different views.[12] The fact is that the materials used by Coedès do allow different interpretations, all of them equally convincing. The content of the inscriptions does not sufficiently illuminate the events which have occurred, and, in addition, it is impossible to comprehend their language entirely. This is also true of the Chinese reports. It is in cases like these that one turns to archaeology for additional materials, in the fervent hope that they will reveal data of decisive importance. Where Shrīwijaya is concerned, the little archaeological material which is available clearly cannot support either Coedès' opinion or the views of his opponents.[13]

We have already mentioned that, apart from inscriptions, written information is also available in the form of literary products. The kingdom of Kĕḍiri, during the period from about 1100 to 1200, for instance, produced such a large number of literary works that this period is known as the golden age of literature. Nevertheless, we do not find anything in these writings regarding the historical events which occurred during that period. However important as literature, this written material is therefore of no importance to historiography.

But the *Nāgarakĕrtāgama,* a poem of the Majapahit period, written by Prapanca in 1365, constitutes a different case. With certain reservations this book can be considered a history of the kingdoms of Singasari and Majapahit from the beginning of the thirteenth to the middle of the fourteenth century. By checking its data against that of the *Pararaton,* although the latter is more a tale than history, and other historical evidence such as inscriptions and caṇḍis, it is possible from the

---

[10] G. Coedès, "Le Royaume de Çrīvijaya," *BEFEO,* vol. XVIII (1918), and "A propos d'une nouvelle théorie sur le site de Çrīvijaya," *JRASMB,* XIV, pt. 3 (1936), 1–9.

[11] At first Shrīwijaya was considered to be the name of a king, i.e., by H. Kern; see his "Inscriptie van Kota Kapur," *Verspreide Geschriften,* VII (The Hague, 1913–1929), 205 ff.

[12] For the varying viewpoints, see Nilakanta Sastri, *History of Sri Vijaya* (Madras, 1949), pp. 31–36.

[13] Cf. the author's paper for the ninth Pacific Congress in Bangkok, 1957, "A Contribution to the Location of Çriwijaya's Ancient Capital," an expanded version of which was presented at the First Indonesian National Science Congress in Malang, 1958, "Tentang Lokalisasi Çrīwijaya," *Laporan Kongres Ilmu Pengetahuan Nasional Pertama* (1958), pp. 245–258.

Nāgarakĕrtāgama to reconstruct with some degree of completeness the history of the kingdoms of Singasari and Majapahit. Nevertheless, the reconstruction which was carefully and seemingly solidly built up was recently torn down by C. C. Berg's attempt to give a new interpretation of existing written sources.[14] This attempt at historical reconstruction, however, was not based on new archaeological evidence, and it had therefore no archaeological basis for support. This may account for the violent reaction of the archaeologist F. D. K. Bosch. Bosch compared Berg's theory with an "unstable tower of hypotheses," of which the top reaches into "a rarified atmosphere where historical truth cannot be present but in an homeopathical dilution." [15]

This sharp criticism was countered by Berg in an equally sharp rejoinder: "I wonder whether Bosch, who is an archaeologist, has occupied himself intensively with the study of Old Javanese." [16] The controversy could, of course, go on endlessly, but in the meantime the main problem—the writing of history as truthfully as possible—still remains unsolved. It is true that the writing of history consists to a large extent of interpreting historical materials, but because those materials generally allow more than one interpretation, it is quite possible for one hypothesis to coexist with other hypotheses. We have seen that the location of Shrīwijaya constitutes a similar problem. It is impossible for archaeology to follow, and even less to support, Berg's view, but at the same time it cannot be denied that because of the insufficiency of historical material archaeology has no grounds on which to refute Berg's interpretation with its far-reaching consequences.

II

We have so far pictured archaeology in a rather negative—though albeit still important—role; it is now time to show the positive contribution that archaeology has made and has to make to Indonesian historiography. An interesting example of this is the discovery of the remains of two buildings within the Canḍi Kalasan, near Jogjakarta:

[14] See, in the first place, "De geschiedenis van pril Majapahit," pt. I, *Indonesië*, IV (1950–1951), 481–520; pt. II, *Indonesië*, V (1951–1952), 193–233; "De Saḍengoorlog en de mythe van Groot-Majapahit," *Indonesië*, V (1951–1952), 385–422; and *Herkomst, vorm en functie der Middeljavaanse rijksdelingstheorie, Verhandelingen der Koninklijke Nederlandse Akademie van Wetenschappen, Afd. Letterkunde,* new ser., vol. LIX, no. 1 (Amsterdam, 1953).

[15] F. D. K. Bosch, "C. C. Berg and Ancient Javanese History," *BKI*, CXII (1956), 1–24.

[16] Berg, "Gedachtenwisseling over Javaanse geschiedschrijving," *Indonesië*, IX (1956), 183. My translation.

the present candi, which is still standing, has turned out to be the third building, erected on top of and around the second one, while within the second building the remains are to be found of the first.[17] There are therefore three Candis Kalasan, and the inscription of A.D. 778 which mentions the construction of the candi must refer to the first building.

This archaeological discovery proved to have further consequences when J. G. de Casparis, on the basis of hitherto unknown historical material—inscriptions which had not yet or only partially been published and translated—succeeded in changing the historical picture of Central Java between the middle of the eighth and the middle of the ninth centuries.[18] According to his view Central Java at that time was ruled by two royal dynasties: the Buddhist Shailendra-wangsha in the southern part and the Shiwa-ite Sanjaya-wangsha in the north. This conclusion is in accord with—and provides an explanation for—the fact that in the northern part of Central Java, Shiwa-ite candis are to be found, while in the southern part are scattered Buddhist candis. De Casparis' picture, further, provides a more convincing solution to the problem of architectural development in Central Java.[19] The existence of three Candis Kalasan opens two possibilities. Did the line of architectural development run from the Diëng (in the northern part of Central Java) and Kalasan I to the present Kalasan III, or were the Diëng and the Kalasan basically different? Because of de Casparis' work it can now be safely assumed that the Diëng and the Kalasan are two separate artistic creations, each with its own line of development. The meeting point between these two lines of development is to be found in the Candi Lara Jonggrang in Prambanan (near Jogjakarta), i.e., after the two dynasties merged through the marriage of Rakai Pikatan of Sanjaya-wangsha with Prāmodarwardhanī of Shailendra-wangsha.[20]

This conclusion has further consequences regarding the placing of the Lara Jonggrang complex within the context of ancient Central Javanese history. The old view placed this complex in the tenth century and

[17] *OV*, 1940, p. 21.

[18] J. G. de Casparis, *Prasasti Indonesia I: Inscripties uit de Çailendra-tijd* (Bandung, 1950).

[19] In many ways, N. J. Krom stresses (see *Inleiding tot de Hindoe-Javaansche kunst* [The Hague, 1923], I, 170–172) that the candis on the Diëng Plateau are the oldest architectural products in Central Java, although the oldest date found at the site is A.D. 809. This gives rise to the difficulty of explaining the course of architectural development, if Candi Kalasan (before the two other candis in it were discovered) which dates from A.D. 778 constitutes an artistic peak.

[20] De Casparis, *Prasasti*, I, 131–132.

connected it with Balitung or his successor Dakṣa.[21] In view of its connection with Pikatan, this complex must originate in the ninth century. There is, moreover, strong epigraphical evidence to support this view. De Casparis found a specification of a caṇḍi complex in an inscription of the year A.D. 856 which showed a great similarity with the Lara Jonggrang complex, and he succeeded in proving that they must be identical.[22] This means that that caṇḍi complex already existed.

De Casparis also makes a brief reference to the existence of short inscriptions on the walls of several buildings of the complex. These inscriptions can, on paleographical grounds, be dated from the ninth century. And among them—*mirabile dictu*—the name Pikatan occurs.[23] Finally, this conclusion also finds corroboration in Poerbatjaraka's study of the Old Javanese *Rāmāyana*.[24] In this book there is also a description of a caṇḍi complex which fits only the Candi Lara Jonggrang.[25] Concerning the *Rāmāyana*, Poerbatjaraka drew the conclusion that it had to originate from the period before Sindok, i.e., before the beginning of the tenth century. This means that regarding the complex itself the dating accords with the findings of de Casparis.

With the change in the dating of the Candi Lara Jonggrang complex from the tenth to the ninth century, the whole picture of the final period of the ancient history of Central Java changes also. This picture will continue to change, with wider and wider implications, every time archaeology succeeds in presenting new materials. A beginning has now been made, and already there is a sequel. In the middle of 1960 an archaeological excavation on the site of the Candi Sewu complex succeeded in revealing an inscription, dated A.D. 792, which mentions the expansion or enlargement of that complex.[26] This information indicates that the Candi Sewu complex existed long before 792 and therefore that the old view which places the complex at the end of the ninth century [27] has to be abandoned.

[21] Krom, *Inleiding*, I, 441–442, and *HJG*, p. 171. See also Stutterheim, "De stichters der Prambanan tempels," *Djawa*, XX (1940), 218–233.

[22] J. G. de Casparis, *Prasasti Indonesia II: Selected Inscriptions from the Seventh to the Ninth Century A.D.* (Bandung, 1956), pp. 280–330.

[23] *Ibid.*, pp. 310–311.

[24] R. Ng. Poerbatjaraka, "Het Oud-Javaansche Rāmāyana," *TBG*, LXXII (1932), 151 ff.

[25] Canto VIII, strophe 43' ff.

[26] This inscription is at present in preparation for publication by the Archaeological Service.

[27] W. F. Stutterheim, "De ouderdom van Tjandi Sewu," *BKI*, LXXXV (1929), 491–496.

Another view which similarly has to be abandoned concerns the question of the spread and growth of Islam in Indonesia, and especially in East Java. The oldest available evidence on the presence of Islam here is a memorial tablet commemorating the burial of Fatimah, daughter of Maimun (better known as Princess Suwari) in Leran (north of Gresik), in the year A.D. 1082, and the tomb of Maulana Malik Ibrahim in Gresik in the year A.D. 1419. Because the value of the first find as historical evidence is still doubtful,[28] it is generally assumed that the spread of Islam in Java started in the fifteenth century.[29]

A few years ago Louis Damais, in his study of the tombstones which were found at the site of the capital of Majapahit, managed to find a number which date back to the golden age of Majapahit under the rule of King Hayam Wuruk (the oldest date carved on the stone is A.D. 1368).[30] Hence it can be established that in the middle of the fourteenth century there was already a Moslem community at the capital Majapahit, in the southern part of town (now the hamlet of Tralaya). This means that in the town of Majapahit, Islam was not unknown. The further conclusion can be drawn that its propagation must have been going on for some time. Furthermore, it should be remembered that the oldest Moslem tombs in Indonesia were imported from Cambay and did not have any headstones, like the oldest tombs in Samudra-Pasai and the one of Maulana Malik Ibrahim. The use of headstones in the tombs of Tralaya, which were, moreover, decorated with ornamental carvings in the contemporary style, therefore clearly shows that Islam as a cultural element had already penetrated and was already accepted in what was still a Hindu society. The use of dates in the Shāka calendar, and not in the Hijrah calendar, written with Old Javanese characters, further strengthens this conclusion.

III

It also sometimes happens that a new discovery quite important, perhaps, from an archaeological viewpoint has no effect whatsoever

---

[28] This doubt relates to the reading of the date and also to the possibility that this memorial stone originates from another place (cf. Krom, *HJG*, p. 452, and also R. A. Kern, "De verbreiding van den Islam," in F. W. Stapel, ed., *Geschiedenis van Nederlandsch Indië* [Amsterdam, 1938–1940], I, 306). It is true that the tomb in Leran is quite recent, and the building housing it does not show convincing indications of its origin in the eleventh century.

[29] This conclusion is based not only on the existence of the tomb of Maulana Malik Ibrahim but also on the reports of Ma-Huan of China, who in the beginning of the fifteenth century came to Majapahit, and on Portuguese reports. .

[30] L. Ch. Damais, "Etudes javanaises: I, Les Tombes musulmanes datées de Trålåjå," *BEFEO*, XLVIII (1957), 353 ff.

on the existing historical reconstruction. There are an extraordinary number of such discoveries, generally accidentally made by the local population; they range from large stone statues to small golden ornaments. A large part of them only serve the purpose of filling museums. Among them there are, nevertheless, some that are very interesting, and if the question of their significance were gone into, it might lead to unexpectedly far-reaching consequences. Let us take, for instance, the discovery of small golden plates in Plaosan, near Prambanan, in 1959. These plates were joined together in the shape of a flat puppet, of which the head was carved to look like a mask. It is especially from this part that the puppet can be identified as a Buddha. The puppet therefore looks like a frontal cover of a Buddha statue.[31] We do not know the significance of this piece; however, in present-day Bali similar objects are to be found—the "adegan" (effigies of wood or palm leaves) and the "ukur" (effigies made of gold or silver chips; also of Chinese coins)—which have something to do with cremation ceremonies.[32] It is therefore possible that this is also true of the object just mentioned.

A very interesting discovery was also made at the end of 1960 in eastern Lombok, a region which has not so far produced any materials from the period of ancient history. This discovery was therefore a thrilling event. What would we learn from it? Not very much, as it turned out. The discovery consisted of four bronze Buddhist statues. Their style is quite old, and one of the statues depicts Buddha in a manner strongly resembling that by which Buddha is pictured at the Borobudur. In the light of this resemblance, the only conclusion which can be drawn is that in the eighth and ninth centuries there were already followers of Mahāyāna Buddhism in the eastern part of Lombok.

Not only with the isolated finds, but also oftentimes even with archaeological excavations, the results have no direct historical significance. This is, for instance, the case with the excavation at the Elephants Cave (Goa Gajah) in Bali. There was a temple in the courtyard in front of the cave. On the right and on the left side of the entrance to the cave are a number of statues which had served as waterspouts. These statues caused us to look for remains which had to do with irrigation. A two years' search (1952–1954) finally disclosed a holy bathing place, exactly underneath the temple, about

---

[31] A similar find was made almost at the same time in Maguwo, near Jogjakarta, but its "mask" did not depict the face of Buddha or of any other deity.

[32] See, e.g., P. Wirz, *Der Totenkult auf Bali* (Stuttgart, 1928).

three and a half meters below the ground. Hence it became necessary
—with the consent of the local population—to tear down the temple
entirely.[33] From an archaeological viewpoint this find was sensational,
but in the absence of any written information or any other indication,
the discovery did not add any new material of historiographical
significance.

IV

Finally, to round out our picture of the significance of archaeology
for historical investigation, one other possibility should be discussed—
that archaeology provides materials which fall short of being of
historiographical significance but are sufficient to help bridge a gap in
available materials.

As we know, the candis and statues of the period before A.D. 950 and
those after that period show a marked difference, so much so that one
can speak of a Central Javanese and an East Javanese style. This
difference seemed to have developed quite suddenly, for from the
period of Sindok (approximately A.D. 950) to the period of Wishnuwardhana (approximately A.D. 1260) no buildings or statues are to be found
which might give an idea of the course of development from Central to
East Java. Several attempts have been made to show that there exists a
direct developmental relationship between those two styles.[34] However,
the evidence in support of this view was insufficient until the discovery
of new material in 1958. In that year an interesting statue of Brahma
was found in Gurah near Kědiri, in a style reminiscent of the Singasari
period. Digging down to five meters below ground level uncovered the
remains of a candi, the stairway of which was ornamented with a
makara (gargoyle).[35] Because the candis in the East Javanese style do
not have makaras, there were therefore two conflicting pieces of
evidence. Only the discovery of a third piece of evidence could decide
the issue. This decisive piece was indeed found *in situ;* it consisted of
an inscribed stone. Although the inscription consisted of only one word
and did not contain any information, it was nevertheless possible
paleographically to determine its date, the eleventh century. This
means that the candi found in Gurah was of the Kědiri period—a

[33] *Laporan tahunan Dinas Purbakala 1954* (Annual Reports of the Archaeological
Service, 1954).

[34] See Krom, *Inleiding,* II, 1–3, and also W. F. Stutterheim, "Oud Javaansche
kunst," *BKI,* LXXIX (1923), 323–346.

[35] The report of this excavation is still in preparation.

period of which the architecture is not known to us—and in this way it constituted a link between the architecture of Central and East Java. Regrettably, of this newly found candi only the base was left, and it was therefore impossible to draw any additional conclusions.

V

In conclusion, we can state once again how important archaeology is for historiography, while from the examples discussed in this article, it also becomes clear why archaeology in Indonesia is with justification concerned primarily with the field of ancient history. Quite obviously this part of Indonesian history is still very dependent on archaeological investigations. Every new archaeological discovery could conceivably give rise to historiographical changes. The cases discussed here sufficiently bear this out. And it is quite possible that eventually the whole of the period of ancient history will have to be rewritten in the light of such new discoveries.

We can therefore only hope that it will be possible for Indonesian archaeology to improve and expand its activities. In order to do so the Indonesian Archaeological Service will have to overcome its shortage of expert and other trained personnel and will have to induce a larger number of talented people to accept the sacrifices which being an Indonesian archaeologist entails.

IV

Epigraphy and Indonesian Historiography

By BUCHARI

Archaeologist, Archaeological Service, Jakarta

I

WHENEVER the ancient history of Indonesia is discussed, one automatically visualizes N. J. Krom's study, *Hindoe-Javaansche geschiedenis,* which was published for the first time in 1926 and later in a revised edition in 1931, because up to the present Krom's study can be regarded as the only reference book on the ancient history of Indonesia. Its title immediately draws our attention, because it gives the impression that Krom deals only with the history of Java in the Hindu period. A closer look reveals that the study also deals with the other islands of the Indonesian Archipelago. The first, deceptive impression is caused by the fact that the largest part of the sources on the period from the eighth to the sixteenth century are to be found in Java, and thus it is only of Java that we can get a picture with any degree of completeness for this period. We know, of course, that the Shrīwijaya Empire, which presumably was centered in Sumatra and which, according to historical sources, flourished between the seventh and the fourteenth centuries, was one of the largest empires in Indonesian ancient history. Unfortunately, because of the small number of sources we are able to obtain only a meager picture of Shrīwijaya. The sole other Indonesian area which can more or less measure up to Java in possession of historical sources is Bali.

On examining the content of Krom's study it is immediately clear that we are faced with an analysis quite different from that to be found in conventional history books. One frequently finds an extensive discussion about the reading or interpretation of a particular word in an inscription or some other historical source or a penetrating evaluation of various theories about a particular problem, on the basis of which Krom then draws his cautious conclusions. But often he does not draw any conclusion at all. In such cases the reader is apparently asked to draw his own conclusions, to choose from the alternatives which Krom presents in his book the one most acceptable to the reader. Such an attitude may give the "outsider" the impression that Krom is afraid to set down his own conclusion.[1]

But such is not the case. Whoever has become acquainted with the study of ancient history in Indonesia knows that Krom does not have any other choice. He knows that the sources on ancient history are, although quite varied in kind as one can see in Krom's book,[2] inadequate in number to enable construction of a complete picture of the course of history. Among these sources the inscriptions, which constitute one of the contemporaneous historical sources, will be the present matter of discussion.

The term inscription refers to historical sources written in ancient times on stone or metal. Most of them are inscriptions ordered to be made by rulers who reigned in various parts of Indonesia since the fifth century. A small number of these inscriptions constitute a kind of judicial decision, commonly known as *jayapattra*. Some of the inscriptions contain lengthy texts, but a number contain only a date or the name of a particular state dignitary.[3] Inscriptions from the Moslem period, which are mostly written on tombstones, ordinarily contain the name of the deceased who is buried at that particular place, information about the date of his death, and some quotations from the Koran.

At present, the preservation, custody, and study of historical sources in the form of inscriptions are the task of the Dinas Purbakala dan Peninggalan Nasional (the Archaeological Service), a section of the Ministry of Education. As a scientific institute, the Archaeological Service has a special branch which is concerned with the study of inscriptions. In the latter office are preserved almost 3,000 estampages of stone and metal inscriptions which have been found in various places in the Indonesian Archipelago. The inscriptions are written in Sanskrit, Old Malay, Old Javanese, Old Balinese, or Arabic. Most of them still

[1] J. G. de Casparis, "Twintig jaar studie van de oudere geschiedenis van Indonesië," *Orientatie*, no. 46 (1954), p. 627.

[2] Krom, *HJG*, pp. 1–33.

[3] J. G. de Casparis, "Penjelidikan prasasti: Tugas ahli epigrafi Dinas Purbakala," *Amerta*, no. 1 (1952), pp. 21–23.

require detailed study because, although many of them have been read, many have as yet been only provisionally transcribed, e.g., the collection of transcriptions by J. L. A. Brandes, which covers 125 inscriptions.[4] In order to obtain a better view of what needs to be done in regard to epigraphy, the study of inscriptions, let us consider the list of inscriptions as arranged by L. Ch. Damais and published in 1952.[5] Of the 290 inscriptions, originating from Sumatra, Java, Madura, and Bali, only 81 have been published in complete transcription and translation together with analyses, 134 have been published only in transcription, while 75 have not been published at all as yet—not to mention inscriptions which do not contain any date, new discoveries which have been made since Damais wrote his article, and inscriptions of the Moslem period which have been practically neglected by scholars. The latter group is represented by about 1,800 estampages at the office of the Archaeological Service. R. Goris made mention of 174 inscriptions found in Bali,[6] while in Damais' list only 67 inscriptions are listed. It becomes clear, then, why Indonesian ancient history is still full of gaps.

In view of the fact that much work has yet to be done in the field of epigraphy, it is to be deeply regretted that until now the Archaeological Service has no more than one epigraphist. The future looks a little more promising, for among the students of the Department of Archaeology, Faculty of Letters, University of Indonesia, several have shown great interest in the study of epigraphy, while one has been working as an assistant with the Archaeological Service since the beginning of 1960. An increase in the number of epigraphists in the near future is felt as an urgent need, because it would be impossible indeed for one epigraphist and one assistant to finish what ought to be done, even if they should dedicate their whole lives to the task. The present task of the epigraphist is not only to study the as yet unpublished inscriptions but also to reexamine all inscriptions which have been published in provisional transcription and then to translate them into a modern language so that other scholars, especially historians, can make use of the information contained in these inscriptions.

A number of difficulties are inherent in the task. Firstly, many of

[4] N. J. Krom, ed., "Oud-Javaansche oorkonden: Nagelaten transcripties van wijlen Dr. J. L. A. Brandes," *VBG*, vol. LX (1913), xx, 267 p. Reference to a particular inscription will be indicated by OJO and a Roman numeral after it.

[5] L. Ch. Damais, "Etudes d'épigraphie indonésienne: III, Liste des principales inscriptions datées de l'Indonésie," *BEFEO*, XLVI (1952), 1–105. The series will be referred to as EEI.

[6] R. Goris, *Prasasti Bali*, I (Bandung, 1954), 2.

these inscriptions are in such a state of deterioration, particularly the inscriptions written on stone, that it is difficult to read them. One has to go over the weathered parts a number of times until a satisfactory reading is found. By mastering the forms of letters with all their coils and curls and by making constant comparisons between the scarcely visible remains of weathered letters and letters which are still distinctly visible, an epigraphist attempts to read as much as possible of those parts of the inscriptions that are worn out. In this connection, inscriptions written in Sanskrit offer some advantage, because they are written in meter form, which enables the epigraphist to make frequent use of the rules of *guru-laghu* as an aid in producing an accurate reading of the problematic parts. Nevertheless, even with perseverance the epigraphist is often confronted with parts of inscriptions which can no longer be read.

The translation of the texts presents other difficulties. Our knowledge of the languages employed in the inscriptions is still insufficient to enable us to get a full understanding of the meaning of the texts. In regard to inscriptions written in Old Javanese we are indeed in possession of comparative material in the form of literary products. But the publication of these manuscripts, although frequently accompanied by a word list, does not give us the desired assistance, because the inscriptions are written in a special language which differs from the language of the *kakawin,* the common literary form. Many terms appear in connection with regulations concerning land, various kinds of taxes, and official positions which are never found in Old Javanese *kakawin* manuscripts. The publication of Old Javanese legal manuscripts, *shāsana,* by philologists may provide great assistance to the epigraphist. It becomes clear, then, that with the advancement in our knowledge of old languages existing translations will have to be continually revised. Correspondingly, all conclusions derived from these translations will have to be reexamined.

II

In general, inscriptions commemorate the investiture of an area as a *sīma,* a freehold, as a royal grant to a particular functionary who has been of particular service to the state or as a royal grant in the interest of a particular sacred monument.[7] The investiture of a new *sīma* was

---

[7] Because most of the published inscriptions are written in Old Javanese, the discussion that follows will rely primarily on inscriptions written in this particular language.

regarded as a very important event, since it concerned change in the status of a piece of land which, in Indonesian society, is always tied in a religio-magic relationship with the group of people living on it. Thus in an inscription extensive information is given as to the exact day, month, and year that the event occurred and as to the person who invested the particular piece of land with *sīma* rights, those who assisted in the ceremony, the kind of rites which were observed, etc. The place where the oath was administered, or the curse hurled at whoever would violate the regulations contained in the inscription, plays a significant role in the inscription itself. Frequently one also finds information concerning the exact boundaries of land invested with *sīma* rights. Whenever a ruler invested a piece of land with *sīma* rights in the interest of a particular functionary, such a functionary was in addition frequently endowed with a number of special rights which were enumerated in the inscription concerned. Most investitures of land with *sīma* rights were performed by a king or by order of a king. In such a case we often find a list of high state functionaries who executed the royal command. But there are also cases where *sīma* rights were granted by state functionaries.[8]

The year and month, which are usually written in complete and accurate form, followed by the names of the king and royal high functionaries, may provide the chronological frame for the writing of history. Based on these pieces of information, knowledge may be obtained in regard to the probable period [9] of reign of a particular ruler, while the place where the inscription has been found may give an idea of the area of authority of the king. It stands to reason that an accurate reading of the dates constitutes an imperative requirement. It has occurred many times that people have confused a particular number with another one, e.g., two has been confused with four, one with

[8] Krom, *HJG*, p. 2.

[9] The exact date of the commencement and conclusion of the reign of a particular ruler cannot be known from the inscriptions. Known are merely the oldest and the most recent date of the reign of a particular ruler. Only a few exceptions are noted, such as the year of the commencement of Rakai Kayuwangi's reign (778 Shāka, according to a stone inscription from Central Java which at present is kept in the Museum of Jakarta, no. D. 28; see J. G. de Casparis, *Prasasti Indonesia,* II [Jakarta, 1956], 289) and the year of the conclusion of the reign of King Dharmmawangsha Teguh and the coronation year of King Erlangga (938 Shāka and 941 Shāka respectively according to the "Calcutta stone"; see H. Kern, *Verspreide Geschriften,* VII [The Hague, 1917], 83–114 [H. Kern's work will be referred to as Kern, *VG*]). The first and last years of the reign of a number of Singasari and Majapahit kings are also known, but not on the basis of information from inscriptions.

six, etc. And when a theory is built on the erroneous reading of a date, chaos may result. An example would be the inscription on the back of the Cāmuṇḍī statue [10] of Ardimulyo (Singasari). Its date, which is indeed written on a weathered part, was first read by Goris [11] and Stutterheim [12] as the year 1254 of the Shāka calendar. Stutterheim, then, connected the inscription with Queen Tribhuwanā of Majapahit and the battles of Saḍeng and Kĕṭa which occurred under her reign, mentioned in the book *Nāgarakĕrtāgama*,[13] while he identified Ganesha and Bhairawa, which are portrayed at the sides of Cāmuṇḍī, as Gajah Mada and Adityawarman respectively. Some other scholars have been carried away by these readings and have formulated their theories. C. C. Berg, among them, wrote about the battle of Saḍeng and the myth of the glory of Majapahit,[14] while J. L. Moens employed the information as a basis for his theory which propounds that Tribhuwanā had a bigamous relationship with Cakreshwara, her consort, portrayed as Bhairawa on the left and Gajah Mada portrayed as Ganesha on the right side of the Cāmuṇḍī statue.[15]

Later on, all these theories were exploded when Damais succeeded in establishing that the exact date is 1214 Shāka and that the inscription

[10] Damais has noted in an interview with the author that the statue is not called Cāmuṇḍā, as its name is read by scholars up to the present time, but Cāmuṇḍī. A closer examination of the estampage kept by the Archaeological Service (no. 2710) gives indeed the reading *cāmuṇḍyāi* a *dativus singularis femininum* form of the word *cāmuṇḍī*. W. F. Stutterheim once read it as *cāmuṇḍau*. He subscribed to the opinion that the word naturally originates from *cāmuṇḍā*, the *āu* being formed by a *samdhi* with the next word, since it is to be regarded as an impossibility that one is faced with a *dualis* form. Furthermore, *cāmuṇḍau* can only be a *dualis* form of the word *cāmuṇḍī*, while such a word has never been known (W. F. Stutterheim, "Oudheidkundige aanteekeningen: xxxix, De zgn. Guhyeçwarī van Singhasāri: Toevoegingen en verbeteringen," *BKI*, XCII [1935], 210). Stutterheim's opinion proved to be incorrect, because the word *cāmuṇḍī* is found as another name of Kālī (Durgā) in G. Jouveau-Dubreuil's study, *Iconography of Southern India*, trans. by A. C. Martin (Paris, 1937), pp. 38–40. In view of this reading, it might have been hoped that C. C. Berg would revise his analysis in regard to Stutterheim's reading of *cāmuṇḍau* which he regarded as a *dualis masculinum* form (C. C. Berg, "Kṛtanagara's Maleise affaire," *Indonesië*, IX [1956], 408–412).

[11] In *OV*, 1928, p. 32.

[12] "De dateering van eenige Oostjavaansche beeldengroepen," *TBG*, LXXVI (1936), 313–317.

[13] *Nāgarakĕrtāgama*, xlix, 3.

[14] C. C. Berg, "De Saḍeng-oorlog en de mythe van Groot Majapahit," *Indonesië*, V (1951–1952), 385–422.

[15] J. L. Moens, "Wiṣṇuwardhana, vorst van Singasari, en zijn Madjapaitse santānapratisantāna," *TBG*, LXXXV (1955), 365–436, particularly pp. 381–386.

should be connected with King Kĕrtanagara.[16] It became even more apparent, after a few additional pieces completed the inscription, that the inscription had no connection with the battle of Saḍeng,[17] because the part which was reconstructed by Stutterheim as *mawuyung yi sa (ḍeng)* actually should have been read *manuyuyi sakaladwīpāntara.*[18]

Such confusion occurs many times when one is faced with copied inscriptions made some centuries after the original inscription was written. As an example, mention can be made of a copper plate of Gĕdangan. The said inscription made in 1289 Shāka [19] contains a copy of an inscription written in 782 Shāka. In the inscription of 782 Shāka,

[16] L.Ch. Damais, EEI: IV, "Discussion de la date des inscriptions," *BEFEO,* XLVII (1955), 151–153. See also F. D. K. Bosch, "Uit de grensgebieden tussen Indische invloedssfeer en oud-inheems volksgeloof op Java," *BKI,* CX (1954), 11–12.

[17] Buchari, "An Inscribed Lingga from Rambianak," *BEFEO,* XLIX (1959), 407. Berg, who later also admitted that the 1214 Shāka reading is right and that the inscription does not contain the word Saḍeng, nevertheless does not want to be convinced that the inscription really does describe the event which occurred in that particular year. According to his opinion, Kĕrtanagara was a "pacifist," who was seeking to establish an alliance with other kingdoms of Nusantara in a peaceful manner in order that they might be able to face together the threat from China. The fact that the inscription contains sentences which, as it were, conjure up a vision of victory through the force of arms can be explained, according to Berg, by regarding it as an "antisymbolic" statement which attempts to nullify the fact that, two months after the event mentioned in the inscription, King Kĕrtanagara met his end in the attack by Jayakatwang. By applying his particular method, Berg declared that the inscription was written in 1253 Shāka, when Majapahit was engaged in a war with Saḍeng in the period of Tribhuwanā's reign. He further stated that by waging this war Tribhuwanā carried out an act which was similar to that of Kĕrtanagara, after its characteristics were changed by "verbal magic." This is the reason why the statue, which he regarded as being named *Cāmuṇḍāu,* in the *masculinum dualis* form, symbolized Tribhuwanā-Kĕrtanagara (Berg, "Krtanagara," pp. 406-409; see also note 46 on p. 416).

[18] According to what the author has seen of the estampage and the photograph (D. P. 20076), the word is clearly *manuyuyi.* The second letter can by no means be read as *wa,* because at the lower part is a vertical line in the middle, a continuation of a descending line from the upper side on the left, which at the base of the letter turns to the left, ascends slightly, turns right on the horizontal line, and then descends again. The letter *wa* does not have a vertical line at the middle of its base, while the straight line in the middle part is always written slantingly, because it runs from the lower right to the upper left. The *anuswāra* sign, which is usually clearly written as a reversed comma, is also not seen above the third letter. But here it is probably a mistake of the sculptor. The third letter should probably be a *la,* so that the correct reading would be *manuluyi.* Such a mistake can be understood because both the letter *la* and *ya* have three legs.

[19] H. Kern, "Over eene Oudjavaansche oorkonde (gevonden te Gedangan, Surabaya) van Çaka 782 (of 872)," *VG,* VII, 19–53. Concerning the year 1289 Shāka, which formerly was read as 1295 Shāka, see Damais, EEI: III, *BEFEO,* XLVI (1952), 76–77.

the name of King Shrī Bhuwaneshwara Wishnusakalatmakadigwijaya Parakramottunggadewa Lokapāla lañcana is mentioned. Such a title was not common in the eighth century of the Shāka calendar; it did not appear until the Kĕḍiri period (eleventh to twelfth century of the Shāka calendar). Because of these facts, and because of a number of other factors in the inscription under consideration commonly found in inscriptions of the Sinḍok-Erlangga period, Krom casts doubt upon the date 782 Shāka as indicated in the inscription. And because at the time of writing his article Krom knew only one Lokapāla, who was the son-in-law of mpu Sinḍok, he suggested that probably the copyist had interchanged the number 7 with the number 8, so that the actual date should have been 872 Shāka.[20] Krom's view was maintained by other scholars until Damais gave evidence that 782 Shāka was indeed the correct date and that there had indeed been a ruler by the name of Lokapāla in the eighth century of the Shāka calendar, a king more commonly known by the name of Rakai Kayuwangi.[21]

Rather exceptional in the ancient history of Indonesia is the use of a calendar other than the Shāka calendar in two stone inscriptions, viz., the inscriptions of Taji and Gatak.[22] These two stone inscriptions promulgated by Dakṣa make use of the Sanjaya calendar. Brandes read these dates as 694 and 693 Sanjayawarṣa,[23] while R. Goris thought them to be 172 or 174 and 176 Sanjayawarṣa.[24] Based on Brandes' reading, Krom noted that the beginning of the Sanjaya calendar would be between A.D. 217 and 226, a period in which Hindus were already found in Java. According to him, we might conclude that this was a Hindu-Javanese calendar, or that it was a calendar originating from India (although there is no reference to it in Indian sources), or, another possibility, that the beginning of the calendar was a fiction, based on imagined calculations.[25] In a note below his explanation, Krom mentioned Goris' reading and remarked that should the reading be correct,

[20] N. J. Krom, "Epigraphische aanteekeningen: VIII, De dateering der oorkonde van Kañcana," *TBG*, LVI (1914), 477–484.

[21] L. Ch. Damais, "Epigrafische aantekeningen: I, Lokapāla-Kayuwangi," *TBG*, LXXXIII (1949), 1–6.

[22] In Damais' list these are mentioned respectively as the inscriptions of Taji Gunung and Timbanan Wungkal (EEI: III, *BEFEO*, XLVI [1952], 50 and 52).

[23] OJO, XXXVI, and OJO, XXXV.

[24] R. Goris, "De eenheid der Mataramsche dynastie," *Feestbundel uitgegeven door het Koninklijk Bataviaasch Genootschap van Kunsten en Wetenschappen bij gelegenheid van zijn 150 jarig bestaan, 1778–1928*, I (Weltevreden, 1929), 202–206. The publication will be referred to as *FBG*.

[25] Krom, *HJG*, p. 191.

the Sanjaya calendar would have begun with King Sanjaya, who indeed was a historical person. But apparently he still clung to Brandes' reading.[26] Goris himself set forth the view that most probably the Sanjaya era commenced with the establishment of a *lingga* by Sanjaya in 654 Shāka, and therefore the years 172/174 and 176 Sanjayawarsa would be the same as the years A.D. 904/906 and 908.[27]

These theories concerning the Sanjaya era were eventually refuted when Damais gave conclusive evidence that the dates in the two stone inscriptions should be read 194 and 196 Sanjayawarṣa and that these dates would be the same as the years A.D. 910 and 913. Thus the Sanjaya era commenced in A.D. 717, probably the time that an event considered to be of paramount importance [28] occurred in the life of Sanjaya, who was to be regarded as *vamshakartā* by succeeding rulers.[29]

The preceding discussion shows how important it is to obtain the correct reading of the dates in an inscription. In this connection, Damais has contributed illuminating studies which have appeared successively since 1951 in a number of issues of the *Bulletin de l'Ecole Française d'Extrême Orient*.[30]

After mention of the dates and their complete dating elements has been made, the inscriptions usually note that at that time the command of the ruler was handed down to a group of high functionaries who conveyed the royal command further to a lower group of functionaries. Based on these informative notes, we may draw the tentative conclusion that there were at least two groups of state functionaries. The first group consisted of four or five people, viz., *rakryān mapatih i hino, rakryān mapatih i halu, rakryān mapatih i wka, rakryān bawang,* and

[26] *Ibid.*, note 1 on p. 191.

[27] Goris, *FBG*, I, 204.

[28] L. Ch. Damais, EEI: II, "La Date des inscriptions en ère de Sañjaya," *BEFEO*, XLV (1951), 42–63. See also F. D. K. Bosch, "Boekbespreking: L. Ch. Damais, 'Etudes d'épigraphie indonésienne'," *BKI*, CXII (1956), 332.

[29] Such a conclusion can be derived from the fact that in one of his inscriptions (Mantyāsih, dated 829 Shāka) Balitung mentioned the kings who had reigned before him, beginning with Sanjaya (W. F. Stutterheim, "Een belangrijke oorkonde uit de Kedoe," *TBG*, LXVII [1927], 172–215). And since Dakṣa's reign the formula *sakweh ta dewata prasiddha maṅraksang kaḍatwan çrī mahārāja ing bhūmi matarām* (OJO, XXX) was used, while Sanjaya used the title of Rakai Matarām.

[30] L. Ch. Damais, EEI: I, "Méthode de réduction des dates javanaises en dates européennes," and EEI: II, "La Date des inscriptions en ère de Sañjaya," *BEFEO*, XLV (1951), 1–63; EEI: III, "Liste des principales inscriptions datées de l'Indonésie," *BEFEO*, XLVI (1952), 1–105; and EEI: IV, "Discussion de la date des inscriptions," *BEFEO*, XLVII (1955), 7–290.

rakryān i sirikan.[31] In the inscriptions of the Majapahit period, only three of them remained, called *rakryān mahāmantri katrīni.* The three highest functionaries of the Majapahit period were *rakryān mahāmantri i hino, rakryān mahāmantri i halu,* and *rakryān mahāmantri i sirikan.*[32] The second group was called *para taṇḍa rakryān ring pakira-kirān.* Up to the present time we still do not know how many people were members of the second group. Probably a detailed investigation, and a comparison of its results with information from Chinese sources, would yield an accurate picture of the groups of state functionaries. In Hsin T'ang-shu (A.D. 618–907), for example, it is noted that in Ho-Ling, also called Chö-p'o, 32 high dignitaries were found.[33] In the notes of the Sung dynasty (A.D. 960–1279) mention is made that there were 3 princes who ruled as viceroys and 4 high functionaries, called *rakryān,* who together administered state affairs as did the ministers in China. Furthermore, there were more than 300 civil servants, assisted by about 1,000 lower functionaries.[34]

Following the date and the list of functionaries concerned, information is given concerning the event commemorated in the inscription, the event being the investiture of a particular area with *sīma* rights. As has been said previously, *sīma* rights could be a royal grant to a deserving functionary, or they could also be a royal grant to the inhabitants of a particular piece of land for the maintenance of a sacred monument. However, these historical events regarded as of great importance by people in ancient times, and therefore commemorated by a royal inscription, do not necessarily concern historians of the present.

Contemporary historians are much more interested in the ensuing information, which concerns the reasons why a particular functionary obtained a royal grant or why a sacred monument was erected. This part of the inscription, usually preceded by the word *sambandhanya,*

[31] Found, among others, in OJO, XII, where the fourth person is called *samgat bawang.* Among the five persons, four are constantly mentioned, these being *rakryān mapatih i hino, i halu* (or *i watutihang*), *i sirikan,* and *i wka.* Sometimes *samgat bawang* is replaced by *samgat* (or *sang pamgat*) *tiruan,* although one need not necessarily draw the conclusion that *samgat bawang* is a synonym of *samgat tiruan.* (These were found, among others, in the copper plate of Poh, dated 827 Shāka. See W. F. Stutterheim, "De inscriptie van Randoesari I," *Inscripties van Nederlandsch Indië,* I [Batavia, 1940], 3–28. The latter publication will be referred to as *INI.*)

[32] Found, among others, on the copper plate of Sukamĕrta, dated 1218 Shāka. See R. Ng. Poerbatjaraka and W. F. Stutterheim, "Oorkonde van Kṛtarājasa uit 1296 A.D. (Penanggungan)," *INI,* I, 33–49.

[33] W. P. Groeneveldt, *Historical Notes on Indonesia and Malaya, Compiled from Chinese Sources* (Jakarta, 1960), p. 13.

[34] *Ibid.,* pp. 16–17.

does indeed contain historical data which can be woven into a historical narrative. In a number of inscriptions this particular part yields invaluable historical data, such as is the case with the stone inscription, better known as the Calcutta stone, of King Erlangga found on Gunung Penanggungan,[35] the copper plate of Gunung Buṭak,[36] and the copper plate of King Kĕrtarājasa found on Gunung Penanggungan and dated 1218 Shāka.[37]

The Calcutta stone, dated 963 Shāka, consists of two parts, one written in Sanskrit, the other in Old Javanese. The part written in Sanskrit contains a chronological list of kings, followed by a report concerning the dissolution of the empire and the fact that Erlangga had to escape into the jungle in the company of his servant Narottama. In 932 Shāka, representatives of the people and priesthood approached Erlangga to submit a request that he govern the empire. This information is succeeded by accounts of Erlangga's victories in his battles with other rulers, which allowed him to reign in peace after 959 Shāka. The part written in Sanskrit is concluded with the report that as a token of faithfulness to his pledge to the gods Erlangga ordered the construction of a hermitage on the slope of Gunung Pūgawat.

The part written in Old Javanese, arranged according to the customary rules of Old Javanese inscriptions, contains a report of the fact that the king had invested two areas, Barahĕm and Capuri, with *sima* rights in order to construct a sacred monument, *dharmma karṣyan*. He ordered these two investitures because he had made a pledge when Java underwent *pralaya* as the consequence of Haji Wurawari's attack in 938 Shāka.[38] This report is followed by an account of Erlangga's experiences in his period of exile with Narottama. After he was invested as king in 941 Shāka, he started again to subjugate lesser kings in the surrounding areas. In contrast to other inscriptions, the part which starts with *sambandha* and relates the experience of Erlangga is written in extended form, so that the part which in other inscriptions occupies an important place, i.e., the part which concerns the status of the area invested with *sīma* rights and the curses upon those who do not respect the ordinances contained in the inscription, consists of only a few lines.

[35] Kern, *VG*, VII, 85–114. The part written in Old Javanese has also been published by J. L. A. Brandes, OJO, LXII.

[36] J. L. A. Brandes, *Pararaton: Het boek der koningen van Toemapel en van Majapahit* (The Hague, 1896), pp. 78–80. Another part is published in OJO, LXXXI.

[37] Poerbatjaraka and Stutterheim, "Oorkonde," pp. 33–49.

[38] The date indicated is the correct date, and not 928 Shāka as in H. Kern's reading. See R. Ng. Poerbatjaraka, "Strophe 14 van de Sanskrit-zijde der Calcutta-oorkonde," *TBG*, LXXXI (1941), 431.

The copper plate of Gunung Butak, dated 1216 Shāka, commemorates a grant by King Kĕrtarājasa Jayawardhana to the *rama* at Kudadu in the form of the village of Kudadu, withdrawn from the *dharmma* authority at Klĕme and invested with rights as an autonomous area in favor of the *rama* of Kudadu and all his descendants until the end of the world. The *rama* at Kudadu received this royal grant because he had been meritorious in providing the king with protection when he was still named Narārya Sanggrāmawijaya, before he became king. At that time, Sanggrāmawijaya was seeking refuge from his enemies, the troops of King Jayakatwang, who had attacked King Kĕrtanagara and destroyed him. This part is related in extended form, covering more than three inscription plates on both sides; it details the experiences of Wijaya from the time he was ordered to expel the enemy, who had already reached Jasun Wungkal, until he was forced to escape because he was surrounded. His retreat—while he was still engaged in fighting, although always on the losing side on account of the greater strength of his enemies—brought him to the village of Kudadu. It became apparent that the *rama* of Kudadu was still loyal to King Kĕrtanagara, for Wijaya was given food and drink and a place to hide. Later Wijaya was escorted by the *rama* of Kudadu to Rembang so that he could sail to Madura. When Wijaya became king, he did not forget the merits of the *rama* of Kudadu, and thus a grant was made consisting of a village invested with *sīma* rights in favor of the *rama* and all his descendants.[39]

The copper plate of Gunung Penanggungan, dated 1218 Shāka, is also an inscription of Kĕrtarājasa Jayawardhana. The inscription commemorates a grant by the king to Panji Patipati mpu Kapat in the form of the Sukāmĕrta land, part of the Pangkah area. Apparently the land concerned was previously a freehold in the interest of a sacred monument, but the king withdrew these rights in order to invest it with *sīma* rights in favor of sang Panji Patipati and all his descendants to the end of the world. Panji Patipati was favored with such a royal grant because of his extraordinary loyalty when, after King Kĕrtanagara's death, Sanggrāmawijaya had to flee his enemies. At that time this loyal subject shared the joys and sufferings of the king, never leaving the side of his master, wandering from jungle to jungle, climbing up and down the mountains, crossing rivers and the sea, holding an umbrella when it rained, and holding a torch when it was dark. He also took part when Wijaya proceeded to take revenge and attacked the enemies who had

---

[39] In the inscriptions it is always stated that the *sīma* investiture is legitimate until the end of the world (*mne hlĕm tkā ri dlāha ning dlāha*).

killed King Kĕrtanagara, until victory was obtained and his master was crowned as king. Apart from the said royal grant, Patipati also received another grant, his father's title, Panji, which he was permitted to use *in toto;* furthermore, he was appointed *dharmmādhikraṇa* with the rank of *dharmmādhyakṣa ring kaçaiwan.* There are also some other pieces of information relating to Patipati's father, who had been loyal to the grandfather of the king, King Jaya Shrī Wishnuwardhana. In conclusion, the account relates that Panji Patipati wished to follow in the steps of his father and that therefore he granted part of his autonomous land in favor of *sang hyang dharmmasīma* at Pagĕr, owned by the king.

These are important pieces of historical information, contained in the part of the inscription explaining the reasons why a particular person was favored with a royal grant or why a sacred monument was built. But when we examine all inscriptions which have been published up to the present time, these three inscriptions prove to be deviations from the rule. Other inscriptions also contain historical information in this particular section, but it is usually rather vague. The inscription of Balitung, dated 827 Shāka,[40] for example, relates that the king favored five *patihs* of Mantyāsih with a grant, because they were meritorious in recruiting people to undertake *buathaji* (= some kind of devotional labor?) during the wedding of the king, because they never failed to honor a number of sacred royal monuments, and because they agreed to the peoples' request to guard the road at the village of Kuning, so that the inhabitants of that village were no longer afraid, etc.

What can be learned from these informative data? We know that the king had a wedding, but whom did he wed? And what is the meaning of this royal wedding in regard to history? Neither of these questions can be answered on the basis of any other inscription. We also do not know why the villagers of *desa* Kuning were afraid. These are some of the difficulties. It is certainly true that the writer of inscriptions did not write for us, people of the present world; he did not consider it of great importance to provide absolutely clear information, because for his contemporaries it was perfectly obvious which royal wedding and which danger threatening the villagers of *desa* Kuning he referred to in the inscription. Those who lived in the succeeding years needed only to know that the piece of land mentioned in the inscription had been invested with *sīma* rights in favor of the five *patihs* at Mantyāsih and all their descendants.

An inscription of King Lokapāla found at Gunung Kidul, dated 802

[40] Stutterheim, "Een belangrijke," pp. 172–215.

Shāka,[41] differs from other inscriptions in that it mentions, immediately after the date and its dating elements, a historical event which concerns Rakryān Mānak, who was abducted by her younger brother, Rakryān Landhayan, and left behind at Tangar and who afterward committed suicide by throwing herself onto the burning piles [42] at Taas. Thereupon, Dyaḥ Bhūmi, who later proved to be the son of King Lokapāla named Dyaḥ Bhūmijaya, fled to the south in the direction of the sea and arrived at the village of Wuatan Tija. The officials of that village protected him and afterward brought him back to the king. The joy of the king was so great that he granted gold and garments to those who brought his son back. Furthermore, *desa* Wuatan Tija was released from the authority of Sang Pamgat Wintri and invested with *sīma* rights in favor of Dyaḥ Bhūmijaya.

Who was Rakryān Mānak, and what was the position of Rakryān Landhayan in the political hierarchy? Of the name Rakryān Mānak (having children) we can speculate that it involves (one of) the king's queen(s) who had given birth to Dyaḥ Bhūmijaya. But this is no more than an assumption, a guess, although based on arguments which are rather strong. Concerning Rakryān Landhayan we do not have any other information than that he was a younger brother of Rakryān Mānak, so that, based on the former assumption, he would have been a brother-in-law of the king. When in another inscription [43] we come across the name of Shrī Mahārāja dyaḥ Waba (read Wawa), son of Kryan Ladheyan *sang lumāh ring alas* (who was entombed in the jungle), the question arises whether Kryan Ladheyan, the father of King Wawa, was the same person as Rakryān Landhayan, brother-in-law of King Lokapāla. No clear reasons are given as to why he abducted his sister and nephew. In this case also, one can only guess.

There are many other examples, such as a number of inscriptions of the kingdom of Kĕḍiri. Among others, mention can be made of a stone inscription from *desa* Pikatan (Blitar), dated 1108 Shāka.[44] In that inscription the investiture of an area as *sīma* land is commemorated, a

[41] Stutterheim, "Epigraphica: II, De oorkonde van Rake Lokapāla uit het Zuidergebergte," *TBG*, LXXV (1935), 437–443.

[42] In the inscription *maturunn-apuy* is written in active form, but W. F. Stutterheim translated it in the passive form, which caused the event to be interpreted differently.

[43] R. Goris, "De Oud-Javaansche inscripties uit het Sri Wedari-Museum te Soerakarta," *OV* (1928), pp. 63–70.

[44] OJO, LXVII.

grant of King Bāmeshwara [45] to the *rama* at Padĕlĕgan, because he had shown his loyalty to the king by offering his life on the battlefield. A stone inscription of *dukuh* Jaring, *desa* Kembangarum (Blitar), dated 1103 Shāka,[46] commemorates the grant of King Kroncaryyadipa to a functionary at Jaring, because he had shown his loyalty to the king by fighting his enemy. And an inscription of Kĕmulan (Trĕnggalek), dated 1116 Shāka,[47] commemorates the grant of King Sarwweshwara to *sāmya haji katandan sakapāt* (?) who succeeded in expelling the enemy which had launched an attack from the east. The inscription states, among other things, that initially the king was forced to leave the palace at Katang-katang but that because of the devotion of the *sāmya haji* (a vassal?) he was able to regain his throne and rule as king of Kĕdiri. These pieces of information would be very valuable to the historian if it were clearly known with whom the king was engaged in the wars mentioned in the inscription and what the nature of these wars was. But no further explanation is available concerning these questions, either in other inscriptions or in any other historical sources.

One can understand, then, why the history of ancient Indonesia is full of fragments which are neither clear nor definite. It is not only because the historical sources are incomplete but also because what we do have in our possession does not provide us with clear information.

Furthermore, as was pointed out in the beginning of the present article, not all historical sources in the form of inscriptions have been published and studied. In this regard mention should be made of inscriptions on the oldest Moslem tombs. The most important are the Moslem tombs in North Sumatra, and Tralaya in the neighborhood of the former center of the Majapahit Empire. The inscriptions on the Moslem tombs in North Sumatra tell us that a Moslem kingdom was already in existence in that particular area in the thirteenth century, the kingdom being the kingdom of Samudra.[48] But up to now the information contained in these inscriptions proves only the historicity of the tradition concerning the kingdom of Samudra found in the *Hikayat Raja-Raja Pasai*, and *Sejarah Melayu*, and cannot as yet be used as a primary source in writing the history of the empire, because only a few

[45] The reading of the king's name is indeed *Bāmeçwara*, and not *Kāmeçwara*. See L. Ch. Damais, "Epigrafische aantekeningen: II, Kāmeçwara I—Bāmeçwara," *TBG*, LXXXIII (1949), 6–10.

[46] OJO, LXXI.   [47] OJO, LXXIII.

[48] J. P. Moquette, "De eerste vorsten van Samoedra-Pasé (Noord Sumatra)," *ROD* (1913), pp. 1–12.

of these inscriptions have been read so far. Probably a thorough investigation of other inscriptions in North Sumatra would yield information which would change our picture of the role of Islam in North Sumatra.[49] It would not be surprising if Moslem tombs older than those of the thirteenth century were found, since Chinese and Arabian sources have mentioned the existence of Moslems in the Indonesian Archipelago in the eighth century.[50] And it seems that the historical value of the inscriptions on the Moslem tombs of Tralaya, although the inscriptions themselves have been known since the middle of the nineteenth century, has as yet not been realized.[51] We know from these inscriptions that in the fourteenth century, the period of Majapahit's greatness, a large number of Moslem people were already to be found in the surroundings of the capital of Majapahit. An intensive study might provide us with a picture of the role of Islam in the process of the downfall of the empire. That Islam had more or less a role in the fall of the empire can be imagined on the basis of the tradition which relates that the fall of the Majapahit Empire was caused by a combined attack by Moslem troops from Demak under the command of Sunan Giri.[52]

It becomes clear, then, that a great part of what is presented in books on the ancient history of Indonesia is actually still conjecture, which at any time may be discarded upon the discovery of new historical sources or a new interpretation of sources which have already been made use of. Let us consider, for example, the account of Balitung.

[49] As has been mentioned previously, the Archaeological Service of the Republic of Indonesia has about 1,800 estampages of inscriptions on Moslem tombs in North Sumatra; the lists of these are found in *OV*, 1913, pp. 22–26, 79–82, 113–114; *OV*, 1914, pp. 43–49, 85–93, 225–229; *OV*, 1915, pp. 51–55, 131–134, 171–173; *OV*, 1916, pp. 27–32, 65–69; *OV*, 1917, pp. 32–35, 106–108. Some of them are known to contain names of sultans, such as can be seen in the reports by J. J. de Vink in *OV*, 1912–1917, and J. P. Moquette, "Verslag van mijn voorlopig onderzoek der Mohammedaansche oudheden in Atjeh en Onderhoorigheden," *OV*, 1914, pp. 73–80.

[50] Groeneveldt, *Historical Notes*, p. 14. See also Wang Gungwu, "The Nanhai Trade: A Study of the Early History of Chinese Trade in the South China Sea," *JRASMB*, XXXI (1958), 70, 75 (and note 19 on this page), 79–80, 92, 96–97, 103–104. Arabian reports on this subject have been compiled by G. Ferrand, *Relations de voyages et textes géographiques arabes, persanes et turques relatifs a l'Extrême Orient du VIIIme au XVIIIme siecles* (2 vols.; Paris, 1913–1914).

[51] L. Ch. Damais, "Etudes javanaises: I, Les Tombes musulmanes datées de Trålåyå," *BEFEO*, XLVIII (1957), 353–415. The article also deals with previous publications about these inscriptions.

[52] Krom, *HJG*, pp. 462–464. See also Brandes, "Pararaton," pp. 183–186, 188–201.

The marriage mentioned in the inscription of Kedu, dated 829 Shāka, was assumed to be a marriage between Balitung and a princess of Central Java, which caused Balitung to gain the throne of Central Java. According to this theory, Balitung was a king who came from East Java, since his oldest inscriptions were found in East Java.[53] On the basis of this theory it was later suggested that Caṇḍi Prambanan, which shows East Javanese elements, was built by Balitung. The theory of Balitung's marriage may be sustained independently from the problem of his origin. But the theory that he was a king from East Java can at present no longer be accepted, or at least should be doubted. After more of Balitung's inscriptions were discovered, the oldest turned out to be an inscription from Central Java.[54] If one cannot regard Balitung as of East Javanese origin, no foundation remains to support the theory that Balitung was the builder of Caṇḍi Prambanan. And, indeed, de Casparis succeeded in proving, after a thorough examination of the facts, that Caṇḍi Prambanan was built by Rakai Pikatan in 778 Shāka.[55]

Another example is provided by the versions according to which Sanjaya, Rakai Panangkaran, and their successors were kings of the Shailendra Dynasty.[56] Owing to the investigations of J. Ph. Vogel,[57] F. H. van Naerssen,[58] and de Casparis,[59] it can now be stated that in the eighth and ninth centuries there were actually two dynasties in Central Java; one was the Sanjaya dynasty, which adhered to the Shiwa religion, while the other was the Shailendra dynasty, which embraced

[53] Goris, *FBG*, I, 202–206.

[54] The stone inscription of Telahap, dated 820 Shāka; the inscription has not yet been published. The date on this stone inscription was read by W. F. Stutterheim as 829 Shāka (*INI*, I, 13), but according to Damais, who based his conclusion on certain dating elements in the inscription, the date should be 820 Shāka (EEI: IV, *BEFEO*, XLVII (1955), 117–118.

[55] *Prasasti Indonesia*, II, 309–311.

[56] N. J. Krom, *De Sumatraansche periode in de Javaansche geschiedenis* (Leyden, 1919). See also W. F. Stutterheim, *A Javanese Period in Sumatran History* (Surakarta, 1929). Although there have been opinions which contradict the validity of such a hypothesis, it has been defended again by R. Ng. Poerbatjaraka, "Çrīvijaya, de Çailendra en de Sañjayavaṁça," *BKI*, CXIV (1958), 254–264. It is only natural that his hypothesis received a severe attack from G. Coedès, "L'Inscription de la stèle de Ligor: Etat présent de son interprétation," *Oriens Extremus*, VI (1959), 42–48, particularly pp. 45–47.

[57] J. Ph. Vogel, "Het Koninkrijk Çrīvijaya," *BKI*, LXXV (1919), 634.

[58] F. H. van Naerssen, "The Çailendra Interregnum," *India Antiqua* (Leyden, 1947), pp. 249–253.

[59] J. G. de Casparis, *Prasasti Indonesia*, I (Bandung, 1950), 131–133.

Mahāyana Buddhism. In this regard, de Casparis has done a great service in throwing light on a very interesting period in the ancient history of Indonesia, although there is still much which is hypothetical.[60]

III

A historian cannot expect all inscriptions to contain complete information such as is the case with the "Calcutta stone" or the inscription of Gunung Buṭak. He has to weave his historical account around a number of facts which are scattered throughout various inscriptions, like a bird which weaves its nest around a number of scattered points on the branches of a tree. But in weaving his account, the historian has to take cognizance of the characteristics and structure of the society which serves as the background of the historical events under investigation. And in this regard the inscriptions do provide much information, although this is the very thing the historian tends to neglect. The matters discussed above comprise only part of the content of an inscription. The other parts, which are sometimes very detailed, provide useful information on the characteristics and structure of old Javanese society.

In these parts one can obtain more detailed information about the status of a *sīma*. Among other things it is stated that a *sīma* land may not be visited by *manilāla drawya haji*, who, until now, have been considered as "taxation officers." Various kinds of taxes are mentioned in inscriptions, such as taxes on livestock traders and on agricultural products. There is also information regarding penalties for the violation of various kinds of regulations which might occur within the boundaries

---

[60] Take, for example, the theory of the existence of ten Shailendra kings in Central Java before the reign of Samaratungga, putting the reign of the first Shailendra king in Java in the beginning of the seventh century A.D. This assumption was connected with G. Coedès' hypothesis that the Shailendra kings in Java very likely originated from Funan which fell also in the beginning of the seventh century (*Prasasti Indonesia*, I, 187–192). One objection to de Casparis' theory is the proposition that Bhānu in the inscription of Hampran (Plumpungan) was one of the Shailendra kings (*Prasasti Indonesia*, I, 4–7, 97–98, 133). The reasons advanced to support the proposition that he was a king and that the inscription of Hampran is a Buddhist inscription are not very convincing. The word *prajā* in the sentence *çrīr-astu svasti prajābhyah* at the beginning of the text of the inscription can mean not only "people" or "subject" but also "creature." Furthermore, de Casparis himself has noted, in the inscription Bhānu does not use the title *mahārāja*, while the Shailendra kings always made use of this particular title. The Buddhist character of the inscription cannot be proved on the basis of the words *dharmma*, *dāna*, and *içabhaktyā*, because the words *dharmma* and *dāna* are also commonly used in Shiwaitic inscriptions, while *Īça*, as one of the names of Buddha cannot be found in the *Amarakoça* (these objections have been advanced by Damais in lectures attended by the author).

of a *sīma* area.[61] In these parts one may also come across information concerning the grant of special privileges to the beneficiary of the royal grant.[62] If such information is collected in a systematic manner, one may obtain a picture of the differences which existed between the common people and the aristocracy, such as the sphere of authority which was exclusively that of the aristocracy.

Thereafter, various functionaries are mentioned, from the top functionaries of the kingdom to the village and religious functionaries who were ordered to execute the investiture of the *sīma* land. Their respective positions can be determined on the basis of the number of *pasok* which each of them received from the beneficiary of the royal grant. An examination of these data might yield a description of the administrative hierarchy of ancient times. In this part one may also find information concerning the presence of *gamelan* musicians, singers, dancers, comedians, etc., who would participate in the investiture ceremony. The names of villages which sent their representatives as witnesses in the investiture ceremony (*wanua i tpi siring pinaka sākṣi*) might often help in locating the *sīma* area. Such information is important because quite often such an area was invested with *sīma* rights in the interests of a sacred monument. And since at present there are still many archaeological remains in the form of caṇḍis, the localization of such a *sīma* land might very probably enable one to identify a caṇḍi, which at present is still in existence, with the sacred monument mentioned in the inscription. Thus *sang kamūlan i bhūmisambhāra*, a sacred monument mentioned in an inscription of Shrī Kahulunnan of Kedu, dated 764 Shāka, has been identified by de Casparis as being the same as Caṇḍi Borobudur.[63]

[61] E.g., in the text of the "Minto stone" (Sangguran), dated 850 Shāka (OJO, XXXI), on the front part of the stone, lines 18–20; *samangkana ikang sukha duhkha kadyāngga ning mayang tan pawwah. walū rumambat ing natar. wipati wangkai kabūnan. rāh kasawur ing da(19)lan. wāk capalā. duhilatĕn. hidu kasirat. hasta capalā. namijilakĕn turuh ning kikir. mamuk. mamumpang. lūdan. tūta(20)n. daṇḍa kudaṇḍa. bhaṇḍihalādi.* Unfortunately the meaning of a great part of these terms is as yet not known.

[62] E.g., in the copper plate of Waharu II (Jenggala), dated 851 Shāka (OJO, XLII): . . . *muwah panugraha çrī mahārāja ri wuañan i samasānak i waharu tankolahulaha acuriña rahina wñi apayuña putih lamba, mwang apras watang. prasaṅgi prasiddhayuga pasilih galuh. dodot nawagraha* (4a) *skul sakurakura, grih sakujur sayub sabatang,* etc.

[63] *Prasasti Indonesia*, I, 160–170. Apart from his theory stating that the word Borobudur originates from the word *Bhūmisam bhārabhūdhara*, a theory which contains many weaknesses, the localization of *sang kamūlan i bhūmisambhāra* at Borobudur can be accepted. Similar to the terms *dharmma nira i salingsiñan* (in-

Then follows the part which describes the climax of the investiture ceremony consisting of the pronouncement of the curse by a religious functionary especially assigned to this task, called *sang (pamgat) makudur*.[64] This section usually starts with the enumeration of the various kinds of offerings required at the ceremony, consisting of the head of a water buffalo, a chicken, an egg, water to wash the feet, needles, shaving knives, nail cutters, a *dandang* (a copper container in which to cook rice), utensils for eating and drinking, and agriculture implements.[65] The function of these offerings is still not clear, with a few exceptions, such as that of the chicken, the egg, and water to bathe the feet. Before *sang makudur* began the ceremony, he washed his feet (and his hands),[66] making use of the prepared water. Afterward, while pronouncing the curse, he slaughtered the chicken and smashed the egg upon *sang hyang kulumpang* (a stone object used in such ceremonies), with the expectation that those who dared to violate the regulations concerning the *sīma* land, as indicated in the inscription, would meet the same fate as the chicken and the egg.[67] The function of the head of the water buffalo *(tandas ning kbo)*, although not explicitly indicated, may be surmised. The head of the water buffalo was presumably buried in the ground at some place on the *sīma*

---

scription of Kurambitan, dated 791 Shāka), *prāsāda i gunung hyang* (inscription of Juruñan, dated 798 Shāka), and others, in which the words Salingsingan and Gunung Hyang are names of places, the word *Bhūmisambhāra* is also the name of a place which later changed into Bumisegara. Probably a change from *bha* into *ga* has no parallel in the development of the Javanese language, but by a kind of "folk etymology" the change from Bhūmisambhāra into Bumisegara can be explained. The word *sambhāra* was later naturally pronounced *sembara* by the Javanese. And because the Javanese did not understand what the word *sembara* meant in conjunction with the word *bumi* (earth), a word was sought which sounded closely similar to the word *sembara*, but which could be understood in conjunction with the word *bumi*, and thus they found the word *segara* (sea). The word Bumisegara is indeed the name of one of the villages at the foot of Borobudur (see *Prasasti Indonesia*, I, note 3 on p. 169).

[64] According to R. Ng. Poerbatjaraka (in an oral statement to the writer), the word *makudur* later became *makutuk* (to curse).

[65] Among the implements were *linggis* (a crowbar), *wadung* (an axe), *rimbas* (?), etc. Up to the present time, people still frequently come across various iron implements stored in a *dandang* (copper rice pot), presumably remains of implements which were reserved for the ceremony investing an area with *sīma* rights (Stutterheim, *INI*, I, 24 ff).

[66] OJO, XXXI, the last part of line 19: *maṅārgha ta sang pinaka wiku*.

[67] A. B. Cohen Stuart, *Kawi oorkonden in fascimile* (Leyden, 1875), no. 1, line 22: *kadyāṅganike hantlū tan waluy i kuruñanya samang-kana ikeng hayam tan waluya matpung gulū nya mangkana tmahana nikanang ñwang umulahulaha susuk ning kudur.* The publication will be referred to as *KO*.

land, a practice which is still observed up to the present day at the commencement of every important undertaking, such as the construction of a bridge or a large building.

In some inscriptions one also frequently finds mention that offerings were *inmas* (given in gold).[68] Quite probably it meant that the person concerned was not required to prepare all these various offerings but could meet the requirements by paying *sang makudur* with gold. Such a description is not strange to contemporary Indonesian society. Whenever a person goes to a medicine man to get medicine or magical formulas, the medicine man requests the preparation of various offerings. And whenever the person concerned feels unable to prepare them, because frequently the required offerings are difficult to get, the medicine man may ask for a substitute in the form of money, so that the person concerned need not bother to seek the required objects.

Sang makudur then arranged the offerings in their proper places,[69] upon which the participants in the ceremony dined together. The dishes served are frequently also mentioned in the inscriptions.[70] After this, *sang makudur* started to pronounce his curse. The function of the curse was to damn whoever dared to violate the regulations concerning the *sīma* land as mentioned in the inscription. In this regard he usually called upon the gods and all the other supernatural beings to assist in punishing violators. One can observe here that, besides believing in the gods of the Hindu pantheon, people then clung to the indigenous belief in the existence of supernatural beings *(danyang)* which protect various places regarded as sacred. A number of inscriptions reveal that deceased kings were also regarded as gods.[71] In this connection one inscription occupies a special place, i.e., the inscription of Balitung of Kedu, dated 829 Shāka.[72] In this particular inscription

[68] Inscription of Mantyāsih, dated 829 Shāka, side B, line 2. In another inscription is found the following sentence: *panumbas i rika sarbwa saji i sang makudur mā su 8* (stone inscription of Hĕring, dated 856 Shāka, OJO, XLVII).

[69] E.g., in the inscription of Kudadu (Gunung Buṭak), plate 11 b.: *pinarṇnah teka saji sañakurug. kadyāṅga ning hayām. hantiga sasiring nya sawidhiwidhāna ning manusuk sīma ring lagi. ṅkāne sor ning witāna.*

[70] Inscription of Mantyāsih, dated 829 Shāka, side B, line 3: *lwir ning tinaḍah haḍaṅan. wök. kidang. wḍus. ginaway samenaka. muang saprakāra ning harang harang ḍeng hasin. ḍeng hañang. ḍeng tarung. muang hurang halahala hantriṇi.* Drinks are also mentioned (KO, no. I, 3, line 12): *luir nikanang ininum tuak. siddhu. ciñca.*

[71] Stone inscription of Sugihmanek, dated 837 Shāka (OJO, XXX), the back side of the stone, lines 27–28: *sakweh ta dewata prasiddha manraksang kadatwan çrī mahārāja ing bhūmi matarām.*

[72] This part is found on side B, lines 7–9, which reads: *ta (7) sak rahyang ta*

there is a list of rulers who reigned before Balitung, beginning with
King Sanjaya who, we know, ruled in the middle of the seventh century of the Shāka era.[73] These names are, quite naturally, of great
importance to the student of history.[74] Apart from this, the information
provides us with indications that our ancestors held to their old indigenous custom of ancestor worship.[75]

Very frequently mention is also made of those who became the object of the curse, i.e., the succeeding rulers *(sang anāgata prabhu)*,
state functionaries, and other persons. Sometimes mention is also made
of people of the four known castes of India, the *brāhmaṇa, kshatriya,
waishya,* and *shudra* castes. Whether mention of these four castes would
imply that Indonesian society of ancient times was also divided into
four castes, with all their aspects as found in Indian society, is not
definitely known. In his investigations, de Casparis came to the conclusion that the Indonesians were not as severe as their Indian counterparts in keeping the boundaries between these castes.[76]

In the end, as the conclusion of the ceremony and as a symbol of
the reality of the investiture of the *sīma* land (*cihnānyan mapagĕh
ikanang susukan sīma)*, the participants "multiplied their leaves."
Probably this means that the participants wrapped the remains of the
dinner in leaves to take home (*mbrĕkat,* Jav.). In some inscriptions

---

*rumuhun. sirangbāsa ing wanua. sang mangdyān kahyaṅan. sang magawai kaḍa-
twan. sang magalagah pomahan. sang tumanggöng susuk. sang tumkeng wanua
gaṇa kadi laṇḍap nyan paka çapatha kamu. rahyang* (8) *ta rumuhun. ri mḍang.
ri poḥ pitu. rakai matarām. sang ratu sañjaya. çrī mahārāja rakai panangkaran.
çrī mahārāja rakai panunggalan. çrī mahārāja rakai warak. çrī mahārāja rakai
garung. çrī mahārāja rakai pikatan* (9) *çrī mahārāja rakai kayuwaṅi. çrī mahārāja
rakai watuhumalang. lwiha sangkā rikā laṇḍap nyān paka çapatha çrī mahārāja
rakai watukura dyaḥ dharmmodaya mahāçambhu.*

[73] The name Sanjaya appears for the first time in the stone inscription of Caṅgal,
dated 654 Shāka (Kern, *VG,* VII, 117–128).

[74] However, whether on the basis of this list one can draw the conclusion that
Balitung was a direct descendant of Sanjaya is still a problem which needs further
investigation. It should be noted in this connection that B. Schrieke's investigation
has resulted in the proposition that Balitung was not a direct descendant of Sanjaya
and that the list of kings which was constructed by Balitung was only a means to
legitimize his position (B. Schrieke, "Breuk en continuiteit in de Javaansche geschiedschrijving," *Gedenkboek 25-jarig bestaan van het rechtswetenschappelijk
hoger onderwijs in Indonesië* [Groningen and Jakarta, 1949], pp. 1–16).

[75] The strength of the indigenous Indonesian element has been demonstrated by
de Casparis, who noted that the Mahāyāna Buddhism of the Shailendra rulers in
Central Java was adapted to the worship of ancestors (*Prasasti Indonesia,* I, 134–
151, particularly pp. 138–140).

[76] J. G. de Casparis, "Sedikit tentang golongan² di dalam masjarakat Djawa
Kuna," *Amerta,* no. 2 (1954), pp. 44–47.

information is found which relates that at the ceremony of the investiture of a *sīma* land, entertainment was furnished in the form of, for instance, *gamelan* music performance, dances, singing, poetry reading *(tembang)*, comedy *(dagelan)*, recitation from a manuscript, etc.[77]

Inscriptions which are grouped in the *jayapattra* category provide information of a different character. Some of them contain decisions regarding lend-lease matters.[78] One of these inscriptions, dated 844 Shāka, is extremely interesting.[79] It contains a decision regarding the citizenship of an individual. In the inscription indicated, mention is made of a sang Dhanādi, an inhabitant of *desa* Wurudu Kidul, which was part of the Halaran area, who was thought to be a *wārga kilalān*, descendant of the Khmer people. In court it was later proved that sang Dhanādi was a native inhabitant *(wwang yukti)*. Proof was gathered by inviting his relatives and other witnesses, scattered over a number of villages, who were regarded as knowing how matters stood, and it turned out that sang Dhanādi's ancestors were really native inhabitants. Another *jayapattra* contains information regarding the sale of land.[80]

IV

These are pieces of information which, if examined thoroughly, would provide interesting insights into the characteristics and structure of the society, religion, and customs of ancient Indonesia. There have already been some pioneers in such studies, among them B. Schrieke,[81] R. Goris,[82] and F. H. van Naerssen.[83] We have only to

[77] F. H. van Naerssen has published the inscription, kept at the Koninklijk Instituut voor de Tropen, Amsterdam, which, among others, contains the following sentence: *macarita rāmāyana* ("Twee koperen oorkonden van Balitung in het Koloniaal Instituut te Amsterdam," *BKI*, XCV [1937], 445).

[78] J. L. A. Brandes, "Een jayapattra, of acte van rechterlijke uitspraak van Çaka 849," *TBG*, XXXII (1889), 98–149; Brandes, *OJO*, XXIX; de Casparis, "A Judgment of Law Dated 860 A.D.," *Prasasti Indonesia*, II, 330–337.

[79] W. F. Stutterheim, "Epigraphica: III, Een Javaansche acte van uitspraak uit het jaar 922 A.D.," *TBG*, LXXV (1935), 444–456.

[80] W. F. Stutterheim, "Transcriptie van twee jayapattra's," *OV*, 1925, Appendix D, pp. 57–58.

[81] B. Schrieke, "Iets over het Perdikan-instituut," *TBG*, LVIII (1917–1919), 391–423; "Uit de geschiedenis van het adatgrondenrecht, I," *TBG*, LIX (1919–1921), 122–190; *Indonesian Sociological Studies*, pt. II, *Ruler and Realm in Early Java* (The Hague and Bandung, 1957), pp. 7–267.

[82] R. Goris, "Enkele historische en sociologische gegevens uit de Balische oorkonden," *TBG*, LXXXI (1941), 279–294.

[83] F. H. van Naerssen, "Twee koperen," pp. 456–460, and "De Saptopapatti," *BKI*, XC (1933), 239–258.

continue their work. Specific knowledge concerning the characteristics and structure of ancient society would prevent the danger of anachronisms, because without such knowledge as a foundation, one is easily tempted to project historical facts of ancient times upon the state of present-day society, which, very likely, respects different norms.

One important problem, according to the author's judgment, which should be solved is the nature of government administration in ancient times. Was the structure of government of those times centralized, or did it consist of a group of smaller kingdoms? [84] The inscriptions provide enough data for an investigation which would solve this particular problem and determine the administrative hierarchy from top to bottom. The author tends to believe that in early Indonesian history there was no centralized form of government, except for the period of the Shailendra kings in Central Java.[85] In this regard a comparison with the structure of government in the Moslem kingdom of Mataram in its period of glory might prove very useful.

Once this question is solved, some historical data might appear in quite a different light. Take, for example, the problem concerning the causes of the transfer of the center of the kingdom of Medang from Central Java to East Java in the middle of the ninth century of the Shāka era, which nowadays is explained by experts as the result of conflict between Shrīwijaya and Medang [86] or of other, i.e. economic, factors.[87] But would it not be possible that an eruption of Mt. Merapi, which was assumed by R. W. van Bemmelen to have occurred in A.D. 1006,[88] actually occurred one century earlier (since a geological investigation cannot be exact in terms of centuries) and was the direct cause of the transfer of the center of authority? This seems possible if we take into consideration that Indonesians of ancient times regarded a natural disaster, such as the eruption of a volcano described by van Bemmelen, as a punishment by the gods (běběnduning djawata).

[84] L. Ch. Damais, "Epigrafische aantekeningen: VIII, Centraal gezag of koninkrijkjes?" TBG, LXXXIII (1949), 22–26.

[85] V. R. van Romondt, "Pidato Pemimpin Seksi Bangungan Dinas Purbakala," a speech given at the ceremony on the conclusion of the reconstruction of Candi Shiwa at Prambanan (Dinas Purbakala Laporan Tahunan; 1953), p. 43.

[86] J. G. de Casparis, Erlangga (Malang, 1958), an inaugural address as professor at the Faculty of Education, University of Airlangga, Malang. Unfortunately we only have a mimeographed copy of his manuscript, so that no page references can be made.

[87] B. Schrieke, "The End of Classical Hindu-Javanese Culture in Central Java," Ruler and Realm, pp. 295–301.

[88] R. W. van Bemmelen, De geologische geschiedenis van Indonesie (The Hague, 1952), p. 67.

The fall of the kingdom of Dharmmawangsha in 939 [89] may also be explained in a different manner. Until now it has been assumed that Haji Wurawari, who attacked Dharmmawangsha from Lwarām, which became the cause of his downfall, was an ally of Shrīwijaya from the Malacca peninsula.[90] The attack has so far been regarded as a revenge attack by Shrīwijaya, who had previously been attacked by Java.[91] But actually not one inscription mentions the role of Shrīwijaya in this event. Why do we conclude that Wurawari was a king from the Malacca peninsula when such a name was not alien in Java? [92] Could not Haji Wurawari have been a vassal in Java, a *bupati,* so to speak (if we use the term of the period of Moslem Mataram), who, for one reason or another, rebelled against his king? If we consider the fact that the attack occurred when King Dharmmawangsha was celebrating the marriage of his daughter, it may be presumed that Haji Wurawari had once requested the hand of the princess but that he had been turned down by the king, a matter which provoked his anger. Such a picture is not entirely strange in Javanese literature. Apart from that, we need not imagine King Erlangga crossing the Straits of Malacca in order to fight back; we need not seek data that would indicate that Haji Wurawari was later given authority over a piece of territory in East Java by Shrīwijaya,[93] which, according to the author's judgment, is not very convincing, if it is realized that it was not Haji Wurawari whom Erlangga regarded as his toughest enemy, but Haji Wĕngkĕr.

V

In the previous paragraphs the author has tried to present a short discussion on epigraphy and has attempted to suggest in what way it may be of assistance to the writing of the history of ancient Indonesia. However, this discussion would appear incomplete if no mention were made here of a lively debate which has recently developed among experts on Indonesian history; we refer to the views of C. C. Berg concerning the value of indigenous Indonesian historical sources, particularly sources from Java, in the writing of Indonesian history. He

[89] Concerning this date, see note 38.

[90] G. P. Rouffaer, "Was Malaka emporium vóór 1400 A.D., genaamd Malajoer? En waar lag Woerawari, Ma-Hasin, Langka, Batoesawar?" *BKI,* LXX (1921), 43, 73, 90–92, 112–125, 133; de Casparis, *Erlangga.*

[91] The attack occurred about A.D. 990–992. See Groeneveldt, *Historical Notes,* pp. 18, 65.

[92] Krom, *HJG,* p. 241. See also *Lijst der voornaamste aardrijkskundige namen in den Nederlandsch-Indischen archipel* (Weltevreden, 1932).

[93] De Casparis, *Erlangga.*

made a study of the value of the *kidungs* [94] as historical sources, and later of other literary products.[95] Finally, he dealt with some inscriptions.[96] In a series of articles, he advanced the idea that Indonesians, particularly the Javanese,[97] did not know historiography in the sense that it is known in China or the West. Thus, in evaluating Javanese historical sources, one should utilize a particular method. One should view these historical sources, whether in the form of books, such as the *Nāgarakĕrtāgama* and the *Pararaton*, the *kidungs*, the *babads*, and other literary works, or in the form of inscriptions, as products of Indonesian culture, and consequently one should view them in accordance with the Indonesian "spirit." Or, in his own words, one should utilize the syntypical method in making use of these historical sources for the writing of Indonesia's history.

His basic idea is acceptable, but the problem is how to apply his idea in practice. It seems that P. J. Zoetmulder is correct in stating that those who live in the present can never entirely become "insiders," can never obtain complete knowledge of elements which are hidden in these historical sources.[98] And for the epigraphist, Berg's idea con-

[94] C. C. Berg, *De Middeljavaansche historische traditie* (Santpoort, 1927); "Iets over de historische Kidung Sorāndaka," *FBG*, I, 22–34; "Rangga Lawe, Middeljavaansche historische roman," *Bibliotheca Javanica*, vol. I (Weltevreden, 1930); "Een nieuwe redactie van den roman van Raden Wijaya: Kidung Harṣa-Wijaya," *BKI*, LXXXVIII (1931), 1–238; "Kidung Sunda," *BKI*, LXXXIII (1927), 1–161.

[95] C. C. Berg, "De Arjunawiwāha, Er-Langga's levensloop en bruiloftslied?" *BKI*, XCVIII (1939), 19–94. Berg reported that the result of his investigations of the *Bharatayuddha* and its connection with King Jayabhaya of Kĕḍiri was lost. But he has advanced his basic ideas about the problem in his book *Herkomst, vorm en functie der Middeljavaanse rijksdelingstheorie, Verhandelingen der Koninklijke Nederlandse Akademie van Wetenschappen, Afd. Letterkunde*, new ser., vol. LIX, no. 1 (Amsterdam, 1953), pp. 24–26 and note 20 on p. 187.

[96] He touched, among others, upon the inscription at the base of the statue of Amoghapasha of Padang Rotjo, dated 1208 Shāka ("Kṛtanagara, de miskende empire-builder," *Orientatie*, no. 34 [1950], pp. 3–32). The Calcutta stone and the inscription at the base of the statue of Akṣobhya of Simpang (Surabaya), dated 1211 Shāka, was mentioned, among others, in "Javanische Geschichtsschreibung," *Saeculum*, VII (1956), 161–181. The inscription on the back of the statue of Cāmuṇḍī, dated 1214 Shāka, was treated in "De Saḍeng-oorlog," pp. 385–422, and in "Kṛtanagara's Maleise affaire," pp. 406–412.

[97] It is certainly true that C. C. Berg limits his study to sources from Java. Probably a penetrating comparison with the local historiography of other ethnic groups in Indonesia will yield interesting results. In this regard there have already been pioneer studies of historical sources consisting of literature from areas other than Java (see de Casparis, "Twintig jaar studie," pp. 643–644, and the bibliography listed on p. 661).

[98] P. J. Zoetmulder, *Kawi dan Kekawian* (Jogjakarta, n.d.), p. 6, later published in its English translation as "Kawi and Kekawin," *BKI*, CXIII (1957), 52.

stitutes a threat to his *raison d'être*, because if the historical data which are only sparsely to be found in the inscriptions cannot be viewed as they are, then what should he abide by? In this connection it might be sufficient to take a look at the result of Berg's investigations and the results of the investigation by J. L. Moens, who, although unable to agree fully with Berg, did make use of Indonesian historical sources in accordance with Berg's ideas. What has been stated by Moens in regard to the genealogical line of King Erlangga [99] and the rulers of Majapahit [100] is sufficient to cast some doubt on the strict applicability of this method.

[99] J. L. Moens, "De stamboom van Erlangga," *TBG*, LXXXIV (1950), 110–158.
[100] J. L. Moens, "Wiṣṇuwardhana," pp. 365–436.

V

Local Traditions and the
Study of Indonesian History

By HOESEIN DJAJADININGRAT

*Late Professor of Islamic Studies, University
of Indonesia, Jakarta*

I

IT can be said that wherever there have been kingdoms in Indonesia,
historical traditions have been maintained. Some of the written traditions have been published, or in some cases their synopsis in Dutch.
Apart from the *Pararaton*, the Book of Kings, written in the Javanese
language of the medieval period,[1] the written historical traditions are
known in Javanese as *babad, sějarah,* and *sěrat kanda* (written stories),
in Sundanese as *sadjarah, tjarita,* and *wawatjan* (reading), and in
Malay as *hikajat, sedjarah, tutur* and *salsila.*

The content of these local traditions usually consists of a glorification
of kings or of one particular king; it may also be an account of the
genesis of a particular kingdom. A tradition of the latter category is,
for example, the *Hikajat Radja-Radja Pase,* as it is known in the

[1] Published and provided with explanatory notes by J. L. A. Brandes, "Pararaton,
of het boek der koningen van Tumapěl en van Majapahit," *VBG,* vol. XLIX
(1897), 314 p.

Achenese language, or, in Malay, *Hikayat Raja-Raja Pasai*.[2] The content of this *hikayat* may be summarized as follows: Two brothers, the eldest being Raja Ahmad and the younger Raja Muhammad, each cleared an area in the jungle in which to establish his own town. Raja Muhammad found a small girl in a big bamboo tree, took care of the girl as his own daughter, and gave her the name of Puteri Betung (Princess Bamboo). Raja Ahmad, in another part of the jungle, came across an old man who pointed out an elephant which every Friday brought a small boy to the bank of a particular river in order to bathe him. Raja Ahmad took the boy, gave him the name of Marah Gajah (Sir Elephant), and further cared for him. The respective foster fathers later arranged the marriage of Puteri Betung and Marah Gajah with each other. Two boys were born in the new family; the eldest was Marah Silu, who became the ancestor of the kings of Pasai.

One day when Marah Silu went out hunting, he heard his hunting dog, Pasai, persistently barking on the top of a hill. Marah Silu made his way to the hill and saw an ant as big as a cat. He caught the ant and ate it. On that particular spot he built a palace, and when his people moved to the hill to settle and live there, they called the place Semudera, a derivation from *semut raya,* big ant. The Prophet Muhammad, who had predicted that such an event would take place, ordered Marah Silu and his people to embrace Islam, when the occurrence of the event became known in Mecca. The Prophet's command was executed. Marah Silu was given the title of Malik al-Sâlih, while the town was called Semudera Dâr-as-Salâm. Malik al-Sâlih built another town, which he called Pasai after his dog, whom, on a hunting trip, he had seen fighting a *pelanduk* (mouse deer). Malik al-Sâlih married a daughter of the Sultan of Perlak and had a son, named Malik al-Zâhir. The further narrative of the *Hikayat Raja-Raja Pasai* is not relevant to the purpose of the present article. J. P. Moquette has published, in his study, a number of photographs of the inscriptions on the tombs of Malik al-Sâlih and Malik al-Zâhir. The inscriptions inform us that Malik al-Sâlih died in the year 696 of the Hijrah calendar (A.D. 1297), and his son died in 726 Hijrah (A.D. 1326).

[2] *Hikayat Raja-Raja Pasai* was published by Ed. Dulaurier as *La Chronique du royaume des rois de Pasey* (Paris, 1849). Aristide Marre translated the *hikayat* into French as *Histoire des rois de Pasey* (Paris, 1849). Afterward, the content of the *hikayat* was compared with the part relating to the kingdom of Samudra-Pasai in *Sejarah Melayu* (also known as *Sulalat al-Salatin,* "The Descendants of Kings") and analyzed by J. P. Moquette, "De eerste vorsten van Samoedra-Pasé (Noord Sumatra)," *ROD* (1913), in connection with the discovery of a number of inscribed tombs near the village of Samudra.

Without the tradition contained in the *Hikayat Raja-Raja Pasai* and *Sejarah Melayu* we would therefore not be in a position to establish the identity of Sultan Malik al-Sâlih.

An example of a local tradition in which one particular king is glorified is given by the *Hikayat Acheh*. Teuku Iskandar, who has published and discussed this tradition in a dissertation entitled *De Hikajat Atjéh*,[3] holds the view that the Dutch translation of the title "Geschiedenis van Atjeh" ('History of Acheh') is not very appropriate. He also considers the term "chronicle," as proposed by H. G. Juynboll[4] and the present writer for *hikayat*, rather misleading. The *Hikayat Acheh* is in Teuku Iskandar's opinion[5] essentially the *hikayat* of Iskandar Muda. It is certainly true that more than half of the said *hikayat* consists of a glorification of Iskandar Muda, 1607–1636, the greatest king of Acheh, but the first part gives an account of a number of rulers of Acheh together with each one's death date, while Iskandar Muda was also a ruler of Acheh. It would therefore in my opinion be correct to refer to the *hikayat* as *Hikayat Acheh*.[6]

In the first part of the *Hikayat Acheh* and in the first part of the section in which Iskandar Muda is glorified, a number of stories are told which by no means could be called history. This is also the case in *Hikayat Raja-Raja Pasai*, which has been summarized above. Such features are common in local historical traditions. In these traditions one comes across myths, sagas, legends, and fairy tales. In his dissertation, *Een achttiende eeuwse kroniek van Wadjo'*,[7] J. Noorduyn points out which elements of the *Hikayat Wajo'* should be classified as myth, legend, and fairy tale and which combine the characteristics of myth and also history. In the *Babad Cĕrbon*,[8] many legendary elements are blended together with actual historical data concerning Sunan Gunung Jati. This makes it difficult to evaluate both these elements properly.

[3] Teuku Iskandar, *De Hikajat Atjéh*, VKI, vol. XXVI (1958).

[4] H. G. Juynboll, *Catalogus van de Maleische en Sundaneesche handschriften der Leidsche Universiteits-bibliotheek*, vol. CCXXXIV (Leyden, 1899).

[5] Teuku Iskandar, *De Hikajat Atjéh*, p. 17.

[6] The word "kroniek" in Dutch has the connotation of history (*geschiedverhaal, geschiedenis*). The *Hikayat Raja Banjar dan Kotaringin*, which does not mention any chronology, has been discussed by A. A. Cense in his dissertation, *De kroniek van Bandjarmasin* (Santpoort, 1928). See also the words "chronique" and "histoire" in French.

[7] J. Noorduyn, *Een achttiende eeuwse kroniek van Wadjo'*, (The Hague, 1955), pp. 32–51.

[8] J. L. A. Brandes and D. A. Rinkes, "Babad Tjerbon," VBG, vol. LIX (1914), 144 p., which contains a summary in Dutch.

However, legends should not be dismissed out of hand as of no historical value; at the same time, the historical parts should be verified by Western records such as Portuguese and, later, Dutch reports.

II

R. A. Kern has only little appreciation, if any, for local traditions. In his chapter in F. W. Stapel's *Geschiedenis van Nederlandsch Indië*, he states: "Whenever a particular fact is established on the basis of other sources, one may sometimes find in the Malay chronicles, buried under heaps of fantasy, some small trace of that particular historical event; but in such cases one can just dismiss the chronicle." [9] As an example, he mentions the story of *Hikayat Raja-Raja Pasai* concerning the marriage of the founder of the kingdom of Pasai with the daughter of the Sultan of Perlak. Marco Polo informs us that Perlak had at that particular time already been converted to Islam. But the *Hikayat Raja-Raja Pasai*, in which the centuries are quite mixed up, does not give us any certainty that this particular event really happened. In his statement Kern, however, does not take account of the fact that it was precisely through this *hikayat* that Moquette was able to determine the identity of Malik al-Sâlih, whose tomb was found not far from the village of Samudra, as has been pointed out above.

P. A. Tiele, who wrote a number of articles concerning the Europeans in the Malay archipelago,[10] does not subscribe to the same opinion. Presenting a summary of the account of Fernão Mendez Pinto's experiences on the island of Java, Tiele expressed some doubts as to the authenticity of part of the account. However, he wrote, since to his knowledge no reference is made to that particular event in any of the Javanese *babads*, it is not possible to determine what should be considered a misconception on the part of Fernão Mendez Pinto.[11] This then serves to show that Tiele had some degree of appreciation for local historical traditions.

Noorduyn also holds a different view. Among the propositions

[9] R. A. Kern, "De verbreiding van de Islam," in F. W. Stapel, ed., *Geschiedenis van Nederlandsch Indië*, I (Amsterdam, 1938), 314. English translations in this chapter are by the author.
[10] P. A. Tiele, "De Europeeërs in den Maleischen Archipel," *BKI*, XXVIII (1880), pt. 4, 310.
[11] *Ibid.*, *BKI*, XXX (1882), pt. 6, 220.

(stellingen) advanced by him in presenting his aforementioned dissertation, the first one reads as follows: "For a description of the history of South-west Celebes the study of the products of Macassarese and Buginese historiography from a philological as well as a historical angle is indispensable."

European and Arabic sources may provide accurate information concerning particular dates when mention of them is made, such as dates on tomb inscriptions, but regarding additional information to be found in them much obviously will have depended on the informant involved. A clear example of such a case is given by T. J. Veltman.[12] Portuguese historians recounted that the kings of Acheh were descendants of a slave. Very likely the Portuguese obtained this story from the king of Pidië (in Malay, Pedir) who sought refuge with the Portuguese in Pasai in 1521, when he was attacked by the king of Acheh.[13] Now, it is an old custom in Acheh, in order to insult someone, to refer to him as being descended from a slave. This was said about the ancestors of Panglima Polem, head of Sagi XXII Mukim, a very powerful man, and about Habib Sennagan.[14] According to Veltman,[15] there are other such examples available.

At Cheribon in 1766 Resident Armenault was told by the four *tumenggung* (ministers) of the four kings of Cheribon that Sunan Gunung Jati, ancestor of the kings of Cheribon, possessed only priestly and not royal authority—that, however, his great grandson who succeeded him at the age of fourteen or fifteen when Sunan Gunung Jati was at an advanced age did hold royal authority. This information is contradictory to the traditions of Cheribon, Bantam, and Priangan, and it is also contradictory to the Portuguese reports which can be connected up with the traditions of Bantam and Cheribon. It seems that the four *tumenggung* intended to improve on the status of their kings, who did not possess much power and who, moreover, were subservient to the Government of the Netherlands Indies.[16]

---

[12] T. J. Veltman, "Nota over de geschiedenis van het Landschap Pidie," *TBG*, LVIII (1919), 29.

[13] On p. 26, *ibid.*, called Ibrahim, while on p. 29 called Ali Moeqajat Sjah.

[14] *Habib* refers to *sajjid*, a title held by the male descendants of Muhammad. In this case, however, the name refers to a religious leader who originated from Pidië and who taught a heretical form of mysticism in the area of Seunagan, south of Meulaboh, West Acheh. See C. Snouck Hurgronje, *De Atjehers*, II (Batavia, 1893–1894), 15.

[15] See note 12.

[16] P. A. Hoesein Djajadiningrat, "Kanttekeningen bij 'Het Javaanse Rijk Tjërbon in de eerste eeuwen van zijn bestaan'," *BKI*, CXIII (1957), 380–392.

III

Western accounts should be compared and related with local traditions in order to get a historical picture. The famous Portuguese historian João de Barros explained in his study *Da Asia* [17] that a certain man from Pasai, named Falatehan, upon his return from Mecca found Pasai occupied by the Portuguese. Falatehan felt that he had no freedom to propagate Islam, and thus he decided to move to Demak where the king was a Moslem. At Demak he was given the honor of marrying one of the king's sisters. With the approval of the king, he moved from Demak to Bantam in order to propagate Islam. When he found the local situation in his favor, he speedily conquered the ports of Bantam and Kalapa, both under the authority of the king of Sunda, with the aid of an army which he had requested from Demak. Barros did not mention the year in which this event occurred. But from his reports concerning the relationship between the Portuguese and the authorities of Sunda at Kalapa, the conclusion can be drawn that the event must have occurred at the end of 1526 or in the beginning of 1527.

F. Mendez Pinto, who has already been mentioned, tells us that in 1546 he and some of his Portuguese friends followed Tagaril, king of Sunda in Bantam,[18] to Demak in response to a summons from the king of Demak, who planned to attack Pasuruan which had not yet been converted to Islam. Upon their return to Demak, some incidents took place as a result of the assassination of the king of Demak. Pinto and his friends thereupon took leave of the king of Sunda.

By connecting the accounts of the two Portuguese with what is written in the *Sějarah Bantěn*, it becomes possible to identify Falatehan and Tagaril as one and the same person—the man who, after his death, was known as Sunan Gunung Jati, ancestor of the kings of Bantam and of Cheribon. It was he who changed the name Sunda-Kalapa into Jayakarta. But among the many names of Sunan Gunung Jati mentioned in the existing local traditions, none resembles in sound or form the name of Falatehan or Tagaril.

One can only speculate that the name Falatehan originated from the Arabic word Fathan, which is still used in Java as a personal name, and that Tagaril originated from Fachril, an abbreviation of Fachrillah, another personal name.[19]

[17] João de Barros, *Da Asia* (Lisbon, 1777), IV, 86.
[18] He referred to Tagaril as king although he knew that Tagaril was under the authority of the king of Demak.
[19] Djajadiningrat, *Critische beschouwing van de Sadjarah Bantěn* (Haarlem,

In order to evaluate Portuguese accounts, it is useful to be familiar
with Islamic terminology in Indonesia. Tomé Pires, who in 1513 took
part in a voyage to Indonesia and called at a number of ports on the
north coast of Java, relates that the master of Cheribon was a person
known as Lebé Uça. The word *lebé* comes from the Tamil language
and refers to a Moslem businessman.[20] In Sundanese the word *lebé*
is still used to refer to (1) a village official who administers religious
affairs (in one of the Javanese dialects and in Indonesian the word
lebai has the same connotation) and (2) a devoutly religious man who
has an extensive knowledge of Islam (similar to the word *leube* in the
Achenese language). When the word was used in 1513 to refer to the
head of the port of Cheribon, it should, of course, be understood in its
original meaning, i.e., a Moslem businessman. Tomé Pires reports that
Lebé Uça, like some other big traders, had a great respect for Paté
Quedir, a proud Javanese trader of noble descent. If it is assumed
that Lebé Uça (the name Uça is certain to have been derived from
Musa, as explained by Kern) was a Tamil, a foreigner in Cheribon, his
humble attitude, even though he was master of Cheribon, toward Paté
Quedir can easily be understood.[21]

Inscriptions on tombs which contain names and dates remain isolated pieces of information when they are not brought into relation
with local traditions. In the village of Leran, in the neighborhood of
Gresik, is a tomb inscribed in old Arabic calligraphy. Moquette, who
has published this inscription, deciphered the name of Fatimah bint
Maimun bin Hibatallah, who met her death in the year 495 Hijrah
(A.D. 1102). It turns out that this particular inscription cannot be
brought into relation with any local tradition. Moquette's conclusion is
an acceptable one, and thus the pieces of information contained in the
inscription indicated above remain isolated pieces of information.[22]

1913); *idem*, "De naam van den eersten Mohammadaansche vorst in West Java,"
TBG, LXXIII (1933), 401–404; *idem*, "Hari lahirnja Djajakarta," *Bahasa dan
Budaja*, V, no. 1 (1956–1957), 3–11, an article which dealt with Soekanto's book,
Dari Djakarta ke Djajakarta; idem, "Tjatatan" under Soekanto's answer, "Tentang
karangan Prof. Dr. P. A. Hoesein Djajadiningrat, 'Hari lahirnja Djajakarta'," *Bahasa
dan Budaja*, V, no. 3 (1956–1957), 3–9; *idem*, "Kanttekeningen."

[20] Ph. S. van Ronkel, "Maleisch Labai, een Moslimsch-Indische term," *TBG*,
LVI (1914), 137–142.

[21] Djajadiningrat, "Kanttekeningen."

[22] J. P. Moquette, "De oudste Moehammedaansche inscriptie op Java n.m. de
de Grafsteen te Leran," *Handelingen van het Eerste Congres voor de Taal-, Land-
en Volkenkunde van Java, 1919* (Weltevreden, 1921), pp. 391–399.

An example of a case in which a local tradition enables us to put a person, whose tomb is found to contain an inscription, in the proper historical context has been given above in the discussion of the *Hikayat Raja-Raja Pasai* and the tomb of Malik al-Sâlih.

In Gresik is located the tomb of Malik Ibrahim, who died in 822 Hijrah (A.D. 1429). According to a plausible analysis of the style of the inscription on the tomb by Moquette, Malik Ibrahim must have come from Kâsjan, Iran.[23]

A number of Javanese traditions—not all of them—refer to Malik Ibrahim as a member of the *wali sanga* (the nine saints), who were the first to propagate Islam in Java. This is difficult to accept. Sunan Bonang, who in *all* traditions is mentioned as one of the *wali sanga* and who, after his father Sunan Ngampel (who himself is usually not included as a member of the *wali sanga*), belongs to the oldest group among them, began to officiate as *wali* in the fourth quarter of the sixteenth century. (This is a conjecture, as no definite date is available.[24])

In his aforementioned article,[25] Kern also rejected these traditions. He noted that the inscriptions on the tomb indicated only that Malik Ibrahim was a Persian. Kern also drew the conclusion that Malik Ibrahim was most likely a respectable businessman, who had "struck it rich," as is evident from his imposing tomb. Moquette, who reproduced the part of the inscription relating to Kâsjan, remarks that the place was eminently suited to train proselytizing traders.[26] In the history of Islam, up to the present, the combination of trader and teacher of religion has not been a strange one. A famous example is Abû Hanîfah, who died in 150 Hijrah (A.D. 767), imam (leader) of the Hanafî sect. He was a trader in textiles although he had a great number of students. A Moslem interpreter of the *hadith* (Islamic traditions) has said that teachers of religion are not allowed to exact payment but are only allowed to accept gifts. In *A Handbook of Early Muhammadan Tradition*,[27] A. J. Wensinck simplified this statement in the entry "Knowledge" to "the teacher may not ask payment."

[23] J. P. Moquette, "De grafsteenen te Pase en Grisee vergeleken met dergelijke monumenten uit Hindoestan," *TBG*, vol. LIV (1912).

[24] B. J. O. Schrieke, *Het boek van Bonang: Bijdrage tot de kennis van de Islamiseering van Java* (Utrecht, 1916), pp. 53, 54. Sunan Bonang is regarded as only an imam.

[25] Kern, "De verbreiding," p. 324.

[26] Moquette, "De grafsteenen te Pase en Grisee," p. 547.

[27] A. J. Wensinck, *A Handbook of Early Muhammadan Tradition* (Leyden, 1927).

In a sixteenth-century Javanese *primbon* [28] mention is made of Sjech Ibrahim Maulana and Sjech Maulana, together with some of his sayings in regard to Islam,[29] while mention of the name Maulana Malik Ibrahim is made in *Sĕjarah Bantĕn*.[30] The term "Sjech," which in general means head or leader, refers in connection with the *tarekat* (religious orders) to its founder, while Maulana, "our lord," refers to *ulama* and/or *wali*, religious leader. If we consider all these facts, we may presume that although it is difficult to include Malik Ibrahim as a member of the *wali sanga* he was certainly a *wali*, a teacher of religion, propagator of Islam in Java whose teachings were transmitted by his pupils until they were eventually recorded in a Javanese *primbon* of the sixteenth century.[31]

In order to be able to make a study of local traditions concerning the beginnings of Islam and the following periods, or of Islamic history in general, a knowledge of Islam is certainly necessary.[32] In discussing the development of Islam in India, Kern wrote: "Unlike the Christians, there were only two alternatives for a Hindu: to be converted to Islam or to be destroyed. This was the rule of the Sjariat. But in reality matters were quite different." [33] This statement has been repeated by Kern in his recent book, *De Islam in Indonesië*.[34] The statement is not correct. In his well-known book,[35] Th. W. Juynboll notes in his discussion about laws regulating slavery that captured *kafir* (heathens) were made slaves, and in his discussion about *jihad* (holy war), it is stated that women, children, aged people, priests, and others who were not able to resist were not to be killed.[36] Kern's error is probably derived from Juynboll's statement, which is too short and therefore not quite accu-

---

[28] Published without translation as a dissertation by J. G. H. Gunning, *Een Javaansch geschrift uit de zestiende eeuw* (Leyden, 1881). Later it was translated and discussed by H. Kraemer, also as a dissertation, *Een Javaansche primbon uit de zestiende eeuw* (Leyden, 1921), while it was reissued in translation with a discussion by G. W. J. Drewes, *Een Javaanse primbon uit de zestiende eeuw* (Leyden, 1954).

[29] Drewes, *Een Javaanse primbon*, pp. 306–326.

[30] Djajadiningrat, *Critische beschouwing*, p. 30.

[31] The exact date is not known; see Djajadiningrat, "Kanttekeningen."

[32] See, as examples, Cense, "Eenige Maleische boeken van Borneo," *De kroniek van Bandjarmasin*, pp. 159–173, and Noorduyn, "4, De Islamiseëring," in "Het historiografisch materiaal," *Een achttiende eeuwse kroniek van Wadjo'*, pp. 93–107.

[33] Kern, "De verbreiding," p. 313.

[34] R. A. Kern, *De Islam in Indonesië* (The Hague, 1947), p. 6.

[35] Th. W. Juynboll, *Handleiding tot de kennis van de Mohammedaansche wet volgens de leer der Sjafi'itische School* (3d ed.; Leyden, 1925).

[36] *Ibid.*, p. 233.

rate and easily misinterpreted. Juynboll stated that *kafir* who were not *ahl-al-Kitab,* "people of the Book," i.e., Jews and Christians, were not allowed to surrender.[37] The holy war against these heathen had to be continued until they were entirely destroyed or converted to Islam.[38]

IV

To conclude these brief notes, a few words might be said about the unconventional value of the chronology used in local traditions. In the *Sĕjarah Bantĕn* it is said that those who were about to attack Pakuan, capital of the kingdom of Pajajaran, left Bantam on Sunday, 1 Muharram, year Alip, *sĕngkala* (Javanese chronogram): *bumi rusak rekèh* or *mangkè iki,* which means 1501 Shāka or A.D. 1579.[39] In *Critische beschouwing van de Sadjarah Bantĕn,*[40] the present author explained that the first day of the seven-day week, the first day of the first month of the Moslem year, and the first year of the *windu* (Javanese cycle of eight years) as dates of particular events can be dismissed as having been made up and as unhistorical. It should be added in this connection that 1501 Shāka was the first year of a new century. H. ten Dam, who will be referred to later, asserted that the year 1501 Shāka and Sunday, 1 Muharram, and the year Alip should be regarded as a whole. This is quite correct. In determining the *numeral* value of the word *rekèh,* the present author said only that it would make no difference whether the given date is right or wrong.[41] Furthermore, that particular date could not have been a Sunday when checked against the *windu* system. This manner of reckoning time, which was decreed by Sultan Agung of Mataram in 1555 Shāka, consists of a small cycle (in Javanese, *windu*) of eight years, in which each year is indicated by an Arabic letter in accordance with a *numeral* value (1st year Alip = 1; 2d year Éhe = 5; 3d year Djim = 3, etc.), and a big cycle of 120 years. When Sultan Agung ordered the beginning of the new calendar (in 1555 Shāka), he decreed that the new calendar should continue the year count of the old calendar so that the first year of the new Javanese-Moslem calendar was 1555, the next year 1556, etc. As the calendar was a lunar calendar, every 120 years a correction had to be made by passing over one day. When no correction was made, each year of the small cycle started with an identical day. When the new calendar was

[37] *Ibid.,* p. 344.   [38] *Ibid.,* p. 348.
[39] Djajadiningrat, *Critische beschouwing,* pp. 35, 132.
[40] *Ibid.,* p. 132.   [41] *Ibid.,* p. 132.

decreed by Sultan Agung, 1 Muharram of the year Alip was Friday. After the correction had been made in 1675 by passing over one day, the year Alip started with Thursday.[42] If this time reckoning had been practiced before 1555 Shāka, it is clear that 1 Muharram, year Alip, 1501 Shāka, could not have been Sunday, such as is indicated in *Sĕjarah Bantĕn,* but must have been Saturday. According to G. P. Rouffaer, one *windu* before 1555 Shāka the *windu* time reckoning was already practiced; the year Alip therefore started with a Friday.

In an article entitled "Verkenningen rondom Padjadjaran," H. ten Dam wrote: "If Djajadiningrat had understood this—or better: if he could have understood this in 1913—it would have become clearer to him why the whole chronology up to and including the period of Molana Jusup has been disarranged." [43] One should make a distinction between "history" and "symbolism." As a historical datum the present author dismissed the chronology in *Sĕjarah Bantĕn;* however, he accepts its "symbolic" value, although he made a mistake by not mentioning it then. The date concerned symbolizes a new age, the Moslem age (although at that time Pakuan had not yet been conquered by Bantam), as is indicated by the chronogram *bumi rusak rekĕh* or *mangkĕ-iki* (the world will presently be destroyed). At the end of his article, H. ten Dam wrote: "Whether something happened and what happened in regard to Pajajaran in 1501 remains for the time being an open question."

Another example of a date which, in the author's opinion, should be considered as symbolic is the *candra-sĕngkala* (chronogram): *sirna hilang kerta ning bumi* (the disappearance of world peace), dated 1400 Shāka (A.D. 1478). It is mentioned in the Javanese *babads* as the date of the fall of the Hindu kingdom Majapahit, brought about by the Islamic kingdom of Demak. That date, obtained from the Javanese traditions, had at first been considered historical. However, later on, among Dutch scholars some refuted it, while others continued to support it, even though the fall was not brought about by an Islamic kingdom but by another Hindu kingdom. According to the latest interpretation of the event,[44] the date cannot be considered historical. The present author considers the date to be symbolical. To support this

---

[42] G. P. Rouffaer, "Tijdrekening," *Encyclopaedie van Nederlandsch-Indië,* IV (1905), 446–448.

[43] H. ten Dam, "Verkenningen rondom Padjadjaran," *Indonesië,* X, no. 4 (1957), 290–310.

[44] H. J. de Graaf, "Tomé Pires' 'Suma Oriental' en het tijdperk van godsdienstovergang op Java," *BKI,* CVIII (1952), 132–171.

contention one should compare the verbal meaning of its chronogram with that of the chronogram in the *Sĕjarah Bantĕn* referring to the downfall of the Hindu kingdom Pajajaran, brought about by the Moslem kingdom Bantam. The first chronogram means "the disappearance of world peace"; the second, "the destruction of the world."

One should also compare the numeral value of the two chronograms. The one (1400 Shāka) indicates the end of an old, the other (1501 Shāka) the beginning of a new, century.

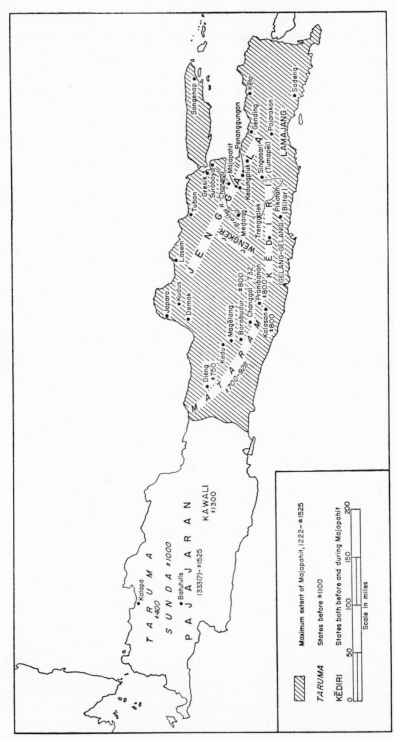

2. Javanese Kingdoms before 1525

VI

The Javanese Picture of the Past[*]

By C. C. BERG

Professor of Austronesian Linguistics, University of Leyden

1. INTRODUCTORY REMARKS

HUMAN language is a product of social intercourse: it presupposes a verbal activity of individuals availing themselves of certain physical and hereditary qualities, as well as a permanent speech community which remains substantially unaffected by comers and goers. The permanent speech community imposes upon its members a permanent complex of speech habits. An analysis of the mass of linguistic forms resulting from these habits shows—apart from such features as are irrelevant to the present discussion—the existence of socialized simple linguistic forms, roughly definable as dictionary units, and the existence of constructions in which those socialized simple linguistic forms function as bricks in buildings. These constructions—sentences and conglomerates of sentences—may be divided into nonsocializing ones and socialized ones. I call the latter constructions "myths." Thus myths are socialized composite linguistic forms as opposed to socialized simple linguistic forms on the one hand and nonsocializing composite linguistic forms on the other side. The term "socialized" refers to a process of socialization; "imposing" is one aspect of this process, the opposite aspect being belief.

Belief is our willingness to take linguistic forms at their face value and to pass them on to others. Normally the objective truth of a myth is of little concern to us. An American boy who is told that "the earth revolves on its axis and around the sun" is likely to believe his teacher in the same way as a Javanese boy of yore who was told that "Bharāda

[*] This article represents a stage in the evolution of the author's theory of the Javanese conception of history and renders his viewpoint of 1959.

87

flew over the country when tracing a line of demarcation through Erlangga's land." If, in connection with myths, the term "credulity" forces itself upon us, we should bear in mind that unconcerned belief in myths is fairly universal. The mythical patterns which mankind has developed, however, are widely divergent, so as to make different speech communities believe very different things.

Although the members of a speech community are committed to their complex of speech habits, the arbitrary character of human language and the underlying hereditary qualities of man account for a marginal freedom which is the cause of linguistic change and the ultimate cause of linguistic differentiation and expansion. The individual deviations which result from this marginal freedom are errors and distortions when judged by a synchronic social standard; if, however, the individual deviation becomes socialized, the very process of socialization transforms the erroneous or distorted form into a habit of the community. In this way socialized variants come into existence. Under certain circumstances it may happen that the coexistence of two socialized variants induces differential fixation, i.e., an individual tendency to use the two forms differently. If this individual tendency manages to become socialized, a new distinction is added to the complex of speech habits. As language constitutes a complex of distinct and distinctive linguistic forms, it owes its existence to an interplay between the individuals' general acceptance of the prevailing complex of speech habits and their marginal freedom to deviate from it. It must be pointed out that variants may also come into existence as a result of linguistic borrowing in intertribal or international intercourse; in such cases the term "synchronic social standard" which has been used above should be replaced by "synchronic and syntypical social standard," though the process remains the same.

A picture of the past is a specific complex of myths in the sense of "myth" defined above, as myths necessarily reflect past experience. As a specific complex of myths, a picture of the past constitutes a part of the speech habits of a community and is subject to the processes described above. Each speech community has, therefore, its own slowly expanding picture of the past; a constant evolution slowly rejuvenates the forms as well as the contents of the picture, in a way comparable to the slow rejuvenation of a vocabulary. To some extent we are able to reconstruct the sequence of the changes which mark this development; satisfactory results, however, are not attainable unless written documents provide us with reliable clues.

The Javanese picture of the past has absorbed a considerable number of Indian myths in the period of Indo-Javanese cultural contacts; this is why we find Indian gods and heroes as royal ancestors in Javanese genealogies. Not only for stories about gods and heroes, however, are the Javanese indebted to the Indians; they also learned from them linear chronology and alphabetic writing. The oldest era in Java is the Shāka era. The Sanskrit name of this era, *çākakāla*, survives in the Javanese form *sĕngkala* which now means "chronogram"; a *sĕngkala* is a combination of ambiguous words which reminds the hearer or reader of some important event in the past and enables him to figure out the Shāka—or, after A.D. 1633, the Shāka/Hijrah—year of its occurrence. Such chronograms might have helped the Javanese in developing a chronologically well-arranged picture of the past even without the aid of an alphabet. As it stands, the Javanese became familiar with an Indian alphabet without developing the need of putting the important facts of the past in the right chronological order. A reasonable hypothesis to explain this fact is that the Javanese appreciation of the newly acquired knowledge did not encourage them to transform their picture of the past into a "chronicle."

The study of Javanese manuscripts and theatrical performances has revealed the existence of texts in *basa kawi* or "poetical style" which reflect, in each separate case, the individual conception of a trained scholar rather than a process of socialization. In many cases we do not know what kind of considerations induced the authors to compose them. Some theatrical performances and the recitation of some texts, however, are certain to have served the purpose of magic, and this is why the thought presents itself that their author, too, may have had this purpose in mind. Observing that words sometimes make human beings behave in accordance with the sense they convey, many people believe words to possess an inherent power which may affect situations and dead objects as well, and priests to possess the gift of handling such powerful words. We call the practice of speaking powerful words "magic" if the speaker himself believes that his words bring about the desired effect. The ancient Javanese did believe in verbal magic, as is evident from stories which we find in their literature. Considering, then, that some Javanese texts are unintelligible unless we suppose the author to have practiced magic, and that many other texts are easier to understand and fit better into a framework of facts if interpreted on the basis of that supposition, we shall have to reckon with the possibility that in Java "poetical style" and magical function were concomitant.

Javanese texts which served a purpose of verbal magic at the time of their birth could in due time become part of the picture of the past, if

circumstances were favorable. But we should not forget that such texts
are potential weapons: if used to strengthen the position of a king, they
must be as disagreeable to his opponents as they are welcome to him,
so that a change of regime could only be detrimental to their survival.
We find, as a matter of fact, remarkable gaps in the chronological distribution pattern of the Javanese charters, as well as stories about the
destruction of ancient books after the rise of Islam. If we take it that
the priestly supporters of a new dynasty destroyed the books and
charters which strengthened the authority of the preceding dynasty,
then this theory explains the gaps in the distribution pattern and at
the same time agrees with what we know about "heresy hunt" in other
parts of the world. It is probable, therefore, that the Javanese picture
of the past reflects—apart from the result of its normal evolution—the
priestly cultivation of verbal magic in a negative as well as in a positive sense.

As a rule the Javanese priests did not inform their readers of the
motives and intentions which underlay their activities. Why, indeed,
should they have done so, as members of a more or less homogeneous
community? Motives and intentions, however, do and did play an important part in shaping the utterances of a speech community. The
modern student of Javanese history who wants to know what really
happened in Java and why things happened as they did, cannot, when
reading Javanese books as possible sources of information, get round
the difficulty of ascertaining their informational value. When trying
to do so he will be confronted with the question as to what were the
author's motives when he wrote or published his book. Since the answer to this question requires some knowledge of the Javanese pattern
of culture, contributions of specialists, and first of all an article on the
Javanese picture of the past, might be helpful, even if it bears the
stigma of prematurity.

The present writer will try to outline the evolution of the Javanese
picture of the past during the period for which written documents are
available. He is quite aware of the provisional character of his contribution, since many texts have not yet been subjected to careful examination.

2. ERLANGGA AND THE EARLY MAJAPAHIT PICTURE OF THE PAST

The object of a priest who performs an act of verbal magic is to
influence the course of events. Events may imply human activities, and

human activities may imply speech; priestly magic, therefore, may be intended to bring about a change in the utterances of the community concerned, the members being expected to conform to the priestly statements. These statements presuppose, therefore, utterances of the speech community which were disagreeable to the priests or their employer. Thus a priestly doctrine is likely to invert a prevailing picture of the present. The broader the gap between the popular picture of the present and the priestly doctrine, the more impressive must be the priestly statement as the instrument of inversion; the use of Sanskrit, of allegories and chronograms, etc., should be seen in this light. It goes without saying that the inversion of historical facts by means of priestly statements is by no means confined to Java.

Bearing all this in mind, we may safely call Erlangga—a Javanese king who ruled in the second quarter of the eleventh century—a usurper, since three texts have been written in order to establish the opposite view, viz., OJO 62, in Javanese, the poem *Arjunawiwāha*, also in Javanese, and a Sanskrit Erlangga hymn. OJO 62 deals with the inauguration of a Wishnu sanctuary destined to be "the *palinggan* of the country, and especially of the many future kings," i.e., to safeguard the interests of Erlangga's dynasty; the sanctuary is said to owe its existence to a solemn and prophetical promise made by Erlangga at the dawn of a new era.[1] In connection with the main theme the author tells a story about Erlangga's initial troubles, enumerates his wars, and describes his final victory. The author of the Sanskrit hymn tells essentially the same story, but instead of hinting at the dawn of a new era he calls Erlangga the son of Udayana and his wife Mahendradattā, the daughter of King Makuṭawangshawardhana, who had been the son of Lokapāla and his wife Īshānatunggawijayā, Īshānatungga's daughter; this Īshānatungga has been identified with the prime minister Sinḍok/ Īshānawikrama who is mentioned in OJO 33 and with King Sinḍok/ Īshānawikramadharmottunggadewa whom we know from a fairly large number of inscriptions dated between 929 and 947 (OJO 37 *et seq.*). The *Arjunawiwāha*, written by a skillful poet and certainly not a specimen of primitive Indo-Javanese poetry, contains the story of the Indian hero Arjuna who, after losing his realm and living a hermit's life in the forest, was invited by the gods to defeat their enemy Niwātaka-

---

[1] OJO = "Oud-Javaansche oorkonden," texts of Old Javanese charters, published in *VBG*, vol. LX (1913), 267 p. *Lingga* is the Sanskrit word for the symbol of procreative power; the Javanese derivative *palinggan* either had the same or almost the same meaning as *lingga*, or was used in the meaning of "*lingga* sanctuary."

waca; he gained a complete victory and, as a result, seven celestial brides whom he enjoyed for seven celestial days in Indra's heaven.

The *Arjunawiwāha* story runs differently in the Sanskrit poem *Mahābhārata* whence it derives, but it fits in with the picture which we find in OJO 62; if we identify Arjuna with Erlangga, Arjuna's seven celestial days suggest the regnal period of a dynasty which, according to the Javanese myths, consists of seven kings. The first of them was Erlangga. As to Īshānatungga, it seems to me that he has been rightly identified with Sindok, but we have as little reason to regard him as Erlangga's historical ancestor as we have reason to regard the goddess Venus as the ancestress of Emperor August: a self-made man simply looks better if he is surrounded by royal or divine ancestors. We do not know what the Indian poet had in mind when he called Erlangga's grandfather Makutawangshawardhana; the name sounds like "successor to the royal family of . . ."—the trouble then being that several Javanese place names could be rendered by *makuta*.[2] Now if one of the three authors avails himself of an allegory in order to transfer Arjuna's invincibility to his own king, and the Indian poet invents a line of ancestors *ad majorem Erlanggae gloriam,* why should we have unconditional faith in what the third man says? Let us simply regard the three documents in question as a literary triptych, a masterpiece in its way: the main panel depicts the founder of the dynasty, one side panel shows his ancestors, the other hints at the prospective successors.

The text of the Erlangga hymn must have been abracadabra to the Javanese of the eleventh century. It may, however, have been explained in Javanese in much the same way as the *Mahābhārata* books, or as Javanese texts have been retold in Madurese and Balinese in later centuries. In the first period of its existence this paraphrase of the Erlangga hymn must have absorbed many Indonesian elements, whereas the genealogical pattern seems to have been modified for different reasons in different times; yet the text which came into existence in this way and which developed into the *Pararaton* version of the early days of Majapahit is sufficiently characteristic to be recognized as the Javanese counterpart to the Sanskrit Erlangga hymn. In the finished product, the *Pararaton,* i.e. "the Dynasty," the ancestor bears his Javanese name; *Sindok* must have been understood as *si Ndok,* and under the influence of various factors developed into *ken*

---

[2] *Makuṭa* (Sanskrit *mukuṭa*), "crown." In Javanese it may also have been used as a word for "bracelet" or "anklet." In that case it may have suggested *galuh* or *gĕlang,* and hence such place names as Galuh, Magĕlang, Gĕgĕlang, Wĕngkĕr, etc.

Angrok. He enters as the incarnation of the late "son of the Lord of Jiput"—an expression which we should very much like to understand, since it points to a picture of the past which is unknown to us. The paraphrase mentions a considerable number of details about Angrok's early years which we do not find in the Sanskrit hymn; however, these details do not reflect a better knowledge of the past, since they derive from an ancient Indonesian myth which depicts the ancestor's struggle for life and power in terms of a child's prenatal existence, the embryo being, according to the ancient Indonesians, in constant danger of becoming the pontianak's victim and helper.[3] Once a king, Angrok manifested himself as the incarnate Shiwa, since Īshāna is one of Shiwa's names. The Javanese attributed two shapes to Shiwa's consort: she was Durgā, the angry one, and Umā, the kind one. Accordingly Angrok was said to have two wives, Ḍĕḍĕs and Umang, and either wife was given four children, in symmetrical groups. In either case the names of two sons suggest the nature of their mother; this reminds us of Īshānatungga's daughter whose name is practically identical with that of her father. The diabolical Durgā being characterized by flaming genitals, Ḍĕḍĕs' two sons were called Wongatĕlĕng Agnibhaya, in approximative translation "danger of the vulvar fire," though Ḍĕḍĕs' vulva was given a softer shine in our story.[4] Among the grandsons we find a Rangga-Wuni, i.e. "vulvar brightness," whose genealogical position roughly corresponds to Makuṭawangshawardhana's position in the Sanskrit hymn; his royal name Wishnuwardhana reminds us of the expression "like the illustrious Wishnu" used in the Erlangga hymn in connection with Makuṭawangshawardhana, according to Kern's translation.

Makuṭawangshawardhana's epithet does not suffice to explain the name of his opposite number, however. The case of Wishnuwardhana is more complicated, and the same holds true for the kings of the fourth and fifth generation. According to the *Pararaton,* the king of the fourth generation was a man who fell a victim to enemy raiders, whereas the king of the fifth generation, his son-in-law, was lucky enough to escape by the skin of his teeth. So far so good. According to the Sanskrit hymn, the lucky son-in-law Erlangga took refuge with the priests, who

[3] Cf. C. C. Berg, "Angrok und das Wochenbettgespenst," *Oriens Extremus,* VI (1959), 5–30. Pontianaks are birth spirits; they attack women in childbed and their babies.

[4] In the oldest version of the paraphrase, Wongatĕlĕng Agnibhaya may have been a girl, corresponding to the Īshānatunggawijayā of the Erlangga hymn. She may have changed into two boys when her name became unintelligible.

recognized him as the future king and helped him to defeat his enemies. This story returns in the *Pararaton* insofar as *Bañak Wiḍe* and "the priests" are equivalent; if we suppose that *bañak wiḍe* was an eleventh-century expression for "the scholars" which lost its transparency when *bañak* fell into disuse as an indicator of the plural, the condensation of "the priests" into the one helper Bañak Wiḍe of the *Pararaton* story becomes understandable.[5] The *Pararaton* does not call the lucky son-in-law Erlangga, however; it calls the murdered king Kěrtanagara/Shiwa-buddha and his son-in-law Wijaya. The Chinese account of the Mongolian raid which struck East Java in 1293 leaves no shade of doubt as to the historicity of Kěrtanagara's violent death and Wijaya's efforts to become his successor. In view of these facts we may safely conclude that the paraphrase of the Erlangga hymn has been applied, in 1294 or one of the following years, to the case of Wijaya, the founder of the dynasty of Majapahit. It is this applicability of an old story to a new situation to which we probably owe the survival of the paraphrase.

In 1294 a royal charter—OJO 81—was issued by King Wijaya's priests which confirms our theory. The story about Wijaya's initial troubles and final victory which we find in OJO 81 runs parallel to the story of OJO 62 so that it is reasonable to regard OJO 81 as a priestly statement proclaiming Wijaya's functional identity with Erlangga, i.e., as an official justification of his usurpation. Moreover, OJO 81 calls Wijaya "a son-in-law in the royal family of Narasingha, Narasinghamūrti's daughter's son, Kěrtanagara's daughter's husband," just as Erlangga had been Makuṭawangshawardhana's daughter's son and husband of the daughter of the "previous king." If we compare this, in the light of the Erlangga documents, to what the *Pararaton* says, it stands to reason that the Wishnuwardhana of the *Pararaton* story and the Narasing-hamūrti mentioned in OJO 81 were identical. The meaning of the names may be an additional argument: *Narasinghamūrti* means "Wishnu's incarnation," and *Wishnuwardhana* means "Wishnu's successor." The argument implies that Narasinghamūrti/Wishnuwardhana was a Makuṭawangshawardhana in terms of the Erlangga hymn.

However, Wishnuwardhana—or, better, Jaya Wishnuwardhana—seems to have been the founder of a new dynasty himself, the dynasty

[5] *Bañak* is "goose" in Javanese and "people," "multitude," "many," in Malay. It may have acquired the meaning "goose" in Javanese under the influence of *angsa* which derives from Sanskrit *waṃça*, "people," and from Sanskrit *haṃsa*, "goose"; cf. the evolution of *bañak ḍalang*, in ancient Javanese probably "the ḍalangs," in modern Javanese an ornament in the shape of a goose, in both cases more or less equivalent to *upacara*. In the Kidung *Rangga-Lawe*, Bañak Wiḍe's second name is āryādhikāra, "Lord Bishop"; this is an additional argument in favor of our theory.

of Singasari which came to an end when Kĕrtanagara was murdered. We have reason to suppose that this usurper—were he and Wijaya Madurese adventurers?—managed to conquer a part of East Java in 1252.[6] After his accession to the throne he, too, may have been celebrated as the Erlangga of the new era, just as Wijaya was in 1294. There is no direct evidence in support of this theory. Two arguments, however, may be put forward in favor of it: *Par.* 18,9 *et seq.*, ascribing to Wishnuwardhana "the elimination of the *lingga* of the lord" which may mean that he put an end to the dynasty protected by Erlangga's *palinggan*, and, secondly, the interpretation of Wishnuwardhana's name, since Erlangga had been the Wishnu of his era. If both Wishnuwardhana and Wijaya were the Erlangga of their days, they must have been regarded as functionally identical. Now the similarity of the main dates of Wishnuwardhana's and Wijaya's regnal periods as we find them in Prapanca's *Nāgarakĕrtāgama* (1365) points to the existence of such a theory; according to Prapanca, Wishnuwardhana arranged the coronation of his son two years after his victory and fourteen years before his death. And so did Wijaya. If this argument is valid, it opens the way toward better understanding of the *Pararaton*. The author of the early Majapahit version of this book could not eliminate Wishnuwardhana from the picture of the past, if Wishnuwardhana and Wijaya were functionally identical as reincarnations of the usurper Erlangga. On the other hand, the functional identity conception was inconsistent with the simple character of the *Pararaton*. Under these circumstances a popular solution which approached the priestly notions may have been preferred: availing himself of the opportunity provided by the synonyms Wishnuwardhana/Narasinghamūrti, the author distinguished a dynasty consisting of Wishnuwardhana and Kĕrtanagara from a dynasty consisting of Narasingha and the kings of Majapahit, deriving both, however, from Dĕdĕs, who was given an additional child by a first lover.[7] From a technical point of view this reconstruction of the paraphrase must have been a rather simple affair, though it was essentially a mutilation of the ancient myth. It must be emphasized, however, that mutilation

---

[6] This seems to be what a chronogram in *Nag.* 15,2 suggests. I do not quite understand the remarks made by Teeuw and Uhlenbeck in "Over de interpretatie van de Nāgarakrtāgama," *BKI,* CXIV (1958), 220. The figures which we find in the Nāgarakĕrtāgama manuscript under the words of the chronogram did not escape Krom's attention; I ignored them at an earlier occasion since I do not take them seriously.

[7] The *Pararaton* calls Dĕdĕs' first lover Tunggul-Amĕtung. Being the last king of the previous dynasty, this man could be associated with the kings of Singasari after Majapahit came to power. Cf. note 38.

of ancient myths is a matter of as little concern to a speech community as the corruption of words. Anyhow, it is in its corrupted form that the *Pararaton* has exercised considerable influence upon poets who had to explain the origin of a new dynasty in later years.

A second major change to which the *Pararaton* owes its own character as compared with the paraphrase of the Erlangga hymn was Bañak Wiḍe's metamorphosis, a metamorphosis which could occur all the more easily since the man started life as a mere proper name, after the sense of the underlying collective noun faded away. According to the *Pararaton* Bañak Wiḍe was a *babatangan* in exile who took revenge by plotting the destruction of his oppressor Kĕrtanagara; after causing Kĕrtanagara's death he became a king in East Java. A *babatangan* is a nonking whose future kingship was predicted by a priest: the prophecy being a magic formula, the *babatangan*'s career must lead up to the predicted situation whatever happens in the meanwhile. Functionally a *babatangan* story as it occurs in Javanese literature is a justificatory statement, and as such it is not essentially different from the type of allegory which we have discussed above. This is why a *babatangan* story could have been told with respect to Wijaya himself, instead of the allegory which identifies him with Erlangga. The fact that both a *babatangan* story, the one concerning Bañak Wiḍe, and an allegory, the one referring to Wijaya, play a part in the Wijaya episode of the *Pararaton* may point to the existence of two East Javanese states in the first decades after the Mongolian invasion.[8] From the point of view of a court priest such a situation must have detracted from the glory of his employer so as to require normalization. The solution found by the author of the *Pararaton* is interesting: he identified Erlangga/Wijaya's protector Bañak Wiḍe and the *babatangan* X so that Wijaya was able to give the *babatangan* Bañak Wiḍe a kingdom as a reward for the services of Bañak Wiḍe/ "the priests." The Wijaya episode of the *Pararaton* ends, therefore, with a story about the partition of the realm; according to this text, Wijaya and the *babatangan* were friends, whereas the variant which has been incorporated into the *Babad Tanah Jawi* calls them brothers, sons of the last king of the previous dynasty.

We now understand why the Story of Calon Arang and the *Nāgarakĕrtāgama* mention a partition effectuated by Erlangga in behalf of his two sons: the functional identity of Wijaya and Erlangga could

[8] The history of early Majapahit is still very obscure. The remarks on this subject which I made in 1951 should be reconsidered.

work the other way as well. The Story of Calon Arang is a kind of biography of Wijaya/Erlangga. The frustratory aspect of the embryonic king takes in this text the shape of Calon Arang, the witch who scourges the country and its inhabitants until the priest Bharāda exorcises her, thus paving the way for the king's glorious manifestation. How closely this myth was akin to the Angrok story is apparent from the fact that the marriage of Calon Arang's daughter and Bharāda's son finds a parallel in the marriage of Bango Samparan's daughter and Lohgawe's son mentioned in the *Pararaton*.[9] The partition story is an anticlimax, unsatisfactory in itself, but understandable as an expression of the author's desire to normalize Wijaya's situation by projecting it into the past, so as to transform Wijaya's activities into an apparent imitation of the policy of his prototype. As to Erlangga's decision, the author explains it as an act of paternal care: he had to give each of his two sons a part of Java after the Balinese priest Kuturan had refused to accept a Javanese ruler, for the time being. The second part of this explanation refers to a situation of the Great Majapahit period rather than of Wijaya's regnal years, as will be seen in the following section.

3. KĚRTANAGARA AND THE DOCTRINE OF GREAT MAJAPAHIT

Under the Queen of Majapahit and her prime minister Gajah Mada a completely new dogma was proclaimed which put an end to the Erlangga/Wishnu cult of the preceding centuries. It was formulated in the text of a Sanskrit inscription on an Akṣobhya statue which represents Kěrtanagara. We read in this Kěrtanagara hymn that "after Bharāda had brought about a partition of the realm and Jaya Wishnuwardhana had restored the unity, the priest Nādajña erected, in 1211 Shāka, a previously erected Akṣobhya statue of Jñānashiwabajra [10] in the graveyard of Wurare, to the interest of the king, the royal family, and everybody else and with a view to the unity of the country." From a linguistic point of view the text is clear, if we divide it into four parts ending with shloka (stanza) 2, 6, 12, and 19 respectively.[11] Gram-

[9] Calon Arang's daughter and Bango Samparan's daughter bear names which suggest that the girls represented Shrī, the goddess Fortuna of the Javanese myths. In Bali, Calon Arang is the queen of the leyaks who have many features in common with the pontianak.

[10] The name means "whose salutary weapon is knowledge." Cf. *Nag.* 43,2 where Kěrtanagara is called Jñānabajreshwara, "the king whose weapon is knowledge."

[11] For Poerbatjaraka's text and translation see "De inscriptie van het Mahākṣobhya-beeld te Simpang," *BKI*, LXXVIII (1922), 426–462. The author's contribution

matically Nādajña is "first person"; he may have written a Javanese
text which was subsequently translated into Sanskrit by an Indian.[12]
The date, corresponding to A.D. 1289, is expressed in a chronogram
which means "revolution" or "new era." *Wurare* seems to be the name
of a babies' graveyard or *pabajangan*, traditionally the place where the
newborn founder of a dynasty, no longer threatened by the pontianak,
manifests himself, rising from the ashes or from the dead, so to say; in
myths it is there that the king of a new era replaces his predecessor.[13]
It should be noted that in the Kĕrtanagara hymn the previous dynasty
is represented by the priest Bharāda; the text calls Kĕrtanagara/Jñān-
ashiwabajra a *muni* so as to make him Bharāda's compeer able to neutralize Bharāda's power and, consequently, to abrogate Erlangga's
partition of the realm. Two problems then remain: why does the author
introduce Jaya Wishnuwardhana with his wife Jayawardhanī and his
son Jñānashiwabajra, and why does the author call the statue a "previously erected" statue?

In order to understand the doctrine expressed in the hymn we must
start, once more, from the consideration that a priestly statement presupposes a totally different popular picture of the present. As far as we
know, the Javanese of the early years of the fourteenth century had
never heard of a unification of Java achieved by either Jaya Wishnuwardhana or his son Kĕrtanagara. Those people who were well informed
knew Kĕrtanagara to have been killed by Kĕḍirian raiders; they may
have ascribed his defeat to his ill-considered Malayu adventure, since
the *Pararaton* refers to his *pamalayu*—historically the mission of 1286 to
be mentioned below—and his defenselessness in the same breath. Still
more people may have known, from personal experience, that Java
suffered from a lack of unity, since the *Pararaton* mentions several wars
and revolts against the founder of Majapahit and his son.

Kĕrtanagara's regnal period coincided with a period of expansion of
the Mongolian empire under Kubilai Khan. Before starting the conquest of South China, Kubilai seems to have come to terms with the
Tibetans; he embraced Tibetan Buddhism, and the Tibetans accepted

is very valuable, but I do not support the view that stanza 13 belongs to the
preceding stanzas, preferring in this respect Kern's older translation in "De Sanskrit-
inscriptie van 't Mahākṣobhya-beeld te Simpang," *TBG*, LII (1910), 99–108.

[12] The words *asuji* and *pakabu* in stanza 14, *sinta* in stanza 15, and *dharmādhy-
akṣa(twa)* in stanza 19 were Javanese terms, unintelligible to non-Javanese
Sanskritists.

[13] Cf. Berg, "Angrok," pp. 16 ff. *Wurare* seems to be the abbreviated form of
awu rare, "children's ashes."

him as their overlord. Since Kĕrtanagara introduced a similar form of Buddhism in Java, we may guess that he followed Kubilai's example in order to acquire the same degree of power so as to be able to protect his country against Kubilai's raiders; the argument here is the same as was used above in connection with Kĕrtanagara and Bharāda. A very remarkable Buddhist sculpture which, according to its inscription, reached the king of Malayu from Kĕrtanagara in 1286 is understandable if interpreted as a symbolic invitation to join an alliance against Kubilai on the basis of Buddhism and connubium. If the interpretation is correct, Kĕrtanagara's policy was a policy of friendly negotiations with some of his neighbors; it had, however, no direct result, since he met an untimely death by the hands of Kĕdirian raiders and since a Mongolian invasion did strike East Java in 1293. This failure explains the *Pararaton* item referred to above; scornful laughter is quicker than unprejudiced appraisal.

The Queen's advisers, in the fourteenth century, may well have been impressed with the broadness of Kĕrtanagara's outlook; at the same time, however, they may have blamed him for not being on his guard against his rivals in Java. If that be true, the advisers' approval of Kĕrtanagara's aims would account for the Great Majapahit interest in Tantric Buddhism, whereas their disapproval of Kĕrtanagara's home policy and the subsequent inability of the first kings of Majapahit to command respect might account for the "correction" which they applied to Kĕrtanagara's behavior. Whatever their motives were, it appears from the first canto of the *Nāgarakĕrtāgama* that Kĕrtanagara was accepted in the fourteenth century as the prototype of Hayam Wuruk/Rājasanagara, and from a comparative study of all the available material that older information about Kĕrtanagara's activities was replaced by later assertions. A real need for unification is likely to have existed in the early days of the Queen's rule. We have reason, therefore, to suppose that Kĕrtanagara's achievements were modified after his death in order to justify the Queen's measures taken in the fourteenth century in the interest of the political unity of Java. In other words, part of Kĕrtanagara's reign was replaced by a period of the Queen's rule in order to create a prototype which could be "adhered to" by the Queen, in a way similar to that discussed at the end of section 2. The period in question lasted twenty years, viz., from 1331 (when Kĕrtanagara's Aksobhya statue "disappeared" from Candi Jajawa, according to *Nag.* 57,4) to 1350, and was followed by a twenty-first year, the year of Rājasanagara/Kĕrtanagara's accession to the throne, 1351. The Kĕrtanagara hymn mentions 1289, which is also a twenty-first year since Wishnuwardhana died in 1268 and the Javanese chronologists put the beginning of Kĕrtanagara's reign in 1269. There is reason, therefore, to suppose that the Aksobhya statue was reerected in 1351 bearing the inscription, and especially the words "I have erected the previously erected one," which changed Kĕrtanagara's life sixty years after his death and justified the Queen's policy. Since Akṣobhya was a peace-loving god, the author did not specify the suppressive measures which constituted the process of unification. Prapanca —as we shall see below—enumerated those measures in his *Nāgarakĕrtāgama,* but he did so on the basis of the Great Majapahit doctrine, so that his information has no historiographical value.

During the period preceding the year 1351 the man who was going to be a *rāja-sanagara,* "a king of the entire kingdom," and the Kĕrtanagara of his era was a mere boy. He was still an *ayam wuruk,* "a young bird," under his mother's wings.[14] The identification process which can be distilled from the Kĕrtanagara hymn shows that the Queen performed the task of unifying the country on his behalf. This is why the Kĕrtanagara hymn mentions Jaya Wishnuwardhana: his was, according to the author, functionally identical with Hayam Wuruk's mother, in his capacity of Kĕrtanagara's historical father. This functional identity was expressed by calling Tribhuwanottunggadewī—in the feminine form, of course—Jaya Wishnuwardhanī, e.g. in OJO 84 and 85, and by calling her Jaya Wishnuwardhana's consort in the Kĕrtanagara hymn; the form of the proper name which is used there, viz. Jaya Wardhanī, seems to be no more than a variant. We may put it in this way since nowhere else in Javanese charters—apart from the case of the "daughters of Kĕrtanagara" which is as exceptional as the present one—does the king appear in the company of his wife or wives.[15]

The Queen was, so to say, officially the Bloody Mary of Javanese history: she did the dirty work which, however inconsistent with the Buddhist ideal, was necessary "for the protection of the world under the sway of Kali," as *Nag.* 43,1 has it. For this reason she was represented in the shape of the aggressive goddess Cāmundā. On her statue one finds an inscription stating that "the goddess was erected because

[14] Was Wishnuwardhana said to be Kĕrtanagara's guardian because of Hayam Wuruk's minority in the years preceding 1351? In that case the charters dated in Wishnuwardhana's regnal period must have been written in the fourteenth century. This problem deserves attention; it cannot be solved here.

[15] For the question of Suhitā's historicity see section 4.

of the King's complete victory, at home and abroad, in 1292"; this inscription, too, subverts historical facts, but in a different way, since it denies that Kĕrtanagara had fallen a victim to the Kĕdirians.[16] The choice of Cāmundā may have been influenced by the Javanese conception that the Queen was a royal pontianak, conjured up by Wijaya's "insulting" partition of the realm; if that be true, the result may have been a fusion of ideas which explains some of the features of the Story of Calon Arang.[17]

The Rājasanagara/Kĕrtanagara identification as well as the double chronology technique of the Great Majapahit doctrine is by now sufficiently clear, but the motive of the politicians of Great Majapahit for diabolizing the Queen awaits further explanation. Their disapproval of Kĕrtanagara's home policy and of the early Majapahit conflicts may have been strong, but the diabolization of the Queen and the subsequent radical change of Kĕrtanagara's picture look, perhaps, a little out of proportion. Thus we must look for some other factor(s) which may have exercised influence.

With an eye on the explanation to be given below it should first be remarked that not only was Rājasanagara declared to be the Kĕrtanagara of his era but he was also proclaimed to be Kĕrtanagara's great-grandson. We have seen in section 2 that OJO 81 calls Wijaya Kĕrtanagara's son-in-law and Narasinghamūrti's grandson. He probably was neither, but even if he was Kĕrtanagara's son-in-law on the eve of the Kĕdirian raid, his bride must have perished; otherwise OJO 81, published as early as 1294, would have mentioned her escape. In order to become Rājasanagara's great-grandfather Kĕrtanagara had, however, to be given a surviving daughter. He was supplied with four, in 1331. These four imaginary ladies were called Wijaya's wives in royal charters which bear the date 1296 and 1304 respectively, although they were not issued before 1331, in my opinion; "the charter of 1304" also calls the ladies "manifestations of the four islands." As far as we know, Wijaya's historical wife was a princess of Champa who had arrived in Java after the Mongolian invasion; she may have been in the company of a princess of Malayu who likewise became

[16] The date, 1292, is based on a different fixation of the "twenty years" in Kĕrtanagara's regnal period. We find this different theory applied in *Par.* 18,11 (where 1272 is the year of Wishnuwardhana's death) and in *Nag.* 49,4 (where 1343 is the year of the Bali war).

[17] Cf. Poerbatjaraka's text and translation "De Calon-Arang," *BKI*, LXXXII (1926), 110–180, and especially pp. 164 ff. where an expiatory ceremony in Girah is mentioned.

Wijaya's wife.[18] Wijaya's international marriage became the prototype
of the royal marriage of certain later myths; it started to exercise its
influence in the days of Great Majapahit, since Kĕrtanagara's daughters
came to stand for "the four islands" and Rājasanagara's marriage became the center of "the three rivers" (apparently a mystical indication
of the three countries involved in Kĕrtanagara's Triple Alliance:
Champa, Java, and Malayu). In a society where symbols played such
an important part nobody would be taken aback by the sudden appearance of "daughters of Kĕrtanagara" who owed their existence to
magical rites.

Now who was the woman whom we have been calling "the Queen":
the princess of Champa or her daughter Tribhuwanottunggadewī?
OJO 84 and 85 tell us that Tribhuwanottunggadewī was a Jaya Wishnuwardhanī; this implies that she was regarded as Hayam Wuruk's
guardian. On the other hand, the Chamese princess disappeared from
the scene in 1350, at the very end of the period of twenty years, and
it was she who, after her death, was said to be Prajñāpāramitā, a peace-
loving Buddhist goddess of the type of Aksobhya. Moreover, the rites
for her deification as Prajñāpāramitā in 1362 were quite pompous and
for a mere dowager rather impressive; her temple in Kamal-Pandak—
where, as we read in *Nag.* 67 *et seq.*, Bharāda was believed to have
landed after drawing his dividing line—had an important political
function, viz., to safeguard the unity of the realm. The extent of the
purification rites of 1362 is understandable, if the princess of Champa
was the Queen who had been a demon for twenty years. In my opinion,
therefore, the Queen must have been Tribhuwanottunggadewī's
mother, the princess of Champa.[19] Prapanca calls her a reverend nun;
this is what she was from the point of view of a man who wrote in 1365,
after the purification rites had been performed.

We know from Javanese stories that the goddess Umā changed into
the diabolical Durgā after committing a mortal sin. The idea behind
these stories is that mortal sins can be forgiven only after a public

[18] Since *Dwārawatī* was more or less a synonym of *Campā* (Champa), the Javanese
often call the Chamese princess *putri Darawati.* We have reason to suppose that *Par.*
24,28 has retained this name in the corrupted form *Darapĕtak* (= *daraputih;* a
copier may have written *daraputi* instead of *darawati*). The *Pararaton* calls the
second princess *Darajingga;* since *putih* is "white" and *jingga* is "orange," the latter
name is obviously modeled on the former one. The Menak-Jingga to be mentioned
in the eleventh paragraph of this section may have come into existence as Darajingga's son.

[19] It is possible, however, that for the Javanese of those days the difference
between the Queen and her daughter was irrelevant.

confession of guilt; a confession of guilt, however, is a manifestation of one's own wickedness, a kind of self-diabolization which is not essentially different from the diabolization performed or proclaimed by a priest. Suppose that the princess of Champa did commit a mortal sin, the sin to suit us best would be regicide. If, indeed, the princess of Champa murdered Jayanagara, the second king of Majapahit, or was indirectly responsible for his death, a new dynasty must have come to power round 1328, and this dynasty could, for obvious reasons, not be a traditional Wishnu/Erlangga dynasty: it had to be anti-Jayanagara, and its political program could only be the opposite of what had been characteristic of the Jayanagara period, viz., a program of emphasis on the necessity of Java's unity. In order to get prepared for purification, the royal murderess had to go through a period of "mortification" during which she belonged to the realm of death, and during that period her prime minister could act the devil incarnate in the field of politics.[20] Since Kĕrtanagara had indicated a new way in Javanese politics and since he was not very popular in the early days of Majapahit, he was in 1331 an acceptable prototype, though his nature had to be changed in order to allow the Queen to "imitate" Kĕrtanagara in accordance with Gajah Mada's political program. A combination of private motives and political considerations might explain the revolution of 1331 better than a purely political vision would.

In official documents we find, of course, no argument in favor of this theory, apart from the fact that the Kĕrtanagara hymn is written in Sanskrit and that Jayanagara is almost completely ignored in the charters of this period.[21] The nonofficial or semiofficial documents, however, provide us with clues. According to the author of the relevant part of the *Pararaton* supplement, Jayanagara was murdered because he wanted to marry his half sisters, whom we know as the Queen's daughters, preventing other suitors from contacting the girls. In the Story of Damar-Wulan we read that the Virgin Queen of Majapahit induced the man who was predestined to become her consort to kill King Menak-Jingga, who had been soliciting her. The most important of these stories, however, is the Story of Shrī Tanjung, Tambapetra's granddaughter, who after being solicited by the king ordered her hus-

[20] Cf. *Par.* 28,20 *et seq.*, where Gajah Mada proclaimed his intention to conquer the "other islands" before *amukti palapa*, i.e., enjoying the rites, viz., of Tantric Buddhism.

[21] It should be noted that a charter of 1323 (OJO 83) calls the king of Majapahit of those days Sundarapāṇḍya. We do not find this name elsewhere.

band to kill the offender; Shrī Tanjung's name might be rendered by "princess of Champa," her grandfather is a "lord of the realm of darkness," and she is said to have undergone several purification rites.[22] The story of Shrī Tanjung is handed down as the second volume of a book the first volume of which goes by the name of Sudamala; in the first volume Kuntī, mother of the Pāṇḍawas, wants to kill her son who is a regicide, in order to be able to establish a new dynasty, and by sentencing her son to death she attains her chief aim, since Sadewa, at the critical moment, delivers Durgā from evil; in myth one mortal sin may easily substitute for the other.[23] The Tantu Panggĕlaran, on the other hand, says that the sin of the princess of Champa was adultery. This is not necessarily incompatible with the other version. However, we shall certainly lose our way if we try to harmonize the details of these kinds of stories. What we are interested in is the possibility of the Queen's diabolization in consequence of a sin which initially was a personal affair but subsequently had important political consequences. It is noteworthy in this connection that, according to the *Pararaton*, the Saḍeng war which Gajah Mada, fully backed by the Queen, undertook in 1331 was a sinful affair as well; we have reason to believe that this war was not the sort of thing Kĕrtanagara would have undertaken, and it may have been the political complement of the Queen's moral crime.

It goes without saying that the preceding remarks do not solve the problems we are confronted with when studying the Great Majapahit picture of the past. We know several texts which seem to owe their existence to the exchange of thoughts that must have taken place among the Javanese in and after the days of the queen of Majapahit; most of them have not yet been studied from the point of view which is relevant here.[24] Thus the only thing to do, for the time being, is to

[22] *Tambapetra*, in the Korawāshrama Tambrapeṭa, derives from Sanskrit *tāmrapreta*, "the copper ghost"; *tāmra*, however, may be used here instead of *tāmragomukha*, "the copper cow's head," i.e. "hell." Tambapetra is said to be blind, i.e., he lives in the world of darkness. We find the story of Shrī Tanjung (edited and translated by Prijono) and the Sudamala (edited and translated by van Stein Callenfels) sculptured on the walls of certain Javanese temples of the fourteenth century; thus we are fairly sure that the texts were functional poetry. Moreover, Cāmuṇḍā's "three rivers symbol" was found among the Shrī Tanjung pictures of Caṇḍi Kĕḍaton.

[23] Cf. Th. Pigeaud, "De Tantu Panggĕlaran, een Oud-Javaansch prozageschrift," text, translation, and notes (The Hague, 1924), p. 185. If Tribhuwanottunggadewī was an illegitimate child, her normal right of succession would be nil and magic rites to replace it all the more necessary.

[24] E.g., the Panji Story, in which Hayam Wuruk's marriage is the main theme. The kakawin *Smaradahana*, too, may be a document of this period.

repeat that our knowledge of the Javanese picture of the past is imperfect. It is necessary, however, to give a brief survey of the relevant
parts of the *Pararaton*. The *Pararaton* reflects the doctrine of Great
Majapahit in the Wijaya episode which was extended, after 1331, with
a story about two daughters of Kĕrtanagara who found their way to
Majapahit, as well as in a supplement dealing with the exploits of
Gajah Mada. As to the story of the princesses, the author says that
Wijaya succeeded in rescuing one of the girls on the day of the catastrophe, whereas her sister had to live for some years a prisoner's life
at the court of Kĕḍiri; Wijaya married her after Bañak Wiḍe had persuaded the "king of the Tatars"—by suggesting the princesses as a
quid pro quo—to come to Wijaya's help and after he had succeeded
in trapping the Mongolian army. As to the stories about Gajah Mada,
the *Pararaton* tells us how he became prime minister, how he conquered Saḍeng in East Java, how he announced his plans to subdue
"the other islands," and how he prevented Hayam Wuruk from marrying a Sundanese princess. The informational value of these stories
varies; they deserve, however, careful attention.

4. PRAPANCA'S *NĀGARAKĔRTĀGAMA*

In 1365 the Buddhist priest Prapanca—possibly Nādajña's son—
wrote a poem which is generally called *Nāgarakĕrtāgama,* "Story of
the Glorious Dynasty." It is clearly a priestly statement, functionally
akin to the *Arjunawiwāha* and the Sanskrit hymns mentioned above;
it is, therefore, an elaborate optative, and as such it consists of a subject describing the situation which was known to the reader and a
predicate expressing the new doctrine which the author wanted to
impose. The situation known to the reader was no real situation, of
course; it was the officially prevailing picture of the past which had
been imposed in 1331. This is why the *Nāgarakĕrtāgama* informs us of
the Great Majapahit doctrine as well as of Prapanca's amendments.
Since many details of the Great Majapahit doctrine escape us, we cannot be quite sure as to what was the poem's subject and what its
predicate. The main point, however, is quite clear.

Tribhuwanottunggadewī's charters mention, in accordance with the
doctrine explained in the previous section, two kings of Singasari, Jaya
Wishnuwardhana and Kĕrtanagara. The *Nāgarakĕrtāgama,* however,
gives a list of four kings of whom Jaya Wishnuwardhana was the third
and Kĕrtanagara the fourth, according to the author. It is reasonable
to suppose, therefore, that the predicate of the *Nāgarakĕrtāgama* was
mainly a statement about the first and the second king of Singasari.

It appears from what has been discussed in section 2 that the early Majapahit reconstruction of the paraphrase of the Erlangga hymn had resulted in Wishnuwardhana's taking Makuṭawangshawardhana's place as Angrok's grandson. Tribhuwanottunggadewī's priests, rejecting the whole Erlangga story and recognizing Kĕrtanagara as a Buddha and a ruler *sui juris*, had taken Jaya Wishnuwardhana into the bargain, as Kĕrtanagara's father who had to act the modest part of guardian. Under favorable circumstances a period of forty years suffices to establish a new doctrine; we need think only of present-day Russia to realize that. When, therefore, in 1359 Prapanca found a document in Ḍarbaru which—to judge from his own narrative in *Nag.* 35 *et seq.*—must have been an early version of the *Pararaton,* he experienced this event as a revelation or as an unexpected affirmation of hearsay.[25] He must have been under the impression that the priests of 1331 had overlooked some kings or made some other mistake, and he may have written his poem in order to correct what he thought to be an error. Prapanca's poem was published in 1365, a year after Gajah Mada's death; the date may be significant since Gajah Mada was not likely to encourage a young poet who intended to modify his doctrine.

It should be emphasized that Prapanca did not reject the doctrine of 1331: he maintained it substantially, and when adding two kings to the existing list he took care not to deviate too far from the established doctrine of Great Majapahit. In the *Nāgarakĕrtāgama* Wishnuwardhana's father is Anusanātha, the Nusapati of the early Majapahit version of the *Pararaton,* and, perhaps, the Lokapāla of the Erlangga hymn.[26] Anusanātha's father, however, is neither the Tunggul-Amĕtung, Ḍĕdĕs' first lover, nor the Angrok of the *Pararaton;* he is a new character, Ranggah-Rājasa. This Ranggah-Rājasa was partly modeled on Wishnuwardhana, since Prapanca ascribed to him the restoration of the unity of Java which Wishnuwardhana had been credited with in 1331/1351; on the other hand, he was called "a nonborn child of the gods, a son of the famous Girīndra." A nonborn child of the gods suggests somebody who after ascending to heaven returns to this world. As *Girīndra* is a synonym of *Shailendra,* the name of the Buddhist

[25] I do not think that the remarks of Teeuw and Uhlenbeck ("Over de interpretatie van de Nāgarakṛtāgama," pp. 225 ff.) on *Nag.* 35,2 are correct, based as they are on a misinterpretation of *Nag.* 35,3,d.

[26] *Nusapati* and *Anuṣanātha* are Javanized forms of Sanskrit *manuṣapati* (or *-nātha*), "king," and synonyms of *lokapāla.* If Wongatĕlĕng Agnibhaya originally was a girl, Nusapati may have played a part in the story from the very beginning; cf. note 4.

dynasty which had preceded Erlangga, Prapanca recognized the dynasty of Singasari and Majapahit as a rejuvenated Shailendra dynasty by a simple act of substitution. By doing so he proved himself a good Buddhist and continued to divert the public attention from Erlangga; the only thing of Erlangga's time he mentioned in the *Nāgarakĕrtāgama* is that king's regrettable partition of the realm. The effect of the reappearance of the Shailendra dynasty could, therefore, only be that the Erlangga dynasty and the period of Wishnuism gradually turned into a blind spot in the Javanese picture of the past.

When ascribing the unification of Java to Ranggah-Rājasa, Prapanca associated the function of unifier with the function of founder of the dynasty. Did or did he not know that Wishnuwardhana had only been a unifier in his capacity of Kĕrtanagara's guardian? There is no definite answer to this question, but it appears from the *Nāgarakĕrtāgama* text that Prapanca was a compromiser. The *Nāgarakĕrtāgama* mentions Wishnuwardhana's guardianship implicitly, and the phraseology of *Nag.* 41,3—where Prapanca introduces Janggala and Kĕdiri as partners—reflects to some extent the unification doctrine of 1331/1351. Moreover, the "well-known chronogram" which contains the date of Wishnuwardhana's conquest of a part of Java, viz. 1253, occurs in the *Nāgarakĕrtāgama,* though it was inconsistent with Prapanca's own new vision; it is perhaps for that reason that we find it not in *Nag.* 41 but in *Nag.* 15 and in a corrupted form at that.[27] As to Kĕrtanagara, he holds a very important position in Prapanca's picture, but not a dominating one, since there is the glory of the Shailendra king in the background. Prapanca ascribes four wars to Kĕrtanagara, two wars against Javanese "rascals," in 1270 and 1280 respectively, and two wars against foreign rulers, a war against Malayu in 1275 and a war against Bali in 1284. Prapanca applies the "double chronology technique" in his poem in that he gives—as we have seen above—parallel sets of dates for Wishnuwardhana and Wijaya; however, he deviates from the specific form of double chronology which we find in the Kĕrtanagara hymn, since he ignores the "ceremony" of 1289 and gives 1343 as the date of the Bali war, instead of 1331 or 1346.[28] The poet describes the events connected with Kĕrtanagara's death and Wijaya's accession to the throne in a circumspect way; still, he does describe them. Kĕrtanagara's four daughters, Wijaya's cousins, remain in the *Nāgarakĕrtāgama* the link between the dynasty of Singasari and the dynasty of Majapahit. Among Wijaya's children Prapanca mentions Jayanagara as well as his

[27] Cf. note 6.   [28] Cf. note 16.

two half sisters; it strikes us that he even admits Jayanagara's victory
in his war against Lamajang, be it in very sober words. He then proceeds to the period of Tribhuwanottunggadewī, informing us of her
accession to the throne and of Gajah Mada's accession to power, in
1329 and 1331 respectively. The latter is also the year of Gajah Mada's
victories in Saḍeng and Kĕta. I am inclined to think that *Saḍeng*
originally suggested Bali as well, in the same way as *Kĕta* suggested
Madura as well, so that the two proper names indicated four wars; a
Bali war is mentioned separately, however, in the last stanza of Prapanca's "story of the dynasty." [29]

On the whole, Prapanca's statement is less radical than the doctrine
of 1331/1351. He seems to have tried to keep the happy mean between
the revolutionary theory of 1331 and the older traditions. As a compromiser he is, of course, an unreliable informant from a modern historian's point of view, but his own colleagues may have regarded him
as remarkably matter of fact. Being a more or less normal product of
Javanese functional poetry, the *Nāgarakĕrtāgama* could exercise a normal influence upon the epigones; its list of Majapahit's dependencies
has achieved fame, and Prapanca's abundant use of chronograms has
been imitated ever since. Last but not least, it is Prapanca who gave
the *Pararaton,* the former paraphrase of the Erlangga hymn, a chance
to survive in the very century of Erlangga's eclipse; it is a trick of
Mother Evolution that the post-*Nāgarakĕrtāgama* version of the *Pararaton* came to contain a sentence which says that Angrok's royal name
was Rājasa!

Apart from this isolated remark, several elements of the final version
of the *Pararaton* derive from the *Nāgarakĕrtāgama,* directly or through
imitation. The story about Angrok's conquest of Kĕdiri in 1222 which
we now find in *Par.* 14,7 *et seq.* reflects Prapanca's "displaced act of
unification" and must, therefore, have been added after 1365; in its
turn this *Pararaton* paragraph has engendered the myth about a "battle
of Gantĕr" which some scholars regard as a landmark in Javanese
history.[30] The dates and chronograms in the *Pararaton*—we find both,
probably by different authors—also betray Prapanca's influence. The
same holds true for the so-called biographical notes, a novum in the
Nāgarakĕrtāgama which seems to have become popular in a short time

[29] I use this term intentionally in order to stress that the cantos 40–49 in my
opinion are the quintessence of the *Nāgarakĕrtāgama.* They have determined the
name of the whole poem as against the faked name suggested by Prapanca himself.
[30] Cf., e.g., Krom, *HJG,* p. 316.

and which may have helped to pave the way toward elementary historiography. It should be remarked, however, that in the fourteenth and fifteenth centuries these notes had a magic function rather than historiographical value; Krom's and Schrieke's efforts to use them for reconstructive purposes may, therefore, have been made in vain. It appears, indeed, from an analysis of the last pages of the final version of the *Pararaton* that the post-Rājasanagara genealogy is a mere imitation of the post-Kĕrtanagara genealogy, on the basis of Rājasanagara's identification with Kĕrtanagara. In the same way as Kĕrtanagara was succeeded by his nephew and son-in-law Wijaya, Rājasanagara, according to the *Pararaton*, was succeeded by his nephew and son-in-law Wikramawardhana; and in the same way as Wijaya was succeeded by his daughter Tribhuwanottunggadewī, Wikramawardhana was succeeded by his daughter Suhitā. Wijaya's conflict with Bañak Wide—his half brother, according to the *Babad Tanah Jawi*—finds a parallel in Wikramawardhana's conflict with his wife's half brother Wīrabhūmi; even the chronograms of *Par.* 26,9 and 31,15 are likely to have been identical.[31] This is why Suhitā's historicity is dubious and Tribhuwanottunggadewī may have been the only queen of Javanese history. On the other hand, it is possible that after Rājasanagara's death the succession was arranged in accordance with the picture of the past; in that case Krom's and Schrieke's efforts or part of them may have been useful. This is one of the many problems which have to be solved and which deserve closer attention for various reasons.

5. THE *BABAD TANAH JAWI*

About 1600 the dynasty which, as far as we know, was descended from Rājasanagara had to make way for the usurper whose descendants have ruled Central Java ever since. We hardly know when and how this revolution took place.[32] For the seventeenth-century picture of the past we have at our disposal the *Babad Tanah Jawi*, a book which functionally belongs to the same category as the *Nāgarakĕrtāgama*; its evolution, however, compares with the evolution of the *Pararaton* since later generations have repeatedly modified the existing version of the text. *Babad Tanah Jawi* is an expression which derives from the *Para-*

---

[31] *Nag.* 48,2 gives 1316 as the date of the Nambi war. Since the chronogram of *Par.* 31,15 is correct and that of 26,9 is corrupt, the *Pararaton* is not likely to have absorbed Prapanca's date before 1425.

[32] De Graaf has recently written two books on the early history of Mataram, availing himself of Javanese materials. Since my approach is fundamentally different, I cannot support his views.

raton: Bañak Wide's Madurese people came to Java (*tanah jawa*) in order to clear (*mbabad*) the forest where Majapahit was going to be built, and (*m*)*babad tanah jawi* hence must have suggested in those days the activity of the founders of Majapahit, or simply "The Foundation of Majapahit." The present section deals with the oldest version to which the title applies in its original meaning. When in the following centuries the text was modified and extended, the title grew inadequate; it was kept up, however, and for this reason *Babad Tanah Jawi* was gradually understood to mean "History of Java."

"The Foundation of Majapahit" refers, however, to the foundation of Mataram. We have seen in section 2 that the story of the foundation of Majapahit was told in OJO 81 in terms of the story of Erlangga's accession to the throne, although some details of the ancient story were replaced by other details in order to suit the situation of Wijaya's days. At the end of section 2 and in section 3 we have discussed some other cases in which the story of the prototype was considerably changed so as to allow the "imitators of the prototype" to have their own way. In section 4 we have made the acquaintance of the *Nāgarakĕrtāgama* whose author tells us the story of Kĕrtanagara; though he knew that Kĕrtanagara was Rājasanagara's prototype, he yet informs us of Rājasanagara's reign as well. The *Babad Tanah Jawi* comes in the same category as OJO 81 in that it tells the story of the foundation of the dynasty of Mataram in terms of the *Pararaton* story of the foundation of the dynasty of Majapahit, adding such details as facilitated the application of the prototype; the number of such details is considerable in the *Babad Tanah Jawi*.[33] The Mataramese poet followed Prapanca, however, in that he tells the story of the foundation of Majapahit, as well as a story of Majapahit which is adapted, in some respects, to the needs of his own days; the prototype, therefore, shows features which can be explained only from the point of view of a seventeenth-century court poet. According to the *Babad Tanah Jawi*, for instance, the founder of Majapahit when roaming about after the catastrophe met a woman who foretold him the future glory of Mataram, when Wijaya's descendants would be kings and she would be their consort. The same holds true for the author's representation of Wijaya: he distinguishes a Bra Wijaya I who is the founder of Majapahit

[33] Remember that the Wijaya episode of the *Pararaton* which the author of the *Babad Tanah Jawi* supposed to be a reliable story of the foundation of Majapahit was originally an Erlangga story. In a way, therefore, the author of the *Babad Tanah Jawi* tells the story of the foundation of Mataram in terms of an Erlangga story.

from a Bra Wijaya II who is the king of the four consorts; in the *Babad Tanah Jawi* this Bra Wijaya II is the last king of Majapahit, and in this capacity he could be considered as the immediate ancestor of both the kings of Demak and the kings of Mataram just as Ḍĕḍĕs is the ancestress of both the kings of Singasari and the kings of Majapahit in the *Pararaton.*[34]

Looking at the *Babad Tanah Jawi* from another point of view, we may observe that the author imitated Prapanca—who made Kĕrtanagara as well as the Shailendra king Rājasanagara's prototype—in proclaiming the king of Mataram to be the new king of Majapahit as well as the Shailendra king of his era. Of these two prototypes the king of Majapahit must have been regarded as the ancestor of many Javanese princes of the fifteenth and sixteenth centuries, since Prapanca's exaggerated picture of the greatness of Majapahit made a deep impression on the Javanese as well as on the non-Javanese Indonesians of those days. As to the Shailendra king, the author must have accepted him as his own king's prototype because of the doctrine Prapanca had launched in 1365. Since we have seen, in section 4, that Prapanca declared Rājasanagara to be descended from Ranggah-Rājasa who was "a nonborn child of the gods, a son of the famous Girīndra," thus combining a parousia theory with a genealogy, we should not be astonished to find that the author of the *Babad Tanah Jawi* likewise combines a genealogy with a story about the reappearance of the Shailendra king.

It is on the principles described in the two preceding paragraphs that the structure of the *Babad Tanah Jawi* is based. The author mentions the ascension of the Shailendra king in the introduction of his book and then proceeds to expatiate on the six dynasties which have ruled over Java after him, viz.,

1) the Erlangga dynasty
2) the dynasty of Pajajaran
3) the dynasty of Majapahit
4) the king(s) of Giri
5) the dynasty of Demak
6) the dynasty of Mataram

in such a way that 1 and 4 run parallel, as well as 2 and 5 and, of course, 3 and 6. This structure does not become transparent, however, unless one takes into account the meaning of the proper names. Now this remark has been made before, since we have seen in section 2 that the Wijaya episode of the *Pararaton* is not wholly transparent

---

[34] Both Nusapati and Patah (the alleged first king of Demak) were born after their mother had become their stepfather's wife.

unless we render *bañak wiḍe* by "the priests." On the other hand, the opaqueness of the term *Bañak Wiḍe* which resulted from a normal evolution of the language was likely to prevent the readers from recognizing the Wijaya episode of the *Pararaton* as an Erlangga story; in the same way Javanese as well as foreign readers must have experienced some difficulty in understanding the *Babad Tanah Jawi* after extensions and modifications had obscured the structure which the author of the original version had in mind. For instance, Dutch scholars of the nineteenth century have put down the first story of the *Babad Tanah Jawi* as a Polynesian myth because they failed to see that *Watu-Gunung* is a Javanese equivalent of Sanskrit *Shailendra* and also because they were not sufficiently familiar with the books which the author of the *Babad Tanah Jawi* knew. It does not matter, of course, whether or not such substitutes are acceptable from a modern linguist's point of view or whether the interpretation of older Javanese literature by the author of the *Babad Tanah Jawi* is correct from the philologist's point of view; what matters is how the Javanese of the seventeenth century interpreted the picture of the past which had been handed down to them.

The Watu-Gunung story is a good specimen of a picture-of-the-past myth, and evidence of the existence of a tenacious oral tradition at that. The starting point must have been a Javanese *Rāmāyana* version, conceived as an allegory which refers to the struggle between Wishnuism and Buddhism; Wishnuism was represented by Erlangga and Buddhism by the Shailendra king, Erlangga being Wishnu and therefore also Rāma, the Buddhist Shailendra king being Rāwana. Watu-Gunung's wife in incestuous wedlock is dewi Sinta, the Sītā of the *Rāmāyana*. When Sinta discovers that her husband is her own son, she urges him to ask a celestial virgin in marriage. By doing so, Watu-Gunung becomes the Niwātakawaca of the *Arjunawiwāha* who wanted to acquire a *widadari*, hence attacked the gods and was finally defeated by Arjuna; since the Rāma/Arjuna combination is specific of Erlangga, it is obvious that the story refers to the period of Erlangga. After Watu-Gunung's death is mentioned, the story takes an unexpected turn, however: the author says that dewi Sinta—though it was she who had planned her husband's ruin—was far from happy when she heard what had happened. On the contrary, she had a crying fit and wept so much that the Lord of Heaven was forced to promise her to revive Watu-Gunung and return him to the earth after three days. On the third day, however, nothing happened, and so dewi Sinta started to weep again. The Lord of Heaven repeated his promise, and this time he did revive Watu-Gunung. Watu-Gunung, however, preferred to stay in heaven, desiring his family to join him. Thus his two wives and Sinta's twenty-seven children ascended to heaven, one a week, in this way constituting the Javanese calendar of thirty *wukus*. As this is a story about the origin of time, the author clearly hints at the beginning of a new cosmic day which followed the Shailendra era, just as the author of OJO 62 had done in 1041. Since the word for "day" is often given a broad interpretation in Javanese myths, we are expected to understand that the three days of the divine promise were the Erlangga era, the era of Singasari, and the era of Majapahit; the king of Majapahit, as we have seen, was said to be a Shailendra king. The conception of Mataram as New Majapahit required, however, a second series of three days, and for this reason Sinta had to weep again in order to bring the king of Mataram into the position of Shailendra ruler of the sixteenth Shāka century. It goes without saying that historically the "divine promise" depends on Prapanca's remark on Ranggah-Rājasa in *Nag.* 40; it is this remark, therefore, which explains Sinta's unreasonable behavior.

We have seen in the preceding section that Prapanca, by choosing the Shailendra king as his employer's prototype and by ignoring Erlangga, turned the Erlangga era into a blind spot. Moreover, Prapanca must have preferred the Buddhist Shailendra king to Erlangga, since Erlangga was the exponent of a different religion. In this way a myth may have come into existence according to which the Erlangga period had been the period of a mysterious realm where a foreign religion prevailed. As a matter of fact, the *Babad Tanah Jawi* says that the king of the "first day" ruled over the spirits, whereas the king of the "fourth day"—who, as we have seen, was functionally identical with the king of the "first day"—is described as a king of the spirits and an apostle of Islam.[35] Now if the kings of the first and the fourth dynasty have been regarded as priests in their capacity of apostle of a "different" religion, later generations may have been unable to distinguish Erlangga from his priest Bharāda. At the same time "the priests" who were Erlangga's supporters in his days of exile according to the author of the Erlangga hymn and the ape Hanuman who was Rāma's helper in his days of exile according to the *Rāmāyana* must have been regarded as functionally identical since Rāma was Erlangga's prototype.

[35] This is why the present-day Javanese believe in the victory of Islam at the end of the period of Majapahit.

Finally, the Javanese could easily mistake "the priest" for "the priests" and vice versa, since formal distinction between singular and plural plays a very modest part in Javanese grammar. Under these circumstances the ape Hanuman, Erlangga's priestly supporters in his days of exile, Erlangga's priest Bharāḍa, Erlangga himself, and the king of the fourth dynasty could coalesce in different ways. We find, indeed, that Bañak Wide's second name is Siyung-Wanara in the *Babad Tanah Jawi* and that the king of the first and the fourth dynasty is called *Prabuset(mata)*; in both cases the meaning of the name in its original form seems to have been "divine ape."[36] On the other hand, a ruler of the spirits replaces Bañak Wide in the *Babad Tanah Jawi* where the author mentions the helper of the king in exile after the catastrophe; it is the Lady of Gunung Kombang who foretells Bra Wijaya I the future.[37] As to Bharāḍa, he took over the function of Erlangga as the man who gave each of his sons a kingdom and who was the predecessor of the kings of Singasari; the author of the *Babad Tanah Jawi* calls him Kaṇḍi-Awan and Rěsi-Gěntayu and provides him with five children instead of two sons.[38]

Rěsi-Gěntayu's son-in-law Amijaya[39] was the first king of Singasari, according to the *Babad Tanah Jawi*. His grandson removed the residence to Pajajaran in West Java. The fourth king of Pajajaran, Paměkas —the word means "the last one," but we easily recognize in him Kěrta-

[36] *Siyung-Wanara* seems to be the corrupted form of *Si Hyang Wānara*, "Divine Ape"; a synonym was *ra-Buset*. After *ra-Buset* had developed the variant *prabuset* and after the Sanskrit word *prabhusaṃmata* ("appreciated by kings" and hence "passionflower") had developed the Javanese variant *prabusetmata*, *prabuset* and *prabusetmata* got mixed up. This is why the king is called Prabuset as well as Prabusetmata and why *prabuset* is now used in Javanese as a word for "passionflower"; cf. the remarks on *bañak* in note 5. In their turn, Dutch Javanists misunderstood *Prabuset* in the nineteenth century, interpreting the name as *prabu Set*, "king Set."

[37] *Gunung-kombang* means "Bumblebee Mountain." The bumblebee is one of the animals which the Javanese regarded as souls of the deceased.

[38] In the *Babad Tanah Jawi* Kaṇḍi-Awan and Rěsi-Gěntayu are father and son; the two names have a common origin, however. One of Kaṇḍi-Awan's five sons is the Tunggul-Amětung of the *Pararaton;* he is said to have been given the function of king of the palm-wine tappers. Cf. the story of the king of the palm-wine tappers in *Sějarah Mělayu* 14,7; in the Malay version he is given the name Ariadikara (*āryādhikāra*, i.e. Bañak Wiḍe; cf. note 5) and proclaimed to be Gajah Mada's compeer. Elsewhere in the *Babad Tanah Jawi* the palm-wine tapper is the unsuccessful pretender.

[39] *Amijaya* is a variant of *Wijaya*. Here, therefore, we meet Wijaya as the son-in-law of the previous king; his place in the royal genealogy is only slightly different. Wijaya the son-in-law, Wijaya the founder of Majapahit, and Wijaya the husband of four consorts are three different characters in the *Babad Tanah Jawi*.

nagara, the (fourth and) last king of Singasari—had a normal son Raden Susuruh and an abnormal son by a concubine who was a *babatangan* and whom his father, therefore, tried to dispose of. The child survived, however, and when he had grown a man he avenged himself and killed Pamĕkas. For this reason difficulties arose between Raden Susuruh and the abnormal son, Bañak Wide or Siyung-Wanara. Susuruh left Pajajaran and went to East Java where he founded Majapahit, whereas Bañak Wide remained in possession of West Java. The version of the *Babad Tanah Jawi* which I am rendering here does not enumerate Bañak Wide's successors in Pajajaran, but we learn from other stories that one of Bañak Wide's descendants was a princess of Pajajaran who became the wife of Sukmul and the mother of Jangkung, i.e. Jan Pieterszoon Coen, the first Governor-General in Batavia. This princess of Pajajaran was called Tanuraga ("the slender-bodied one," Durgā) and had flaming genitals. She is, of course, functionally identical with Ḍĕḍĕs in whom we recognized Durgā in section 2; Ḍĕḍĕs was the ancestress of the kings of Majapahit, Tanuraga was the ancestress of the "kings" of Batavia. It was, therefore, in order to engender the dynasty of Batavia that Amijaya's grandson removed his residence to Pajajaran, according to the *Babad Tanah Jawi;* when the germ developed, the "normal" king returned to East Java and founded Majapahit.

This leads us to the question of the Mataramese interpretation of Kĕrtanagara's Triple Alliance which—as we have seen before—played a part in the political ideology of Majapahit as well, the three powers then being Champa, Majapahit, and Malayu. Being impressed with the pronouncements of the statesmen of Majapahit and apparently believing them to render the truth, Añakrakusuma, the founder of the dynasty of Mataram who is generally called Sultan Agung, "the Great," made an effort to unite the entire island of Java under his scepter and to make himself obeyed by the other islands. This happened in the first decades of the seventeenth century. Añakrakusuma, however, failed to bring about the unification of Java because, after his conquest of East Java, he did not succeed in breaking the resistance of the Dutch in Batavia so that Bantam, a kingdom on the northwestern coast of Java, remained inaccessible to him. This failure did not detract from the mythical validity of the doctrine of 1331/1351 in the period after Añakrakusuma's campaign against Batavia; in the eighteenth century the kings of Mataram, Kartasura, etc., still claimed to be the lords of the whole of Java and the other islands. After 1628/1629, however, it became an ideological necessity—long before it was a political necessity—to take into account the position of the Dutch. To this purpose the Triple Alliance doctrine could render yeoman service. Regarding Islam and the Dutch East India Company in Batavia as two foreign powers, the Mataramese priests inserted stories in the *Babad Tanah Jawi* which were to convey that the ruler of Champa had been converted to Islam and that his Moslem son was serving the king of Majapahit. A similar story was told in connection with the Dutch East India Company. According to the *Sĕrat Baron Sĕkĕnḍer*, the Spanish merchant Baron Kawit-Paru had twelve wives; after abnormal conception eleven wives gave birth to eleven sons, whereas the youngest wife gave birth to twins, Sukmul and Sĕkĕnḍer. After many adventures which finally brought them to Java, Sukmul married Tanuraga so as to become the ancestor of the Dutch "kings" of Batavia, whereas Sĕkĕnḍer entered the service of the king of Mataram. Sĕkĕnḍer is the Iskandar Dhū 'l-Ḳarnain of Moslem tradition who, in his turn, developed from Alexander the Great; according to the *Sĕjarah Mĕlayu*, Iskandar Dhū 'l-Ḳarnain was the founder of the dynasty of Malayu, so that it was easy enough for Javanese scholars who were acquainted with that Malay book to connect the dynasty of the "kings" of Batavia with Malayu.

The *Babad Tanah Jawi* consists of many stories; in order to be understood many of them require a high degree of familiarity with ancient Javanese literature. I have mentioned a few of them in order to draw the reader's attention to the importance of this book for our knowledge of the Javanese picture of the past, while regretting that I must exclude many other stories from the discussion, as well as the whole set of stories which has been added to the original *Babad Tanah Jawi* in later years. It should be repeated, however, that the *Babad Tanah Jawi* is also characterized by a genealogical structure. This genealogical structure does not quite fit in with the dynastic pattern discussed above. The oldest version of the genealogy must have enumerated seven kings preceding Bra Wijaya I, seven kings of Majapahit, and seven descendants of Bra Wijaya II who preceded Añakrakusuma. This three times seven structure was enlarged in later years so as to become a seven times seven structure. This enlarged structure was extended once more when Adam and six descendants were added in order to satisfy the curiosity of the Moslem community. The original genealogy was not only extended; it must also have been modified by scholars of the seventeenth and eighteenth centuries in order to be made subservient to the interests of later kings.

6. FINAL REMARKS

A picture of the past is a complex of myths, and as such it exists everywhere and in any period of human history. This is why a final section should deal with the picture of the past which is in vogue with the present-day Indonesians. For various reasons, however, the author of this article must refrain from endeavoring to write that final section.

It must be repeated here that even our efforts to reconstruct the older picture of the past could give only provisional results. Our views depend on our knowledge of such documents as have been published and on some additional knowledge of documents in manuscript. A considerable number of manuscripts in different Indonesian languages are waiting for scholars to read and analyze them. It is more than probable that several ancient Javanese books which are described in the catalogues as "loan myths" from Indian literature will prove to bear on episodes of Javanese history, in one way or another. Furthermore, we find abundant evidence of information handed down in oral tradition in priestly families, constituting something midway between the written documents and the oral tradition of the larger community. I do not know to what extent this priestly tradition still is a source of knowledge; it seems useful to try to find out.

Useful reading for people who are interested in the subject of this contribution is Brandes' appendix to his *Pararaton* edition, Djajadiningrat's book on the *Sějarah Bantěn,* and Schrieke's *Ruler and Realm in Early Java.* The present author has published his views in essays which have appeared since 1927, modifying his conclusions as often as continued research forced him to do so. Unfortunately, there is no common view as to the value of the theories which have been launched hitherto. On the other hand, that is the normal *choc des opinions* to which a French proverb ascribes the mysterious power to produce truth.

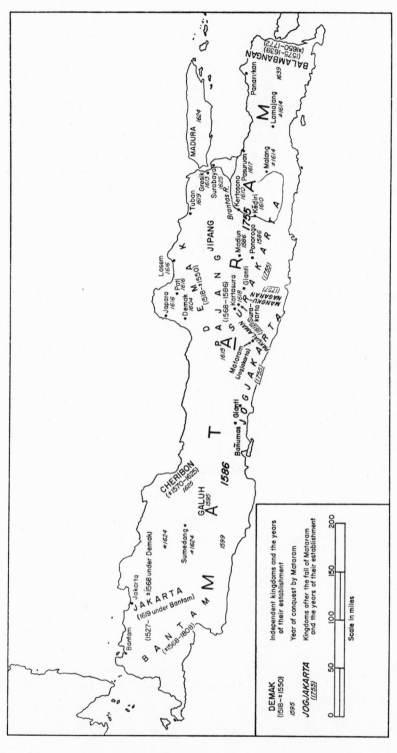

3. Javanese Kingdoms after 1525

BANTAM
Bantam
Jakarta
JAKARTA
(1527–
(±1568–1808)
(1619 under Bantam)
±1568 under Demak

Sumedang •
±1624
±1624

CHERIBON
(±1570–1625)
1625

GALUH
A 1595

1599

T
A
M
A
T
A

Bañumas •
Giánti

JOGJAKARTA
(1755)

Mataram
(Joglakarta)
1615 (1618 ±1586)

DADAJANG
A
K
E ((1518–±1550)

Japara
1616 •
• Pati
1616
• Demak
1604 (1518–±1550)

Lasem
1616

K

Tuban •
1619

Gresik
1613
• Surabaya
1625

MADURA
1624

JIPANG

A
S
U
R
A
B
A
J
A

MANGKU-
NAGARAN
(1757)

Sura-
karta
±1618

Giánti
1618 •

Madiun
1586 • R.

Brantas R.

Kertosono
1610
• Pasuruan
1617

Kediri
1610

Ponorogo
1586

1755
A
K
A
R
T
A

A

• Malang
±1614

M

• Lamajang
±1614

Panarukan

BALAMBANGAN
(1575–1639)
(±1650–1772)
1639

Kartasura
(±1618)

DEMAK
(1518–±1550)
1595
JOG.JAKARTA
(1755)

Independent kingdoms and the years
of their establishment

Year of conquest by Mataram

Kingdoms after the fall of Mataram
and the years of their establishment

Scale in miles
0   50   100   150   200

VII

Later Javanese Sources and Historiography

By H. J. de GRAAF

Formerly lecturer in the Modern History of the Indonesian Peoples, Universities of Indonesia and Leyden

THERE is no other Javanese work of literature with which the outside world became acquainted as early as the *Babad Tanah Jawi*, the so-called Javanese State Chronicles. No other work of New Javanese literature has been the object of such lengthy and serious labor as this astounding book. But even more study and energy will have to be devoted to it before we can gain a clear and relatively complete view of this book, its purposes, composition, history, and original form.

Already the Dutch envoy to the Court of Mataram, Rijklof van Goens (1619–1681), later Governor-General, in his "Corte Beschrijvinge van 't Eijland Java" (in *De vijf gezantschapsreizen van R. v. Goens* [The Hague, 1956]), could report that the Javanese were extremely knowledgeable about their past, since they were in possession of "oude comediën, geschriften, ende 't verhael van veel ouder tijden" (old comedies, manuscripts, and the accounts of much earlier times) than any of the "Maleijers, Balijers, Macassaren, Amboineesen, Molucaenen, Borneoten, Sumbawers, Soloreesen" (p. 184). However, van Goens was not yet able to identify any specific work by name.

More than a century later (1779 and subsequently), the first Dutch translation of a Javanese work of literature appeared—a translation of the first parts of the State Chronicles, published in the first three issues of the *Verhandelingen van het Bataviaasch Genootschap* (*VBG*), through the initiative of the Reverend Josua van Iperen, member of

the Board of the Batavian Society. The translation itself was made by
the official translator of the Dutch East India Company, a man named
Gordijn.

In 1807, the famous governor of Java's East Coast, Nicolaas Engel-
hardt, ordered a complete translation into Dutch of a chronicle found
in his residency of Semarang, the *Sĕrat Kanda,* a manuscript closely
related to the *Babad Tanah Jawi.* Unfortunately this valuable manuscript never reached the printing presses, and at first only a small
circle of interested persons was able to profit from the translation. Not
until the beginning of the present century did this remarkable book
start to draw attention.

Yet, although only very limited portions of the Babad had appeared
in print, these manuscripts had already exerted their influence. Lieutenant Governor Thomas Stamford Raffles, during the British interim
rule (1811–1816), had devoted much attention not only to the improvement of Java's rural tax system but also to Javanese culture; he utilized
much material derived from the Babad in his famous *History of Java.*
He was able to do so thanks to his friend and collaborator, Panembahan Natakusuma of Sumenep (Madura). Through Raffles' work,
many historical data from *babad* lore became known to the world.

Following in the footsteps of Raffles was the self-taught and enthusiastic historian J. Hageman whose two-volume *Handleiding tot de
kennis der geschiedenis, aardrijkskunde, fabelleer en tijdrekenkunde
van Java* (Manual of the Knowledge of History, Geography, Mythology
and Chronometry of Java; Batavia, 1852) drew extensively from Java's
traditions. Unfortunately his uncritical and inexpert use of the material
brought it into temporary discredit.

More lasting success was achieved by J. J. Meinsma, an instructor
at the Institute for the Training of Civil Service Officials for the Indies
in Delft, with his *Babad Tanah Djawi, tekst en aantekeningen* (The
Babad Tanah Jawi, Text and Annotations; The Hague, 1874–1877).
A two-volume work, this book was an abridged edition in prose of a
Babad text composed by Kertapradja. The purpose of this abridged
version was not so much to promote more knowledge of history among
aspiring civil service officials as to provide them with simple reading
material in Javanese and also to familiarize them with the mores,
customs, and views of the Javanese.

Although this work did not cover the entire scope of the Babad
—it ran only up to the Javanese year of 1647 (A.D. 1723)—it did serve
to increase acquaintance with Javanese historical writings. Although

initiates were well aware of the fact that the Babad material was much more extensive—reaching into the year 1743 and therefore containing much more information—for lack of a complete edition of the real Babad this abridged prose-version, otherwise a very useful edition, had to serve for a period of seventy years.

A number of private publishers brought out several editions of babad manuscripts—including a three-volume *Babad Tanah Jawi* running up to 1685 and published by the Van Dorp publishing company (Samarang and Surabaya, 1917). But these unscholarly editions, mainly intended for Javanese readers, did not succeed in permanently distracting the attention of experts on Javanese from the so-called *Babad Meinsma*, which not only saw the light of several editions but which was even provided with a (Javanese) alphabetical index by the scholar J. L. A. Brandes.

An additional stimulus to the Babad study came with the publication of the *Babad Meinsma* in Roman script, accompanied by a translation into Dutch made by W. L. Olthof and provided with an alphabetic register compiled by A. Teeuw. This edition was published at the initiative of the Koninklijk Instituut voor Taal-, Land- en Volkenkunde (The Hague, 1941).

Finally, an edition of the "Great Babad" in its entirety was published by the Balai Pustaka (government publishing house for popular literature) in thirty-one small volumes in Javanese script; it was unfortunately unaccompanied by an index, which rather seriously restricted its usefulness. Although World War II limited the circulation of this edition outside Indonesia, any future study of the *Babad Tanah Jawi* must henceforth in the first place take into consideration this Balai Pustaka issue, and not the abridged Meinsma version.

All the existing editions have not been able to meet the needs of scholarly research. A critical, scholarly edition, provided with a Western-language translation and with a name index, would be essential for a thorough study of the *Babad Tanah Jawi*. That so far we have had to make do with such defective Babad editions is actually ridiculous, particularly when this is compared with what is available in other branches of philology—in Latin, Hebrew, and Greek philology, for instance. An additional and aggravating circumstance is the fact that the complete Balai Pustaka text has, since 1950, been unobtainable in Indonesia.

Nevertheless, for a further study of Javanese history, the Babad is indispensable. It is impossible and it would be irresponsible to undertake the study of the history of the Javanese people without a thorough knowledge of native source material, among which the Babad is by far the most important. Let us hope that this will be increasingly realized and that interest will continue to grow at such a rate that a valid and scholarly edition, or at least an index to the Balai Pustaka edition, will no longer be an impossibility.

Although besides the widely scattered and numerous manuscripts there have been only a few and imperfectly printed editions available, the investigation into the nature and composition of the Babad has proceeded without hesitation. After the uncritical glorification of the Babad by Raffles and Hageman, Dr. Brandes was one of the first to shed some light on this work. We have already mentioned his index, the compilation of which naturally brought him in contact with the material of the entire Babad. Brandes discussed rather elaborately the nature of the Babad in his annotations to his edition of the *Pararaton* ("Pararaton of het boek der koningen van Tumapël en van Majapahit," ed. by N. J. Krom, 2d ed., *VBG*, vol. LXII [1920]). In this work Brandes proposed the thesis that the older Babad "could from a certain viewpoint be considered a handbook of Javanese literature as well as a historical narrative" (p. 209). Brandes, in short, found that it contained numerous genealogical data, but he did not encounter any dates, and therefore thought of the manuscript as a "manual for the poet." In Brandes' opinion, stories were added in chronological sequence, and eventually there emerged manuscripts which "as a matter of course, as it were, presented themselves as historical tales, particularly because of the fact that the ruling monarchs traced their ancestry to heroes mentioned in those old stories" (p. 210).

In this connection the question could be raised whether such an older Babad had ever actually existed and whether its oldest editor had not started from the onset to record, collect, and arrange all kinds of oral traditions and had not finally compiled them into a book with the naïve conviction of thus having produced a proper historical work.

A renewed attempt to deal with the Babad problem was made a few years later by Hoesein Djajadiningrat in his invaluable doctoral thesis, *Critische beschouwing van de Sadjarah Bantĕn* (A Critical Review of the *Sĕjarah Bantĕn;* Haarlem, 1913).

He was of the opinion that in dealing with Javanese babads the works or parts of works which pertain to later periods should not be considered as regular history *books* but rather as historical *sources* and that the historical value of those works should therefore not be overestimated.

However, Djajadiningrat further contended, these books should be highly appreciated because they provide opportunities to gain knowledge about "the views and emotional condition of the Javanese or of particular groups of the population during a specific period" (p. 307).

Important are the author's attempts to date specific parts of the *Babad Tanah Jawi* and to attribute those parts to authors known to us from Javanese literary traditions. Grateful use was made in these efforts, of "post eventum prophecies."

Following this procedure, Djajadiningrat discerned in the *Babad Tanah Jawi* three stages:

1) the Kraton Mataram and the preceding period up to 1677, completed by Pangeran Adi Langu II shortly after 1705
2) the Kraton Kartasura from 1677 till 1718, completed under Sunan Mangkurat IV (1718–1727) by Carik Bajra (later promoted to Tumenggung Tirtawiguna)
3) The Kraton Kartasura from 1718 till 1743, completed after 1757 under Sunan Paku Buwana III (1749–1792), probably also by the same Carik Bajra.

It seems to me that in this connection the question should also be investigated of whether indeed Pangeran Adi Langu II is to be considered the first author-editor of the *Babad Tanah Jawi*; in other words, whether he did not have predecessors.

A quarter of a century later the problem of the Babad was taken up again by Professor C. C. Berg in his "Javaansche geschiedschrijving" (his contribution to the *Geschiedenis van Nederlandsch Indië*, vol. II ed. by F. W. Stapel [Amsterdam, 1938], pp. 5–148). This first attempt of Berg to solve the Babad problem was followed after the war by a long series of articles by him in several publications, many of which more or less touched upon the problem. Special attention should be given to Berg's article in *Indonesië* (VIII, [1955], 97–128), "Twee nieuwe publicaties betreffende de geschiedenis en geschiedschrijving van Mataram," which was continued in successive issues.

In his first article, Berg cautioned that the historical value of the *Babad Tanah Jawi* should not be overestimated. He saw in that Babad in the first place a device to add to the king's power. "The literary form is often of greater importance than the need of conveying factual knowledge" (p. 145). Berg said he was only able to find fragments which could be employed by Western observers as sources of information. "Generally speaking, the usefulness of Javanese manuscripts to Western historians is inversely proportional to their value for the Javanese people" (p. 147). In subsequent studies Berg continued to adhere to this thesis. For instance, in the above-mentioned article published in *Indonesië*, Berg arrived at conclusions which questioned the historical reality of certain persons who so far had been considered historical figures—such as the founder of the Mataram dynasty, Panembahan Senapati and his son Panembahan Krapyak. This would place Sultan Agung not only at the zenith of that dynasty but also at its starting point.

With this contention Berg came into conflict with the present author, who in a public lecture on October 19, 1953, entitled "On the Origins of the Javanese State Chronicles" attributed to the Javanese a much stronger sense of history, which conclusion, he felt, could be drawn from a review of the Babad itself. Even the sense for chronology among the Javanese, so often underestimated, proved to be quite vivid, as evidenced by the existence of date lists already referred to by Raffles. The editors of the Babad very likely made grateful use of these lists, of which four are at our disposal. As far as it has been possible to check them against European data, the lists of dates have shown a surprising degree of accuracy. It could therefore be assumed that the date lists may, despite the inaccuracies or deliberate distortions which can be found in places, contain valuable historical data about periods prior to the arrival of Westerners. It even appeared not impossible that within the four date lists known to us a fragment of a similar list is contained which can be dated back to the kingdom of Demak.

Professor Berg and this author have continued the exchange of opinions on this issue, but on important points our views have not come closer to each other. Naturally, the views of this author will be brought out more prominently in this article, referring for further details and evidence to the above-mentioned public lecture and also to his article "De historische betrouwbaarheid der Javaanse overlevering" (The Historical Reliability of Javanese Traditional History), *BKI*, CXII (1956), 55–73.

It seems to me that most researchers, in undertaking the study of the Babad, have made the mistake of starting with the beginning of this massive volume. They were probably prompted to do so because they needed those first pages of the Babad for information and clarification regarding the last centuries of Hindu-Javanese civilization. This investigation proved generally rather disappointing, and not without reason. For it can be readily assumed that the oldest material, chronologically most remote from the later authors of the Babad, must have suffered worst in transmission—unless the miracle can be assumed that during the seventeenth century in Mataram such pre-Islamic writings as the *Pararaton* were still widely known. In my opinion, there are hardly any indications in that direction. As a result of continuous oral transmission, the oldest material takes on a mythological character. Furthermore, there is the possibility that the older material has been rewritten or reedited more frequently by later editors as compared to the newer material, which was recorded as late as the eighteenth century, soon after the actual events.

No wonder, then, that these older Babad parts, which have been most seriously studied, have yielded little of historical value and therefore have led the researchers into the temptation of underestimating the historical qualities of the *entire* Babad.

It appears to me, therefore, that it would be more useful for the historian examining the Babad to start not with the beginning but rather with the middle or the end of the book. But for this purpose the most accurate possible knowledge of events, conditions, and circumstances in Mataram in the course of the seventeenth and eighteenth centuries is required in order to find out to which influences the Babad text was subjected during that period. Regarding the seventeenth century we have, at present, some knowledge of this; regarding the eighteenth century, hardly any. However, the available material in manuscripts and archives, either in Dutch or in Javanese, is considerable in quantity.

Armed with knowledge about the time and conditions under which the *Babad Tanah Jawi* came into being and working back from the most recent parts toward the oldest, one would have the best chance to unveil the secret of this book. It would probably be a lengthy and laborious task, in view of the extensive material which must be consulted. Of this, the little, albeit very useful, material which was published by J. K. J. de Jonge almost a century ago in his *De opkomst van het Nederlandsch gezag in Oost Indië* (The Hague and Amsterdam, 1862–1888) is utterly insufficient for the purpose.

Let us review what, following this method, has been achieved so far with regard to the *Babad Tanah Jawi*. With regard to the genesis of the Babad, there are for the moment only a few external data, which have already been utilized by Djajadiningrat, viz., the assertion in *Javaansche samenspraken* of J. F. Winter, Sr. (3d ed.; Amsterdam, 1882), that the Javanese babads—including the *Babad Mataram* and therefore reaching into the year 1677—were made by Pangeran Adi Langu II during the Kartasura period (1680–1743). Adi Langu's work was continued by

Carik Bajra from Surabaya who later became Tumenggung Tirtawiguna. He was a well-known figure, not only in the kraton cities of
Kartasura and Surakarta but also in Batavia, where, as envoy, he paid
his respects. An additional piece of information comes from the Reverend Josua van Iperen, who, as we know, published the first translation into Dutch of the early portion of the Babad. The translator,
Gordijn, supposedly bought the Javanese manuscript in 1750 from his
Javanese teacher, Ki Sutaprana.

Subsequently, we can compare the *Babad Tanah Jawi* with similar
works, such as the *Sějarah Bantěn*, which has been dealt with by
Djajadiningrat and which undoubtedly drew considerably on an earlier
Babad edition. The months-long stay of a number of Bantam envoys
in Mataram in 1650 was presumably of importance in this connection.

We also could place the Babad next to the works of such Dutch
authors as Rijklof van Goens, who visited the court city five times
(1648–1654), and the Reverend François Valentijn (1666–1727), both
of whom made references to Javanese historical traditions.

It is almost certain that van Goens obtained his information from
Mathijs Pietersen, a shipmate who had spent years in a Javanese prison
(1632–1646) and who had thus learned Javanese. The Reverend Valentijn obtained his information from the secretary of Mangkurat II, Sura
Wikrama, who was elevated to this position in 1680.

For a check on the historical references in the Babad, historical data
found in manuscripts of the Portuguese and the Dutch can be employed. While the Portuguese, who rarely touched Java in their voyages, were not very informative, the Dutch provided rather abundant
information. In this way it is sometimes possible to discern a historical
kernel in seemingly rather improbable Babad stories—for instance, in
the incident of Sultan Agung with the *kidang* (deer), which we can
ascertain and even date (1624) thanks to information extended by the
Dutch envoy H. de Haen. We also find a mention of the reportedly
multilingual port officer of Japara, Kyai Marmagati, whose signature in
Arabic characters even appears on a document at the Landsarchief
(now the National Archives) in Jakarta.

While Western sources often lack knowledge of the exact condition
or circumstances surrounding events, their chronology is usually excellent, often exact to the day. This enables us to check the traditional
chronograms or *candra sěngkala* of reported events; and where such
chronograms are lacking, we can at least determine the correct sequence of events. Generally, in cases where such checking was possible,

only a few discrepancies have been found, which is to the credit of the sense of history of the Javanese.

In cases where checking is possible, genealogical data also display a high degree of accuracy. It seems that at an early stage there was already a vivid interest in genealogy, a characteristic not foreign to Westerners, as evidenced by the large number of genealogists in our archives. Already in older times it seems that people tried to reconstruct and record family trees, and the most famous among those, the *Sĕjarah Dalem* (Semarang, 1902), has been of the greatest value to this author. Genealogies enable us to trace the exact family relations between various persons, which is of the greatest importance in Javanese society.

Actually, we should study the text of the babads *critically*. But because only very recently has a single and complete edition of the Great Babad been available, philologists have not had much time to compare this text with other printed texts or manuscripts; in fact, nothing has yet been done in this respect. We must therefore necessarily refrain from considering the Babad text from the viewpoint of a linguist; instead we might view the Babad as a historian, a historian armed with information obtained from other sources, particularly from Dutch sources.

Careful scrutiny will disclose that some parts of the Babad are more historically and more realistically written than other parts. Myths seem to play a much smaller and incidental role in those parts than in the other. This we may ascribe to the length of time between the actual occurrence of events and their recording. Presumably accounts of recent events will be clearer and more accurate than of events which occurred decades before. Based on this proposition, we can therefore assume that a "realistic" account was the labor of a contemporary author shortly after the actual occurrence of the described event.

With only one extraordinary exception, the period from 1600 to 1635 has been described with considerable accuracy and in good chronological order. The description of the succeeding period is vague, confused, superficial, and "mythical," after which the historical narrative again acquires realistic traits. We can therefore assume the activities of an author not too long after 1635.

There are some more indications in this direction. In the Babad story, the rulers of Demak and Pajang have been given the title of sultan, a title which, according to Portuguese sources, these two rulers never carried. They were probably never more than a *pangeran* or a *panem-*

bahan, and the sultan title was probably conferred on them afterward. Now, there is only one brief period in which this posthumous promotion was possible, viz., during the five years that the ruler of Mataram —later known as Sultan Agung—carried the sultan's title. This serves to strengthen the assumption that the first edition of the *Babad Tanah Jawi* was completed during the last years of the rule of Sultan Agung, i.e., between the years 1641 and 1646.

Moreover, it was also during that period that Mataram reached its greatest territorial extension, reaching from Palembang to the Straits of Bali, while relations were also established with Jambi and Banjermasin. Now the *Babad Tanah Jawi* contains accounts of most of those regions named, and it is certainly striking how much emphasis has been placed on the westernmost territories of Priangan and Palembang. In contradiction to the actual course of events, Majapahit is purportedly established from the Sunda regions. This text further reports that the first ruler of Demak originated from Palembang, and not from Gresik, as the Portuguese assure us. Accounts from Priangan, Demak, Kudus, Mataram, Pajang, Sèla, Surabaya, and Giri are also incorporated.

It seems that this "collecting" habit is typical of the Mataram dynasty. Of lowly origin, this dynasty collected all kinds of attributes to heighten its prestige and to outdo the nobler families in the coastal regions. Titles (first pangeran, followed by susuhunan, and finally sultan) were collected, and also heirlooms, units of bodyguards, and magical objects like cannons. Why therefore not also historical traditions, or what were considered as such?

Special attention should be given to the accounts originating from Surabaya, because we have knowledge about their presumable transmitter, Pangeran Pekik (+ 1659), son of Surabaya's last ruler (dethroned 1625) and a refined and erudite coastal gentleman who must have conspicuously contrasted with the still little-civilized Mataram. Not only are those accounts extensive, but they contain traditions of Majapahit which Mataram must therefore have received from Surabaya.

These accounts of traditions of Surabaya are so numerous and so extensive that at first I thought we were dealing with a lost work of Surabaya history. But in a letter, Dr. Djajadiningrat expressed his differing opinion, indicating that these Surabayan data, and, similarly, the accounts regarding Palembang, Priangan, Kudus, Demak, etc., probably originated from oral traditions.

Although until 1636 Mataram was on hostile terms with Giri, even

Giri traditions were incorporated into the *Babad Tanah Jawi*. This vindicates what we have already suspected on the basis of other data, i.e., that in the meantime Mataram had come to establish peace with the priest-rulers of this remarkable, often so intensely fought-against, little clerical state.

No trace can be found of an edition of the Babad of the years 1624 or 1633, as alleged and defended by Berg. Furthermore, in that critical war year, 1624, Mataram's ruler must have had many other things on his mind besides the composition of the state's chronicles.

Who did compose this first Babad between 1641 and 1646? In view of the frequent Dutch assertion that "papists" often acted as scribes at the Mataram courts, it can be readily assumed that we should look for the author among the ranks of the prominent Moslem scribes. Now, the founding father of the hereditary priest-rulers of Adi Langu, Sunan Kalijaga, was prominently depicted by the Babad as assisting the founder of the Mataram Dynasty, Panembahan Senapati. A short biography of this famous and saintly sage was even included in the *Sĕjarah Bantĕn* (pp. 25–26), which must have drawn extensively upon the Babad. From Dutch sources we know that the Mataram court was on very friendly terms with the rulers of Adi Langu. It is therefore quite probable that besides Pangeran Adi Langu II in the beginning of the eighteenth century a predecessor of this venerable gentleman half a century earlier had devoted his labors to the composition of a *Babad Tanah Jawi*.

Pangeran Adi Langu II must have brought about a decisive change in this first Babad. Not only must he have brought the Babad story up to 1677—the fall of the Kraton Mataram—but he must also have drastically changed passages in the already-finished text, viz., those regarding the role of the erstwhile hostile Pajang. Mataram's new kraton, Kartasura, was established not too far from the site of the once famous Kraton of Pajang, which had been totally destroyed by Mataram (1618). Pajang's role now was shown in a much more favorable light.

A much larger number of songs than had been originally the case were devoted to Pajang; and Pajang's last ruler, Adiwijaya, who came to a fateful end, was pictured much more sympathetically, and a parallel was drawn between the last days of this ruler and those of Mataram's Sunan Mangkurat I Tegalwangi. Furthermore, accounts of Pengging, located on the other side of Kartasura and, according to archaeological data, clearly an older and once famous community, were incorporated in the accounts of Pajang.

To Carik Bajra, who continued the Babad during the rule of Mangkurat IV, fell the precarious task of proving that in 1677 Sunan Mangkurat II had rightly been made Susuhunan instead of his brother
Pangeran Puger; and, secondly, Bajra had also to provide incontestable
proof that it was the full right of Pangeran Puger to succeed his brother
Mangkurat II to the throne rather than the latter's own son, the so-
called Sunan Mas. Carik Bajra exhibited great skill in carrying out this
difficult task.

It was probably the same Carik Bajra—meanwhile promoted to
Tumenggung Tirtawiguna—who in his old age was given the task of
bringing the *Babad Tanah Jawi* up to the fall of the Kartasura kraton
in 1743. This time he had to give special consideration to the Purbaya
family because the mother of the then ruling Sunan Paku Buwana III
was a descendant of this family. It was therefore probably Bajra who
in the Babad attributed to Pangeran Purbaya miraculous deeds, allegedly performed during the siege of Batavia in 1628–1629—miracles
Purbaya's most observant contemporaries had not even noticed.

Similarly, Purbaya, who had played a highly dubious political role
during the rule of his nephew Mangkurat I, was given a hero's death
as a loyal follower of his king during the battle of Gegodog, on October
13, 1676.

In this fashion, until very recent times, older parts of the Babad
have been purposely changed or added to. This was prompted by the
fact that old manuscripts had previously been used as political weapons, and it was therefore desirable to alter those manuscripts in such
a way that the policies of the Mataram rulers could find their justification in them.

We have already pointed out how the issue of the succession of
rulers was ably defended by Carik Bajra. But other political actions
also required justification: for instance, the transfer of the kraton from
its original founding place in Mataram to Pajang and also the alliance
with the Dutch, which did not meet with the approval of many.

Alleged prophecies put in the mouths of such authoritative and
venerable persons as Sultan Agung were therefore of decisive importance. When reading and studying the *Babad Tanah Jawi,* one has
to keep constantly in mind the occasional polemical character of this
manuscript, which defended certain premises, not always with the
strictest adherence to facts. It should also be taken into consideration
that, apart from the manuscripts of their predecessors and some date
lists, Babad authors had to rely on oral narratives which were often

strongly partisan. It is therefore not surprising that those manuscripts do not always show the impartiality of the historian, which until recently was considered a necessary adornment of any historical work. Careful reading and continuous comparison with other sources, preferably Western, are therefore highly recommended. If this is taken into account, the babad literature will yield a rich treasure of data and insights—if not of the era described in the text, then at least of the era of its author.

There is no doubt about the sacral character of the babad literature. I was informed that the late Sultan of Jogjakarta, Hamengku Buwana VIII, would never have the Babad read to him without having first dressed in special ceremonial attire. Babad critique in the fashion sometimes conducted by Westerners is not always agreeably received, as, similarly, Christians would not be appreciative of a scientific treatment of the Bible text which did not take sufficiently into consideration the Bible's character as Holy Scripture.

On the other hand, the esteem for the Babad cannot be compared to the veneration the Old Testament enjoyed among the Jews who carefully guarded the purity of its text. Several variants of the Babad are in existence, which agree on the main outlines but which contain hundreds of minor differences. Neither are the manuscripts treated with secrecy, as is sometimes the case with *pusakas* (heirlooms) of the realm or with certain sacred graves. This sacral aspect may not at first have been present but could have grown gradually with the increased esteem for this book which contains the history of the ruling dynasty.

I doubt whether any Javanese manuscripts have been purposely destroyed, as has sometimes been assumed. In this country, neglect is sufficient to cause the complete loss of a manuscript. Humidity and bugs will see to this. Only repeated copying will save a manuscript from speedy destruction. But who would copy a manuscript for which interest had waned?

After the completion of the great *Babad Tanah Jawi,* the Javanese continued to write the history of their people. Several works were completed which should be considered as supplements and sequels to the Babad.

First there is the *Babad Petjina,* which narrates the fall of the kraton of Kartasura at the hands of mutinous Chinese and their followers (1743).

Then there is the great *Babad Gianti,* written by the famous Javanese poet Radèn Ngabéhi Jasadipura. It relates the war of partition between

Surakarta and Jogjakarta and the adventures of Mangkubumi, the first prince Mangkunagara (1757–1796). The Balai Pustaka publishing house has issued a good edition of this work, supplemented with maps and name index (Batavia Centrum, 1937–1939). This work could become an important source about an era of which so many Dutch documents are already available.

Then there is also a Javanese babad of which C. Poensen has provided us with a lengthy abstract under the titles "Mangkubumi (1755–1792)" and "Amangku Buwana II (Sepuh) (1792–1828)," both on sultans of Jogjakarta.

In succession to this work is the precious *Babad Dipanagara*, written by the great rebel himself during his exile (1830–1855). Starting with the first man, Adam, Dipanagara relates the history of Java as he knew it from the traditions of the court, and, about one-third through the book, he embarks upon an account of the fortunes of the Jogjakarta sultanate. The main part of this book consists of Dipanagara's personal memoirs, which are of considerable interest.

Meinsma considered this book of the highest value in learning about "the ways of thinking and the historical concepts of the Javanese." "Seen from this viewpoint, the value of such a source for historical critique cannot easily be overestimated," he wrote (report on the *Babad Dipanagara*, in *Notulen van het Bataviaasch Genootschap*, XV [1877], 89–95).

P. J. E. Louw, who diligently studied the *Babad Dipanagara* before writing his six-volume *De Java-oorlog, 1825–1830* (The Java War; Batavia and The Hague, 1894–1909), commented:

One reads Dipanagara's narrative with increasing interest, and one is often struck by the really important information it provides, particularly with regard to political relations. Unhesitatingly we would attribute such a high historical value to the *Babad Dipanagara* that any history of the Java War could undoubtedly be branded as highly incomplete if it had not utilized the *Babad Dipanagara* as a source. [I, 94]

In the light of such testimony, then, it is difficult to deny the Javanese any sense of history. It is therefore amazing that in this period of such great admiration for this warrior, the *Babad Dipanagara* attracts so little attention. The few editions published under this title by Western publishers have been sold out, and copies, as usually is the case with such works, are now very hard to find. The only Dutch translation available is in manuscript. For his *Java War*, Louw has written an extract of the *Babad Dipanagara* which clearly shows the importance of this manuscript.

It would be very useful labor indeed if not only this authentic and biographical *Babad Dipanagara* but all historical writings of the Javanese were published, even as a simple text publication, though provided with a name index. Only after this had been done, and after the rich archives of the Dutch East India Company had been consulted, would it be possible to write the history of this island and this people.

Besides the *Babad Tanah Jawi*, its additions, and its sequels, there are also various other historical writings with a more pronounced local character. These manuscripts have not been the object of such great care as has been the Babad text, whose fortunes were so closely linked to the Mataram Dynasty. Only a few of these manuscripts were later reedited or continued, while many show familiarity with the Babad traditions or are connected up with them.

We have already mentioned the *Sĕjarah Bantĕn*, of which Djajadiningrat in his excellent thesis has provided us with such a valuable abstract. The great role this book used to play in the family of the author has been demonstrated by the memoirs of the author's brother, Pangeran Aria Achmad Djajadiningrat.

There are also a *Babad Cĕrbon*, published by D. A. Rinkes (*VBG*, LIX [1911], 144 pp.), and a *Babad Pasir*, dealing with Bañumas, which has been translated by J. Knebel (*VBG*, LI, pt. 1 [1900]).

A *Sĕrat Babad Gresik* was preserved in manuscript, though of only recent origin, and contains the traditions regarding the old priest-rulers of Giri.

Several babads have been written about Balambangan, that ancient tiny Hindu kingdom in the eastern corner of Java. The best among them is probably the *Babad Tawangaloen*, of which Th. Pigeaud has given us an extract and a discussion (*TBG*, LXXII [1932], 216–267).

The historical value of these local writings, however, differs considerably, important though they sometimes may be because they furnish additional information outside the official babad material. The majority, however, have not gone much further than the collection of often very valuable folk traditions. The *Sĕjarah Bantĕn* still most nearly resembles a systematic chronicle dealing with successive generations.

A survey of the historiographical activities of the Javanese during the entire Moslem period will show strikingly that those activities came into full play coincident with the rise of the new state of Mataram (around 1640), and finally came to a decline together with the person who made the last attempt to assign to his house and to his religion a much greater role than the one which various circumstances forced them to play.

This historiography covers a period of almost two centuries, and it has not only described the vicissitudes of fortune of Java's royal dynasties but has itself undergone that same fate. This historiography deserves to be treasured as a precious heritage by the Javanese and to be utilized further with newer methods.

As, in the struggle to regain independence, it was thought necessary to follow in the footsteps of the last great Javanese fighter under the old constellation, it should at present be proper, now that arms have been laid down, to follow him also, though in a more modern and scholarly fashion—on the equally steep path of Javanese Historiography.

SOME JAVANESE HISTORICAL TEXTS
(complete or in extract)

Babad Cĕrbon

Rinkes, D. A., ed. "Babad Tjerbon: Uitvoerige inhoudsopgave en noten door wijlen Dr. J. L. A. Brandes, met inleiding en bijbehoorende tekst" (*Babad Cĕrbon:* Detailed Summary and Notes by the Late Dr. J. L. A. Brandes, with Introduction and Accompanying Text), *VBG*, vol. LIX (1911–1914), pt. 2, 144 pp.

Babad Dipanagara

Dipanagara, Pangeran Arya. *Serat Babad Dipanagara Karanganipun swargi . . . piyambak.* (History of Dipanagara: An Autobiography). 2 vols. Surakarta, 1908–1909.

Babad Gianti

Jasadipura. *Babad Gijanti, Serat Babad Soerakarta ingkang oegi nama Babad Gijanti* (History of Surakarta, Also Called History of Gianti). 21 vols., with index. Batavia, 1937–1939.

Babad Pasir

Knebel, J., ed. "Babad Pasir, volgens een Banjoemaasch handschrift, met vertaling" (*Babad Pasir,* According to a Bañumas Manuscript, with Translation), *VBG*, vol. LI (1900), pt. 1, viii, 332 pp.

Babad Petjina

Poenika serat Babad Petjina, anjarijosaken doek ri kela bedahipoen ing nagari Kartasoera (History of the Chinese Revolt and of the Fall of Kartasura). Semarang, 1874.

Babad Tanah Jawi

Babad Tanah Jawi. 31 vols. Batavia, 1939–1941.

Olthof, W. L., tr. *Babad Tanah Jawi in Proza* (*Babad Tanah Jawi* in Prose). The Hague, 1941. Javanese history until the year 1647 of the Javanese calendar; under assignment of the Koninklijk Instituut. From the edition published by J. J. Meinsma, index by A. Teeuw. (This is a translation of the *Poenika Serat Babad Tanah Jawi wiwit saking Nabi Adam* listed below.)

Poenika Serat Babad ing Tanah Jawi . . . ingkang njaosi babonipun . . . raden panji Jaja-Subrata (History of Java with Particular Reference to Raden Panji Jaja Subrata). 3 vols. Semarang and Surabaya, 1917.

Poenika Serat Babad Tanah Jawi wiwit saking Nabi Adam doemoegi ing taoen 1647 (History of Java from the Time of Adam to the Year 1647). The Hague, 1941.

Sĕjarah Bantĕn

Djajadiningrat, Hoesein. *Critische beschouwing van de Sadjarah Banten: Bijdrage ter kenschetsing van de Javaansche geschiedschrijving* (Critical Appraisement of the *Sĕjarah Bantĕn*: Contribution to the Characterization of Javanese Historiography). Haarlem, 1913.

Sĕjarah Dalem

Padma-Susastra. *Sadjarah Dalem pangiwa lan panengen, wiwit saka Kandjeng Nabi Adam tumeka Karaton lan Ngajogja-Karta Adiningrat* (History of the Kings from the Time of Adam until the Period of the Jogjakarta Kraton). Semarang and Surabaya, 1902.

Untitled manuscript, excerpts

Poensen, C. "Amangku Buwana II (Sepuh), Ngajogyakarta's tweede sultan (Naar aanleiding van een Javaansch handschrift)" (Amangku Buwana II, Jogjakarta's Second Sultan, with Reference to a Javanese Manuscript), *BKI*, LVIII 1905), 73–346.

——. "Mangkubumi, Ngajogyakarta's eerste sultan (Naar aanleiding van een Javaansch handschrift)" (Mangkubumi, the First Sultan of Jogjakarta, with Reference to a Javanese Manuscript), *BKI*, LII (1901), 223-361.

READING LIST ON
NEW JAVANESE HISTORIOGRAPHY

Berg, C. C. "Javaansche geschiedschrijving" (Javanese Historiography), in F. W. Stapel, ed., *Geschiedenis van Nederlandsch Indië*, II, 5-148. Amsterdam, 1938.

——. "Twee nieuwe publicaties betreffende de geschiedenis en de geschiedschrijving van Mataram" (Two New Publications on the History and Historiography of Mataram), *Indonesië*, VIII (1955), 97-128.

Djajadiningrat, H. *Critische beschouwing van de Sadjarah Bantěn.* (See above, *Sějarah Bantěn.*)

Graaf, H. J. de. "De historische betrouwbaarheid der Javaanse over-levering" (The Historicity of the Javanese Traditions), *BKI*, CXII (1956), 55-73.

——. *Over het onstaan van de Javaanse Rijkskroniek* (On the Origins of the Javanese Royal Chronicle). Public lecture at the Royal University at Leyden, 19 October 1953.

Krom, N. J., ed. "Pararaton (Ken Arok), of het boek der koningen van Tumapěl en van Majapahit" (Pararaton [Ken Arok] or the Book of Kings of Tumapel and Majapahit; 2d ed.), *VBG*, LXII (1920), 208ff.

VIII

Origins of South Celebes
Historical Writing

By J. NOORDUYN

Linguist, Bible Society, Bogor, Indonesia

I

Comparison of the best-known local traditions of historical writing in Indonesia will bring to light some typical differences among them as to style, subject matter, and attitude to history, even if one allows for geographical and language differences. Taking the *Babad Tanah Jawi* as a typical example of Javanese historical writing, I want to mention here only two things which characterize it in contradistinction to South Celebes historical writing: the abundant mythological components and the prophecies which form an essential part of its structure.

The discussions on this subject over the last years have made it clear that the mythological elements in Javanese historical writing pose intricate problems of interpretation for the investigator. These mythological elements not only are found in the form of long imaginary dynastical genealogies and miracle tales concerning what perhaps might be called legendary times but even are present in a tale such as the siege of Batavia in 1629, which according to Berg is an instance of contemporaneous historical writing whereas de Graaf believes it to date some fifty years later. In this tale we read of a minister of the Javanese king who flies through the air and ruins a city wall by merely pointing at it. Also in these later parts of the *Babad* the fate of the dynasty or the course of history is often foretold by perspicacious people several decades beforehand.

Turning from Java to South Celebes, one feels as though one were coming into quite another climate. The Buginese and Macassarese chronicles occasionally even reveal tendencies quite opposite to the Javanese. Their writers have clearly tried to disassociate themselves from the mythological and legendary elements that they had to include because they found them in their sources. If they had to tell about a certain queen of Bone who was taken away by a whirling fire from heaven which ascended the stairs of her palace while she was sitting in the garret, they make it clear by repeatedly inserting such words as "it is said" or "according to the story" that they would not take responsibility for the tale. Or when it is told that a king of Sidenreng wanted at any cost to buy a crocodile which, as rumor had it, usually had golden excrements, the writer relates with dry humor the disappointment of the buyer who did not get what he expected.

Mythological elements certainly are not absent in South Celebes chronicles, but usually they are confined to the very first part of the writing. There we find the so-called *manurung* tales which explain the origin of the dynasty as founded by a king and queen descended from heaven. But even in these cases the tale is told in a quite matter-of-fact way and purely from the human side. The chronicle of Bone, for instance, relates that in the time before there was a king the country was once hit by earthquakes, lightning, and thunder, lasting for a whole week. After these natural phenomena had finally ceased, a man was seen standing in the center of the plain, clad wholly in white. This man was thought to be a *manurung* ("descended one"). So all the people gathered and resolved to ask him to become their king, for until then there had been only trouble and dissension among them. But when they approached him for this purpose, he proved not to be the *manurung* himself but only his servant. When he got their firm promise that they would take his master as their king, he at last led them to the real *manurung*. They found him clad in yellow, sitting on a flat stone and surrounded by other servants who held his yellow umbrella, his fan, and his betel box. Thereupon he consented to accept full power as king of Bone and was solemnly inaugurated as such by the people.

It is a noteworthy feature of such a tale that the first king's descension from heaven is presupposed and alluded to by the word *manurung* but about the actual event itself nothing is related.

Another chronicle, that of Tanete, starts by relating that some people of a little village, Pangi, once upon a time while hunting came to the top of a mountain and saw there a jar full of water. They concluded that there were probably people on the mountain, and after a while they really found a man and a woman, who apparently lived on fish which were brought to them by birds. As the villagers thought them to be *manurungs*, they asked them to become their king and queen. But the two people refused to descend to the villages. After some time, however, they agreed to give their daughter in marriage to the head of one of the villages, if the people promised always to bring them certain products of the wood, no matter where they would settle. When after many years the man and his wife with their sons at last founded a new settlement near the coast, this relation with Pangi and the other villages was renewed. But they themselves did not become the king and queen of the settlement which was the later Tanete. They had to ask the king of neighboring Segeri to take that function, because he was of truly royal blood, though at the same time subordinated to the kingdom of Goa. The descendants of the two people from the mountain became viceroys.

It will be clear from this rather intricate story that it is primarily meant to explain the position of the dynasty of viceroys and the existing historical relations of Tanete with some inland villages and with the kingdoms of Segeri and Goa.

Such stories with comparable explanatory elements are not confined to historical literature. They presumably are connected with every community, small or large, which has its own object of worship. An interesting example was found by Chabot during his sociological studies in Borongloe, a small part of the kingdom of Goa. A stone was its center of worship, and a short tale explained the origin of the stone as well as the relation of Borongloe to Goa and to a neighboring community. Such a common object or center of worship, together with the story about it, acts as a means to increase the internal coherence of the community, and therefore to foster the expansion of the community's power.

It is understandable, therefore, why stories about *manurungs* and the like had also to be included in local chronicles whenever somebody set himself to write down the history of his country.

Prophecies after the manner of the Javanese *Babad Tanah Jawi* we seldom or never come across in South Celebes chronicles. One example from South Celebes is a little story about Arung Singkang which, however, has not been incorporated in any of the chronicles but can be found only in a separate small manuscript. In the eighteenth century this Arung Singkang, who was a man with quite an interesting personality, played an important role in the history of the kingdom of

Wajo'. Though of Wajorese noble birth, he had sought his fortune on the east coast of Borneo and had assembled there a rather considerable force of some forty large ships with a devoted group of Buginese warriors. At a given moment he sailed home to Wajo', which at the time was more or less subjected to Bone, the principal ally of the Dutch East India Company in South Celebes. His large force caused no little consternation in Wajo' and Bone, the more so when he asked permission to go ashore. By all means Bone and Wajo' wanted to avoid this, but their force did not suffice to stop him. In our little story we are told that Arung Singkang, not getting permission to go ashore, sailed away to the opposite shore of the Bone bay. On a little island there he met a person, called "the big scabby one," who urged him to go back to Wajo', because he surely would liberate Wajo'. So Arung Singkang returned, and afterward he did succeed in going ashore and driving the Bonese troops out of Wajo'. He was finally even able to cause the relations of Wajo' with the Dutch to become juridically uncertain because a new contract remained unsigned. Thus the prophecy he had acted upon according to this story certainly can be said to have come true.

This little story does not relate the issue forecast by the prophecy. The events of the following years we find in some chronicles of Wajo' and in a rather extensive and detailed piece of writing about Arung Singkang. There no prophecies are mentioned. On the contrary, the writers have confined themselves to recording facts: the actions of the leading personalities, the words spoken in official diplomatic negotiations, etc.

In general, South Celebes historical writing is characterized by a certain terseness and matter-of-factness. Most of the chronicles are comparatively short.[1] Fifty pages would be considered quite long. Many of them are much shorter. One of the reasons may be that their writers were assuredly not poets, while most of the long Javanese historical writings are poetical works. Historical poems are not wholly absent in South Celebes literature, but the local chronicles always are written in a rather dry and nonliterary prose style, which often even makes a piecemeal impression.

This especially applies to chronicles such as those of Goa and Tallo',

[1] The historical writings usually called "chronicles" form the central part of South Celebes historical literature. They were designated by a special term (Macassar: *pattorioloang;* Buginese: *attoriolong*), meaning "the things concerning the people of former times." This shows that they were regarded as the historical writings par excellence.

in which the facts related are not given in strictly chronological order. Instead they are grouped in sections of related subjects. Only the main chapters are in chronological order, since each of them covers the time of one of the successive kings. But within these chapters an order of subject matter is more or less strictly adhered to. Successively mention is made of the names of the king, i.e., his personal name, his title of nobility, his title as an appanage prince, and his royal name; then his age at the time of several important events of his life and the number of years he reigned; then the wars he waged, the kingdoms and places he subdued, and the pacts he concluded; after that the wives he married and the children he had; thereafter sometimes the new techniques or customs which for the first time came into use during his reign. Finally, there is usually some appreciation of his character and capacities before the chapter is concluded with his death and his posthumous name.

That the writer indeed had a fixed scheme of subject matter in mind while composing his chronicle becomes especially clear—as Cense has remarked—from the occasional statement that there was nothing to relate about some of these subjects. The writer apparently felt obliged to say so expressly, and he told the reader, for example: "On this subject I cannot say anything because I have not found any notes about it, and nobody whom I asked for information could help me."

This method of composition gives a sure guarantee of the accuracy of the composer and the reliability of his work. But, on the other hand, the lack of chronological data connected with it represents a serious drawback to its usefulness as source material.

Other chronicles though chronologically arranged throughout also show a lack of precise chronological data. Dates nearly always are missing, even when they are known from other Buginese or Macassarese sources. Sometimes only the number of years that elapsed between two events is mentioned. But there are also chronicles, for instance the long chronicle of Tanete, that lack even these data. There events are connected only by phrases such as "after some time" or "after some years." In this regard too there is an essential difference from Javanese historical writing. The typical Javanese chronogram, consisting of a date disguised in words that have figure value and abundantly used in some Javanese chronicles, is completely unknown in South Celebes. More affinity seems to exist with Malay historical writing. There too one often looks in vain for dates.

It seems to have become a literary requirement not to mention dates

in the more or less official local chronicles. Perhaps this may be attributed partly to the influence of the ordinary folk tale of indigenous
or foreign origin, in which dates are never to be expected. It might also
be possible that this chronicle style goes back to times when no chronology was yet in use. Then there is the possibility that the precise
dates were thought to be sufficiently and more properly preserved in
other kinds of writing, as in the so-called diaries.

All this does not mean, however, that there are no writings containing dates. The long piece about Arung Singkang mentioned above is
a clear example. In that, almost every event is dated by means of the
Moslem or European day and month or by the number of days elapsed
since the event previously mentioned. Thus it becomes possible to
make up an exact time table from day to day over a number of years
during the period covered by the story of Arung Singkang.

From an example such as this it will be clear that there must have
been independent and contemporaneous sources which contained these
dates and which could be used by any history writer. The method of
the chronicle writer then was to take over the data from this source
without the dates which formed its frame. In the case of the Arung
Singkang story mentioned, the data were connected into a continuous
story interspersed with dates.

There is every reason to suppose that these sources in question were
the historical "diaries"; for the diaries as we still have them are usually
books wherein days and months were written down beforehand for
a number of years, while for each day some space was left open to be
filled with notes. Several valuable diaries of this kind, used by kings
of Bone and containing interesting historical information, are preserved but still need to be edited.

The only diary edited so far is the Macassarese one of Goa and Tallo',
which mainly covers the seventeenth century and the first part of the
eighteenth century. Apparently it has been handed down from one
generation to the next, each continuing to make historical notes about
his own time. There are indications that sometimes earlier parts were
touched up in later times. Occasionally some notes were added later
on, and sometimes persons are called by names which they got only
after their death. But on the whole it is clear from their very detailed-
ness that the larger part of the notes are really contemporaneous. One
example may suffice to illustrate the way in which important pieces of
information were put down. They are always very short, exact, and
particularly detailed as to dates: in the year A.D. 1638/A.H. 1049 it was

recorded that "on Wednesday the 15th of June, the 12th of Shaffar, at one o'clock, the king Tu-ammenanga-rigaukanna Sultan Alaudin died."

In this way all kinds of events were briefly recorded. The royal diaries contain information not only about births, marriages, deaths, and other happenings in the royal family and about state affairs, war expeditions, pacts, and visits but also about such extraordinary natural phenomena as eclipses, earthquakes, and comets or such occurrences as the arrival of an elephant presented to the king by a Portuguese merchant—in short, all things which in one way or another were considered interesting or important.

This habit of keeping diaries—there are also several private ones, and in the Malay colony at Macassar there were even diaries kept in Malay—seems to have been confined to South Celebes and the peoples that underwent cultural influence from there. In neither the Javanese nor the Malay cultural area do we ever hear of this kind of literature. Perhaps the Javanese so-called year *babads* are nearest to the Buginese and Macassarese diaries, but they are far less detailed in their dates. The Javanese *primbons* might possibly be compared with the notebooks from South Celebes; but in this case too there is a real difference in content, the *primbons* being primarily collections of religious and particularly mystical speculation.

In South Celebes there seems to have been a real urge for recording all sorts of facts, especially perhaps in the heyday of the Macassarese and Buginese cultural expansion. Data concerning very practical and material things such as weapons, fishing implements, houses, ships, financial matters and inventories, laws, and customs have been recorded on pages of diaries left open for the purpose, as well as in separate notebooks. There exist translations of Spanish works on artillery and the making of gunpowder. Buginese maps of the sea with precise geographical annotations have been found.

In this wider sphere of general attitude and interest we obviously must note the attention to historical recording—chiefly the keeping of diaries but also the writing of chronicles and other historical literature. It was an urge to save from oblivion all sorts of things worth knowing that drove many people to write history. In the introduction to several chronicles the writers have expressly said so and have briefly stated why they undertook to record the past. The chronicle of Goa, for instance, declares: "The recording is done only because it was feared that the old kings might be forgotten by their posterity; if people were ignorant about these things, the consequences might be that either we would consider ourselves too lofty kings or on the other hand foreigners might take us only for common people."

No doubt much of the material we now find included in the chronicles was first recorded for very practical reasons, outside the sphere of pure historiography. This means, for instance, that pacts concluded between states or negotiations conducted between them were immediately recorded in writing for use again later in practical politics. We know, in fact, of several instances which show that historical documents were used in political deliberations. At the same time, however, these written records were eventually included in writings on history and in this way became parts of the historical literature.

Summing up our argument so far, we might say that South Celebes historical writing in several respects proves to be in close congruence with the region's whole culture—to be firmly rooted in it and, at least partly, to originate directly from it. This of course merely gives some indication as to the ultimate origin of the phenomenon as such. But in a negative sense it can be said that there are several essential and striking differences from other Indonesian historical writing such as Javanese historiography. This seems to exclude any strong influence from outside as a simple explanation of its origins.

II

Besides these typological considerations of a general nature, there remains the task of inquiring in a more detailed way into the origins of this tradition of historical writing. The actual facts of time, place, and contributing circumstances must be made an object of investigation, if there is to be any progress in our understanding of origins and development. This task is not an easy one. In the first place, we have to rely wholly on the products of South Celebes historical writing itself, since we are carried back into times for which no detailed outside information concerning South Celebes is available. The Portuguese, it is true, already had some superficial contacts with this region in the sixteenth century, but what they have to tell us about it is very little and of a rather general and fragmentary nature.

Furthermore, precisely for that century the diaries, our valuable sources for later times, are still lacking. The earliest one does not date before the beginning of the seventeenth century. Information concerning earlier times is contained only in some of the local chronicles. None of these writings themselves, moreover, was composed in the sixteenth century. The earliest chronicles that are still extant were written in the course of the seventeenth century.

In spite of this scarcity of material and the uncertainty concerning its value, we will try to trace some important lines of historical development which may lead us back to the beginning of the sixteenth century and to the time when historical writing began. The chronological data contained in the oldest chronicles will be the footholds for our steps along this way.

Thus we must work on the presumption that these chronological data are reliable if we want to get anywhere, even though there is no way to demonstrate whether they are right or not beyond the fact that they show no internal contradiction. We assume, in the second place, that reliable chronological data in some way or other originate from contemporaneous sources.

At the same time there will be opportunity to illustrate in somewhat greater detail what kind of historical information one may expect to get from these chronicles and diaries and how it may lend itself to historical research. Some of the main developments of the history of South Celebes will be briefly outlined.

If we start from what is known, we must begin with the time when Islam was adopted in South Celebes, i.e., the beginning of the seventeenth century, because from this time come the first fixed full dates, which later may become the starting point for gradually working backward chronologically.

In ascertaining the right date for the Islamization of South Celebes, I will make use of the results contained in an earlier publication in Dutch, for until recently there has existed some confusion about this date in the literature concerned. Several European writers mention a precise date—and some of them even add the day and the month— for the Islamization of Goa and Tallo' which were the first states on South Celebes to adopt Islam officially. But these dates mentioned vary from 1603 to 1606. A similar confusion seemed to exist in Macassarese sources, for the diary edited gives 1603, the chronicle of Goa 1606, and that of Tallo' 1605. Most of the former statements proved to be finally based on one of the Macassarese sources. Moreover, an old Dutch East India Company report about a visit to the town of Macassar in 1607 fixed the Islamization "some four years ago."

As usual, the diary of Goa and Tallo' gives only a very short communication of one sentence: "The king and one of his brothers adopt Islam." Since this same sentence occurs also in the chronicle of Tallo' in the chapter on King Karaeng Matoaya who at the time was also chancellor of Goa, we may conclude that it was he who took the initiative in this change of religion. This is corroborated by the Arabic name he adopted on this occasion—Abdullah Awwal-al-Islam, which means Abdullah the first Moslem.

The diary mentions not only a year but also a double date, according to both the Christian and the Moslem calendar, the eve of Friday the 22d of September A.D. 1603, the 9th of Jumad I A.H. 1015. This information, however, proves to contain some errors: these dates of both calendars indeed coincided, but actually in the year A.D. 1605/A.H. 1014, and the day of the week was a Thursday. These data are sufficient to assume that the figure 3 in the diary as well as the 6 in the chronicle of Goa are scribes' errors and that the year 1605 was meant in both cases. Incidentally we may remark that John Crawfurd in his book of 1819 gave this same year.

Apparently in this year the king of Tallo' and chancellor of Goa personally embraced Islam, and his example was soon followed by the king of Goa, Alaudin, who was much younger and honored his chancellor as his father. The diary reveals, however, that it was not until the year 1607 that "the first Friday service was held at Tallo', when we adopted Islam." Presumably the completion of the official Islamization of the whole state took some two years.

It is at any rate quite incompatible with Macassarese and Buginese information when some modern Dutch historians say that as early as 1606 the Buginese state of Bone was compelled by Goa to adopt Islam, or even that this event took place twice, a second time in 1611. The latter date proves to be the right one. The former is caused by an old mistake originating from the Dutch report of Admiral Speelman, who gathered his information on South Celebes at Macassar about the year 1668. We here meet with an instance of the regrettable neglect by traditional Dutch colonial historians of the historical sources from Celebes itself, for these sources contain sufficient data to enable the historian to establish the main happenings in the years following the adoption of Islam in Goa and Tallo'.

It is true that Goa sent military expeditions to the Buginese countries to force them to embrace Islam, after they had rejected Goa's exhortation to do so voluntarily. But these wars were not started before the year 1608. The first expedition was successfully met by the combined forces of the three largest Buginese states, united in the Tĕllumpochcho alliance: Bone, Wajo', and Soppeng. But the following year Sidenreng and Soppeng were compelled to give in under a second assault; Wajo' followed in 1610; and Bone, the largest and most powerful among them, was the last, in 1611. The Buginese chronicles go into much detail about the particulars of these Islamic wars, about the route the expeditionary armies took, about how the battles were fought, about the reasons for the Buginese defeat and other relevant happenings. The development outlined here on the base of Buginese sources gives a quite trustworthy picture of the course of events of these years.

For Goa the result of its military enterprise meant more than the fulfillment of a holy duty. Now for the first time it had succeeded in definitively subjecting all Buginese princedoms—and particularly Bone, its old rival on the peninsula. Apparently internal dissension, occasioned by wavering attitudes with regard to Islamization, which was the official objective of Goa's war, had hastened the defeat of the princedoms. Vassals of Wajo', for instance, went over to Islam without any resistance. The king of Bone himself solemnly embraced Islam when his country was still undefeated, and for that reason he was deposed by his people.

In this way Goa had in fact finally established its hegemony on the peninsula for which it had fought during the larger part of the previous century without complete success. The whole of the Macassar-speaking area and large parts of the Buginese region were already in one way or another dependent on Goa. Even Wajo', one of the larger Buginese states, had been compelled to acknowledge Goa as its master over a long period, until it united with Bone in the Tĕllumpochcho alliance. Only Bone had been able, until its Islamization, to resist Goa's power, although there had been many wars between these big two, in which Goa, conspicuously, was always the assailant. Indeed, the main thread running through the whole history of South Celebes was this struggle for hegemony, in which Goa took a leading role until it was defeated by the Dutch East India Company in 1668. After that time Bone took its place. As Chabot has remarked, this struggle for hegemony was a special case, on the highest level of society, of the "opposition" phenomenon which characterizes and pervades the whole society of South Celebes.[2] Here lie the origins of the never-ceasing struggles among

[2] Social relations at different levels of South Celebes society were found by Chabot to be characterized by some form of "opposition" among individuals or groups, more or less manifestly directed at the enlargement of their prestige and power. H. P. Fairchild's definition of "opposition," quoted by Chabot, runs: "resistance to or efforts to prevent or offset the efforts or ideas of another person or group, not necessarily accompanied by attitudes of anger or purpose to destroy or injure the opponent" (*Dictionary of Sociology* [New York, 1944]).

the many states of the peninsula. Here too lie, consequently, the reasons why historical writing never has attempted to cover the history
of the whole peninsula as a unity. It has always remained divided into
many different local traditions.

The data concerning the history of the sixteenth century which we
may learn from these several chronicles are numerous and rather detailed. But as far as exact chronology is concerned, there is occasionally some confusion as to sequence of events and frequently no information at all as to dates.

The chronological data contained in the chronicle of Bone, for instance, reach back no more than some thirty years before the Islamization of the state in 1611. To establish the years of the kings who reigned
during this time, we may start with the king who was deposed in this
year, just before the defeat of Bone. That this really happened in 1611
or A.H. 1020 is further corroborated by the data about the years of his
successor, Matinroe-riTallo'. The chronicle of Bone says that Martinroe-
riTallo' reigned for twenty years, and the diary of Goa and Tallo'
mentions his death in the year 1630 or A.H. 1040.

It can be seen from these latter data that the twenty years mentioned
in the chronicle were meant as Moslem, i.e., lunar, years, which in this
case differ from our era by one year. Whether, however, the years
mentioned for the times before the Islamization were also lunar years
remains to be seen. For the years of the kings of Bone it happens to
make no difference, because their reigns were rather short.

The deposed king had been reigning only for some months, for his
predecessor, the queen Matinroe-riSidenreng, had gone to the newly
Islamized Sidenreng in the year after the Islamization of Wajo', which
took place in 1610. She too adopted Islam there, but shortly afterward
fell ill and died. She had reigned for nine years, which would be from
1602 to 1611.

Her predecessor, her father Matinroe-riBĕttu, had reigned for seven
years, thus from 1595 to 1602. His predecessor, his cousin Matinroe-
ria'denena, was killed by his people because of his cruelty and tyranny,
after he had been king for eleven years. Therefore he reigned from
1584 to 1595. The years of the preceding king, Bongkangnge, are not
given. We learn only that he died two years after he had concluded
the Tĕllumpochcho alliance with Soppeng and Wajo'. Thus we at least
know that this important Buginese alliance dates from the year 1582.
The years of two of the predecessors of Bongkangnge are given, but
it is impossible to turn them into fixed dates. The only thing we know

for certain is that Bongkangnge already was king during the war between Bone and Goa which ended in 1655 according to Macassarese data.

Up to this point the identification of the calendar in use during pre-Islamic times is not vital. But because for the chronology of Goa it does make a difference whether we reckon with lunar or with solar years, this problem has to be tackled first. There are not, however, many concrete data which can shed light on the question. I know, in fact, of only one admittedly rather small indication, in the diary of Goa and Tallo', that indeed a solar calendar was used.

The first dates contained in this diary are of a somewhat different nature from all later ones. Mentioned are only the years of the Christian and of the Islamic calendar—but no days or months. The births of some princes and kings of Goa and of Tallo' are noted, with the age they eventually reached. The writer of the diary makes clear, by repeatedly using the word "presumably," that he is not quite certain about these dates. And in fact they contain some obvious errors, for the two calendars do not tally. It is said, for instance, that King Alaudin of Goa was born in the year 1586, which coincides with A.H. 994/995, and the Moslem year 996, which is A.D. 1587/1588.

All this leads us to suspect that these dates were not contemporaneous data but were calculated at a later time. It is not difficult to detect how they were calculated. The precise dates of the deaths of these princes were known—they are to be found in the diary itself—and also their ages at the time of death. Thus someone apparently subtracted the figure of their ages from the years of their deaths, in the case of both calendars. In this way one necessarily obtained contradictory results, because of the difference between solar and lunar years. Our example illustrates it: King Alaudin died in the year 1639/1049 at the age of fifty-three. If we perform the subtraction, we get as a result precisely the years mentioned for his birth. Which of the two is the right one, the Moslem or the Christian, depends upon whether his fifty-three years were lunar or solar.

Among these first dates in the diary there is one which is not contradictory and cannot be calculated in the way described. It presumably is contemporaneous and possibly contains a valuable hint for the solution of our problem. It is told that in August of 1600/1009 Karaeng Pattingalloang, a prominent Tallorese prince, was born and that he reached the age of fifty-four years. His death is recorded in the diary in the year 1654/1064. It is clear from these figures that these fifty-four years tally with the Christian era and not with the Islamic one, and consequently were solar years.

From these facts we may perhaps infer that in Goa not only were both calendars already known before the actual adoption of Islam but also that the Christian calendar, or at least one of solar years, was used by preference. It seems advisable at any rate to take the chronological data concerning the sixteenth century as though it were reckoned in solar years. The results will prove more satisfactory, moreover, if we calculate according to the Christian, rather than the Moslem, calendar.

If we therefore now proceed to discuss the chronology of the kings of Goa as we have done for those of Bone and if we start with King Alaudin, already several times mentioned, we may assume that he indeed was born in 1586. According to the chronicle of Goa he was seven years old when he became king (1593). He had reigned for twelve years when he adopted Islam (1605), and he died after having reigned for forty years in 1639. As can be seen, these dates are in accordance with the results obtained above, especially as to the year 1605 for the Islamization of Goa and Tallo'.

His predecessor was his older brother Tunipasulu', who was fifteen years old when he became king but was deposed two years later and died twenty-four years afterward in exile on the island of Buton. Thus the reign of Tunipasulu' lasted only from 1591 to 1593. During this time the second period of wars between Goa and Bone ended with the peace of Meru, which was to last until the Islamic wars.

It was Alaudin's father, Tunijallo', who led several military expeditions against Bone and Wajo' during the decade after these Buginese states and Soppeng in 1582 concluded the Tĕllumpochcho alliance, which was expressly directed against the rising power of Goa. He was, however, never successful in these wars, and on the way to his last assault he was murdered by a slave. Tunijallo' was twenty years old when he came to the throne and reigned for twenty-five years, thus from 1566 to 1591.

Tunibatta, father of Tunijallo', reigned for only forty days, since both he and his older brother Tunipalangga, who preceded him, died in the first war with Bone. The expedition which Tunipalangga led against Bone resulted in great disaster for Goa. During the fights in the country of Bone, Tunipalangga, the king of Goa, fell ill and had to leave his troops. He was brought back to Goa and died there soon afterward. His younger brother Tunibatta immediately took over the reign and went to Bone. But in the ensuing battle near the capital of

Bone he was killed and the Goarese troops were utterly defeated. Thereupon the king of Tallo', who was there in the army, took over command and made peace with Bone. Goa and Bone then concluded the pact of Chalĕppa', which fixed among other things the Tangka River as their common boundary. Tunipalangga was thirty-six years old when he became king, and he reigned for eighteen years. Thus his reign lasted from 1548 to 1566, and his birth date was 1512.

Tunipalangga's father, Tumapa'risi'-kallonna, reigned for thirty-six years, i.e., from 1512. He might be called the first historical king of Goa, for though we hear of several other kings before his time, the chronicle writer knows almost nothing about them except their names. This king Tumapa'risi'-kallonna laid the foundation for Goa's later powerful position by turning it from a little village community into one of the largest states of South Celebes. He is reported to have waged war against several places which we have known for a long time as integral parts of the state of Goa but which at that time were apparently still independent petty kingdoms, as Goa itself had once been. All the places he conquered were made vassals of Goa. Only one of them, the neighboring Tallo', was united with Goa in an alliance, and since that time it has remained a faithful and very close partner of Goa. More or less during the same period the other large states, such as Bone and Wajo', seem to have been formed in the same way. In their continuing expansion they naturally soon met as rivals and thus a struggle for hegemony set in.

One of the little places subjected by Tumapa'risi'-kallonna was Garrisi'. In this connection the chronicle makes an interesting remark. It reports that Garrisi' was conquered in the same year that the Portuguese conquered Malacca. Since this happened in the year 1511, we are confronted by some curious problems and possibilities.

In the first place, we here have a synchronic date *in optima forma* which connects the older chronology of South Celebes with the known European and Asian history. It is quite imaginable that it was remembered and recorded on purpose. If this is true, it must necessarily date from the year itself or from shortly afterward at the latest. The fall of Malacca was an important event which must have created great consternation in the Indonesian world, particularly in commercial circles. The rumor of it must have spread quickly throughout Indonesia and would soon have reached the most important ports. It is known that in the beginning of this century South Celebes, particularly Macassar, already had commercial relations with Malay and Javanese countries. The Portuguese merchant Tomé Pires, who was at Malacca and Java between the years 1512 and 1515, reports in his *Suma Oriental* about the brisk trade of South Celebes. The Macassarese chronicles also give some data about these relations. And early contacts with Java are borne out by some place names in the neighborhood of Goa which resemble Javanese names. Garrisi' itself is an example, for it is the Macassarese form of the Javanese Grĕsi' (Gresik) which was one of the important East Javanese ports of that time.

There is, however, a second consideration: if Tumapa'risi'-kallonna was the king of Goa who conquered Garrisi' in the same year as the fall of Malacca, it is impossible that he ascended the throne in 1512, as was the result of our exposition above. This year must be 1511 at the latest. But in that case the chronology of Goa must somewhere contain a mistake of one year. At least some of the dates we have established on the basis of chronicle data must be placed one year earlier. But we do not know where the error begins. We will remain on the safe side if we say that a certain number of dates of sixteenth-century Goarese chronology contain an uncertainty factor of one year. This uncertainty is perhaps best explained by the fact that the figures given in the chronicle are all whole years. The neglect of months and days may easily have resulted in a shortage of one year in a century. It is remarkable that the uncertainty is not greater than this.

If, then, this synchronic date of 1511 has helped us to correct a mistake in the chronology established, it must be pointed out that this year is at the same time the earliest date of South Celebes history which can be reached on the basis of the historical writing originating from there. So this year also marks the beginning of South Celebes chronology. Considering this fact we may surmise that it has also served the Macassarese historians themselves as their starting point for establishing the chronology of their history.

Because these historians used a calendar of solar years, it seems unlikely that they got their information on this point from the Moslem Malays. There remain the possibilities of Portuguese or Javanese influence.

As long as there are no more exact details available concerning the calendar which was used in pre-Islamic times, it will be difficult to decide this question. Some manuscripts make mention of an old Buginese calendar which would have been in use "before the Portuguese calendar was adopted," as we are told. It contained twelve solar months, called with names of Sanskrit origin; but their sequence differed from the Indian or Javanese. Some of these names perhaps show

Javanese influence, e.g., *Posia*, Jav. *Posya*, Sanskrit *Pausa*. In addition, an old Buginese week of twenty days contains some names of Javanese provenance, e.g., *Wage* and *Berukung* (Jav. *Wurukung*). But we do not know whether these calendars were ever commonly used, though occasionally they are found also in later diaries, along with the Islamic and European calendars. There are, moreover, no traces of similar calendars among the Macassars.

The Macassarese and Buginese names for the European months show clearly, in their oldest form, their Portuguese origin, e.g., *Janeru*, *Pabereru, Marasu, Abarili, Mayu, Juñu*, and *Julu*. Therefore it is certain that the European calendar was borrowed from the Portuguese. But again we do not know when.

Since the writing of history presupposes the ability to write, we may, finally, devote some attention to the question when the art of writing became known in South Celebes. The writer of the chronicle of Goa several times mentions written records precisely concerning the beginning of the sixteenth century. First he says, about some earlier kings, that he cannot report anything of their actions, their wives, or their children, because at that time there were not yet writings *(lontara')*. Secondly, he reports, about King Tumapa'risi'-kallonna, that no details about his wars were put down in the written records *(lontara')*, apart from the bare fact that he waged wars—and, we may add, the names of the places he conquered. Thirdly, we find recorded that in the time of the same king the Macassar script *(lontara')* was invented by his minister and *shahbandar* Daeng Pamette'. It remains uncertain how far tradition is to be trusted in this case, since no special investigation has been made into the history of this script. But because it belongs to the family of Indonesian scripts which ultimately stem from India, it is clear at any rate that it dates from pre-Islamic times. Besides features of its own it shows some resemblance to Sumatran scripts.

These local traditional beliefs all purport to fix the beginning of writing in general and of historical writing in particular in the time of this same king, i.e., within three decades after the year 1511. It must be left to prolonged investigations to discover whether it was indeed this time which saw the birth of South Celebes historical writing.

At this point we must leave the questions we have sought to answer. By no means have we with full clarity established the origins of this intriguing phenomenon. We could do no more than argue some of the possibilities and point out some contributing factors. Perhaps this very plurality of factors is the most useful result that has come from this effort. The historical conjunction of the adoption of an Indian script and a Portuguese calendar by a people with a keen interest in this world and its affairs may have given rise to a type of historical writing which in any case has developed independently along its own lines.

We hope we have shown at the same time that here lies an object of scientific research which is fully capable of repaying the trouble taken to unravel its problems. May it help to inspire especially Macassar and Buginese historians to follow in the steps of their forefathers and to delve into the rich manuscript collections that are to be found at Macassar, Jakarta, and Leyden—to mention only the most prominent ones—in order to bring the facts and developments of their history and their historical writing into the full light of the tropical day.

BIBLIOGRAPHY

Cense, A. A. "Enige aantekeningen over Makassaars-Boeginese geschiedschrijving." (Some Notes on Macassar-Buginese Historiography), *BKI*, CVII (1951), 42–60. Detailed characterization of the genres of South Celebes historical writing by an authority on matters of South Celebes culture.

——. "Makassaars-Boeginese prauwvaart op Noord Australië in vroeger tijd" (Macassarese and Buginese Proa Shipping to North Australia in Early Times), *BKI*, CVIII (1952), 248–264. The oldest references to Macassarese and Buginese fishers regularly sailing to the north coast of Australia together with details from Macassarese informants.

——. "De verering van Sjaich Jusuf in Zuid Celebes" (The Worship of Sheikh Yusuf in South Celebes), *Bingkisan Budi*. Leyden, 1950. pp. 50–57. Information about a seventeenth-century Macassarese mystic, his religious influence, and the homage paid to his grave in the present time.

Chabot, H. Th. *Verwantschap, stand en sexe in Zuid Celebes* (Kinship, Class, and Sex on South Celebes). Groningen and Jakarta, 1950. 277 p. Results of a sociological investigation in a Macassarese village before and after World War II; contains an extensive bibliography of South Celebes.

Kern, R. A. "Proeve van Boegineesche geschiedschrijving" (A Specimen of Buginese Historiography), *BKI*, CIV (1948), 1–32. A Buginese historical poem from the first half of the nineteenth century partly translated and compared with Dutch sources.

Le Roux, C. C. F. M., and A. A. Cense. "Boegineesche zeekaarten van den Indischen archipel" (Buginese Sea Maps of the Indian Archipelago), *Tijdschrift van het Aardrijkskundig Genootschap,* LII (1935), 687–714.

Ligtvoet, A. "Transcriptie van het dagboek der vorsten van Goa en Tallo met vertaling en aanteekeningen" (Transcription of the Diary of the Kings of Goa and Tallo' Together with a Translation and Notes), *BKI,* XXVIII (1880), 1–259. Important edition and translation of the greater part of the Macassarese royal diary; notes from Dutch sources.

Matthes, B. F. *Boeginesche chrestomathie* (Buginese Chrestomathy). 3 vols. Macassar and Amsterdam, 1864 and 1872. Text in Buginese script of the chronicle of Bone on pp. 468–498; notes in vol. III.

——. *Kort verslag aangaande alle mij in Europa bekende Makassaarsche en Boeginesche handschriften* (Short Description of All Macassarese and Buginese Manuscripts in Europe Known to Me). Amsterdam, 1875. 100 p.

——. *Makassaarsche Chrestomathie* (Macassarese Chrestomathy). 2d ed. Amsterdam, 1883. Texts in Macassarese script of the chronicles of Goa and Tallo' on pp. 146–203; notes at the back, pp. 1–30.

Niemann, G. K. *Geschiedenis van Tanete: Boeginesche tekst met aanteekeningen (History of Tanete:* Buginese Text Together with Notes). The Hague, 1883. 172 p. Text in Buginese script edited from manuscripts at Leyden.

Noorduyn, J. *Een achttiende-eeuwse kroniek van Wadjo'* (An Eighteenth-Century Chronicle of Wajo'). The Hague, 1955. 332 p. Text and translation of one of the Buginese chronicles of Wajo', together with an introduction on the Buginese language and the history of Wajo'.

——. "Een Boeginees geschriftje over Arung Singkang" (A Short Buginese Writing about Arung Singkang), *BKI,* CIX (1953), 144–152. An episode from the career of Arung Singkang.

——. "De Islamisering van Makasar" (The Islamization of Macassar), *BKI,* CXII (1956), 347–366.

IX

Some Malay Historical Sources:

A Bibliographical Note

BY J. C. BOTTOMS

Lecturer in Malay, School of Oriental and
African Studies, University of London

FOR material on the history of Indonesia one naturally turns first to Java, Sumatra, and the other islands.[1] Here in all its richness and variety Indonesian culture, throughout various stages, developed and flourished. In some places, history is there for all to see: in great monuments and sculpture and in present-day manifestations of that culture. For other places and other periods we have the major historical lit-

---

[1] It has not been possible for the present writer to consult even a majority of the works mentioned in this chapter, which should be regarded as a preliminary reconnaissance in this field. Most of the information has been compiled from the catalogues of Malay manuscripts and other similar sources referred to in the list at the end of this article. The most important of these are: H. H. Juynboll, *Catalogus van de Maleische en Sundaneesche handschriften der Leidsche Universiteits-Bibliotheek* (hereafter cited as *Juynboll Cat. Leyden MSS*); P. S. van Ronkel, "Catalogus der Maleische handschriften in het Museum van het Bataviaasch Getnootschap van Kunsten en Wetenschappen" (hereafter cited as *Van Ronkel Cat. Bat. Gen. MSS*); P. S. van Ronkel, "Catalogus der Maleische handschriften van het Koninklijk Instituut voor de Taal-, Land- en Volkenkunde van Nederlandsch-Indië" (hereafter cited as *Van Ronkel Cat. Kon. Inst. MSS*); and P. S. van Ronkel, *Supplement-Catalogus der Maleische en Minangkabausche handschriften in de Leidsche Universiteits-Bibliotheek* (hereafter cited as *Van Ronkel Suppl. Cat. Leyden MSS*). In the catalogues may be found further information about individual works which it has not been possible to include in this short survey. Much information has also been drawn from Sir Richard Winstedt's "A History of Malay Literature."

I wish here to express my most grateful acknowledgments to these sources in extenuation of the fact that in the body of the paper the source of my information has not always been recorded, since to do so would have introduced a mass of short footnotes of little interest to the general reader. Where source references are given in footnotes, only short references are normally provided, since at the end of the chapter there is a list of the main materials used, with bibliographical details.

erary sources in Old Javanese or Middle Javanese such as the *Pararaton* and *Nāgarakĕrtāgama* dealt with by Professor Berg, Dr. Zoetmulder, and Dr. de Graaf. Elsewhere in this volume, too, are presented the valuable—but secondary because foreign—source materials to be found in English, Portuguese, Dutch, Japanese, and Chinese historical records.

Malay sources—in this context, historical writings in the Malay language—fall curiously between the entirely native and the entirely foreign type of source material just referred to. Written in the language which was the direct ancestor of modern Indonesian, *Bahasa Indonesia*, these Malay sources are yet partly alien, for though some of them remain central to the Malay world as a whole, others now appear to be peripheral to the general current of historical development in Malaysia since the end of the eighteenth century, the time at which the peninsular and archipelagic sections of Malaysia drifted finally apart.[2] Drifted, perhaps, is not quite the word—were forced apart, rather, for the peninsular and Indonesian areas, each caught up in an earlier extensive Far Eastern version of the *Drang nach Osten* of the Western powers, inevitably followed the lead and consequently the divergence of their colonial patrons, the British and the Dutch.

Thus, two areas which formed an ethnic and cultural whole were artificially separated more or less by historical accident, for if the British or Dutch had never come to the East they might never have been divided; or if either of the two Western powers had held influence over both areas, these might well have grown together in strength and unity in the process of forming the inevitable opposition to colonial rule and in the pursuit of ultimate independence. Be that as it may, colonial intervention proved a more permanent and final divider than might have been thought, and the two territories have since been separate, whatever possibilities the future may hold in store.

HISTORICAL BACKGROUND

Let us then summarize, at the expense of some oversimplification, the main historical relationships which have existed between Malaya and Indonesia.[3]

[2] "Malaysia" is here used to mean the total area formed by "Malaya" (the Malay Peninsula and adjacent islands) and "Indonesia" (Java, Sumatra, the islands including Celebes, and Borneo). None of these three terms is used in any modern political sense. "Malay" means pertaining to the *Malay* people, language, literature, etc.; "Malayan" to the combined peoples and cultures of *Malaya* as a whole, i.e., including aborigines and immigrant Indians, Chinese, Europeans, and Eurasians; "Malaysian" means pertaining to the whole area, culture, etc., of *Malaysia*.

[3] For fuller accounts the reader is referred to R. Le May, *The Culture of South*

1) The first is an ethnic rather than a historical relationship—simply, that the Malaysian peoples of Malaya and Indonesia had a common origin. Few are agreed as to exactly where this was, when it was, or how the migrations took place. Southwest China as the place and between 2000 and 1000 B.C. as the date of the main migration are perhaps most generally accepted. But the common racial, territorial origin is, within broad limits, agreed, and with it the fact of a common basic cultural tradition.

2) It is clear from the work done on the prehistory of Indonesia (by van Heekeren) and of Malaya (by M. W. F. Tweedie) that the identity of racial origin was prolonged with a similarity of life, culture, and behavior in both areas during the prehistoric period that followed, and on into the earlier centuries of the Christian era.

3) We know little of the first 500 years A.D. except that Indian and other traders made contacts in Indonesia and perhaps set up small trading communities there in or adjacent to existing settlements and that this early influence came mainly from South India.

4) The first historical period of which we have reasonable knowledge is that of the Buddhist empire of Shrīwijaya, centered on Palembang in Sumatra but extending its control over a large part of Java and over the Malay Peninsula as far north as Kedah and the southern Thai states. This period from A.D. ca. 600 to A.D. ca. 1300 was the time during which Indian influence, both Buddhist and Hindu, was most widely, if relatively thinly, spread in Southeast Asia.

5) The Majapahit Empire which replaced Shrīwijaya was Hindu and centered in East Java. Its power lasted into the late fifteenth century, and it is very probable that in the fourteenth century the southern and eastern states of the Malay Peninsula accepted its suzerainty.

6) The impact of Islam, felt first in North Sumatra toward the end of the thirteenth century, spread during the next century to Malacca, to other places in the Peninsula, and to Java and other places in the archipelago. This was a further cultural factor held in common, as was to be the impact of the West some 400 years later.

7) When from about 1400 until 1511 Malacca became the center of the Malay world, various states of Sumatra, though not Java, together with some Borneo and island territories admitted the suzerainty of Malacca.

East Asia (London, 1954), chs. ii, v, and vi; to D. G. E. Hall, *A History of Southeast Asia* (London, 1955), chs. i-iv, x, xi, and xvii, and the other authorities cited there; or to Sanusi Pané, *Sedjarah Indonésia* (6th ed.; Jakarta, 1955), which is a textbook for use in Indonesian schools.

8) From the end of the sixteenth century, on a broad view, the Malay world collapses into its component parts and was not to any degree reunited until bound together, temporarily and artificially, into the two main groupings under British and Dutch rule. Acheh, Mataram, Riau, and the Bugis all had their short days in the sun, but none lasted long nor were they able to turn their short-lived power into any form of permanent dominion.

9) The colonial period, say ca. 1650 to ca. 1950, is included for the sake of completion, but this is a period of historical dissociation rather than association. Superficial contacts there were, within the superimposed colonial patterns; but there was no real and active bond between the people of one country and that of another except the feeling of a shared heritage and a common nostalgia for the golden age that was past—the *zaman bahari* so frequently referred to in Malay vernacular literature.[4]

We have thus summarily divided Indonesia's long history into separate periods, but it is important to remember Schrieke's injunction, in his *Ruler and Realm in Early Java,* that these periods must not be studied in isolation from each other, and the basic continuity of history ignored.

MALAY AND INDONESIAN LANGUAGE AND LITERATURE

It will therefore be seen that for almost the whole of their long histories the various parts of Malaysia have been animated and affected by similar trends and influences. As a result both Indonesian and Malay historical sources are useful and complementary for the general history of the Malaysian area. In addition, Malay sources have a particular value for Indonesian historians in that, in providing a provincial rather than a metropolitan view, they allow the historian to view his subject from a fruitful, because unusual, angle; just as the early morning or late evening sun, rather than the bright noonday glare, gives the best light for observing a carved inscription on stone. These sources also provide particular information about some of the outlying areas in the Indonesian geographical complex as well as evidence of the foreign policies pursued by the earlier Indonesian colonial powers of Java and Sumatra.

---

[4] It was this folk memory of a "golden age" that Sukarno so adroitly and effectively contrasted with the "dark present" and the hope of a luminous and "promising future" in the early days of his work for Indonesian independence. See Bambang Oetomo, "Some Remarks on Modern Indonesian Historiography," p. 75.

There is a further preliminary aspect to be discussed before we can usefully consider the Malay texts themselves. We have mentioned the historical relationship between Indonesia and Malaya; we should now see how that relationship was expressed in terms of language and literature. Indeed, since there is often uncertainty today about the connection between modern Malay and modern Indonesian, it will be no bad thing to deal briefly with their earlier relationship. In fact, the answer is very simple: the two languages were previously one and the same. That single language, though it contained dialectal differences, was called Malay; the Indonesian term, *Bahasa Indonesia*, has been used only since 1928.[5] Malay was not widely spoken as a first language in all the areas where Indonesian is now spoken; its main and original areas were East Sumatra, Malaya, and the Riau-Lingga Archipelago. But it was also spoken as a lingua franca throughout the Malaysian area.[6] As a member of the main Malayan or Indonesian branch of the Malayo-Polynesian, or Austronesian, family of languages it is also linguistically allied to the large number of languages which are spoken by smaller groups of people throughout the Malayo-Poly-nesian area;[7] in Malaya itself there are some dozen other dialects, only partly Malay, spoken by aboriginal groups;[8] in Sumatra there are yet some ten other languages and dialects,[9] and this is to take only the two areas which, as stated above, are regarded as the *loci classici* of the Malay language. In the midst of this variety of tongues, Malay, in either its present or an earlier form, has probably been the pre-dominant language of Malaysia (in spread, if not in total number of speakers) for at least 1,300 years.[10] In the last thirty years, however,

---

[5] A. Teeuw, *Pokok dan Tokoh* (Jakarta, 1955), p. 34.

[6] "A person who can speak Malay can be understood from Persia to the Philippines" (F. Valentijn, *Oud en Nieuw Oost Indiën* [8 vols.; Dordrecht and Amsterdam, 1724–1726], V, 310 [translated]). Cf. also: "Tesnière estimates [from statistics for the year 1925] that Malay is native to some three million people, but is spoken as a foreign language, especially in commerce, by some thirty millions" (L. Bloomfield, *Language* [London, 1958, reprint of 1935 ed.], p. 45).

[7] Bloomfield, *Language*, p. 71.

[8] W. W. Skeat and C. O. Blagden, *Pagan Races of the Malay Peninsula* (London, 1906), II, 379–413, 432–472.

[9] P. Voorhoeve, *A Critical Survey of Studies on the Languages of Sumatra* (The Hague, 1955).

[10] This is to judge from stone inscriptions alone, for these are the only written materials for these early times. Inscriptions have been found, written in Old Malay, dating from the seventh century A.D. mainly in Sumatra but in two cases also in Java. We do not know to what extent a spoken form of Malay, spread by immigrants, seafarers, and traders, may also have existed in these and other parts during and earlier period. See G. Coedès, "Les Inscriptions malaises de Çrivijaya," *BEFEO*,

Malay has been left behind by the tremendous development of Indonesian which is now a more effective instrument of expression and communication in the modern world. Thus, although *Bahasa Indonesia* was originally primarily a political concept, it has since become a valid linguistic one.[11]

A language held partly in common meant to some degree a common literature, and thus we find works in Malay, in both prose and verse, being written in places as far apart as Malacca, Acheh, Pasai, Riau, Java, Borneo, the Celebes, and the Moluccas at various times. Malay was by no means the only literary language to be found in this area. Java has a literature of its own, in Old and Middle Javanese dating back to the tenth century, and richer both in quality and in quantity than the works of Malay literature to which it has made a considerable contribution.[12] Sumatra not only gave to Malay a rich store of vernacular folk legend and culture but was itself at times the center of thought and writing in the Malay language, as well as of writings in its other vernaculars. Together with works of specifically Malayan provenance there is therefore a considerable body of literary material in Malay.

Malay literature goes back, in written form, at least to the fifteenth century. In the *Sejarah Melayu* (or Malay Annals) which will be referred to later, there is an account of how on the night before the expected Portuguese assault on Malacca in 1511 the young Malay warriors, nervous and excited at the thought of the coming clash, kept their martial spirit at fever pitch by reading one of two famous Malay epic stories, then in the possession of the Sultan, which they borrowed specially for the purpose. These two stories—the *Hikayat Muhammad Hanafiah* and the *Hikayat Amir Hamzah*—thus appear to have existed in written form before 1511 and were well known at that time.[13]

XXX (1930), 29–80, and J. G. de Casparis, *Inscripties uit de Çailendra-tijd* (Bandung, 1950) and *Prasasti Indonesia II: Selected Inscriptions from the 7th to the 9th Century A.D.* (Bandung, 1956).

[11] In the last few years, and especially since independence in Malaya (1957), Malay has made great strides and has narrowed the gap between itself and Indonesian. In the opinion of the writer, the two languages (as they are now considered) are bound to grow together again after their temporary estrangement.

[12] R. M. Ng. Poerbatjaraka and Tardjan Hadidjaya, *Kepustakaan Djawa* (Jakarta and Amsterdam, 1952). On Javanese influence on Malay literature, see Winstedt, "A History of Malay Literature" ch. iv.

[13] P. 168 of C. C. Brown's translation of the *Sejarah Melayu* (see note 39 below). These two *hikayat* (tale, story) are adaptations of Persian epics dealing with early Islamic heroes. There is nothing specifically Malay about them except the language.

There is no evidence, but a strong presumption, that written material in Malay existed for some centuries before this in Sumatra and that in its original oral form the material of old Malay literature is older still. In it, we find versions and echoes of stories and characters that have been current in the East, especially in India, since about the fourth century B.C. and almost certainly this is the very material which passed by word of mouth, through many centuries, until it was embodied in some of the written works we now have. Some of these written works have been collected and put in written form only during the last ninety years: [14] yet more material, indeed, is still only in an oral form and has not been recorded in writing.[15]

HISTORICAL WORKS IN MALAY

Of historical works in Malay, John Leyden, a brilliant Oriental scholar and friend of Raffles who unfortunately died in Batavia in 1811 at the age of thirty-six and was thus prevented from increasing the valuable contributions he had already made to early Malay scholarship, has this to say:

There are many *Malayu* compositions of a historical nature, though they are not so common as the classes that have been enumerated; such as the Hikayat Rajah bongsu, which I have not seen, but which has been described to me as a genealogical history of the Malay Rajahs. The *Hikayat Malaka,* which relates the founding of that city by a *Javanese* adventurer, the arrival of the Portuguese and the combats of the Malays with Albuquerque and the other Portuguese commanders. The Hikayat Pitrajaya Putti, or history of an ancient Raja of Malacca, the Hikayat Achi, or history of Achi or Achin in Sumatra and the Hikayat Hang Tuha, or the adventures of a Malay Chief during the reign of the last Raja of Malacca, and the account of a Malay Embassy sent to Mekka and Constantinople to request assistance against the Portuguese. Such historical narratives are extremely numerous, indeed there is reason to believe that there is one of every state or tribe; and though occasionally embellished by fiction, it is only from these that we can obtain an outline of the Malay history and of the progress of the nation.[16]

Malay historical works are not perhaps "extremely numerous" as Leyden supposed, but there are at least some fifty or more separate

[14] E.g., the folk romances such as the folk version of *Hikayat Seri Rama* collected by Sir William Maxwell before the turn of the century; and *Hikayat Malim Dewa, Hikayat Malim Deman,* and *Hikayat Awang Sulong Merah Muda* collected by R. O. Winstedt and A. J. Sturrock in the first three decades of the present century.

[15] The present writer, in 1958–1959, recorded in Trengganu a number of long stories of this genre which may not previously have been written down.

[16] J. Leyden, "On the Languages and Literature of the Indo-Chinese Nations," in *Asiatic Researches,* X (5th ed.; London, 1811), 179–180.

works, and as Leyden implies, in the absence of other written historical records the value of these histories is enhanced.

There is a generally accepted surmise that the earliest extant Malay historical work was written sometime in the fifteenth century, but as it exists only in a single nineteenth-century manuscript, it is not possible to be certain.[17] Indeed, the general situation with Malay manuscripts of any kind is that they exist mainly in nineteenth-century copies; there are a fair number dating from the eighteenth and seventeenth centuries, and a total of a dozen or so from the second half of the sixteenth century.[18] Dates of composition of the works contained in these manuscripts are a matter of surmise.

Regarding the Malay historical texts to be mentioned, I must make it clear that I am dealing with works written in Malay about Malaysia and primarily only with those that more or less specifically set out to be histories. I shall also include, in less detail, reference to four other categories of material of historical interest: autobiographical works, mainly of the nineteenth century; descriptive poems, dating from the seventeenth to the nineteenth century and containing accounts of contemporary or earlier events; codes of law; and diaries, personal letters, and memoranda. I shall also venture to suggest later that many other works of old Malay literature might yet yield valuable historical material to the painstaking and cautious inquirer.

It is difficult to know in what order to present the historical works to the reader. It is unfruitful to follow the historical order adopted on pages 157–159 above, as many Malay histories start with seemingly fantastic accounts of legendary beginnings and slowly grow more useful and accurate as they approach the writer's own period. To follow the successive periods through each of the various works would mean a great deal of useless and irritating repetition. It is equally impossible to follow the dates of composition of the histories themselves, since these are largely unknown. I have therefore compromised by grouping the works on a territorial basis, dealing first with works on the Malay Peninsula (following alphabetically the modern division into states), then with those on Indonesia and Borneo. This method is not entirely successful, as many works deal with more than one area, but it is probably the most satisfactory for our purposes.

A word needs to be said about the provenance and availability of the texts to be described.[19] Most of them are still in the great libraries

---

[17] This is the *Hikayat Raja-Raja Pasai;* see pp. 174–175 below.
[18] A. Teeuw, "The History of the Malay Language," p. 149.
[19] It is hoped that the reader who has merely a general interest in this subject will

at Leyden, Jakarta, London, Cambridge, Oxford, and Paris where they were originally lodged by the Dutch, British, and French scholar-travelers who first collected them.[20] A small proportion of these manuscripts has been published in the *Jawi* original, a few in romanized Malay *(Rumi);* fewer still—to be counted on the fingers of both hands —have been translated, usually only in extract, into English, Dutch, French, or German, nearly always in the journals of learned societies, and especially in the Journal of the Straits Branch (from 1923, the Malayan Branch) of the Royal Asiatic Society *(JRASSB* and *JRASMB* in references) to whose line of distinguished editors all workers in this field owe a great debt.[21] Of what has been published, much is now out of print and unobtainable; very often the bare texts are all that have been published without editorial annotation and introductory matter. Similarly, regarding the status, dating, authorship, and provenance of these works; their textual comparison, collation, and history; and questions of orthography, graphology, and physical characteristics—of all this something exists, scattered through the manuscripts themselves, the catalogues, and the journals just referred to. But this material is elusive and, when found, sometimes confusing, so that there is a crying need for it to be collected and associated definitively with the texts with which it deals. This process has already been undertaken for a number of texts by Dutch scholars, but the number of important texts requiring this treatment is still large.[22]

It may be that, in the past, attention has rightly centered on the importance of getting the texts published, without worrying too much

---

bear with references to Malay histories which may be available only in manuscript form in some museum or university library. I have thought it proper to include this material, together with some more detailed information about the manuscript versions in certain cases, because, although the existence of these manuscripts is not widely known, these texts are often easily and cheaply obtainable through the microfilming service now usually operated by such institutions.

[20] I am sorry not to have been able to include references to the Malay and Indonesian collections in the State Library in Berlin, though I understand from Miss L. T. Kho of the University of Singapore Library who was recently in Munich that most of the Malay manuscripts (the Schoemann Collection) are now to be found in the University Library of Tübingen.

[21] Although beginner's Dutch has enabled me to use the Dutch catalogues of Malay manuscripts, it has not enabled me to examine many of the relevant articles in the great Dutch journals, particularly the *Bijdragen tot de Taal-, Land- en Volkenkunde (van Nederlandsch-Indië)* published at The Hague, and the now-defunct *Tijdschrift voor Nederlandsch Indië* published at Groningen. Both these journals and the later *Indonesië* published at The Hague, are rich quarries for workers in this field and contain some of the texts mentioned in this chapter.

[22] E.g., the histories of the Riau-Lingga Archipelago, which are variously de-

about their critical status and description. But in our present historiographical context this paraphernalia is vital to the historian, for without it he cannot assess the true character or value of the text he is considering. In this present state of knowledge, then, it will be clear that much of what follows about the individual histories—based as it is on existing published materials—is inadequate and could usefully be supplemented by a careful examination of the individual texts.

MALAYA

Johore

To start with the histories of the South of the Peninsula, there are several Malay histories of Johore, which has received more attention from Malay historians than most of the Malay States. A Jawi text of a *Hikayat Negri Johor* has been printed in full (31 pages) and edited by Winstedt with an English outline and some notes.[23] There are several manuscripts of this text, which gives an account of Johore history from 1672, when Johore was taken by the Raja of Jambi, up to the early nineteenth century, ending with an attack on Perak by the Raja of Selangor.[24] There is also a *Sha'er Perang Johor* of some thirty pages recording seventeenth-century events in Malacca and Johore and an account of an embassy from Johore to Patani.[25] There is a recent *Hikayat Johor* by Captain Haji Mohamed Said (formerly private secretary to His Highness the late Sultan) published in Singapore by the Methodist Publishing House in 1916.[26] This is mainly about Sultan Abu Bakar, the grandfather of the present Sultan.

---

scribed (referred to on pp. 175–178) and which can only be satisfactorily sorted out by comparison of the actual manuscripts.

[23] *Hikayat Negri Johor:* Jawi text and outline in English, R. O. Winstedt, ed., *JRASMB,* vol. X, pt. 1 (1932); the text is collated from the two MSS from the Van Ronkel catalogue listed in note 24.

[24] *Hikayat negri Djohor:* MS no. CCXLI in *Juynboll Cat. Leyden MSS,* in Jawi; MSS nos. CCCLV (*Hikayat Negeri Djohor*) and CCCLVI (*Hikayat Negari Djohor*) in *Van Ronkel Cat. Bat. Gen. MSS* (it is perhaps one of these two Jawi MSS which is quoted by R. J. Wilkinson in *JRASMB,* IX, pt. 1 [1931], 28–29). There is also a microfilm of *Hikayat Negri Johor* in the University of Malaya Library.

[25] *Sja'ir Perang Djohor:* MS no. XIX in *Juynboll Cat. Leyden MSS,* in Jawi. Note that in the main body of this chapter the titles of all the historical texts mentioned are standardized in the normal peninsular Malay romanized spelling. In the footnotes, however, to facilitate reference in libraries and catalogues, the titles are recorded in the form given in the actual text or catalogue reference.

[26] *Hikayat Johor,* by Capt. Haji Mohamed Said bin Haji Suleiman (Singapore, 1930 [7th impression]).

Kedah (and Perlis)

The main work is the *Hikayat Marong Maha Wangsa* (or *Hikayat Mĕrang Mahawangsa*), better known as the Kedah Annals.[27] There is not very much history in this in spite of the beguiling English title which has been given to it.[28] Winstedt says of it:

Were it not for a colophon giving a list of Kedah rulers, a preface copied from later recensions of the "Malay Annals" and the borrowing of the Arabic title of those chronicles, the Hikayat Merong (or Marong) Mahawangsa would never have been styled the "Kedah Annals" or accepted as serious history.[29]

And again:

Critical scholarship has exposed it as a farrago of folk-tales, where the Prophet Solomon is called the master of Vishnu's Garuda and stories from the *Ramayana*, the *Katha Sarit Sagara* and the *Jataka* collection appear as authentic history. The discovery of the names of kings of Sri Vijaya and Kadaha has exploded its early genealogies, and even its siting of Langkasuka is disputed, though the frequent changing of the capitals of Perak and Johore should make critics cautious. The work is full of omissions, gross anachronisms and errors.[30]

Also to be found in this work is the popular Kedah legend about Raja Bersiong, which is connected with a number of existing place names in the Baling District of Kedah, as well as an account of the founding of the adjacent state of Perak. Parts of this work have been translated into English, with notes by Lieutenant Colonel James Low, though in these notes of 1849 the historical content of the text is taken much more seriously than Winstedt considers justified today.[31]

The *Sejarah Negri Kedah* is a mainly fabulous history very similar to the *Hikayat Marong Maha Wangsa* just mentioned and is probably another version of it.[32] The work is variously described in the manuscript as *Sejarah negri Kedah Zamin Turan* and *Salalat as-Salatin* and

[27] *Hikayat Marong Maha Wangsa* ("*The Kedah Annals*"): romanized text, A. J. Sturrock, ed., *JRASSB*, vol. LXXII (1916).

[28] Neither this work nor the *Sejarah Melayu*—sometimes known as "The Malay Annals"—is an annal in the strict sense of the word, i.e., a yearly chronicle of events. See Brown in the introduction to his translation of the latter (see note 39), p. 7, where he refers to "annals" as "a popular mistranslation" of the word *sejarah*.

[29] Winstedt, "A History of Malay Literature," p. 110.

[30] R. O. Winstedt, "Malay Chronicles from Sumatra and Malaya," p. 26.

[31] *The Kedah Annals*: extracts translated into English with extensive notes by Lt. Col. James Low, in J. R. Logan, ed., *Journal of the Indian Archipelago*, vol. III (Singapore, 1849; separately reprinted, Bangkok, 1908).

[32] *Sedjarah Negeri Kedah*: MS no. CCCLXXIX in *Van Ronkel Cat. Bat. Gen. MSS*, a Jawi text of 256 pp.

according to the doxology was written in the reign of Sultan Muazzam Shah ibni Sultan Shah. In the collection of Malay manuscripts which Sir William Maxwell gave to the Royal Asiatic Society in London there is also a work entitled *Silsilat al Salatin* which contains a genealogical history of the kings of Kedah.[33] In the British Museum there is an 84-page work entitled *Sultan Maulana* which is a verse romance telling the history of Sultan Maulana Ahmad Tadjuddin of Kedah and the Siamese attacks on Kedah and Patani.[34] Finally, on Kedah, there is a microfilm in the University of Malaya Library entitled *Peringatan Raja-Raja Kedah,* as well as two modern published works—*Al-Tarikh Silsilah Negri Kedah* by Mohamed Hasan (Penang, 1928) and *Salasilah atau Tawarikh Kerajaan Kedah* by Wan Yahya (Penang, 1913).

Kelantan

There is a reference to a *Salasilah Negri Kelantan,* but there are no details of it available. There is a book entitled *Rengkasan Cherita Kelantan* by Haji Nik Mahmud; [35] and a fragment of the History of Trengganu and Kelantan by Haji Abdullah, a court historian in Trengganu, has been published in romanized Malay, with an English translation and notes by H. Marriott.[36] This describes the struggle between Kelantan and Trengganu in the late eighteenth and the early nineteenth century. The *Hikayat Patani* used by Newbold in his book and in his possession early in the last century may still be in existence.[37] Newbold said it contained an account of the founding of Patani and quotes from it the names of early members of the Kelantan royal dynasty; and it may contain other material useful for Kelantan history.

---

[33] *Silsilat al Salatin:* in the Maxwell Collection of the Royal Asiatic Society, London. This MS is numbered 16 in C. O. Blagden, "List of the Malay Books Bequeathed to the Society by the late Sir W. E. Maxwell K.C.M.G." (hereafter cited as *Blagden*). In respect of manuscripts in the Library of the Royal Asiatic Society in London I have used for convenience the numbers under which they are listed in *Blagden.* However, each manuscript also has its own number in the collection to which it belongs, e.g., Raffles 18, Maxwell 118, Farquhar 4.

[34] *Sultan Maulana:* MS no. 19 in G. K. Niemann's note on the British Museum MSS ("De Maleische handschriften in het Britsch Museum").

[35] *Rengkasan Cherita Kelantan,* by Haji Nik Mahmud bin Ismail (Kota Bharu, 1934).

[36] *Fragment of the History of Trengganu and Kelantan* (no Malay title given), by Haji Abdullah: romanized Malay text and English translation by H. Marriott, *JRASSB,* vol. LXXII (1916).

[37] *Hikayat Patani:* Jawi MS formerly in the possession of T. J. Newbold and mentioned in his *British Settlements in the Straits of Malacca* (London, 1839), II, 68–69.

Malacca

In considering the Malay kingdom of Malacca, we come to the one Malay history which is both wholly available in English and has also been translated, in part or entirely, into other European languages. This is the *Sejarah Melayu*, which is also considered to be the finest work in peninsular Malay literature. As in this survey we are mainly interested in such works as a tool for the historian and are therefore closely concerned with the editing and translating of historical texts, there is one important point which can profitably be made in considering this work and in trying to determine the kind of editorial work which needs to be done on other works of the same kind to make them more widely available to historians.

The *Sejarah Melayu* was first translated into English by John Leyden;[38] more recently it has been translated by C. C. Brown.[39] The latter version, though it raises the general question as to the most suitable English style in which a "period" work may be projected to the modern reader, is all that one asks of a good translation: it is accurate and complete, reads well, and maintains something of the style and atmosphere of the original. There is an important lesson here for anyone contemplating the translation of a historical text. The translator has confined himself, as a language man, to providing a translation —with detailed and excellent notes on certain textual and linguistic difficulties. He has not attempted to edit the text historically as well but has provided the English material on which the historian can now work: he is in the position of a technical witness in a court case who has given his impartial and expert testimony and now leaves it to the judge or jury to make of it what they will. In any plan for dealing with these Malay histories and making them available to a greater number of people, there are, ideally, two separate stages of work: first, to translate them into English with adequate textual and linguistic notes; secondly, to edit, annotate, and evaluate the resulting English translation from the historical point of view. A third alternative—perhaps the best of all—is the editing and evaluation of these Malay histories *in Malay or Indonesian.* This last is really the best answer, for it would cater to a new generation of historians who will not normally work in a European language, and it would help to throw off that Europocentric

---

[38] *Sejarah Melayu* ("The Malay Annals"): English translation by J. Leyden, *The Malay Annals* (London, 1821).

[39] *Sejarah Melayu* or "*Malay Annals*": English translation and notes by C. C. Brown, *JRASMB*, vol. XXV, pts. 2 and 3 (1952).

approach of which Professor D. G. E. Hall justly complains in the introduction to his *A History of South-east Asia.*

When the historian is not working in his own language, it appears almost inevitable that the work of processing and evaluating vernacular texts of this kind should be the task of more than one type of worker in the field of Southeast Asian historiography. For the texts are relatively so few that corroboration is always difficult and sometimes impossible; the mixture of myth and reality is so pervasive; and the presentation and very nature of the material are so optative, as Berg has called it [40]—so much what the writer would have *liked* it to be rather than what it was—that the historian using such texts needs a preternatural awareness of possible twists and distortions, a masterly grasp of every apparently insignificant detail of his period and area, and an unusually alert and suspicious surveillance of his sources. To command all these qualities and a thorough knowledge of several source languages as well is the privilege of a number of distinguished workers in this field, but in general the most fruitful method of tackling this problem may well be to base it on close cooperation between the linguist and the historian, so that whereas only the historian can evaluate such sources—the second of the two stages mentioned above—the first, i.e., translation, should ideally be undertaken by linguist and historian together.

Of the *Sejarah Melayu* and Malay histories in general, Wilkinson has the following pertinent remarks to make:

We can easily criticize the various Malay histories and prove that their chronology is unreliable and that many of their legends are only echoes from Indian and Persian literature, but we need not, on that account, discard Malay chronicles as altogether worthless. The *Sejarah Melayu* has the merits and failings of all anecdotal history; it may often sacrifice truth to the point of a story or the interests of a pedigree, it adorns many anecdotes with unreliable details as to private interviews and secret conversations that could never have transpired, but it must be true to the ideas and to the spirit of its age. It gives us a very life-like picture of the times. It tells us tales of the tyranny and profligacy of the old Malay Kings, of the corruption of the Court, of the bribery of the officials, of murders and judicial trials, of feuds, vendettas, intrigues and elopements, and of the attitude of the people to all these episodes.[41] We may not be specially interested in the fate of "Tun Mi

[40] C. C. Berg, "Javanese Historiography—A Synopsis of Its Evolution," p. 16.

[41] This catalogue of undiluted violence and nastiness is quite out of character with Wilkinson's normally sympathetic and fairminded approach to his subject; and it omits account of the qualities of humor, courage, nobility, and commonsense kindliness also described in the *Sejarah Melayu.*

the Hairy Caterpillar" and other gentlemen of that sort,[42] but we are deeply concerned in the settings of the tales—the details that come out incidentally about etiquette, about houses and clothing, about industries, about judicial procedure, and about the Government of the country. Such matters are of very real importance to the scientific historian who cares more about the condition of the people than about the biographies of individual Kings.[43]

As Sir Richard Winstedt has said:

The author of the "Malay Annals" is not only a mediaeval scholar but also proves the value of some historians being literary artists. His artistry has left us a vivid picture of a port thronged with Indian traders, Hindu and Muslim as well as settlers from China, Java and Sumatra. There are life-like vignettes of Tamil archers, Pathan horsemen, bibulous mahouts and Indian missionaries self-important but cowardly in battle. There are wonderful portraits of the old chief who put gold dust along skirting and panelling for his grandchildren to play with, of a Prime Minister too diplomatic to go abroad in a litter given him by his Sultan, of another who had a long pier glass and consulted his wife on the set of his hat.[44]

In his recent work entitled *Indigenous Political Systems of Western Malaya* (p. 7), J. M. Gullick, in speaking of the *Sejarah Melayu,* says: "But its main significance in the context of social analysis is that Malay literature and history served to transmit the traditions and values of the community, more especially of its ruling class."

The text of the *Sejarah Melayu* has been published several times in both Jawi and romanized Malay, in some cases with short extracts translated into English. The *Sejarah Melayu* edited by T. D. Situmorang and Professor A. Teeuw, has an excellent introduction and notes in Indonesian.[45] Among several other editions of this classic there is the romanization in *JRASMB*,[46] which is the text translated by C. C. Brown; and it has also been translated, mainly in extracts, into French (by Devic [47] and Marre [48]) and German (by Overbeck [49]). There are many manuscripts of this work in various collections.

[42] Tun Mi Ulat Bulu is a nickname for one of the nobles at the court of Sultan Mahmud Shah.

[43] R. J. Wilkinson, *Papers on Malay Subjects; Literature: History,* pp. 33–34.

[44] Winstedt, "Malay Chronicles from Sumatra and Malaya," pp. 25–26.

[45] *Sedjarah Melaju:* Indonesian romanized edition, with introduction and notes by T. D. Situmorang and A. Teeuw (Jakarta, 1952).

[46] *Sejarah Melayu:* romanized text, R. O. Winstedt, ed., *JRASMB,* vol. XVI, pt. 3 (1938).

[47] *Sedjarat Malayou:* French translation with notes by L. M. Devic in his *Légendes et traditions historiques de l'Archipel Indien* (Paris, 1878).

Apart from the *Sejarah Melayu*, which is the main source for the Malay kingdom of Malacca as well as an important one for the history of the Malay Peninsula and the Malay world as a whole, there is little historical material in Malay on Malacca. In a work entitled *Asal Raja-Raja Melayu* in London there is a general genealogical chronology of the Malay kings with sketches of the history of Naning in Malacca and Muar in Johore.[50] There is also a list of Malacca governors and resident councilors from about 1717 to 1855 and "a good deal about the relations of the Malays with the Dutch Government of Malacca." [51] In an untitled manuscript of the Royal Asiatic Society in London which also contains an account of the attack on Indrapura (Pahang) by *todak* fish —a sort of swordfish or gar pike also mentioned in the *Sejarah Melayu* —there is an account of the first arrival of the Portuguese in Malacca.[52] An English translation of this latter portion was made by Raffles and published.

Negri Sembilan

On the Negri Sembilan all that has been found while preparing this chapter is *Aturan Sungai Ujong*, edited by R. N. Bland, which appeared in 1895,[53] and a recorded legend from Johol (no Malay title) in *Papers on Malay Subjects, Second Series; Johol* (1941), pp. 72–74. But neither of these is a history. See also the *Asal Raja-Raja Melayu* mentioned above. Probably the reason for this paucity of material is that Negri Sembilan has been largely colonized by Minangkabau and other peoples from Sumatra who have retained their own histories and legends.

[48] *Malaka: Histoire des rois malays:* French translation of short extracts from the *Sejarah Melayu* by A. Marre, with some useful footnotes (Paris, 1874).

[49] *Sejarah Malayu* (Die Chronik der Malaien): German translation, abridged and adapted, by H. Overbeck in his *Malaische Weisheit und Geschichte*, with introductory and explanatory matter (Jena, 1927).

[50] *Asal Raja-Raja Malayu:* in the Maxwell Collection of the Royal Asiatic Society, London; noted and numbered 8 in *Blagden*.

[51] *Blagden* says this manuscript is dated A.H. 1242 = 1826, but in view of the list of governors and resident councilors up to 1855, this date can apply only to part of the manuscript.

[52] MS Raffles 32, Royal Asiatic Society, London, in Jawi; see H. N. van der Tuuk, "Short Account of the Malay Manuscripts Belonging to the Royal Asiatic Society" (hereafter cited as *Van der Tuuk*). The English translation by Raffles appeared in *JRASSB*, vol. IV (1879).

[53] *Aturan Sungai Ujong:* romanized text edited by R. N. Bland, *JRASSB*, XXVIII (1895), 53–72.

Pahang

On Pahang there is a *Hikayat Pahang* which was widely used and translated by the late Dr. W. L. Linehan in his "History of Pahang." [54] An untitled manuscript which is in the possession of Sir Richard Winstedt and which has been described by him was probably written in Pahang and contains information about Pahang royal regalia, ceremonies, and customs, in addition to references to 'Abdu'l Jalil, Sultan of Johore (1699–1719), 'Abdu'l Jamal Temenggong (ca. 1750), and the founding of Singapore by Raffles.[55]

Patani

See under Kelantan above.

Perak

The *Misa Melayu* is an interesting account written by a Raja Chulan of events in Perak in the late eighteenth century especially during the reign of Sultan Iskandar (1750–1764).[56] It contains information about the relations of Perak with the Dutch and about the Bugis in Selangor and also a long poem about a trip round the Perak coast made by Sultan Iskandar.

Casual details throw light on Perak's trade and politics. The writer mentions the sale of two cannons by the master of an English ketch in return for tin-ore, and talks also of royal trading with India in elephants. There are references to a lodge maintained by the Dutch on the estuary of the Perak river to enforce their monopoly of the purchase of tin and to the signing of a treaty with a Dutch commissioner. . . . Throwing much light on life in a Malay state two centuries ago, the *Misa Melayu* eschews folklore and is one of the more realistic of Malay chronicles.[57]

This work was edited by Sir Richard Winstedt and published in Singapore in 1919 but is now difficult to obtain. The poem, however, has been recently published under the title *Sha'er Pelayaran Sultan Iskandar Perak*.[58] An English summary and notes had been written earlier

[54] *Hikayat Pahang*: English extracts *passim* in W. Linehan, "History of Pahang," *JRASMB*, vol. XIV, pt. 2 (1936); unpublished romanized version with Dr. C. Gibson-Hill, editor of *JRASMB*, at Raffles Museum, Singapore; Jawi microfilm in the University of Malaya Library.

[55] MS belonging to Sir Richard Winstedt; notes and an English summary by Winstedt, *JRASMB*, XI, pt. 2 (1933), 161–165.

[56] *Misa Melayu*, by Raja Chulan bin Raja Hamid: text edited by R. O. Winstedt (Malay Literature Series, 15, Singapore, 1919).

[57] Winstedt, "Malay Chronicles from Sumatra and Malaya," p. 26.

[58] *Sha'er Pelayaran Sultan Iskandar Perak*: A. Talib bin Haji Ahmad, ed., romanized Malay (Kuala Lumpur, 1959).

by Sir William Maxwell,[59] who also quotes several long translated extracts in his article "The Dutch in Perak." [60]

There is a useful group of half a dozen or so further works on Perak, in most of which there is probably a good deal of duplicated material. Several of these manuscripts were collected by W. E. Maxwell during his service in Perak toward the end of the last century and were later presented by him to the Royal Asiatic Society in London, where they now are. The *Hikayat Salasilah Perak* starts, like many other Malay histories, from Alexander the Great and goes up to Sultan Ala'eddin Mansur Shah Iskandar Muda.[61] A further history of Perak from the death of the last Sultan of Malacca down to A.D. 1777 and retailing the relations between Perak and the Dutch Government of Batavia is also at London,[62] together with a number of others [63] and a supplement commissioned by Maxwell during his service in Perak and probably written by one Raja Haji Yahya of Blanja, Perak, which completes the royal genealogy down to 1882.[64] This last has been translated into English by Maxwell.[65] The *Hikayat Shamsu'l-Bahrain*, though not a history, was widely considered in Perak to be an account of the ancient kingdom of Bruas in Perak, and local place names were identified in it.[66] There are no other written sources for the old kingdom of Bruas so this *hikayat* might prove useful, though otherwise it has the appear-

---

[59] *Misa Melayu:* English summary and notes by W. E. Maxwell, *JRASSB*, II (1878), 187–193.

[60] *Misa Melayu:* English extracts in W. E. Maxwell, "The Dutch in Perak," *JRASSB*, IX (1882), 258–266.

[61] *Hikayat Salasilah Perak:* MS no. XX in *Van Ronkel Cat. Kon. Inst. MSS* (from W. E. Maxwell—probably a copy of one of the MSS mentioned below), in Jawi; this is referred to by Maxwell in his article "The History of Perak from Native Sources," *JRASSB*, vol. I (1878).

[62] *A History of Perak* (no Malay title): in the Maxwell Collection at the Royal Asiatic Society, London; noted and numbered 25 in *Blagden*.

[63] Four MSS in the Maxwell Collection, Royal Asiatic Society, London, as described and numbered in *Blagden*: (a) *A Genealogical History of the Kings of Perak*, no. 24 (3); "A full and accurate genealogy of the Perak Royal family"— Winstedt. (b) *A Genealogical Account and Lists of the Kings of Perak*, no. 44 (2); "An inaccurate list of Perak rulers and chiefs"—Winstedt. (c) No. 44 (3) of 12 p., another paper on the same subject. (d) No. 105, which contains a history of the Perak rajas as well as a shortened version of the *Sejarah Melayu* and was partly translated into English (perhaps by Maxwell) in *JRASSB*, vol. IX (1882).

[64] *Silsilah Raja-raja yang di dalam Negri Perak*, ? by Raja Haji Yahja: in the Maxwell Collection, Royal Asiatic Society, London; noted and numbered 103 in *Blagden*.

[65] *Silsilah Raja-raja yang di dalam Negri Perak*, ? by Raja Haji Yahja: translated into English by W. E. Maxwell, *JRASSB*, vol. XIV (1884).

[66] *Hikayat Shamsu'l-Bahrain:* MS no. 61 in *Van der Tuuk*, in Jawi.

ance of a typical Hindu-style story full of magic and mythology.[67]

Perlis

See Kedah above.

Selangor

Although some information on Selangor is contained in a number of texts mainly dealing with other areas,[68] there is not much else to be found. *Kenang-Kenangan Selangor,* published in 1937 by Abdul Samad bin Ahmad, is based on the reminiscences of an old Selangor chief of the days before British intervention.

Trengganu

In addition to the work already referred to under Kelantan, there is a long anonymous Jawi poem published at Kuala Trengganu that gives the history of Sultan Zainal Abidin III and is entitled *Sha'er Tawarikh Zainal Abidin yang Ketiga.*[69] A modern history of the state, *Mengkaji Sejarah Trengganu,* was published in Jawi in 1954 by Haji Mohamed Salleh.[70] There are numerous references to Trengganu events and personalities in some of the later Riau histories, when these two areas were closely related.

INDONESIA AND BORNEO [71]

The oldest known Malay history—probably composed in the fifteenth century—is the *Hikayat Raja-Raja Pasai,* of which there is Dulaurier's

[67] Maxwell, "The History of Perak from Native Sources," pp. 86–88.

[68] See the texts cited in notes 23, 56, 74, and 110.

[69] *Sha'er Tawarikh Zainal Abidin yang Ketiga,* by "T. D. K. dalam Kota Maziah": in Jawi, 2 vols. (Singapore). Where, as in this case, the date or place of publication or type of text (i.e., Jawi or romanized) is not stated, it is not known to the writer.

[70] *Mengkaji Sejarah Trengganu,* by Haji Mohamed Salleh: in Jawi, 2 vols., illustrated (Singapore, 1954).

[71] Both the editors and the author of this chapter had hoped to include references to, and an assessment of, the historical works in Malay dealing with Indonesia and Borneo. To have done so in any detail, however, would have added half as much again to this chapter. Lack of time and space alike have prevented this, but short notes are included on a few of the known texts. The main justification for omitting the rest is that since many of them have already been used by Dutch and Indonesian historians, it was thought more fruitful at this stage to bring to notice works of mainly peninsular provenance which might not be so well known in an Indonesian context. Of course, some of the latter may be familiar to Indonesians as *Indonesian* rather than *Malay* works, happily shared as they are by both peoples. *A fortiori,* and again with great regret, it has not been possible to refer to a number of modern historical and quasi-historical works written in Indonesian.

Jawi text and an unsatisfactory romanized version in *JRASSB*, now out of print.[72] In French there is a translation by Aristide Marre, with useful footnotes and appendices.[73] Marre also prints, at the end of his version, a translation of the chapter on Pasai in the *Sejarah Melayu*. The latter is derived from the *Hikayat Raja-Raja Pasai*, and it is useful to be able to compare two accounts of the same events. The main use of the Pasai history to the historian of Malaysia is its account of how Islam first came to Sumatra, together with some rather vague geographical detail on the interior of Sumatra. The dominating influence of Indian traders at this time (i.e., between about 1290 and 1350) is indicated by several incidents, including one describing the mining of Sumatran gold under Indian direction. There is emphasis throughout on the marvelous and legendary, which is obviously important to the author and his readers or listeners. This is a characteristic which continually recurs in later Malay histories. Although we may reject this aspect of the work, some of the details—quite unimportant to the author and therefore not likely to have been exaggerated or distorted —may well provide useful evidence to historians. The late Dr. A. H. Hill of the University of Sydney, who published the translation of the *Hikayat Abdullah* referred to on page 184 below, completed a new romanization and translation of this work which was published in *JRASMB*, vol. XXXIII, pt. 2 (1960).

There is a useful but complex group of works dealing with the Riau-Lingga Archipelago, Johore, and the Bugis. First must come the *Tuhfat al-Nafis* (or "Precious Gift") by Raja Ali bin Raja Ahmad of Riau. The full Jawi text is published in *JRASMB* with an English summary by Winstedt.[74] This Raja Ali was the grandson of the famous warrior Raja Haji Ali and thus was himself in the direct line of Bugis and Riau history; moreover, as a noble and an educated person of his time, familiar with court life and traditions, he was in an excellent position to collect his materials. His book was begun in 1865, and although he recapitulates the early history of Singapore, Malacca, and Johore from the usual legendary material, it is mainly valuable for Riau and South Malaya history from the end of the seventeenth century until just short of the date of composition; and it has the additional interest of provid-

---

[72] *Hikayat Raja-Raja Pasai:* Jawi text of 159 pp. in E. Dulaurier, *Collection des principales chroniques malayes*, vol. I (Paris, 1849); romanized text, J. P. Mead, ed., *JRASSB*, vol. LXVI (1914).

[73] *Histoire des rois de Pasey:* French translation with notes and appendixes by A. Marre (Paris, 1874).

[74] *Tuhfat al-Nafis*, by Raja Ali Haji bin Raja Ahmad of Riau: Jawi text, R. O. Winstedt, ed., *JRASMB*, vol. X, pt. 2 (1932).

ing a Malay account of events of which Dutch and English records also exist. There is information about Selangor, the Dutch, English, and Bugis, and a number of genealogical trees. The author exhibits a sense of value in relation to his sources and by no means accepts them uncritically. This work is also a work of value from a literary point of view, as Raja Ali Haji is one of the most important figures in later Malay literature. In 1958 a gazetteer of the many geographical names in the *Tuhfat al-Nafis*, with notes on each, was compiled as an academic exercise by an Honors student at the University of Malaya;[75] and in 1959 a similar academic exercise was written on the Arabic influence in the language of this Malay work.[76]

The same author, Raja Ali Haji, wrote a *Silsilah Melayu dan Bugis* of which the full Jawi text was recently printed by the Government Printer, at Johore Bahru, by royal command,[77] and of which English excerpts had previously been published by H. Overbeck.[78] Written in 1866, partly in prose and partly in verse, this is an account of Bugis ascendancy in Borneo, the Riau Archipelago, and the Malay Peninsula down to 1737.

The foregoing are the two main works on this area, but the histories of Riau and the Bugis form a complicated group which it is difficult to sort out. There are at least a dozen works in this group. Of some of these, there are a number of manuscripts, some no doubt identical and others varying in differing degrees, so that it is impossible to say which contains the same work and which contain different works, without all being carefully collated and compared. The several separate works and the comparatively numerous manuscripts still extant indicate the importance of the Johore-Riau Lingga area in the latter part of the eighteenth century and the nineteenth century, and this may in turn have encouraged historical writing dealing with that area. Certainly during the latter century this kind of writing appears to have been popular and relatively widespread.

These Riau histories go under a variety of names, and sometimes the

[75] Mohamad bin Anas, "Geographical Notes to the Tuhfat al-Nafis" (unpublished academic exercise in typescript, Department of Malay Studies, University of Malaya, 1958).

[76] Ismail bin Abdul Rahman, "The Arabic Influence in Tuhfat al-Nafis" (unpublished academic exercise in typescript, Department of Malay Studies, University of Malaya, 1959).

[77] *Silsilah Melayu dan Bugis*, by Raja Ali Haji bin Raja Ahmad of Riau: Jawi text (Johore Bahru, 1957).

[78] *Silsilah Melayu dan Bugis*, by Raja Ali bin Raja Ahmad of Riau: English excerpts by H. Overbeck, *JRASMB*, vol. IV (1926).

same manuscript bears more than one of these names as a title or description. Such titles are *Sejarah Raja-Raja Riau*,[79] *Hikayat Riau*,[80] *Salsilah Keturunan Raja Bugis*,[81] *Aturan Setia Bugis dengan Melayu*,[82] and *Sejarah Raja-Raja Melayu*.[83]

The *Hikayat Upu Daeng Menambon* tells the story of the prince of that name who was the first Buginese raja of Mampawah in Borneo and founded the family of the Raja Mudas of Riau in the first half of the eighteenth century.[84] For later Riau history an untitled manuscript in the Leyden collection may be useful.[85] Of the twelve chapters in this work, five contain the history of Riau from the time of the Bugis troubles in 1819 to the return of Sultan Abd-ur-rahman from Trengganu in 1823. Two other untitled Leyden manuscripts are worth mentioning as they contain information about the history and customs of the Malay and Riau rajas and both were written at Riau in the early part of the nineteenth century.[86] Before leaving the Riau-Lingga Archipelago

[79] *Sejarah Raja-Raja Riau:* (a) English outline by R. O. Winstedt, *JRASMB*, vol. XI, pt. 2 (1933), of a Jawi MS belonging to the former Batavian Society in Jakarta (MS no. CCCLVIII in *Van Ronkel Cat. Bat. Gen. MSS*); see also (d) below. This work also contains information on Pahang and Trengganu. (b) This similar and perhaps identical Jawi MS romanized as *Sadjarah Radja-Radja Riau* contains a history of Riau down to A.D. 1752 and of the alliance between the Malays and Bugis (MS no. 107 in *Van Ronkel Suppl. Cat. Leyden MSS*). (c) A third similar but later Jawi MS with the same title (romanized as *Sjadjarah Radja-Radja Riouw*) is MS no. XIX in *Van Ronkel Cat. Kon. Inst. MSS.* (d) There are five other Jawi MSS with this same title (romanized *Sjadjarah Radja Radja Riouw*) in *Van Ronkel Cat. Bat. Gen. MSS* (MSS nos. CCCLVIII-CCCLXII); see (a) above and also the text cited in note 81 below.

[80] *Hikayat Riau*, by Raja Muda Ali bin al-Marhom Raja Ja'afar: MS no. 106 in *Van Ronkel Suppl. Cat. Leyden MSS;* Van Ronkel says this Jawi text, unlike the *Sejarah Raja-Raja Riau* and the *Aturan Setia Bugis dengan Melayu* (see note 79 above and note 82 below), is more a chronological account of events of mainly local interest in Riau, Lingga, Selangor, and Malacca from about A.D. 1672 to 1845.

[81] *Salsilah Keturunan Raja Bugis:* this is how MS no. CCCLXII in *Van Ronkel Cat. Bat. Gen. MSS* describes itself in the exordium and should perhaps be regarded as its title, *faute de mieux* (see also note 79 [d] above); in Jawi.

[82] *Aturan Satiya Bugis dengan Malayu:* MS no. CCXXXVII in *Juynboll Cat. Leyden MSS*, described there as recounting Malay history from 1718 to 1784; Jawi MS dated 1824. A Jawi extract has been published in A. Meursinge's *Maleisch Leesboek* (Leyden, 1842–1868), III, 72.

[83] *Sjadjarah Radja-Radja Melajoe:* Jawi MS no. CCCLIV in *Van Ronkel Cat. Bat. Gen. MSS;* this mainly follows the *Sejarah Melayu* but also contains some later history of Johore, Riau, Lingga, and Siak.

[84] *Hikayat Upu Daeng Menambon:* MS no. CCLIII in *Juynboll Cat. Leyden MSS*, in Jawi.

[85] MS no. CCCLIX in *Juynboll Cat. Leyden MSS*, in Jawi.

[86] MSS nos. CCLXIII and CCLXIV in *Juynboll Cat. Leyden MSS*, both in Jawi, but the former also has a romanized transcription.

there is one further work to be mentioned, which belongs to a category of works to be discussed later. This is a narrative poem called *Sha'er Sultan Mahmud di-Lingga*.[87] It is a rhymed account, over a hundred pages long, of Sultan Mahmud Muzaffar Shah ibni Marhum Lingga and his family and his journey to Mecca.

One of the most notable works of Malay literature is the *Bustan a's Salatin* begun at Acheh in 1638 by Shaikh Nuru'ddin al-Raniri, a scholar from the Gujerat.[88] Although primarily a work on general Islamic history and ethics, in the second of its seven books there is a chapter on Acheh containing, as Winstedt says, "a precise chronicle of its rulers and immigrant missionaries"; and another chapter of this book contains some information, mainly derived from the *Sejarah Melayu*, on Malacca and Pahang.

Several other works on Acheh use the historical portion of Shaikh Nuru'ddin's work as a source, while at least another, which has been given the title *Geschiedenis van den Atjehoorlog*,[89] is a translation into Batavian Malay of a much later Achehnese work fully described by Snouck Hurgronje.[90] There is also a *Sha'er Perang Acheh*[91] which has been described by Hurgronje as "a nonsensical Malay poem."[92] The latest work in this field is *De Hikajat Atjéh* by Dr. Teuku Iskandar (1958) which contains a romanized version of the text of *Hikayat Acheh* (120 pages) with notes and introduction in Dutch.[93]

There are also Malay historical texts dealing with Bangka, Barus, Bencoolen, Brunei, Jambi, various parts of Java, Lampong, Macassar,

---

[87] *Sjair Soeltan Mahmoed di Lingga:* MS no. CDLXXI in *Van Ronkel Cat. Bat. Gen. MSS,* in Jawi; another copy is MS no. 193 in *Van Ronkel Suppl. Cat. Leyden MSS* under the title *Sjair Soeltan Mahmoed.*

[88] *Bustan a's-Salatin,* by Shaikh Nuru'ddin al-Raniri: R. J. Wilkinson, ed., 2 vols. (Singapore, 1899–1900); there is a microfilm of the Jawi text in the University of Malaya Library, and a Jawi extract in G. K. Niemann, *Bloemlezing uit Maleische geschriften* (The Hague, 1907), vol. II.

[89] *Geschiedenis van den Atjehoorlog* (no Malay title): MS no. 115 in *Van Ronkel Suppl. Cat. Leyden MSS,* romanized.

[90] C. Snouck Hurgronje, *The Achehnese* (2 vols.; London, 1906), II, 106. Historical works dealing with Acheh *in Achehnese* are fully dealt with on pp. 80–121 of the work cited. For other *Malay* works dealing with Acheh see H. Djajadiningrat, "Critisch overzicht van de in Maleische werken vervatte gegevens over de geschiedenis van het Soeltanaat van Atjeh," *BKI,* LXV (1911), 135–265.

[91] *Sha'er Perang Acheh:* lithographed (Singapore, 1912).

[92] Hurgronje, *The Achehnese,* II, 102. Hurgronje, whose comment was first published in 1893–1894, perhaps saw an earlier version of the 1912 lithograph of this work, which is the only edition that has come to notice.

[93] *De Hikajat Atjéh:* romanized and edited text by Teuku Iskandar, *VKI,* vol. XXVI (1958).

Montrado, the Moluccas, Palembang, Pasemah, Sambas, Siak, Ternate, and a number of other places. It is necessary to do little more than mention the main Bornean chronicles, the *Salasilah Kutai* [94] and *Hikayat Raja-Raja Banjar dan Kotaringin*,[95] as these have been extensively examined and edited by C. A. Mees and A. A. Cense respectively, with an additional commentary by W. Kern on the former. Of the *Salasilah Kutai*, however, Dr. C. Hooykaas has said in his *Perintis Sastra:*

> This genealogy records few genuine events, and its contents are far less important than those of the *Sejarah Melayu*. Its value lies more in the non-historical material to be found in it; for people's thoughts and feelings in those former times are very clearly drawn, as are the descriptions of palace ceremonial and dress customs.[96]

And the same author, in a later work, notes that "The *Salasilah Kutai* has been commented upon in the philological sense, but the commentary on its meaning has still largely to be written, by a social anthropologist or a student of the phenomenology of religion, and only then a historian can use it for a picture of the past." [97]

This percipient remark indeed applies, to a greater or lesser degree, to almost all the works under discussion, and we will now go on to consider the main reasons for this.

SOME MALAY IDEAS OF HISTORY

Now that the Federation of Malaya is independent, more and more people are interested in the background of the country and in learning something of its history, literature, and general culture. Although in the past the greatest services to Malay scholarship have been rendered almost exclusively by "expatriates" such as Marsden, Leyden, Raffles, W. E. and C. N. Maxwell, Wilkinson, and Winstedt, paradoxically the very fact of British protection and intellectual interest has previously inhibited the growth of local interest and activity in these fields. Much

[94] *Salasilah Kutai* (De kroniek van Koetai): romanized text (148 pp.), edited with notes by C. A. Mees (Santpoort, 1935); commentary by W. Kern in *VKI*, vol. XIX (1956).

[95] *Hikayat Radja Bandjar dan Kotaringin:* MSS nos. CCXLIII and CCXLIV in *Juynboll Cat. Leyden MSS*, Jawi texts of 298 and 264 pp. respectively, and Juynboll also mentions a text of 148 pp. in romanized Malay (MS no. CCXLV); three other MSS of this work are described in *Van Ronkel Suppl. Cat. Leyden MSS*, pp. 40–41, and eight in *Van Ronkel Cat. Bat. Gen. MSS*, pp. 270–274; commentary by A. A. Cense, *De kroniek van Bandjarmasin* (Santpoort, 1928).

[96] C. Hooykaas, *Perintis Sastra* (Jakarta, 1953), pp. 135–136 (translated from Indonesian by the present writer).

[97] *Idem*, "A Critical Stage in the Study of Indonesia's Past," p. 324.

of the present written history has been written through Western eyes, in terms of Western concepts, and from non-native sources. And even when native sources have been used, the approach has still sometimes been made from a Western viewpoint. This has been true for both Malaya and Indonesia.[98]

Thus, at present, questions are being asked by a new generation of historians and students as to what Malay sources exist for the study of the history of Malaya and Indonesia and to what extent such sources might offer material for one of those fresh interpretations which, occurring as they do with each new generation, keep history alive, moving, and meaningful. These sources do exist, as we have seen, and were widely used by the previous generations of writers just mentioned. But as can be seen from the footnotes, for the most part these Malay sources have not yet been translated; and they are normally difficult of access, being preserved in the great museums and libraries in manuscript form, usually in Jawi script. Thus, though they may contain material of use to the modern historian, the latter cannot or does not use them, either because he does not know Malay or because he may not be aware of the existence of the material. It is to try and alleviate this frustrating situation that the present tentative bibliographical essay has been written.

However, before we can know what Malay historical works can mean to us, we must first know what they meant to the Malays. History to the Malay has not until recently been either a science or an art, but an entertainment. Accuracy, completeness, and organized exposition were not the vital principles; what best pleased were legend, fantasy, and a pleasant hotchpotch of court and port gossip. We get an inkling of this from the several Malay words for "history" which have already appeared in this essay. At the present time, the preferred equivalent for the English word "history" is the Arabic *tawarikh*. This means history as university departments of history know it.[99] But the much more popular word, with a longer and more distinguished record in Malay literature, is *sejarah* (originally = family tree, now history generally),

[98] The classic attack on this approach is that of J. C. van Leur, *Indonesian Trade and Society*. Van Leur's work, together with that of C. C. Berg and G. J. Resink, in this context has recently been discussed by Justus M. van der Kroef, in "On the Writing of Indonesian History," and by Soedjotmoko, in *An Approach to Indonesian History*.

[99] Haji Zainal Abidin bin Ahmad (Z'aba) notes in his article "Recent Malay Literature" that it was the publication of R. O. Winstedt's schoolbook *Tawarikh Melayu* (Singapore, 1918) that first popularized the Arabic word for history, introducing the scientific concept and divorcing it from a largely legendary context.

and this means history as the Malay has always seen it—a mixture of truth and legend, fantasy and fact, entertainment and instruction. This fairly describes, for instance, the *Sejarah Melayu,* and we would, in addition, do well to remember that though, as we have seen, there is now a fairly large corpus of written works of Malay history, again, almost certainly, historical material has also been handed down, for centuries, by oral tradition. From an oral process of this kind we naturally cannot expect accuracy or reliability. The third Malay word (from an Arabic word for "chain") very frequently used in connection with Malay histories—*salasilah, salsilah, silsilah*—meaning "genealogy," illustrates a particular type of history, dear to the Malays, which traces the descent of families, particularly royal families, back as far as memory can stretch, and often, indeed, as far as imagination can stretch too since they can lead directly back to Alexander the Great and, in extreme cases, Adam.[100] The fact that the words *hikayat* and *cherita, chetera,* or *cheritera* (= story, tale) are also fairly indiscriminately applied to "histories" helps to indicate their partly fictional nature.

By contrast, the word "history" in this context now postulates not only scientific methods but also a certain degree of intellectual development in society: the ability to stand outside oneself and look in with a sense of impartial interest and understanding, the ability to regard oneself as a passing phenomenon with both earlier and later connections, as part of a continuous but constantly changing human process —and not least to realize that history is development with compound interest rather than a genealogical process of simple addition. Such a realization, such a sense of history, we do not find in Malay histories until the nineteenth century and then only in isolated cases.[101] But to

[100] The Greeks did the same. "The Greeks liked to establish connections with the past and did so by genealogies, but such genealogies were often created for political or personal reasons and their variety alone invited suspicion" (C. M. Bowra, *The Greek Experience* [London, 1959], p. 177). It is interesting to note that that good Malay Greek Alexander the Great—*Iskandar Dzu'l Karnain* (Alexander the Two-Horned)—achieved his sobriquet in a similar way. When he visited Egypt "and desired to consolidate his position in the eyes of the Egyptians, he went to the oasis of Amon and there went through a ceremony by which, though already a grown man, he became the son of Amon, and wore the curved horns of the Theban ram as proof of his divine descent" (M. Murray, *The Splendour That Was Egypt* [London, 1951], p. 126).

[101] However, as Dr. Noorduyn tells us elsewhere in this volume, the keeping of chronicles and personal and court diaries—implying a nascent historical sense—appears to have been a relatively common Macassarese and Buginese practice from the eighteenth, perhaps the seventeenth, century. See also Soedjatmoko, *An Approach to Indonesian History,* p. 5.

whatever type most Malay histories belong, we also find in them information of local alliances, uprisings, wars, and foreign policies; stories and notes on the lives, livelihoods, trades, and travels of the local people and their neighbors; and the unconscious illustration of group attitudes and influences. From this, history certainly can be extracted by the expert historian who has a wide knowledge of the facts, fancies, and documents of his area and period and who by this knowledge is properly equipped to check constantly the wilder flights of fantasy of the Malay historian of the past.

There is an interesting contrast here with Chinese historiography. Although in China history was written from a much earlier date, the Chinese dynastic histories initiated in the first century B.C. demonstrate a continuous pattern of historical writing from then until A.D. 1911. Apart from a certain stultifying rigidity of approach and the adoption of scientific method, the main characteristic of these histories is said to be the detached impartiality with which events are recorded and the lack of interpretative or deductive comment. This impartiality needed physical courage as well as intellectual integrity.

The historians of China . . . were often called upon to brave the wrath of unworthy rulers. Once in the 6th century B.C., when a commander of the palace guard, named Ts'ui Chu . . . killed the Prince of Ch'i for having deprived him of a beautiful woman, the official historian recorded the incident in one sentence: "Ts'ui Chu murdered Duke Chuang," whereupon Ts'ui Chu took the tablet from the archives and had the historian executed. Then a brother of the historian renewed the record, only to suffer death himself. When a second brother presented himself, brush in hand, Ts'ui saw that he truly stood condemned, and the record was made.[102]

This may be contrasted with the narrower and more pliant attitude of the Malay court historian who in this respect was much nearer to his European contemporary than to his Chinese colleague. Thus Professor Teeuw in his introduction to the *Sejarah Melayu* compares the chronicler with the Javanese court historians of whom he says:

The authors of these compositions do not seek any "objective realism in history"—for them, realism is not important. What is important is reality as it concerns their own prince and as seen through the prince's eyes, the eyes of one who is himself the very navel and center of his state. Not only, therefore, do we fail to find realism in these works—it would be foolish to expect

[102] Han Yu-Shan, *Elements of Chinese Historiography* (Hollywood, 1955), p. 5. Cf. the English historian Matthew Paris (died 1259): "If I tell the truth, I offend many; if I tell falsehoods, I offend God."

such a historian to observe objectively in any Western sense. His own experience of life and the world around him must determine, to an absolute degree, what he sees and how he sees it. The result is a type of historical writing which conforms to the environment and viewpoint of the writer; and this can only mean deep respect and praise for his prince. Episodes which do the royal personage less than justice are skipped or minimized; the royal genealogy is streamlined; the identification of the prince with his distinguished ancestors is zealously guarded.[103]

There is another factor, noted by Wilkinson, which detracts from the strictly historical value of Malay historical writing. In the same way that Aristotle regarded history as being ancillary to, and less philosophical than, poetry, the Malays have also regarded history as being ancillary to, and less important than, theology. "To him [the well-read Malay] history is a branch of theology; the superior interest attaching to ancient chronicles is due to the fact that they help to elucidate allusions in the Koran." [104]

This view partly accounts for the way in which historical and theological sections may be found juxtaposed in many Malay works and for the way in which the two kinds of material, plus legendary material, are so often mixed. It is clear that the Malay does not see history, the Greek "historiē" (inquiry), as a separate concept valid in its own right, for which an individual approach and a special technique are appropriate. It is seen only as an ancillary activity and as such has to make its own way as best it can. In modern jargon, the Malay historical writer was "committed" from the start, firstly, by virtue of writing and observing only within a subjective situation as described by Professor Teeuw and, secondly, because he had no allegiance to any historical absolute of the kind illustrated by the incident in Chinese historiography just described.

Thus, though it may rarely be possible to take historical writing in Malay at its face value, providing we have adequate knowledge of the writer, his circumstances, and attachments and a certain amount of known data by which to measure any individual degree of aberrance, historical value may yet be found in it. Professor Berg's writings are

[103] Situmorang and Teeuw, *Sedjarah Melaju*, p. ix (translated from Indonesian by the present writer).

[104] R. J. Wilkinson, *Malay Beliefs*, p. 43. Cf. the Indian view of history: "History was important to the average Indian only for the light which it could throw on the personal truths of the Hindu philosophy and as a record of exemplary lives" (J. E. van Lohuizen-de Leeuw, "India and Its Cultural Empire," in D. Sinor, ed., *Orientalism and History*, p. 49).

the classic exposition of this situation applied to Indonesia; [105] but the situation itself is not peculiar to Malaya and Indonesia. The problem was stated in general terms in relation to the philosophy of history by R. G. Collingwood and is inherent in all historical writing and thinking, wherever it takes place.[106]

OTHER MATERIAL OF HISTORICAL VALUE

There are four other categories of material that would certainly repay investigation by historians. Indeed, they might prove more reliable than the works that specifically set out to be histories, for unlike the latter many of them are not written from a particular dynastic standpoint and thus the suspicions and safeguards which have just been discussed do not apply to them with quite the same force. This comment particularly applies to the first and third categories that follow —the former consisting mainly of autobiographical reportage and the latter of legal manuals which generally seek only to codify and record existing law and custom.

The first is that containing the autobiographical accounts of the lives and voyages of Malay writers and personalities in the last century. Munshi Abdullah's autobiography, the *Hikayat Abdullah*,[107] is well

[105] For a short summary see Berg, "Javanese Historiography—A Synopsis of Its Evolution."

[106] R. G. Collingwood, *An Autobiography*. "I began by observing that you cannot find out what a man means by simply studying his spoken or written statements, even though he has spoken or written with perfect command of language and perfectly truthful intentions. In order to find out his meaning you must also know what the question was (a question in his own mind and presumed by him to be in yours) to which the thing he has said or written was meant as an answer" (p. 31). "Now, the question 'To what question did So-and-so intend this proposition for an answer?' is an historical question, and therefore cannot be settled except by historical methods. When So-and-so wrote in a distant past, it is generally a very difficult one, because writers (at any rate good writers) always write for their contemporaries, and in particular for those who are 'likely to be interested,' which means those who are already asking the question to which an answer is being offered; and consequently a writer very seldom explains what the question is that he is trying to answer. Later on, when he has become a 'classic' and his contemporaries are all long dead, the question has been forgotten; especially if the answer he gave was generally acknowledged to be the right answer; for in that case people stopped asking the question, and began asking the question that next arose. So the question asked by the original writer can only be reconstructed historically, often not without the exercise of considerable historical skill" (p. 39). See also Collingwood's posthumous *The Idea of History*.

[107] *Hikayat Abdullah*, by Abdullah bin Abdul Kadir Munshi: romanized text, introduction, and notes, R. A. Datoek Besar and R. Roolvink, eds. (Jakarta, 1953); English translation and notes by A. H. Hill, *JRASMB*, vol. XXVIII, pt. 3 (1955); an earlier English translation of certain parts by a contemporary of Abdullah is J. T. Thompson, *Hakayit Abdullah* (London, 1874).

known, as is his account of a voyage in 1838 up the east coast of Malaya in *Kesah Pelayaran Abdullah* [108]—of which a pleasant English translation has been published by A. E. Coope.[109] But the fact that his son, Mohammad Ibrahim Munshi, was interpreter to Sir Andrew Clarke and wrote an account of his experiences is less well known. This was called *Kesah Pelayaran Mohammad Ibrahim Munshi,* and a Jawi edition has recently been reprinted by the Government Printer in Johore Bahru.[110] In this work there is information on early tin mining, Ngah Ibrahim and Raja Muda Abdullah in Perak, Sultan Abdul Samad at Langat, a Tuan Irvine, A. M. Skinner, and the Pangkor Engagement of January 1874. An unpublished account of a similar kind is referred to by Haji Zainal Abidin bin Ahmad in his chapter on Modern Developments in Winstedt's "A History of Malay Literature." This is *Hikayat Hikmat,* a Jawi manuscript of about 1870 relating the travels of a Christian Batak in Malaya and Sumatra. This may contain useful material and might be worth investigating if the manuscript, which was at the Sultan Idris Training College at Tanjong Malim in Perak, survived the Japanese occupation.

The second category is that of the descriptive poems which became popular in the last century. There are many of these. From a historical point of view the most interesting appear to be the following. There are four about nineteenth-century events in Singapore, the first two by Abdullah Munshi. The *Sha'er Singapura Terbakar* or *Sha'er Singapura di-makan Api* was composed by Abdullah, according to his own account, during and immediately after the great fire of February 13, 1830, in which he himself lost most of his own possessions.[111] Copies of this poem and his other one, *Sha'er Kampong Gelam Terbakar,*[112] about the 1847 fire, are now scarce. Two anonymous works on Singapore are *Sha'er Kampong Boyan di-makan Api*[113] and *Sha'er Bah Singapura.*[114] One short epic poem which takes us back to Malacca in 1784 is the

[108] *Kesah Pelayaran Abdullah,* by Abdullah bin Abdul Kadir Munshi: romanized text (Singapore, 1949 [6th ed.]).

[109] *Kesah Pelayaran Abdullah,* by Abdullah bin Abdul Kadir Munshi: English translation by A. E. Coope, *The Voyage of Abdullah* (Singapore, 1949).

[110] *Kesah Pelayaran Mohammad Ibrahim Munshi,* by Mohammad Ibrahim Munshi: Jawi text (Johore Bahru, 1956).

[111] *Sha'er Singapura Terbakar,* by Abdullah bin Abdul Kadir Munshi: published in Jawi and romanized Malay at different times in Singapore; MS versions are nos. 199 and 200 in *Van Ronkel Suppl. Cat. Leyden MSS* and no. CDLXXIII (*Sja'ir Singapoera Dimakan Api*) in *Van Ronkel Cat. Bat. Gen. MSS.*

[112] *Sha'er Kampong Gelam Terbakar,* by Abdullah bin Abdul Kadir Munshi: Jawi text, lithographed (Singapore).

[113] *Sha'er Kampong Boyan di-makan Api:* Jawi text, lithographed (Singapore).

[114] *Sha'er Bah Singapura:* Jawi text, lithographed (Singapore).

Sha'er Raja Haji—a story of that Buginese prince (the grandfather of
the author referred to on page 175 above) who was killed as he attacked
the Dutch in Malacca fort.[115] Of the poem, W. E. Maxwell, who romanized it, with notes and a useful English translation of the Dutch
account by Netscher of this event, says: "The literary merit of the
poem is not great, but it is of considerable historical interest and will
be valued in Malacca as the work of some local bard of the last century, who celebrated in the best language he could command the successful repulse of the raid attempted on his native city." [116]

As Maxwell notes, the names of persons, including those of the
Dutch commanders who led the attack in which the Malay hero of
the ballad lost his life, are given, so that it may be a work contemporaneous with the events which it describes.

In the libraries at Leyden and Jakarta there are mid-nineteenth-
century manuscripts entitled *Sha'er Perang Siak* about Bengkalis in
Siak and the war with Johore; [117] *Sha'er Moko-Moko*,[118] a family chronicle of Moko-Moko in West Sumatra; *Sha'er Pangeran Sharif Hashim* [119]
on the Banjermasin war of 1861–1863; and several others of considerable historical interest; as well as the seventeenth-century *Sha'er Speelman*,[120] about the war with Macassar, of which an annotated edition
and English translation are being prepared by Dr. C. Skinner of the
University of Malaya, and the *Sha'er Kompeni Welanda berperang dengan China*.[121] There is also the *Sha'er Himup* (Imhoff), which describes
seventeenth-century Jakarta and the Dutch-Chinese troubles in the
middle of the next century and of which extracts have been given by
Dr. Hooykaas in his *Perintis Sastra*.[122]

[115] *Sha'er Raja Haji:* romanized text and comment by W. E. Maxwell, *JRASSB,*
XXII (1890), 173–224.
[116] *Ibid.,* p. 174.
[117] *Sja'er Perang Siak:* MSS nos. 195 and 196 in *Van Ronkel Suppl. Cat. Leyden
MSS;* cf. MS no. CDLXX in *Van Ronkel Cat. Bat. Gen. MSS,* but entitled *Sja'ir
Radja Siak,* in Jawi.
[118] *Sja'ir Moko-Moko:* MS no. 190 in *Van Ronkel Suppl. Cat. Leyden MSS,* Jawi
text of 32 pp.
[119] *Sja'ir Pangeran Sjarif Hasjim:* MS no. XVIII in *Juynboll Cat. Leyden MSS,*
Jawi text of 95 pp.; see also MS no. CDLXII in *Van Ronkel Cat. Bat. Gen. MSS* and
MS no. 191 in *Van Ronkel Suppl. Cat. Leyden MSS* (both with the title *Sja'ir
Perang Bandjarmasin*).
[120] *Sja'ir Sipelman* (Speelman): MS no. XVI in *Juynboll Cat. Leyden MSS* contains 6 pp. embodying the first 139 distichs of this poem. (See p. 193 below.)
[121] *Sja'ir Kompeni Welanda berperang dengan Tjina:* J. Rusconi, ed., Utrecht
dissertation (Wageningen, 1935); E. J. van den Berg, ed., Leyden dissertation
(1936).
[122] *Sja'ir Emoep* (Imhoff): MS no. CDLX in *Van Ronkel Cat. Bat. Gen. MSS,*

Thirdly, another useful quasi-historical source comprises the codes of traditional law and custom (variously called *Hukum Kanun, Undang-Undang, Adat*) written in Malay, many of which have been published in *JRASSB* and *JRASMB* and one, the important *Ninety-nine Laws of Perak*, in the *Papers on Malay Subjects*.[123] Some of these must be mentioned. One is the *Adat Raja Raja Melayu* edited by van Ronkel.[124] This work was commissioned by Governor de Bruin of Malacca from the *Kapitan Melayu* about 1779 and was taken down in dictation from one Lebai Abdul Muhit who was reported to be the last and sole repository of the ancient customs of the Malay kingdom of Malacca. Two texts of this kind that have been recently published are *Undang-Undang Sungai Ujong* (in Negri Sembilan) with a romanization and translation by Sir Richard Winstedt and Dr. P. E. de Josselin de Jong,[125] and the *Maritime Laws of Malacca* collated and published by the same editors from no fewer than thirteen manuscripts with various Malay titles.[126]

Similar codes exist for various Sumatran territories, e.g., Bencoolen, Jambi, Indragiri, and Palembang; and these are based on the Malacca law, with local modifications. The most recent publication of this type is an edition of *Adat Acheh* by G. W. J. Drewes and P. Voorhoeve from a manuscript in the India Office Library in London.[127] It is not possible to give a full account here of these legal codes and digests, but some of them are among the earliest Malay manuscripts now extant, so that

---

Jawi MS of 381 pp.; romanized extracts in Hooykaas, *Perintis Sastra*, pp. 401–408 (*Sja'ir Himup*).

[123] *Ninety-nine Laws of Perak* (no Malay title): edited and translated into English by J. Rigby, *Papers on Malay Subjects*, vol. II, pt. 2 (Government Printer, F.M.S., 1908).

[124] *Adat Radja-Radja Melajoe:* P. S. van Ronkel, ed., Jawi text and introduction in Dutch (Leyden, 1929); the text is collated from three MSS of the Royal Asiatic Society, London (? including Farquhar 4 and 10 in *Van der Tuuk*).

[125] *Undang-Undang Sungai Ujong:* romanized text and English translation by Sir Richard Winstedt and P. E. de Josselin De Jong, *JRASMB*, vol. XXVII, pt. 3 (1954), from MSS Maxwell 118 and 118A, Royal Asiatic Society, London.

[126] *The Maritime Laws of Malacca* (under various Malay titles): romanized text and English translation by Sir Richard Winstedt and P. E. de Josselin De Jong, *JRASMB*, vol. XXIX, pt. 3 (1956), collated from thirteen MSS in the Royal Asiatic Society, London (Raffles and Maxwell Collections), Leyden University Library, and the Royal Military Academy at Breda, the Netherlands. One of these Raffles MSS is probably that translated by Raffles himself and said to have been published in the *Asiatic Researches;* the translation was later reprinted in *JRASSB*, vols. III and IV (1879).

[127] *Adat Atjèh:* facsimile Jawi text of 174 p., edited and introduced by G. W. J. Drewes and P. Voorhoeve, *VKI*, vol. XXIV (1958).

for this reason, too, they are particularly valuable. Details may be found in the catalogues referred to in the list at the end of the chapter.

Fourthly, for the historian in search of original documents the later sections of these same catalogues of Malay manuscripts may repay attention. Most of them have a small section of *varia* mentioning the original Malay letters, diaries, and memoranda to be found in these great collections, and it is clear from even the short descriptions there given that some of them should be of value to the historian. For the most part they appear to be diplomatic exchanges and local administrative instructions from the Netherlands East Indies authorities to the local potentates in Johore, Riau, and other places and vice versa.[128]

CONCLUSION

After this short survey of the works available—or all that have come to notice—and some assessment of their value, let us see what is missing. To start with, it is clear that for the period before the middle of the eighteenth century our sources are very few—the *Sejarah Melayu, Hikayat Raja-Raja Pasai,* the *Bustan a's Salatin, Hikayat Acheh, Sha'er Speelman,* several legal codes, and the legendary opening of nearly every Malay history or pseudo-history—this is all we have to go on. For the period from, say, 1750, there is a lot of material about Johore, the Bugis, and Riau when activity and power in the Malay world were centered in that area. The best of this material is the *Tuhfat al-Nafis,* which sets a new standard in Malay historiography and is, like the other similar works, happiest and most reliable in dealing with relatively recent dates. From the time of *Tuhfat al-Nafis,* i.e. the 1860's and 1870's, very few historical works have been produced in Malay that specifically set out to be careful, considered history. Territorially, there is very little on Negri Sembilan, Selangor, and Penang, and this is unexpected for Selangor at least; surely there is a Malay history extant of this state? Clearly, we are due for a renaissance in this particular field, as in the realm of peninsular Malay literature generally.[129]

Finally, there is no doubt that, providing proper mental safeguards

---

[128] Dr. H. A. Lamb, Department of History, University of Malaya, and Mr. E. H. S. Simmonds of the School of Oriental and African Studies in London have both informed me verbally that there is material of this nature in Malay concerning the southern Malay states of Thailand and the northern states of Malaya in the National Library in Bangkok.

[129] "Part of the difficulty arises from the present paucity of indigenous materials and scholarship. Presumably when the historical commissions such as those created in recent years in Burma . . . and Thailand . . . begin to publish their material, some redress may be expected even if such historical writing proves to be over-

are applied, the historian can learn much—at any rate about the general nature of society—not only from the sources already mentioned but from many old works of Malay literature of an entirely fictional nature.[130] Hardly any of these older works can be dated; and in any case a high proportion of the total corpus does not directly concern Malaysia, being adapted versions or translations of Indian, Persian, or Arabic originals. But it is a characteristic of the more original works of old Malay and Indonesian literature that their background and spirit are often intensely, almost exultingly, local, and in the case of the works in the corpus of Panji tales [131] (which mainly concern Java), such folk romances as *Hikayat Malim Deman, Hikayat Awang Sulong Merah Muda*, the historical prose epic *Hikayat Hang Tuah*, and many others, the social historian can surely find material to fill what must at present be very large gaps. Writing mainly of folk material of this kind, Sir Richard Winstedt said as long ago as 1910:

The places and persons they refer to may be historical but are generally obscure or forgotten. We can only make deductions on very broad lines. Rhapsodists will always declare how their tales have historical sequence, though they will add they have lost the links or forgotten how the sequence should run. It is hopeless probably ever to connect the threads. Can the disconnected tangled threads lead us anywhere? [132]

I believe they can, provided the material is carefully and cautiously examined; and I see no reason why substantial works with entrancing titles such as the following (or their equivalent in Malay or Indonesian) should not flow from the pens of our historians—"A Social History of

---

weighted on the nationalist side, as has been true in some instances in India" (Frank N. Trager, "Recent Southeast Asian Historiography," pp. 359–360).

[130] For the historian and sociologist dealing with the modern period, Indonesian literature since 1920 is also of the greatest value and interest and has already received considerable attention. While twentieth-century Malayan writing in Malay is poorer in quality and is in general much less rewarding (the times, after all, have not been so emotionally and intellectually stirring in Malaya as in Indonesia), some of it should be of similar interest, though it is not, so far as the present writer is aware, being much worked on from this angle at present. See A. H. Johns, "Indonesian Literature and the Social Upheaval," *Australian Outlook*, XIII, no. 4 (1959), 293–303, and also Ismail bin Hussein, "Pengarang-pengarang Melayu di-Singapura selepas Perang Dunia II (1945–1958)"; (unpublished academic exercise in typescript, Department of Malay Studies, University of Malaya, 1959).

[131] Much work has already been done on the historical background of the Panji tales by Dutch scholars, notably C. C. Berg, J. Brandes, and W. H. Rassers.

[132] R. O. Winstedt, "The History of the Peninsula in Folk Tales," pp. 183–184.

the Malays," "Everyday Life in Fifteenth-Century Malacca," "The Malay Kingdom of Malacca," "The Great Days of Acheh"—once these Malay sources have been tapped and interpreted anew.

If a general personal view may be expressed in concluding, I do not myself think it is a matter for regret that Malay historical writing errs on the side of gossip rather than chronology. The important dates, generally speaking, can be established by other means—by archaeological evidence or from foreign sources. The kind of material not so found is exactly that characteristic of Malay historiography—social material, detailed physical descriptions of places and things, implicit revelations of group attitudes and conflicts. If carefully checked and evaluated (as inspiringly illustrated, in the case of mainly non-Malay sources, in the works of van Leur and Schrieke), this material helps more than anything else to answer the questions of modern historical research, which is rightly more concerned with social, economic, and conceptual backgrounds than with the simple chronology of political events.

MAIN MATERIALS USED

Berg, C. C. "Javanese Historiography—A Synopsis of Its Evolution," in D. G. E. Hall, ed., *Historians of South East Asia*, pp. 13–23.

Blagden, C. O. "List of the Malay Books Bequeathed to the Society by the late Sir W. E. Maxwell K. C. M. G.," *JRAS*, 1899, pp. 121–129.

Browne, E. G. *A Handlist of the Muhammadan Manuscripts in the Library of the University of Cambridge*. Cambridge, 1900.

———. *A Supplementary Handlist of the Muhammadan Manuscripts in the Libraries of the University and Colleges of Cambridge*. Cambridge, 1922.

Cabaton, A. *Catalogue sommaire des manuscrits indiens, indo-chinois et malayo-polynésiens*. Paris, 1912.

Cheeseman, H. R. *Bibliography of Malaya*. London, 1959.

Collingwood, R. G. *An Autobiography*. Oxford, 1951; first published London, 1939.

———. *The Idea of History*. London, 1946.

Hall, D. G. E., ed. *Historians of South East Asia*. London, 1961. See also under Berg, Hooykaas, Oetomo, and Winstedt.

Hooykaas, C. "A Critical Stage in the Study of Indonesia's Past," in D. G. E. Hall, ed., *Historians of South East Asia*, pp. 313–325.

Journal of the Malayan Branch of the Royal Asiatic Society. Singapore, 1923 to date.

Journal of the Straits Branch of the Royal Asiatic Society. Singapore, 1878–1922.

Juynboll, H. H. *Catalogus van de Maleische en Sundaneesche handschriften der Leidsche Universiteits-Bibliotheek*. Leyden, 1899.

Kroef, J. M. van der. "On the Writing of Indonesian History," *Pacific Affairs*, XXXI, no. 4 (Dec., 1958), 352–371.

Leur, J. C. van. *Indonesian Trade and Society: Essays in Asian Social and Economic History*. The Hague, 1955.

Logan, J. R., ed. *Journal of the Indian Archipelago*, vols. I-IX. Singapore, 1847–1855.

——. *Journal of the Indian Archipelago*, new ser., vols. I-IV. Singapore, 1856–1859.

Niemann, G. K. "De Maleische handschriften in het Britsch Museum," *BKI*, 3d ser., VI (1871), 96–101.

Oetomo, Bambang. "Some Remarks on Modern Indonesian Historiography," in D. G. E. Hall, ed., *Historians of South East Asia*, pp. 73–84.

Poerbatjaraka, R. M. Ng., P. Voorhoeve, and C. Hooykaas. *Indonesische handschriften*. Bandung, 1950.

Ronkel, P. S. van. "Aanvulling der beschrijving van de Maleische en Minangkabausche handschriften . . . in het bezit van het Koninklijk Instituut voor de Taal-, Land- en Volkenkunde van Nederlandsch-Indië," *BKI*, CIII (1946), 555–606.

——. "Account of Six Malay Manuscripts of the Cambridge University Library," *BKI*, 6th ser., II (1896), 1–53.

——. "Beschrijving der Maleische handschriften van de Bibliothèque Royale te Brussel," *BKI*, 7th ser., VI (1908), 501–520.

——. "Catalogus der Maleische handschriften in het Museum van het Bataviaasch Genootschap van Kunsten en Wetenschappen," *VBG*, LVII (1909), 1–515.

——. "Catalogus der Maleische handschriften van het Koninklijk Instituut voor de Taal-, Land- en Volkenkunde van Nederlandsch-Indië," *BKI*, 7th ser., VI (1908), 181–248.

——. *Supplement-Catalogus der Maleische en Minangkabausche handschriften in de Leidsche Universiteits-Bibliotheek.* Leyden, 1921.

Sinor, D., ed. *Orientalism and History.* Cambridge, 1954.

Soedjatmoko. *An Approach to Indonesian History: Towards an Open Future.* (Cornell Modern Indonesia Project, Translation Series.) Ithaca, 1960.

Teeuw, A. "The History of the Malay Language," *BKI*, CXV, pt. 2 (1959), 138–156.

Trager, F. N. "Recent Southeast Asian Historiography," *Pacific Affairs* XXX, no. 4 (Dec., 1957), 358–366.

Tuuk, H. N. van der. "Short Account of the Malay Manuscripts Belonging to the Royal Asiatic Society," *JRAS*, new ser., II (1866), 85–135.

——. "Kort verslag van de Maleische handschriften in het East India House te London," *Tijdschrift voor Nederlandsch Indië*, I (1849), 385–400.

University of Malaya Library. Unpublished list of Malay MSS and microfilms.

Wilkinson, R. J., ed. *Malay Beliefs.* Leyden, 1906.

——. *Papers on Malay Subjects,* 1st and 2d ser. Kuala Lumpur and Singapore, 1907–1927. Especially the section *Literature: History.*

Winstedt, R. O. "A History of Malay Literature," *JRASMB*, XVII, pt. 3 (1939), 1–243.

——. "The History of the Peninsula in Folk Tales," *JRASSB*, LVII (1910), 183–188.

——. "Malay Chronicles from Sumatra and Malaya," in D. G. E. Hall, ed., *Historians of South East Asia*, pp. 24–29.

——. "Malay Manuscripts in the Libraries of London, Brussels, and The Hague," *JRASSB*, LXXXII (1920), 153–161.

——. *Tawarikh Melayu: An Anthology of Malay History.* London,

1958. (This is a different book from that mentioned in note 99 on p. 180.)

Zainal Abidin bin Ahmad, Haji. "Modern Developments" (a separate chapter in Winstedt's "A History of Malay Literature," *q.v.*).

————. "Recent Malay Literature," *JRASMB*, XIX, pt. 1 (1941), 1–20.

The seventeenth-century historical poem formerly called the *Sha'er Speelman* (see p. 186) has now been aptly renamed *Sja'ir Perang Mengkasar* by Dr. Skinner. He has collated, transcribed, translated, and edited the two previously known London and Leyden MSS in his recently published edition of this text, which he ascribes convincingly to the authorship of Entji' Amin, the Sultan of Goa's Malay secretary. (*Sja'ir Perang Mengkasar*, by Entji' Amin: romanized and edited text, with English translation *en face*, by C. Skinner, *VKI*, vol. XL [1963]. Based on a London Ph.D. thesis.) This volume, which embodies extremely high standards of scholarship and layout, will be a model for all future editors.

X

Chinese Historical Sources and Historiography

By TJAN TJOE SOM

*Professor of Chinese, University of
Indonesia, Jakarta*

THOSE who want to make a study of the history of the relations between Indonesia and China from Chinese sources are confronted with
the following problems: which are the sources to be used; are they
original, i.e., direct records of actual travelers; in those records what
are the facts and what are the fancies; are their topographical descriptions and their dates reliable; what do their many strange names of
persons and places stand for? [1]

The general problem of Chinese historical sources is their over-
abundance. Those bearing on the relations between China and other
countries, including Southeast Asia and Indonesia, are no exception.

It may be expected that anybody wanting to collect material on
Chinese history should first turn to the *Dynastic Histories,* twenty-six
in number if the *New History of the Yüan Dynasty* and the *Draft
History of the Ch'ing Dynasty* are included. They represent the continuous history of China from the earliest antiquity down to the end
of the Manchu Dynasty in 1911.[2]

---

[1] The insufficient material in the libraries at Jakarta makes it very difficult to
compose an article which would meet the necessary bibliographical demands. In the
present, far from complete, article I have therefore to a great extent been obliged
to draw on previous bibliographical studies and rely on their information where the
actual works are unavailable.

[2] For a list of the first twenty-five *Dynastic Histories,* cf. Yang Lien-sheng, *Topics
in Chinese History* (Cambridge, Mass., 1950), pp. 32–38; for the *Draft History of
the Ch'ing Dynasty* cf. Ch. S. Gardner, *Chinese Traditional Historiography* (Cambridge, Mass., 1938), pp. 97–99.

The composition of these *Histories* in general follows the same pattern. There is first the section called the "Basic" or "Imperial Annals," which record in chronological order all the acts of the reigning emperors. Then there is a section which usually consists of genealogical tables of the Imperial clan and important ministers; further, a section containing essays on divers special subjects such as rites, music, astronomy, law, economy, etc.; and, lastly, a large section with biographical chapters of eminent persons. It is in this biographical section that the chapters on foreign countries and peoples are also found. They occur in all the *Dynastic Histories*, with the exception of the *History of the Ch'ên Dynasty* (557–589) and the *History of the Northern Ch'i Dynasty* (550–577).

The composition of the *Dynastic Histories*, however, is such that a subject is not exhausted with the chapter specially devoted to it. Scattered through the other chapters and sections may be found supplementary material bearing on the subject in question. It often corroborates the story told in the special chapter but sometimes also confuses or even contradicts it in some of the details. For instance, what we read in the chapter on foreign countries may be repeated or supplemented or perhaps contradicted by what we find in the biographical chapters of the men who were somehow connected with the travels and in the "Basic Annals" which record audiences with foreign envoys and contain edicts and memorials relating to foreign travels. It is thus necessary to read through the whole of the *Dynastic Histories* in order to gather all material relevant to a given subject, and it is not sufficient for that purpose to restrict the reading to the chapters dealing specifically with it.

The reason why the *Dynastic Histories* are composed in this particular way is probably as follows. The history of each dynasty had, of course, to be written on the basis of the original documents. These documents were of different kinds, written by different officers and kept by different offices. Being too bulky, they could not be published in their unwieldy entirety but had to be edited into some more tractable form. The *Dynastic Histories* are to be seen as the final digests of original documents, or archives, each section having as source a special collection of archives. Thus the "Basic Annals" are based on the *Shih lu (Veritable Records)*, which were again reeditions of the *Ch'i chü chu (Diaries of Activity and Repose)*, reports of all the events at court in minute detail. The other sections of the *Dynastic Histories*, viz. the "Tables," the "Essays," and the "Biographies," are again, each of them, compilations based on other collections of documents.[3]

The sources for the compilation of the chapters on foreign countries, occurring in the "Biographies," seem also to have been prepared separately. During the T'ang Dynasty (618–906), in any case, there was an office which "was charged with interviewing tribute-bearing envoys of foreign countries, informing itself of the geography of these countries, the customs and attire of the people, the distance over which the tribute came, and the names of their chieftains."[4] In fact, since the Han Dynasty (206 B.C.–A.D. 220) there seem always to have been hostelries for foreign guests at the capital and special offices for the translation of foreign languages.[5]

All the documents were finally deposited in a special office, as archives upon which to edit the *Dynastic Histories*. The task of editing, however, following ancient Chinese traditional scholarship, is chiefly to make a choice out of the wealth of material, altering as little as possible the wording of the texts and so preserving as far as possible their authenticity. Thus it is that the same event may be entered in different chapters and sections in different ways and presented from different angles, according to the documents which supplied the material. At the same time the text of the *Dynastic Histories* retains its authentic character as a primary source.

Admitting the authentic character of the *Dynastic Histories*, however, we would still like in special cases to consult the original archives themselves. Unfortunately they have not survived, with a few exceptions such as the *Ta t'ang ch'uang yeh ch'i chü chu (Diary of Activity and Repose of the Establishment of the T'ang Dynasty)*,[6] the *Shun tsung shih lu (Veritable Record of the T'ang Emperor Shun-tsung)*,[7] the *Ming shih lu (Veritable Records of the Ming Dynasty)*,[8] and the *Ch'ing shih lu (Veritable Records of the Manchu Dynasty)*.[9] These

[3] Cf. Gardner, *Chinese Traditional Historiography*, pp. 88–96.

[4] See Bernhard S. Solomon, *The Veritable Record of the T'ang Emperor Shun-tsung* (Cambridge, Mass., 1955), p. xxv.

[5] See P. Pelliot, "Le Hō̈ja et le Sayyid Husain de l'Histoire des Ming: Appendice III, Le Sseu-Yi-Kouan et le Houei-T'ong-Kouan," *T'oung Pao*, XXXVIII (1948), 207–290.

[6] See Woodbridge Bingham, "Wên Ta-ya, the First Recorder of T'ang History," *Journal of the American Oriental Society*, LVII (1937), 368–374.

[7] Translated by Solomon; see note 4.

[8] E.g., cf. W. Franke, "Zur Kompilation und Ueberlieferung der Ming Shih-lu," *Sinologische Arbeiten*, I (1943), 1–46; "Weitere Beiträge zur Kompilation und Ueberlieferung der Sing Shih-lu," SA, II (1944), 1–29; "Nachtrag zur Kompilation und Ueberlieferung der Ming Shih-lu," SA, III (1945), 165–168.

[9] E.g., cf. Knight Biggerstaff, "Some Notes on the *Tung-hua lu* and the *Shih-lu*," *Harvard Journal of Asiatic Studies*, IV (1939), 101–115.

extant works represent the documents from which the "Basic Annals" drew their material. The other documents, forming the material for the other sections of the *Dynastic Histories*, have also largely disappeared, but for the Ch'ing Dynasty there are still huge collections of archives.[10]

It would in itself be a formidable task, for the purpose of research (e.g. on the study of the relations of China with foreign countries), to hunt through the whole of the *Dynastic Histories* and the *Veritable Records*. There are, however, still other sources.

The particular character of the *Dynastic Histories* has long since induced Chinese scholars for convenience' sake to compose works which would present the material in a more systematic way. In this way were published, for instance, the *Chi shih pên mo*, continuous accounts of important historical events; the *hui yao*[11] and the *t'ung*,[12] which contain descriptions of government institutions including the official relations with foreign countries, the first for one dynasty separately, the second including several dynasties; the *lei shu*, *Encyclopaedias* arranged according to subject matter and dealing also with foreign countries.[13] The arrangement of these works makes it easier to consult them for any subject we want to investigate, and even if they have not the authentic character of the *Dynastic Histories*, but to a large extent are based on them, they also contain much new material from sources which have since been lost.[14]

The several thousand *Local Gazetteers* are also important historical sources. These are not only geographical descriptions of specific areas but also local histories, which give detailed information about promi-

[10] Cf. Gardner, *Chinese Traditional Historiography*, p. 95, note 18.

[11] The *hui yao* of the Western Han (206 B.C.-A.D. 8), the Eastern Han (25-220), the Three Kingdoms (220-265), the T'ang (618-906), the Five Dynasties (907-960), the Sung (960-1279), and the Ming (1368-1644) all contain chapters on foreign countries. We may also mention the *hui tien* of the Ming and the Ch'ing dynasties, which contain chapters describing the tributes presented by foreign envoys.

[12] The *t'ung tien* by Tu Yu (735-812), the *t'ung chih* by Chêng Ch'iao (1104-1162), and the *Wên hsien t'ung k'ao* by Ma Tuan-lin (thirteenth century) with their seven supplements (cf. Têng Ssŭ-yü and Knight Biggerstaff, *An Annotated Bibliography of Selected Chinese Reference Works* [rev. ed.; Cambridge, Mass., 1950], pp. 147-156). Chapters on foreign countries occur in all, except the *Ch'ing ch'ao t'ung chih*.

[13] E.g., *I wên lei chü* (end of sixth century), *T'ai p'ing yü lan* (end of tenth century), *Ts'ê fu yüan kuei* (beginning of eleventh century), *Yü hai* (end of thirteenth century), and *Ku chin t'u shu chi ch'êng* (beginning of eighteenth century).

[14] E.g., two works compiled in the third century by K'ang T'ai, the *Wu shih wai kuo chuan* (*Accounts of Foreign Countries of the Wu Period*) and the *Fu nan chi* (*Record of Fu-nan*), have been lost, but passages from them are quoted in the *I wên lei chü* and the *T'ai p'ing yü lan*.

nent people born in the area, among whom may be those who have been to foreign countries or have had some indirect contact with them.

And of course there are the accounts written by the travelers themselves or by their friends, as well as geographical books written by people who were for some reason interested in foreign countries without going there themselves. We may mention the accounts given by Buddhist pilgrims, such as Fa Hsien, Hsüan Tsang, and I Ching; [15] other important, still extant, works are the *Ling wai tai ta,* published in 1178 by Chou Ch'ü-fei, the *Chu fan chih,* with preface dated 1225, by Chao Ju-kua, the *Tao i chih lüeh,* published ± 1350, by Wang Ta-yüan.[16]

In view of the vastness of Chinese literature, any serious study based on original sources is an immense task. In the case of the study of the historical relations between China and other countries, it would be impossible, or at any rate unsatisfactory, to restrict oneself to one country or one region, since the geographical descriptions often refer to one another, and many names and expressions, such as those relating to foreign customs and products, obscure in one chapter, may be clarified in another. It is, therefore, essential that such an over-all study should begin with the collection of all relevant material. This, however, is only feasible with a large library, and we know the inadequacy of most of the Chinese libraries outside China. A good solution would be to publish a new edition of the whole of the sources, from those con-

[15] Fa Hsien traveled from 399 to 414, Hsüan Tsang from 629 to 645, I Ching from 671 to 695. A photolithographic reprint of a Sung edition of the *Fa hsien chuan* was published in Peking in 1955, so also of a Ming edition of the *Ta t'ang hsi yü chi* of Hsüan Tsang. The work on Fa Hsien is also called *Fo kuo chi;* there are translations, e.g. by J. Legge, *A Record of Buddhistic Kingdoms* (Oxford, 1886), by H. A. Giles, *The Travels of Fa Hsien* (Cambridge, Eng., 1923), and by Li Yung-hsi, *A Record of the Buddhist Countries* (Peking, 1957). The book on Hsüan Tsang's travels was translated, e.g. by S. Beal, *Buddhist Records of the Western World* (London, 1906). I Ching's two travel works are the *Ta t'ang hsi yü ch'iu fa kao shêng chuan* and the *Nan hai chi kuei nei fa chuan,* both occurring in the Chinese Tripiṭaka (Nanjio Catalogue, nos. 1491 and 1492); translations are by Ed. Chavannes, *Mémoire composée à l'époque de la grande dynastie T'ang sur les Religieux Éminents qui allèrent chercher la loi dans les pays d'occident* (Paris, 1894), and J. Takakusu, *A Record of the Buddhist Religion as Practised in India and the Malay Archipelago* (Oxford, 1896).

[16] The *Chu fan chih* has been translated from the Chinese and annotated by Friedrich Hirth and W. W. Rockhill, *Chau Ju-Kua: His Work on the Chinese and Arab Trade in the Twelfth and Thirteenth Centuries* (St. Petersburg, 1911). There is a modern edition of the *Chu fan chih,* revised and annotated by Fêng Ch'êng-chün (Peking, 1956), and of the *Tao i chih lüeh,* revised and annotated by T. Fujita (1915). Only the *Tao i chih lüeh* is the account of an actual traveler.

tained in the *Dynastic Histories, Veritable Records, Encyclopaedias, Gazetteers,* etc., down to the separate works by actual travelers and stray notes contained in the innumerable essays by Chinese scholars.

In this connection I may refer to a publication of the Central Academy for the Study of Minorities in Peking, entitled *Li tai kê tsu chuan chi hui pien* (*Collection of Accounts concerning Various People throughout History*), edited by Chien Po-tsan, Ch'ên Shu, Sun Yüeh, Ch'u Mingshan, Wang Kung-liang, and Wu Hêng. Two parts in three volumes appeared in May, 1958, August, 1958, and March, 1959, respectively. The work, to be complete in four parts, will contain all the chapters on foreign tribes and foreign countries of the *Dynastic Histories.* According to the preface in the first volume, relevant material from the other sections of the *Dynastic Histories* will be published in subsequent series. Further, it is planned to publish collections of material concerning foreign countries from other sources (e.g., works based on what the travelers saw themselves or heard from others, special books based on archives, notes found in the *Local Gazetteers,* the *t'ung k'ao* and the *hui tien,* collections of literary writings, essays, and inscriptions). It need not be said that the completion of this project will greatly facilitate the practical problem of Chinese sources.

A comprehensive edition of all available Chinese sources would enable us to make a fresh start in the study of the historical relations between China and foreign countries. Nobody will deny that our present knowledge, especially of the older periods, is rather confused, in spite of, or perhaps because of, the great quantity of research done by so many eminent scholars, Western as well as Oriental.[17] Only to read through their articles contained in the numerous journals is an arduous job; besides, they offer so many conflicting theories that without a knowledge of the Chinese original texts further research based on a choice of these theories would probably lead to greater confusion.

Chinese texts dealing with foreign peoples are as a rule not difficult to read. Mostly they are a rather dry enumeration of the countries visited, with a matter-of-fact description of their customs and products; it is easy to distinguish these facts from the few fancies which now and then occur, for instance, the cliché story in the *Hsin t'ang shu* about the queen of Ho-ling under whose beneficent rule "objects lost in the streets were not picked up" or the ancient legend told in the *Chu fan*

[17] E.g., cf. the hundreds of books and articles in Japanese quoted in *Research in Japan in History of Eastern and Western Cultural Contacts* (Japanese National Commission for UNESCO; 1957).

chih about San-fo-ch'i, where out of a sudden rent in the earth tens of thousands of buffaloes emerged and ran up the hills in crowds. The dates which various accounts give of one event may sometimes be conflicting. These need not be inherently wrong but may depend for their chronological entries on various original documents which have registered the event; and with this evidence a plausible reconstruction may, in fact, be built up, as has been satisfactorily done with the dates of Chêng Ho's travels.

The chief difficulty lies in the identification of the geographical names, particularly in the older texts before the Sung Dynasty, for the elucidation of which no, or very few, documents exist in the countries concerned. In those texts the names are sometimes hopelessly obscure, while their geographical indications may mean almost anything. There are two ways to arrive at an identification: one is philological, i.e., a reconstruction of the ancient sound of the Chinese character with the help of historical phonology, which is the method preferred by Sinologists; the other is geographical, i.e., a reconstruction on the basis of the indication of situations and distances given by the text. Both methods should, of course, complement each other, and actually they are both used even by the staunchest philologist or the staunchest geographer. It is when the two methods lead to different results that the one abides by a philological decision and the other by a geographical; or when they lead to no results that one resorts to guessing or even to a radical altering of the indications in the text. Thus, based on its sound, P'o-li is seen by Schlegel as (Pulau) Puli, by Pelliot as Bali, by Moens as Pati; [18] because of its topographical description, Groeneveldt, who reads the text wrongly, sees in P'o-li the island of Sumatra, while Bretschneider takes it for Borneo.[19] And so in a passage which describes the shadow of a gnomon falling southward at the summer solstice, Pelliot suggests reading "northward" and "winter-solstice." [20] In Chia Tan's description of Ho-ling as situated four to five days east of Fo-shih, Moens proposes changing east into "west." [21]

When two people from two foreign countries speaking two foreign languages try to understand each other and write down in their own

[18] G. Schlegel, "Geographical Notes, III," *T'oung Pao*, IX (1898), 274–286; P. Pelliot, "Deux Itinéraires de Chine en Inde à la fin du VIIIe siècle," *BEFEO*, IV (1904), 285; J. L. Moens, "Çrīvijaya, Yāva en Katāha," *TBG*, LXXVII (1937), 363.

[19] W. P. Groeneveldt, *Historical Notes on Indonesia and Malaya, Compiled from Chinese Sources* (Jakarta, 1960), p. 84, and also *VBG*, XXXIX (1880), 84; E. V. Bretschneider, quoted by Pelliot in "Deux Itinéraires de Chine en Inde," p. 284.

[20] Pelliot, "Deux Itinéraires de Chine en Inde," p. 294.

[21] Moens, "Çrīvijaya," pp. 352–353.

script the foreign sounds they hear, the result will depend on many factors, first of all a correct tongue and an accurate ear. In addition, there are circumstantial factors: the region from which the speaker originates, which will give his pronunciation a peculiar flavor; the status he has, which will decide his choice between an official name and a colloquial one; the region from which the hearer comes, which will decide the way he transposes the sounds heard; the status he has which, in the case of Chinese, will decide the characters he uses to represent the foreign sounds. Some characters for some reason seem to come more readily into general use, even if they do not represent the foreign sound adequately. Knowledge of foreign countries is gained by direct or indirect contact. The direct contact of Chinese with foreigners took place in different ways: foreigners coming to China as envoys or traders pretending to be envoys, or Chinese going to foreign countries as traders, pilgrims, or envoys. Here again it depends on the people how the sounds will be pronounced and transcribed: envoys, because of their political interests, and pilgrims, because of their religious interests, will probably, more than traders, pay attention to the correct spelling of the names of places and personages. Traders will usually transcribe the names they hear into their own dialects; envoys will probably have to take into account the language at court. With indirect contact the factor of uncertainty in the transcription of foreign sounds is, of course, greater; names, even if originally correctly understood, are apt to change in the course of more than one transmission.

There is, however, method in the madness, and it would be wrong to assume that the Chinese just wrote down every foreign name they heard as it suited their immediate mood and fancy and that, therefore, we have the right now to follow their example and invent our readings arbitrarily and unsystematically, using the modern Peking pronunciation of the Chinese characters and hunting for some name which resembles it, however remotely.[22] On the other hand, I think it somewhat exaggerated to bar any identification which does not strictly adhere

[22] For attempts at elucidating the Chinese system of transcriptions I may mention S. Julien, *Méthode pour déchiffrer et transcrire les noms sanscrits qui se rencontrent dans les livres chinois* (Paris, 1861); F. Hirth, "Chinese Equivalents of the Letter R in Foreign Names," *JRAS North China Branch*, XXI (1886), 214–223; G. Schlegel, "The Secret of the Chinese Method of Transcribing Foreign Sounds," *T'oung Pao*, 2d ser., I (1900), 1–32, 93–124, 219–253; O. Franke, "Grundsätzliches zur Wiedergabe fremder Länder- und Ortsnamen im Chinesischen," in *Sitzungsberichte der Preussischen Akademie der Wissenschaften*, vol. XV (1934); J. R. Hamilton, "Etude des transcriptions chinoises du turc au Xe siècle," Appendix to *Les Ouïghours à l'époque des Cinq Dynasties d'après les documents chinois* (Paris, 1955).

to the severe laws of historical phonology. These laws, after all, have not yet been universally accepted,[23] and our knowledge of the transition periods of Archaic and Ancient Chinese is not yet perfect. Neither do we know whether even in the offices of translators the transcription of names relating to the Southern Sea countries was done or examined by competent linguists, as was the case with Buddhist Sanskrit names and terms. A practical step would probably be to make a list of all the names occurring in Chinese sources with their sounds in Ancient Chinese and the modern dialects. Such a list would, in any case, bring some order into the chaos caused by the transcriptions used by the scholars—English, French, German, and others, each according to his own system—all so bewildering to non-Sinologists.

I may, by way of illustration, conclude this article with a list of works on Chêng Ho. The list is only of a tentative character and does not pretend to be exhaustive.

A. Inscriptions giving particulars of Chêng Ho's ancestry, life, and dates of voyages (cf. Hsiang Ta, Chu Hsieh, Pelliot, and Duyvendak in the works mentioned below under F2, F4, G11, and G15).
   1. Inscription on Chêng Ho's father's grave, made in 1405, published in the *Tien i* by Yüan Chia-ku in 1923.
   2. Inscription in the Palace of the Celestial Spouse at Lung-chiang, Nanking, dated 1416.
   3. Inscription of Ch'üan-chou in memory of Chêng Ho's sacrifice before starting on his (fourth) voyage, dated 1417.
   4. Inscription in the Palace of the Celestial Spouse at Liu-chia-chiang, Chiangsu, dated 1431.
   5. Inscription in the Palace of the Celestial Spouse at Ch'ang-lo, Fuchien, dated 1431.
   6. Inscription in the Great Mosque of Hsi-an, dated 1523.
   7. Inscription in Ceylon in three languages, dated 1409.
B. *Veritable Records of the Ming Dynasty (Ming shih lu)*. The chapters dealing with the reigns of Ch'êng-tsu (1403–1424), Jên-tsung (1425), and Hsüan-tsung (1426–1435).
C. *History of the Ming Dynasty (Ming shih)*.
   1. The sections in the "Basic Annals" on the reigns of Ch'êng-tsu (1403–1424), Jên-tsung (1425), and Hsüan-tsung (1426–1435).

[23] Cf. the difference of opinion concerning the ancient pronunciation of *Yeh t'iao* between R. A. Stein and P. Demiéville: R. A. Stein, "Le Lin-yi, sa localisation, sa contribution à la formation du Champa et ses liens avec la Chine," *Han hiue* (Bulletin du Centre d'Etudes Sinologique de Pékin), vol. II (1947), and Demiéville's review of Stein, *T'oung Pao*, XL (1951), 346.

2. The biography of Chêng Ho in the "Biographies" section.

3. The chapters on foreign countries in the "Biographies" section.

D. Works on Chêng Ho's voyages by his companions.

1. *Ying yai shêng lan,* compiled in 1451 by Ma Huan, who accompanied Chêng Ho on three of his voyages and described twenty countries. There is a printed edition, revised and annotated by Fêng Ch'êng-chün, preface 1934, reprinted Shanghai, 1955.

2. *Hsing ch'a shêng lan,* compiled in 1436 by Fei Hsin, who accompanied Chêng Ho on four of his voyages and described twenty-two countries which he had visited himself and twenty-two of which he had heard. There is a printed edition, revised and annotated by Fêng Ch'êng-chün, preface 1936, reprinted Shanghai, 1954.

3. *Hsi yang fan kuo chih,* compiled in 1434 by Kung Chên, who accompanied Chêng Ho on his seventh, and last, voyage (1431–1433) and described twenty countries. The work, long considered to be lost, has lately been recovered and is now in the Peking National Library (see Hsiang Ta, below under F2, p. 564, additional note 2).

4. *Wu pei chih,* collection of maps by Mao Yüan-i, preface 1621, in which as ch. 240 are to be found twenty-four maps describing Chêng Ho's voyage routes, probably drawn by his navigating officer.

E. Works by Ming authors containing material partly taken from the works mentioned above.

1. *Ch'ien wên chi,* compiled by Chu Yün-ming (1460–1526), occurs in the *Chi lu hui pien.*

2. *Hsi yang ch'ao kung tien lu,* compiled in 1520 by Huang Hsing-tsêng, occurs, for example, in the *Yüeh ya t'ang ts'ung shu.*

3. *Hai yü,* compiled in 1536 by Huang Chung, *Ssŭ k'u ch'üan shu* edition.

4. *Huang ming ssŭ i k'ao,* compiled in 1564 by Chêng Hsiao, occurs in the *Wu hsüeh pien.*

5. *Shu yü chou tzŭ lu,* compiled in 1583 by Yen Ts'ung-chien, Palace Museum edition.

6. *Tung hsi yang k'ao,* compiled in 1618 by Chang Hsieh, *Ssŭ k'u ch'üan shu* edition.

7. *San pao t'ai chien hsi yang chi,* compiled in 1597 by Lo Mou-têng (a romantic account of Chêng Ho's travels), several editions.

F. Studies on Chêng Ho by modern Chinese authors.

1. Liang Ch'i-ch'ao, *Chêng-ho chuan*, compiled in 1906, in *Yin ping shih chuan chi*, vol. IX, Shanghai, 1941.
2. Hsiang Ta, *Kuan-yü san-pao t'ai-chien hsia hsi-yang ti chi-chung tzŭ-liao*, compiled in 1929, reprinted in *T'ang-tai ch'ang-an yü hsi-yü wên-ming*, Peking, 1957.
3. Fêng Ch'êng-chün, *Chêng-ho hsia hsi-yang k'ao* (translation of Pelliot's article; see below under G9), Peking, 1955.
4. Chu Hsieh, *Chêng Ho*, Peking, 1956.
5. Chêng Hao-shêng, *Chêng-ho i-shih hui-pien*, Shanghai, 1948.
6. Kam Seng Kioe, *Sam Po* (in Indonesian, description of Chêng Ho's temple at Semarang, includes his biography), Semarang, no date.

G. Studies on Chêng Ho by Western scholars.
1. W. F. Mayers, "Chinese Explorations of the Indian Ocean during the Fifteenth Century," *China Review*, III (1874–1875), 219–225, 321–331, and IV (1875–1876), 61–67.
2. W. P. Groeneveldt, "Notes on the Malay Archipelago and Malacca," *Verhandelingen van het Genootschap van Kunsten en Wetenschappen*, vol. XXXIX (1879). Republished under the title *Historical Notes on Indonesia and Malaya*, Jakarta, 1960.
3. G. Phillips, "The Sea-Ports of India and Ceylon," *JRAS North China Branch*, XX (1885), 209–226, and XXI (1886), 30–42.
4. G. Phillips, "Mahuan's Account of the Kingdom of Bengala," *JRAS* (1895), 523–535, and "Mahuan's Account of Cochin, Calicut, and Aden," *JRAS* (1896), 341–351.
5. W. P. Groeneveldt, "Supplementary Jottings," *T'oung Pao*, 1st ser., VII (1896), 113–134.
6. G. Schlegel, "Geographical Notes," *T'oung Pao*, 1st ser., IX (1898), 177–200, X (1899), 33–52, and 2d ser., II (1901), 107–138, 167–182, 329–377.
7. W. W. Rockhill, "Notes on the Relations and Trade of China with the Eastern Archipelago and the Coast of the Indian Ocean during the Fourteenth Century," *T'oung Pao*, XVI (1915), 61–159, 236–271, 374–392, 435–467, 604–626.
8. J. J. L. Duyvendak, *Ma Huan Re-examined*, Amsterdam, 1933.
9. P. Pelliot, "Les grands voyages maritimes chinois au début du XVe siècle," *T'oung Pao*, XXX (1933), 237–452.
10. T. Yamamoto, "Chêng Ho's Expeditions to the South Sea under the Ming Dynasty," *Tōyō gakuhō*, XXI, no. 3 (1934), 1–45; no. 4, 36–86.

11. P. Pelliot, "Notes additionnelles sur Tcheng Houo et sur ses voyages," *T'oung Pao*, XXXI (1935), 274–308.

12. P. Pelliot, "Encore à propos de voyages de Tcheng Houo," *T'oung Pao*, XXXII (1936), 210–222.

13. J. V. Mills, "Malaya in the Wu-pei-chih Charts," *JRASMB*, XV, pt. 3 (1937), 1–48.

14. J. J. L. Duyvendak, "Sailing Directions of Chinese Voyages," *T'oung Pao*, XXXIV (1938–1939), 230–237.

15. J. J. L. Duyvendak, "The True Dates of the Chinese Maritime Expeditions in the Early Fifteenth Century," *T'oung Pao*, XXXIV (1938–1939), 341–412.

16. J. J. L. Duyvendak, "Voyages de Tcheng Houo," *Monumenta Cartographica Africae et Aegypti*, vol. IV, Leyden, 1939.

17. W. Z. Mulder, "The Wu pei chih Charts," *T'oung Pao*, XXXVII (1942), 1–14.

18. J. V. Mills, "Notes on Early Chinese Voyages," *JRAS* (1951), 3–25.

19. J. J. L Duyvendak, "A Chinese *Divina Commedia*," *T'oung Pao*, XLI (1952), 255–316.

20. J. J. L. Duyvendak, "Desultory Notes on the Hsi-yang-chi," *T'oung Pao*, XLII (1953), 1–35.

Since the above article was written, some five years ago, several new publications on our subject have appeared in China. Among these are *Chung-wai chiao-t'ung shih-chi ts'ung-k'an* (Collection of Historical Documents on the Relations between China and Foreign Countries), under the editorship of Hsiang Ta, and published by the Chung-hua shu-chii, Peking. The collection will consist eventually of 42 books. Four books in three volumes appeared in 1961, viz., *Chêng ho hang hait'u* (Maps of Chêng Ho's Voyages, facsimile edition of chapter 240 of the *Wu pei chih* by Mao Yüan-i, see above under D4); *Hsi yang fan kuo chih*, by Kung Chên (based on a manuscript in the Peking National Library, see above under D3); *Shun fêng hsiang sung*, a work of the sixteenth century, and *Chih nan chêng fa*, a work of the beginning of the eighteenth century (both based on manuscripts in the Bodleian Library, Oxford, and edited in one volume under the title *Liang-chung hai-tao chen-ching* [Two Treatises on Sailing Directions]).

XI

Recent Japanese Sources for Indonesian Historiography

By KOICHI KISHI

Senior Specialist, Research Division, Institute of Asian Economic Affairs, Tokyo

I

VERY little has been done as yet with source materials in Japan relating to the occupation period, 1942–1945. They are, however, a rich source of information indispensable, of course, for an examination of Japanese Military Government policy and useful also for information on any analyses of conditions in Indonesia during the war years, particularly with reference to preparations for the Proclamation of Independence.

It is to be hoped that the following listing of these materials will be of help to the non-Japanese-speaking student in giving him at least a general idea of what may be found and where to find it and will thus encourage foreign scholars to undertake research in this period. Foreign scholars may be assured of the full cooperation of the agencies holding these documents in matters of access and translation.

In the second section of this article, I have listed and described some of the recent research by Japanese scholars in Indonesian history.

A. Documents concerning the fundamental policies of the Japanese Military Government in occupied Indonesia during the period 1942–1945.

 1. *Nanpō Senryōchi Gyōsei Jisshi Yōryō* (General Principles for the Administration of the Southern Occupied Territories), decided upon at a liaison conference between the Headquarters and the Government, Nov. 20, 1941.

 2. *Senryōchi Gunsei Jisshi ni kansuru Rikukaigun Chuō Kyōtei*

(Basic Agreement between the Army and Navy concerning Military Administration of the Occupied Territories), decided upon Nov. 26, 1941.

3. *Nanpō Keizai Taisaku Yōkō* (Principles for Economic Policies for the Southern Area), decided by the ministers concerned on Dec. 12, 1941, and reported at a liaison conference between the Headquarters and the Government, Dec. 12, 1941.

4. *Senryōchi Gunsei Shori Yōryō* (Principles for the Military Administration of the Navy's Occupied Territories), March 14, 1942.

5. *New Guinea Gunsei Jisshi Yōkō* (Principles for the Military Administration in New Guinea).

6. "Java no Gunsei Shidō Yōryō" (Guiding Principles for the Military Administration in Java), *Djawa Shinbun*, Feb. 3, 1943.

7. *Sumatra Gunsei Jisshi Yōryō* (Principles for the Military Administration of Sumatra), 25th Army, April 27, 1942.

8. *Nanpō Keizai Rikugun Shori Yōryō* (The Army's Economic Policies in the Southern Area), June 5, 1943.

The fundamental policies of the Japanese Army concerning the military administration of Indonesia can be divided into two parts. Documents 1, 2, and 3 mentioned above deal with the over-all policies, while 4, 6, 7, and 8, which are based on them, deal with the principal policy for the military administration of the areas occupied respectively by the Army and the Navy. Document 5 is based on 4 and applies only to New Guinea.

All these fundamental policies of military administration were prescribed uniformly except that each reflects special regional concerns. The essential aims of military administration were the restoration of public order, rapid acquisition of important resources for national defense, and the self-support of the operating forces. These three aims determined the basic policy of military administration, and the economic and housing policies were geared into them. The economic policy, as outlined in Document 3, was directed at obtaining resources important to the continuation of the war, at establishing the self-sufficiency of the Great East Asia Co-prosperity Sphere, and at building up Japanese economic strength through these two means.

These materials are in a collection of the Ohkuma Institute of Social Sciences, Waseda University, and the Military History Section (Senshi Shitsu) of the Defense Board also has a collection.

In the "Plan for the Administration of the Southern Occupied Territories," the first of the fundamental policy documents listed in section

A, there is a separate section concerning the position of the southern occupied territories, including Indonesia, after the war. The intentions of the Japanese are further clarified in the following documents in section B.

B. Documents giving the central and on-the-spot opinions concerning the future of the southern occupied territories which played an important role in the decisions of the military administration.

    1. *Senryōchi Kizoku Fukuan* (Plans for the Future of the Occupied Territories), Jan. 14, 1943.

    2. *Gunsei Sōkan Shiji* (Instructions of the Inspector General of Military Administration), Aug. 7, 1942.

    3. Osamu Shūdan, *Java no Kizoku ni kansuru Iken* (*Osamu* Command, Proposal concerning the Future of Java).

Documents 1 and 2 are very important in that they clarify Japan's aims in the Pacific war. It was the intention that strategically important but thinly populated regions where independence was not likely in the near future would become Japanese colonies. But this policy was a military secret during the war, and therefore public discussion of the matter was forbidden at the time.

In Document 3 relating to the future of Java, it is said that Java was to be given high-level autonomy, but not independence, after the war. This proposal aroused considerable discussion, as the question of Indonesian independence or autonomy had not been raised by the Japanese Imperial Headquarters.

These documents, like the ones indicated above, are to be found at the Ohkuma Institute of Social Sciences, Waseda University, and also at the Military History Section (Senshi Shitsu) of the Defense Board.

C. Documents of the Central Government concerning the problem of Indonesian independence.

From 1943, when the Japanese Army displayed signs of defeat, to August, 1945, the Japanese Central Government had continual discussions about Indonesian independence because of strategic needs to secure Indonesia. Most of the documents on this matter were burned at the time of surrender, but a part of them still exist.

    1. Gaimushō Sōmukyoku Sōmuka (General Affairs Section, General Affairs Bureau, Foreign Ministry), *Tōindo Kankei Dai 1 Gō: Tōindo Dokuritsu Shisaku ni kansuru Ken* (Document no. 1 concerning the East Indies: On the Policy concerning the Independence of the East Indies).

2. ——, *Tōindo Kankei Dai 2 Gō: Java tō no Dokuritsu ni kansuru Ken* (Document no. 2 concerning the East Indies: Concerning the Independence of Java, etc.).

3. ——, *Tōindo Kankei Dai 4 Gō: Tōindo Dokuritsu ni kansuru Ken* (Document no. 4 concerning the East Indies: Concerning the Independence of the East Indies).

4. ——, *Tōindo Kankei Dai 5 Gō: Tōindo Dokuritsu Sochi ni kansuru Ken* (Document no. 5 concerning the East Indies: Concerning Measures for the Independence of the East Indies).

5. ——, *Tōindo Kankei Dai 6 Gō: Tōindo Dokuritsu Shidō ni kansuru Ken* (Document no. 6 concerning the East Indies: Concerning the Preparations for the Independence of the East Indies).

6. Gaimushō Nanpō Jimu Kyoku Seimuka (Political Section, Southern Affairs Bureau, Foreign Ministry), *Tōindo Dokuritsu Kankei Kimitsu Shorui* (Secret Documents on Indonesian Independence), July-Aug., 1945.

These documents are kept at the Ohkuma Institute of Social Sciences, Waseda University.

D. Osamu Shūdan Gunshireibu (The Military Headquarters of the *Osamu* Command, *Zen Jawa Kaikyō Jōkyō Chōsasho* (Research Report on the Conditions of Islam in All Java), 1943, 388 pp.

This report seems to have been translated into Japanese by an Indonesian scholar at the request of the occupation forces in Java for the study of Javanese Islam. My guess is that it was from a survey of the Kantoor van Inlandsche Zaken (Office of Native Affairs).

It is a research report on the conditions of Islam in various places as a means for analyzing the special character of Javanese Islam. That is, it describes the history of the propagation of Islam, the organization and beliefs of Javanese Islam, mysticism, and Islamic religious functions and customs. In "A Research Report on the Situation of Islam in All Java in 1942," which is the main subject, the author presents a statistical survey on the numbers of hadjis, followers of mysticism, mosques, persons who had been in Mecca, and Islamic schools and teachers.

E. Jawa Shinbunsha, *Jawa Nenkan* (Java Yearbook).

This was compiled by Jawa Shinbunsha founded in Java by the Asahi Press during the occupation. It offers materials on all the political, economic, social, and legal problems in Java during the occupation and has become the main source for *De Japanse bezetting van Indonesië en haar volkenrechterlijke zijde* (Leyden, 1954), by A. A. Zorab.

The *Jawa Nenkan* is now preserved at the Asahi Press, Tokyo.

F. Periodicals published by the Japanese during the occupation.

Indonesia was divided into two parts: Java and Sumatra were ruled by the Army during the occupation, while Borneo, Celebes, and the region to the east of them were ruled by the Navy. As media of mass communication in these areas, there were five newspapers which were published under the supervision of the Military Government. These were the *Jawa Shinbun* in Java, the *Borneo Shinbun* in Borneo, the *Celebes Shinbun* in Celebes, the *Sumatra Shinbun* in Sumatra, and the *Ceram Shinbun* in the Ceram area. The *Jawa* and the *Borneo Shinbun*, the *Celebes Shinbun*, and the *Ceram Shinbun* were taken charge of respectively by the Asahi Press, the Mainichi Press and the Yomiuri Press. The Dōmei Press edited the *Sumatra Shinbun* with the cooperation of domestic local newspapers in Japan. They contain very important materials relating to the daily development of military administration. The Asahi Press (Tokyo) has the *Djawa* and the *Borneo Shinbun* from the beginning issue of December 8, 1942, to March 20, 1945. The Mainichi Press (Tokyo) has copies of the *Celebes Shinbun* for almost the same period. Regarding the other two periodicals, I do not think they are to be found in Tokyo.

Shin Djawa (New Java) was the only magazine in the occupied area, and it was published up to no. 6 by Jawa Shinbunsha. As many people concerned with the military administration presented their opinions and articles in this periodical, it is a very important document. It is now kept at the Asahi Press.

G. 1. Shunkichirō Miyoshi, *Jawa Gunsei Ryakushi* (A Short History of the Military Administration in Java).

Memoirs of many people who participated in World War II have been made public, but comparatively few persons in charge of military administration took note of military administration. This memoir of Miyoshi Shunkichirō's is about important questions of military administration which he encountered from March, 1942, when he landed on Java, to January, 1946, when he came back to his native country. It also concerns his direct contacts with Indonesian leaders on important political matters. It is particularly valuable as a source of information on *Putera*, the Javanese Youth Organization, and on the problem of preparation for independence.

2. Shigetada Nishijima, *Dai 3 no Shinsō* (The Third Truth; unpublished manuscript).

This is the translation of Adam Malik's *Riwajat dan Perdjuangan Sekitar Proklamasi Kemerdekaan Indonesia,* with Nishijima's comments and corrections appended to each section. Since Nishijima was behind the scenes during the events surrounding the Proclamation of Independence, August 17, 1945, this is the most important of the Japanese memoirs relating to Indonesia.

3. Shizuo Miyamoto, *Jawa Shūsen Shori Ki* (Memorandum on Actions in Java at the End of the War).

Jawa Shūsen Shori Ki is a document by Commander Miyamoto, a staff officer of the 16th Army, on the Japanese Army's surrender in Java and on operations and military administration in Java up to that time.

II

There are only a few scholars in Japan who are engaged in the study of Indonesian history, and their field is rather limited. Among the studies based upon consultation of original data, the following are noteworthy. They appeared after 1945 and are concerned with various problems dealing with the period of the East India Company and with modern political history.

A. Research articles using Chinese materials.

The following two articles were based upon consultation of materials in classical Chinese (which cannot be used fully by Western scholars because of linguistic difficulties):

1. Tomosaburo Niwa, "Gen Seiso Jawa Ensei Zakkō: Tokuni Gunshi narabini Kaisen no Kazu ni tsuite" (Impressions on the Expedition of Yüan Ancestors to Java—Especially on the Number of Soldiers and Battleships), *Shigaku Kenkyu,* LIII (Jan., 1954), 57–63.

2. Kozo Tasaka, "Jawa Boruneo Kaikyō-shi Josetsu" (An Introduction to the History of Islam in Java and Borneo—as a part of an introduction to the history of Islam in Southeast Asia), *Tohogaku Ronshu,* IX (Oct., 1954), 59–74.

The latter investigates Islam in the area east of Java and Borneo before the fifteenth or sixteenth century and concludes that the history of Islam in Java does not date back as far as the latter half of the tenth century and that Indonesian converts continued to increase in

number from the fifteenth century. It also suggests that special attention should be paid to the conversion of Chinese merchants in Indonesia.

B. Research articles using documents of the period of the East India
   Company.

Dr. Seiichi Iwao, professor at Tokyo University, who is the leading
scholar in this field and who made a study of Japanese towns in South
Asia before the war, is the author of the book, *Nanyo Nihonjin Machi
no Kenkyu* (A Study of Japanese Towns in the South Seas; Tokyo, 1940,
367 pp.). He used documents in the archives in The Hague and in
Jakarta, which were written in Middle Dutch. In addition, he has written the following articles:

1. Seiichi Iwao, "17 Seiki Batabia Ijū Nipponjin no Dorei Torihiki"
   (The Japanese in Batavia during the Seventeenth Century and
   Their Slave Trade), *Tohogaku Ronshu*, I (Feb., 1954), 26–55.
2. Seiichi Iwao, "Amboina no Shoki Shinamachi ni tsuite" (The
   Early Chinese Community in Amboina), *Toyogakuho*, XXXIII,
   no. 3 (Aug., 1951), 1–43.
3. Seiichi Iwao, "17 Seiki Batabia Ijū Nipponjin to Kin'yū-gyo"
   (The Japanese in Batavia during the Seventeenth Century and
   Their Financial Business), *Nihon Gakushiin Kiyo*, II, no. 1
   (March, 1956), 1–20.
4. Seiichi Iwao, "Senreibo o tsūjite mitaru Batabia no Nipponjin"
   (The Japanese in Batavia as Seen through the Baptismal Records), *Tohogaku*, I (1951), 76–94.
5. Seiichi Iwao, "On the Epistle of an Annamese King Asking
   Reinforcements of the Dutch Governor General of the East
   Indies" (in English), *Toyogakuho*, XXXVI, no. 4 (March, 1954),
   1–24.

Besides these, Akira Nagazumi, a younger scholar and a research
worker in the Oriental Library, has published the following outstanding article:

6. Akira Nagazumi, "Oranda no Tōindo Keiei Shoki ni okeru Sham
   Bōeki no Yakuwari" (The Role of Trade with Siam in the Early
   Stage of Dutch Administration of the East Indies), *Toyogakuho*,
   XXXIX, no. 2 (Sept., 1956), 189–222.

As to the East India Company, the following article was written by
Professor Ryosei Kobayashi of Senshu University:

7. Ryosei Kobayashi, "Shokuminchi Tōchi Keiei no Ichi-ruikei:

Oranda Tōindo-gaisha no Baai" (An Example of Colonial Administration and Management—the Dutch East India Company), *Seikei Ronso,* IX, no. 5 (March, 1956), 1–31.

C. Research articles on modern political history.

Concerning Indonesia in the Dutch colonial days of the nineteenth century, however, there are few studies which are worth noticing.

 1. Ryosei Kobayashi, "19 Seiki ni okeru Oranda no Indoneshia Shokumin Seisaku" (The Dutch Colonial Policy toward Indonesia during the Nineteenth Century), *Senshu Daigaku Ronshu,* I (Jan., 1952), 1–14.

During the twentieth century, Indonesia awoke nationally and stood at a turning point in its history. In connection with various problems relating to this independence there are the following articles:

 2. Ryosei Kobayashi, "Indoneshia Dokuritsu no tameno Tōsō" (Indonesian Struggle for Independence), 1949, 45 pp. included in the *Keizaigaku Zenshu,* Tokyo, 1949.

 3. Ryosei Kobayashi, "Indoneshia no Minzokushugi Undo" (The Nationalist Movement in Indonesia), *Shakai Kagaku,* vol. XI (Jan., 1948).

 4. Mikio Sumiya, "Ajia no Nashonalizumu" (Asian Nationalism: Three Types as Exemplified by Indonesia), *Tōyō Bunka—Oriental Culture,* X (Aug., 1952), 12–36.

 5. Kenzo Tsukishima, "Indoneshia ni okeru Gōgisei to Senseisei" (On the Political System of Some Malaysian Tribes at the Time of the Dutch East Indies), *Tōyō Bunka—Oriental Culture,* XI Nov., 1952), 27–67.

Among these four articles, Professor Ryosei Kobayashi's "Indonesian Struggle for Independence" is important reading for the study of the nationalist movement in Indonesia after the war. Mikio Sumiya's article, which criticizes Professor Kobayashi's views, is noteworthy.

Concerning Indonesia during the period of the Japanese occupation from 1942 to 1945, the year in which modern Indonesia began, there have been many studies made by Western scholars, but very few by Japanese. A recent landmark is the study made at the Social Science Research Institute, Waseda University, which was launched in 1956 through a grant from the Rockefeller Foundation. In this study, entitled "The Impact of the Japanese Military Government on Indonesian Independence," an attempt was made to be as objective as possible —by analyzing Western and Indonesian views on the one hand and

Japanese on the other. The study was published in June, 1959, under the title "The Japanese Military Administration in Indonesia."

    6. Koichi Kishi, Shigetada Nishijima, and others, Ohkuma Institute of Social Science, Waseda University, *Indoneshia ni okeru Nihon Gunsei no Kenkyu* (A Study of the Japanese Military Administration in Indonesia), Tokyo, 1959, 630 pp. (collection of related materials, pp. 529–603, and Bibliography, pp. 605–630).

There exists only one article, mentioned below, which deals with important problems in relation to the armed opposition against the Netherlands for the four years from the time of the Proclamation of Independence to the transfer of sovereignty in 1949, as well as with the interference of the United Nations.

    7. Masaru Yanaihara, "Ringajati Kyōtei" (The Linggadjati Agreement), *Mita Gakkai Zasshi*, April, May, and June, 1953, pp. 67–78, 72–85, and 64–75.

D. Others.

Lastly, the following is an excellent article which deals with the studies made by Christian missionaries in Indonesia during the Dutch colonial days.

    1. Takashi Nakamura, "Tōindo ni okeru Kirisutokyō Senkyōshi no Gakuteki Kiyo" (Academic Contributions of Christian Missionaries in the East Indies), *Nihon Bunka*, XXVIII (1950), 33–81.

The writer aims, in this article, at elucidating the efforts made by missionaries to study scientifically Indonesian culture, devoting space to the academic activities of the missionaries Jan Frederik Gerrit Brumund (1814–1863), Caspar Adam Laurens van Troostenburg de Bruijn (1829–1902), Dr. Benjamin Frederik Matthes (1818–1908), Albertus Christiaan Kruijt (1859–1949), Nicolaus Adriani (1865–1926), and others.

An Indonesian history written by a Japanese scholar is very rare. There exists only one, mentioned below.

    2. Ryosei Kobayashi, *Tonan Azia Shakai no ichi Ruikei—Indonesia Shakai Keisheishi* (A Stereotype of Southeast Asian Society—A History of the Formation of Indonesian Society), Tokyo, 1949, 166 pp.

Dr. Kobayashi studied the historical process of the formation of Indonesian society. His study stood on the assumption that the impact of foreign cultures has not been so crucial as is usually thought and thus that the present structure of Indonesian society derives from the original indigenous institutions. He argues, therefore, that a firm understanding of its social structure must be based on a study of the emergence and development of its society.

This book is divided into nine chapters. Chapter I is the introduction; Chapter II contains a study of society under Hindu political power. Chapter III deals with society under the Islamic political powers. Chapters IV–VIII deal with the historical development of Indonesian society under the Dutch regime, and Chapter IX is the conclusion.

Approximately fifteen years ago, Namposhi Kenkyu Kai (Society for Southern Asian Studies) was organized at Tokyo University under the direction of Dr. Tatsuro Yamamoto. This society has been of considerable importance in promoting the study of South and Southeast Asian history. Prior to World War II, South and Southeast Asian history was studied merely as a part of general Oriental history and, with the exception of the works of a few scholars, drew primarily on Chinese history source materials. Little work was done in South and Southeast Asian history on a country-by-country basis.

Since the war, following the lead of the Western countries—and particularly the United States—Japan has also devoted more attention to the study of the history of the newly emerging countries of this area, including of course Indonesia. However, there was no Japanese journal devoted to South and Southeast Asian history until 1959, when, with the financial aid of the Harvard-Yenching Institute, Namposhi Kenkyu Kai brought out the first issue of *Namposhi Kenkyu* (Southern Asia). This journal enables South and Southeast Asian historians to publish the results of their research and writing; and in the volume issued in 1960 there appeared two articles on Indonesian history. One was Norio Tanaka, "Oranda Tōindo Kaisha no Seibu Jawa ni okeru Gimu Kyushutsu Seido (verplicht leverantiën) ni tsuite" (On "Forced Deliveries" in West Java under the Dutch East India Company), *Namposhi Kenkyu,* II (1960), 81–130. The second was Shijiro Nagaoka, "17–18 Seiki Batavia Tōgyo to Kakyo" (Sugar Manufacturing and the Chinese in Batavia during the 17th and 18th Centuries), *Namposhi Kenkyu,* II (1960), 131–156.

Both articles are studies of the economic problems of Java during the period of the Dutch East India Company in the seventeenth and eighteenth centuries. The first deals with the development and implementation of the "forced deliveries" system in West Java and its impact on the native society. The second describes Chinese sugar manufacturing in West Java before the introduction of the Western sugar industry and discusses the monopolistic sugar-purchasing policy of the Company in the eighteenth century and its impact on the economic life of the Chinese in Batavia.

XII

Some Portuguese Sources
for Indonesian Historiography

By C. R. BOXER

Camoens Professor of Portuguese, King's College,
University of London

IN the course of his famous castigation of the second and third volumes of Dr. Stapel's *Geschiedenis van Nederlandsch Indië* for the Europe-centric outlook which dominated most of that work, the late J. C. van Leur observed: "In this connection it is impossible to overrate the significance for early Indonesian history of Portuguese source materials, for they give a picture of the Indonesian world before any European influence was really at work." [1] More recently, an English historian of Southeast Asia has written:

With the coming of the Portuguese to South-east Asia at the beginning of the sixteenth century the first serious attempts were made to carry out what we might call regional surveys of the area. These surveys had their limitations; they were somewhat hasty and superficial, and rather coloured by prejudice: but on the whole they were extremely informative, generally honest, and as scientific as could be expected of European travellers coming for the first time face to face with the strange peoples and civilizations of another continent over four hundred years ago. [2]

Perhaps these claims are pitched rather high, but they do indicate that a survey of some Portuguese sources for the history of Indonesia may prove useful. This can most conveniently be done by discussing briefly (1) the official chroniclers for the early period of direct Portuguese

[1] J. C. van Leur, *Indonesian Trade and Society* (The Hague, 1955), pp. 261–262.
[2] Brian Harrison, *South-east Asia: A Short History* (London, 1954), pp. 54–55.

contacts (ca. 1511–1650), (2) other secular narrative and eyewitness accounts, and (3) the missionary literature. By way of conclusion we will glance at the principal modern works in this field and mention some Spanish sources.

João de Barros (ca. 1496–1570) may be termed the first great "colonial" historian and pioneer Orientalist. He was also a good classical scholar and a very capable administrator. Apart from a voyage to Guinea in 1522, he seems never to have left Portugal; but he had a life-long interest in the lands and peoples of Asia which his official position enabled him to gratify. From 1525 to his retirement in 1567 he held high office in the Casa da India, or India House, for most of the time as factor (*feitor*), a post corresponding to Crown agent for the Portuguese colonies. As such, he saw all of the official and most of the unofficial correspondence which passed between the authorities at Lisbon and their subordinates in the East; and he met all the leading officials, merchants, and adventurers who lived to return home. He also handled all the business relating to the dispatch of the annual India fleets and the disposal of their return cargoes. He was thus able to procure Persian, Arabic, Indian, and Chinese books and manuscripts, engaging educated slaves or freemen of those nationalities to translate them for him. The manuscripts included the (since lost) Persian chronicle of Turan Shah and an Arabic chronicle of Kilwa. He also tried to obtain a chronicle of the Malay rulers of Malacca, but in this, unfortunately, he was unsuccessful. Nevertheless, he was able to secure and record the story of Parameswara as the founder of Malacca.

As Factor of the India House, Barros spent his scanty leisure hours in compiling his great chronicle of *Deeds Done by the Portuguese in Their Discovery and Conquest of the Seas and Lands of the East,* eventually published under the collective title of *Decadas da Asia.* The first draft of this truly monumental work was finished in 1539, but he was still making additions ten years later, and publication did not begin until 1552. The second volume was printed in 1553, and the third followed in 1563, but the fourth was not edited from Barros' unfinished draft until 1615. These four volumes take the story only as far as 1538, the work being continued by Diogo do Couto as described below. Barros also wrote in draft a number of more specialized works dealing with Asian geography, commerce, and navigation, to which he makes frequent reference in his *Decadas,* but these unfortunately disappeared after his death. As a foremost recipient of royal patronage from his earliest youth, as a prominent functionary of the Crown, and as the official chronicler of the deeds of the Portuguese in the Indies for the benefit and the emulation of posterity, Barros naturally tended to soft-pedal or slur over their misdeeds, although he neither lacked a critical sense nor did he excuse their misconduct on all occasions. He was a convinced and wholehearted "imperialist" in the nineteenth-century sense of the term, firmly believing that Portugal had a divine mission to spread its religion and its rule by forcible measures in certain circumstances. Such an attitude was almost inevitable in his age and with his education (there was no Las Casas at the Portuguese Court), and it was largely offset by his genuine interest in the civilizations of Asia and their varying geographical and economic backgrounds.

China was the country which fascinated João de Barros most, but he has some interesting things to say about Southeast Asia in general and Indonesia in particular. He gives us an excellent account of Siam, being the earliest writer to throw light on the doings and habits of the Thai people, as distinct from recording the pomp and ceremony of the internecine wars of their kings, which alone were supposed by the Thai annalists to constitute history. He also anticipated Sir Henry Yule by over three centuries in his tentative identification of Marco Polo's Caugigu with Laos. His description of Sumatra fills one of the biggest gaps in Polo's *Travels* and was probably the fullest and most accurate account of that island which appeared in print until the publication of Valentijn's encyclopedic *Oud en Nieuw Oost-Indien* in 1724. His description of Java is both more superficial and more erroneous, since he ascribed a Chinese origin to the Javanese and made the western region (Sunda) a separate island, while acknowledging that the Javanese themselves regarded the island as one. He expressly states that he had given a much fuller account of Java in his great "Geography," which, as noted above, disappeared after his death. This is all the more to be regretted since this work likewise contained a wealth of economic information. It may be said to have anticipated in some ways Milburn's *Oriental Commerce* (London, 1813) and Crawfurd's *Descriptive Dictionary of the Indian Islands and Adjacent Countries* (Edinburgh, 1856). Both these authors, incidentally, quote freely and approvingly from Barros' *Decadas*, even at that distance of time. Where Barros' published work can be compared with the original documents, it stands the test well. The present-day historian of Indonesia has no reason to quarrel with Crawfurd's observation of a century ago that "for the time in which he lived, Barros certainly made a faithful and judicious use of his opportunities." [3]

[3] Crawfurd, p. 40. For further details on Barros as a pioneer Orientalist and historian of Asia cf. C. R. Boxer, *Three Historians of Portuguese Asia: Barros, Couto*

We have insufficient space to consider the other chroniclers in detail, but this is hardly necessary. Their outlook, advantages, and limitations were basically those of João de Barros, and they must be used in much the same way. They were all—with the possible exception of António Bocarro, who had been a crypto-Jew for many years—convinced that Portugal had a divine mission to spread Christianity in the East, if necessary by militant means; they were all incapable of appreciating Islam or the Moslem viewpoint; they were primarily interested in recounting the exploits of their own countrymen and were only secondarily concerned with the Asian peoples with whom they fought or traded; they were all prevented from carrying criticism too far by virtue of their official positions. On the other hand, most of them had access to records and correspondence, much of which has since perished. Some of them spent many years in the East, and they wrote about much of it from personal knowledge though only one of them, Fernão Lopes de Castanheda (1500–1559), actually visited Indonesia and got as far as the Moluccas.[4]

Of course, they differed in emphasis and ability among themselves. Diogo do Couto (ca. 1543–1616), who became the first keeper of the archives at Goa and continued the *Decadas* of João de Barros, also followed his predecessor's practice of consulting Asian traditional history and source material, when he could do this through the medium of interpreters. He was much more outspokenly critical than Barros, and his *Dialogo do soldado prático* (Dialogue of the Veteran Soldier) is probably the most vitriolic denunciation of Portuguese behavior in Asia which was ever penned. Not surprisingly, it was not printed until nearly two centuries after his death.[5] Castanheda, though he visited Indonesia, has less to say about the indigenous kingdoms than João de Barros; and though his work can be used to check that of the latter, it is written from a narrower viewpoint. By the time that António Bocarro

---

and Bocarro (Macao, 1948), pp. 6–12; I. A. Macgregor, "Some Aspects of Portuguese Historical Writing of the Sixteenth and Seventeenth Centuries on South East Asia," in D. G. E. Hall, ed., *Historians of South East Asia* (London, 1961), pp. 179–186.

[4] First published in 1551–1561, the most convenient edition of Castanheda's *Historia do descobrimento e conquista da India pelos Portugueses* is that published at Coimbra, 4 vols., 1924–1933.

[5] In 1790, to be exact; but there is a better modern edition edited by M. Rodrigues Lapa, *Diogo do Couto: O soldado prático; Texto restituido* (Lisbon, 1937). For Couto and his *Decadas* cf. the articles cited in note 3 above, together with C. R. Boxer, *The Tragic History of the Sea, 1589–1622* (Hakluyt Society, vol. CXI; London, 1959), pp. 30–42.

compiled his encyclopedic "Livro do Estado da India Oriental" (Book of the State of East India) in 1635, the Portuguese were no longer a power in Indonesia, but he has an interesting account of Malacca.[6] The "History" of the Moluccas during the governorship of Sancho de Vasconcellos which has been ascribed to Bocarro is not by him but merely has a forwarding note from his pen.[7] Braz de Albuquerque's uncritical life of his great father, though valuable for its account of Malacca at the time of the Portuguese conquest in 1511, is of much less value than the collected edition of the letters and dispatches of Affonso de Albuquerque published at Lisbon in 1884–1915.[8]

All these chroniclers, and others who could be mentioned, understandably concentrated their attention on events in Malayan waters, with Malacca as the center of interest, and secondarily on the Moluccas, particularly Ternate, Tidore, and Ambon. About the rest of Indonesia they have relatively little to say; and some islands such as Borneo, Madura, and Timor receive only an occasional mention. In a day of small mercies, however, the heart is thankful for scraps, and in the absence of any other outside accounts, even a casual remark or chance observation in one of these books may be of value to an Indonesian historian looking for clues to check some doubtful points in his country's history. In this connection we may cite Albuquerque's mention of a Javanese navigational chart which showed Brazil and the Cape of Good Hope and his tribute to the skill of Javanese shipwrights. Unfortunately, few of these works are available in modern and well-indexed editions to facilitate the task of the researcher, but what can be done with them is shown by P. A. Tiele's lengthy series of articles, "De Europeërs in den Maleischen Archipel, 1509–1623," published serially in *BKI* (1877–1887). Since, however, consultation of this work is likewise by no means easy, it remains a prime desideratum for some competent person to go through all the Portuguese chronicles and to publish an annotated translation of all the references to Indonesia, on the lines of

[6] Translated and annotated by W. G. Maxwell, "Barretto de Resende's Account of Malacca," *JRASSB*, no. 60 (1911), pp. 1–24. For Bocarro and his work in general see C. R. Boxer, "António Bocarro and the 'Livro do Estado da India Oriental,'" reprinted from *Garcia de Orta: Numero especial* (Lisbon, 1956).

[7] "Historia de Maluco no tempo de Gonçalo Pereira Marramaque e Sancho de Vasconcellos, 1565–1579," recently published by Artur de Sá, *Documentação para a historia das missões do padroado portugues do Oriente: Insulíndia,* IV (Lisbon, 1956), 164–474.

[8] Braz de Albuquerque, *Comentarios do grande Affonso de Albuquerque* (Lisbon, 1557 and 1576) and *Cartas de Affonso de Albuquerque seguidas de documentos que as elucidam* (6 vols.; Lisbon, 1884–1915).

the task performed for Ceylon by Donald Ferguson in his *History of Ceylon from the Earliest Times to 1600 A.D., as Related by João de Barros and Diogo do Couto.*[9]

There are two works of outstanding importance for the history of Indonesia in our second category of other secular narratives and eye-witness accounts. The first of these is the *Suma Oriental* of Tomé Pires, which gives us a fascinating picture of conditions in Southeast Asia when the Portuguese first appeared on the scene and before Indonesia had been much affected by European enterprise. There is no need to stress the importance of this work here, since it has been utilized by all recent historians, and it is available in Armando Cortesão's scholarly edition for the Hakluyt Society, which contains both the original Portuguese text and an annotated English translation.[10] Less well known, and made available in a reliable text only very recently, is Gabriel Rebello's "Description of the Moluccas," which therefore deserves more than a passing mention.[11]

The "Informação" of 1569 is divided into three parts. The first gives a detailed description of the Moluccas and their natural history, with a more summary account of Halmaheira and other islands to the east. This is the best and fullest description of the Spice Islands which we have from the pen of a Portuguese. Rebello not only was a careful and accurate observer but also seems to have had a smattering of the Ternate vernacular. He describes the manners and customs of the people of the Moluccas, their physical characteristics, their dress and deportment, their sports and pastimes, as well as their religious beliefs. His

[9] Forming vol. XX, no. 60, of the *Journal of the Ceylon Branch of the Royal Asiatic Society* (Colombo, 1909).

[10] A. Cortesão, ed. and trans., *The Suma Oriental of Tomé Pires: An Account of the East, from the Red Sea to Japan, Written in Malacca and India in 1512–1515* (Hakluyt Society, 2 vols.; London, 1944).

[11] Gabriel Rebello, "Informação das cousas do Maluco dada ao Senhor Dom Constantino da Bragança," dated 1569 and first printed from a defective and in-adequate copy in the *Collecção de noticias para a historia e geografia das nações ultramarinas*, VI (Lisbon, 1856), 143–312, but without any notes or critical comment. This version is reprinted, but with corrections and notes, in Artur de Sá, *Documentação . . . Insulíndia*, III (Lisbon, 1955), 345–508. It is preceded, pp. 192–343, by the publication of an earlier draft of Rebello's work, entitled "Historia das ilhas de Maluco," dated Chaul, Oct. 31, 1561, which is printed here for the first time. Further detailed information concerning other manuscript versions of Rebello's "Informação" of 1569, including a contemporary copy in the present writer's collection, will appear in vol. VI of Artur de Sá's *Documentação*, now in press. Cf. also G. Schurhammer, S.J., *Die Zeitgenössischen Quellen zur Geschichte Portugiesisch-Asiens und seiner Nachbarländer zur Zeit des hl. Franz Xaver, 1538–1552* (Rome, 1962), pp. 462, 512.

account of Ternate is especially valuable, as he lived there for many years and knew everyone of importance from the Sultan down. He is surprisingly observant in his account of the local flora and fauna, which can bear comparison with those made centuries later by scientific naturalists, such as Wallace and Guillemard, who have visited those islands. The second part relates the history of the Portuguese discovery of the Moluccas and of their disputes with the Spaniards over the sovereignty thereof. As a patriotic Portuguese he is very critical of the Spaniards, and the first chapter of the "Informação" contains an attack on Gonzalo Hernández de Oviedo for errors about the Spice Islands which that chronicler allegedly perpetrated in his famous *Historia general y natural de las Indias,* published in 1535–1537. The third and final part of the "Informação" describes the captaincy of Bernaldim de Sousa at Ternate (1549–1552). Rebello admittedly wrote this work largely to justify de Sousa's conduct, so that the tone of this section is anything but impartial. He is also an apologist for Sultan Hairun of Ternate, perhaps with more reason.

Diogo do Couto confessedly depended on Rebello's manuscript for most of his own narrative of events in the Moluccas. The "Informação" has also been used by a few modern writers on Indonesia, but always in the faulty and unreliable Lisbon edition of 1856, for want of any other. Now that Padre Artur de Sá has given us two vastly superior texts in his *Documentação,* it is to be hoped that some scholar will publish an annotated English translation. The late R. S. Whiteway had already completed such a version from the 1856 text, but I have not been able to discover what became of this manuscript after his death.[12]

Manuel Godinho de Erédia (1563–1623) was the son of a Portuguese captain and a princess from Macassar. Born at Malacca and educated by the Jesuits there and at Goa, India, he later became government cosmographer in the Indo-Portuguese capital. He was an eccentric but talented character whose work on Southeast Asia and Indonesia is well known to us through the scholarly editions by Janssen and Mills.[13] A noble family in Portugal possesses what may be termed for want of a

[12] Whiteway announced his completion of this work in the *Revista de historia* (16 vols.; Lisbon, 1912–1928), II (1913), 53–54, but he died before he could publish it.

[13] L. Janssen, *Malaca, l'Inde Méridionale et le Cathay: Manuscrit original auto-graphe de Godinho de Erédia* (Brussels, 1882); J. V. Mills, "Erédia's Description of Malacca, Meridional India and Cathay," *JRASMB,* vol. VIII (1930), pt. I. There is also an unpublished cosmographical sketch of Northern India and Gujerat, dated 1611, by Godinho de Erédia in the British Museum (Add. Mss. 9854, fls. 77–81).

better name a commonplace book *cum* atlas of Manuel Godinho de Erédia, with many more maps, drawings, and sketches than those hitherto published. So far as I can recollect from a cursory examination of this codex which I made some ten years ago, the text does not equal the illustrations in interest; but in any event its forthcoming publication should add something to our historical knowledge of Indonesia, as Godinho de Erédia was naturally very interested in that region.[14]

Before dealing with the missionary literature which was concerned with Indonesia, a brief mention may be made of Fernão Mendes Pinto's famous *Peregrination*, which does not fall easily into any particular category. There will never be general agreement among historians as to what degree of credibility can be attached to Pinto's fascinating but highly controversial literary masterpiece. He must always have an interest for Indonesian historians, however, as he purports to describe events in Java and Sumatra, such as a campaign of the Moslem ruler of Demak against the Hindu king of Pasuruan, about which we otherwise know little or nothing. The only thing that can be said with certainty is that Pinto was a frequent visitor to Malacca and that even if he did not visit Indonesia, he can still have got his information from those who did. It is also certain that even when Pinto is narrating historical events in which he himself took part, he never fails to embroider the facts to a greater or lesser degree.[15]

Portuguese culture during the sixteenth and seventeenth centuries was preponderantly a clerical culture, particularly from about the middle of the sixteenth century when the Jesuits and the Inquisition were firmly established in the mother country and in most of her overseas settlements. Higher education became increasingly concentrated in the hands of the Jesuits, who were, for a time at any rate, among the best teachers in Europe, while the direct and indirect censorship exercised by the Inquisition largely determined what books could be published and what works readers could dare to read. As for education in the overseas empire—and there was a surprising amount of it—this was even more the monopoly of the religious orders in general and of

[14] Cf. Jorge Faro, "Manuel Godinho de Erédia, Cosmógrafo," reprinted from *Panorama*, 2d ser., nos. 13–14 (Lisbon, 1955).

[15] The critical literature on Pinto and his *Peregrinaçam*, first published at Lisbon in 1614, is extensive, but it will suffice to cite the following: G. Schurhammer, S.J., *Fernão Mendes Pinto und seine Peregrinaçam* (Leipzig, 1927); G. le Gentil, *Fernão Mendes Pinto: Un Précurseur de l'exotisme au XVI siècle* (Paris, 1947); A. J. Saraiva, *Fernão Mendes Pinto* (Lisbon, 1958).

the Jesuits, from 1542 onward, in particular. Persons of a studious or intellectual turn of mind naturally tended to gravitate into one or another of the religious orders, which also offered the best prospect of worldly as well as spiritual advancement to ambitious youths of humble origin. The Church, to its credit, was not so insistent on nobility of blood (*nobreza de sangue*) as a reason for promotion and advancement as the Crown was inclined to be. For these and other reasons, the clergy were usually a good deal better educated than the laity, and the latter automatically regarded the former as the literary and learned class. Here again, the Jesuits generally skimmed the cream of youthful talent, since they were careful to pick out the most promising youths, and their system of training was much more thorough and rigorous than that of the other religious orders or of the secular clergy.[16]

This preponderantly clerical culture strongly colored all sixteenth- and seventeenth-century Portuguese writing, and it is particularly noticeable in the almost comical mixture of ignorance and unfairness with which all religions other than Roman Catholic Christianity were treated. This prejudice was particularly marked as regards Islam, and two typical examples will suffice. Diogo do Couto, who was one of the most intelligent men of his time and who took considerable trouble to study the history of Asian peoples from their own written and oral sources, could still write of an incident in the 1546 siege of Diu when the Moslem assailants allegedly carried a banner "on which was painted the figure of Mahomet, as hideous and terrifying as were his works." João dos Santos, who lived as a Dominican missionary for many years in East Africa and who has left us one of the best-informed accounts of that region, after describing briefly the differences between the four principal Moslem sects, added, "but they are all infamous and lying, and as distant from the truth as is the dark night from the clear and beautiful day."[17] I do not mean to imply that such deep-rooted prejudices were confined to Portuguese chroniclers, for they were shared by the overwhelming majority of all Europeans, whether Protestant or Catholic, while Moslem writers doubtless exhibited similar bias against Christians. But in view of the exaggerated claims which are sometimes

[16] The best historical survey of Portuguese culture is that by António José Saraiva with a number of other writers, *História da cultura em Portugal* (3 vols., Lisbon, 1950–1962). For the culture of "Portuguese Asia" in its prime cf. Josef Wicki, S.J., "Zum Humanismus in Portugiesisch-Indien des 16 Jahrhunderts," reprinted from *Analecta Gregoriana*, LXX (Rome, 1954), 193–246.

[17] Diogo do Couto, *Decada,* vol. VI (Lisbon, 1612), Book I, ch. v; João dos Santos, O.P., *Ethiopia Oriental* (Evora, 1609), pt. I, Book 5, ch. i.

made nowadays for the objectivity and reliability of the old missionary writers,[18] it is well to remember that they were the children of their age, which was one of religious bigotry, as against the political and national hatreds which divide the world today.

The old missionary literature relating to Indonesia is not of the same standard as that relating to, say, China, Japan, or India. This is partly because Portuguese power was never firmly established east of Malacca, their foothold in the Moluccas being always insecure. Save for the annual galleon which went to fetch the cloves from Ternate, and later from Ambon, communications with Goa and Malacca were relatively infrequent and irregular. The sixteenth-century Portuguese in the Spice Islands were left very much to their own devices, a fact of which their captains repeatedly complained. After the loss of the Moluccas to the Dutch in 1605, and still more after the conquest of pro-Portuguese Macassar by the Hollanders sixty years later, Portuguese influence in Indonesia was reduced to Timor, Solor, and the eastern tip of Flores (Larantuka). Even here it was of a tenuous description for many years, and Timor and Solor were not officially claimed as dependencies of the Portuguese Crown until 1681,[19] although some of the local *datus* had acknowledged Portuguese suzerainty long before. The first governor of Timor, Antonio Coelho Guerreiro, did not land in that island until February, 1702, and he was closely besieged in Lifao for most of his term of office. His successors likewise exercised only nominal control over most of the island, and the Portuguese who frequented that region were limited to a few sandalwood traders from Macao and a handful of Dominican missionary friars. They seldom amounted to as many as a hundred white men before the nineteenth century, and in 1750 there were only eight, apart from a few friars, on Timor. This in turn meant that the missions in Indonesia were

---

[18] S. R. Welch, in *Portuguese and Dutch in South Africa, 1641–1806* (Johannesburg, 1951), p. 147, and elsewhere in his six-volume history of the Portuguese in Africa, is always making absurd claims of this kind. He terms Santos' *Ethiopia Oriental* (1609) a "literary and scientific masterpiece" and states that there were many more Portuguese works of this kind on Africa. As noted above, *Ethiopia Oriental* is certainly a remarkable and informative book; but it was the only one of its kind, its literary merits are not outstanding, and its author (like most of his contemporaries) was a firm believer in witchcraft and sorcery.

[19] Panduronga Pissurlencar, ed., *Assentos do Conselho do Estado da India, 1659–1695*, IV (Goa, 1956), 352, where "As ilhas de Timor e Solor de que he capitammor Antonio Hornay provido por este Gouverno da India" are mentioned for the first time (12.ix.1681) among the possessions of the Portuguese Crown in Asia, which were always enumerated whenever a viceroy or governor-general at Goa handed over his office to his successor.

always starved of men and supplies and that the literature about them was for the most part correspondingly sparse and poor.

Despite obvious deficiencies, however, it would be a great mistake to ignore this missionary literature altogether. As I have had occasion to remark before, in the day of small mercies the heart is thankful for scraps; and since reliable written records about so much of Indonesia are so scant, such of the old Portuguese accounts as have survived may sometimes help the modern historian. Very valuable in this connection is the serial publication of the Portuguese records relating to their missionary activities in Indonesia now being undertaken by Padre Artur Basilio de Sá, a missionary of many years' experience in Timor.[20] The value of his *Documentação* is enhanced by the inclusion of many documents which are primarily of military, economic, or social interest. They thus give a complete picture (insofar as the original documentation has survived) of Portuguese activities in this area; and they likewise contain many incidental notices of the peoples with whom they came into contact. In this connection, attention may be drawn to the voluminous account of Sancho de Vasconcellos' activities in Ambon and the neighboring islands during the last quarter of the sixteenth century. Although mainly concerned with chronicling the doughty deeds (and misdeeds) of his hero, the anonymous author of this account, who was also a companion-in-arms of Vasconcellos, incidentally sheds a good deal of light on the nature of the interisland rivalries which existed before the Portuguese came and which were inevitably exacerbated by their presence.[21]

The value of the surviving Jesuit accounts of this period is already familiar to us from the work of Father Wessels.[22] The modern historian can only regret that with the Jesuits' departure from the Indonesian

---

[20] *Documentação para a história das missões do padroado português do Oriente: Insulíndia* (5 vols.; Lisbon, 1954–1958). These five volumes cover the period 1506– 1597, and a sixth volume is expected shortly, to be followed by others in regular succession. Padre de Sá is also the author of an interesting little work, *A planta de Cailaco, 1727* (Lisbon, 1949).

[21] Artur de Sá, *Documentação . . . Insulíndia,* IV, 164–454. This "Historia" was written about 1600 and unfortunately was not available to Dr. J. Keuning when he wrote his interesting article "Ambonnezen, Portugezen en Nederlanders: Ambon's geschiedenis tot het einde van de zeventiende eeuw," *Indonesië,* IX (1956), 135– 168. Incidentally, the "Historia" of ca. 1600 contains the earliest reference in a European work (that I know of) to the term *Merdeka,* there applied under the form of *merdequa* to the class of Indonesian freemen whom the Dutch subsequently called *Mardijkers* (Sá, *Documentação,* p. 244).

[22] *De geschiedenis der R. K. Missie in Amboina, 1546–1605* (Nijmegen, 1926), and later articles in various historical periodicals.

mission field after the Dutch capture of the Moluccas he is forced to depend on the far less reliable and methodical Dominican narratives, as it was to the Order of Preachers that missionary work in the Lesser Sunda Islands was exclusively entrusted by the Portuguese Crown. There are, of course, some welcome exceptions to the credulous miracle-mongering which disfigures so much of the Dominican writing on this region. One of these is Fr. Miguel Rangel's account of Solor and the neighboring islands in 1633, and another is Fr. António de Encarnacão's narrative of the three-cornered struggle between Timorese, Portuguese, and Dutch some thirty years later.[23] Both of these original editions are exceedingly rare but they are or will be included in Padre Artur de Sá's *Documentação*.

Apart from a diffuse and unreliable Dominican mission history by various hands, entitled *Historia de São Domingos, particular do Reino e conquistas de Portugal* (4 vols.; Lisbon, 1623–1733), no Portuguese work relating to Indonesia worth mentioning was published between 1665 and the appearance of Affonso de Castro's *As possessões Portuguesas na Oceania* (Lisbon, 1867), just over two centuries later. Castro had been one of Portuguese Timor's more successful and conscientious governors, and the lapse of nearly another century has not diminished the value of his book in many respects. The documents printed on pages 185–295 of this work are still indispensable to the student of Timor's history, and nothing of importance in this field was added until the publication of two books by A. Faria de Morais in 1933–1934. These are useful for the selection of documents from the Goa archives which Faria de Morais published therein, but he was a jejune and rambling writer who did not make the best use of this material.[24]

Much more satisfactory in every way are the well-documented works on the history of the Portuguese in the Lesser Sunda Islands, which are now in the course of publication by Commandante Humberto Leitão.[25] This author is a retired Portuguese naval officer, who after

[23] *Relações summarias de alguns serviços que fizeram a Deos, e a estes Reynos, os Religiosos Dominicos, nas partes da India Oriental nestes annos proximos passados* (Lisbon, 1635), pp. 20–35, Rangel's report dated Malacca, 13.xii.1633; António da Encarnação, O.P., *Breve Relaçam das cousas que nestes annos proximos fizerão os Religiosos da Ordem dos Pregadores e dos prodigios, que succedérão nas Christandades do Sul, que correm por sua conta na India Oriental* (Lisbon, 1665).

[24] *Subsídios para a história de Timor, 1511–1769* (Bastorá-Goa, 1934); *Solor e Timor* (Lisbon, 1944).

[25] *Os Portugueses em Solor e Timor de 1515 a 1702* (Lisbon, 1948); *Vinte e oito anos de história de Timor, 1698 a 1725* (Lisbon, 1952). Other volumes are in preparation.

serving for a long time on Timor, has spent the last decade in research on the relevant documents preserved in the Arquivo Histórico Ultramarino (Overseas Historical Archive) at Lisbon. His works are conscientiously written and full of new material. Taken in conjunction with the *Documentação* of Padre Artur de Sá, they undoubtedly provide a rich field for investigation by contemporary Indonesian historians. Unfortunately, unlike the *Documentação*, Commandante Leitão's books are not indexed, but this is a defect which one hopes will be remedied in future volumes. There are a number of other modern works by Portuguese writers which deal mainly or partly with the history of Timor, but they are of little importance in comparison with the works of Padre de Sá and Commandante Leitão, who have made use of them where necessary. Mention may be made, however, of a short but suggestive essay by Ruy Cinatti, *Esboço histórico do sândalo no Timor Português* (Lisbon, 1950), which contains some interesting historical facts about the cultivation of the sandalwood tree in Timor which are not to be found elsewhere. Cinatti has also written on prehistoric rock paintings in Timor.

The reader will gather from the foregoing that the archival sources for the history of the Portuguese in Indonesia—and hence for Portuguese accounts of or references to Indonesia which might interest that country's historians—are in process of being divulged in a satisfactory fashion. For the benefit of those who cannot wait until the works of Padre de Sá and Commandante Leitão have been completed or who wish to carry out research on their own account in the Portuguese archives, we may mention the following facts. The oldest and largest archive, that of the Torre do Tombo at Lisbon, is not adequately catalogued, and the seeker for documents on Indonesia can best orientate himself by consulting Padre de Sá's *Documentação*, the *Zeitgenössischen Quellen zur Geschichte Portugiesisch-Asiens und seiner Nachbarländer zur Zeit des hl. Franz Xaver, 1538–1552* (Rome, 1962) of Padre G. Schurhammer, S.J., and the informative articles of the late I. A. Macgregor in *JRASMB*, XXVIII, pt. 2 (May, 1955), especially pages 44–45, 120–122. Most of the relevant documents in the other main Portuguese archive, the Arquivo Histórico Ultramarino at Lisbon, are not older than the early seventeenth century. They are filed chronologically in boxes and bundles with the geographical indications "Timor," "India," etc. As regards the Arquivo Histórico do Estado da India at Goa, the documents therein are all properly filed and catalogued as explained by Panduronga Pissurlencar, *Roteiro dos Arquivos da India Portuguesa* (Bastorá-Goa, 1955). The great majority of these records likewise do not go further back than the early seventeenth century, and some of those dealing with Timor are indicated in C. R. Boxer, "A Glimpse of the Goa Archives" (*Bulletin of the School of Oriental and African Studies*, XIV [1952], 299–324). Attention may also be drawn to the documents from many archives, both Portuguese and foreign, admirably calendared and indexed in the *Boletim da Filmoteca Ultramarina Portuguesa* (8 vols.; Lisbon, 1954–1963).[26]

Since the regions of Indonesia with which the Portuguese were most directly concerned were the Moluccas for the period 1515–1605 and the Lesser Sunda Islands from about 1605 onward, both printed Portuguese books and unpublished Portuguese records are likewise primarily concerned with those regions and periods. During the years 1615–1665, however, the Portuguese occupied a privileged position in Macassar, where the presence of their traders from Goa, Malacca, and Macao was greatly encouraged by the local sultans, who sought in this way to strengthen their own position against the growing power of the Dutch East India Company. Readers of Dr. F. W. Stapel's *Het Bongaais verdrag: De vestiging der Nederlanders op Makassar* (Groningen, 1922) may recall the name of the Portuguese merchant-adventurer, Francisco Vieira de Figueiredo, who played such an important role as the councilor, friend, and envoy of successive rulers of Macassar from 1642 to 1665.[27] There is a good deal of unpublished material relating to Vieira de Figueiredo's activities at Macassar in the archives at Jakarta, Goa, and The Hague, as well as at Lisbon and London. From his headquarters at Negapatam and Macassar, he maintained mercantile and economic connections with Macao, Manila, Cambodia, Siam, Larantuka, Solor and Timor, Japara, Batavia, and Bantam, to say nothing of Malacca ,Goa, and the Coromandel Coast. The English at Madras referred to him in 1652 as "an eminent fidalgo and known friend of ours in the South Seas." [28] Dominie Baldaeus described him as "een man

[26] This most useful publication is still in progress. For further information on the Portuguese archives and their contents, especially those of Lisbon, see the articles of Virginia Rau and Bailey Diffie in *Proceedings of the International Colloquium on Luso-Brazilian Studies, Washington, D.C., October 15–20, 1950* (Nashville, Tenn., 1953), pp. 181–213; A. da Silva Rego, *Licões de Metodologia* (Lisbon, 1963), pp. 31–48.

[27] C. R. Boxer, "Francisco Vieira de Figueiredo e os Portugueses em Macassar e Timor na época da Restauração, 1640–1668," reprinted from the *Boletim Ecclesiastico de Macau*, Ano 36 (Macao, 1940), pp. 727–741. Cf. also H. Leitão, *Os Portugueses em Solor e Timor de 1515 a 1702* (Lisbon, 1948), pp. 193–205.

[28] Commonwealth Relations Office (ex-India Office), London, *Original Corre-*

van groot aanzien ende een van de voortreffelijkste Kooplieden in India." [29] As early as 1634 the viceroy of Portuguese India had criticized him for being more friendly with the Hindus of Negapatam than with his own fellow countrymen,[30] and he certainly remained on terms of friendly intimacy with the Moslem rulers of Macassar, fervent Roman Catholic though he was.[31] It is seldom easy to distinguish when he was mainly operating on his own account and when he was chiefly acting on behalf of the great ones of Macassar; but undoubtedly many of his ventures were undertaken in partnership with the latter. He also acted as the Sultan's diplomatic agent on more than one occasion, voyaging in this capacity to Goa, Siam, and Bantam. Francisco Vieira de Figuei-redo was a Portuguese equivalent of such outstanding seventeenth-century Asian entrepreneurs as Mir Jumla, the merchant-regent of Golconda, or the Malaya family in Pulicat. A more detailed study of his career, which I hope to make one day, may well bring to light some new facts concerning the economic and political rivalry between Jan Compagnie and the "haantjes van den Oost" (the fighting cocks of the East) as the Dutch termed their formidable opponents in South Celebes.

Portuguese relations with the Sultan of Mataram during this same period were neither so close nor so cordial as they were with Macassar, but the "Livros das Monções" (Books of the Monsoons) and "Livros dos Reis Vizinhos" (Books of the Neighboring Kings), which comprise the correspondence of the Crown with the viceroy of Goa, contain some relevant material on this subject, and the same can be said of the proceedings of the viceregal consultive council at Goa, which have recently been published.[32] Dislike of the Dutch was, of course, the bond between the two erstwhile enemies; but although Goa and Ma-

---

spondence 2246, letter from Fort St. George, Madras, to the Court of Directors, Jan. 14, 1952. My colleague Dr. D. K. Bassett informs me that there are numerous references to Francisco Vieira de Figueiredo's activities in Indonesia in the old Bantam Records of the English East India Company at the CRO.

[29] Ph. Baldaeus, *Beschryving van het machtige eyland Ceylon* (Amsterdam, 1672), p. 141.

[30] "Em espessial hum Francisco Vieira que mais comunicação tem com os gentios que com christãos" (*Diario do Conde de Linhares, vice-rei da India* [Lisbon, 1937], p. 121).

[31] Fr. Domingo Fernandez Navarrete, O.P., *Tratados historicos, politicos, ethicos, y religiosos de la monarchia de China* (Madrid, 1676), pp. 329–330.

[32] Panduronga Pissurlencar, ed., *Assentos do Conselho de Estado da India* (5 vols.; Bastorá-Goa, 1953–1958). The volumes cover the period 1618–1750. For the "Livros das Monções" and "Livros dos Reis Vizinhos" see Pissurlencar's *Roteiro* cited above.

taram exchanged envoys on more than one occasion, nothing much
came of their projected anti-Dutch alliance, except for the fact that the
Susuhunan provisioned Malacca with rice whenever the small Javanese craft could run the gauntlet of the Dutch blockade of that fortress.
At the Sultan's request, the viceroy sent him a present of four Moslem
virgins (presumably Indian or Arab) in 1634, "richly dressed in cloth
of gold with many jewels." [33] The viceroy had previously made lavish
offers of military and naval assistance against the Dutch, which he
well knew were impossible of fulfillment, but, as he wrote to his king,
"It is convenient that we should lead him [the Sultan] on from one
hope to another until God improves the times, and meanwhile he should
be encouraged to go on. For we have always plenty of opportunity to
make excuses, since necessity has made us masters of them as regards
the neighboring kings." [34] Needless to say, Sultan Agung was not de-
ceived, but he continued to help Malacca insofar as he could, if only
out of enlightened self-interest.

The reader may recall that Portugal and Spain formed a dual mon-
archy from 1580 to 1640, and although the respective colonial admin-
istrations and spheres of influence of the two Iberian crowns were kept
distinct during this period, the Spanish archives naturally contain a
wealth of information about Portuguese colonial possessions as well
as their own. This is particularly true of the archives at Simancas and
Seville, the Archivo de Indias in this last-named city being remarkably
rich in documents on the Philippines. These in their turn often include
material relating to Indonesia, more especially for the period when the
Spaniards were established in Ternate and Tidore (1606–1663). [35] An
account of Acheh compiled in 1584 by the Portuguese Bishop of Malacca, Dom João Ribeiro Gaio, has survived obscurely in a contemporary
manuscript translation; and the voluminous correspondence of Don

[33] *Diario do Condo de Linhares*, p. 183, under date of Sept. 26, 1634.

[34] Viceroy to Crown, Nov. 2, 1632, *apud* Pissurlencar, *Assentos*, I, 418.

[35] *Catálogo de los documentos relativos á las islas Filipinas existentes en el Archivo de Indias de Sevilla por D. Pedro Torres y Lanzas, precedido de una historia general de Filipinas por el P. Pablo Pastells, S.J.* (10 vols.; Barcelona, 1925–1934) cover the period down to 1660. Cf. also A. R. Rodriguez Moñino, "Bibliografía hispano-oriental: Apuntes para un catálogo de los documentos referentes a las Indias Orientales de las Colecciones de la Academia," *Boletín de la Academia de la Historia*, XCVIII (Madrid, 1931), 417–475; C. R. Boxer, "Some Aspects of Spanish Historical Writing on the Philippines," in D. G. E. Hall, ed., *Historians of South East Asia* (London, 1961), pp. 200–213. For a guide to Spanish archives in general, see E. J. Burrus, S.J., "An Introduction to Bibliographical Tools in Spanish Archives and Manuscript Collections Relating to Hispanic America," in *Hispanic-American Historical Review*, XXXV (1955), 443–483.

Gerónimo de Silva, the Spanish governor of Ternate in 1612–1617, has been printed in a series which is certainly not easy of access in Southeast Asia.[36]

The research worker looking for documents dealing with Indonesia must therefore also take Spanish libraries and archives into account, particularly since they did not suffer a loss comparable to that of the destruction by earthquake and fire of the Casa da India at Lisbon on November 1, 1755. The administration of the Portuguese African and Asian overseas possessions had been centralized in the Casa da India from early times, and the annihilation of this institution in the catastrophe of 1755 is particularly regrettable for the early sixteenth-century records from the Moluccas and Malacca which disappeared in the flames along with many others on that memorable All Saints' Day.

Nevertheless, as indicated above, despite the loss of the great bulk of the early Portuguese documents relating to Indonesia, sufficient material is left to justify the sending of a qualified Indonesian scholar with a good knowledge of Portuguese and Spanish to investigate the Iberian libraries and archives, when time and funds permit. Such a mission of historical research would probably last for a year or two at least. Even though no revolutionary discoveries are likely to ensue, I have little doubt that many interesting facts would be gleaned concerning Indonesia's past in the days when men fought, intrigued, and chaffered for souls and spices, as they do nowadays (*mutatis mutandis*) for oil.

Since 1958, when this article was written in its original form, two major works have been published which show what good use can be made of Portuguese manuscript and printed sources for the history of Indonesia in the sixteenth century. They are as follows: M. A. P. Meilink-Roelofsz, *Asian Trade and European Influence in the Indonesian Archipelago between 1500 and About 1630* (The Hague, 1962); and Georg Schurhammer, S.J., *Franz Xaver. Sein Leben und seine zeit.* Zweiter Band: *Asien 1541–1552,* Erster Halbband: *Indien und Indonesian, 1541–1547* (Freiburg im Breisgau, 1964), especially pp. 599–803.

[36] "DeRotero y relaçion que don joan ribero gayo obispo de Malaca hizo de las cosas de achen," cited in C. R. Boxer, "A Late Sixteenth-Century Manila MS," *JRAS,* April, 1950, p. 40; "Correspondencia de don Gerónimo de Silva con Felipe III, el Rey de Tidore, y otros personajes, 1612–1617, sobre el estado de la Islas Molucas," *Colección de Documentos Inéditos para la Historia de España,* LII (Madrid, 1868), 5–439.

XIII

Dutch Historical Sources

By GRAHAM IRWIN

Associate Professor of History, Columbia University

FOR students of Indonesian history a knowledge of Dutch and of Dutch source materials is essential. Nearly all official documents and most private memoirs and descriptive accounts of the country that have appeared during the past three hundred and fifty years are written in that language. Sources in other languages are obviously important too, as the chapter headings of the present volume indicate. But Dutch must be regarded as preeminent. Without it, research in *any* aspect of Indonesian history is impossible. Even when the materials themselves are in other languages—Sanskrit, for example, or Old Javanese—the student will find that the best, and often the only, commentaries on the sources are in Dutch, and these commentaries he will neglect at his peril.

Nevertheless, a large proportion of Dutch source materials may, at first sight, appear irrelevant in the context of *Indonesian* history. What concern have I, the Indonesian historian is entitled to ask, with the records of a non-Indonesian people? Official Dutch accounts surely portray Dutch, not Indonesian, life and actions. They are written from a European, not an Asian, point of view. From them I cannot hope to learn what, primarily, I want to know, which is the story of the development of my own people during a period of alien rule.

These are cogent objections, but they are answerable. In the first place, the sheer mass of Dutch sources, both manuscript and printed, should be emphasized. The leather-bound volumes of the records of the Dutch East India Company, ranged along the shelves of the State Archives in The Hague, alone number over twelve thousand. The records of that Company's successor, the Netherlands Indian Govern-

ment—some bound, some still in the bundles in which they were originally tied—are ten times as numerous. It would be strange if so vast
an accumulation did not contain information on at least some non-
European subjects—information, moreover, which cannot be obtained
from any other source. Secondly, Dutch officials in Indonesia, from
the earliest days onward, had many interests and responsibilities outside the day-to-day business of commerce and administration. In the
seventeenth century, when European ignorance of Asia was much
greater than it is now, the servants of the East India Company had to
provide their masters in Holland with minute descriptions of the Indonesian scene, so that decisions taken at home might be based on something better than guesswork. Later, when the Netherlands Indian
Government was administering the whole country, its officials had to
submit reports on any and every detail of local law and practice that
came to their notice. Once again, the subject was that government
policy might be meshed with the needs of time and place, and not
unwittingly colored by prejudice or misconception. On the whole, these
tasks were performed more competently by Dutch officials in the East
than by those of any other colonial power, presumably because the
Dutch officials were the best trained. Their voluminous reports are
available now for the historian to consult if he has the desire (and, it
must be added, the patience). Thirdly, Holland, though possessing a
vast colonial dominion, was only a small nation. "The Colonies" bulked
far larger in the Dutch imagination than in, for example, the British
or the French. In nineteenth-century Holland educated opinion was
fairly well informed on the problems of Indonesia, and a relatively high
proportion of Dutchmen had personal experience of the country. In
the same period British ignorance of and French indifference to colonial affairs were proverbial. In the nineteenth century, too, whereas
Britain found its best market for manufactures not in its existing possessions but in its former colony of the United States, the economies of
Holland and Indonesia became, by contrast, more and more closely
bound together as the century wore on. The result of this comparatively high degree of cultural and economic integration was that Dutch
comment on Indonesian affairs, if not always unbiased, was usually
expert and exact.

It is in the light of these considerations that Dutch sources for Indonesian history must be viewed. In the Dutch archives the research
worker will find much that is of interest only to historians of Holland
itself and much more that is directly related only to the more theoreti-

cal aspects of the history of colonial policy. With neither of these subjects will a modern Indonesian historian be primarily concerned. But
among an admittedly large quantity of irrelevant material in the colonial archives lies the true stuff of Indonesian history. To reject the
Dutch sources, whether through prejudice or ignorance, on the ground
of inappropriateness would be very foolish. Until these sources are more
thoroughly and systematically examined than has been possible so far,
the detailed history of Indonesia from 1595 to 1942 will not be written.

THE PERIOD OF THE EAST INDIA COMPANY, 1595–1800

In evaluating the worth of a historical document the historian must
apply certain criteria. He must, for example, bear in mind the known
or presumed purpose of its author. Was the document a piece of propaganda, designed to obscure or mislead rather than illumine? Did the
author give untrue information because he feared punishment or ridi-
cule if he told the truth? If so, the document will be *deliberately* false,
and the historian will know how to assess it. But perhaps the writer
of the document simply did not know what he was talking about, or
had been told wrong, or had placed an incorrect interpretation on an
observed event. In that case, the document will be *unconsciously* false,
and the historian, as before, will be able to make the appropriate
allowances.

Secondly, it is a generally agreed maxim that one must be chary of
accepting published reports as more trustworthy than unpublished ones
—provided the latter are authentic. A confidential diplomatic dispatch
is more likely to be reliable than a newspaper story. Here again, the
vital consideration is the writer's purpose. A diplomat will not know-
ingly mislead his home government, even if the news he conveys is
unpalatable. But a newspaper editor may print untruths deliberately.
Probably the "perfect" piece of historical evidence is a locked diary,
never intended for other eyes than the writer's own.

Measured against these criteria, the records of the Dutch East India
Company stand up well. An intensely secretive organization, the Company never disclosed its affairs to the public until, at the end of its
life, it was forced to do so by approaching bankruptcy. Throughout
its existence it acted independently of the home government in the
Netherlands, which had little control over its general policy and
none at all over the detailed implementation of that policy. (This
tradition of secrecy lasted long after the Company was wound up;
until a Liberal government insisted on the practice in 1848, the authori-

ties at Batavia did not even have to make an annual report to the States-General.) Entirely absent from the Company's records, therefore, is the element of propaganda. There was never any question of publication except when the Company itself wanted it, and consequently no fear of public opinion. If thousands of Javanese died in a famine, if an expeditionary force was decimated because of bad generalship, these facts were duly reported home, but they were not revealed. The Dutch nation only learned about Indonesia what the Company thought it ought to know.

This line of argument must not, of course, be pressed too far. Although officials of the Company, when submitting their reports, did not have to beware of possible public censure, they did have to answer to their superiors, and the directors of the Company at Amsterdam, the famous "Seventeen Gentlemen," were not easy taskmasters. The Company's officials obviously could not disclose their own errors and failings without the fear of any retribution at all. This is why there is little detailed information in the Dutch Company records, or indeed anywhere else, on such matters as the extent of private trading or the size of the bribes known to have been accepted by company servants from Asian traders and Indonesian princes. But such falsifications and omissions fell within the sphere of essentially "Dutch" activities; they are part of the internal history of the Dutch East India Company. Where "Indonesian" questions were under review, an official did not need to misrepresent the true situation since he could not normally be blamed if things had gone wrong. It therefore seems reasonable to assume that, after due allowance is made for ordinary human carelessness, the seventeenth- and eighteenth-century official Dutch accounts of Indonesian customs, institutions, and manners, and of Southeast Asian politics and trade, are as free from distortion and inaccuracy as they well can be.

This point is strengthened when it is remembered for what purpose the Dutch came to the East. Before the nineteenth century their only abiding interest was trade. They did not propound theories of colonization; they had no doctrine of a master race. Although staunch Calvinists, they felt no urge to convert "Moors" to Christianity. They were businessmen, not crusaders and, unlike the Portuguese, they never allowed religious prejudice to outweigh commercial advantage. Their attitude to Indonesia and Indonesians was always levelheaded and matter of fact, and their recorded descriptions of Indonesian life are correspondingly free from bigotry and racial antagonism.

Finally, the records of the Company may be commended because of the value they possess as checks on indigenous Indonesian chronicles. Scribes at Indonesian courts rarely found it necessary to give a precise date even to events of conspicuous importance like the death of a sultan or the birth of an heir to the throne. In the Indonesian chronicles may be found the more detailed description of the event itself. But the contemporary Dutch account, while treating the same event more briefly, will give an exact time and place. From the Dutch records, moreover, can sometimes ‘be determined whether or not a court scribe is telling the truth. As is well known, Indonesian court chroniclers often had to suppress the facts of past history when these were unflattering to their present masters. Dutch Company officials were, of course, under no such disability.

It is now time to turn to the Dutch East India Company records themselves. They may be divided for convenience into two sections: manuscripts and published materials.

A. Manuscripts

The manuscript records of the Dutch East India Company, known as the "Koloniaal Archief, 1594–1803," are preserved in the State Archives, The Hague. They comprise approximately 12,050 volumes. Of these more than half may be ignored by the historian of Indonesia, since they relate to domestic affairs in Holland and to outlying factories of the East India Company in China, India, the Cape of Good Hope, Persia, etc.

In the purely Indonesian context the collections of most value are as follows:

1. The Records of the "Voorcompagniën" (vols. 1–107). These are papers relating to the so-called "wilde vaart" of the Dutch in Indonesian waters and elsewhere between 1595, the year of the first voyage of Cornelis de Houtman, and 1602, the year of the formation of the East India Company. In recent years, however, a great deal of detailed research has been done on these early voyages, and the student would be well advised to consult the modern published versions of them (especially the "Works" of the Linschoten-Vereeniging) before making an assault on the original manuscripts.

2. The Domestic and Commercial Papers of the Amsterdam Chamber (vols. 108–494, 4386–4453, and 4458–4464). These include the minutes of meetings of the Seventeen, the recorded decisions of that body, the minutes of meetings of the Amsterdam Chamber, and the letters

and instructions sent by the Seventeen to their subordinates in the East.

3. The Resolutions of the Governor-General and Council of the Indies (vols. 558–743). In these volumes are to be found the text of decisions taken by the Governor-General in Council from November 30, 1613, to December 31, 1791. The decisions themselves are often of little interest, since they may merely record, for example, the transfer of an official from one post to another. But prefixed to the actual resolution is usually a long preamble, giving the history of the events upon a consideration of which the resolution was based. These preambles may consequently be used to check the accuracy of the other sources.

4. The "Out" Letter Books of the High Government at Batavia (vols. 744–955). These consist of copies of letters, orders, and instructions sent by the Governor-General in Council to subordinate governments throughout Indonesia and elsewhere between July 19, 1622, and December 31, 1792.

5. The "Brieven en Papieren Overgekomen, 1602–1794" (vols. 960–3877). There are 2,918 volumes in this series, and, for the purpose of the general historian of Indonesia, they form by far the most valuable part of the Koloniaal Archief.

They consist, in the first place, of the originals of letters, reports, memorials, etc., written by the High Government at Batavia to the Seventeen in Amsterdam. Particularly useful are the so-called "Generale Missiven"—reports furnished regularly (usually at the end of March and/or December of each year) on the state of the Dutch possessions in the East. Each "missive," which may be anywhere from 100 to 2,000 folio pages long, contains sections on the various outlying factories and ends with a summary of the financial position and prospects of the Company as a whole. A typical "Generale Missive" will have sections of from five to twenty pages on each of the following: Ambon, Banda, Ternate, Macassar, Banjermasin, Timor, Palembang, Jambi, China, Japan, Malacca; and somewhat longer sections on the West Coast of Sumatra, Ceylon, Bengal, Coromandel, Malabar, Surat, Persia, the various parts of Java, and Batavia. The sections always follow this particular order.[1]

Secondly, the "Brieven Overgekomen" contain copies of letters and

[1] Professor W. Ph. Coolhaas has undertaken the task of editing selections from the Generale Missiven for the "Rijks Geschiedkundige Publicatiën" series of the Netherlands Ministry of Education. His first volume appeared in 1960: *Generale missiven van Gouverneurs-Generaal en Raden aan Heren XVII der Vereenigde Oostindische Compagnie, Deel I: 1610–1638* (The Hague, 1960).

reports received by the Governor-General in Council from his subordinates. From 1661 onward these were grouped together in annual volumes under the title "Batavia's Inkomende Briefboek." Basically, the volumes are made up of the letters written each year to Batavia by the heads of the various outlying governments and factories. But also included are copies of reports and recommendations by special commissioners and other officials on detached diplomatic and trading missions and copies of the more important dispatches from subordinate officials to their local governors or directors.

The number of volumes in the "Brieven Overgekomen" for each year remains steady at some five or six up to about 1675 and from then on increases to an average of thirty or more from 1730 until the series ends in 1794.

It cannot be denied that, even for those whose first language is Dutch, the manuscript records of the East India Company are often very hard to decipher and, when deciphered, harder still to comprehend. The most difficult documents are, naturally enough, the oldest. In the early seventeenth century, Gothic script was normally used in the Netherlands and, as a consequence, in Indonesia as well. At that period many shorthand abbreviations were employed and capital letters might be written in a number of different ways. By modern standards the style of the authors of official dispatches in those days was clumsy and verbose. Sentences were extremely long, the subject of the sentence was often omitted, and punctuation, when used at all, was erratic. On the other hand, a kind of official jargon was early adopted, leading to considerable stereotyping of diction and phraseology, and the Company's officials did not, on the whole, employ a large vocabulary.[2] From about 1680 onward the manuscripts present fewer difficulties because cursive or Latin script was by then becoming increasingly common. Eighteenth-century handwriting, compared to seventeenth, is nearly always a pleasure to read.

B. Published Materials

No precise dividing line can be drawn between "primary" and "secondary" historical material. It depends on the time of writing, on the subject under consideration, and on the point of view. An account of

[2] In this connection two useful aids to research may be mentioned: J. Verdam's *Middelnederlandsch handwoordenboek* and H. Brouwer's *Beknopte handleiding tot de kennis van het Nederlandsche oude schrift.*

the structure of seventeenth-century Indonesian trade, written in 1950, is a secondary authority; a discourse on the same subject, written in 1650, must be regarded as primary. Similarly, a contemporary description of an eighteenth-century shadow play may have been based on hearsay and, from the point of view of a historian of the Javanese theater, is therefore a secondary source and perhaps of little merit. If, however, the author of the description unintentionally reveals his own attitude toward theatrical performances in general, the value of his account as a piece of historical evidence changes, and a modern social historian might well find in it primary material of great value.

This being so, it is obvious that *everything* written in Dutch about Indonesia is liable to have primary significance for *some* modern historian. It is equally obvious that to list all such sources here would be impracticable. (It would also be unnecessary, since adequate bibliographies are available.) In this section, therefore, attention will be drawn only to the major published sources, and particularly to collections of original documents. These collections are the foundation on which specialist historians, using other materials as appropriate, can build their own particular edifices. They constitute the best starting point for a course of research, since the manuscript records of the Dutch East India Company are not only more difficult to handle than published works but, at least for historians outside Holland, much less accessible.

1. J. K. J. de Jonge and others, eds., *De opkomst van het Nederlandsch gezag in Oost-Indië: Verzameling van onuitgegevene stukken uit het oud-koloniaal archief (1595–1814)*. This substantial work was published between 1862 and 1909 in two series, with a supplement. The first series consists of documents relating to the pre-Company voyages, the founding and development of the East India Company, and the extension of Dutch influence in Java. The second series, which was edited by P. A. Tiele and J. E. Heeres and is subtitled *Bouwstoffen voor de geschiedenis der Nederlanders in den Maleischen Archipel*, deals with the Company's possessions in Indonesia outside Java. The work comprises nineteen parts, usually bound in thirteen volumes.

De Jonge's *Opkomst*, though one of the earliest to appear, is still probably the most useful single collection of Dutch Company documents published so far. All kinds of documents are included: dispatches from the Governor-General to the Seventeen, reports by commanders of outlying factories to Batavia and by subordinate officials to their superiors within those factories, instructions issued by the Governor-

General to governors, presidents, and commanders, copies of agreements made between the Company and Indonesian rulers, translations of letters from Indonesian rulers to the government at Batavia, and texts of diaries kept by commissioners on special duty. From the technical point of view, however, the collection has one weakness. Many documents are given in extract form only, and it is not clear on what principle the editors worked when making their selections. But this blemish detracts only slightly from the value of the work as a whole.

2. J. A. van der Chijs and others, eds., *Dagh-Register gehouden int Casteel Batavia* (31 vols., published between 1887 and 1931). This series reproduces the daybook or journal of the Dutch East India Company's Batavian headquarters for various years between 1624 and 1682. After 1682 the journal continued to be entered up, but so far publication has not been carried beyond that date. There are, moreover, several gaps in the text already issued, since for some years between 1624 and 1682 no journal has survived. The text is, however, continuous for the period 1662–1682.

The *Dagh-Register* may be compared to a rag bag, since all kinds of information were thrown into it more or less indiscriminately. Alongside an entry listing the number of prahus in Batavia harbor on a particular day may appear the text of a communication from the Governor-General in Council to the Sultan of Ternate. Summaries of proceedings in the Council of the Indies are included, as also are précis of dispatches received from the heads of company posts in the Outer Islands. Statements of future policy are given, together with the reasoning behind decisions taken. As would be expected, there is a minute record of events in Batavia itself during the whole period under review. The indexes at the end of each volume, however, are neither complete nor accurate and should be used with caution.

3. J. E. Heeres and F. W. Stapel, eds., *Corpus Diplomaticum Neerlandico-Indicum* (published in six parts between 1907 and 1955 by the Koninklijk Instituut voor Taal-, Land- en Volkenkunde). In this series are collected together all contracts, agreements, and treaties entered into by the Dutch East India Company on the one side and the Asian princes with whom the Company had commercial relations on the other.

The precise terms of the privileges granted by or exacted from Indonesian rulers are not perhaps of vital interest today. But from the texts of contracts in the *Corpus Diplomaticum* much more may be learned than the details of the Company's system of monopoly. The titles and ranks of the contracting parties are usually given in full.

With these before him the historian can determine such matters as the relative importance of various court ministers in a particular state; the text may indicate, for example, that a *laksamana* is of greater consequence than a *bĕndahara*. From the terms of a monopoly contract, moreover, may be deduced the economic circumstances of the Indonesian contracting state—its wealth, its products, and even the extent of its business acumen and the political sophistication of its rulers. Finally, the details of financial and other privileges exacted by the Company from Indonesian rulers often give a clue to the nature of the indigenous fiscal and revenue systems that were operating before the Dutch arrived. (It may be added that the introductory notes prefixed to the texts of the contracts are models of brevity and relevance.)

4. H. T. Colenbrander and W. Ph. Coolhaas, eds., *Jan Pietersz. Coen: Bescheiden omtrent zijn bedrijf in Indië* (7 parts in 8 vols., published between 1919 and 1953). This collection is wider in scope than its title suggests. When the documents it contains were selected, the test applied was that they should be originated by or addressed to J. P. Coen and the committees and councils of which he was a member. But Coen was no ordinary man. The quantity of dispatches, suggestions, pleas, demands, and curses that flowed from his pen during his service in the East was prodigious. Between 1614 and 1629 (the period with which these volumes are concerned) very little can have occurred in Indonesia, at least in the sphere of Dutch activities, with which Coen was not in some way involved. The publication of *Jan Pietersz. Coen* has probably made these fifteen years the best-documented segment of Indonesian history.

5. Pieter van Dam, *Beschryvinge van de Oostindische Compagnie* (7 vols., 1927–1954; vols. 1–6 edited by F. W. Stapel; vol. 7 by C. W. Th. baron van Boetzelaer van Asperen en Dubbeldam, Rijks Geschiedkundige Publicatiën 63, 68, 74, 76, 83, 87, and 96).

Pieter van Dam was secretary of the head office of the Dutch East India Company at Amsterdam from 1652 to 1706, an astonishing span of fifty-four years. It may safely be said that no man of his time knew more about the inner workings of the Company than van Dam. In July, 1693, he was commissioned by the Seventeen to write a "definitive and exact description" of the administrative and trading methods of the Company from its foundation to date. The result was his monumental *Beschryvinge*, which took him nearly eight years to complete.

The work is divided into five books, of which the first four are reproduced in the seven published volumes. The fifth book, which related to controversies between the Netherlands and Great Britain, has not survived.

Of the four extant books, the second is of particular interest to historians of modern Indonesia. Book I is concerned exclusively with the Company in Europe, Book III with the minutiae of administration, and Book IV with the affairs of the Dutch Reformed Church. Book II, however, is a detailed political, military, and economic history of all territories from the Cape of Good Hope to Japan with which the Company was in contact between 1602 and the end of the seventeenth century. Van Dam's was the first attempt to set the operations of the Dutch East India Company against a world background. His work has its weaknesses: the writer had never been to the East and makes many errors both of fact and of interpretation. But the *Beschryvinge* will continue to be, as it long has been, a rich quarry for historians of Indonesia.

6. *Werken uitgegeven door de Linschoten-Vereeniging.* The Linschoten Society began issuing its reprints of early Dutch voyages in 1909, and over fifty volumes have appeared so far. Of these about a third are directly related to Indonesia. The texts are easy to use because of the excellent indexes published in two parts in 1939 and 1957 under the title *Tresoor der zee- en landreisen.* With the aid of this index (which should be used in conjunction with the glossary in Pieter van Dam's *Beschryvinge*), many problems involving place-name identification, the fixing of weights and measures, and the relative values of different local currencies may be satisfactorily solved.

Another set of voyages worthy of mention is the *Reisebeschreibungen,* published by S. P. l'Honoré Naber in thirteen volumes between 1930 and 1932. This series contains descriptive accounts of the East and West Indies written between 1602 and 1797 by German officials and military men in the service of the Dutch East and West India companies. As Germans, the writers could and did criticize their Dutch employers when the need arose, and their narratives constitute one of the few nonpartisan sources for Indonesian history in company times that we possess.

THE PERIOD OF THE NETHERLANDS INDIAN GOVERNMENT, 1816–1942

So far, we have been considering only such source materials for Indonesian history as have come down to us from the time of the Dutch East India Company. In the latter part of the eighteenth century that Company rapidly declined. It failed to recover from the financial blows it suffered during the Anglo-Dutch War of 1780–1784. In 1796 the directors were forced to surrender their powers to a committee appointed by the pro-French revolutionaries who in the previous year had seized control of the Netherlands, and on December 31, 1799, the Company ceased to exist.

The next sixteen years saw the French and then the British in control of Dutch possessions in Indonesia. Until 1811 the Dutch were still the nominal rulers, but the real master of the Indian Archipelago, as of Holland itself, was Napoleon. In September, 1811, Java fell to the British, who held it until 1816, in which year all former Dutch possessions in the archipelago were restored to Holland in accordance with the Convention of London. The "Netherlands Indian Government," inaugurated in Batavia on August 19, 1816, remained the lawful Dutch authority in the Indonesian islands until it was expelled by the Japanese in 1942.

The new government brought to Indonesia a different type of administration from anything that had gone before. The East India Company had been a profit-conscious mercantile enterprise, concerned to the exclusion of nearly everything else with buying and selling. It possessed no *mission civilisatrice*, no urge to interfere with the way of life of the peoples with whom it carried on business. It encouraged production for export but, except to a limited extent in the case of Java coffee and sugar, did not organize it. By contrast, the Netherlands Indian Government of the nineteenth and early twentieth centuries was an entrepreneur on the grand scale. Under its auspices Indonesia was gradually transformed into a Western-style production machine. In the process, plantation agriculture, social services, and a measure of industrialization were introduced, and government ordinances and regulations began to impinge on millions of Indonesians whose ancestors had hardly been aware that the Dutch East India Company existed.

These changes are reflected in the surviving records of the Netherlands Indian Government's administration. Whereas in company times a clear distinction can be drawn between documents that relate to the Company itself and those that bear on indigenous Indonesian history, official records from 1816 onward are not only more mixed in content but more comprehensive in scope. The role of the Company in Indonesian affairs was very largely that of an outsider; only with reluctance did it allow itself to become a participant. The Netherlands Indian Government, on the other hand, was "the State." Very little that went on in the country, from the building of mosques to the digging of village wells, did not sooner or later come under its scrutiny. In consequence, its records relate to every aspect of Indonesian political, economic, and social life.

With regard to nongovernmental sources the position is similar. From the seventeenth and eighteenth centuries few materials apart from East India Company documents survive, because the Company was the only Dutch organization active in the area. But in the nineteenth and twentieth centuries all kinds of nongovernmental entities came into existence: commercial firms, trade unions, political parties, banks, insurance companies, shipping lines, mining concerns, import and export agencies, schools, missionary societies, and so on. The majority of these organizations were Dutch or, at any rate, Dutch-speaking. All were in close contact with Indonesian affairs, and their records must be regarded as original Dutch source materials for Indonesian history.

It is not practicable to list all such materials. In the following section, therefore, the aim will be, first, to describe the manuscript records of the Netherlands Indian Government (in the State Archives, The Hague); secondly, briefly to draw attention to the major official publications of the period of 1816–1942; and, thirdly, to indicate two aids to research with the assistance of which a knowledge of the nongovernmental sources may be obtained.

A. Manuscripts

The archives of the former Ministry of the Colonies fall into two main sections: the records of the Ministry itself and copies of the transactions of the Netherlands Indian Government transmitted to Holland from Batavia.

1. The records of the Ministry of the Colonies. The series known as the "Gewoon Archief" (Ordinary Archive) comprises the day-to-day incoming and outgoing correspondence of the Ministry on all matters not regarded at the time as confidential or secret. The 1,906 bundles which refer to the years 1814–1849 are located at the main repository in Bleijenburg, The Hague. Those referring to 1850–1900 (5,250 bundles) are housed in an auxiliary repository at Schaarsbergen, near Arnhem, but may be consulted in The Hague by arrangement. The records of the Ministry after 1900 are not open to public inspection.

Of greater interest to Indonesian historians is the "Geheim Archief"

(Secret Archive). In the nineteenth century many topics were classed as secret which, given similar circumstances, would not be placed in such a category today. The "Geheim Archief" is therefore richer in general information than its name implies. It includes, among other things, discussions of future policy, expressions of opinion on past government actions, and accounts of negotiations with foreign states and individuals. Indeed, anything which, if made public, might have even slightly embarrassed the administration seems to have been relegated to the "Geheim" rather than the "Gewoon Archief." This naturally leads one to suppose that the former is the more reliable, because the more uninhibited, source.

Other records of the Ministry of the Colonies which bear on Indonesian history include the "Kabinetsarchief," which contains the personal transactions and decisions of successive colonial ministers, and some thirty private collections of documents deposited in the State Archives by officials who served under the Netherlands Indian Government or by their descendants.

2. The records of the Netherlands Indian Government. The "East Indian Decrees," the title by which the transactions of the Netherlands Indian Government are known, are catalogued under four headings. First, they are divided into "ordinary" and "secret" decrees; secondly, into decrees by the Governor-General in Council ("in Rade") and decrees by the Governor-General acting alone ("buiten Rade"). By the Regeeringsreglement of 1836 the Council of the Indies ("Raad van Indië") was deprived of its executive functions and became a purely advisory body. From that date, therefore, all decrees were promulgated by the Governor-General acting alone. Before 1836, however, the Governor-General was empowered to take decisions on his own responsibility on some matters but not in all. Consequently, the decrees up to 1836 appear under the two headings "in Rade" and "buiten Rade."

The following is a list of the various collections of East Indian Decrees as subdivided in the State Archives:

Letters from Commissioners-General of the Netherlands Indies, 1816–1828; Transactions and Decrees of Commissioners-General of the Netherlands Indies, 1816–1817 and 1826–1828; Secret Decrees of the Commissioners-General, 1816–1819.

Decrees of the Governor-General of the Netherlands Indies in Council, 1819–1836.

Secret Decrees of the Governor-General of the Netherlands Indies in Council, 1819–1834.

Decrees of the Governor-General of the Netherlands Indies, Acting
Alone, 1814–1849.

Decrees of the Governor-General of the Netherlands Indies (East
Indian Decrees), 1830-1932.

Secret Decrees of the Governor-General of the Netherlands Indies,
Acting Alone.[3]

B. Official Publications

The Netherlands Indian Government's annual reports to the States-
General, known as the *Koloniale Verslagen,* appear as a supplement to
the *Staatscourant* (published in Holland) from 1851/2 onward. Official
facts and figures and the details of laws, royal decrees, and government
ordinances and regulations applicable to Indonesia may be obtained
from the *Almanak van Nederlandsch-Indië* and the *Staatsblad van Nederlandsch-Indië,* the *Bijblad op het Staatsblad van Nederlandsch-Indië,*
and the *Javasche Courant.* Budget announcements, debates on colonial
affairs, policy statements, and much other incidental information may
be found in the *Handelingen der 1e en 2e Kamer der Staten-Generaal*
(The Dutch "Hansard"). The *Handelingen van den Volksraad,* or
"Transactions of the People's Council," were published from 1918 onward, the year in which the Volksraad, or Parliament, of the Netherlands Indies was inaugurated. Much material for legal, social, and
economic history may also be found in the annual reports of the various
Netherlands Indian Government departments.

C. Research Aids

Finally, two publications may be mentioned which together give a
reasonably complete picture of the printed sources available in Dutch
for Indonesian history. Both list secondary as well as primary materials, but the references given are sufficiently detailed for the one to
be distinguished from the other in most cases.

The first is the *Catalogus der Koloniale Bibliotheek van het Koninklijk Instituut voor de Taal-, Land- en Volkenkunde van Nederlandsch-
Indië en het Indisch Genootschap* (4 vols., 1908–1937). In this catalogue are mentioned very nearly all the historical publications on the
Dutch colonies that appeared up to and including the year 1935. It
may therefore be regarded as an almost complete bibliography of
Indonesian history as written to that date.

[3] For further information on the manuscript records of the Netherlands Indian
Government, see Graham Irwin, *Nineteenth-Century Borneo* (The Hague, 1955),
Appendix "A."

A second valuable research aid is J. C. Hooykaas and others, eds., *Repertorium op de koloniale litteratuur* (11 vols., 1877–1935). This work is a *catalogue raisonné* of all articles in periodicals, journals, and transactions of learned societies dealing with Dutch overseas territories and published in those territories or in Holland itself between 1595 and 1932. Dutch periodical literature is notably rich in original source materials. In the learned journals, a check list of which is provided in the *Repertorium*, are to be found numerous translations of Indonesian chronicles, various collections of documents, and the original minutes and reports of many conferences and government commissions of inquiry.[4]

In the foregoing analysis our purpose has been to describe those sources for Indonesian history which are written in the Dutch language. Because of the nature of the relationship between Holland and Indonesia over the past three and a half centuries, many of these sources are likely to seem unduly "Europocentric" and, in the context of today, irritatingly partisan. But, as has been suggested above, it would be disastrous if such sources were disregarded on that account alone. The duty of the historian of modern Indonesia vis-à-vis the Dutch sources is to separate the true metal from the dross. He will find the task a rewarding, if exacting, one.

READING LIST

Published Collections of Documents

Chijs, J. A. van der, ed. *Nederlandsch-Indisch plakaatboek, 1602–1811.* 17 vols. Batavia, 1885–1900.

---

[4] Since this paper was written, D. G. E. Hall, ed., *Historians of South East Asia* (London, 1961), has appeared. In this volume there is valuable comment on the various types of Dutch language source material for Indonesian history: Chapter 11, J. G. de Casparis, "Historical Writing on Indonesia (Early Period)"; Chapter 15, H. J. de Graaf, "Aspects of Dutch Historical Writings on Colonial Activities in South East Asia with Special Reference to the Indigenous Peoples during the Sixteenth and Seventeenth Centuries"; and Chapter 16, W. Ph. Coolhaas, "Dutch Contributions to the Historiography of Colonial Activity in the Eighteenth and Nineteenth Centuries." Professor Coolhaas has also recently published *A Critical Survey of Studies on Dutch Colonial History* (The Hague, 1960).

Chijs, J. A. van der, and others, eds. *Dagh-Register gehouden int Casteel Batavia*. 31 vols. The Hague and Batavia, 1887–1931.

Colenbrander, H. T., and W. Ph. Coolhaas, eds. *Jan Pietersz. Coen: Bescheiden omtrent zijn bedrijf in Indië*. 8 vols. The Hague, 1919–1953.

Dam, Pieter van. *Beschryvinge van de Oostindische Compagnie*. Ed. by F. W. Stapel and C. W. Th. baron van Boetzelaer. 7 vols. The Hague, 1927–1954.

Heeres, J. E., and F. W. Stapel, eds. *Corpus Diplomaticum Neerlandico-Indicum*. 6 vols. The Hague, 1907–1953.

Jonge, J. K. J. de, and others, eds. *De opkomst van het Nederlandsch gezag in Oost-Indië*. 13 vols. The Hague, 1862–1909.

Mijer, P., ed. *Verzameling van instructiën, ordonnanciën en reglementen voor de Regeering van Nederlandsch-Indië vastgesteld in de jaren 1609–1836*. Batavia, 1848.

Naber, S. P. l'Honoré, ed. *Reisebeschreibungen von deutschen Beamten und Kriegsleuten im Dienst der Niederländischen West- und Ost-Indischen Kompagnien, 1602–1797*. 13 vols. The Hague, 1930–1932.

Realia: Register op de generale resolutiën van het Kasteel Batavia, 1632–1805. 3 pts. Batavia, 1882–1886.

Periodicals and Learned Journals

Bijdragen tot de Taal-, Land- en Volkenkunde (to 1950 *van Nederlandsch-Indië*). The Hague, 1853–. Cited as *BKI*.

Djåwå: Tijdschrift van het Java-Instituut. Weltevreden, 1921–1941.

Indische Gids, De. Amsterdam, 1879–1941.

Indonesië. The Hague and Bandung, 1947–1957.

Koloniale Studiën. Weltevreden, 1916–1941.

Koloniaal Tijdschrift. The Hague, 1912–1941.

Tijdschrift voor Indische Taal-, Land- en Volkenkunde. Batavia and Jakarta, 1853–1957. Cited as *TBG*.

Verhandelingen van het Bataviaasch Genootschap van Kunsten en Wetenschappen. Batavia, 1825–1950. Cited as *VBG*.

Verhandelingen van het Koninklijk Instituut voor de Taal-, Land- en Volkenkunde. The Hague, 1938–. Cited as *VKI*.

General Histories

Colenbrander, H. T. *Koloniale geschiedenis*. 3 vols. The Hague, 1925–1926.

Fruin-Mees, W. *Geschiedenis van Java.* 2 vols. Weltevreden, 1919–1920.

Gonggrijp, G. *Schets ener economische geschiedenis van Nederlands-Indië.* Haarlem, 1949.

Graaf, H. J. de. *Geschiedenis van Indonesië.* The Hague and Bandung, 1949.

Kat Angelino, A. D. A. de. *Staatkundig beleid en bestuurszorg in Nederlandsch-Indië.* 2 pts. in 3 vols. The Hague, 1929–1930. In an abridged form published in English as *Colonial Policy,* Amsterdam and Chicago, 1931.

Krom, N. J. *Hindoe-Javaansche geschiedenis.* 2d rev. ed. The Hague, 1931.

Stapel, F. W., ed. *Geschiedenis van Nederlandsch-Indië.* 5 vols. Amsterdam, 1938–1940.

Stapel, F. W. *Geschiedenis van Nederlandsch-Indië.* 2d ed. Amsterdam, 1943.

Vlekke, B. H. M. *Geschiedenis van den Indischen Archipel.* The Hague, 1947.

For Reference

Atlas van tropisch Nederland. The Hague, 1938.

Encyclopaedie van Nederlandsch-Indië. 8 vols. The Hague, 1917–1939.

XIV

English Sources for the Modern Period of Indonesian History

By JOHN BASTIN

Lecturer in Southeast Asian History, School of Oriental and African Studies, University of London

I

BECAUSE of the long domination of Indonesia by the Netherlands it is too often assumed that the printed and documentary sources relating to modern Indonesian history are all in the Dutch language. It is of course true that, when considered against the vast Dutch literature, English contributions to Indonesian studies have been minor;[1] yet one should not forget that the real beginnings of Indonesian historiography are to be found not so much in the work of the early Orientalists at Leyden or in the writings of Valentijn as in the massive histories which were published by the British scholars Marsden, Raffles, and Crawfurd, at a time when Indonesian studies attracted little attention in the Netherlands. And if these early histories have long since been superseded by the voluminous writings of Dutch scholars, there still remains an impressive body of English documentary material relating to various aspects of Indonesian history. It tends nowadays to be forgotten that before they were expelled from West Java in 1682 by Sultan Abunasr Abdulkahar the British were actively engaged in trading transactions in many parts of the archipelago and that until

---

[1] This essay is concerned only with works by British and American scholars, although occasional reference is made to studies published in English by other nationals. English studies relating to British Borneo and to the old period of Indonesian history are also excluded from consideration. The essay was written in 1958 and therefore takes no account of recently published books and articles.

early in the nineteenth century they maintained extensive territorial settlements in West Sumatra. Furthermore, during the latter part of the Napoleonic wars they controlled virtually the whole of Indonesia, and even after 1824, when the Treaty of London obliged them to withdraw from West Sumatra, they continued to have commercial dealings with the northern and eastern parts of that island by way of Penang and Singapore. The documentary sources concerning these varied activities of the British in Indonesia furnish valuable information about the country and its people during the early phase of Western expansion into Southeast Asia.

II

The first main body of English records relating to Indonesia are the narratives of the early voyages made to Asia by groups of private London traders or, after 1600, by merchants of the newly constituted East India Company. The most important of these accounts have been published in part in Richard Hakluyt's *The Principal Navigations, Voyages, Traffiques & Discoveries of the English Nation* (London, 1598–1600) and Samuel Purchas' *Hakluytus Posthumus or Purchas His Pilgrimes* (London, 1625) or *in extenso* by the Hakluyt Society of London. For historical purposes they can be considered as complementary to the more valuable Dutch narratives, which were published in the late sixteenth and early seventeenth centuries or in recent years by the Linschoten-Vereeniging; but even in themselves they constitute an interesting mass of material about the places visited by the British traders during the early period of Western intercourse with Indonesia.

The narrative of John Davis, who was chief pilot in Cornelis de Houtman's fleet,[2] and the accounts of the second voyage of Sir James Lancaster to Indonesia in 1601–1603 [3] throw some light on the internal affairs of the sultanate of Acheh during the rule of Sultan 'Ala'u'd-din Ri'ayat Shah, as well as on Achehnese relations with the Portuguese in Malacca and with the Malay state of Johore. The narrative of the voyage of Sir Henry Middleton, which was first published in London in 1606 and since then on two separate occasions by the Hakluyt So-

[2] Purchas (Glasgow, 1905), II, 306–326; A. H. Markham, ed., *The Voyages and Works of John Davis the Navigator* (Hakluyt Society; London, 1880), 1st ser., LIX, 132–156.

[3] Purchas, II, 392–437; C. R. Markham, ed., *The Voyages of Sir James Lancaster, Kt., to the East Indies* (Hakluyt Society; London, 1877), 1st ser., vol. LVI; W. Foster, ed., *The Voyages of Sir James Lancaster to Brazil and the East Indies, 1591–1603* (Hakluyt Society; London, 1940), 2d ser., vol. LXXXV.

ciety,[4] contains an interesting eyewitness account of the last stage of the Dutch-Portuguese conflict in the Moluccas and some important information about the relations between the rulers of Ternate and Tidore.[5] The accounts of other of the East India Company's voyages to Indonesia, especially *The Journal of John Jourdain, 1608–1617* (Hakluyt Society; Cambridge, 1905), also provide details about early Anglo-Dutch activities in the Moluccas. Most of the information from these narratives,[6] however, concerns North Sumatra, the West Sumatra pepper ports of Tiku and Priaman, and the sultanate of Bantam.

Similar printed and documentary sources regarding Indonesia at this period are the reports and letters of Britishers actually resident in the country. Many of these have been published in F. C. Danvers and W. Foster's *Letters Received by the East India Company from Its Servants in the East, 1602–17* (London, 1896–1902) and in W. Foster's *The English Factories in India, 1618–69* (Oxford, 1906–1927); others may be found scattered among the records of the India Office Library, London, especially in the *Collection of Original Correspondence from India, with Collateral Documents Originating at Any Places between England and Japan.* Two related series of printed documents, *A Calendar of the Court Minutes, etc., of the East India Company, 1635–1679* (Oxford, 1907–1938) and *Calendar of State Papers, Colonial Series, East Indies . . . 1513–1629* (London, 1862–1884), contain extracts from the Court Books and other records of the Company, together with relevant material preserved in the Public Record Office, London. The main body of this material, however, relates to the Indian subcontinent and not to Indonesia.

Of the actual printed descriptions of Indonesia at this time, none

---

[4] B. Corney, ed., *The Voyage of Sir Henry Middleton to Bantam and the Maluco Islands* (Hakluyt Society; London, 1855), 1st ser., vol. XIX; W. Foster, ed., *The Voyage of Sir Henry Middleton to the Moluccas, 1604–1606* (Hakluyt Society; London, 1943), 2d ser., vol. LXXXVIII.

[5] Direct British contact with this part of Indonesia was made in 1579 by Sir Francis Drake. See Hakluyt, XI (Glasgow, 1903–1905), 124–130; Purchas, II, 141–145; and R. C. Temple, ed., *The World Encompassed and Analogus Contemporary Documents concerning Sir Francis Drake's Circumnavigation of the World* (London, 1926).

[6] See W. Foster, ed., *The Voyage of Thomas Best to the East Indies, 1612–14* (Hakluyt Society; London, 1934), 2d ser., vol. LXXV; R. C. Temple, ed., *The Travels of Peter Mundy, in Europe and Asia, 1608–1667* (Hakluyt Society; London, 1919), 2d ser., vols. XLV and XLVI; W. H. Moreland, ed., *Peter Floris His Voyage to the East Indies in the Globe, 1611–1615* (Hakluyt Society; London, 1934), 2d ser., vol. LXXIV; and W. Foster, ed., *The Voyage of Nicholas Downton to the East Indies, 1614–15* (Hakluyt Society; London, 1939), 2d ser., vol. LXXXII.

is perhaps more fascinating than Edmund Scott's *An Exact Discourse of the Subtilties, Fashishions* [sic], *Pollicies, Religion, and Ceremonies of the East Indians, as well Chyneses as Javans, there abyding and dweling . . . at Bantam,* which was first published in London in 1606, republished by Purchas, and later by the Hakluyt Society.[7] Scott was for a time in charge of the East India Company's first trading factory at Bantam, and his *Discourse* contains some acute observations on the people of West Java and on the way of life of the early European residents in Indonesia.

Other documentary material relating to West Java, Borneo, the Celebes, and the Moluccas, down to the year 1682, may be found in various volumes of *Factory Records, Home Miscellaneous Series,* and other deposits of records in the India Office Library, London, as well as in odd collections in the Arsip Negara, Jakarta, and the Algemeen Rijksarchief, The Hague. Although these records shed very little light on Indonesian habits and customs, they do contain a wealth of information about economic conditions in the archipelago at this period, so that it is surprising that they have been neglected for so long by both Dutch and British historians. Happily, in recent years the bulk of this early English documentary material, including the Court Minutes and Letter Books of the East India Company, has been examined by D. K. Bassett for his London University doctoral thesis, *The Factory of the English East India Company at Bantam, 1602–1682,* and by the Danish historian, K. Glamann, whose monumental *Dutch Asiatic Trade, 1620–1740* was published in The Hague in 1958. These two works help fill a gap which has hitherto existed in studies pertaining to modern Indonesian economic history.

III

The abandonment of the Bantam factory in 1682 forced the English East India Company to concentrate its activities upon Sumatra, especially upon the west coast which yielded large quantities of pepper. In 1685 a settlement was formed at Bencoolen, and subsidiary outstations were established further along the coast. With varying fortunes these settlements remained intact until 1824, and the voluminous records connected with their administration provide a very rich source of information for this part of Indonesia during the late seventeenth, eighteenth, and early nineteenth centuries. The 162 volumes of the *Sumatra Factory Records* in the India Office Library have never been

[7] Purchas, II, 438–496; Foster, ed., *Middleton,* 81–176.

subjected to detailed investigation, although the Dutch scholar, P. Wink, who made a particular study of certain aspects of Bencoolen history,[8] published some of the early records in *TBG*, LXIV (1924), 461–520. Another series of documents, embracing the whole period of British rule, is now being published by the University of Malaya Press.

An interesting collection of the private letters of Joseph Collet (who was the Deputy Governor of Bencoolen responsible for the building of Fort Marlborough in 1714) was edited by Professor H. H. Dodwell in 1933 under the title *The Private Letter Books of Joseph Collet* (London and New York, 1933). These letters give a delightfully informal account of life in West Sumatra during the early part of the eighteenth century, as well as a few references to British relations with the Indonesian rulers. Some additional information on this particular subject will be found in William Dampier's *A New Voyage round the World*, which appeared in seven editions in London between 1697 and 1729, and in Alexander Hamilton's *A New Account of the East Indies* (Edinburgh, 1727). These two works and Dampier's *Voyages and Descriptions* (London, 1699) also contain some informative details about Acheh at the end of the seventeenth and beginning of the eighteenth century. Other eighteenth-century English contributions to Sumatran studies include Charles Miller's "An Account of the Island of Sumatra," which was published in volume LXVIII of the *Philosophical Transactions* of 1778, and William Marsden's *History of Sumatra*.

Marsden's remarkable book, which was published in London in 1783, republished in the following year, and revised and republished in 1811, was the first full-scale work on Indonesia in the English language, so that its importance can scarcely be exaggerated. Its scope, however, far exceeded what today we would properly ascribe to the bounds of true history, for it contained not only "an account of the government, laws, customs, and manners" of the Sumatran people but also a description of the island's "natural productions" and its "ancient political state." Strangely, its value is in no way diminished by this; indeed, it was precisely because Marsden interested himself in Indonesian languages, customs, and laws, and considered that these subjects lay within the broad purview of his *History*, that he is now regarded as one of the pioneers of the study of Indonesian linguistics and cus-

---

[8] "De onderafdeeling Lais in de Residentie Bengkoeloe," *VBG*, LXVI (1926), 1–131; "De ontwikkeling der inheemsche rechtspraak in het gewest Benkoelen," *TBG*, LXIX (1929), 1–50.

tomary *(adat)* law.[9] Because of its importance in these fields it is surprising to learn that although the book was translated into German in 1785 and into French three years later, no Dutch edition has ever been published. In Great Britain it had a considerable influence and directly inspired the early-nineteenth-century Orientalists Raffles and Crawfurd, both of whom held Marsden in high esteem.

As Lieutenant Governor of Bencoolen between 1818 and 1824, Raffles was responsible for a considerable widening of Western knowledge about the geography, peoples, and natural history of Sumatra. He undertook arduous exploratory journeys into the southern and central districts of the island, sponsored the work of the Baptist missionaries in the Batak regions, and encouraged his subordinates to contribute papers on Sumatran and other Indonesian subjects to a journal which was published locally at Bencoolen. The two volumes of *Malayan Miscellanies,* which appeared between 1820 and 1822, contain papers on Pulau Nias, the annals of Acheh, the *undang-undang* (laws) of Moko-Moko, and cannibalism among the Bataks. Raffles also directed that detailed investigations be made into Indonesian society in the Bencoolen districts, and the reports of these investigations, which were published in *Proceedings of the Agricultural Society Established in Sumatra 1820* (Bencoolen, 1821), contain more accurate and penetrating observations on Indonesian society than might generally be supposed. When brought into relation with other published English manuscript sources, such as "William Jack's Letters to Nathaniel Wallich, 1819–1821," *JRASSB,* LXXIII (1916), 147–268, and *The Journal of Thomas Otho Travers (1813–1820)* (Memoirs of the Raffles Museum, Singapore, no. 4; 1957), and with the later Dutch accounts by Nahuijs, Francis, Verploegh, and de Stuers,[10] these reports furnish us with an extraordinarily rich source of information about this part of Indonesia during the early nineteenth century. Other contemporary English accounts of Sumatra were B. Heyne's *Tracts, Historical and Statistical, on India; . . . also, An Account of Sumatra* (London, 1814); M. H. Court's *Relations of the British Government with . . . Palembang* (London, 1821);

[9] C. van Vollenhoven, *De ontdekking van het adatrecht* (Leyden, 1928), pp. 14–19; J. Gonda, "William Marsden als beoefenaar der taalwetenschap," *BKI,* XCVIII (1939), 517–528; J. Gonda, "Taalbeschouwing en taalbeoefening," *BKI,* XCIX (1940), 44–52. See also P. Wink, "De bronnen van Marsden's adatbeschrijving van Sumatra," *BKI,* LXXX (1924), 1–10.

[10] Colonel Nahuijs, *Brieven over Bencoolen* (Breda, 1826); E. A. Francis, "Benkoelen in 1833," *Tijdschrift voor Neêrlands Indië,* IV (1842), 417–450; P. H. van der Kemp, "Eene bijdrage tot E. B. Kielstra's opstellen over Sumatra's Westkust," *BKI,* XLVI (1894), 257–320, 525–615.

T. Horsfield's "Report on the Island of Banka (1814)," *JIAEA*, II (1848), 299–336, 373–427, 705–725, 779–824; R. Burton and N. Ward's "Report of a Journey into the Batak Country, in the Interior of Sumatra, in the Year 1824," *Transactions of the Royal Asiatic Society*, I (1827), 485–513; J. Anderson's two books, *Mission to the East Coast of Sumatra in [1823]* (Edinburgh, 1826) and *Acheen, and the Ports on the North and East Coasts of Sumatra* (London, 1840); and G. F. Davidson's *Trade and Travel in the Far East* (London, 1846).

Since the early nineteenth century, English contributions to Sumatran history have been few. The former superintendent of the India Office Records, F. C. Danvers, wrote a curiously erratic article entitled "The English Connection with Sumatra," in the *Asiatic Quarterly Review*, I (1886), 410–431; A. Wright and T. H. Reid in *The Malay Peninsula* (London, 1912) added some new details about the early years of the British settlement at Bencoolen; C. J. Brooks wrote an article "English Tombs and Monuments in Bencoolen," in *JRASSB*, LXXVIII (1918), 51–58; and R. J. Wilkinson, who made many notable contributions to Malayan studies, published two brief articles on Bencoolen in the *JRASMB*, XVI (1938), 127–133, and XIX (1941), 101–119. The second part of J. Bastin's *The Native Policies of Sir Stamford Raffles in Java and Sumatra* (Oxford, 1957) briefly analyzes the effects of the British pepper system on the West Sumatran cultivators during the late eighteenth and early nineteenth centuries, and there are some studies by American scholars of the Sumatran pepper trade during approximately the same period. The most important of these are G. G. Putnam's *Salem Vessels and Their Voyages: A History of the Pepper Trade with the Island of Sumatra* (Essex Institute; Salem, Mass., 1924), 1st ser., and Dr. J. W. Gould's three-part article "Sumatra—America's Pepperpot, 1784–1873," *Essex Institute Historical Collections*, XCII (1956), 83–152, 203–251, 295–348. J. D. Phillips' *Pepper and Pirates: Adventures in the Sumatra Pepper Trade of Salem* (Boston, 1949) and *Salem and the Indies* (Boston, 1947) are only popular works.

In addition to these studies, there are a small number of articles on Acheh, including T. Braddell's "On the History of Acheen," *JIAEA*, V (1851), 15–25; G. P. Tolson's "Acheh, Commonly Called Acheen," *JRASSB*, V (1880), 37–50; and D. F. A. Hervey's report "Achin Piracy," *JRASMB*, V (1927), 316–323. On the subject of piracy one may refer here to W. Bradley's little-known work, *The Wreck of the Nisero and Our Captivity in Sumatra* (London, 1884), and the official *Blue Books: Correspondence [and Further Correspondence] respecting the Wreck* of the "Nisero," and the Detention of Her Crew by the Rajah of Tenom, which was published in six volumes in London during 1884. There are also a few comparative studies of certain aspects of Malayan and Indonesian history, such as C. A. Gibson-Hill's "On the Alleged Death of Sultan Ala'u'd-din of Johore at Acheh, in 1613," *JRASMB*, XXIX (1956), 125–145; Sir Richard Winstedt's "The Early Rulers of Perak, Pahang and Acheh," *JRASMB*, X (1932), 32–44; "Negri Sembilan: The History, Polity and Beliefs of the Nine States," *JRASMB*, XII (1934), 37–111; and "The Chronicles of Pasai," *JRASMB*, XVI (1938), 24–30. The only other contributions made by British scholars to the modern period of Sumatran history lie within the more general field of Islamic studies. Sir Richard Winstedt's "The Advent of Muhammadanism in the Malay Peninsula and Archipelago," *JRASSB*, LXXVII (1917), 171–175, and G. E. Marrison's "The Coming of Islam to the East Indies," *JRASMB*, XXIV (1951), 28–37, discuss the early spread of Islam in the archipelago; and the related subject of the diffusion of Sufi doctrines in Sumatra has been treated by R. L. Archer in *JRASMB*, XV (1937), 1–126, and in *Muslim World*, XXVIII (1938), 231–238, and, more recently, by A. H. Johns, whose London University doctoral dissertation, "Malay Sufism as Illustrated in an Anonymous Collection of 17th Century Tracts," has been published in *JRASMB*, XXX (1957), 1–111. The same writer's "Aspects of Sufi Thought in India and Indonesia in the First Half of the 17th Century," *JRASMB*, XXVIII (1955), 70–77, and Sir Richard Winstedt's "Some Malay Mystics, Heretical and Orthodox," *JRASMB*, I (1923), 312–318, may also be usefully consulted.

IV

One of the most disappointing features about English contributions to Indonesian history is that so little use has been made by scholars of the voluminous English manuscript material of the early nineteenth century. Other than such contemporary publications as W. Vaughan's *The Narrative of Captain David Woodward and Four Seamen, who lost their ship . . . and surrendered themselves up to the Malays, in the island of Celebes; containing . . . an account of the manners and customs of the country* (London, 1804) and an *Illustrated Account of Captain Cole's Splendid Achievement in the Capture of the Island of Banda* (London, 1811), there is almost nothing of a historical nature that has appeared in English on the eastern part of Indonesia. Of the India Office Library records only a journal of the British expeditionary force sent against the Moluccas in 1796 has been published, and that by the Dutch scholar, J. E. Heeres; [11] the remainder of the records concerning the British administration of eastern Indonesia have, for the most part, attracted little attention. A brief account of the fall of the Moluccas will be found in C. N. Parkinson's *War in the Eastern Seas, 1793–1815* (London, 1954),[12] and H. R. C. Wright has discussed certain aspects of Moluccan spice production during this period in a part of *JRASMB*, vol. XXXI (1958).

Until recent years, the early-nineteenth-century English records relating to Java, which are deposited in the India Office Library, the British Museum, and the Royal Asiatic Society Library, London, and in the Algemeen Rijksarchief, The Hague, and the Arsip Negara, Jakarta, had also escaped detailed examination, and even yet there has not been extracted from them much of their rich content regarding the political, social, and economic organization of Java during the period of British rule (1811–1816). Of the India Office Library holdings, the *Java Factory Records*, especially the volumes containing the Public Consultations of the British colonial government, are, of course, invaluable, as are many of the documents in the *Raffles Collection* and in *Dutch Records A;* but perhaps the most interesting series of records are those which were collected by Colonel Colin Mackenzie during his stay in Java [13] and which are now generally designated as the 1822 and Private collections of the Mackenzie manuscripts. In 1916 C. O. Blagden published a comprehensive catalogue of these two collections, and reference should be made in the first instance to this, as it provides an excellent introduction to the whole of the Mackenzie manuscripts.[14] There exists in the India Office Library a printed, but unpublished, catalogue of the Class division of the manuscripts, but the Miscellaneous section, which is relatively unimportant, still remains unclassified. Insofar as it concerns Indonesia, the Mackenzie collections contain English translations of Javanese and Malay manuscripts, translations of a number of early-nineteenth-century Dutch works on Indonesia, dynastic lists of Javanese regents, and statistical tables and descriptive

[11] "Eene Engelsche lezing omtrent de verovering van Banda en Ambon in 1796," *BKI*, LX (1908), 249–368. The journal has been partly published in *JRASSB*, VII (1881), 51–74.

[12] Published as a companion volume to his *Trade in the Eastern Seas, 1793–1813* (Cambridge, 1937).

[13] W. C. Mackenzie, *Colonel Colin Mackenzie, First Surveyor-General of India* (Edinburgh and London, 1952), pp. 101–170.

[14] *Catalogue of Manuscripts in European Languages Belonging to the Library of the India Office: The Mackenzie Collections—The 1822 Collection & the Private Collection* (Oxford, 1916), I (i).

accounts of many districts in Java and Madura at the beginning of the nineteenth century. In addition, there are a number of descriptions, and water-color paintings, of Javanese antiquities which were uncovered and restored during the period of British rule. Some of the paintings are extraordinarily interesting and have recently been catalogued by Mrs. M. Archer.

In the British Museum there are also a number of manuscripts referring to early-nineteenth-century Java. The volume "Papers Relating to Java, circa 1815" (Add.MSS. 30353) contains John Crawfurd's "A Short Sketch of the Native History of Java," together with his penetrating study "Remarks on the Nature and Condition of Landed Tenures under the Native Governments of Java" which was written in 1813. Another volume, entitled "J. Crawfurd, Papers on Java, Cochin China, etc., 1811–1823" (Add.MSS. 33411), includes reports by various writers on Bangka, Bantam, Kedu, and Borneo, which were used by Crawfurd in his numerous publications. It is worth noting that in the British Museum (Add.MSS. 45272) there is a volume of Raffles' secret letters written between January and March, 1812, which really form a continuation to those in the *Raffles Collection* XIII, in the India Office Library.

In the Library of the Royal Asiatic Society, London, there is a bound volume entitled "Java Antiquities" containing a number of assorted manuscripts, including extracts from the private journal of Raffles' assistant, Captain G. P. Baker, who was responsible for recording and surveying many of the ancient monuments of central Java. A companion volume, "Java Antiquities—Craufurd" [*sic*], includes manuscript versions of a number of papers on the monuments of Java which were written by Crawfurd at this period and subsequently published. A third volume in the Royal Asiatic Society's Library contains a set of documents dealing with the internal troubles of the Javanese courts during 1811–1812, but these are mainly duplicates of documents which may be found in a more accessible form in the *Java Factory Records* and in other collections of the India Office Library. Similar duplicates of English manuscripts are scattered among many of the private collections in the Algemeen Rijksarchief, The Hague, although there is occasionally to be found an original document which is not represented in any of the London collections.

In the Arsip Negara, Jakarta, there are some important collections of English manuscripts, including the invaluable land revenue and judicial proceedings of the British colonial government. Before the last

war the former director of the archives, F. de Haan, made a thorough
investigation of these and other records with the object of writing a
definitive account of the British period in Java, but he died before the
work was completed. His "Personalia der periode van het Engelsch
bestuur over Java, 1811–1816," *BKI*, XCII (1935), 477–681, was, however, a useful by-product of painstaking and assiduous research.

Of the early-nineteenth-century English printed accounts of Java,
the outstanding one is, of course, Raffles' *History of Java*, which was
first published in two quarto volumes in London in 1817 and republished thirteen years later in octavo form with an index. Like Marsden's
History of Sumatra, Raffles' book comprised much that was not strictly
historical, including chapters on the geography, agriculture, manufactures, and commerce of Java. But the historical section in the second
volume marked an important step forward in Western historiography
of Indonesia, as it extended the existing limits of Javanese history
backward from the sixteenth century to the period of traditions and
legends. Despite the numerous faulty transcripts and translations of
Javanese inscriptions and texts, *The History of Java* remained the
standard work on the subject until nearly the end of the nineteenth
century, when the steady stream of publications by Dutch scholars
superseded it. In certain respects, Raffles' earlier work, *Substance of a
Minute . . . on . . . the Establishment of a Land Rental on the Island of Java* (London, 1814), was as important a contribution to Indonesian studies as *The History of Java*, because it was the first serious
attempt to come to grips with the confused subject of Javanese land
tenures; and, although Raffles' bias in favor of peasant proprietorship
often led him to erroneous conclusions, the book nevertheless places
him, along with Marsden, in the forefront of the pioneers of the study
of *adat* law in Indonesia.[15]

Raffles' revival of the Bataviaasch Genootschap van Kunsten en
Wetenschappen (Batavian Society of Arts and Sciences)—the oldest
learned society of its kind in Asia—gives him an equally honored place
among the early patrons of Oriental studies in Indonesia. In the two
volumes of the *Verhandelingen van het Bataviaasch Genootschap van
Kunsten en Wetenschappen* (*VBG*), which were published under his
auspices in 1814 and 1816, there are a number of English contributions,
including C. Mackenzie's "Narrative of a journey to examine the remains of an ancient city and temples at Brambana [*sic*] in Java," J.
Crawfurd's "An inscription from the Kawi . . . taken from a stone

[15] Van Vollenhoven, *De ontdekking van het adatrecht*, pp. 24–31.

found in . . . Surabaya," and Raffles' "Copies of two of the ancient inscriptions on copper plates dug up in the vicinity of Surabaya." The two discourses which Raffles gave before the society in 1813 and 1815 are also printed in these volumes.

Other English publications of this period include W. Thorn's *Memoir of the Conquest of Java* (London, 1815), which contains some interesting, although not always accurate, historical information on various places in Java, as well as an account of the British military operations at Palembang in 1812; C. Assey's *Review of the Administration, Value, and State of the Colony of Java with Its Dependencies* (London, 1816), which generally reflects Raffles' ideas on questions of colonial policy and administration; and the various official publications of the British Government in Java, such as the *Java Government Gazette* (Batavia, 1812–1816), *Proclamations, Regulations, Advertisements, and Orders, printed and published on the Island of Java, by the British Government* (Batavia, 1813–1816), *The Java Annual Directory and Almanac, for 1814* (and *for 1815* and *for 1816*) (Batavia, 1814–1816), and an untitled volume of documents concerning the charges preferred by Major General R. Gillespie against Raffles' administration, which was printed at Batavia in 1815. In a somewhat different category there are J. J. Stockdale's *Sketches, Civil and Military, of the Island of Java and Its Immediate Dependencies* (London, 1811) and G. A. Addison's *Original Familiar Correspondence between Residents in India, including Sketches of Java* (Edinburgh, 1846), which includes a number of private letters written in Java during the period of British rule. More important than these is Lady Sophia Raffles' *Memoir of the Life and Public Services of Sir Thomas Stamford Raffles*, which was first published in London in 1830 and republished in two octavo volumes five years later. The book is of considerable value as it contains a large number of Raffles' private letters and public dispatches, although these have often been so badly edited that in matters of detail it is unwise to rely too heavily upon the text.

The later English secondary accounts of Raffles and the British period in Indonesia are far from being impressive. The biographies of Raffles—D. C. Boulger, *The Life of Sir Stamford Raffles* (London, 1897); H. E. Egerton, *Sir Stamford Raffles* (London, 1900); J. Cook, *Sir Thomas Stamford Raffles* (London, 1918); R. Coupland, *Raffles, 1781–1826* (Oxford, 1926); and E. Hahn, *Raffles of Singapore* (London, 1948)—all have grave shortcomings, mainly because the writers made little use of the records in the India Office Library. Raffles' most recent biographer, C. E. Wurtzburg, went to considerable pains to have voluminous extracts taken from some of these records, but unfortunately he did not incorporate much of this fresh information in his book *Raffles of the Eastern Isles* (London, 1954). H. R. C. Wright's two articles, "Muntinghe's Advice to Raffles on the Land Question in Java," *BKI*, CVIII (1952), 220–247, and "The Freedom of Labour under Raffles's Administration in Java (1811–16)," *JRASMB*, XXVI (1953), 104–112, are critical studies, as are the two preliminary monographs, *Raffles' Ideas on the Land Rent System in Java* (VKI, vol. XIV; 1954), and *The Native Policies of Sir Stamford Raffles in Java and Sumatra* (Oxford, 1957), by J. Bastin; but these studies generally relate only to Raffles' policies, so that there is yet really nothing in English which gives as comprehensive an account of Java during the British period as H. D. Levyssohn Norman's *De Britsche heerschappij over Java en onderhoorigheden (1811–1816)*, which was published in The Hague as long ago as 1857.

The same thing is true of studies about Anglo-Dutch relations in the Indonesian Archipelago during the Napoleonic and post-Napoleonic period. A. C. Baker's "Some Account of the Anglo Dutch Relations in the East at the Beginning of the 19th Century," *JRASSB*, LXIV (1913), 1–68; H. R. C. Wright's "The Anglo-Dutch Dispute in the East, 1814–1824," *Economic History Review*, III (1950–1951), 229–239; J. Bastin's "Raffles and British Policy in the Indian Archipelago, 1811–1816," *JRASMB*, XXVII (1954), 84–119; and P. N. Tarling's "The Relationship between British Policies and the Extent of Dutch Power in the Malay Archipelago, 1784–1871," *Australian Journal of Politics and History*, IV (1958), 179–192, and the early chapters of his Cambridge University doctoral dissertation, "British Policy in the Malay Peninsula and Archipelago, 1824–1871," *JRASMB*, vol. XXX (1957)—all are very useful as far as they go, but they can hardly be said to have replaced the massive articles of the Dutch scholar P. H. van der Kemp, which were published in the *Bijdragen tot de Taal-, Land- en Volkenkunde (BKI)* during the 1890's and early decades of this century.

V

Although Marsden and Raffles had confined their studies largely to Sumatra and Java, British attention had already been directed to other parts of the Indonesian Archipelago, particularly to Borneo. This island had been a center of British commercial activity in the early days of the East India Company,[16] and British interest in it had been revived during the second half of the eighteenth century by the proposals of Alexander Dalrymple to found an entrepôt at Balambangan.[17] This interest had been kept alive, to some extent, by British private traders like John Hunt and officials like Raffles, who wanted to create a British sphere of influence in western Borneo; but it was really not until the 1840's, when James Brooke's actions in Sarawak created some attention at home, that British scholars became aware of the island as a potential field for scientific study.

Before this time, the only English contributions to Borneo studies were John Leyden's "Sketch of Borneo," which was published in *VBG*, vol. VII (1814), and in J. H. Moor's *Notices of the Indian Archipelago and Adjacent Countries* (Singapore, 1837); and J. Hunt's "Sketch of Borneo, or Pulo Kalamantan," which appeared in *Malayan Miscellanies*, in Moor's *Notices*, and, appropriately, as it apparently exerted some influence on Brooke, in H. Keppel's *The Expedition to Borneo of H.M.S. Dido* (London, 1847). Since Brooke's period, English studies on western (British) Borneo have been relatively voluminous, but as they fall outside the scope of this essay they cannot be listed here. Mention should be made, however, of J. R. Logan's pioneering papers, "Notices of European Intercourse with Borneo Proper Prior to the Establishment of Singapore in 1819," "Traces of the Origin of the Malay Kingdom of Borneo Proper," and "Notices of Chinese Intercourse with Borneo Proper Prior to the Establishment of Singapore in 1819," which were published in *JIAEA*, II (1848), 498–512, 513–527, 611–615; C. A. Gibson-Hill's "Documents Relating to John Clunies Ross, Alexander Hare," *JRASMB*, XXV (1952), 1–306, which discusses, *inter alia*, the attempts made in the early nineteenth century to establish a British settlement at Banjermasin; and G. Irwin's *Nineteenth-Century Borneo: A Study in Diplomatic Rivalry* (VKI, vol. XV; 1955), which deals with the reactions of the Dutch to British activities in western Borneo.

VI

Borneo was included within the scope of John Crawfurd's *History of the Indian Archipelago*, which was published in three octavo vol-

---

[16] J. Willi, *The Early Relations of England with Borneo to 1805* (Langensalza, Beyer, 1922); T. C. P. Edgell, "English Trade and Policy in Borneo and the Adjacent Islands, 1667–1786" (unpublished Master of Arts thesis, University of London, 1935). See also D. Beeckman, *A Voyage to . . . Borneo* (London, 1718).

[17] V. T. Harlow, *The Founding of the Second British Empire, 1763–1793* (London, 1952), I, 70 ff.

umes in Edinburgh in 1820. In his book, Crawfurd attempted to go beyond the limited framework of Marsden's and Raffles' works by taking the whole of the Indonesian Archipelago, the Philippines, and the Malay Peninsula as his subject matter; in practice, however, he focused so much attention on Java that Raffles, who reviewed the book in the light of his own *History of Java*, complained that Crawfurd's work contained not a single fact that was new to him.[18] Crawfurd's work was also unoriginal in the sense that it was as firmly rooted as its predecessors in a philosophy of history which embraced all aspects of knowledge. Thus a reader has to proceed through the whole of the first volume, devoted to such subjects as the character of the people, their arts and methods of agriculture, and through half of the second before he will be treated to anything that can reasonably be defined as history proper; and having proceeded so far, he will doubtless be dismayed to read that, in the opinion of the author, Indonesian history is too "defective in interest and dignity to demand the solemn and continuous narrative of regular history." [19] For all that, the *History of the Indian Archipelago* was an important book mainly because it established the "Indian Archipelago" as an intelligible field of historical study.[20]

Crawfurd's book brought the term "Indian Archipelago" into general vogue, and it was used in the titles of a number of English books which appeared soon afterward. In 1837 J. H. Moor published his *Notices of the Indian Archipelago and Adjacent Countries*, which included articles on Malayan and Indonesian subjects by himself and other contemporaries, as well as a few papers by older scholars, and in the same year George Windsor Earl published in London his popular work, *The Eastern Seas, or Voyages and Adventures in the Indian Archipelago*. The term was also used by J. R. Logan in the title of his *Journal of the Indian Archipelago and Eastern Asia*, which he edited in Singapore between 1847 and 1862. Among the many important papers published in that *Journal* were Logan's "The Present Condition of the Indian Archipelago," I (1847), 1–21, which contains some general ob-

[18] Interestingly, the Dutch edition of Crawfurd's *History*, which was published at Haarlem in 1823, expressed the limited scope of the book in a subtitle: *De Indische Archipel: In het bijzonder het eiland Java, beschouwd. . . .*

[19] II, 285.

[20] B. Harrison, "English Historians of 'The Indian Archipelago': Crawfurd and St. John" (Historical Writing on the Peoples of Asia: South East Asia Seminar, London, 1956; since published in D. G. E. Hall, ed., *Historians of South East Asia* [London, 1961], pp. 245–254).

servations on the history of the region; T. Braddell's "The Ancient Trade of the Indian Archipelago," and "The Europeans in the Indian Archipelago in the 16th and 17th Centuries," new ser., II (1858), 237–277, 313–335; and Spencer St. John's "Piracy in the Indian Archipelago," III (1849), 251–260.

The last-named contributor—Spencer St. John—became involved in the affairs of the archipelago during the middle decades of the nineteenth century. He was a personal friend of James Brooke and in 1855 succeeded the White Rajah as British Consul General to the native states of Borneo. Two years previously his brother, Horace St. John, had published in London his two-volume *The Indian Archipelago: Its History and Present State*. Horace St. John's imagination had been early stirred by Brooke's exploits, and from the perspective of London, he had discovered "a romance" in the history of the Indonesian islands. What he meant by history, however, was nothing more than the development of European trade and conquest,[21] so that, except for a brief introduction on the origin and diffusion of the Malay peoples, his book is confined largely to Western activities in the Indonesian region from the Portuguese period down to the middle of the nineteenth century. Yet, perhaps because of its singleness of theme, and certainly because of its copious references to all the available English printed sources, the book today appears to be a more modern work than any of the books of his contemporaries. It remains important as a source for the history of piracy in the Indonesian Archipelago during the first half of the nineteenth century and is still worth reading as the first detailed English account of the Dutch colonial system in Indonesia.

St. John's work was followed two years later by Walter M. Gibson's *The Prison of Weltevreden; and a Glance at the East Indian Archipelago* and *Sketches in the East Indian Archipelago*, both of which were published in New York. A year later again Crawfurd published *A Descriptive Dictionary of the Indian Islands & Adjacent Countries*, in place of a second edition of his *History*, and in 1857 F. Boucher's *The Indian Archipelago* appeared. Both these works were published in London, and in the succeeding three decades a spate of books on the archipelago were published there, including A. S. Bickmore's *Travels in the East Indian Archipelago* (1868), A. R. Wallace's *The Malay Archipelago* (1869), W. H. D. Adams' *The Eastern Archipelago* (1880), H. O. Forbes's *A Naturalist's Wanderings in the Eastern Archipelago* (1885), and Anna Forbes's *Insulinde: Experience of a Natural-*

[21] I, preface vii, v.

ist's Wife in the Eastern Archipelago (1887). As their titles indicate, these were not historical works, but they are of general interest to the historian in providing him with a particular type of Indonesian source material of the second half of the nineteenth century.

Other nineteenth-century English studies of Indonesia are the travel books *De Zieke Reiziger; or Rambles in Java and the Straits (in 1852), by a Bengal Civilian* (London, 1853), H. Yule's *Sketches of Java* (London, 1862), and W. B. Worsfold's *A Visit to Java* (London, 1893) and the works on the Dutch colonial system which were written by English visitors to Java. Among these are J. W. B. Money's *Java: or, How to Manage a Colony* (London, 1861) and H. S. Boys's *Some Notes on Java and Its Administration by the Dutch* (Allahabad, 1892). Money's book, which was dedicated to the former Dutch Governor-General, J. van den Bosch, was so influential in creating in Great Britain a climate of opinion favorable to the Culture System that it was not until the end of the nineteenth century that any serious challenge was offered to his interpretation by English scholars. Around the turn of the century, however, coinciding with the high tide of liberalism and, in Great Britain, with the mounting anti-Dutch feeling engendered by the Anglo-Boer conflict in South Africa, the earlier colonial policies of the Dutch in Indonesia began to come under the sharp criticism of some English writers, including Raffles' biographers, Boulger and Egerton. The main liberal onslaught on the Culture System, however, was left to a young American scholar, Clive Day, who in 1904 published what is perhaps the most stimulating book ever written in English about the Dutch colonial system in Indonesia.

VII

Day's book, *The Policy and Administration of the Dutch in Java* (New York, 1904), was heralded in 1900 by two articles on the Culture System which he contributed to the February and May issues of the *Yale Review*. These articles, under the title "Experience of the Dutch with Tropical Labour: (i) The Culture System, (ii) Abolition of the Culture System and Transition to Free Labour," constituted the first scholarly criticism of the Culture System in the English language; and, although Day's opinions have a strong liberal bias, they have continued to find general support not only among later English writers but also among a large number of Dutch scholars. This is partly due to the fact that the articles were incorporated by Day into his book which, in its Dutch translation, had the good fortune to be prescribed as a text for the Leyden University Indological faculty. Its influence on liberal Dutch scholarship is therefore impossible to calculate. The book deserved its high reputation because its appraisal of Dutch policy and administration in Indonesia was based on a meticulous analysis of the available Dutch literature and because it suggested a number of interesting avenues of research, many of which, unfortunately, have never been fully explored.

In 1909 the vast *Twentieth Century Impressions of Netherlands India* was published in London, and this contained a long introduction by Arnold Wright on the history of Indonesia. Wright was a painstaking and accurate historian, who in 1912 wrote an important pioneer study of British rule in Malaya [22] and five years later produced an exceedingly well-written book entitled *Early English Adventurers in the East,* in which he examined, among other things, the Ambon "massacre." But his historical introduction to *Twentieth Century Impressions of Netherlands India,* although it contains some interesting factual information, is too much of an occasional piece to demand anything other than passing notice.

Quite otherwise is D. M. Campbell's two-volume *Java: Past and Present,* which was published posthumously in London in 1915. Unlike other British scholars, Campbell had the advantage of an intimate knowledge of Indonesia gained from a lifetime's residence in the country. During the twenty-three years he spent in Java he served as British Vice-Consul and as a member of the Gewestelijke Raad of Semarang and of the Semarang Chamber of Commerce. He devoted something like seven years to the actual writing of his book, which was intended to describe the country of Java, its people, history, antiquities, and economic products. When Campbell died in 1913, the historical sections had been completed, and these, together with chapters on flora, fauna, and industries of Java, together with miscellaneous notes on the people and political and social life in Java, were published by his widow. Campbell's book is a virtual treasure house of out-of-the-way information on the history of Java, but the lack of documentation often makes it impossible to distinguish highly speculative opinions from conclusions based on obscure, though, one suspects, accurate factual information.

Since the appearance of Campbell's work there have been published a number of books in English on Indonesia mainly by American,

[22] A. Wright and T. H. Reid, *The Malay Peninsula: A Record of British Progress in the Middle East* (London, 1912).

or Dutch-American, scholars, but most of these have been concerned
with history only insofar as it was considered necessary to illustrate
contemporary Indonesian political, social, economic, and religious
themes. Amry Vandenbosch's *The Dutch East Indies*, which was first
published in California in 1933, Rupert Emerson's *Malaysia: A Study
in Direct and Indirect Rule* (New York, 1937), J. O. M. Broek's *Economic Development of the Netherlands Indies* (New York, 1942), and,
more recently, George McT. Kahin's *Nationalism and Revolution in
Indonesia* (Ithaca, N.Y., 1952), J. M. van der Kroef's *Indonesia in the
Modern World* (Bandung, 1954–1956) and *Indonesian Social Evolution* (Amsterdam, 1958), and H. J. Benda's *The Crescent and the Rising
Sun* (The Hague, 1958) are all cases in point. Except for an occasional
article by van der Kroef [23] and articles on more recent Indonesian
history, such as P. W. van der Veur's "E. F. E. Douwes Dekker: Evan-
gelist for Indonesian Political Nationalism," *Journal of Asian Studies*,
XVII, no. 4 (1958), 551–566, recent American scholarship has ignored
the historical field and concentrated upon the contemporary Indonesian scene. If this is not in itself surprising, the decline of the traditional indological studies in the Netherlands makes the future
prospect for Indonesian history seem somewhat alarming.

Nor is the situation likely to be saved by British historians of Southeast Asia, for their interest in Indonesia is for the most part incidental.
Since the appearance in 1939 of J. S. Furnivall's *Netherlands India: A
Study of Plural Economy*, nothing has been published in Great Britain
which compares with his original and penetrating analysis of the nineteenth and early twentieth centuries.[24] C. R. Boxer has published a
few articles, including "Cornelis Speelman and the Growth of Dutch
Power in Indonesia, 1666–1684," *History Today*, VIII, no. 3 (1958),
145–154, and his profound scholarship in other Asian fields has thrown
incidental light on aspects of Indonesian history; V. Purcell in *The Chinese in Southeast Asia* (Oxford, 1951) has given us a historical account
of Chinese activity in Indonesia from earliest to modern times; G. C.
Allen and Audrey G. Donnithorne in *Western Enterprise in Indonesia
and Malaya* (London, 1957) have provided some knowledge of the
economic history of Indonesia during the nineteenth century; and B.
Harrison in *South East Asia: A Short History* (London, 1954) and D.

[23] "Prince Diponegoro: Progenitor of Indonesian Nationalism," *Far Eastern
Quarterly*, VIII (1949), 424–450; "The Colonial Deviation in Indonesian History,"
East and West, VII (1956), 251–261.
[24] Compare the other important work by Furnivall, *Colonial Policy and Practice:
A Comparative Study of Burma and Netherlands India* (Cambridge, 1948).

G. E. Hall in *A History of South-east Asia* (London, 1955) have broken new ground by attempting to integrate Indonesian history into a broader Southeast Asian framework. But research and writing on Indonesian history by Britishers has not been attempted at that fundamental level which has for so long distinguished Dutch scholarship in this field. With one or two exceptions, it is true to say that the most significant English contributions to Indonesian historiography were made in the early nineteenth century—by Marsden, Raffles, and Crawfurd.

XV

Soviet Sources
for Indonesian History

By RUTH T. McVEY

Research Associate, Cornell Modern Indonesia Project,
Cornell University, Ithaca, New York

IT has been only in recent years that the Soviet Union has had substantial contact with Indonesia, and therefore the amount of Russian scholarly research on that country has not been large. On the other hand, Soviet periodicals printed more articles on Indonesia than on any other Southeast Asian country prior to World War II; and since the ending of that war they have treated Indonesia with a frequency second only to that of Vietnam. Moreover, the international character of communism has ensured Russian interest in that important component of the Indonesian revolutionary movement. Not only did Soviet opinion on the Indonesian situation have a major influence on Indonesian Communist policy, but Indonesian revolutionaries published articles and pamphlets while in the USSR, furnishing accounts which supplement usefully the few existing sources on the early period of the independence movement. Soviet comments on the Indonesian situation during the revolutionary period are of interest because of the role played by the Soviet Union in the United Nations debates and because of the continuing controversy concerning the Indonesian Communist Party's policies at this time. Finally, in recent years Russian scholars have produced an increasing number of works on Indonesia which are useful not only as reflections of the Soviet Government's attitude toward that country but as historical studies in their own right.[1]

[1] I am indebted to Dr. E. P. Zakaznikova of the USSR Academy of Sciences'

Although the quality of Russian research on Indonesia has been highest in most recent times, it is not Soviet publications of this period which are of the greatest importance to the historian but rather the sources published before World War II, when the USSR had virtually no contact with Indonesia or, for that matter, with any of the Southeast Asian countries. There are two reasons for this apparent paradox. In the first place, a number of Indonesian leaders—most of them members of the Indonesian Communist Party (PKI)—spent some time in the Soviet Union during the 1920's and 1930's and published books, pamphlets, and articles in the course of their sojourns. We might also note that many of the early Dutch participants in the Indies Communist movement published articles on that subject in the Comintern organs. Secondly, Indonesian Communist leaders took an active part in the meetings of the Comintern and its affiliated organizations, and the publications of these bodies provide valuable insights into the thinking of the Indonesian left revolutionary leaders and their relations with the Third International and the Dutch Communist movement.

The contributions of Indonesian revolutionaries to Soviet and Comintern publications do not, of course, properly represent Soviet contributions to Indonesian historiography. However, since writings by the Indonesian left revolutionary leaders of the colonial period are hard to come by today and since they contain in some cases quite important contributions to Indonesian history, I shall take the liberty of including them in this survey. The major work in this category is a book written by Tan Malaka, *Indoneziia i ee mesto na probuzhdaemsia Vostoke* (Indonesia and Its Place in the Awakening East). Malaka, having been exiled from the Netherlands Indies in 1922, traveled to Holland and then to Russia, where he attended the fourth Comintern congress in November of that year. Following the meeting, he relates in his autobiography, he was asked by the Comintern to write a book describing Indonesia's historical, economic, and political situation, to supplement the International's scanty sources of information on that country.[2] How much of the resulting work was completely Tan Malaka's is a bit of a problem, as he relates that he was told that he was to provide the facts and the Russians would fill in the analysis.[3] At any rate,

Institute of the Peoples of the East for reading the draft of this essay and providing valuable corrections and additions. She is not, of course, responsible for the analysis presented here.

[2] Tan Malaka, *Dari Pendjara ke Pendjara*, I, 95, 102.

[3] *Ibid.*, p. 102.

the book was favorably received in Soviet reviews [4] and had two editions, the first appearing in 1924 and the second a year later.[5] Tan Malaka also published a number of articles in Comintern-affiliated organs. They include "Communism in Java" (written together with the Dutch PKI leader Bergsma), which appeared in *International Press Correspondence* (the Comintern newspaper, usually shortened to *Inprecorr*; vol. III, no. 56, Aug. 16, 1923). He was particularly active in contributing to the Profintern (Red International of Labor Unions) bulletin *Krasnyi internatsional profsoiuzov*.[6] Among his publications in that organ are "Holland: The Affiliation of the NAS to the RILU" (vol. III, no. 4, April, 1923); "Indonesia: The Contract Coolies" (vol. III, no. 2, Feb., 1923); "Indonesia: The Labor Movement" (vol. III, no. 5–6, May–June, 1923); "The Workers in the Sugar Industry on the Island of Java" (vol. III, no. 5–6, May–June, 1923); and, together with Van Reesem, "The Labor Union Movement in Indo-China [*sic*] (the Dutch East Indies)" (no. 10, Oct., 1922).

Musso, an Indonesian Communist leader who spent much of his career in exile in Russia, published two pamphlets on Indonesia while in that country: *Indoneziia—koloniia gollandskogo imperializma* (Indonesia, a Colony of Dutch Imperialism), which was published in Moscow in 1931 by the Central Committee of the International Red Aid (TsK MOPR), and *Prinuditel'nyi trud v Indonezii* (Forced Labor in Indonesia), which appeared in 1930. The latter booklet is particularly interesting for the account it gives of the attempts to organize plantation workers' unions in the 1920's, efforts in which Musso himself had taken a major part. Musso also wrote a number of articles for the *Eastern and Colonial Bulletin*, an organ which was published from 1927 to 1931 by the Profintern.[7] Among them are the following: "How the Sugar Capitalists Exploit the Javanese Peasantry and Workers" vol. I, no. 6, Nov. 15, 1927); "The Consolidation of the Nationalist Organizations in Indonesia" (vol. I, no. 10, March 15, 1928); "The Role

[4] See reviews by B. Puretskii in *Pechat' i Revoliutsiia*, no. 1, 1926, p. 214, and Kim, in *Novyi Vostok*, no. 10–11, 1925, pp. 325–326.

[5] The book, which was translated into Russian from the Dutch original, was published in 1924 by Krasnaia Nov' and in 1925 by the state publishing house, Gosizdat.

[6] Reference is here to the Russian edition, but, like most Comintern-affiliated organs, this periodical also appeared in German, French, and English versions.

[7] The bulletin was published in Russian, English, French, and German editions, the content of which varied slightly. Reference here is to the English edition; the Russian edition is entitled *Vostok i kolonii*.

of the Agents of the Amsterdam International in Indonesia" (vol. I, no. 13, May 15, 1928); "How the Dutch Imperialists Are Treating the Indonesian Toiling Masses" (vol. I, no. 15, June 15, 1928); "The Millions Profits of Indonesia" (vol. I, no. 18, Aug. 1, 1928); "The Role of the Agents of the Amsterdam International in Indonesia" (vol. I, no. 23, Oct. 15, 1928); "White Terror in Indonesia" (vol. II, no. 2–3, Feb.– March, 1929); "Conflict between the Nationalists and Social Democrats in Indonesia" (vol. II, no. 4–5, April–May, 1929); "May First in Indonesia" (vol. II, no. 4–5, April–May, 1929); "New Laws against Revolutionary Movements Enacted in Indonesia" (vol. II, no. 11, Nov., 1929); "Strike Movement in Indonesia after the Uprising" (vol. III, no. 1–2, Jan.–Feb., 1930); and "Protest against the Australian 'Labour' Government Handing Over Indonesian Communists Who Escaped from Exile" (vol. III, no. 4–5, April–May, 1930).

In addition, Musso published a number of articles in *Inprecorr;* these include "The Foreign Capital of Indonesia" (vol. VIII, no. 29, May 31, 1928); "The National Parties and the Workers' Organisations of Indonesia" (vol. IX, no. 27, June 7, 1929); "How the Social Democrats Betray the Workers in Indonesia" (vol. VIII, no. 29, May 31, 1928); "The White Terror in Indonesia" (vol. IX, no. 13, March 8, 1929); "The 'Victory' of the Berlin International in Indonesia" (vol. XI, no. 37, July 9, 1931); and "The Situation in Indonesia" (vol. XII, no. 2, Jan. 14, 1932). For the Profintern journal *Mezhdunarodnoe rabochee dvizhenie* he wrote: "How the Sugar Magnates Are Exploiting the Javanese Peasants and Workers" (no. 45–46, 1927); "New Stage in the Politics of the Dutch Government in Indonesia" (no. 32–33, 1929); "The Activity of the Supporters of the Profintern in Indonesia" (no. 49–50, 1929); "The Arrests of Leaders of the National Liberation Movement in Indonesia" (no. 2, 1930); "How the Influence of Amsterdam Is Penetrating Indonesia" (no. 5, 1930); "The 'Labour' Government of Australia Hands Over Indonesian Communists Who Escaped from Banishment" (no. 15, 1930); and "The Uprising on the Dutch Cruiser 'Zeven Provinciën'" (no. 2, 1933). In *Krasnyi internatsional profsoiuzov,* another Profintern organ, he published: "The October Revolution and the Revolutionary Movement in Indonesia" (no. 11, 1927); and "The Sharpening of the Crisis and the Tasks of the Revolutionary Workers of Indonesia" (no. 16, 1931). Finally, an article by Musso on "Indonesia and the Chinese Revolution" was published in the first issue of the *Pan Pacific Worker* (July 1, 1927).

Darsono's publications for the Comintern include "The Situation of the Indonesian People's Movement," *Kommunisticheskii internatsional* (no. 9, Nov. 9, 1926 [hereafter cited as *KI*; the English edition is titled *Communist International*]), an important critique of the PKI's policies which appeared just before the Communist revolt on Java. He also wrote "The Struggle for Rubber," a discussion of the competition between Indonesian smallholder and foreign estate producers (*KI*, no. 1, 1927). Under the name of Kijai Samin, Darsono published "The Uprising in Java and Sumatra (Indonesia)," *KI* (vol. VIII, nos. 3 and 5, March 29 and April 12, 1927); "New Storms Gathering in Indonesia," *KI* (vol. VIII, no. 38–39, Sept. 29, 1927); "Dutch Imperialist Terror in Indonesia," *Inprecorr* (vol. VIII, no. 57, Aug. 31, 1928); and "The Situation in Indonesia," *Inprecorr* (vol. VIII, no. 68, Oct. 4, 1928), this last being a co-report on the revolutionary movement in the colonies presented to the sixth Comintern congress. Darsono's report to the Comintern meeting was also published as "Dutch Imperialism in Indonesia and the Struggle of the Indonesian Communist Party," in *O revoliutsionnom dvizhenii v koloniiakh i polukoloniiakh* (Concerning the Revolutionary Movement in the Colonies and Semicolonies; Moscow, 1929).

During his long exile in the Soviet Union, Semaun wrote two brief works on his homeland. *Indoneziia v tsepiakh imperializma* (Indonesia in Imperialist Chains) was published by the Profintern in 1927 and also appeared in a German translation put out by the Comintern's Berlin publishers.[8] The second pamphlet, *Indoneziia: Sotsial'no-ekonomicheskii ocherk* (Indonesia: A Socioeconomic Outline), was brought out in Moscow by the publishing house for political literature (Politizdat) in 1940. More important for the historian than these writings are the articles Semaun wrote for Comintern organs in 1925–1927, since these present interesting critiques of the PKI's policy and reactions to the first news of the Indonesian uprisings. They are "The National Movement and the Communist Party of Indonesia (the Dutch East Indies)," *KI* (vol. VI, no. 5, 1925); "International Imperialism and the Communist Party of Indonesia," *KI* (vol. VI, no. 11, 1925); "The Trade Union Movement in Indonesia," *Krasnyi internatsional profsoiuzov* (no. 3, March, 1926 [hereafter cited as *KIP*]); "The Labor Movement in Indonesia in 1925," *Mezhdunarodnoe rabochee dvizhenie* (no. 3, 1926); "The Rebellion in the Dutch East Indies," *Inprecorr* (vol. VI, no. 84, Dec. 2, 1926); "On the Uprising on Java," *KIP* (no. 1, Jan., 1927); and "Indonesia in

[8] Semaoen, *Indonesien hat das Wort!* (Berlin and Hamburg: Carl Hoym Nachf., 1927).

1926," *Mezhdunarodnoe rabochee dvizhenie* (no. 6, 1927). In addition, Semaun published "Indonesia" in *Krest'ianskii internatsional* (no. 10–12, 1924 [the organ of the Farmers' and Peasants' International, or Krestintern]); and "Terror and the Trade Union Movement in Indonesia," *Revoliutsionnyi transportnik* (no. 9–10, 1925).

Finally, we should include among the works by Indonesian revolutionaries a lengthy pamphlet, *The Peasants' Movement in Indonesia*, which was first published for the Krestintern in Berlin in 1926 and appeared in a Russian translation (*Bor'ba krest'ianstva Indonezii*) issued by the Soviet state publishing house (Gosizdat) in 1927. The author of the pamphlet signed himself "S. Dingley"; but he was evidently an Indonesian, and the Netherlands Indies Government, in justifying its banishment of Iwa Kusumasumantri a few years later, charged that he had written it. Since the Dutch authorities were anything but reluctant to link Indonesian revolutionary leaders with the Comintern, this claim should not be accepted unquestioningly; but since Iwa Kusumasumantri worked as Semaun's assistant and was living in Moscow at the time the booklet was written, his authorship is not completely unlikely. The pamphlet is of considerable interest because it reviews at length the development of the revolutionary movement among the peasantry and presents an important criticism of the policies which the PKI had been following in mobilizing agrarian support.[9]

The published records of the Comintern meetings are also valuable sources of information on the early development of the Indonesian revolutionary movement. It is preferable to consult the German editions of these, at least for the 1920's, as they are the most complete and accurate versions. The protocols of the second (1920) Comintern congress are important for their account of the role played by Sneevliet, the Dutch founder of the Indonesian Communist movement, who appeared at that meeting under the name Maring and who, as secretary to the congress's commission on the national and colonial question, did much to shape early Comintern policy in Asia. On the floor of the congress he argued for international Communist approval of the strategy

---

[9] I have seen one reference to another work by Dingley, *Statement of the Anti-Ribut*, but have been unable to locate a copy of it or to find any further bibliographical information on it. It seems to have been an English-language pamphlet, published about 1925 or 1926—perhaps also by the Krestintern. Its title would indicate that it dealt with the problem of combating rural strong-arm opposition to the PKI, a matter of considerable concern to the Indonesian Communists at that time. In view of the importance of the subject, it is a particular pity that this account—if it really existed—seems to have vanished into limbo.

undertaken by the Indonesian party, and he presented a lengthy report on the Indonesian revolutionary movement which was later published by the Comintern.[10]

The records of the two major Comintern meetings which followed the second congress—the First Congress of the Peoples of the East, in 1920, and the third Comintern congress, in 1921—yield nothing of direct interest concerning Indonesia, though the first of these was attended by Sneevliet and the second by Darsono. The First Congress of the Toilers of the Far East, held in early 1922, made up for this neglect, however. It was attended by Semaun, who presented a lengthy and detailed account of the development of the Indonesian labor movement; this was included in the Russian edition of the congress's report (*Pervyi s"ezd revoliutsionnykh organizatsii Dal'nego Vostoka* [Moscow and Petrograd, 1922]). The fourth Comintern congress, in late 1922, also yielded interesting material, for there Tan Malaka took part in an attack on the Comintern leadership, which he accused of downgrading the colonial question; he also quarreled with the Dutch party spokesman over the role played by the Netherlands Communists in the Indonesian movement and conducted a heated but futile struggle to secure Comintern backing for Pan-Islamism.

Tan Malaka also attended the Pacific Transport Workers' Conference, which took place in Canton in June 1924 under Comintern and Profintern sponsorship; he seems, however, to have attended the meeting not as a delegate from Indonesia but as an agent for the International in Southeast Asia.[11] The Indonesian delegation itself was made

[10] H. Maring, "Niederländisch Ost-Indien: Bericht für den zweiten Kongress der Kommunistischen Internationale," in *Berichte zum zweiten Kongress der Kommunistischen Internationale* (Hamburg: Verlag der K.I., 1921).

[11] At the meeting, Tan Malaka was appointed to head a contact bureau for transport workers' unions in the Far East. In this capacity, he published an English-language journal called *The Dawn* for about a year. Obviously, this publication is of interest to the historian of the Indonesian revolutionary movement; but I have been unable to locate any copies of it. Similarly, I have not seen issues—except the first —of the *Pan-Pacific Worker*, which was put out by the Pan-Pacific Trade Union Secretariat, an organization established in 1927 in Shanghai. Since Indonesia was represented on the secretariat by Musso, a PKI leader who was most prolific in contributing to the International's publications at the time, it would seem likely that the *Worker's* pages contained a number of articles on the Indonesian situation. I am informed by Dr. Zakaznikova that the following numbers of the journal are available at the Fundamental'nyi bibliotek obshchestvennykh nauk in Moscow: vol. I, nos. 1–11, published in Hankow in 1927; vol. I, no. 12, Shanghai, 1928; and vols. I (1930) and II (1932), published in Vladivostok. The same library has vols. I–V (1928–1932) of an Australian edition of the *Worker*, published by the Pan-Pacific Relations Committee of the Australian Council of Trade Unions, Sidney.

up of the PKI leaders Alimin and Budisutjitro, who were described in the Comintern representative's report on the conference [12] as having assumed a left revolutionary stand which they were persuaded only with difficulty to modify. Since the following December the PKI resolved to undertake a major party reorganization aimed at setting off a rebellion, a decision which has frequently been attributed to the Canton conference, these observations as to the Indonesians' attitude are of distinct interest. For the same reason, the records of the fifth Comintern congress, held in June–July, 1924, are of importance to Indonesian history. That gathering's decisions concerning party reorganization were, we find, followed in some parts at the PKI's December conference but rejected in others: the Comintern congress, for example, reserved high praise for the PKI-sponsored mass organization, Sarekat Rakjat, while the December conference voted to dissolve that movement.[13]

The next Comintern congress, the sixth, took place in 1928 and thus after the ill-fated Indonesian rebellion of 1926–1927. Although the defeat of the uprisings meant the end of communism's significance in colonial Indonesian history, the congress's records are of interest because of the considerable attention paid to the rebellion and the PKI's policies—both commenting on the party's past mistakes and dictating a new program—and because of the controversies which arose there between individual members of the Indonesian delegation and the Comintern leadership. Finally, at the seventh and last Comintern congress, in 1935, Rustam Effendi presented a report on the Indonesian situation, analyzing it in terms of the Popular Front which the International had then resolved to espouse.

This listing of sources for the early Indonesian revolutionary movement is necessarily a cursory one. It does not give the numerous articles on Indonesia written for Comintern and Profintern publications by Dutchmen who were connected with the PKI or by other non-Indonesian writers. Neither have we discussed the plenary sessions of the

[12] G. Voitinsky, "First Conference of the Transport Workers of the Pacific," *Inprecorr*, vol. IV, no. 65, Sept. 11, 1924.

[13] We might also note that Semaun, the Indonesian representative to the Comintern meeting, published a lengthy report on it for the benefit of the Indonesian Communists—an account which is of critical importance in evaluating the relationship of the International's policies to the PKI's decision to undertake a revolt (Semaoen, *Rapotan Hal Kongres² di Moskou dan Hal Konferentie di Hamburg* [mimeograph; n.p., n.d.]; the meetings referred to in the title are the fifth Comintern congress, the third Profintern congress, and the European equivalent of the Pacific Transport Workers' Conference, all three of which Semaun attended).

Comintern executive (ECCI), some of whose published records also contain valuable materials on Indonesia. These are of particular interest after 1924, when the ECCI sessions began to replace the Comintern congresses as the principal forums for the International's discussions. (We might note that Semaun, Darsono, Tan Malaka, Musso, and Rustam Effendi were at one time or another members of the ECCI, and Semaun and Musso belonged to its presidium.) The records of Profintern meetings also contain references to Indonesia; they generally duplicate the Comintern materials but sometimes present new and useful information. We might expect that the Krestintern, by reason of its agrarian orientation, would have produced materials of interest on Indonesia; but its publications were concentrated on East and Central Europe, and, except for "Dingley's" pamphlet and a few scattered articles, it did not deal with events in the Indies. An occasional article on Indonesia may be found in the publications of the International Red Aid (the official financial backer of Communist movements) and the Young Communist International (the Comintern's Youth arm).

After 1928, the collapse of the Indonesian Communist movement, the increased difficulty of contact with the Indies, and the diminishing role of the Comintern itself all combined to reduce the significance of the International's importance as a source of materials on Indonesia. Its postwar descendant, the Cominform, was concerned primarily with European Communist affairs, and its organ, *For a Lasting Peace, for a People's Democracy*, contained almost nothing of direct significance for Indonesia. The publications of other Soviet-oriented international organizations, such as the World Federation of Trade Unions, World Peace Council, International Union of Students, and World Federation of Democratic Youth, contain occasional articles on Indonesia, but these are generally of marginal importance for historical purposes if only because they deal with a period in which more detailed and accurate information is available directly from Indonesian sources. The international journal *Problems of Peace and Socialism* (*World Marxist Review*) has occasionally published important articles by PKI leaders, however.

After the 1920's the most important discussions of Indonesia appearing in publications issued in the USSR were those by Soviet scholars. As can well be imagined, Russian research on Indonesia began under severe handicaps. Not only was there no direct contact with the country during the colonial period, but Russia had had no tradition of interest in Southeast Asia to start out with.[14] Prior to the October Revolution, academic work on the Orient had concentrated on Central Asia and the northern Far East and was chiefly concerned with the classical fields of archaeology, linguistics, and ancient history. Many of Russia's Asia specialists fled the country following the revolution and civil war; others were unacceptable to the Soviet regime, and the rest had to learn to adjust their work to the Marxist view. A whole new approach to Asian studies had to be developed in line with Marxist-Leninist philosophy and in the service of the world revolution—a process which involved not only a change in the interpretation of existing subjects of study but also a shift in emphasis from classical fields to contemporary socioeconomic lines. Under these conditions it is little wonder that Soviet work on Indonesia in the period before World War II was generally of secondary quality and that the historical studies produced were more notable for their polemical than for their scholarly content.[15]

In general, Soviet writings on Indonesia from this time fall into three broad categories: those which dealt with the economic development of the area under Dutch rule, with an eye to pointing out the evils of imperialist domination; those which interpreted the development of the independence movement according to the current Comintern attitude toward nationalism; and those—appearing mostly in the 1930's—which emphasized the danger of Japanese encroachment.

The major foundation for academic research and publication on Asia was the All-Union Scientific Association for Oriental Studies, which formed a part of the USSR Academy of Sciences. Its journal during the 1920's was *Novyi Vostok* (The New East), which included various articles and reviews dealing with Indonesia. In addition, its ten-volume *Bibliografiia Vostoka* (Bibliography of the East), issued between 1932 and 1937,[16] is of considerable value both for its references

[14] A listing of prerevolutionary Russian writings on Indonesia may be found in *Bibliografiia Iugo-vostochnoi Azii* (Bibliography of Southeast Asia; Moscow: Izdatel'stvo vostochnoi literatury, 1960); most of them deal with geography, ethnography, and travel. See especially pp. 19–21, 26, 130–133, 134–137, 138–141, and 144.

[15] For an account of the development of Soviet Orientology in this period, which discusses the difficulties outlined above, see A. A. Guber, "Twenty-five Years of Historical Research in the USSR on the Countries of the East," in the collection *Dvadtsat' piat' let istoricheskoi nauki SSSR* (Twenty-five Years of Historical Science in the USSR; Moscow and Leningrad, 1942). It should be remarked that Professor Guber's major writings of the prewar period form a notable exception to my generalization regarding the quality of early Soviet studies of Indonesia.

[16] A previous volume of the same name was published by the association in 1928 and covered writings which appeared from 1917 to 1925.

to Soviet publications on Indonesia and for the indication it gives of the types of Western works on the area which were then being received in the Soviet Union.

At the end of the 1920's, the association's functions were restricted to the classical subjects of Orientology, and new foundations were given the task of conducting political-economic research on the contemporary East. From 1927 to 1937, the Scientific Research Association for the Investigation of National and Colonial Problems published the journal *Revoliutsionnyi Vostok* (The Revolutionary East); [17] this institute also published the series *Materialy po natsional'no-kolonial'-nym problemam* (Materials on National-Colonial Problems), which contained a number of studies dealing with Indonesia. In addition, the association put out a bibliographical bulletin of journal articles on the non-Soviet and Soviet East (*Bibliograficheskii biulleten' zhurnal'nykh statei po zarubezhnomu i sovetskomu Vostoku*). From 1934 to 1938 the State Social-Economic Publishing House issued *Tikhii okean* (Pacific Ocean), a "political-social-economic journal" devoted to the Far East and particularly concerned with the threat of Japanese expansion in that area. Finally, a series of collections of essays on colonial countries was published in 1933 and 1935 by the colonial division of the Institute of World Economics and World Politics under the title *Kolonial'nye problemy* (Colonial Problems).

Of the scholars working on Indonesia under the auspices of these organizations, by far the most eminent and prolific was A. A. Guber, a historian who is still the dean of Soviet specialists on Southeast Asia. His major work, *Indoneziia: Sotsial'no-ekonomicheskie ocherki* (Indonesia: Social-Economic Features) was published in 1932 and again in 1933.[18] He also collaborated with the Dutch Communist authority on Indonesia, S. J. Rutgers, in a historical study of colonial Indonesia (*Indonesië* [Amsterdam: Pegasus, 1937]). In addition, Professor Guber published a work on the colonial regimes in Indonesia and Indochina, *Indoneziia i Indokitai* (Moscow: Ogiz, 1942), contributed a chapter on "The Agrarian Question in Indonesia" to the symposium *Agrarnyi vopros na Vostoke* (The Agrarian Question in the East; Moscow:

[17] At the time of the journal's founding, its sponsor's title was the Scientific Research Association attached to the J. V. Stalin Communist University of the Toilers of the East.

[18] The book was issued in 1932 by the State Social-Economic Publishing House (Gossotsekiz), Moscow and Leningrad, and in 1933 as vol. IX of the *Trudy* (Works) of the Scientific Research Association for the Investigation of National-Colonial Problems.

Mezhdunarodnyi Agrarnyi Institut, 1933), and published a pamphlet on the Indonesian revolutionary movement (*Indoneziia* [Moscow: Molodaia gvardiia, 1932]).

Professor Guber also wrote a large number of journal articles on Indonesia during the colonial period. Among those of interest to the historian we may list "Indonesia," *Materialy po natsional'no-kolonial'-nym problemam* (no. 1, 1932 [hereafter cited as *MNKP*]); "The Class Differentiation of the Peasantry in Indonesia," *Revoliutsionnyi Vostok* (no. 9–10, 1930 [hereafter *RV*]); "The Crisis and the National Liberation Movement in Indonesia," *MNKP* (no. 4–5, 1932); "The Appearance of Dutch Imperialism," *MNKP* (no. 7, 1933); "The World Economic Crisis and Some of Its Results in Indonesia," *RV* (no. 3, 1934); "The National Liberation Movement in Indonesia," *RV* (no. 3–4, 1932; no. 1, 1933); "Concerning Two Trends in the Development of Capitalism in Indonesia," *Kolonial'nye problemy* (no. 3–4, 1935 [hereafter *KP*]); "The Situation of the Working Class in Indonesia," *RV* (no. 4–5, 1928); "The Revolutionary Movement in Indonesia at the Present Stage," *RV* (no. 5, 1933); "The Deepening of the Economic Crisis in Indonesia and the Nationalist Organizations," *MNKP* (no. 6, 1933); "The Uprising in the Indonesian Colonial Fleet and the Revolutionary Movement in Indonesia," *MNKP* (no. 3, 1933); and "Towards a History of Dutch Penetration in Indonesia," *Uchenye zapiski Moskovskogo gosudarstvennogo pedagogichekogo instituta* (vol. III, 1941).

Other contributors of political and historical articles on Indonesia in this period included I. V. Mil'gram, "On the Question of the National Liberation Movement in Indonesia," *Tikhii okean* (no. 3, 1936 [hereafter *TO*]); N. Frantsevich, "The Sarekat Islam," *RV* (no. 4–5, 1928); A. Gal'perin, "The Economic Efforts of the National-Revolutionary Movement in Indonesia," *Novyi Vostok* (no. 25, 1929 [hereafter *NV*]); "The Dutch East Indies," *NV* (no. 20–21, 1928); and "Japanese Expansion into Indonesia, the Malay States, and the Philippines," *TO* (no. 1, 1934); I. Vanin, "The Fate of the Dutch East Indies," *NV* (no. 5, 1924); A. E. Kudriavtsev, "The East Indies Problem in England in the Seventeenth Century," *Uchenye zapiski Leningradskogo gosudarstvennogo pedagogicheskogo instituta* (vol. XI, 1938); O. Zabozlaeva, "The Struggle of the Powers for the Dutch East Indies," *Mirovoe khoziaistvo i mirovaia politika* (no. 6, 1940), and "The Dutch Indies after the Occupation of Holland," *Mirovoe khoziaistvo i mirovaia politika* (no. 3, 1941); and K. Petrovskii, "The Fate of Indonesia," *Bol'shevik* (no. 9, 1940). In addition, the Central Committee of the International Red Aid issued a pamphlet on the Zeven Provinciën uprising: N. Volchanskaia, *"Potem-kin" gollandskogo flota* (The "Potemkin" of the Dutch Fleet; Moscow: TsK MOPR, 1933).[19]

Finally, we may list some articles of interest but of uncertain parent-age: A., "National-Reformist Youth Organizations in Indonesia," *MNKP* (no. 3, 1934); Ardzheno ["Ardjuno"?], "Causes of the Uprising in the Indonesian Fleet," *KP* (no. 1, 1933); "Anglo-Dutch Agreement for the Defense of Their Rule in the Far East," *TO* (no. 1, 1938); "The Movement against Japanese Aggression in the Countries of the South Seas," *TO* (no. 3-4, 1937); "Indonesia: Economic Crisis; Revolutionary Movement," *MNKP* (no. 1, 1931); and "The Response to the Japanese Intervention in China in the Philippines and Indonesia," *MNKP* (no. 3, 1932).

Indonesia is also dealt with at some length in volume IV of *Agrarnyi vopros i krest'ianskoe dvizhenie; spravochnik* (The Agrarian Question and the Peasant Movement; a Guidebook; Moscow: MAI, 1937); in Kh. Eiduss, *Ocherk rabochego dvizheniia v stranakh Vostoka* (Outline of the Labor Movement in the Countries of the East; Moscow: Gosizdat, 1922); in V. Balabushevich, L. Geller, and Kh. Eiduss, *Rabochie organi-zatsii Vostoka: Kitai, Iaponiia, Indiia, Indoneziia* (Labor Organizations of the East: China, Japan, India, and Indonesia; Moscow: Gosiz-dat, 1927); in *Novaia istoriia kolonial'nykh i zavisimykh stran* (Modern History of the Colonial and Dependent Countries; Moscow: Gossotse-kizdat, 1940); in *Mirovoe professional'noe dvizhenie* (World Labor Union Movement; Moscow and Leningrad: Gosizdat, 1927); in U. Hay-ama, *Rabochee dvizhenie v koloniiakh Vostoka* (The Labor Movement in the Colonies of the East; Moscow and Leningrad: Gosizdat, 1930); and in *Mezhdunarodnoe profdvizhenie za 1924–1927gg.* (The Inter-national Labor Union Movement, 1924–1927; Moscow: Izdatel'stvo Profinterna, 1928).

A relatively large number of articles on Indonesia appeared in 1940 and 1941, Soviet interest no doubt having been quickened by the threatening war in the Pacific. At this time the first comments on Indo-nesia appeared in agitators' guidebooks, indicating that the Indonesian situation was considered a topic for general political discussion: "The Struggle for the Dutch Indies," *Sputnik agitatora* (no. 18, 1940); E. Narovlianskaia, "The Dutch Indies (Indonesia)," *Propaganda i agitat-siia* (no. 9, 1940); "The War Measures of the Dutch Indies," *Sputnik*

---

[19] This booklet was reissued in revised form in 1934 under the title *Vosstanie v voennom flote Gollandskoi Indii* ("The Uprising in the Dutch Indies Naval Fleet").

agitatora (no. 11, 1941); and N. Lazarev, "The Netherlands Indies," *Sputnik agitatora* (no. 3, 1942). The USSR's own involvement in World War II soon reduced Soviet attention to nil, however, except for a few descriptions of the Pacific war theater.

The postwar period brought a rapid revival of interest in the area. The revolution against the Dutch brought Indonesia to the center of world attention, and Russia's role as a major power backing the Republic in the United Nations gave it for the first time a direct diplomatic interest in that country. Soviet publications during the revolutionary period reflected Russia's diplomatic concern to the exclusion of almost all other aspects of Indonesian affairs. These writings were of two sorts: those—the majority—which were intended for an international audience, and those aimed primarily at Soviet readers. Their main content was essentially the same, emphasizing the USSR's selfless support for the Indonesian cause, denouncing the Dutch, and painting the Americans as perfidious mediators whose real intentions were to establish their own hegemony over the area. Those publications oriented toward the home audience tended to give a somewhat broader background on the history of Indonesia, which was then still an area unknown to most Russians.

Articles intended for foreign readers can be found chiefly in *New Times* (*Novoe Vremia*), a news magazine which has been published in the major languages since 1945; comments on Indonesian current events appeared with considerable frequency in this source during the course of the revolution. Among the writings designed for home consumption, we find articles appearing for the first time in such popular magazines as *Ogonek*. Public lectures on the Indonesian question were given in Moscow, and two pamphlets were produced from them: A. A. Guber, *Natsional'no-osvoboditel'noe dvizhenie v Indonezii* (The National Liberation Movement in Indonesia; Moscow: Pravda, 1946), and A. A. Guber, *Voina v Indonezii* (The War in Indonesia; Moscow: Pravda, 1947). Indonesia was also given a prominent place in other pamphlets comprising public lectures: V. A. Avarin, *Politicheskie izemeneniia na Tikhom okeane posle Vtoroi mirovoi voiny* (Political Developments in the Pacific since the Second World War; Moscow: Pravda, 1947), and A. A. Guber, *Krizis kolonial'noi sistemy posle Vtoroi mirovoi voiny* (Crisis of the Colonial System Following the Second World War; Moscow: Pravda, 1947).

Interestingly enough, few studies of Indonesia appeared in Soviet academic and party journals during the revolutionary period, in spite of the importance which Indonesia had assumed. Among those that were published we find V. Vasil'eva, "Events in Indonesia," *Mirovoe khoziaistvo i mirovaia politika* (no. 1-2, Jan.–Feb., 1946); A. Leonidov, "Indonesia and the Struggle for National Independence," *Sovetskoe gosudarstvo i pravo* (no. 2, 1946); E. Martin, "Indonesia and Holland," *Sovetskoe gosudarstvo i pravo* (no. 9, Sept., 1947); A. A. Guber, "Imperialists—the Suffocators of Freedom and Independence of the Peoples (On the Events in Indonesia)," *Bol'shevik* (no. 19, 1947); brief summaries of three reports by A. A: Guber to various institutes of the Academy of Sciences: "The Great October Socialist Revolution and Indonesia," *Vestnik Akademii nauk SSSR* (no. 1, 1948), "The October Revolution and Indonesia," *Voprosy istorii* (no. 4, 1948), and "India and Indonesia," *Voprosy istorii* (no. 10, 1947); I. Plyshevskii, "The Communist Party of Indonesia Is Struggling for the Freedom and Independence of Its Country," *Partiinaia zhizn'* (no. 1, Jan., 1948); and V. Vasil'eva, "The Struggle for the Democratic Development of the Indonesian Republic," *Voprosy ekonomiki* (no. 1, March, 1948).

Russian publications of this period are, in general, useful as indications of the Soviet attitude toward the diplomatic and military development of the Indonesian revolution and not as sources of information on what transpired within the Republic at this time. Of the articles listed in the paragraph above, only the last two deal to any extent with internal Indonesian politics, and reports on Indonesia in the Soviet press were also notably devoid of references to events within the Republic. The principal reason for this would seem to be a lack of information on the subject; during the revolution, we must remember, Russia had almost no contact with the Indonesian scene in spite of the Republic's independent state. Moreover, while the Soviet Union was certain that it supported the Indonesian battle against the Dutch, it does not seem to have been so sure of its attitude toward the political forces within the Republic, nor does it appear to have been very knowledgeable of what the relationship of these forces was.[20]

The Madiun Affair served to chill the Russians' enthusiasm for the Republic's government and to remove for the time being any doubts concerning the category in which its leaders should be placed. In consequence, the interpretation of the Indonesian revolution presented

[20] For interesting miscalculations of the Republic's political leanings, see E. Zhukov, "The Sharpening of the Crisis of the Colonial System," *Bol'shevik*, no. 23, Dec. 15, 1947, pp. 52, 57, and V. Vasil'eva, "The Struggle for the Democratic Development of the Indonesian Republic," *Voprosy ekonomiki*, no. 1, March, 1948, p. 81.

in Soviet publications from 1949 to 1952 differed considerably from earlier analyses; Sukarno and Hatta, for example, now appeared as the villains rather than the heroes of the revolutionary drama. Since the political character of the Indonesian government was no longer in question so far as the Russians were concerned, there was a greater amount of assertiveness on domestic political conditions. At the same time, the ending of the revolution and the cooling of Soviet-Indonesian relations caused general concern with the area to drop.

New Times and the WFTU organ, *World Trade Union Movement*, are the major sources of accounts on Indonesia in the 1949–1952 period. No articles on the subject appeared in the major academic and party journals, though *Voprosy ekonomiki* (no. 10, 1949) contains a summary of a report by A. A. Guber on "The National Liberation Struggle in Indonesia" made to a joint session of the Academy of Sciences' Pacific Institute and Institute of Economics. Professor Guber also wrote a chapter on "The Indonesian People in the Struggle for Independence," which appeared in *Krizis kolonial'noi sistemy; natsional'no-osvobodi-tel'naia bor'ba narodov vistochnoi Azii* (Crisis of the Colonial System; the National Liberation Struggle of the Peoples of East Asia; Moscow: Tikho-okeanskii institut, 1949). This study is of considerable importance in Soviet historiography of Indonesia, since it represents a first analysis of the Indonesian independence struggle in terms of Mao's strategy in the Chinese revolution, which the Soviet Union then felt to be the pattern for all Communist movements in Asia.

Three pamphlets published during this period also deal with Indonesian affairs: V. Ia. Vasil'eva, *Natsional'no-osvoboditel'naia bor'ba v stranakh Iugo-vostochnoi Azii* (The National Liberation Struggle in the Countries of Southeast Asia; Moscow: Pravda, 1949); I. L. Khaliuta, *Indoneziia* (Indonesia; Moscow, 1949); and I. P. Plyshevskii, *Indoneziia 1945–1949 godov* (Indonesia, 1945–1949; Moscow, 1951).

Up to this time, only a very small number of histories of the Far East had been published in the Soviet Union. In the immediate postwar period, only one such work was published which touched on any event in Indonesia: V. Ia. Avarin, *Bor'ba za Tikhii okean: Iapono-amerikanskie protivorechiia s kontsa XIXv.* (The Struggle for the Pacific: The Japanese-American Conflict since the End of the Nineteenth Century; Moscow: Gospolitizdat, 1947). Beginning in the early 1950's, however, an increasing number of histories of the Far East began to appear, interpreting that area's past in terms of the then-current Soviet ideological and political position. Those which touch on Indonesia include *Mezhdunarodnye otnosheniia na Dal'nem Vostoke, 1870–1945gg.* (International Relations in the Far East, 1870–1945; Moscow: Gospolitizdat, 1951); B. Rodov, *Rol' SShA i Iaponii v podgotovke i razviazyvanii voiny po Tikhom okeane 1938–1941gg.* (The Role of the USA and Japan in the Preparation and Outbreak of the War in the Pacific, 1938–1941; Moscow: Gospolitizdat, 1951); *Novaia istoriia stran zarubezhnogo Vostoka* (Modern History of the Countries of the Non-Soviet East; vols. I and II, Moscow: Izdatel'stvo Moskovskogo universiteta, 1952); V. Ia. Avarin, *Bor'ba za Tikhii okean; agressiia SShA i Anglii, ikh protivorechiia i osvoboditel'naia bor'ba narodov* (The Struggle for the Pacific; the Aggression of the USA and England, Their Conflicts and the Liberation Struggle of the Peoples; Moscow: Gospolitizdat, 1952); and *Uglublenie krizisa kolonial'noi sistemy imperializma posle Vtoroi mirovoi voiny* (The Deepening of the Crisis of the Colonial System of Imperialism Following World War II; Moscow: Gospolitizdat, 1953; see especially the chapters by V. A. Maslennikov and V. Ia. Avarin).

About 1953 the Soviet attitude toward Asian neutralism began a shift from the unfavorable to the enthusiastic, and Russia's relations with Indonesia, which had itself assumed a less pro-Western stand, became rapidly more congenial. Interest in and contact with Indonesia increased; the number of Russian scholars who specialized in Indonesian studies expanded rapidly, and the scope of their studies broadened considerably. Moreover, the post-Stalin ideological thaw, when coupled with the USSR's diplomatic bid for neutralist friendship, allowed Soviet scholars greater freedom in interpreting the history, economics, and politics of the area. As a result, there has been a marked increase in the quality as well as in the quantity of Soviet studies on Indonesia, an improvement noticeable particularly in the publications of the late 1950's. A good deal still remains to be done, since prior to 1960 very few of the Soviet Indonesia specialists had been in that country even for a short period of time, and library resources in the USSR are still quite limited. (It is only in very recent times, for example, that a broad selection of Indonesian newspapers has been available in the Soviet Union for academic research.) However, since intensive efforts are now being made by the Russians to overcome these difficulties, we may expect that, barring radical changes in the political situation, Soviet academic publications on Indonesia will continue to increase in depth and general scholarly interest.[21]

[21] Some idea of the sort of library materials available to Soviet scholars may be gotten from A. B. Belinskii, "Indoneziiskii fond" (The Indonesian Collection), in

As we have seen, writings on Indonesia prior to the most recent period were concerned overwhelmingly with current politics, economics, and recent history. While these subjects remained the prime area of concentration, an increasing number of publications on cultural, scientific, and linguistic questions have appeared since about 1955. Several collections of Indonesian folk tales have been published in Russian translation, as well as works by Indonesian novelists, short-story writers, and political figures; the latter include President Sukarno, D. N. Aidit, and Njoto.²² A Russian translation of Djuana and Sulwar, *Tatanegara Indonesia,* has been published with an introduction by L. Ia. Dadiani, a specialist on Asian governmental and juridical systems (*Gosudarstvennyi stroi Indonezii* [Moscow: Izdatel'stvo inostranoi literatury, 1959]); and the Indonesian government paper on the Jungschlaeger and Schmidt affair, *Subversive Activities in Indonesia,* has appeared in Russian translation, also with comment by Dadiani (*Podryvnaia deiatel'nost' v Indonezii* [Moscow: Izdatel'stvo inostranoi literatury, 1958]). Articles by Indonesians have appeared with some frequency in Soviet magazines and in such international organs as *World Trade Union Movement* and *World Student News* (the latter is the journal of the International Union of Students); they are generally brief and deal in a popular manner with current Indonesian events. Finally, the Soviet Union issued books commemorating President Sukarno's 1956 visit to the USSR (*Prebyvanie Presidenta Respubliki Indonezii Sukarno v Sovetskom soiuze* [The Visit of President of the Republic of Indonesia Sukarno to the Soviet Union; Moscow: Izogiz, 1956]) and President Voroshilov's 1957 trip to Indonesia (*Prebyvanie K. E. Voroshilova v Kitae, Indonezii, Vietname i Mongolii* [The Visit of K. E. Voroshilov to China, Indonesia, Vietnam, and Mongolia; Moscow: Gospolitizdat, 1957]).

Among the Soviet monographs published on Indonesia in the recent period are D. V. Bekleshov, *Indoneziia; ekonomika i vneshnaia torgovlia* (Indonesia, Its Economy and Foreign Trade; Moscow: Vneshtorgizdat, 1956); A. P. Kholopova, *Indoneziiskaia respublika* (The Indonesian Republic; Moscow: Znanie, 1956); V. I. Perov, *Nezavisimaia Indoneziia* (Independent Indonesia; Moscow: Gospolitizdat, 1956); L. Ia. Dadiani, *Cosudarstvennyi stroi Indonezii* (The Structure of the

---

Vostokovednye fondy krupneishikh bibliotek Sovetskogo Soivz; stat'i i soobshcheniia (Moscow: Izdatel'stvo vostochnoi literatury, 1963), which describes the collection at the library of the Institute of the Peoples of the East in Moscow.

²² We might note that in 1961 a Russian translation of Sukarno's *Sarinah* went into its second edition; and in the same year a collection of his principal speeches and articles, *Indoneziia obviniaet* (Indonesia Accuses), appeared in a third edition.

Indonesian State; Moscow: Gosudarstvennoe izdatel'stvo iuridicheskoi literatury, 1957); G. Kessel'brenner, *Zapadnyi Irian—neot'emlemaia chast' Indonezii* (West Irian, an Inalienable Part of Indonesia; Moscow: Gospolitizdat, 1958); Ia. N. Guzevatyi, *Indoneziia, geograficheskii ocherk* (Indonesia, a Geographic Outline; Moscow: Geografgiz, 1958); N. Nikolaeva, *Indoneziia—ekonomicheskii-geograficheskii ocherk* (Indonesia: An Economic-Geographic Outline; Leningrad: Obshchestvo po rasprostraneniiu politicheskykh i nauchnykh znanii RSFSR, 1958); V. A. Val'kov, *Indoneziia zashchishchaet svoiu nezavisimost'* (Indonesia Defends Its Independence; Moscow: Znanie, 1959); Ia. N. Guzevatyi, *Ekonomika sovremennoi Indonezii* (The Economy of Contemporary Indonesia; Moscow: Sotsekiz, 1960); V. A. Val'kov, *Indoneziia na puti nezavisimogo rasvitiia* (Indonesia on the Path of Independent Development; Moscow: Izdatel'stvo Instituta mezhdunarodnykh otnoshenii, 1960); A. K. Lavrent'ev, *Tainaia voina protiv Indonezii* (The Secret War against Indonesia [on American involvement in attempts to overthrow the Indonesian government]; Moscow: Izadatel'stvo sotsial'no-ekonomicheskoi literatury, 1960); V. Ia. Arkhipov and O. N. Kulikov, *Finansy i banki Indonezii* (Finances and Banks of Indonesia; Moscow: Gosfinizdat, 1960); G. Kessel'brenner, *Zapadnyi Irian* (West Irian; Moscow: Gospolitizdat, 1960); V. I. Antipov, *Indoneziia; ekonomiko-geograficheckie karakteristiki* (Indonesia; Economic-Geographic Characteristics; Moscow: Geografgiz, 1961). We should also mention the Russian translation of an important Chinese work on recent Indonesian history: Chang Chao-tsiang, *Politika i ekonomika poslevoennoi Indonezii* (The Politics and Economics of Postwar Indonesia; Moscow: Izdatel'stvo inostranoi literatury, 1958). The Russian edition provides extensive annotation and a concluding chapter by L. Ia. Dadiani bringing up to date the original study, which was first published in Peking in 1956.

In 1961 the Academy of Sciences sponsored the publication of a major survey, *Respublika Indoneziia* (The Republic of Indonesia; Moscow: Izdatel'stvo vostochnoi literatury, 1961). The volume consists of essays by Soviet scholars on various aspects of Indonesia since 1945: O. I. Zabozlaeva, "The Struggle of the Indonesian People for Full Independence"; E. P. Zakaznikova, "The Labor Movement in the Republic of Indonesia"; G. S. Shabalina, "The Struggle for Economic Independence and the Economic Policy of the Indonesian Government"; K. V. Novikov, "The Development of National Industry"; Iu. A. Sotnikov, "Agriculture and the Agrarian Question"; O. A. Kharmalov, "Foreign Trade"; V. V. Sikorskii, "The Literature of Independent

Indonesia"; and V. A. Zharov and O. N. Kondrashkin, "Friendship and Cooperation between the Soviet Union and the Republic of Indonesia." In his introduction to the book, A. A. Guber provides a brief sketch of the development of the independence movement under the Dutch; Zabozlaeva's lengthy chapter carries the story from the Japanese occupation to 1960. Unfortunately, the latter essay is one of the weaker sections of this generally most interesting book, having been written with a heavy ideological hand which tends to oversimplify and at times distort the account of events.

Of the numerous articles appearing on Indonesia in this period, we shall list only those of the most substance and interest to the historian and political scientist. These include O. I. Zabozlaeva, "The Formation of the Working Class in Indonesia," in *Kratkie soobschcheniia Instituta vostokovedeniia* (no. 20, 1956); Iu. G. Barsegov, "West Irian Must Be Returned to Indonesia," *Sovetskoe gosudarstvo i pravo* (no. 9, 1956); V. Val'kov, "Indonesia on the Road to Independent Development," *Mirovaia ekonomika i mezhdunarodnye otnosheniia* (no. 5, Nov., 1957); N. F. Bulygin, "Concerning the Reunion of West Irian with Indonesia," *Sovetskoe vostokovedenie* (no. 1, 1957); O. I. Zabozlaeva, "Great October and the National Liberation Struggle of the Indonesian People, 1917–1927," in the collection *Velikii Oktiabr' i narody Vostoka* (Great October [the Bolshevik Revolution] and the Peoples of the East; Moscow: Izdatel'stvo vostochnoi literatury, 1957); D. V. Bekleshov, "Indonesia," in the collection *Zarubezhnye strany: Politichesko-ekonomicheskii spravochnik* (Foreign Countries: A Political-Economic Handbook; Moscow: Gospolitizdat, 1957); V. I. Billik, "Republic of Indonesia," *Prepodovanie istorii v shkole* (vol. XIII, no. 1, Jan.–Feb., 1958; this article concerns the teaching of Indonesian history in Soviet schools); Iu. A. Sotnikov, "Indonesia," in the collection *Agrarnye otnosheniia v stranakh Vostoka* (Agrarian Relations in the Countries of the East; Moscow: Akademiia nauk SSSR, Institut vostokovedeniia, 1958); O. I. Zabozlaeva, "West Irian," in the collection *Poslednye kolonii v Azii* (The Last Colonies in Asia; Moscow: Izdatel'stvo vostochnoi literatury, 1958); E. P. Zakaznikova, "The Labor Movement in Indonesia, 1918–1926," in the collection *Iugo-vostochnaia Azii, ocherki ekonomiki i istorii* (Southeast Asia, Economic and Historical Outlines; Moscow: Izdatel'stvo vostochnoi literatury, 1958); E. I. Gnevusheva, "'Budi Utomo' (Noble Aim): On the Fiftieth Anniversary of the First National Organization in Indonesia," *Sovetskoe vostokovedenie* (no. 5, 1958); "From the History of the National-Liberation Struggle of the Indonesian People (from the 1820's to the 1870's)," *Istoricheskii arkhiv* (no. 2, March–April 1958; documents, with an introductory article by O. F. Solov'ev); A. A. Guber, "On the Question of the Special Characteristics of the Formation of Classes and Parties in Colonial Indonesia," in the collection *Novaia i noveishaia istoria* (Modern and Recent History; Moscow: AON pri Tsk KPSS, 1959); A. G. Pirozhkova, "Indonesia," in the collection *Vneshnaia torgovlia SSSR so stranami Azii, Afriki i Latinskoi Ameriki* (The Foreign Trade of the USSR with the Countries of Asia, Africa, and Latin America; Moscow, 1958); Iu. A. Sotnikov, "On Colonial Traces in the Agrarian Structure of Indonesia," *Sovetskoe vostokovedenie* (no. 4, 1958); L. E. Karunovskaia, "Pre-Islamic Beliefs in Indonesia," *Trudy Instituta etnografiii* (vol. LI, 1959); M. Andreev, "The Development of State Capitalism in Indonesia," *Problemy vostokovedeniia* (no. 6, 1959); V. Arkhipov, "Indonesia on the Path toward Strengthening Its Economy and Finances," *Finantsy SSSR* (vol. XX, no. 20, July, 1959); A. M. Model', "Fifteen Years of Indonesian Independence," *Problemy vostokovedeniia* (no. 4, 1960); L. Ia. Dadiani, "The Political and Governmental System in Indonesia during the Japanese Occupation," *Uchenie zapiski kafedri gosudarstva i prava Instituta mezhdunarodnykh otnoshenii* (no. 1, 1960); Iu. A. Sotnikov, "Some Features of the Social and Economic Development of the Indonesian Outer Islands on the Eve of Their Enslavement by the Imperialists, Late 19th and Early 20th Centuries," *Kratkie soobshcheniia Instituta narodov Azii i Afriki* (no. 43, 1960); B. Il'ichev, "In the Vanguard of the Struggle for the Unity and National Independence of the Indonesian People," *Partiinaia zhizn'* (no. 9, May, 1960); V. Arkhipov, "Economic Problems in Contemporary Indonesia," *Mirovaia ekonomika i mezhdunarodnye otnosheniia* (no. 8, Aug., 1960); M. S. Likhunov, "The Efforts of the Indonesian People to Establish Their Independent State," *Sovetskoe gosudarstvo i pravo* (no. 12, Dec., 1960); P. Anan'ev, "Agrarian Law in Indonesia," *Mirovaia ekonomika i mezhdunarodnye otnoshenaii* (no. 1, Jan., 1961); and V. Ia. Kubenok, "Cooperation of the Soviet Union with Indonesia," *Vneshnaia torgovlia* (vol. XLI, no. 5, May, 1961).

Indonesia is also dealt with in the following works: *Mezhdunarodnye otnosheniia na Dal'nem Vostoke (1840–1949gg.)* (International Relations in the Far East [1840–1949]; Moscow: Gospolitizdat, 1956; a revised edition of the volume on International Relations in the Far East, 1870–1945, published in 1952); *Polozhenie sel'skogo khoziaistva i krest'ianstva v koloniiakh i drugikh slaborazvitykh stranakh* (The Position of Agriculture and the Peasantry in Colonies and Other Under-developed Countries; Moscow: Izdatel'stvo Akademii nauk SSSR, 1958); B. A. Shabad, "Exposition of the Core of the Colonial Policy of Imperialism in Contemporary Bourgeois Historiography," *Voprosy istorii* (no. 2, 1958); *Vsemirnaia istoriia* (World History; 10 vols.; Moscow: Gospolitizdat/Sotsekgiz, 1955–1959); V. Ia. Avarin, *Raspad kolonial'noi sistemy* (The Collapse of the Colonial System; Moscow: Gospolitizdat, 1957); V. Ia. Vasil'eva, *Raspad kolonial'noi sistemy imperializma* (The Collapse of the Colonial System of Imperialism; Moscow: Izdatel'stvo Akademiia nauk SSSR, 1958); *Problemy ekonomiki stran Iugo-vostochnoi Azii* (Economic Problems of the Southeast Asian Countries; Moscow: Izdatel'stvo vostochnoi literatury, 1959); N. A. Simoniia, *Naselenie kitaiskoi natsional'nosti Iugo-vostochnoi Azii* (The Chinese Population of Southeast Asia; Moscow: Izdatel'stvo Instituta mezhdunarodnykh otnosheniia, 1959); *Problemy industrializatsii suverennykh slaborazvitykh stran: Azii, Indiia, Indoneziia, Birma,* (Problems of the Industrialization of Sovereign Underdeveloped Asian Countries: India, Indonesia, Burma; Moscow: Izdatel'stvo Akademii nauk SSSR, 1960); V. Ia. Arkhipov, *Inostrannyi kapital v ekonomike stran Iugo-vostochnoi Azii* (Foreign Capital in the Economy of the Countries of Southeast Asia; Moscow: Gosfinizdat, 1960); *Strany Vostoka nakanune evropeiskogo zavoevaniia* (The Countries of the East on the Eve of the European Conquest; Moscow: Izdatel'stvo vostochnoi literatury, 1961); G. L. Bonarevskii, *Vozniknovenie kolonial'noi sistemy imperializma* (The Rise of the Colonial System of Imperialism; Moscow: Izdatel'stvo vostochnoi literatury, 1961); *Agrarnye reformy v stranakh Vostoka* (Agrarian Reforms in the Countries of the East; Moscow: Izdatel'stvo vostochnoi literatury, 1961); *Agrarno-krest'ianskii vopros v stranakh Iugo-vostochnoi Azii* (The Agrarian and Peasant Question in the Countries of Southeast Asia; Moscow: Isdatel'stvo vostochnoi literatury, 1961); *Agrarno-krest'ianskii vopros v suverennykh slaborazvytykh stranakh Azii: Indiia, Birma, Indoneziia* (The Agrarian and Peasant Question in Sovereign Underdeveloped Countries of Asia: India, Burma, Indonesia; Moscow: Izdatel'stvo Akademii nauk SSSR, 1961); G. A. Martysheva, *Iugo-vostochnaia Aziia posle vtoroi mirovoi voiny* (Southeast Asia since World War II; Moscow: Sotsekgiz, 1960).

The listing of Soviet sources which has been presented here is necessarily a sketchy one, particularly for the period since 1955; it serves only as a guide to the major publications and an indication of the sort of work on Indonesia which has been undertaken in the Soviet Union.

For more complete bibliographies on the subject, see I. I. Korel',
*Natsional'no-osvoboditel'naia bor'ba v Indonezii, V'etname, Malaie i
Birme: Rekomendatel'nyi ukazatel' literatury* (The National Liberation
Struggle in Indonesia, Vietnam, Malaya, and Burma: A Recommended
Bibliography; Leningrad: Gosudarstvennaia publichnaia biblioteka im.
M. E. Satlykova-Shchedrina, 1950); M. N. Talantova, *Uglublenie kriz-
isa kolonial'noi sistemy imperializma posle Vtoroi mirovoi voiny; reko-
mendatel'nyi ukazatel' literatury* (The Deepening of the Crisis of the
Colonial System of Imperialism Following the Second World War; a
Recommended Bibliography; Moscow: Izdatel'stvo gosudarstvennoi
biblioteki SSSR im. V. Lenina, 1955); A. Belen'kii, "Soviet Scholarly
Works on Indonesia," *Narody Azii i Afriki* (no. 4, 1961); and *Bibliografiia Iugo-vostochnoi Azii* (A Bibliography of Southeast Asia;
Moscow: Izdatel'stvo vostochnoi literatury, 1960). The last-named
compilation is the most useful, carrying its listing, which is devoted
exclusively to Russian-language sources, from Czarist times through
1958. It is well arranged and quite complete, though I have noted some
omissions in the prewar period, the most striking being the absence of
all Tan Malaka's writings. The scholar who does not command Russian
but wishes to know what has been published in the Soviet Union may
refer to the U.S. Library of Congress's *Monthly Index of Russian Ac-
quisitions,* which provides English translations of titles. If he does not
wish to plow through these hefty tomes, he may find some succor in
my *Bibliography of Soviet Publications on Southeast Asia* (Southeast
Asia Program, Cornell University, Data Paper no. 34; Ithaca, N.Y.,
1959), which carries the listing to July, 1958. Since 1960, the Soviet
periodical *Novaia sovetskaia i inostranaia literatura po stranam zarubezhnogo Vostoka* (New Soviet and Foreign Literature on the Countries
of the Non-Soviet East) has appeared, with current listings of works
on the area.

Articles on Indonesian current events may be found in considerable
quantity in *New Times, World Trade Union Movement, International
Life,* and *Aziia i Afrika segodnia;* the latter two periodicals provide
rather more sophisticated accounts. *International Life (Mezhdunarod-
naia zhizn'),* which began in 1954, is intended for a foreign audience
and hence appears in several major languages. *Aziia i Afrika segodnia*
(Asia and Africa Today) was begun in 1957 by the then Oriental Institute of the USSR Academy of Sciences as *Sovremennyi Vostok* (The
Contemporary East); its title was changed to the present one in 1961.
Both *International Life* and *Aziia i Afrika segodnia* include from time
to time articles by Indonesians on current Indonesian affairs.

The historian will probably find the following Soviet journals the best current sources for scholarly articles on Indonesia and other countries of the non-Soviet Far East, although such writings are by no means restricted to them. Of primary importance are the publications of the former Institute of Oriental Studies of the USSR Academy of Sciences (since August, 1960, the institute has undergone several changes of title and organization and is currently divided into the Institute of the Peoples of Asia and the Institute of the Peoples of Africa): *Kratkie soobschcheniia* (Brief Reports), *Uchenye zapiski* (Notes of the Profession), and *Narody Azii i Afriki* (Peoples of Asia and Africa; formerly titled *Problemy vostokovedeniia*). Other periodicals of importance are *Voprosy istorii* (Problems of History) and *Vestnik istorii mirovoi kul'tury* (Journal of the History of World Culture), published by the Institute of History, USSR Academy of Sciences; *Mirovaia ekonomika i mezhdunarodnye otnosheniia* (World Economics and International Relations), issued by the Institute of World Economics and International Relations of the Academy of Sciences; *Vneshnaia torgovlia* (Foreign Trade), published by the Ministry of Foreign Trade of the USSR; and *Voprosy ekonomiki* (Problems of Economics), the journal of the Academy of Sciences' Institute of Economics. Most of these publications now provide English summaries of their major articles.

Since the completion of the above survey, Indonesia has been treated in various regional and world histories published in the USSR. O. I. Zabozlaeva wrote a section on the Indonesian independence movement during the colonial period for the *Istoriia mezhdunarodnoi rabochego i natsional'no-osvoboditel'nogo dvizheniia* (History of the International Workers' and National Liberation Movements; Moscow: Izdatel'stvo VPSh i AON pri TsK KPSS, 1962, Part II), a work composed under the auspices of the highest Communist Party school. Another recent collective history, A. A. Guber and A. N. Kheifets, eds., *Novaia istoriia stran zarubezhnogo Vostoka; uchebnik dlia pedagogicheskikh institutov* (Modern History of the Countries of the Non-Soviet East; Textbook for Pedagogical Institutes; Moscow: Uchpedgiz, 1961), treats Indonesia's history from the seventeenth century to 1918. The work, intended for those preparing to teach Asian history courses of middle school level, grants a separate chapter to the Dutch colonization of Indonesia but otherwise integrates its consideration of the area into a general record of events in the Far East. Iu. V. Maretin wrote the chapters on Indonesia in the companion volumes *Novaia istoriia stran zarubezhnoi Azii i Afriki* (Modern History of the Countries of Non-Soviet Asia and Africa) and *Noveishaia istoriia stran zarubezhnoi Azii i Afriki* (Recent History of the Countries of Non-Soviet Asia and Africa), published respectively in 1959 and 1963 by the Leningrad University Press. Maretin's contributions, which cover the period to 1917 in the first volume and to 1961 in the second, include critical surveys of the major published sources on the history of the periods concerned.

In recent years, considerable emphasis has been placed by Soviet scholars—particularly those of the University of Leningrad—on the historiography of Asia. At a meeting of Soviet Asia specialists in 1963 papers were read by M. Movchaniuk on "Contemporary Indonesian Historiography of the Uprising Led by Diponegoro (1825–1830)" and by Iu. V. Maretin on "The Historiography of the Padri Wars in West Sumatra in the First Half of the Nineteenth Century (From the History of the Religious and National-Liberation Struggle in Indonesia)".[23] An essay by A. S. Shin, "Some Questions of the Indonesian Revolution in the Interpretation of American Historians," published in the collection *Protiv fal'sifikatsii istorii Vostoka* (Against the Falsification of the History of the East; Moscow: Izdatel'stvo vostochnoi literatury, 1961), devotes most of its attention to the writings of George McT. Kahin. A series on "The Contemporary Historiography of the Countries of the Non-Soviet East" (*Sovremennaia istoriografiia stran zarubezhnogo Vostoka;* Moscow: Izdatel'stvo vostochnoi literatury) is being published, and Southeast Asia is one of the areas to be covered. The first volume, on China, appeared in 1963; it is devoted largely to a critique of interpretations by Western historians.

Recent Soviet writings on Indonesia have continued to center on the period since the transfer of sovereignty and to deal primarily with foreign relations and economic problems. Among the works on foreign affairs, Iurii Aleshin's *Sovetsko-Indoneziiskie otnosheniia v 1945–1962 godakh* (Soviet-Indonesian Relations from 1945 to 1962; Moscow: Izdatel'stvo Instituta mezhdunarodnykh otnoshenii, 1963) provides a useful account of the development of diplomatic, economic, and cultural relations. M. A. Andreev, *Likvidatsiia ekonomicheskikh pozitsii golland-*

[23] N. A. Kuznetsova and V. N. Nikiforov, "From the Conference of Specialists on the History of the Countries of Asia and Africa," *Voprosy istorii,* June 1963, pp. 107–109. According to this account, the conference criticized Asia specialists outside Leningrad for having paid insufficient attention to historiography, and it was decided to hold biennial conferences on the subject in order to help overcome this weakness. Both Movchaniuk and Maretin were from the University of Leningrad.

skogo imperializma v Indonezii (The Liquidation of the Economic Position of Dutch Imperialism in Indonesia; Moscow: Sotsekgiz, 1962), analyzes the events surrounding the 1957 takeover of Dutch enterprises; I. A. Skryl', "The Struggle of the Indonesian People for Peace," in the collection *Bor'ba narodov Azii za mir* (The Struggle of the Peoples of Asia for Peace; Moscow: Izdatel'stvo vostochnoi literatury, 1962), is concerned with foreign policy from 1945 to 1961 and especially with the interpretation of "positive neutrality." Relations with America are dealt with, by M. M. Pevzner and Ia. Rezema, in the Indonesia section of *Politika SShA v stranakh Iuzhnoi Azii* (The Policy of the USA in the Countries of Southern Asia; Moscow: Izdatel'stvo vostochnoi literatury, 1961); and in A. S. Shin, "U.S. Imperialism and the West Irian Problem," in the symposium *Kolonializm, zleishii vrag narodov Vostoka* (Colonialism, Worst Enemy of the Peoples of the East; Moscow: Izdatel'stvo vostochnoi literatury, 1962).

Recent studies of the prerevolutionary period include A. B. Belen'kii, "From the History of the National Liberation Movement in Indonesia; the Indische Partij," *Narody Azii i Afriki*, no. 2, 1963; and E. I. Gnevusheva, *V strane trekh tysiach ostrov; russkie uchenye v Indonezii* (In the Land of Three Thousand Islands; Russian Scholars in Indonesia; Moscow: Izdatel'stvo vostochnoi literatury, 1962). The latter is a popularly written but very informative little book on Russian academic visitors to Indonesia in the nineteenth and early twentieth centuries. It describes the attempts of N. N. Miklukho-Maklai, who explored New Guinea, to interest the Russian crown in establishing a protectorate there, and the careers of a succession of naturalists who worked at the botanical gardens in Bogor (a regular fellowship for this purpose was established by the Tsarist academy of sciences in 1897). References are provided to their works on Indonesia and to related materials from the Archive of Russian Foreign Affairs.

Another recent and extremely interesting book utilizing archival materials in the USSR is A. A. Guber *et al.*, eds., *Politika europeiskikh derzhav v Iugo-Vostochnoi Azii (6oe gody XVIII—6oe gody XIX v.); dokumenty i materialy* (The Politics of the European Powers in Southeast Asia [from the 1760's to the 1860's]; Documents and Materials; Moscow: Izdatel'stvo vostochnoi literatury, 1962). The volume consists largely of dispatches from Russian diplomats in England, Holland, and Spain concerning the situation in Indonesia, Burma, and the Philippines; the archive location and number of each item are provided, the overwhelming majority of the materials being from the Archive of Rus-

sian Foreign Affairs. The work, which is intended to have a sequel
dealing with events to 1900, grew, according to the introductory essay
by its editors, from the compilation of similar collections of documents
on Tsarist relations with India, China, and Mongolia. It was felt that
although Russia had had no direct relations with Southeast Asia the
materials in Soviet archives could throw additional light on the penetration of the area by the European powers. There are 196 items on Indonesia, comprising about half the book; they are in the original Russian
or French, and are arranged chronologically under the following classifications: Anglo-Dutch rivalry in Sumatra (1763–1764); the fourth
Anglo-Dutch war and the crisis of the Dutch East India Company
(1782–1796); the policy of the European powers in Indonesia in the
era of the Napoleonic wars (1802–1810); colonial policy in Indonesia
in the period of the restoration of Dutch power and the Diponegoro
rebellion (1814–1829); and the colonial policy in Indonesia in the
period of the Cultivation System (1833–1869).[24] Indices of personal
and geographical names are supplied.

In concluding I might also mention, as an indication of the growth
of Soviet interest in Indonesian history, that a fictionalized biography
of Diponegoro has been published for younger Soviet readers: M. A.
Kolesnikov, *Diponegoro* (Moscow: Molodaia gvardiia, 1962).

[24] A good part of the items on Indonesia concern the perennial financial difficulties of the Dutch East India Company and the Netherlands Indies government;
this emphasis drew fire from one Soviet reviewer, who argued that a commentary
on the documents should have been provided lest the reader conclude the Dutch
had not in fact been making great profits at Indonesian expense. He also complained that the attempts of the late-eighteenth-century American bourgeoisie to
expand into Indonesia had not been sufficiently stressed by the compilers of the
collection. N. A. Khalfin, review in *Voprosy istorii*, May 1963, pp. 126–127.

XVI

Use of Anthropological Methods in Indonesian Historiography

By KOENTJARANINGRAT

Professor of Anthropology, University of Indonesia, Jakarta

METHODS OF CULTURAL ANTHROPOLOGY

THE methods of anthropology, particularly cultural anthropology, can be classified according to the specific approaches prevailing in the subdisciplines of anthropology. The subdisciplines that exist in the area of cultural anthropology are (1) prehistorical archaeology, (2) ethnolinguistics, and (3) ethnology. Two specific approaches to the study of culture have developed within the field of ethnology: (1) the diachronic and (2) the synchronic.[1] The terms "descriptive integration," referring to diachronic studies, and "generalizing approach," referring to synchronic studies, are often used.[2]

At Indonesian universities Indonesian [3] prehistory has always been considered a subdivision of Indonesian archaeology (e.g., Indonesian cultural history covering the period of prehistory up to the decline of the Hindu-Indonesian civilization),[4] and it has never, as yet, been connected with Indonesian cultural anthropology. Thus it differs, in its affinities, from prehistory in countries such as Great Britain, South Africa, Australia, the United States, Mexico, and the Soviet Union,

[1] About thirty years ago, when these two research approaches were beginning to develop, they constituted two opposing schools in anthropology.
[2] R. L. Beals and H. Hoijer, *An Introduction to Anthropology* (New York, 1953), pp. 10–11.
[3] By Indonesia is meant, in the present article, the area within the boundaries of the Republic of Indonesia.
[4] The study of Hindu-Indonesian civilization is similar to that of classical archaeology, Egyptology, Mesopotamian archaeology, etc., in that an important part of its approach is philological.

where it has always been considered a part of anthropology. For this reason the relationship between history and prehistory in Indonesia will not be treated in this section on anthropological methods.

Ethnolinguistics has been a section of anthropology in Indonesia from the beginning. Two ethnolinguistic methods have been developed recently which should be useful in the study of Indonesian prehistory: (1) the method of investigating the geographical spread of related languages through an anlysis of their basic vocabularies; (2) the method of lexicostatistical dating, a method for determining at what point in the past two related languages diverged from a common parent language on the basis of the percentage of basic vocabulary shared by the two languages.[5] Since the above-mentioned methods are more particularly applicable to the study of prehistory than to the study of history, they will not be discussed more specifically.

Descriptive integration (also called the diachronic approach) in ethnology has as its aim the acquisition of an understanding of man and his behavior by reconstructing his origin, development, and spread as well as the various intercultural contacts that have taken place throughout time on this earth. In such studies the findings obtained by the methodologies used in prehistorical archaeology, ethnolinguistics, ethnology, and even physical anthropology are all incorporated and integrated into one body of knowledge. The central data incorporated into this descriptive integration, however, are ethnographic data. It is for this reason that, in terms of methodology, descriptive integration studies belong specifically to the field of ethnology, even though, in terms of aims, those studies belong to the field of prehistorical archaeology. Several methods have also been employed to analyze Indonesian ethnographic data in order to obtain a descriptive integration of the cultural history of the peoples of Indonesia. The most important of these methods is one, based upon *Kulturkreise* and *Kulturschichten,* that classifies Indonesian cultural elements into certain categories in order that the diachronic relationships among them may be observed. Since the methods of descriptive integration, like those of ethnolinguistics, are more particularly applicable to the study of Indonesian prehistory than to the study of Indonesian history, they will not be discussed more specifically.[6]

[5] An excellent review article on the development of the method of lexico-statistical dating is to be found in D. H. Hymes, "Lexico-statistics So Far," *Current Anthropology,* I (1960), 3–44.

[6] I have discussed the application of these methods to Indonesian ethnographical data in another book (cf. Koentjaraningrat, *Beberapa Metode Anthropologi dalam*

The generalizing approach (also called the synchronic approach) in ethnology has as its aim an understanding of the basic principles of human culture within the framework of contemporary living cultures. This understanding can be obtained by isolating the general unifying principles which underlie the cultural diversity observable in the thousands of contemporary societies of the earth. The methods used in the generalizing approach can be divided into two categories. The methods of the first category aim at an intensive inquiry [7] concerning a limited number of contrasting societies and cultures (three to five at most). The methods of the second category aim at comparing a limited number of restricted cultural elements from the largest possible number of societies and cultures (two to three hundred or more). These methods of the second category, generally known as cross-cultural methods, are being used increasingly at the present time. In actual practice the anthropologist does not separate the two methodologies but always uses the one to amplify and assist the other. Several specific methods of this generalizing approach to ethnology are of great significance to historiography. These specific methods will be discussed in relation to Indonesian historiography in the succeeding sections.

ANTHROPOLOGICAL DATA AND METHODS USEFUL TO HISTORIOGRAPHY

All methods used in writing the history of a people attempt to "fill in" as much as possible [8] of the background of every event that appears in the historical sources. In this attempted "filling in," a number of anthropological methods, especially those of the "generalizing approach category," can be very useful. Among the methods which we consider important to historiography in general and to Indonesian historiography in particular are (1) the method that explains the process of the assimilation of foreign elements in a culture-contact situation in terms of the "principle of integration" and the "principle of function"; (2) the functional method in the study of the community; (3) the functional method in the study of mythology; and (4) the genealogical method of interviewing informants. In addition to the four methods mentioned above,

Penjelidikan[2] *Masjarakat dan Kebudajaan di Indonesia* [Jakarta, 1958], pp. 248–258).

[7] Regarding the term "intensive inquiry," see S. F. Nadel, *The Foundations of Social Anthropology* (Glencoe, 1951), pp. 6–7.

[8] Compare this with what has been stated about the boundaries of the study of history by J. Huizinga, *De wetenschap der geschiedenis* (Haarlem, 1937), p. 10.

it will be found that use of the large compilation of data on Indonesian peoples and cultures will shed light on many of the problems of Indonesian historiography. We can thus mention point (5), data which appear in Indonesian ethnographic studies, as an additional source to be explored by Indonesian historiography.

The principle of integration and the principle of function. Studies of culture contact have, after a long development, recently become a center of interest for many anthropologists. Among the many problems of culture contact there are several which concern the processes for the adaptation and assimilation of alien cultural elements. These include the problem of why some alien cultural elements are assimilated with ease into a native culture while others are assimilated with great difficulty and the problem of why some native cultural elements are easily displaced and some displaced only with difficulty by alien elements.

Various scholars have advanced different theories attempting to reach an understanding of these problems. E. C. Parsons, for instance, suggested that "a foreign complex is established in its entirety only when it can be fitted into an old form of behavior and is compatible with existing emotional attitudes." [9] This opinion, which can be designated as an opinion based on the principle of integration, is subscribed to by many other scholars. In addition, there are scholars who state that a culture element cannot change easily if that particular element has an important function in the society concerned. This conception, which is based on the theory of function, is formulated by A. L. Kroeber. [10]

According to the anthropological viewpoint, study of the problems mentioned, even though focusing only on particular cultural elements, requires a thorough understanding of the social systems into which those elements are potentially assimilable Contact between two cultures results essentially in a merging of social groups and, of course, of individuals within these groups. This conception is considered very important by anthropologists. Further, in analyzing acculturation problems, anthropologists usually pay special attention to the forms, organization, and world views of particular social groups, such as kin groups, social classes, economic and occupational groups, etc., within the cultures under study.

The functional method in the study of the community. At about the same time that the functionalist approach to field work was becoming established, around 1920, a new concept in the study of the commu-

[9] E. C. Parsons, *Mitla, Town of the Souls* (Chicago, 1922), p. 536.
[10] A. L. Kroeber, *Anthropology* (New York, 1948), p. 402.

nity was being developed. In accordance with this concept, the investigator, when describing a culture, tends more and more to restrict himself to a group of people in a particular locality which is viewed as a complete entity, and he attempts to collect most of his data from that particular locality. Through the intensive study of a single community of limited size, the investigator attempts to see that community as a systematic whole.

The community, as a systematic whole, can be viewed from a variety of angles. First, in viewing the activities of the people of the community as they wring a living from, and in general come to grips with, the forces of nature that form the environment of the community, it may be seen as an ecological system. Second, as a system of interpersonal relations in the society, the community may be seen as a social system. Third, as a system of the ways in which its members interpret their surroundings and the universe, the community may be seen as a system of world view. Fourth, as a system of the feelings and attitudes of human minds confronted by their surroundings, the community may be seen as a system of personality adjustments. Thus a view of the community from any of the four aspects mentioned will give the research worker a deep understanding about forms of humanity.[11]

The functional method in the analysis of mythology. The study of mythology has not, as yet, developed into an independent discipline. It has always been conducted within the framework of other disciplines, such as philology, history, psychology, anthropology, etc., as a special research tool or as a special field of study. Thus the various interested scholars have developed different methods, congruent with the specific views of their individual disciplines, for the analysis of mythology.

One method often used by anthropologists to analyze mythology is based on the assumption that sacred stories are the embodiment of the ideals, the thoughts, and the views of life, etc., which motivate the physical as well as the spiritual activities of the society concerned. Hence the principles underlying those sacred stories have become the key for understanding the principles of the greater part of the society and culture in which these myths exist.

The components of this so-called functional approach to the study of mythology were actually suggested by a great figure in the history

---

[11] The various terms concerning the aspects of community mentioned in this paragraph are taken from R. Redfield's study, *The Little Community: Viewpoint for the Study of a Human Whole* (Chicago, 1956).

of anthropology, Sir James Frazer. However, the functional approach
was clearly formulated by the proponent of functionalism, B. Malinowski.[12] It is to be regretted, however, that the data which he used to
support his ideas were drawn from only one society, the Trobriand
Islands. Malinowski, in contrast to scholars who had previously analyzed mythology, collected sacred stories *in situ*, as they were told,
and not from manuscripts or informants separated from the social
context of the storytelling situation. He observed that among the great
variety of stories of the Trobriand Islanders there was a collection of
myths, which was regarded by them as constituting one special category, called the *liliu*. These sacred myths were not regarded merely
as symbolic stories, as history, or as explanations attempting to account
for conspicuous phenomena but were regarded as a guide for sacred
ceremonies, as a standard of morals, and as a guide for many other
activities in that society.[13]

The genealogical method. This is a particular method of interviewing
which was conceived by W. H. R. Rivers when he undertook research
among the ethnic groups of the islands in the Torres-Straits region
between Irian (New Guinea) and Australia as a member of the Cambridge Torres-Straits Expedition in 1898. The method, which was ex-
pounded for the first time by Rivers in an article in the *Journal of the
Royal Anthropological Institute*,[14] consists of an interview which records the origin or genealogy of a number of individuals in the society
under investigation. The original aim of the method was the collection
of kinship terms in a particular language in order to analyze the kinship system of speakers of that language.[15] Later it was shown that
such an interview could also be used to gather information about many
other elements, phenomena, and events surrounding the interviewed
individuals in their society.[16]

[12] B. Malinowski explained his ideas on the analysis of mythology in an article
which he dedicated to J. Frazer (B. Malinowski, "Myth in Primitive Psychology,"
Magic, Science and Religion and Other Essays [New York, 1954], pp. 93–148).

[13] *Ibid.*, p. 108.

[14] W. H. R. Rivers, "A Genealogical Method of Collecting Social and Vital Statistics," *Journal of the Royal Anthropological Institute of Great Britain and Ireland*,
III (1900), 74–82.

[15] This approach is based on the assumption that a relationship exists between a
particular system of kinship terminology and the kinship system of the group that
uses that system of terminology. This assumption, introduced by L. H. Morgan in
the middle of the nineteenth century and later developed by other scholars, is one
that is important to the methodology of social anthropology.

[16] That the genealogical method serves not merely as a technique for collecting
the kinship terms of a particular people but also as a key which can unlock the gate

In addition, the genealogical method can also provide information about happenings that took place two, three, and sometimes four generations previously. Individuals in the society who provide the research worker with the names of relatives in the second or third ascending generations often still remember incidents that took place during the lifetimes of those relatives. Of course, the more generations that separate the informant from a relative in his genealogy, the less precise and reliable is the information that can be obtained by this method. However, by carefully cross-checking the information received from a number of individuals, data concerning social incidents and phenomena surrounding the individuals recorded in these genealogies can be collected which can provide the basic material for a reconstruction of community history.

Data in Indonesian ethnographic studies. Thousands of books and articles on the various peoples, cultures, and environments in Indonesia may be easily found because almost all of them have been compiled in large bibliographies. One of these bibliographies, comprising ten volumes, the *Repertorium op de literatuur betreffende de Nederlandsche kolonien,*[17] was compiled by the Ministry of Colonial Affairs in the Netherlands; it contains all articles which were written about Indonesia between 1595 and 1932. A short, one-volume bibliography, which is handier to use, was originally compiled by the American anthropologist R. Kennedy and has since been expanded into two volumes by H. T. Fischer and T. W. Maretzki. This *Bibliography of Indonesian Peoples and Cultures* (1955) contains most articles about Indonesia, especially those written during the period between 1800 and 1950.

It is regrettable, however, that only a small part of the vast compilation of written material on Indonesia is of scientific quality.[18] This is due to the fact that until the beginning of the twentieth century most reports on Indonesian peoples and cultures were casually written

of a community's social and cultural secrets, secrets that would otherwise remain hidden and could only be guessed at from the outside, has also been remarked upon by J. Kruyt in "Iets over de genealogische methode van ethnologisch onderzoek," *Mededeelingen: Tijdschrift voor Zendings-Wetenschap,* LXVIII (1924), 329.

[17] Translated into English: Repertory of the Literature regarding the Dutch Colonies (The Hague, 1895–1934).

[18] A Dutch anthropologist, C. Nooteboom, once made a remark in regard to the quality of ethnographic literature about Indonesia; he said: "Die eerbiedwaardige hoeveelheid literatuur over de volkenkunde van Nederlandsch-Indie blijkt bij gebruik soms zeer gering van kwaliteit en soms zeer onbetrouwbaar" (C. Nooteboom, "Volkenkunde en koloniale praktijk," *Koloniaal Tijdschrift,* XXIX [1940], 506).

by people with no knowledge of ethnological concepts and methods. The authors of those reports can be divided into five categories:

1) European travelers and sailors who have been visiting the Indonesian Archipelago since the end of the fifteenth century.

2) Christian missionaries who have been living among Indonesian ethnic groups since the end of the seventeenth century.

3) language experts who were sent to Indonesia by religious institutions in the Netherlands in order to translate the Bible into the various Indonesian local languages.

4) natural scientists who were sometimes sent to Indonesia to conduct scientific expeditions in order to gather data about the soil, natural environment, and the inhabitants of the tropics.

5) officials of the East India Company and Dutch and British colonial administrators in Indonesia.

Ethnographic work resulting from the application of modern methods of field work and data organization has appeared only since about 1920. As a matter of fact, there are some ethnographic reports about Indonesia, written in the period preceding 1920, which contain some of the characteristics of professional ethnographies. However, the majority of the professional ethnographies have been written by W. Schmidt's students who were scholars of the Societas Verbi Divini missionary organization, by American and German anthropologists, by *adat* law scholars, or by scholars who were students of J. P. B. de Josselin de Jong of Leyden.

It is true that Indonesian anthropology still lacks modern ethnographic studies for many Indonesian ethnic groups. A great deal has yet to be done in this field.

PROBLEMS IN INDONESIAN HISTORIOGRAPHY

There are a number of problems in Indonesian historiography which can be analyzed with substantial aid from ethnographic data and the anthropological methods mentioned in the preceding section. The most important of these problems are:

1) the understanding of the processes of the assimilation of alien cultural elements, particularly Hindu and Moslem elements, into Indonesian cultures

2) the search for data to "fill in the background" of historical events which have been extracted from historical sources such as charters, old manuscripts, sculptures, drawings, etc.

3) the reconstruction of local histories in Indonesia

4) the search for information concerning the original meaning and function of various kinds of historical objects and cultural elements from historical times

How various scholars have made fruitful use of the anthropological methods mentioned in the preceding section as an aid in shedding light on these problems will be discussed further in the following sections.

THE UNDERSTANDING OF ASSIMILATION IN INDONESIAN HISTORY

For a considerable time the problem of the processes of the adaptation and assimilation of Hindu and Moslem cultural elements has caught the attention of students of Indonesian history. Some principal questions which can be raised in relation to this problem are: (1) Why were only some elements of alien cultures assimilated into the cultures of Indonesia, and, conversely, why were a great many native cultural elements never, or only very slowly, eradicated by the influence of alien cultural elements? (2) What was the social structure and the social context in which the adaptation and assimilation processes occurred? (3) Why were the Hindu and Moslem cultures the only ones that had an impact on native Indonesian cultures, while very little or nothing came from Chinese and other cultures? No doubt these principal questions can be broken down again into many detailed questions which can all serve as objects of special investigation. But one should be reminded that all these questions constitute complexes which are closely related to each other.

The methods and theories used to answer these questions also cannot be separated from one another. They have, of course, to be taken from various disciplines such as archaeology, philology, economics, sociology, and so on, but it is quite clear that anthropology is able to make a valuable contribution since these questions belong basically to the problem of acculturation.

(1) *The assimilation of alien cultural elements.* Students of Indonesian history, who have been preoccupied with this question for a long time, chiefly in regard to the influence of Hindu culture on native Indonesian cultures, have nearly always made use of ideas based upon the principle of integration mentioned on page 302 above to solve this problem. Two of the most prominent of these students have been W. F. Stutterheim and W. H. Rassers.

W. F. Stutterheim, a student of Indonesian philology and archaeology, attempted to explain why such great epics as the *Rāmāyana* have become so popular among various peoples in Indonesia. The principle of integration appeared in Stutterheim's method of reasoning when he came forward with the explanation that the Rāma stories in Indonesia were influenced not by the classical epic of *Rāmāyana* as composed by Vālmiki but by folk stories about Rāma which contained many elements and motifs similar to those found in Indonesian folk stories. This explains why the Indian stories of the hero Rāma were readily assimilated into Indonesian cultures and transformed into folk stories about the Indonesian hero Rāma.[19]

W. H. Rassers was another scholar who made use of the aforementioned theory concerning the principle of integration. He offered an opinion about the problem of the syncretism of the competing Shiwa and Buddha religions in the Hindu-Indonesian civilization. According to this scholar, these two religions were easily assimilated into Indonesian cultures, and above all into Javanese literature and mythology, because Javanese society was built on the foundation of a moiety system, with a social dualism and a customary spirit of competition between these two sections of their society. Such a social structure gave the Javanese the opportunity to classify the Shiwa religion and all matters connected with it in one moiety and the Buddha religion and all matters connected with it into the other moiety. These two religions, which in their land of origin had contested with each other, became integrated into Javanese culture because of their identification with the moiety competition which constituted such a vital element in the ancient Javanese social structure. This resulted in the syncretism of Shiwa-Buddhism in Indonesia.[20]

(2) *The social structure in which the processes of adaptation and assimilation occurred.* In the past, several historians who have tried to explain the processes of cultural contact between the Hindu and Indonesian cultures have neglected the social structure and the social context in which those processes occurred. These scholars, Mookerji, C. C. Berg, J. L. Moens, and N. J. Krom, and their theories were critically

[19] W. F. Stutterheim, *Rāma-Legenden und Rāma-Reliefs in Indonesien* (Munich, 1925).
[20] W. H. Rassers, "Siva and Buddha in the East Indian Archipelago," in *Pañji, the Culture Hero: A Structural Study of Religion in Java* (The Hague, 1959); this article first appeared as "Çiva en Buddha in den Indischen Archipel," *Gedenkschrift uitgegeven ter gelegenheid van het 75-jarig bestaan van het Koninklijk Instituut voor de Taal-, Land- en Volkenkunde van Nederlandsch-Indië* (The Hague, 1926), pp. 222–253.

reviewed by F. D. K. Bosch in the first part of his inaugural address as professor of Indonesian archaeology at the University of Leyden.[21] Even before Bosch, J. C. van Leur, a scholar in history and Indology, had criticized the theories of these scholars as being too speculative, because they reconstructed the processes of cultural contact and acculturation without taking into consideration the social backgrounds of these merging human societies. In addition, van Leur changed the Europe-centric viewpoint in the study of history by presenting the scholarly world with a new understanding of the magnitude and extent of the international trading activities of Asian peoples, as well as the social matrix in which those activities took place, long before West Europeans began to develop international trade in Asian seas in the sixteenth century.[22]

The new understanding provided by van Leur corresponded to Bosch's views concerning the process of culture contact between the Hindu and Indonesian cultures.[23] Bosch announced his point of view for the first time in 1919. Later he expanded his theory in the inaugural address mentioned. In addition to an understanding of the international trade of the Asian peoples prior to the sixteenth century, Bosch possessed a thorough knowledge of the social organization of Buddhism and of the various schools of Hindu religion. In the beginning Buddhism, especially the Tantrayana disciplines, and later folk forms of Hindu religion, such as the Shaiva-Siddhanta form, came to Indonesia from southern India along the Asian trade routes. Nevertheless, the activities of south Indian traders along the Indonesian coastal areas were essentially of no importance to the actual processes of the assimilation of Buddhist and Hindu cultural elements into Indonesian cultures. There have been many other peoples, such as the Chinese, who have carried out extensive trading activities in the Indonesian area, but they have had little discernible influence on the cultures of Indonesia.[24] It would be correct to say that the only link between these

[21] F. D. K. Bosch, *Het vraagstuk van de Hindoe-kolonisatie van de Archipel* (inaugural lecture, University of Leyden [Leyden, 1946]), pp. 3–44.

[22] J. C. van Leur, *Indonesian Trade and Society* (The Hague and Bandung, 1955).

[23] In a lecture presented to a conference on the *taal-, land- en volkenkunde* of Java, held in Solo in 1919, Bosch stated that the existing Hindu culture in Indonesia constituted a culture of books, a culture which was brought by people who were versed in these Sanskrit books (F. D. K. Bosch, "Een hypothese omtrent den oorsprong der Hindoe-Javaansche kunst," *Handelingen van het Eerste Congres van de Taal-, Land- en Volkenkunde van Java* [Weltevreden, 1921], pp. 93–169).

[24] This matter has also been clearly indicated by van Leur, *Trade and Society,* pp. 100–103. He described in detail the communication channels along which

other traders and the religious propagators, who deliberately carried knowledge from southern India to the upper strata of local societies in Indonesia, was the fact that they made use of the same trade routes. This deliberate religious propagation was a result of the innate missionary power in Buddhism. Apart from Bosch's theory, this process can be observed in the history of the propagation of Buddhism in Tibet, China, Korea, Japan, Ceylon, Thailand, Cambodia, etc. In Indonesia, Bosch further states, these religious propagators, who had been carried on trading ships from southern India, first succeeded in influencing the kings and court circles of some of the many kingdoms which existed in Indonesia. Thus appeared the *bhiksu* orders in Indonesian societies. Many of the priests of these orders later went to India to visit the holy cities of the land of the origin of Buddhism, either on pilgrimage or to intensify their knowledge of the scriptures at the great monasteries, such as that of Nalanda near Rajagrha. Some of these priests who had gone to that holy land returned to Indonesia carrying a more extensive knowledge of Buddhist religion, literature, and art. This process went on until approximately the seventh century when Buddhism, for a variety of reasons, began to decline in India, where it eventually disappeared in the tenth century. At that time various folk forms of Hinduism began to flourish in India. Later these forms spread to Indonesia along the same routes and in the same manner as had Buddhism.

Such was the approximate social background of acculturation between Indian and Indonesian cultures as reconstructed by Bosch on the basis of his extensive knowledge of the social systems of Buddhism and the other religions of India. In its main outlines, Bosch's can be regarded as the most acceptable reconstruction of the process of the diffusion of Indian cultures. Our understanding of this process can, the writer thinks, be even more refined if we have an understanding

---

Hindu cultural elements flowed, but he did not specifically discuss further the processes of merging and acculturation. He did, indeed, indicate how the Javanese rulers legitimized their position as kings with the aid of religious leaders from India (pp. 103–104), but from his description we are still not clear as to how these rulers came originally to know of the Hindu customs and as to precisely why they gave their court ceremonies a Hindu character. The fact that these rulers based the mode of their court life on Hindu models indicates that they were already under the influence of Hindu culture. It is this preliminary process of penetration of Hindu influence into Java which still poses a problem for us. This process was not studied by van Leur, because the matter was indeed outside his field of investigation—trade in Asia—but it has been the specific concern of F. D. K. Bosch.

not only of the social system of Buddhism but also of the societal systems of the peoples of southern India in general, since that is the area where Buddhism and the aforementioned forms of Hinduism were prevalent. Essentially, a religion is not merely a system of beliefs, philosophies of life, ideals, etc., which are laid down in sacred books and separated from the realities of life but also constitutes a system of group activities and a system of human behavior in the reality of social life. Knowledge of the societal system of rural societies in southern India can, among other methods, be provided by anthropological stud- ies. It stands to reason that anthropology would not be able to recon- struct the exact circumstances of the peoples in southern India from the period of the development of Buddhism and Hinduism in the first century to the tenth century; however, knowledge provided by an- thropological studies would be able to give a "general idea"[25] of the social foundation and framework of southern Indian villages in ancient times. Among the social scientists who have studied rural communities in southern India, anthropologists have played a major role. Among them, for example, M. N. Srinivas, E. K. Gough, A. R. Beals, and D. G. Mandelbaum have contributed articles about village life, the caste system, agricultural organization, etc., of village areas in Gujerat, My- sore, Tanjore, and others.[26] The information contained in these articles can be used to deepen and refine our understanding which, in its main outlines, has been given to us by Bosch.

Apart from Bosch's study, a deeper understanding of the problem of the assimilation of alien cultural elements into Indonesia is to be gained from the aforementioned study of van Leur. His study gives us a penetrating insight into a basic difference between the processes of Hindu and Moslem cultural influence on Indonesian societies, which had been previously regarded by scholars as two similar processes. Van Leur called our attention to the fact that the religion of Islam had been employed as a political tool by the trading kingdoms of northern Su- matra and the coastal trading kingdoms of northern Java to destroy the powerful Hindu-Indonesian kingdoms in the fifteenth century. The political and economic aspects of the diffusion of Moslem influence in Indonesia, especially in Java, give us a conception of why Moslem

[25] With the term "general idea" the writer has translated the term "*algemene voorstelling*" of G. W. Locher, "Huizinga en de culturele antropologie," *BKI*, CXIV (1958), 181.

[26] Some of these articles have been collected in a book entitled *Village India*, edited by McKim Marriot (Chicago, 1955).

culture did not at all change the foundations of society and the philosophy of life of the Javanese people. The process of the diffusion of
Moslem cultural elements into Indonesia was explained by van Leur
as being the result of the propagation of the religion of Islam.[27] In
regard to the problem of acculturation between the Moslem and Indonesian cultures, B. Schrieke, another anthropologist, held a point of
view which in its main outlines corresponds to that of van Leur. In
addition, Schrieke also considered the swiftness of the spread of Islam
in Indonesia to be a result of the competition in proselytizing activities
between Islam and Christianity, an outgrowth of the Crusades, in Asia
in general and in Indonesia in particular.[28]

Here one can see how an understanding of the social background
of the merging cultures can lead us to a clearer conception of an
acculturation problem. This holds true not only for acculturation problems involving Indian and Indonesian cultures, or Moslem and Indonesian cultures in the past, but also for those involving European and
Indonesian cultures at the present time.

(3) *The limited influence of Chinese cultural elements in Indonesia.*
The question of why only Hindu and Moslem cultures influenced the
native cultures of Indonesia and of why these native cultures were
not, or were to only a limited extent, influenced by, for instance, Chinese cultural elements is a question which, as far as the writer knows,
has received little attention from scholars working in Indonesia. But
there can be no doubt that an answer to this question would be an
important addition to our knowledge of Indonesian history. Such an
answer could be obtained only by an understanding of the social background and the social structure of the cultures concerned. It might be
said that question 3 is essentially an extension of question 2. Thus when
we want an answer, for example, to the question of why Hindu culture
influenced Indonesian cultures while Chinese culture did not, even
though both had contact with Indonesian cultures for a similar length
of time and under similar circumstances, the answer can be obtained
through a comprehension of the differences that existed in terms of
the organization of social groups such as kin groups, economic and
occupational groups, social classes, etc., between the peoples involved.
Thus the answer to the question which we posed previously will be
gained through a knowledge of the societal system of the Chinese in

[27] Van Leur, *Trade and Society,* pp. 110–116.
[28] B. Schrieke, *Indonesian Sociological Studies,* pt. II, *Ruler and Realm in Early
Java* (The Hague and Bandung, 1957), pp. 232–236.

Indonesia. G. W. Skinner, again an anthropologist, has made an extensive study of this matter.[29]

THE SEARCH FOR DATA "TO FILL IN THE BACKGROUND" OF HISTORICAL EVENTS

A large part of Indonesian historiography, especially that dealing with the period preceding the era of the Dutch East India Company, has been written by scholars of Indonesian philology. Their historiography, which utilizes charters, old Javanese literary manuscripts, architectural remains, etc., as its main sources, has produced lists of rulers and of events which took place in royal court circles in Sumatra and Java. In addition, Indonesian historiography of the period after the arrival in Indonesia of the Dutch East India Company is the product of historians who have made too much use of notes made by Dutch seamen, of the archives of the Dutch East India Company, and of information gathered from colonial government reports. This has resulted in a history of Dutch activities in Indonesia. We do not, of course, deny the merits of these scholars regarding the study of Indonesian history. Even though the research methods of these philologists and historians can generate only lists of political events in royal court circles, those lists can provide us with a framework for the further study of Indonesian history. Similarly, many parts of the history of the Dutch East India Company and of the colonial history written by Dutch historians can also be of much value to Indonesians. The contact situations between Dutchmen and Indonesians, described in these histories, especially constitute particular points which can be used as a preliminary framework for a more intensive study of Indonesian history. As we have pointed out earlier, in the second section of this chapter, the writing of the history of a particular people should as much as possible attempt to "fill in" the framework of political events which, in the first phase, has been extracted from the historical sources. Of course, in such an attempt history cannot stand on its own. The historian J. Huizinga has indicated how history requires the aid of other sciences "to fill in its background"; and these sciences do not consist only of

[29] The study, which contains the results of the investigations undertaken by Skinner from 1956 to 1958 in Indonesia, has not yet been published, but the results of such investigations undertaken in Thailand—the investigation of the Chinese community, especially in Bangkok—have been published in *Chinese Society in Thailand* (Ithaca, N.Y., 1957) and *Leadership and Power in the Chinese Community of Thailand* (Ithaca, N.Y., 1958).

theology, law, linguistics, economics, sociology, etc., but also of *vol-kenkunde* or ethnology.[30]

When we now consider this problem in the field of Indonesian historiography, it immediately becomes clear that anthropology can be most useful to Indonesian historiography by sketching in the social background of historical events. Of the numerous issues connected with this particular problem, only a few can be mentioned here as examples: (1) the question of the socio-politico-economic forms of the Indonesian states between the eighth and the nineteenth century; (2) the question of the societal system of folk life in the various villages scattered over the entire Indonesian Archipelago; (3) the question of the forms and processes of the socio-politico-economic relationship between court circles and rural societies in all Indonesian states during the whole of Indonesian history; (4) the question of the principles and foundations of ancient Indonesian societies in general.

(1) *The socio-politico-economic forms of Indonesian states.* This question has received attention from a few scholars such as Schrieke and, subsequently, van Leur and W. F. Wertheim.

Schrieke dealt with such questions as the premises on which the confirmation of a royal dynasty was rationalized in the minds of the Javanese in ancient times; the nature of the cleavages which split the ancient kingdoms of Java into fragments which were shaped by the geographical features of the island; the slow communications between the various parts of these kingdoms because of bad road conditions and the stratified bureaucratic system of the ancient Javanese kingdoms; and the position and functions of various officials in these kingdoms, such as *shahbandar*,[31] *bupati*,[32] etc.

Van Leur developed considerable insight into the differences in the features and types of socio-politico-economic organizations existing between the various ancient states in Indonesia, such as those that existed between the Hindu-Javanese kingdoms and Shrīwijaya, which had often been neglected in the historical studies of philologists.[33]

Wertheim, who has approached the study of the processes of accul-

[30] Huizinga, *Wetenschap*, p. 10.

[31] All analyses of the aforementioned problems are contained in Schrieke, *Ruler and Realm*, pp. 1–267.

[32] The analysis of the position of the *bupati* (regent) in the governmental system of the ancient kingdoms of Java until the colonial period is to be found in B. Schrieke, "The Native Rulers," *Indonesian Sociological Studies*, pt. I, *Selected Writings* (The Hague and Bandung, 1955), pp. 167–221.

[33] Van Leur, *Trade and Society*, pp. 109–110.

turation in Indonesian society through an intensive investigation of the history of the developmental processes in Indonesian society, has also provided us with a rich variety of material concerning the socio-politico-economic forms of organization in the ancient Indonesian states.[34]

Although Schrieke and van Leur did not particularly employ anthropological techniques in these studies,[35] their understanding of the social background of Indonesian history was certainly a result of, among other things, their knowledge of anthropological data and methods.[36] They were also convinced of the significant role that anthropology could play in studies of exactly such a nature.[37] And even though Wertheim did not specifically recognize the importance of anthropology in providing a social background for Indonesian history,[38] in essence he did make use of data and methods which are normally considered anthropological.[39] It is certainly true that anthropological data and methods provide comparative material which is useful in

[34] W. F. Wertheim, *Indonesian Society in Transition: A Study of Social Change* (The Hague, 1956; a second, revised edition was published in Bandung in 1959).

[35] B. Schrieke, among others, utilized data from historical documents, reports, and accounts of journeys and voyages undertaken by officials of the Dutch or English civil service who had been in contact with the Indonesians of former times. These materials are gathered, for instance, in state archives, in various collected works concerning the development of the colonial government in Indonesia, or have been published as individual books.

[36] Schrieke himself, originally a philologist specializing in Islamic manuscripts, had also intensified his anthropological knowledge and had lectured in this field at the Law School in Jakarta, 1924–1929. Consult his biography in E. J. Lindgren, "Obituary, Bertram Johannes Otto Schrieke, 1890–1945," *Man*, XLVIII (1948), 113–117, and J. Kunst, "In Memoriam Prof. B. J. O. Schrieke," *Cultureel Indië*, VII (1945), 3–6.

[37] E.g., cf. Schrieke, *Ruler and Realm*, pp. 3–5, and van Leur, *Trade and Society*, pp. 54–56.

[38] E.g., Wertheim, *Indonesian Society*, pp. vii–ix.

[39] As a matter of fact, Wertheim's statement is caused not by his ignorance of anthropology *an sich* but by the fact that he terms his study a sociological study. The writer is of the opinion that Wertheim's study can also be called an anthropological study. The old division of labor, by which sociology investigates only modern societies and anthropology only primitive and isolated cultures, can no longer be supported. In the last thirty years, the scope of anthropology has been expanded to include the study of modern societies. The writer agrees that this is not the place to thresh out the problem of the allocation of exclusive domains of subject interest to anthropology and sociology respectively, especially in terms of Indonesian subject matter. It is necessary to state here that anthropology and sociology at present have the same aims in studying the problems of modern Indonesian society and that each of the two sciences now utilizes some methods which were specifically developed by the other.

these studies. The body of knowledge which has been gathered during the last half century by anthropologists concerning the basic principles of the socio-politico-economic structures of the autonomous states in the various parts of Indonesia will provide us with an abstraction of the "general picture" of the basic principles of the socio-politico-economic structures of the Indonesian states in general and will add to the historian's understanding of the basic principles of the socio-politico-economic structures of the Indonesian states in former times.

(2) *The societal system of folk life in various villages scattered over the entire Indonesian Archipelago.* This question can be subdivided into many detailed questions. Ethnographic data, which have been or are being recorded in the various areas of Indonesia, will be very useful in supplying answers to these detailed questions.[40] It can even be said that it is not ethnographic data from Indonesia alone, but also ethnographic data from countries outside Indonesia, which can add to the general understanding of students of the history of Indonesian rural societies. The results of functional community studies can be very important in the context of our problem. A great many studies have already been made in Indonesia which concentrate on the community as a social system. However, as far as we know, no social research has been undertaken as yet which concentrates on the community as an ecological system. In this connection it is necessary to mention that an understanding of the ways in which people who depend on soil cultivation in tropical jungle regions endeavor to adjust their social organization to the diversity of their natural environments can constitute a body of knowledge which may be very useful to students of Indonesian history. Not too long ago, a system of soil cultivation known as swidden agriculture was practiced not only in Sumatra, Borneo, Celebes, Ambon, Banda, etc., but in large parts of Java as well. In this type of soil cultivation the peasants clear gardens in the jungle. After three or four years they are forced to abandon these gardens because the crops have exhausted the soil and to clear new plots in the jungle. This process is continually repeated. The study of little communities whose subsistence is based on swidden agriculture has not been accorded the attention in Indonesia that it has received in other regions of Southeast Asia and the Philippines. Two studies which concentrated on swidden agricultural societal systems in the Philippines were made by C. C.

[40] This has also been admitted by W. F. Wertheim. Cf. *Indonesian Society*, p. 12.

Frake, in a Subanun community on Zamboanga,[41] and by H. C. Conklin among the Hanunoo of Mindoro.[42] These two studies can be regarded as important applications of anthropological research techniques to acquire an understanding of societies based on swidden agriculture. We may imagine the existence of some similarities between the social systems of the Subanun and Hanunoo peoples of today and those of the village (rural) peoples of the Indonesian kingdoms in ancient times.

(3) *The relationship between court society and rural society.* This question, which concerns the forms and processes of the socio-politico-economic relationships that existed between court society and rural society in all Indonesian states during the whole of Indonesian history, also constitutes a problem which can be analyzed with the aid of anthropological data. A knowledge of the pertinent anthropological data may aid the historian in his Indonesian historiographical studies and may help him to evaluate and, if necessary, to discard various speculative theories concerning events in Indonesian history. One such speculative theory explained the transfer of the power center of the Hindu-Javanese kingdom from Central to East Java at the end of the tenth century as being the result of a natural disaster.[43] This particular question was subjected to a penetrating investigation by Schrieke, who took special cognizance of the economic and social factors which may have been responsible for the shift.[44] In this connection Schrieke advanced certain suggestions concerning the relationship between the center of the state and the villages. He paid particular attention to the dual role of the village as a supplier of rice, which was used at the center for both consumption and export, and as a source of the manpower needed in the construction of the hundreds of temples which were built in Central Java in the ninth and tenth centuries. Apparently the extreme demands for temple labor eventually depleted the ranks of village rice producers, and the agricultural base of the kingdom crumbled, with the subsequent transferal of the center of power to East Java. Apart from Schrieke's studies, the study by Wertheim,

[41] C. C. Frake, "Social Organization and Shifting Cultivation among the Sindangan Subanun" (unpublished manuscript, New Haven, 1955).

[42] H. C. Conklin, *Hanunoo Agriculture: A Report on an Integral System of Shifting Cultivation in the Philippines* (Rome, 1957).

[43] Such speculative theories have been suggested by scholars such as D. van Hinloopen Laberton, N. J. Krom, and others.

[44] Schrieke, *Ruler and Realm*, pp. 285–301.

mentioned above, can also be regarded as one which paid much attention to the forms and processes of the socio-politico-economic relationship that existed between court and rural society. In both the aforementioned studies of Schrieke and Wertheim, ethnographic and anthropological data were used for comparative purposes.[45]

(4) *The principles of ancient Indonesian society.* This question can be approached, among other methods, by a functional analysis of the mythological stories which exist in different parts of Indonesia. In the second section we have seen how this method was developed by anthropology. Presently we shall see how this method has been extensively applied in Indonesia. However, since this matter has been discussed in another work,[46] the development of this particular method in Indonesia will be treated only briefly in the next paragraphs, in order to save space.

It was an anthropologist, W. H. Rassers, who first used the functional method in an analysis of Indonesian mythology. The object of his interest was the collection of Javanese myths known as the Panji tales. Applying concepts and theories which had been developed by E. Durkheim, Rassers reached the conclusion that the Panji stories of Java contain a great many elements which apparently serve as guiding principles for many Javanese social activities in both the upper and lower strata of society. He reasoned that in ancient times (the prehistoric era, according to Rassers) [47] these stories were considered to symbolize the basic division of the divine ancestors into two groups, which Rassers called phratries [48] and which had dual functions in relation to each other. In many situations elements of close cooperation between the two groups could be discerned, while in other situations competition and strife, regulated by customary rules, existed between them. Integrated with the phratry system were other elements, such as totemism and initiation ceremonies, and a primitive classification system according to which many nonhuman things were classed as belonging to one or the other of the two phratries. These principles of social structure exerted, according to Rassers, such a deep influence

---

[45] Wertheim, in discussing the system of relationships that existed between master and servant in Java in ancient times, for example, compares it with the system of relationships existing between master and servant among the Macassarese, as described in H. Th. Chabot's ethnographic study (Wertheim, *Indonesian Society*, p. 231).

[46] Cf. Koentjaraningrat, *Beberapa Metode*, pp. 368–427.

[47] Cf. W. H. Rassers, *De Pandji-Roman* (Leyden and Antwerp, 1922), p. 329.

[48] In anthropology the two primary social groups into which such a society is divided are termed moieties.

on the Javanese mind in former times that most of the old literature embodied dualistic elements. The dualistic principle of ancient Javanese society was embodied not only in the structure and subject matter of various myths and other literary products but also in other Javanese elements such as the *wayang* (shadow play), the principles upon which both royal palaces and common dwellings were constructed, the symbolic meaning of the kris (Javanese dagger), of batik designs, of sculpture, and so on.[49]

Rassers' method of analyzing Javanese mythology as a means for acquiring an understanding of a number of principles which underlay ancient Javanese society has received much criticism from scholars of various disciplines. On the other hand, his method has been applied by a group of anthropologists, viz., J. P. B. de Josselin de Jong and some of his students. Josselin de Jong even extended Rassers' method by adding some methodological elements which he derived from B. Malinowski's functional approach to the analysis of mythology. Some of Josselin de Jong's students have applied his method in various regions in Indonesia. These include J. P. Duyvendak in West Ceram, H. J. Friedericy in Macassar and the Buginese region, F. A. E. van Wouden in the eastern Lesser Sunda Islands and Buol (North Celebes), H. Schärer in South Borneo, G. J. Held in the Geelvink Bay region in West Irian (western New Guinea), Koes Sardjono in Java, etc. Although we cannot accept the conclusions of these scholars without qualification, in general their contributions should be taken into consideration by scholars who deal with Indonesian history since, in their general outlines, these interpretations provide some understanding of the principles underlying the ancient Indonesian *beschavingsvormen* or forms of culture.[50]

THE PROBLEM OF RECONSTRUCTING LOCAL HISTORIES IN INDONESIA

That present-day Indonesian history is overly Java-centric in character is generally realized now. Certainly most people will agree that a real understanding of the historical development of the Indonesian people can be obtained only through a broad knowledge of the life ways and local histories of all Indonesian ethnic groups. It has been

[49] Cf., for instance, Rassers' article "On the Javanese Kris," in *Pañji, the Culture Hero*, pp. 217–299, and also in *BKI*, XCIX (1940), 501–582.

[50] J. P. B. de Josselin de Jong, *De Maleische Archipel als ethnologisch studieveld* (Leyden, 1935), p. 6.

primarily philologists who, in the course of analyzing manuscripts containing historical records relating to ethnic groups in local regions, have produced data which could be very useful in the compilation of local histories. Thus we are supplied with information concerning the histories of the Achehnese state by C. Snouck Hurgronje, of Bantam by R. A. H. Djajadiningrat, of Banjermasin by E. B. Kielstra, A. A. Cense, and J. C. Noorlander, of the various kingdoms in South Celebes by J. A. Bakkers and G. K. Niemann, and of Kutai by C. A. Mees, and in the same way mention could be made of various other local histories.

In addition to that provided by philologists, much data relating to local histories has been provided by aliens, such as colonial civil service officials and Christian missionaries, who have lived for long periods of time in local areas. It is probable that ethnographic data obtained from the various ethnic groups in Indonesia could prove to be a valuable source of information relating to local histories. If anthropologists pay attention to the historical data that is available in their local areas, anthropology could be of much use to Indonesian historiography.

We might again call attention to the genealogical method which was discussed in the second section above (see p. 304). This technique can prove particularly useful in the collection of data relating to local histories. We have seen how the investigator, while collecting genealogies, may often be able to obtain some information concerning events that took place during the lifetime of kinsmen who appear in the genealogies of his informants. When informants are thus able to describe events which occurred four generations previously, the investigator has obtained information concerning the nature of the society under investigation as it existed a century or more in the past. The accuracy of the statements may be tested by comparing the genealogies and historical remembrances of a number of informants. A community history which comes into being in such a manner can, of course, be supplemented by various other data, such as local written documents and information embodied in local folklore, or by comparing materials from neighboring communities.[51] Anthropologists who have recently been making investigations in Indonesian regions have always obtained much information about such local histories. The writer had the opportunity personally to observe how the anthropologist G. J. Held gathered a great amount of data concerning the history of the king-

[51] How such a community history can be designed and constructed is described in Redfield, *Little Community*, pp. 96–112.

doms of Dompu and Bima in Sumbawa by using the genealogical method in informant interviewing.[52]

INFORMATION CONCERNING THE ORIGINAL MEANING OF HISTORICAL OBJECTS

The function of a historical object whose original use is no longer known may sometimes be explained through study of ethnographic material. Thus a related object or complex of elements found among different ethnic groups may help the historian's understanding of the object in question. This comparative method has already been successfully used by some scholars in their study of Indonesian history.

One such study was made by W. F. Stutterheim in his article "Some Remarks on Pre-Hindu Burial Customs on Java." [53] Among the Hindu remains of the tenth and eleventh centuries in Java were a number of small stone objects mounted on pillars. The shapes of the first objects discovered were reminiscent of Sundanese rice granaries, and the objects, thought to be altars, were duly named after the rice granaries. Subsequently other stone objects on pillars were found that were not shaped like rice granaries and did not have suitable space for holding offerings.

In attempting to disassociate these objects from their supposed use as altars, Stutterheim first compared them with the bamboo altars used for offerings to Dewi Shri in West Java and Bali today. The impermanent material of these altars contrasted sharply with the durability of the stone "altars." Furthermore, Stutterheim observed that throughout contemporary Bali all altars, temples, houses, and other structures associated with daily life were constructed of impermanent materials. Stone was used only for durable construction, especially for funerary monuments. The stone "rice granaries," then, were conceivably connected with the well-established Hindu-Javanese veneration of royal dead. Throughout Central and East Java there are remains of Hindu stone structures, most of them built to commemorate deceased royalty. A stone casket buried within the monument itself contained the bodily remains (ashes or bones) of the deceased kings; on top of this

[52] G. J. Held undertook field work in Sumbawa in 1954 and 1955.

[53] W. F. Stutterheim, "Iets over prae-Hinduistische bijzettingsgebruiken op Java," *MKAWAL*, new ser., II (1939), no. 5, 105–140; available in English as "Some Remarks on Pre-Hindu Burial Customs on Java," *Studies in Indonesian Archaeology* (The Hague, 1956), pp. 65–90.

casket a portrait statue in the incarnation of a deity was erected.[54] In searching for ethnographic data to substantiate the connection between the stone "granaries" and funeral customs, Stutterheim observed that in the present day among various ethnic groups in Indonesia the dead are deeply venerated. Elaborate ceremonies attend the final deposition of bodily remains, at which time the deceased soul is said to be released from its earthly bonds. Stone images are often erected to commemorate the deceased; the bones of the dead are exhumed after preliminary burial or exposure and are then placed in special vessels. Among the Dyaks of Kalimantan, bones are finally placed on top of a post, in an urn or small wooden coffin which is then covered by a lid or a small wooden house. The Toraja of Celebes use stone coffins which are sometimes shaped like houses. Near their graves the Batak of Asahan place posts topped by carved vases or urns. Occasionally for a woman of high birth, a small house is erected on top of the post. Stutterheim, who feels that the origin of this practice was non-Hindu and probably East Asiatic, sees the Batak custom as an absolute parallel to the small stone houses on posts of tenth- and eleventh-century Java. He concludes that the Hindu stone houses were undoubtedly used for the deposition of ashes, a conclusion made possible by his comparative use of ethnographic material.[55]

Another scholar who has applied the comparative method to historical and ethnographic data in Indonesia is C. C. Berg, who has attempted to explain the historical background of court literature written in Javanese royal court circles of the Hindu-Indonesian and Moslem-Indonesian periods.[56] He observed the existence of various unusual elements in this literature, such as words or sentences which did not fit into context, the frequent occurrence of magical rays as a motif, tales about heirlooms (*pusaka*) which were collected into sacred books,

[54] For example, the statue of Wishnu sitting on a Garuda, a statue which originates from Caṇḍi Belahan and which, according to Rouffaer, has been given the facial features of King Erlangga of Kĕḍiri by its sculptors.

[55] In his study, Stutterheim does not give a clear description of the Toraja and Dyak burial caskets which he used for comparison with the "rice granaries"; nor does he indicate the sources of his information regarding them. He also neglects to mention among which of the many Toraja and Dyak groups these vessels were observed. It is only in his discussion of the urns and houses on pillars of the Batak people in Asahan (Tano Jawa) that he cites the source of his information, an article by the American scholar H. H. Bartlett, "The Grave-Post (anisan) of the Batak of Asahan," *Papers of the Michigan Academy of Science, Arts and Letters*, I (1921), 1–58.

[56] C. C. Berg, "Javaansche geschiedschrijving," in F. W. Stapel, ed., *Geschiedenis van Nederlandsch Indië* (Amsterdam, 1938–1940), II, 5–148.

Chart 1. The relation of anthropology and Indonesian historiography

Subdisciplines of anthropology	Specific approaches	Anthropological methods	Problems in Indonesian historiography which can be explained with substantial aid from anthropological methods
Prehistorical archaeology	—	—	
Ethnolinguistics	Structural linguistics	—	—
	Comparative linguistics	Lexicostatistics	Understanding of the diffusion of foreign cultures into Indonesia in prehistorical periods
	Descriptive integration	Kulturkreis method	Understanding of the diffusion of foreign cultures into Indonesia in prehistorical periods
		Analysis of adaptation of cultural elements	Understanding of the processes of adaptation and assimilation of Hindu and Moslem cultural elements into Indonesian culture
Ethnology	Generalizing approach	Functional analysis in community studies	Filling in of the social background of Indonesian historical events
		Functional analysis of mythology	Abstracting of the principles of ancient Indonesian societies
		Genealogical method of interview	Reconstruction of local histories in Indonesia
		Indonesian ethnographic data	Gathering of information concerning the meaning of historical objects
			Filling in of the social background of Indonesian historical events
			Reconstruction of local histories in Indonesia

and the Javanese court author's dual role as a religious functionary and poet. Berg then compares these elements with ethnographic data [57] about magical practices and supernatural beliefs, especially those relating to strange voices and mysterious sayings, curses, and oaths and the connection between these utterances and the increase of a chieftain's magical power. He concludes that court literature had once served a magical function; it was used to safeguard the magical power of the king, in whose body the power of the state and its people was vested. Thus contact with objects possessing magical power (such as the *pusaka*) helped to maintain the king's own power; the reading of sacred books communicated to him the power contained in mysterious words and sentences.

Unfortunately neither of these two scholars has applied comparative ethnographic data systematically. Stutterheim fails to provide exact documentation for his ethnographic sources, while Berg does not give enough clear examples from various Indonesian peoples. However, this method of comparing historical and ethnographic data can provide us with a more extensive understanding of various historical objects whose function and meaning often seem enigmatic.

CONCLUSION

In the preceding discussion, which is summarized in the accompanying Chart 1, the writer has attempted to demonstrate how anthropological methods, in particular those in the "generalizing approach" category, could be applied to Indonesian historiography. An attempt has also been made to demonstrate the ways in which anthropological methods have been used by scholars in the study of Indonesian history. In the short space of this article it has been impossible to enumerate, one by one, all the scholars who have made use of these methods. Only the most important have been mentioned as examples.

It is beyond doubt that Indonesian historiography and Indonesian anthropology have been frequently in the past, and will continue in the future to be, closely connected with each other, for it is anthropology that provides the social background to historical events. In the absence of knowledge concerning such social background, a considerable part of Indonesian history, as it is known from such sources as inscriptions, old manuscripts, and archival materials, would be reduced

[57] For his ethnographic data, Berg probably relied more on knowledge accumulated over the years, which had been synthesized in his mind, than on actual ethnographic studies.

to dynastic lists and the recounting of political events. Such a situation would not advance us toward the goal of the study of Indonesian history, which is an understanding of Indonesian culture and society. The existence of a "filled in" history of Indonesia would help to dispel many misconceptions that Indonesians might have about themselves and would prevent them from adopting such views as those expressed in the following quotation:

The mild, natural environment . . . the lack of winter and the need to work hard during the summer in order to be able to make it through the cold months have affected the economic sense of the people [read: Indonesians] unfavorably and influenced their personality deeply. . . . has brought about the lack of individualism in the past and in the present, and this is the key to the understanding of Indonesian society and history.[58]

It is not such factors as the mild natural environment and the lack of individualism which constitute the keys to the understanding of Indonesian social problems. Rather, it is through an understanding of the social processes which have activated Indonesian society from the bottom to the top during the course of its history, of the developmental processes generated by the assimilation into Indonesian society of elements borrowed from the various alien cultures with which it has come into contact over the centuries, and of the developmental processes peculiar to each of the local societies in Indonesia that the secrets of Indonesia's social problems can be unlocked.

[58] This view has been expressed by G. Gonggrijp, *Schets ener economische geschiedenis van Nederlands-Indië* (Haarlem, 1949). Author's translation.

XVII

The Significance of the Study of Culture and Religion for Indonesian Historiography

By P. J. ZOETMULDER

Professor of Old Javanese, Gadjah Mada
University, Jogjakarta

LIVING in nature and being himself part of nature, man, from his birth until his death, is constantly seeking to express his life form. Together with his fellow men he forms part of a larger unit of human society, in a reciprocal process of give and take, and he constructs, within the limits of a particular part of the globe and within a particular time span in world history, the way of life which characterizes that society. This way of life we call culture.

With the passing of time, cultures withdraw into the past away from the knowledge of living man, disappearing first into the dusk and finally into the darkness where human memory has no access. The science of history attempts to reclaim those cultures from that darkness and place them under the spotlight of the present, resembling as closely as possible their former appearance.

Past events had their places in those past cultures. Despite their uniqueness and despite the fact that they happened once, never to be repeated again in exactly the same way, those events were partially determined by that specific way of life of which they formed part and from which they themselves derived many of their characteristics. Past events cannot be viewed in the present in their former realities unless we know the totality of which they were once part.

Cultures are therefore the objects of the science of history both as manifestations of human life in the past and because of their influence on past events.

It is clear, however, to all who have made a study of cultures that such a study is impossible without a knowledge of the history of religions. Cultural history and religious history are two fields of research which are not distinctly separate from one another. It is impossible to comprehend a culture without knowing the forces which permeated and gave life and form to that culture. Only in secular cultures without intrinsic ties to religious concepts or convictions would such be possible. But do such cultures exist? Those who study the history of Western countries of the last centuries and think they have found a completely secularized culture should keep their eyes open for religious elements which either are visibly present in that culture or can be brought to the surface with a little digging. At any rate, there are no doubts about this in the case of all other known cultures—those still existing as well as those which have been laboriously reclaimed from the past. To them applies what Christopher Dawson said in his Gifford Lectures in 1947:

Religion is the key of history. We cannot understand the inner form of a society unless we understand religion. We cannot understand its cultural achievements unless we understand the religious beliefs that lie behind them. In all ages the first creative works of a culture are due to a religious inspiration and dedicated to a religious end.[1]

Indonesian historiography deals with a field of research where culture has been formed to a high extent by religion. The resulting problems are manifold. We shall attempt to bring forward some of them. And since a choice has to be made, we shall limit ourselves to one period of ancient Javanese history.

Professor C. C. Berg has occupied himself with that particular terrain of research for the past twenty years. An impressive list of publications has been the result of his studies.[2]

---

[1] Christopher Dawson, *Religion and Culture* (London, 1948), p. 50.

[2] From about thirty titles by C. C. Berg we will mention here only those which have an immediate bearing on the discussion that follows: "Javaansche geschiedschrijving" in F. W. Stapel, ed., *Geschiedenis van Nederlandsch Indië*, Vol. II (Amsterdam, 1938); "Kṛtanagara, de miskende empirebuilder," *Orientatie*, no. 34 (July, 1950); "De evolutie der Javaanse geschiedschrijving," *MKAWAL*, new ser., vol. XIV, no. 2 (Amsterdam, 1951); "De geschiedenis van pril Majapahit," I and II, *Indonesië*, vols. IV (1950–1951) and V (1951–1952); "De Saḍeng-oorlog en de mythe van Groot-Majapahit, *Indonesië*, vol. V (1951–1952) (these three *Indonesië*

Berg starts from the contention that the old viewpoint of Indonesian historiography, so eminently represented by Krom, should be abandoned. This does not mean, however, that those predecessors were not convinced of the necessity of familiarizing themselves with past cultures in order to understand the history of those times. Such is almost axiomatic to all who claim the name of historian. But their critics contend that their familiarity with historiographical methods which had been proved valid in Europe made them undertake their studies of Indonesia with preconceived views—views which are hardly applicable to this terrain and which make it impossible to gain the proper insight.

Obviously such criticisms have a different character when directed to scholars who have undertaken the study of Indonesian history of the period before the arrival of Europeans here and when directed to those who have studied Indonesia's history of the last four or five centuries. In the latter case, the criticism means that they have placed the emphasis on the wrong aspects. To them, Indonesia's history is first and foremost the history of Europeans in Indonesia, and of their contacts with the Indonesian people, viewed from a European viewpoint and based mainly on European sources. That this criticism is just does not require further elaboration.

For the historiography of the preceding centuries matters are different. The historians viewed the sources through European eyes, employing European criteria although the sources were largely of Indonesian origin. The result was that the emerging picture became distorted, because the sources were made to convey meanings that were never intended. A number of them were disregarded because their language was considered senseless from a historical viewpoint. The historians did not realize that, in choosing a particular position and calling it *the* historical point of view, they had made themselves unable to catch the sense that was there.

What Berg opposed was what he called "anatypical historiography, historiography going against the pattern of the culture under study." What he promoted and tried to implement was "syntypical study of

---

articles will be cited in the text as I, II, and III); *Herkomst, vorm en functie der Middeljavaanse rijksdelingstheorie, Verhandelingen der Koninklijke Nederlandse Akademie van Wetenschappen, Afd. Letterkunde,* new ser., vol. LIX, no. 1 (Amsterdam, 1953) (subsequently cited as *HVF*); "Gedachtenwisseling over Javaanse geschiedschrijving," *Indonesië,* vol. IX (1956); "Kṛtanagara's 'Maleise Affaire,'" *Indonesië,* vol. IX (1956); "Javanische geschichtsschreibung," *Saeculum,* vols. VII (1956) and VIII (1957). Translations in this chapter are mine.

the history of a people, in which its own historiography is viewed as one of the elements of its cultural pattern" (III 416 s).

We thought it necessary to expound all this by way of introductory orientation. What we will consider now is this:

What are the problems and difficulties Indonesian historiography finds when, confronted with Java's antiquity, it is convinced that knowledge of culture and religion should provide the key?

The task is clear, and it is the task of historiography in general: attempt to penetrate into the heart of a culture in order to understand its outward manifestations. This involves the task, correctly considered in a preliminary article by Berg, of reading the sources the way they were meant to be read and therefore viewing them as specific cultural manifestations and as component parts of that culture. From realizing this task to realizing the difficulties connected with it, however, is but a small step. To mention but one: we should read the sources using our knowledge of the cultural pattern, yet how can we comprehend that pattern if not from the sources? This looks somewhat like a vicious circle, which could make it impossible for us ever to gain a complete knowledge of the past. But it may be possible to make progress by way of trial and error, by trying whether this particular road will lead us to more light, and returning to start all over again if it has come to a dead end. We can thus attempt to change the vicious circle into a spiral.

Our starting point, then, should be a certain amount of knowledge of the culture in question, obtained through reading the sources. Armed with that knowledge, we go back again to the sources, using them now more than before as specific manifestations of that culture and as such having their own way of conveying information to us. Thus we may find new and unsuspected data which will help to improve and perfect our conception of the culture under investigation.

But it is obvious that there is one condition that has to be fulfilled first: we must be able to read the sources. To state it simply, we must understand what is said. We must know the vocabulary, we must know what a specific structure or idiom wishes to convey. In short, we must know Old Javanese. Those who have studied ancient Javanese works must sadly admit that our knowledge of that language is still highly insufficient. Yet a certain degree of mastery of the language used in those sources should be the foundation for a satisfactory study of culture and religion.

Should we therefore suspend our research until that basic condition is fulfilled? This would be too radical a decision and would exaggerate the pessimism which has been caused by our insufficient knowledge of the language. Furthermore, there is also an element of reciprocity in this. What we know about the culture—with reasonable certainty— will be helpful to us in interpreting the language. But we must be continually aware that the question mark will have to be used frequently in our studies. We should be satisfied if in the course of our researches a number of those question marks can be erased. There is no doubt, alas, that plenty of them will remain.

There is yet another field which the historian of Javanese culture cannot leave unexplored. Indonesian culture is not an isolated phenomenon. This culture is part of a larger whole. It has its ties with, and is continually influenced by, the cultures of South and Southeast and East Asia, particularly for the period which is the object of our study. The progress made in the studies of those cultures outside Indonesia offers opportunity to increase our knowledge of Indonesian culture. Obtaining a more than superficial knowledge of them forms part of the task of the Indonesian historian. The difficulty confronting us in this aspect is: where does what is common to them end, and where does the specific start? There is a danger that continually presents itself: elements found elsewhere seem to fit nicely into the Indonesian pattern, and are therefore supposed to be present here too, though real proof is lacking. What is needed once again is: a copious stock of question marks and the suppression of one's desire to jump to rash conclusions which may later prove to be ill-founded.

This may sound all very general and therefore also very vague. We cannot do better than to try to clarify matters by means of some concrete examples.

In a series of three articles Berg has subjected one century of ancient Javanese history to a profound investigation.[3] The period under study is that which extends from the middle of the thirteenth to the middle of the fourteenth century, the period of the rule of the Singasari kings Jayawishnuwardhana and Kĕrtanagara and the kings of Majapahit Kĕrtarājasa (Wijaya), Jayanagara, and Rājasanagara (Hayam Wuruk).

Unlike the preceding centuries for whose knowledge we have to depend almost exclusively on inscriptions, the events in this period have been recounted in the *Pararaton,* a number of *kidungs* (called more or less appropriately "historical novels" by Berg) and the *Babad Tanah Jawi.* No shortage of sources, one should say. But for the research

[3] See the preceding note, the articles in *Indonesië,* vols. IV and V.

worker it means also no shortage of problems, given the different and even contradictory versions of the same events in those works. The *Nāgarakĕrtāgama* gives an entirely different view of Kĕrtanagara if compared to the *Pararaton,* and Kern concluded "that either the poet (Prapanca) or the chronicle (*Pararaton*) is not telling the truth." [4] But increased knowledge of culture and religion brought clarification to this point. The article of J. Moens, published in 1924 [5]—it has become a classic on this matter—indicated that in Java and Sumatra in this era we are dealing with a form of tantrism, a Bhairawa cult, which "with reasonable certainty can be assigned a place among the numerous sects of Kālacakratantra Buddhism." The descriptions of the death of Kĕrtanagara, so different in the *Pararaton* and in the *Nāgarakĕrtāgama,* turn out to be two versions of the same event, i.e., the fact that Kĕrtanagara died during the performance of some tantric ceremonies he participated in, but are treated from different viewpoints.

In this case, knowledge of particular religious forms found outside Indonesia, combined with Indonesian archaeological data, provided the key that made the written sources, inscriptions as well as literary works, more accessible. In turn, these shed more light on the specific cultural-religious form of society at that time.

Berg has continued this approach. Combining data obtained from outside Indonesia with those from Indonesian sources, he placed Indonesian politics of these days within the larger framework of Southeast Asia, at that time threatened from the north by an invasion of the Mongol emperor, Kubilai Khan—himself an ardent follower of tantrism. Berg arrived at the conclusion that in 1275 Kĕrtanagara "promulgated a far-reaching imperialistic program, probably by the way of receiving a consecration as a Bhairawa" (I 483). This plan intended the mobilization of the forces in Southeast Asia, uniting them into an alliance under the leadership of Kĕrtanagara himself, in particular by means of connubial relations with Champa and Malayu. However, this should not be viewed through eyes which are accustomed to the history of European alliances, undertaken mainly because of exclusively political considerations. In Europe the export of princesses was an approved method of establishing political ties through marriage. In Kĕrtanagara's case it was in the first place an export of *ṣakti,* magical power, taking the form of an exchange of *yoginīs,* the female partners

[4] H. Kern, *Verspreide Geschriften,* VIII (The Hague, 1918), 21.

[5] J. L. Moens, "Het Buddhisme op Java en Sumatra in zijn laatste bloeiperiode," *TBG,* vol. LXIV (1924).

in the circle rites of the Bhairawa cult and as such bearers of *ṣakti* or magical power. In the consecration ceremony of 1275, Kĕrtanagara had obtained the divine status of Bhairawa and through this demoniacal incarnation had become the embodiment of demonic powers enabling him to vanquish hostile forces—of which there were so many in that *kali* era—and to carry out his program against those forces centered outside Indonesia.

In ensuing Bhairawa rituals, which included sexual union with the *yoginīs,* the *ṣakti* was given additional strength, and the *yoginīs* could therefore preeminently be considered to be the bearers of that magical power. It is thus quite probable that such *yoginīs* came first into consideration when the exchange of princesses for the purpose of strengthening political alliances was contemplated. For the political and sacral aspects were inseparably linked together, as may be clear from what was said above.

After Kĕrtanagara's death came the well-known interlude of Wijaya's adventures: the arrival of the Mongol expedition; the founding of a new kraton on the uncultivated grounds of Trik; Wijaya's clever manipulations exploiting the Mongols against Kĕḍiri, but later turning against them and driving them out. Under the name of Kĕrtarājasa, Wijaya became the new ruler in the new kraton, and the Majapahit Empire was founded.

The sources call Wijaya a son-in-law of Kĕrtanagara. Romantic accounts in some of them mention two daughters of Kĕrtanagara, while they speak in addition of two princesses from Malayu. Two inscriptions (of 1296 and 1305) as well as the *Nāgarakĕrtāgama* give four daughters of Kĕrtanagara as having been Kĕrtarājasa's consorts; and the 1305 inscription states that Kĕrtarājasa is united with them, who embody the essence (*prakĕrti*) of Bangli, Malayu, Madura, and Tanjungpura (i.e., the four *nusāntaras*), "as a god with his goddesses" (Berg translates: "in a divine unio mystica").

Berg gives his reasons for doubting whether it is possible that Kĕrtanagara's one daughter—Wijaya's wife before the fall of Singasari—could have survived the turbulent periods during and after that fall. Berg also doubts the historic authenticity of the romantic story concerning the interlude, too short a span of time to contain so much. All this, combined with the possibility of reconciling the seemingly conflicting data of the *Nāgarakĕrtāgama* and the *Pararaton,* made Berg see the information concerning Kĕrtanagara's four daughters in a different light. Viewing them now from his ideas on the Bhairawa cult, he proposes to assume that they were not natural daughters of Kĕrtan-agara, but "daughters" created in the circle rites of the Bhairawas. The four *nusāntaras* were, so to speak, "spiritual children" begotten through the *yoga* of the Bhairawa cult. By making a number of *yoginīs* into Kĕrtanagara's "daughters," by having them represent these territories, and by uniting himself with them in the circle rites, he reinforced through sacral means his ties with these *nusāntaras*.

Here again we find religion and politics. inseparably united. But in this instance there is a difference in emphasis from what we saw hap-pening under Kĕrtanagara. At that time, in a way, the sacral was made subservient to political necessity. The threat of the Mongol attack was, in the first place, a political threat. The countermeasure, establishing an alliance between the threatened nations, was also a political act. But this act was reaffirmed and strengthened by devices on the sacral level.

Obviously the political threat must have decreased after the failure of the Mongol expedition. Why, then, continue the program which by that time might have been considered obsolete? Because there was fear for the consequences if such things were not done, fear for the conse-quences of a sacral nature. Berg states: "The consecration which was carried out in 1275 must have meant for the Javanese of that period the unleashing of tremendous magical powers, which—if not directed toward the projected target—would constitute an extremely great danger to the entire society" (I 498). There were therefore sacral con-siderations which forced them to continue a certain political course even after the original political demands were urgent no more.

And when, some thirty years later, the rulers of Majapahit wanted to abandon them altogether, we notice that a complex pattern of meas-ures was taken with the intention of neutralizing whatever dangers might result from the change of the political course. And all of them were of a religious character, because they were prescribed, not by political considerations but by sacral ones. We refer in this connection to the plan of Gajah Mada to undertake an expedition against Bali, and all that resulted from it.

Viewed from a political standpoint only, such a plan would seem very easy to realize. With a sufficient superiority of forces—and it should not have been too difficult a task for Majapahit to recruit them—the small neighboring island would be easily conquered without too much trouble. But such a view would not be the Indonesian or Java-nese view of those days. Such a view would have been "anatypical" and probably anachronical too. For this plan, though seemingly so easy from a political point of view, was loaded with consequences, and dangerous consequences at that. It was completely contrary to Kĕrtanagara's program. Now that program may have appeared outdated, as far as its political aims were concerned. But from the sacral viewpoint it was still very much alive. The conception as well as the continuation of Kĕrtanagara's policy was closely linked to the rituals of the Bhairawa cult. If something was to be undertaken which was contrary to it —in this case the conquest of one of the *nusāntaras,* Bali—those rituals would have to be temporarily neutralized. This, Berg contends, was the actual meaning of Gajah Mada's well-known oath refraining from *amukti palapa,* an expression which has intrigued historians from the beginning and which has placed before them a difficult problem. Gajah Mada declared that he would not take part in the circle rites until after the surrender of Bali, and with that proclamation he opened a period in which no rituals were carried out, a period of interdict, as Berg succinctly calls it. In his divine existence Kĕrtanagara was living on as the powerful protector of the program he had initiated, but now he was made to enter a temporary ritualistic death, to be recalled to life after the passage of the interdict through another ritual. The Aksobhya statue, representing Kĕrtanagara's first divine existence, was removed from the temple, Caṇḍi Jawi, thus marking the deviation from Kĕrtanagara's peaceful policies.

Ritual prescribes that the *shrāddha* ceremony, through which the soul of the deceased king is freed from all earthly bonds and given its full divine existence, must be preceded by a preparatory period of twelve years. In that period the temple site is chosen and consecrated, the temple is built, and other preparatory rituals are performed. The interdict period and with it Kĕrtanagara's second death began in 1331. Now if the expedition against Bali, which constituted the deviation from Kĕrtanagara's program, had come to a successful end, would it then have been possible to perform the new *shrāddha* ceremony twelve years after the beginning of the interdict, i.e., in 1343? As far as the prescribed waiting time is concerned, there was apparently no objection to that. How then is it to be explained that, according to available sources, the renewed deliverance ceremony in Candi Singasari did not take place before 1351? There can only be one reason: the time condition had been fulfilled, but not so the preparatory rituals, which in the ordinary course of events would have been performed during that time. For it was an interdict; and they made no exception to the rule that no rituals of the tantric cult could be carried out in that closed period.

Thus after the passage of the twelve years of full interdict there followed another period, which may be conveniently called a semi-interdict. The ban on tantric ceremonies had been lifted; the preparations could go ahead; but Kĕrtanagara had to wait till all the conditions for his reinstallation as divine protector had been fulfilled. So it was not until 1351 that the second *shrāddha* ceremony was performed, and from now on Gajah Mada too could take part in the circle rites. He could *amukti palapa* again.

Guided by Berg's publications, we have gone through a century of old Indonesian history. It was—understandably so—an incomplete picture. We could not even give the balanced outlines of the history of that period. For it was with a specific aim that we treated it and we had to make our choice accordingly. But we hope not to have done too much injustice to what Berg constructed with a wealth of material. Our aim was to give an example of how religion, culture, form of government, and politics can be so closely connected that none of these fields can be fully understood without understanding all the others. Without knowledge of the special forms of religion believed in and practiced by the circles in whose hands lay the government of the empire of Majapahit and who determined its politics, it is impossible to understand the sources and attempt to draw a sketch of that century.

It is not our purpose here to discuss in detail the acceptability of the picture. Nor do we need to mention the modifications introduced in it afterward by Berg himself as a result of his further studies. The account given above is, as it seems to us, sufficient proof of the significance of cultural history and religious history for Indonesian historiography. Without these disciplines it appears to be simply impossible.

While the task of historiography is clear, the difficulties, as we mentioned before, are many and serious. Using the same foregoing example we will attempt to touch on some of them.

We must approach our sources armed with knowledge of the culture and religion of our period and region. A mere general knowledge is not enough. This has been clearly demonstrated from Berg's construction. Moens made us clearly realize what we had perhaps been vaguely aware of, but not acted upon sufficiently: that if we are dealing with Buddhism, Shiwaism, and Wishnuism in Java during that period, our general knowledge of those religions, obtained from more or less classical sources as found outside Java, would not be sufficient. What we are dealing with here is a particular form of tantrism in which those religions manifest themselves, very often blending into each other. This was made apparent from the literary sources and even more so from the sculpture of that period. In his investigations Moens has made ample use of comparison with what he had found in the studies of the tantric cults and doctrines in India. The method may be considered sound and very illuminating, but still there is a danger inherent in it: we might too readily accept those data as equally applicable to Indonesia, even though such has never been conclusively proved, as yet. We must constantly remain aware of the degrees of certainty those data possess. Are they of foreign origin only and does, consequently, their applicability to Indonesia constitute a working hypothesis? Or are they confirmed by Indonesian data as well, and to what extent?

To cite an example: Moens contends that the tantrism in Java was "almost certainly" the same as the tantrism of the Kālacakra sect of Buddhism. This will cause no harm if we keep on realizing that what we mean by using this term is: the Kālacakra cult or a related form of tantrism. To my knowledge, Javanese as well as Sumatran sources are not familiar with the Kālacakra figure. We may, for the sake of convenience, use the term Kālacakra Buddhism—the lengthy circumlocution being too clumsy stylistically. But all conclusions derived from what is characteristic in Kālacakra Buddhism, as it is found elsewhere, will have to remain in the realm of pure hypothesis if applied to Indonesia, until confirmed by Indonesian data.

This applies to a much larger extent when we attempt to determine the actual contents of the Indonesian form of tantrism. In Berg's exposition of the religion of Kĕrtanagara and his successors as well as in his probing of the impact it may have had on their political activities, the circle rites play a dominant role. Now, what do we know about the existence of those rites in Indonesia? Next to nothing. For a direct and positive indication we have to rely on *Nāgarakĕrtāgama* 43,3. There, among the religious activities by which the king (Kĕrtanagara) furthered the well-being of the world, *ganacakra* is mentioned. But we are completely in the dark about its concrete meaning.[6] We have an account of a very recent tantric ceremony in Tibet[7] and read there that on the fourth day of the ceremony an oblation is offered to the terrifying deities, that oblation being called *ganapūjā*. Now this might indicate a direction in which to seek for the answer to the question of the meaning of the *ganacakra* ritual, but it is a very vague indication

---

[6] Cf. *HVF* 151.

[7] H. von Glasenapp, *Buddhistische Mysterien* (Stuttgart, 1940), p. 142.

indeed. Whatever else is said concerning the circle rites in Singasari and Majapahit is part of the "key theory" used to interpret the available material.[8] And it has to go a long way.

"Enlightened by Moens" says Berg, "we know that yoga was practiced in the form of a ritual of which sexual union between the Lord of the Circle and his female partners, the *yoginīs*, formed a part." But do we *know* this? Even "we can assume with probability" would be a strong expression. I do not think that Indonesian sources, as far as we know them now, give any direct indications of the mere existence of *yoginīs*, let alone the details of their participation in the circle rites, the role they played therein, the regulations they were subjected to, the purpose it served. That is not to say that we could *expect* to find information in our sources and, consequently, from the absence of any mention are entitled to draw the conclusion that such rituals did not occur in Indonesian tantrism. Evidence *ex silentio*, even though handled with great care, is no conclusive evidence, particularly as we have to assume the incompleteness of our sources. And the more so is this true where tantric rituals are concerned, whose secrets have always been very closely guarded.

But the fact remains that we simply do not know anything about them, about their rules, their purpose, their powers, and how such powers can be neutralized. I remember from conversations with Moens —shortly before his death—that he, basing himself on literature obtained from outside Indonesia, rejected the possibility that the Lord of the Circle could unite himself with several *yoginīs*. Of course it is possible that it nevertheless did occur in Kālacakra tantrism or that it was characteristic of Javanese tantrism, but we have no evidence. Was it possible to create "daughters of Kĕrtanagara" through ritual ceremonies? Berg states: "Those who remember that people who live in the sphere of magic and religion place identity obtained through ceremonies and rituals above natural relations would have little objection to the fact that among the Javanese living in 1300 somebody was called 'daughter of Kĕrtanagara,' although she was not his daughter in the natural sense" (I 488). I do not know to what extent religion and magic in the Majapahit of those days placed identity through consecration above natural relations. I do not know whether the "Javanese from 1300"—sufficiently initiated into the secrets of the cult—would have been utterly amazed or would have nodded in understanding when told about the "creation of Kĕrtanagara's daughters."

[8] Cf. *HVF* 154.

Logic prescribes extreme caution when taking the step from the "possible" to the "actual" (*a posse ad esse*). Although such a step will not give us certainty, it is a step we must often take if we are compelled to have recourse to working hypotheses. It will be a just step, if it is a cautious one. But the dangers increase and the warnings have to sound the louder, if it is the "possibility" itself which becomes a hypothesis. This applies equally to many other aspects of the case study we chose to illustrate the difficulties one has to cope with in this field of investigation. Did the consecration which is assumed to have taken place in 1275 really unleash magical forces of such a nature and to such an extent that they would become extremely dangerous the moment their original aim vanished? Was it possible to neutralize those forces through the suspension of the circle rites and through having the king —previously exalted into the Bhairawa status and surviving in a divine existence—die another death to be resurrected later? Does this all fit as a "possibility" within the logical framework of the way of thinking prevalent in the culture and religion of those days? Only someone initiated in the rituals of that particular form of tantrism, living in and acting according to that special way of thinking, would be able to furnish the answer. As long as no more data are available to us, it will, I am afraid, be impossible for us to find the answer ourselves.

Now I must state that it would be unfair if we considered the account of the conditions existing in the period as given by Berg to be a mere reconstruction, cleverly conceived but separate from the available material. On the contrary, it grew out of a really comprehensive study of all the available sources, and not of only part of them. It is a theory which aims at doing full justice to them and attempts to combine all the material—often heterogeneous and seemingly contradictory—into an acceptable and comprehensible whole. Its very success in doing that would be its vindication. Berg himself has compared it to a jigsaw puzzle (II 197). If the pieces of the puzzle are brought together in such a way that they fit one another, a picture will emerge. If this picture does not too closely resemble a product of abstract art, it can be accepted with probability that the method employed in putting the pieces together has been correct. However, we should always be aware that we are dealing with a special kind of jigsaw puzzle. The pieces have no definite or permanent forms; they consist of data provided by the available sources and then, to fill in the many open spaces left, of postulates and reasonings that have been given their appropriate form. It is obvious that the probability that the emerging picture is the correct one will be inversely proportionate to the number of pieces falling under this second category. For in one way or another they have been "made to fit." As to the data obtained from the sources, there will always remain a considerable amount of uncertainty too, owing to our lack of knowledge of the language they were written in. Hence many a translation is bound to remain a groping interpretation. To consider the pieces of this category as having a definite and permanent form so that we can employ them without further manipulations, with all the possibilities of error inherent in them, would be self-deception.

In this connection we want to bring forward two examples.

The Bhairawa consecration of Kĕrtanagara in 1275 constitutes a very important event in the history of Singasari and Majapahit, as reconstructed by Berg. If indeed *Nāgarakĕrtāgama* 41,5 has the meaning his interpretation gives it, we would have a positive piece of information of great value. *Kadewamūrtin* would then indicate the deification brought about at a given moment through tantric ceremonies, and subsequent *ngūni* would say that such a ceremony had taken place long before.

Taking another view, Bosch [9] translated *kadewamūrtin* into "status of deified ruler," without making any mention of *ngūni*. It is not our intention to discuss this matter here at length, for it would fall outside the scope of this article. We wish only to indicate how the knowledge of Old Javanese should bring the solution. Is it *possible* that the word *kadewamūrtin* is used in the sense of "to be made a dewamūrti," i.e. as a passive verbal noun, or *should* it mean "the dewamūrti state"? In the latter case this passage of the *Nāgarakĕrtāgama* could not be used as positive indication of a consecration having taken place in 1275. But then also the meaning of *ngūni* in this context should be checked again. Thus we arrive at a number of questions concerning the meaning of Old Javanese words and their idiomatic usage, but the answers, much as we would like to have them now, will be obtained only through further study of the language.[10]

[9] F. D. K. Bosch, "C. C. Berg and Ancient Javanese History," *BKI*, vol. CXII (1956).

[10] In this particular case I am inclined to agree with Bosch. At the, unfortunately, only other place in which I found *kadewamūrtin* (*Sutasoma* 74,6), it means beyond doubt "the being a dewamūrti." The use of *ka-* . . . *-n* in a passive verbal noun is unknown to me. *Ngūni* could belong to the following part, so: "earlier" from Prapanca's viewpoint. That it need not mean "a considerable time earlier" the way Berg has it, but that it could indicate "anytime before," even if that time has only "just" passed, can be proved with many examples. But that is not very important here. It only serves to deflate a small additional argument. However, we are now

A second example is the famous, almost notorious, passage in the *Pararaton* which reports the story of Gajah Mada pledging himself to refrain from *amukti palapa* until the conquest of the *nusāntara* was achieved. In Berg's presentation of the events as given above such a conquest would mean a flagrant violation of Kĕrtanagara's political program and as such would be in direct contradiction to the circle rites which produced the *ṣakti* needed for the implementation of that program. Now, says Berg, "the phrase *amukti palapa* allows an interpretation which would be in accordance with this conclusion. Derived from *lapa* (hunger), *palapa* can be interpreted as 'the practice of mortification.' In the same sense we find the Sanskrit *brata,* and this, in turn, can be used to indicate the circle rites" (II 199).

Whether this interpretation is acceptable is a matter of Old Javanese philology, and only knowledge of this language can furnish the answer. An absolute denial of the validity of this interpretation is probably impossible, particularly if one takes into account the possibility that in the esoteric field of tantrism obscure circumscriptions cannot be excluded. However, other arguments are required which, based on passages where a similar or analogous use of the word is found, should add to the probability of the translation. But such passages have not yet been produced. That the prefix *pa-* can be added to *lapa* in the sense of hunger; and that from "being hungry" we may pass to "practicing mortification" and from there to "performing the circle rites"; that *brata* is used to indicate those rites—this all is too speculative to be accepted without additional evidence.[11]

It seems therefore not safe to conclude from the words *amukti palapa* that with them Gajah Mada promulgated the beginning of an interdict. Whether this phenomenon fits into the then-existing cultural and religious patterns and would be acceptable to the way of thinking of those days remains equally uncertain. We know as yet so very little about it. The sources are rare, and their language has become only partially accessible to us.

---

going too far afield in the realm of Old Javanese philology to be of interest to those who are mainly concerned with Indonesian historiography.

[11] Regarding places where *palapa* should be considered, I have found so far: *Rāmāyana* 25,90 and 25,91; *Bomakāwya* 56,1; *Sumanasāntaka* 19,2, 28,28, and 45,6; *Sutasoma* 4,8; *Sārasamuccaya* 423 and 424; *Kidung Harṣawijaya* 4,85 and 5,148; *Kidung Sunda* 1,31. In all these places, however, it would be possible, and in some cases obligatory, to read the form as *palapan.* None of these places, however, supports the translation, or the connection with *lapa,* "hunger." In this connection see A. Teeuw and E. M. Uhlenbeck, "Over de interpretatie van de Nāgarakṛtāgama," *BKI,* CXIV (1958), 210–237.

But this applies equally to the character of these sources and to the spirit in which they want to be read. The main object of Berg's studies is to shed more light on those aspects. To him this is much more interesting than writing a new history of Indonesia or part of it. His articles could rightly carry the same title as this paper, "The Significance of the Study of Culture and Religion for Indonesian Historiography," but then first in the sense of: for the knowledge of Indonesian historiography of former days, the days of Prapanca and the writer(s) of the *Pararaton*. Only after *this* significance is fully realized and understood can contemporary Indonesian historiography expect to do fruitful work. For it will then have acquired the "syntypical" orientation, the only correct one.

We have stated earlier that unquestionably Indonesian historiography should adopt such a viewpoint. We have also pointed out the difficulties which will be encountered. We will now, by way of conclusion, elaborate on some of them.

Commenting on Krom's "anatypical" approach, Berg states: "The unacceptability of Krom's analysis is already apparent in his first chapter. In that chapter Krom makes two different evaluations of the *Nāgarakĕrtāgama* and the *Babad Tanah Jawi*, rather than departing from the premise that both works are the products of one and the same culture" (III 417). Without going into the question of the correctness of Krom's evaluation of those sources, I wonder whether two different products of the same culture could never be dissimilar in value.

We are, it seems, touching upon a fundamental difficulty. We will hardly ever be able to enter into the culture of the past, to relive it, as it were, to such a degree that it will be possible to put ourselves into their way of thinking and reason from their premises, so that we can decide, in the majority of the cases that present themselves, whether within the pattern of that culture something is obvious, probable, or a sheer absurdity. And that is true not so much because the way of thinking of the present researcher is moving along such different lines that it makes him unable to follow those of the past. To follow particular lines of thinking, different from one's own, those lines must be visible with reasonable clarity, and such clarity is lacking here. Continued study of culture and religion should help us in this matter and should shed more light on the problems. But I am afraid that we will never be more than remote from our aims, and the certainties obtained through this method will therefore be few and far between.

Much has become clearer since Berg started his studies in this field with his contribution titled "Javaansche Geschiedschrijving" in Stapel's *Geschiedenis van Nederlandsch Indië*. We have learned to take into consideration the magical function of a book, and also that an author can make his literary magic serve the cult of the king. However, when did a person write purely for the pleasure of the story or for the satisfaction of having wrought a literary creation, and when did he write to fulfill magical purposes and to what rules was that magic bound—if one can speak of rules in a field so far removed from reason? These are all questions which will remain unanswered for a long time, if not forever.

To cite but one example of the many that could be brought forward: we may be convinced that Sanskrit was used to add to the magical powers of a book. Can we therefore say that whenever Sanskrit was used it was for the purpose of augmenting that magical power? Or can we assume that the more Sanskrit is used, the greater will be, *ceteris paribus*, the magical effect of the book in question? Does the presence of Sanskrit quotations in certain passages of the *parwa's*, for instance, indicate the desire of the author to imbue them with special magical powers? I think that such conclusions are not justified because there are no rules here which are generally applicable and also because it is incorrect to assume that all actions are the conscious and logical results of the underlying premises.

Even the use of the term "patterns of culture" poses certain dangers. We might be unconsciously prompted to assume that some conspicuous aspects of a culture that strike us particularly as characterizing its pattern must be considered as dominant and as always determining the actions of the people living in that culture. It is known that cultural anthropology is only rarely able to avoid this pitfall entirely. Those who are captivated by systems of classifications will see classifications everywhere; those who are captivated by magic will see man everywhere as the *homo magicus*. The dangers are twice as great in the case of extinct cultures, because there in most cases the possibility of verification will be lacking.

To avoid such dangers, we will be compelled to use many more question marks than we actually wish to. The Indonesian historiographer must admit many uncertainties and doubts, and the readability of his works will suffer by it. He will not, however, sacrifice his scientific integrity and the conscientious fulfillment of his task to readability.

The purpose of this paper is to show that the study of both culture and religion is part of his task and also that the difficulties encountered along the course of carrying it out are many. The assistance of those who occupy themselves with the study of Old Javanese will be indispensable for this particular part of Indonesian history and will be a *conditio sine qua non* for the success of his work.

XVIII

The Sociological Approach

By W. F. WERTHEIM

Professor of The Modern History and Sociology of Southeast Asia,
Municipal University of Amsterdam

UNTIL 1930 there was a good deal of confusion about the character of what was called "Hindu colonization" in Java. Besides the "Greater India" concept of some Indian historians, who simply attributed the Hindu influence in large parts of Southeast Asia to political domination from India—this, however, found no corroborating evidence in historical sources—there was a view more generally accepted among Dutch historians that Hindu influences in Indonesia could be fully accounted for by the presence of large colonies of Indian traders, some of whom had assumed power as Hindu kings.

In 1934, however, a young Dutch sociologist, J. C. van Leur, demonstrated that the latter view was equally inadequate.[1] If one kept in mind the kind of society the Hindu-Javanese in the early centuries of the Christian era were living in, one arrived at the conclusion that the Hindu-Javanese civilization could never have been brought there by plain Indian traders. In view of the kind of people the traveling traders from India were—peddlers, crowded in large numbers on the ships and in the harbors—it seemed to van Leur improbable that they had been the transmitters of Brahman hierocratic civilization which was the essence of Hindu influence on Java. The social distance between the trader class and the rulers was, in van Leur's view, much too wide to make such a hypothesis probable. The places where the Hindu culture was centered also contradict the traditional view: the Hindu influence did not make itself felt primarily along the coasts of Java, where the

---

[1] J. C. van Leur, *Indonesian Trade and Society: Essays in Asian Social and Economic History* (Selected Studies on Indonesia by Dutch Scholars, vol. I; The Hague and Bandung, 1955).

traders were to be found in large numbers, but in the courtly centers in the interior. It is there that one has to look for the remains of the grandiose Hindu temples.

According to van Leur the transmitters of Hindu civilization were a small group of influential Brahmins, who were summoned by Indonesian princes to their courts for their powers of consecration and perhaps also their chancellory skills. Their work was, as in India, above all the legitimation of the ruling dynasty, the provision of mythological sanction to genealogy and tradition. Thus, sociological analysis according to the "idealtypic" method propagated by Max Weber helped van Leur to arrive at a reinterpretation of the published sources on Hindu-Javanese history. It was a great victory for the sociological approach as such that his findings were essentially corroborated by research independently undertaken by Professor Bosch with a different method, that of archaeology and the history of art.[2] Van Leur's success in challenging the view generally held among Dutch historians is an outstanding example of the significance of the sociological approach to Indonesian historiography.

However, van Leur was not the first to apply a sociological analysis to Indonesian history in line with Max Weber's methodology. Already in 1919, the Dutch socialist D. M. G. Koch had attempted to analyze the Indonesian nationalist movement in terms of the sociology of religion, as elaborated by Max Weber in *The Protestant Ethic and the Spirit of Capitalism*.[3] Koch concluded that a parallel could be drawn between the Sarekat Islam movement and Protestantism as it had developed in Western Europe in the fifteenth and sixteenth centuries. In both instances, according to Koch, an incipient bourgeoisie attempted to build up a new ideology, more in harmony with the requirements of their way of life. Whereas in the years of the rise of Protestantism in Holland the cloth manufacturers had led the way in developing a new attitude toward religious values, in Java the Sarekat Islam movement had been inaugurated by batik industrialists and traders. In both instances, a new attitude toward labor,[4] interpreted in religious terms, was one of the most important signs of a new *Wirtschaftsgeist*, which became transparent in the religious outlook of the social groups concerned.

[2] F. D. K. Bosch, *Het vraagstuk van de Hindoe-kolonisatie van de Archipel* (inaugural lecture, University of Leyden; Leyden, 1946).

[3] Translation by Talcott Parsons (New York, 1930).

[4] Cf., for the different attitude toward labor in general, J. Romein, "Het arbeidsbegrip in Oost en West," in *In de ban van Prambanan* (Amsterdam, 1954).

This sociological interpretation of the Indonesian nationalist movement was included in an official report which was published anonymously.[5] This first attempt to apply a sociological methodology to Indonesian society met with much criticism on the part of the Dutch-language press, and the colonial government was accused of having published a "Marxist" paper.[6] It was not to remain the only occasion when critics would appear to overlook the difference between quasi-Marxist stereotyped evolutionism and Weberian idealtypic analysis giving full scope to social environment and the constellation of time factors.[7]

The two above examples of sociological analysis illustrate the different function of this methodology according to the period of Indonesian history to which it is applied. For more recent times the sociological approach merely adds a new frame of reference and contributes to a deeper insight, without disclosing new unknown facts. But for the earlier periods, where source materials are scarce and not seldom obscure, ambiguous, or unreliable, the sociological approach may open up completely new vistas, as was the case with van Leur's "new look" at Hindu-Javanese history.

The only sociologist who has occupied himself with early Indonesian history as intensively as with more recent periods is the late professor B. Schrieke.[8] In his studies dealing with contemporary history,[9] he provides the reader with many illuminating insights into the dynamic forces operating in Indonesian society, without pretending, however, to shed new light upon the historical chain of events. Insofar as he brings to light facts hitherto unknown, he is applying the usual historical method. The sociological approach is, nonetheless, useful in providing a new enlightening interpretation of facts of common knowledge or in focusing attention on historical occurrences previously neglected or overlooked. For example, Schrieke's analysis of those

[5] *Mededeelingen omtrent onderwerpen van algemeen belang* (Weltevreden, 1920); see also D. M. G. Koch, *Verantwoording: Een halve eeuw in Indonesië* (The Hague and Bandung, 1956), pp. 108 ff.

[6] Koch, *Verantwoording*, pp. 112 ff.

[7] Clifford Geertz, in his review of W. F. Wertheim, *Indonesian Society in Transition*, in *Indonesië*, X (1957), 85, 87.

[8] See vols. II and III of the Selected Studies on Indonesia by Dutch Scholars: B. Schrieke, *Indonesian Sociological Studies*, pt. I, *Selected Writings* (The Hague and Bandung, 1955), and *Indonesian Sociological Studies*, pt. II, *Ruler and Realm in Early Java* (The Hague and Bandung, 1957).

[9] The most important one is "The Causes and Effects of Communism on the West Coast of Sumatra," in *Selected Writings*, pp. 83–167.

social groups in Minangkabau either sympathetic or inimical to the Communist movement, in a period of transition from traditionalism to individualism, may help the reader to have a better understanding of the motive forces behind the revolutionary actions of January, 1927.

The fruitfulness of Schrieke's approach to earlier periods of Indonesian history, however, still exceeds the significance of the contribution he made in his treatment of recent developments. A good instance is provided by his discussion of the political structure of the seventeenth-century kingdom of Mataram.[10]

From Schrieke's description of that kingdom, the picture arises of a true "patrimonial bureaucratic state," in the Weberian sense.[11] As is the case in nearly every pre-Napoleonic state, "the component parts of the kingdom display a loose coherence." [12] Mangkurat I (1646–1677) made an energetic attempt to put the idea of the "state" into practice. Whereas his predecessor, Sultan Agung (1613–1646), had forced the subjected local princes to remain at the court and attempted to tie them through marriage alliances in order to keep them under control, thus transforming the independent landed aristocracy into a court nobility, Mangkurat I applied other means, listed by Weber, to check centrifugal tendencies. After having summoned the subjected aristocracy to court, he deliberately destroyed the whole group "and placed the administration of the provinces in the hands of *ministeriales,* whom he constantly replaced in order to nip in the bud any aspirations to independence." [13]

Mangkurat attempted to bring about certain innovations of the state structure. He made an effort to introduce taxation in money in order to transfer its revenue from the provinces to the central government and made foreign trade a state monopoly. But the attempt to form a state out of a society based on a goods economy and with an underdevel-

---

[10] Schrieke, *Ruler and Realm,* in particular pp. 217 ff. See also "The Native Rulers," in *Selected Writings,* pp. 167–223.

[11] See Max Weber, *Wirtschaft und Gesellschaft* (2d ed.; Tubingen, 1925), III, 679–752. It is a pity that these highly important sections from Weber's work have never been translated into English.

[12] Schrieke, "The Native Rulers," p. 184. This centrifugal tendency in premodern bureaucratic structures is a strong argument against K. A. Wittfogel's thesis that the "Asian bureaucracies" presented a picture of centralism and "total power" (see his *Oriental Despotism: A Comparative Study of Total Power* [New Haven, 1957]). On the contrary, those states showed a high degree of decentralization, if only because the central ruler had to leave both the profit and the burden of administration largely to provincial governors, local princes, or semi-independent satraps.

[13] "The Native Rulers," p. 184.

oped system of communications inevitably failed, and ended in a debacle.[14] But it is curious to note that Mangkurat I, who was painted in traditional history writing in the blackest of colors, appears from Schrieke's analysis as an innovator who was, in some respects, even ahead of the contemporary Company's rule which restored the *ministeriales* to a position of an old-style landed aristocracy.

It is more important still that in Schrieke's view conditions in the Moslem kingdom of Mataram were not essentially different from those prevalent in earlier centuries. From the political structure as he found it in the seventeenth century Schrieke tried to read back into the pages of history dealing with earlier "patrimonial bureaucratic states" in Java, on which we are not so well informed, and his analysis helps to illuminate what must have taken place in those earlier times. It is a great advantage of the sociological, "idealtypic" approach that it helps to reconstruct conditions prevailing in periods on which source materials are scarce and obscure.

Schrieke concludes (and his conclusion would appear to be essentially valid for any "patrimonial bureaucratic state," or any "hydraulic society" for that matter!) that

whatever system was applied—whether the landed nobility were retained as vassals, members of the royal family were established as local administrators, or the territory was put in charge of officials,—the ties which held the various parts of the realm together were always comparatively loose. What we have found taking place during the reign of Sultan Agung can be expected just as well during the reign of an Ayam-Wuruk, a Ěrtanagara, a Jayabhaya, an Erlangga, or a Sinḍok.[15]

It seems to me that the typology of the early Indonesian bureaucratic structures as elaborated by Schrieke may provide a clue to solving the dissensions among historians about the extent of Majapahit's rule.

While according to traditional history writing the empire of Majapahit extended its rule, at the pinnacle of its glory, over a large part of the archipelago, this view has been recently challenged by Professor Berg, who doubts whether Majapahit ever achieved supremacy over other islands than Java, Madura, and Bali.[16]

A sociological approach to this problem may reduce the dispute to a matter largely of terminology. If one keeps in mind the type of political power held by the rulers of those early kingdoms, it becomes

---

[14] *Ibid.*, pp. 184–185.   [15] Schrieke, *Ruler and Realm*, p. 221.

[16] C. C. Berg, "De Saḍeng-oorlog en de mythe van Groot Majapahit," in *Indonesië*, V (1951–1952), 385 ff.

evident that any idea of an empire comparable with our modern national states would appear an anachronism. The only territory where the ruling prince held real power comprised the crown lands (*nagaragung*) surrounding his kraton. In more distant regions, the actual ruler was a provincial governor, whether he was a relative of the prince, a member of the native landed aristocracy, or a *ministerialis* appointed by the prince. It was the governor with his underlings who were entitled to levy taxes and services from the subjected rural population.

In general, his main obligation toward the sovereign was to pay homage and tribute at the yearly ceremony in the court capital, described with such a wealth of color in the *Nāgarakĕrtāgama*. In addition, he had to provide labor and military assistance when summoned by the ruling prince. The periodical inspection tours through the country by the sovereign and his retinue, also related in the *Nāgarakĕrtāgama*, were mainly intended to impress his power upon the governors and the local population and to ensure that the former would not skip their obligations toward the ruler. The spies sent out from the kraton in all directions served to report to the king any indications that the governors might be behaving too independently. If necessary, a military expedition was sent out to remind the vassal of his obligations.

Under such conditions the distinction between "internal" and "international" relations was a fluid one. There was a sliding scale of relationships between rulers, ranging from complete subordination to full equality. The rulers, who considered themselves the pivots of the world (*Paku Buwana*), were prone to consider a trade mission sent by a prince "abroad" a tribute duly paid to their supreme power. Nevertheless, in order not to lose face, they would entertain the mission in a liberal manner and offer precious gifts in return. But for the historian it is difficult to decide where political rule ends and where plain trade begins. Schrieke describes in a colorful manner how the kings of seventeenth-century Mataram attempted to impose their power upon the coastal rulers outside Java, as "lords of thirty-three islands," and how those rulers attempted to shirk the obligation of making a personal appearance and to send ambassadors instead, to the susuhunan's displeasure.[17]

In this light it seems as inappropriate to imagine an empire of Majapahit extending its power over the whole archipelago as to deny a certain subordination of the Sumatran coastal rulers to the king of Majapahit, evidenced by the punitive expedition after the ruler of

[17] Schrieke, *Ruler and Realm*, pp. 221 ff.

Shrīwijaya had attempted to establish direct relations with the Chinese emperor, an event duly recorded in the Ming chronicles.[18] It is impossible to conceive the ancient world in terms of clear-cut national boundaries as exemplified by our maps dividing up the whole world into political units colored yellow, green, or pink. The modern state of Indonesia has as little relationship to early Majapahit as present-day "Smaller Europe" to the medieval Roman kingdom of Charlemagne, the only real link being in either case a powerful political myth.[19] Thus, the sociological approach may help the historian to achieve a relativistic view of early political structures in Indonesia, in the same way as an approach from the angle of international law may help him achieve a more balanced conception of the Dutch-Indonesian colonial structure.[20]

A different approach which could equally be called, with some reservations, a "sociological" one has been followed by a few writers who treat Indonesian history from a Marxist point of view. An outstanding example of this kind of treatment is to be found in a study written by Rutgers, a Dutch Marxist, in cooperation with Guber, a Russian historian.[21] In this work an attempt was made to interpret Indonesian history in terms of class struggle and dialectics, on the lines of historical-materialist thought. In a few interesting pages the authors, for example, take issue with van Leur's view of precolonial Indonesia. According to the writers, some Indonesian coastal kingdoms were on the verge of a truly capitalistic evolution in the direction of a bourgeois society when Dutch colonial monopolistic policy, supported by naval military power, nipped in the bud such autochthonous tendencies.[22] The general contribution of this approach to Indonesian history consisted in deflecting the attention from purely incidental facts largely dealing with personalities to the underlying dynamic social forces rooted in the basic economic structure.

Finally, some special attention has to be devoted to de Kat Angelino's

[18] W. P. Groeneveldt, "Notes on the Malay Archipelago and Malacca," *VBG*, XXXIX (1880), 69.

[19] G. J. Resink, "Tussen de mythen," *De Nieuwe Stem*, VII (1952), 346 ff.

[20] G. J. Resink, "Veronachtzaamde uitspraken," *Indonesië*, VIII (1955), 1 ff.; *idem*, "Onafhankelijke vorsten, rijken en landen in Indonesië tussen 1850 en 1910," *Indonesië*, IX (1956), 265 ff.; *idem*, "Uit het stof van een beeldenstorm," *Indonesië*, IX (1956), 433 ff.; *idem*, "Een cadens van Colijn," *Indonesië*, X (1957), 246 ff.

[21] S. J. Rutgers and A. Guber, *Indonesië*, pt. I (Amsterdam, 1937). See also the postwar publication by S. J. Rutgers, *Indonesië: Het koloniale systeem in de periode tussen de eerste en de tweede wereldoorlog* (Amsterdam, 1947), which was intended as a continuation of the former work.

[22] Rutgers and Guber, *Indonesië*, pp. 37 ff., in particular pp. 51 ff.

magnum opus, which was more or less intended as an official view of the aims and policies of the Netherlands Indies Government.[23] Although not dealing with Indonesian historiography in particular, it was still a significant attempt to analyze many aspects of social development in Indonesia on the basis of a broad knowledge of recent literature on sociology and cultural anthropology. For example, Durkheim was quoted to support the author's view that Indonesian rural life was moving from a status of uniform "mechanic solidarity" toward "organic solidarity" in a more diversified society.[24] Very enlightening is his treatment of the character of towns in premodern Asia. He quotes Oswald Spengler's words: "Sie sind Mittelpunkte des Landes, aber sie bilden innerlich keine Welt für sich. Sie haben keine Seele." In general, they are mere agglomerations of villages and separate quarters.[25]

Yet whereas the works of van Leur and Schrieke, despite some outmoded aspects, are still of absorbing interest to the present-day reader, de Kat Angelino's contemporary work, notwithstanding its positive qualities and the high level of learning to which it bears testimony, reeks of dust and camphor. Evidently sociology cannot stand a blend with official ideology. Sociology, if it is to serve any purpose, has to be independent and critical.

At the time when Koch, Schrieke, and van Leur published their pioneering studies, sociology was only beginning to get a foothold in the Dutch academic world. Since World War II, sociology has become the vogue of the day. Thus, it is understandable that a much greater number of scholars, both Indonesian and others, have devoted themselves to sociological studies with respect to Indonesia. However, whereas in the prewar studies sociology had won its greatest successes in its application to early history, the postwar studies of this kind have dealt mostly with more recent periods of Indonesian history. This can be partly accounted for by the fact that sociological analysis of recent periods has sometimes been linked up with actual field research. For example, Clifford Geertz's analysis of the nonaristocratic elements of Javanese society in terms of a *santri* civilization centered in the bazaars as opposed to an *abangan* sphere characterized by the people's clinging to Javanese tradition, their stress upon communal values, and their "shared poverty" pattern was derived from the field research undertaken by a team of the Massachusetts Institute of Technology engaged

[23] A. D. A. de Kat Angelino, *Staatkundig beleid en bestuurszorg in Nederlandsch-Indië* (2 pts. in 3 vols.; The Hague, 1929–1930); in an abridged form published in English as *Colonial Policy* (Amsterdam and Chicago, 1931).

[24] Dutch ed., I¹, 109. [25] *Ibid.*, p. 117.

in the "Modjokuto" project.[26] Ten Dam's analysis of the processes underlying social stratification and a differentiation of cultural values according to social status within a village in western Java was derived
from the field work undertaken under his guidance by a team of students at the Faculty of Agriculture in Bogor.[27] In the last few years the
number of studies based on field research in Indonesia, some of them
by Indonesian scholars, has appreciably increased.[28]

But quite apart from actual sociological research, the postwar generation of sociologists has felt much attracted by historical developments of the past hundred years, on which source materials are
abundant. Recent literature on social developments deals extensively
with such aspects as the colonial stratification system,[29] the Islamic
reform movement,[30] the process of urbanization,[31] the evolution of

[26] Clifford Geertz, "Religious Belief and Economic Behavior in a Central Javanese Town: Some Preliminary Considerations," in *Economic Development and
Cultural Change*, IV (1956), 134 ff.; *idem, The Social Context of Economic Change:
An Indonesian Case Study* (M.I.T. paper, Cambridge, Mass., 1956); *idem, The Development of the Javanese Economy: A Socio-cultural Approach* (M.I.T. paper,
Cambridge, Mass., 1956); *idem, The Religion of Java* (Glencoe, 1960). Studies
by other members of the team have been published since, and several of them are
still to appear.

[27] H. ten Dam, *Desa Tjibodas* (Bogor, 1951); *idem*, "Coöpereren vanuit het
gezichtspunt der desastructuur in desa Tjibodas," *Indonesië*, IX (1956), 89 ff. (English translation in *Indonesian Economics: The Concept of Dualism in Theory and
Policy* [Selected Studies on Indonesia by Dutch Scholars, vol. VI; The Hague,
1961], pp. 347 ff.).

[28] See, for example, Selosoemardjan, *Social Changes in Jogjakarta* (Ithaca, N.Y.,
1962); Leslie H. Palmier, *Social Status and Power in Java* (London, 1960); Donald
E. Willmott, *The Chinese of Semarang: A Changing Minority Community in Indonesia* (Ithaca, N.Y., 1960); Kampto Utomo, *Masjarakat Transmigran Spontan
Didaerah W. Sekampung (Lampung)* (Spontaneous Transmigrants' Settlements in
the Way Sekampong Department of the Lampong Area; doctoral thesis, Faculty of
Agriculture, University of Indonesia, Jakarta, 1957).

[29] R. Kennedy, "The Colonial Crisis and the Future," in R. Linton, ed., *The Sci-
ence of Man in the World Crisis* (New York, 1945), pp. 306 ff.; D. H. Burger,
"Structuurveranderingen in de Javaanse samenleving," *Indonesië*, vols. II and III
(1948–1949 and 1949–1950); W. F. Wertheim, *Indonesian Society in Transition: A
Study of Social Change* (2d rev. ed.; The Hague and Bandung, 1959); L. Palmier,
"Aspects of Indonesia's Social Structure," *Pacific Affairs*, XXVIII (1955), 117 ff.

[30] C. A. O. van Nieuwenhuijze, *Aspects of Islam in Post-colonial Indonesia: Five
Essays* (The Hague and Bandung, 1958); Harry J. Benda, *The Crescent and the
Rising Sun: Indonesian Islam under the Japanese Occupation, 1942–1945* (The
Hague and Bandung, 1958); Clifford Geertz in his various studies on "Modjokuto";
Wertheim, *Indonesian Society.*

[31] Wertheim, *Indonesian Society;* Geertz, in his various "Modjokuto" studies; The
Siauw Giap, "Urbanisatieproblemen in Indonesië," *BKI*, CXV (1959), 249 ff. See
also *The Indonesian Town: Studies in Urban Sociology* (Selected Studies on Indo-

labor relationships,[32] differentiation of social roles according to age group and sex,[33] and many other aspects of Indonesian society. Whereas the approach of prewar sociologists was largely inspired by Weber's methodology, modern writing on Indonesian society is profusely making use of the conceptual framework and terminology developed by Anglo-Saxon schools of sociological thought. I mention the "color caste" terminology, adopted by the present author from American writers on the Negro problem; Geertz's attempt to analyze social change in Java in terms of Talcott Parsons' theory of social interaction; [34] or Willmott's effort to fit in his materials with theories of socio-cultural change developed by American scholars.[35]

In some cases new or somewhat modified conceptual tools have been developed by sociologists dealing with the Indonesian scene. The "shared poverty" concept elaborated by Geertz and the "mestizo culture" coined by the present writer are both a case in point. Highly significant are Clifford Geertz's attempts to develop Goldenweiser's concept of "involution" as a useful tool of understanding the process of increasing rigidity in Javanese society [36] or his effort to apply a "more dynamic functionalist approach" to Javanese society than usual among social anthropologists in order to deal more adequately with processes of social change.[37]

The suggestion by the present author of a historical chain from communities via individuals toward modern collective organizations to replace the traditional *Gemeinschaft-Gesellschaft* scheme proposed by Tönnies may be seen as an attempt to refine the framework of recent social history. In the same vein a historical sequence is being constructed from status according to birth via status based on achievement toward status derived from membership in collective organi-

---

nesia by Dutch Scholars, vol. IV; The Hague and Bandung, 1958) for significant prewar studies on this subject.

[32] Bruno Lasker, *Human Bondage in Southeast Asia* (Chapel Hill, N.C., 1950); Wertheim, *Indonesian Society*.

[33] G. Bateson and M. Mead, *Balinese Character: A Photographic Analysis* (New York, 1942); Cora DuBois, *The People of Alor: A Social-Psychological Study of an East-India Island* (Minneapolis, 1944); H. Th. Chabot, *Verwantschap, stand en sexe in Zuid-Celebes* (Groningen and Jakarta, 1950); W. F. Wertheim, "De generatiestrijd buiten de Westerse cultuurkring," *De wereld der mensen, Sociaalwetenschappelijke opstellen aangeboden aan Prof. Dr. J. J. Fahrenfort* (Groningen and Jakarta, 1955), pp. 108 ff.

[34] See C. Geertz, "Ritual and Social Change: A Javanese Example," *American Anthropologist*, LIX (1957), 32–54.

[35] Willmott, *op. cit.*, pp. 303 ff.　　[36] Geertz, *The Development*, pp. 29 ff.

[37] Geertz, *Ritual and Social Change*, pp. 34–35.

zations.[38] The traditional view of society as a complex and fully integrated structure is being replaced by one which starts from the assumption that there exist opposing value systems and veiled protest elements against the dominant system of hierarchy in any social structure.[39] This concept of the existence of "counterpoints" in any society, more often than not manifesting themselves in a veiled form, may prove a significant contribution to the study of historical processes. For example, the interpretation of messianic cults as disguised movements of social protest may add to our insight into such phenomena.[40]

At the same time, this type of sociological analysis may draw attention to source materials hitherto largely neglected. Myths, tales, or fiction may provide strong indications for the existence of such counterpoints against the dominant hierarchical values. Sundanese tales of the *kabayan* type reveal the existence of a hidden protest against the prevailing class hierarchy and the domination of the elders. Jokes common in Balinese theater performances may disclose an institutionalized form of reaction against the rigid social order.[41] The *Lay of Jaya Prana* gives a vivid expression to hidden discontent with the imposed caste order of Balinese society.[42] With many reservations, modern fiction may equally provide material which is useful for sociological and historical analysis of Indonesian society.[43]

Thus it would seem as if the sociological approach had made an

[38] This view is somewhat related to Talcott Parsons' distinction between allocation of status by ascription and by achievement; but the historical sequence suggested is a departure from Parsons.

[39] W. F. Wertheim, "Het contrapunt in de samenleving," *Weerklank op het werk van Jan Romein; Liber amicorum* (Amsterdam, 1953), pp. 210 ff. See also *idem*, "De generatiestrijd buiten de Westerse cultuurkring," *loc. cit.*; *idem*, "La Société et les conflits entre systèmes de valeurs," *Cahiers internationaux de sociologie*, XXVIII (1960), 33 ff.

[40] Peter Worsley, *The Trumpet Shall Sound: A Study of "Cargo Cults" in Melanesia* (London, 1957).

[41] Wertheim, "Het contrapunt in de samenleving," *loc. cit.*

[42] C. Hooykaas, *The Lay of Jaya Prana: The Balinese Uriah* (London, 1958), p. 33: "The writer is a low-caste man"; p. 35: "A *Sudra* comes into the poem." In my opinion Jef Last has rightly interpreted this popular drama as a play with a revolutionary tendency, opposing the popular hero to the *ksatrya* ruler and his retinue: Jef Last, "Djajaprana, tragedie in 5 acten naar een Balisch gegeven," *Indonesië*, VII (1953–1954), 381 ff. See, for the role of the Jayaprana myth in postwar Indonesia, H. J. Franken, "The Festival of Jayaprana at Kalianget," in *Bali: Studies in Life, Thought, and Ritual* (Selected Studies on Indonesia by Dutch Scholars, vol. V; The Hague and Bandung, 1960), pp. 233 ff.

[43] Lily Clerx, *Mensen in Deli: Een maatschappijbeeld uit de belletrie* (paper published by the Sociological-Historical Seminar for Southeast Asia, University of Amsterdam, no. 2).

unqualifiedly positive contribution to Indonesian historiography. Still, it becomes increasingly evident that the advantages to be derived from this approach have also certain limitations. It is significant that two of the prewar classics presented in this article as outstanding examples of sociological analysis have been recently submitted to a thorough criticism by well-qualified *pur sang* historians.[44]

One of the main themes of van Leur's analysis of Indonesian society is the wide gulf allegedly existing between the ruling aristocracy of the coastal towns supplemented by a restricted patrician class conforming as far as possible to the aristocratic way of life, who all were incidentally engaged in trading as owners or participants of cargoes and ships, and the numerous class of peddlers, actively engaged in professional trade, who crowded the ships and traveled along with their bundles and loads, representing, as a rule, a high value in a small volume.

The *popolo grosso* as opposed to the *popolo minuto* has been a significant element in both van Leur's interpretation of Hindu-Javanese history and his view on later periods of Indonesian history.

A Dutch historian, Mrs. M. A. P. Meilink-Roelofsz, has recently attempted to test van Leur's picture of early Indonesian trade and society on the basis of historical sources, among them Tomé Pires' *Suma Oriental*, in a doctoral thesis defended at the University of Amsterdam.[45]

Without attacking van Leur's general view of the social structure of early Indonesian society Dr. Meilink still succeeds in establishing that the gulf assumed by van Leur is much less absolute and unbridgeable than alleged in his work. According to Pires' description of early-fifteenth-century Malacca—which had not yet been unearthed at the time of van Leur's and Schrieke's writing—there was a gradual scale leading from the small peddler to the merchant-gentleman, who was included by van Leur with the *popolo grosso* as a patrician whose way of life was nearly aristocratic. Dr. Meilink also points out that not all the traders traveling with their cargoes belonged to the peddler type. There were many who leased a *petak*, a part of the ship's hold,

---

[44] See for the relation between general concepts and detailed historical research in general J. M. Romein, "The Common Human Pattern: Origin and Scope of Historical Theories," *Journal of World History,* IV, no. 2 (1958), 449 ff.

[45] M. A. P. Meilink-Roelofsz, *Ancient Trade and the European Influence in Indonesia between 1500 and 1630* (The Hague, 1962); see also *The Suma Oriental of Tomé Pires and The Book of Francisco Rodrigues,* ed. and trans. by Armando Cortesão, in works issued by the Hakluyt Society (2 vols.; London, 1944).

from the *nachoda* (captain). Further, Dr. Meilink does not agree with van Leur that the trade carried on in Southeast Asia was exclusively one of high-quality goods. Bulk trade had equally its place in the general trade movement.

All in all, the main objection of Dr. Meilink to van Leur's view is that in his effort to draw an idealtypic picture of early Indonesian society he has too much forced the historical facts to fit his theory, tending to neglect the fine shades.

Although the idealtypic approach is not intended to provide a true picture of "reality," in its tendency to simplify reality in order to make it accessible to our comprehensive faculties it still may seduce its followers into distorting the object matter of historians. Historical science, in its stress upon the incidental flow of events, is less prone than sociology to indulge in sweeping generalizations which have an attractive look but are not immune from the danger of too far a departure from the firm ground of historical evidence.

However, if we think of the sweeping generalizations by the historians van Leur was coming up against in his writings—for instance, the "Hindu colonization" of Java!—we begin to doubt whether sociologists are the only ones who are in danger of indulging in unwarranted simplifications.

In general, it can be stated that the sociological approach is especially dangerous in fostering oversimplification, when sociologists attempt to analyze social reality in terms of a dichotomy. *Gemeinschaft-Gesellschaft, popolo grosso-popolo minuto, santri-abangan,* landowners–landless people, Western-Eastern, universalism-particularism—these are a few of the distinctions used in current sociological literature dealing with Indonesia. By and large, such distinctions have only a heuristic value to promote a certain initial understanding and to formulate a working hypothesis for further research. As a rule, such a dichotomy will prove, in the long run, too rough for a deeper understanding, and a more graded scale of possibilities will have to be elaborated to leave room for the fine shades. Especially for a more dynamic approach, as required for modern historiography, the tools of sociology may still be too primitive.

A second example of historical criticism of prewar sociological studies is to be found in van Niel's analysis of the Sarekat Islam movement.[46] Van Niel takes issue with Koch's attempt to view Sarekat Islam pri-

[46] R. van Niel, *The Emergence of the Modern Indonesian Elite* (The Hague and Bandung, 1960), p. 103, pp. 113 ff.

marily as a bourgeois movement comparable with sixteenth-century Protestantism. In his opinion, which is based on an impressive body of biographical information on the leading nationalists of that period, the term bourgeois would appear less appropriate to designate a social group mostly belonging to the *pryayi* elite and in general not engaged in trade but in white-collar functions. In this case, the criticism by the historian is primarily leveled against a tendency of sociologists to look for historical parallels and to reduce phenomena from societies far apart in space and time to an aggregate denomination.

But again the sociologists were not the only ones, or the first, to draw parallels. It was the historian Geerke who thought fit to compare Coen with Mussolini; [47] and it is the historian de Graaf who draws a comparison between the disintegration of the Mataram Empire and similar developments in Western Europe during the early Middle Ages.[48] Comparison of processes in Indonesian history with similar processes elsewhere may yield fruitful insights, provided that the categories used are truly universal and that the simplifying, idealtypic characterization is being refined by taking full account of the time factor, discussed by Professor Romein in this volume. The historian could, in this way, help and correct the sociologist who may tend to look too much for generalities and to overlook specific factors.

Thus, the ultimate value of the sociological approach to historiography has still to be established. Nevertheless, its influence upon Indonesian history writing is already undeniable. The fact that a doctoral dissertation has been written by a historian with the outspoken aim of testing the sociological hypothesis of van Leur is significant of the importance attached to his views in historical circles. Sociologists are likely to continue their efforts to treat Indonesian history from a sociological point of view. But modern historians are equally likely to insert sociological viewpoints in their treatment of Indonesian history.[49] If they do not, their work is bound to be thought, as it were, incomplete.[50]

Modern thinking is so much imbued with sociological elements and jargon that present-day historians will inevitably be influenced by so-

[47] H. P. Geerke, *Jan Pieterszoon Coen: De baanbreker in ons Indië* (Utrecht, 1929), p. 230.

[48] H. J. de Graaf, *Geschiedenis van Indonesië* (The Hague and Bandung, 1949), p. 207.

[49] See, for example, Benda, *The Crescent and the Rising Sun,* and van Niel, *The Emergence of the Modern Indonesian Elite.*

[50] As is the case with de Graaf, *Geschiedenis van Indonesië.*

ciological thought, even though they remain, rightly, critical toward specific theories and views expressed by sociologists. They will, in the fashion of Monsieur Jourdain, write sociology even without knowing it.

Whether the historians accept or reject concrete theories or views emanating from sociologists, the sociological approach has forever added a new dimension to historiography.

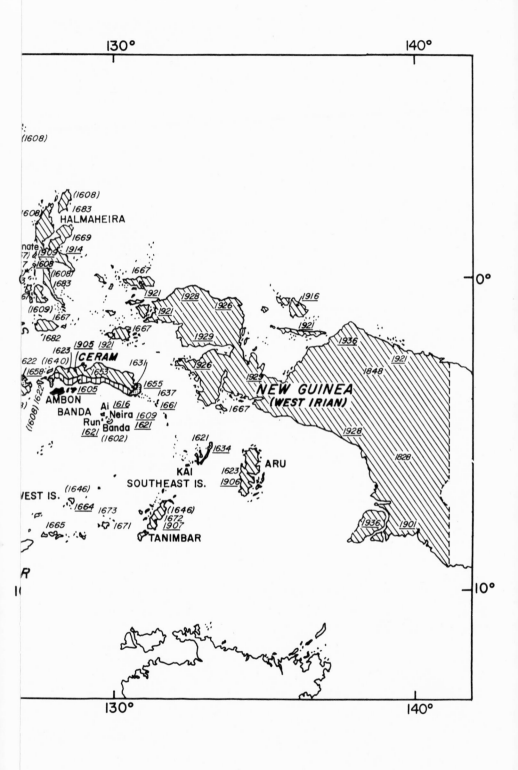

XIX

The Significance of the History of International Law in Indonesia

By G. J. RESINK

Research Professor, Faculty of Law and Social Sciences,
University of Indonesia, Jakarta

THE history of international law in Indonesia has an old and rich reality and is a young and poverty-stricken science. We shall speak first of its age and richness, insofar as this reality can be shaped briefly into words. Following this, we shall describe its youth and its poverty, which subject will be swiftly exhausted. Finally, we shall touch on the history of international law as a "usable past"—the daring term is Herbert J. Muller's [1]—in order to consider its usefulness for the future historiography of Indonesia.

I

The history of international law in Indonesia is as honorably old as the history of Indonesia in general, insofar as it rests upon written records. Indeed, the most ancient of those records which bear on Indonesian history contain their aspect of international law. They derive from Chinese sources and concern what seem to be Indonesian deliveries of tribute and probable Chinese presentation of gifts, part of Indonesian-Chinese international relations of two thousand years ago. They include reports of a mission sent by an Indonesian state to the Heavenly Kingdom about the year A.D. 132.[2]

---

[1] Herbert J. Muller, *The Uses of the Past* (3d ed.; New York, 1957), p. 38. Its last chapter bears the striking title "The Uses of the Future."

[2] D. G. E. Hall, *A History of South-east Asia* (London, 1955), p. 15.

Since that time, Indonesian diplomatic missions have existed as a known institution until the present century. Even then, the State Gazettes (Staatsbladen) of the Netherlands Indies still mentioned envoys of the Indonesian states sent to the Government of the Netherlands Indies —a practice which lasted until 1910 in the case of the Indonesian realms outside Java and until 1913 in the case of the Princely Territories (*Vorstenlanden*). These envoys were received with gun salutes or other ceremony; and from 1862 there was a "native master of ceremonies" appointed to serve as a sort of *chef de protocol* for their reception.[3]

In addition to this diplomatic intercourse between the Indonesian realms and that entity which legislation, administration of justice, and jurisprudence have labeled the state of the Netherlands Indies, there existed in South Celebes an inter-Indonesian exchange of diplomatic representatives between the Buginese states, which seem to have maintained until about the beginning of this century what was, according to Korn, "a well-organized envoy system provided with diplomatic immunities." [4]

Inasmuch as the existence of diplomatic intercourse is probably the most striking evidence of international legal relations, it would not be unjust to refer in the title of this essay to the age of Indonesia's history of international law as being eighteen centuries or even two thousand years old. We shall not make this claim, however; for the history of international law in Indonesia dates in its richness only from the sixteenth century—but then it flowers with a sudden completeness that has only recently been brought to the light of history.

Before that century we must, as far as treaties are concerned, make shift with the assumption that the marriages of King Kameshwara (1117–1130) and Princess Kirana—which reunited Kĕḍiri and Jenggala —and of Kĕrtarājasa with a princess of Champa, and of Jayasimhawarman III with a Javanese princess about the year 1292 represented international agreements. In the sixteenth century, however, we suddenly find ourselves able to refer to both European-Indonesian and inter-Indonesian treaties—the latter being concluded in Celebes, as was pointed out not long ago in Noorduyn's dissertation, a pioneering work in this respect. While these were mostly bilateral undertakings, the Tellumpotcho treaty between Wajo', Bone, and Soppeng, which dates

---

[3] See Staatsblad 1910 no. 661 concerning the kingdoms outside Java; Staatsblad 1913 no. 307 for the "Vorstenlanden"; Bijblad 1125 from 1862 for the "Inlandsche Ceremoniemeester" (native Master of Ceremonies).

[4] V. E. Korn, "Oosterse visie op westers bewind," *BKI*, CXIII (1957), 21.

from approximately 1582, is to the best of our present knowledge the oldest collective treaty. The best known of the multilateral pacts is the treaty of Bonggaya, made in 1667 and renewed in 1824, which until the end of the last century guaranteed the independence of the Indonesian states in South Celebes as "allied powers" (*bondgenoot-schappelijke landen*) in the eyes of Netherlands Indies government officials and judges.[5] Better known are the multilateral treaties between the Balinese kingdoms in the nineteenth century, as most recently dealt with in Korn's book on *adat* law mentioned in note 43.

Since that sixteenth century, a part of the history of Indonesian international law can be found in the many hundreds of treaties and other international agreements and contracts, a good half thousand of which, it is estimated, the Indonesian Republic had to recognize as binding upon itself in 1949.[6]

Although there may be doubt that the Brantas River formed an international boundary after the division of Erlangga's realm in about 1042, this uncertainty does not seem to exist in the case of the River Tangka, which was declared to be the border in the Chaleppa Treaty of 1555 between Bone and Goa. We may question whether the Ping-girraksa, the famous stone wall whose remains can be seen to the south of Gunung Kawi, marked an international boundary or whether the territorial limits which the Prince of Puni requested the Emperor of China to determine in the beginning of the fourteenth century were ever actually delineated. It is, however, certain that the borders of the Macassarese and Buginese princedoms had already been described in the sixteenth century and that the boundaries of the large states were more or less permanently fixed.[7] Since then, the demarcation and abolition of boundaries, border disputes, the regulation of border traffic, and all that goes with such matters have been problems of real import.

[5] Hall, *A History of South-east Asia*, pp. 64, 73, regarding the marriage treaties. For a more detailed discussion of the Celebes treaties see J. Noorduyn, *Een Achttiende-eeuwse kroniek van Wadjo* (The Hague, 1955), p. 68, on the Tellum-potcho treaty, and, further, my article "Eeuwen volkenrecht in Indonesië," *Indonesië*, X, no. 6 (1957), 447. This article gives a list of the most important publications on the history of international law in Indonesia up to 1957, and in my short review "Penjelidikan mengenai sedjarah hukum internasional di Indonesia" (Research on the History of International Law in Indonesia) in *Berita Madjelis Ilmu Pengetahuan Indonesia* (issued by the Council for Sciences of Indonesia), II, no. 6 (1958), 7, is supplied a list of literature up till *medio* 1958.

[6] H. F. Luiking, *De dienst van scheepvaart in Indonesië* (dissertation, Jakarta, 1954), p. 257.

[7] In my article mentioned in note 5, a more detailed discussion is given on pp. 444–446.

Although even before the sixteenth century there must have been officials who presented foreigners to the prince, defended their interests before him, or acted as the heads of foreign communities in the country,[8] it is only in that century that we find more certain evidence concerning those functionaries who appeared under the name of *shahbander* in Pajajaran,[9] Goa, and the Uliasser Islands.[10] These officials frequently held judicial power over the foreign community, in addition to their above-mentioned international-legal administrative functions; and at the same time they often had legislative authority in the sense that they could conclude international agreements with foreigners. These remarkable persons, who may have existed as early as the time of Majapahit, can still be found represented at the end of the nineteenth century in the first two novels of Joseph Conrad, for the Sulunese Babalatchi—diplomat, statesman, harbor master, introducer of foreigners, and defender of their interests before the ruler of Sambir in East Borneo—shows all the features which apply to this multiplicity of functions in international relations.[11]

It is also in the sixteenth century that we hear for the first time of a miniature corps of diplomats in the state of Wajo'[12]—a "foreign service" which appears to have been unique, since Indonesian history has otherwise produced evidence only of emissaries *ad hoc*. Again, it is in that century that we first hear of the existence and solution of international disputes on the islands of Java and the Celebes,[13] a phenomenon which has since proved to be lasting.

[8] Concerning the "djuru Kling" on Java, see Krom, *HJG*, pp. 264–304; and concerning the *shahbandar* in Majapahit, see H. J. de Graaf, *Geschiedenis van Indonesië* (The Hague, 1949), p. 80, which mentions no source.

[9] H. ten Dam, "Verkenningen rondom Padjadjaran," *Indonesië*, X, no. 4 (1957), 296, mentions a *shahbandar* from the year 1521, who receives the Portuguese and who plays a role in the conclusion of treaties.

[10] Noorduyn, *Wadjo'*, p. 76, concerning Goa, and J. A. van der Chijs, *De vestiging van het Nederlandsche gezag over de Banda-eilanden* (Batavia, 1886), pp. 1–10 for the Oeliassers (Oeliasser Islands); the *shahbandar* of Neira was also a judge (in a counsel) in disputes between foreigners, p. 10.

[11] See Joseph Conrad, *Almayer's Folly* (1895) and *An Outcast of the Islands* (1896), in Present Collected Ed. (Dent, 1947), pp. 38 (prime minister, harbourmaster, financial adviser, general factotum), 58 (statesman), 59 (diplomatist), and (Dent, 1949) 364 (*shahbandar*).

[12] Noorduyn, *Wadjo'*, pp. 55, 316.

[13] My essay named in note 5 discusses this more deeply, with the grateful acknowledgment to Noorduyn's dissertation and de Graaf's biography of Senapati, *De regering van Panembahan Sénapati Ingalaga* (VKI, vol. XIII; 1954), which has reviewed our knowledge of the settlement of international disputes to the middle of the sixteenth century.

Finally, it is at the end of the sixteenth century that we first learn of what is called nowadays "territorial sea." On Banda, before anchoring in waters which were under the communal right of disposal of the coastal states, it was necessary to approach the *shahbandars* for permission to trade in return for payment in specified duties, an arrangement which could be negotiated with the *shahbandars* as an (international) agreement.[14] The territorial sea and the activity of the *shahbandars* in one role or another have never since been absent from Indonesia's shores.

From the sixteenth century, not only was international law in Indonesia especially rich, but it also extended beyond the Asian world alone, by reason of its becoming involved in that world-embracing international law for which the Portuguese and Spaniards laid the first foundations. Thus, while we may say that until the sixteenth century international law in Indonesia knew only an Asian milieu, it came to rest thereafter in a European-Asian setting, in which the European role steadily grew at the expense of the part played by non-Indonesian Asia. So far as the Indonesian constellation of states is concerned, we find that in the seventeenth century Achehnese emissaries journeyed to Prince Maurits in the Netherlands, while diplomatic missions from Mataram sailed to Portuguese Goa,[15] and Bantamese ambassadors were sent to King James II of England.[16] In the nineteenth century we see Sibolga and Tapanuli conclude a triple alliance with the British [17] and an Achehnese ambassador depart for Constantinople to call for Turkish protection against the Netherlands.[18]

The internationally divided world of Indonesian realms, states, and lands of "Indian princes and peoples," to use the phrase employed by the Government Regulation (Regeringsreglement) of 1854 to describe that Netherlands Indies which appeared as a subject of international law in its relations with those princes and peoples, persisted until about 1910. Indeed, even at the end of the last century, in 1895, the Supreme

[14] Van der Chijs, *De vestiging*, pp. 1 ff.

[15] For the Achehnese ambassadors to Prince Maurits see de Graaf, *Geschiedenis*, p. 300; and for the ambassadors from Mataram to Portuguese Goa in 1634 see B. Schrieke, *Indonesian Sociological Studies*, pt. I, *Selected Writings* (The Hague and Bandung, 1955), pp. 61 and 19.

[16] C. R. Boxer, "Cornelis Speelman and the Growth of Dutch Power in Indonesia, 1666–1684," *History Today*, VIII, no. 3 (March, 1958), 152.

[17] Korn, "Oosterse visie," p. 20.

[18] H. Fievez de Malines van Ginkel, *Overzicht van de Internationaal-rechtelijke Betrekkingen van Nederlandsch-Indië (1850–1922)* (dissertation, Leyden, 1924), p. 21.

Court recognized as independent little states on Sumba; [19] and in the same year the prominent authority on constitutional law, Margadant, still referred to the rulers of Jogjakarta, Surakarta, Goa, Lombok, "and many others" as "self-governing, independent rulers." [20] In 1897 the no-less-well-known jurist Nederburgh disparaged certain "areas of the Indies"—in a geographic sense—"even in our 'sphere of interest'" as being "completely independent for us or bound to us only through alliance." [21] In 1899 a Resident wrote that, outside of a specified area, Jambi could be viewed as "fully independent"; while in 1907 Colijn announced in his famous official memorandum on "Political and Administrative Management in the Outer Possessions" that central Sumatra, the interior regions of Borneo, the country of the Torajas, and the miniature states existing on Flores and Sumba "are, according to the prevailing viewpoint," situated "outside the Netherlands Indies" and were to be considered independent. Colijn's attitude was expressly shared in an official atlas published in 1907 by order of the Colonial Ministry in the case of the Batak lands, the Dalu-dalu and Rokan lands, and other areas in central Sumatra." [22]

As counterparts of the envoys from these states, who were sent abroad on specified occasions—say once in every three years or on an *ad hoc* basis [23]—were the more permanent diplomatic representatives maintained by the Netherlands Indies Government in the nineteenth century: commissioners to the Princely Territories until 1850 and to Lombok until 1890, emissaries sent to the states of South Bali in the time before their subjugation in 1906–1908, and (lastly) the Residents of Asahan and Pontianak, who continued to be announced as "representatives" until 1910, just as they had been in Jambi ever since 1643. In the selfsame Jambi, an Assistant Resident continued to function under the title of "political agent" until 1903. From the memoirs of a former Resident of Surakarta, published in 1956, we can see how at least this particular government official of the 1920's considered the Residents in the Princely Territories to be "representatives" of not only the Indies Government but even of the Netherlands itself; their office was "largely of a representative sort," and indeed it seemed to him

[19] See my article "Onafhankelijke vorsten, rijken en landen in Indonesië tussen 1850 en 1910," *Indonesië*, IX, no. 4 (1956), 284, 286.

[20] C. W. Margadant, *Verklaring van de Nederlandsch-Indische strafwetboeken* (Batavia, 1895), p. 192.

[21] J. A. Nederburgh, *Wet en Adat*, I, pt. 1–2 (Batavia, 1897), 123.

[22] See H. Colijn, *Politiek beleid en bestuurszorg in de buitenbezittingen*, pt. I (Batavia, 1907), pp. 179–180, and my essay referred to in note 19, p. 285.

[23] See my essay named in note 5, pp. 441 ff.

after accepting that office that it was "considerably more representative" in character than he had already feared.[24]

In the treaties, agreements, and contracts between the state of the
Netherlands Indies and the Indonesian realms a distinction was made
between subjects of each party, and it was only after 1910 that another
differentiation appeared—that made between subjects of the state
(*land*) and subjects of the region (*landschap*). Dutch recognition of a
distinct nationality for persons and vessels from the Indonesian states
was doomed to vanish after 1910—but not completely so,[25] and in
Dutch treaties concluded that very year with Sweden and Montenegro
the Indonesian *nations indigènes* were still expressly exempted from
the most-favored-nation clause on the grounds that they received or
could expect still greater facilities from the Netherlands.[26] These European treaties thus served as a backhanded recognition that the Indonesian states were subjects of international law. This status was also
recognized directly in the treaties which bound those realms to and
yet separated them from the state of the Netherlands Indies in that it
was provided that they were to maintain "peace and friendship" with
other states and were not to engage in hostilities with those realms
without the "knowledge or permission of the Government." [27] If it is
sufficient for the existence of a state in international law that it maintains international relations with at least one other state—indicated
by a number of the rules and institutions of international law, valid
for such relations—these acknowledgments of the legal personality of
the Indonesian states in treaties between the Netherlands and other
European powers and in the treaties between Indonesian realms and
the state of the Netherlands Indies should serve to justify the claim
that the history of international law in Indonesia in its European–
Asian setting did not come to an end until about 1910.

At that time, the state of Netherlands India perished as a result of

[24] For ambassadors sent from and to Bali see Colijn, *Politiek*, pt. II A (1909), pp.
188–189, and Miguel Covarrubias, *Island of Bali* (New York, 1950), p. 33, together
with J. Kersten, *Bali* (3d ed.; Eindhoven, 1947), p. 177. For the commissioners in
the Princely Territories and on Lombok, see my essay referred to in note 5, and for
the Residents see my article "Conflictenrecht van de Nederlands-Indische staat in
internationaal-rechtelijke zetting," *BKI*, CXV (1959), 8–9, as well as M. B. van der
Jagt's *Mémoires* (The Hague, 1956), pp. 301, 313, and 327.

[25] For a more detailed discussion, see my essay "Een cadens van Colijn," *Indonesië*, X (1957), 247–248.

[26] See my essay named in note 19, pp. 286–287.

[27] H. J. Spit, *De Indische zelfbesturende landschappen* (dissertation, Leyden,
1911), p. 141 (Art. 8 of the Model Uniform Contract of 1875), p. 148 (Art. 8 of the
Model Celebes Contract of 1904), and p. 156 (Art. 10 of the Model Contract for the
East Coast of Sumatra, 1906).

its own expansion into the sphere of influence allowed it by England on Borneo and by Portugal on Timor; with this also ended the resident status of the Netherlands Indies as "a variant of the subject status," according to Logemann,[28] although in the 1920's the State Gazette (Staatsblad) was still to make mention of a Netherlands Indies subjectship [29] and of a "State Regulation." In doing so, it harked back to the time when a smaller Netherlands India, though it was a part of the Dutch state, or a Dutch colony, when seen from the point of view of Netherlands or in the light of Dutch legalistic thinking and Dutch constitutional law, was, when approached from the viewpoint of its position in Indonesia and in international law and legal practice, acting alongside and on a level with the "native states of the Eastern Archipelago in friendship with the Dutch Government," clearly marked off up till 1915 by the "Indian Tariff Act" from the "Netherlands Indian possessions" (Staatsblad 1910 no. 79 juncto Staatsblad 1915 no. 219, Art. 2, sub 2, b).

After 1910 there follow thirty-five years in which Netherlands India was the one large colony which, while it maintained international legal relations and in some cases even was a party in its own right to certain treaties, had no right at all to diplomatic representation and knew consuls only in the capacity of trade commissioners.[30] The colony's status as a subject of international law was thus a derived subjectivity, a fact which is all the more striking in that it was precisely in those decades that the international setting of the Netherlands Indies relations in international law became in reality a global one. Via the Netherlands these relations stretched out to states in every corner of the world, and thus even to those which were not already represented in the League of Nations, such as the United States and in certain periods Germany, Japan, and Russia. In addition, the appearance in international law of Australia and South Africa as separate "international personalities" brought the colony into indirect international relations with them, as can be seen in boundary treaties with the first-named dominion and from the appointment of trade commissioners to the other.[31]

[28] J. H. A. Logemann, "De afbakening van rechtsmacht tussen gouvernements-rechter en landschapsrechter," *Indisch Tijdschrift van het Recht*, CXLVII (1938), 426.

[29] C. van Vollenhoven, *Staatsrecht overzee* (Leyden, 1934), pp. 84–85.

[30] F. M. Baron van Asbeck, "L'Elément international aux Indes Néerlandaises," "*Grotius*," *Annuaire international pour 1935*, pp. 30–31.

[31] For the development of the dominions as "international personalities," see J. G.

When in 1945 the Republic was declared, it had been thirty-five years since a Landraad (NI Tribunal for Indonesians) had declared for the last time that the little realm of Goa was "foreign territory . . . in the juridical sense." The newborn republic quickly secured numerous sorts of recognition which had significance in international law. Those ranged from the acknowledgment made in 1946 by Netherlands Indies judges of verdicts passed in 1945 by the republican Pengadilan Negeri (First Instance Court) in cases involving Dutch subjects [32] to complete *de jure* recognition as a state by Asian powers following the conclusion of the Linggadjati Agreement in 1946.[33] It is, however, only since the acquisition of United Nations membership in 1950 that Indonesia's international relations directly or indirectly—through the world organization—have reached out to states in all parts of the globe. This membership, however, has brought Indonesia into such interdependence with other states that the isolated and undisturbed independence enjoyed by many an Indonesian state half a century ago seems almost touching. These states had been, to be sure, within the sphere of "influence" or "interest" [34] of the Netherlands or the Netherlands Indies, but we would be guilty of an anachronistic misconception if we were to refer to them as satellite states for that reason. Dutchmen and Indonesians who ask distrustfully just what their independence actually means, betray an uneasiness over the real significance of present Indonesian or Dutch independence rather than a doubt concerning the independence or the right of existence in international law which the Indonesian states earlier enjoyed. Indeed, the independence and right of existence asserted by such small states as Montenegro and Luxemburg, and by the members of the German Confederation and the little states of Italy prior to their unification in the nineteenth century, were just as indubitable in Europe as were the similar rights of the Indonesian states at that time. In the view of leading Dutch jurists up until Kleintjes in 1911, those states had to be viewed as

Starke, "The Commonwealth in International Affairs," in Rae Else Mitchell, ed., *Essays on the Australian Constitution* (Sydney and Melbourne, 1952), pp. 291, 303 ff.

[32] Judgments of the Landraad in Bandung of May 8, 1946, and the Court of Appeals in Batavia of Sept. 10, 1946, in *Indisch Tijdschrift van het Recht* (1947), respectively pp. 164–167 and pp. 22–24. See also R. D. Kollewijn, "Erkenning van door de rechters van de Indonesische Republiek gewezen vonnissen," *Nederlandsch Juristenblad*, 1946, pp. 681–686.

[33] See Ali Sastroamidjojo and Robert Delson, "The Status of the Republic of Indonesia in International Law," *Columbia Law Review*, XLIX (1949), 345.

[34] See my essay named in note 25, p. 252.

"foreign powers" in the sense in which Article 59 of the Netherlands Constitution of 1887 defined that term.[35]

We thus see that, while the history of international law in Indonesia took place in an Asian milieu prior to 1511 and from that year to about 1910 in a European-Asian setting, it became after the first decade of our century a global history for the colony of Netherlands India—a history, however, in which the colony participated only vicariously through the Netherlands. Finally, through acquiring membership in the United Nations in 1950, a history of direct and global relations was embarked on by the Indonesian Republic, in the fullness of its own perfection as a subject of international law.

Whoever may wish to divide this historical periodization with other dates may do so without much difficulty. Mohammad Ali, for example, has proposed 1911 as a cutoff year, because it was then that the last Short Declaration (Korte Verklaring) was signed and because, we might add, it was in that year that the deposed Sultan of Riau protested in the *Straits Times* about the ending of what he considered to be a protectorate recognized by international law. However, if we may judge on the basis of isolated facts of this sort, we might just as well hold the year 1915 to be a crucial one, since at that time the "native states of the Eastern Archipelago in friendship with the Dutch Government" passed forever out of the "Indian Tariff Act" and since at that same time "the last independent territory on the island of Sumatra" was, according to a Dutch newspaper, absorbed into the Government of the East Coast of Sumatra. In the same fashion, we can name 1917 as the final year in which Indonesian international law existed in a European-Asian setting, because in 1918 were discarded those criminal codes for Europeans and Natives which still mentioned the Netherlands Indies as a subject of the law of war—thus as a state —and its allies in the archipelago as similar subjects of international law.[36] However, though we can thus disagree, especially about the dates marking the end of an era, it does not seem possible to doubt that the setting in which the history of international law in Indonesia took place expanded from an Asian to a European-Asian to a truly global international environment. It owes its age to the Asian period and its richness to the times which followed after.

[35] For a more detailed discussion, see my article "Uit het stof van een beeldenstorm," *Indonesië*, IX, no. 6 (1956), 435.

[36] See H. W. C. Borderwijk, *Rechtspersoonlijkheid der Nederlandsche koloniën* (dissertation, Leyden, 1905), pp. 273, 276; see also pp. 154 and 157 for the term "state."

II

It is characteristic of both the poverty and the youth of the history of international law in Indonesia as a science that attention has been devoted to that history in its Asian setting almost solely by Orientalists; and they have concentrated chiefly on diplomatic relations within the larger framework of political history. It was not until the appearance of a singular study written in 1953 by Yamin, a jurist who based his work on the findings of these scholars, that attention was granted to what the author called—in a completely uncustomary phrase—the "external" diplomatic law of Majapahit.[37] An essay in which he promised to discuss the "internal" diplomatic law of Majapahit has nowhere been published, very probably because the writer himself was aware that he would have had to differentiate between the "world of Majapahit," great but divided internationally into states or nations, and the significantly smaller realm of that name which maintained diplomatic relations with these smaller and weaker states.

No less typical of the history of Indonesian international law as a science is the fact that the scholars who have written on such prominent treaties of the European-Asian period as the pacts of Painan (1663) and of Bonggaya (1667) and on the famed embassies of Rijckloff van Goens and François Tack to Mataram in the seventeenth century have been, respectively, de Leeuw, Stapel, Ottow, and de Graaf, all of them historians and not jurists.[38] Although it was a jurist, Heeres, who published the first two parts of the *Corpus Diplomaticum Neerlando-Indicum*, the compilation of hundreds of Dutch East India Company treaties, it was the historian Stapel and the Indologist Coolhaas who completed the collection; and it was the Orientalist Cense who first made known the Goan counterpart of that *Corpus*, the *Ulukanaja*. Jurists like Massink and Filet, Sandbergen and Schmitz—who wrote respectively on the princedoms of Madura, on the Princely Territories, and on the Company's laws concerning the nationality of ships and desertion—did indeed go back to the seventeenth and eighteenth centuries, but they did not devote more than a few words to international

[37] Muhammad Yamin, "Hukum duta Indonesia dalam zaman Madjapahit, 1293–1525," *Antara Bangsa*, I, no. 1 (1953), 50–61.

[38] W. J. A. de Leeuw, *Het Painansch contract* (dissertation, Amsterdam, 1926); F. W. Stapel, *Het Bonggaais verdrag* (dissertation, Leyden, 1922); W. M. Ottow, *Rijckloff Volkertsz van Goens: De carrière van een diplomaat* (dissertation, Utrecht, 1954); H. J. de Graaf, *De moord op Kapitein François Tack* (dissertation, Leyden, 1935).

law, simply because they were not enough concerned with it and generally kept their gaze fixed on history and constitutional law.[39]

Van Kan, who dredged forth two volumes of material *Uit de rechtsgeschiedenis der Compagnie* (From the Legal History of the Company),
was able to dig up from the Company's collection of Positive Orders
sixteen topics of international law which were relative to those orders,
but he left these subjects themselves untouched. Verzijl, too, pointed
out the significance of the materials on Indonesian colonial history
for the general history of international law, but he also left those
sources uninvestigated.[40]

The history of international law in the nineteenth century has been
seen more clearly by such contemporary juridical dissertation writers
as de Sturler; [41] but after 1910 the view of such young Ph.D.'s as Spit
in 1911 and Fievez de Malines van Ginkel in 1924 was so captured by
the image of one great Netherlands Indies and its development in
history and constitutional law that they almost completely ignored that
international law in the archipelago which had been recognized and
taken into account by contemporary Netherlands Indies legislation,
judicature, and jurisprudence until the second half of the nineteenth
century and the first decade of the twentieth.[42]

To be sure, it was during this period that van Vollenhoven was

[39] Five parts of the *Corpus Diplomaticum* appeared in *BKI*, vols. LVII (1907),
LXXXVII (1931), XCI (1934), XCIII (1935), and XCVI (1938), while pt. VI appeared separately in 1955. For the *Ulukanaja* see A. A. Cense, "Enige aantekeningen over Makassaars-Boeginese geschiedschrijving," *BKI*, CVII (1951), 42–
60; see further H. Massink, *Bijdrage tot de kennis van het vroeger en tegenwoordig
bestuur op het eiland Madoera* (dissertation, Leyden, 1888); P. W. Filet, *De
verhouding der vorsten op Java tot de Ned.-Indische regeering* (dissertation, Leyden, 1895); F. J. H. W. Sandbergen, *Nederlandsche en Nederlandsch Indische
scheepsnationaliteit* (dissertation, Leyden, 1931); J. P. G. Schmitz, *Recht-
historische bijdragen tot de kennis van het materieële en formeele strafrecht van
toepassing op de dienaren van de Vereenigde Oost-Indische Compagnie, voor-
namelijk betrekking hebbende op het delict van desertie* (dissertation, Utrecht,
1938), ch. ii, sec. 4, pp. 117–126, and sec. 5, pp. 126–128, which contains the curious treaty between the Company and Goa of 1773 about the extradition of de-
serters. This treaty is unjustly excluded from pt. VI of the *Corpus Diplomaticum*.

[40] See J. van Kan, *Uit de rechtsgeschiedenis der Compagnie, II* (Bandung, 1935),
69, and J. H. W. Verzijl, "Volkenrechtsgeschiedenis," *MKAWAL*, new ser., XVI,
no. 2 (1953), 46.

[41] J. E. de Sturler, *Het grondgebied van Nederlandsch Oost-Indië in verband met
de tractaten met Spanje, Engeland en Portugal* (dissertation, Leyden, 1881), p. 27.

[42] See H. J. Spit, *De Indische zelfbesturende landschappen* (dissertation, Leyden,
1911), and my criticism in the essay named in note 19, pp. 276, 279–280, 286–287,
289. See, further, van Ginkel, *Overzicht*, and my criticism of this work in
"Veronachtzaamde uitspraken," *Indonesië*, VIII, no. 1 (1955), 6, 7, and 10.

systematically making a place for *adat* (customary) international law in his famous work on adat law; but the facts he presented on this subject were scarce at best, filling less than three pages for each adat area. If we glance into Korn's rich book on the adat law in Bali, in its second edition of 1932, we see that the adat law of nations on that island alone occupied a little over five large pages; and in Dormeier's dissertation on the smaller adat law area of the Banggai Archipelago, written in 1947, a whole chapter (no. VI) of fifteen pages was devoted to adat international law.[43]

The fact that adat international law became categorized under the single heading of customary law resulted in its removal from the purview of those who observed international law in Indonesia not solely in an inter-Indonesian or regional setting but also in a wider, truly international environment. It is clear from Soeripto's otherwise excellent dissertation on the legal codes of the Princely Territories (1928) how little this pupil of van Vollenhoven was able or willing to do this, even though the codes, indigenous Javanese regulations from the eighteenth and nineteenth centuries, betray so many international legal aspects in both their form and content that we must consider them to have been written not merely for quasi-international but for regular international affairs and disputes in which foreigners and subjects of the prince were involved.[44] How little van Vollenhoven himself saw the history of the law of nations in Indonesia in its wider, truly international setting is apparent from his book *Du droit de paix*, in which, out of all Indonesian international law, he considers only one institution from the Minangkabau area of the late nineteenth century to be worthy of mention in the history of the general law of peace.[45]

It is not until van Asbeck, Kollewijn, and Logemann that we find reference to contemporary or recent international law, and this in a time in which the Netherlands' one great colony was taking part in a world-embracing—and thus incontrovertibly international—law of nations. It was van Asbeck, the first professor of international law in Indonesia at the Law School in prewar Batavia, who outlined the

[43] C. van Vollenhoven, *Het adatrecht van Nederlandsch-Indië*, (2d unrev. ed.; Leyden, 1931), 235–236, 260, 279, 289–290, 308–309, 317, 333, 353, 360, 375–376, 388, 407–408, 427–429, 443, 479–480, 566, 676, 726; V. E. Korn, *Het adatrecht van Bali* (2d ed.; The Hague, 1932), pp. 437–442; J. J. Dormeier, *Banggaais adatrecht* (dissertation, Leyden), published in *VKI*, VI (1947), 173–184.

[44] Soeripto, *Ontwikkelingsgang der Vorstenlandsche wetboeken* (dissertation, Leyden, 1929).

[45] C. van Vollenhoven, *Du droit de paix* (The Hague, 1932), p. 21.

international legal, economic, geopolitical, and demographic position of the Netherlands Indies.[46] Kollewijn was to refer to the international private law background of the internal conflicts of law (*intergentiel recht*),[47] while Logemann pointed out the international-legal consequences implied in the existence of the status of Netherlands Indies subject and subject of the Indonesian states prior to 1910.[48] Even so, later research has shown that these scholars, too, did not observe the recent history of international law closely enough to be able to draw much from it, although there were enough reminiscences of that recent past in their own time.

Those reminiscences of the history of international law in Indonesia before 1910 did not merely concern subject status and the nationality of vessels.[49] The "long contracts" and the "short declarations" concluded with the self-governing territories—partly made available in print in 1929 by the Department of the Interior [50]—continued to be referred to as "treaties" in the Indies State Regulation (Indische Staatsregeling), and the exceptional rights enjoyed by Netherlands subjects in those territories were still called "extraterritorial" rights even though by then there was every reason to cease doing so. Indeed, it seemed impossible for people of a later time to imagine how deep-going the application and effect of international private law principles had been prior to 1910 in the field of what was at first called quasi-international and later conflicts of law (*intergentiel recht*) concerning rights on the soil and mixed marriages; nor have they appreciated its impact on the area of that extraordinary international private law, later called interregional law, which showed points of contact both to private law in the "realm in Europe" and to the many kinds of private law of the Netherlands Indies realm.[51]

It is only since 1950 that the history of international law in Indonesia has appeared to grow noticeably toward maturity as a science —at least wherever the international legal surroundings, immediate

[46] Van Asbeck's articles "L'Elément international aux Indes Néerlandaises," "*Grotius*," *Annuaire international pour 1935*, and *The Netherlands Indies' Foreign Relations*, published by the National Council for the Netherlands and the Netherlands Indies of the Institute of Pacific Relations, on the occasion of the Virginia Study Conference of that institute in 1939.

[47] R. D. Kollewijn, *Intergentiel recht: Verzamelde opstellen* (The Hague, 1955).

[48] Logemann, "De afbakening van rechtsmacht tussen gouvernementsrechter en landschapsrechter," *Indisch Tijdschrift van het Recht*, CXLVII (1938), 399 ff.

[49] Colijn, *Politiek*, pt. II B (2d ed.; 1914), pp. 73, 75, and 130–131; and my essay named in note 25, pp. 246–248.

[50] See *Mededeelingen van de Afdeeling Bestuurszaken der Buitengewesten van het Departement van Binnenlandsch Bestuur*, Ser. A, no. 3 (1929).

[51] See my article cited in note 24, pp. 1–39.

and global, have provided the scope and spiritual climate for this. It has been mostly Dutch jurists who have scientifically investigated the Indonesia-Dutch Union Statute [52] and various other recent events and phenomena with relevance to international law; and they have done this not merely in articles or symposia [53] but also in dissertations and other books specifically devoted to the problem.[54] He who sees history as beginning a fraction of a second ago shall consider what took place after 1950 or 1942 to be part of the history of international law in Indonesia, even though it belongs not to the dead past but to the still-living present. Whoever sees events begin to be history only before 1942 or before 1910—"begin" in the sense of the "backward-working" method used by Karl Löwith in his *Meaning in History* [55] and applied to Indonesia on a lesser scale by Hooykaas in his *Perintis Sastera* [56]— will at least concede that in 1955 the dissertations of Alders and Noorduyn brought the history of international law in Indonesia to maturity as a science concerning the reality of the more distant past.

Alders' dissertation is completely devoted to the international arbitrations between the Indonesian states and the VOC before 1700; and it has produced more material from one century than van Boetzelaer (1929) was able to find for all Dutch international arbitrations from 1581 to 1794.[57] Heeres had pointed out to van Boetzelaer the importance of the material contained in the company treaties, but it was

[52] See E. Utrecht, *Pengantar dalam Hukum Indonesia* (4th ed.; Jakarta, 1957), p. 357, note 135.

[53] See, for example, the contributions referring to Indonesia in *Volkenrechtelijke opstellen,* published in honor of Professors B. M. Telders, F. M. Baron van Asbeck, and J. H. W. Verzijl (Zwolle, 1957), and in *Symbolae Verzijl,* presented to Professor J. H. W. Verzijl on the occasion of his seventieth anniversary (The Hague, 1958).

[54] See, among others, A. A. Zorab, *De Japanse bezetting van Indonesië en haar volkenrechtelijke zijde* (dissertation, Leyden, 1954); E. C. Sohns, *Arbeidsrecht, arbeidsconventies en de samengestelde staatsvorm: De ontwikkeling van Nederlands-Indië tot de Verenigde Staten van Indonesië en de betrekkingen met de Internationale Arbeidsorganisatie* (The Hague, 1950); and E. P. F. Tervooren, *Statenopvolging en de financiële verplichtingen van Indonesië* (The Hague, 1957). There are also various articles on Indonesia in the *Nederlands Tijdschrift voor Internationaal Recht,* while some dissertations have dealt in part with Indonesia; see among others the list of literature in my essay cited in note 5, pp. 467–468, note 82.

[55] Karl Löwith, *Meaning in History: The Theological Implications of the Philosophy of History* (Chicago, 1949).

[56] C. Hooykaas, *Perintis Sastera* (Jakarta, 1951).

[57] See E. O. van Boetzelaer, *Nederlandsche internationale arbitrages tussen 1581 en 1794* (dissertation, Leyden, 1929), supplemented by my essay "Nederlandse internationale arbitrages waarbij de Compagnie betrokken is geweest," *Tijdschrift van het Recht,* 1948, pp. 271 ff., and L. W. Alders, *Internationale rechtspraak tussen Indonesische rijken en de V.O.C. tot 1700* (dissertation, Nijmegen, 1955).

more than a quarter of a century before they were worked through by Alders. And the admirable dissertation by Noorduyn—Orientalist again and no jurist—brought to sudden light material on sixteenth-century inter-Indonesian international law [58] of such significance that we may view that era as of decisive importance for the expansion and development of international law in Indonesian history from both a Europe-centric and an Indonesia-centric point of view.

In spite of all this, the history of international law remains a needy science. It is, in fact, in want of much more support from scholarly workers—jurists as well as historians, Orientalists as well as sociologists. Without those who can point the way to the comprehension and interpretation of the materials which are at hand and on which such history must be based, it will remain sickly even in maturity. Indonesian historians will not, however, have to call on the unknown goddess to whom van Vollenhoven directed himself in the "Invocation" to his book *Du droit de paix;* for they can turn, more in Indonesian character and with greater justification, to the familiar Dewi Saraswati with his words "Chante-moi donc, o déesse, cette histoire trop longtemps négligée afin que notre génération tourmentée se regarde dans ce précieux miroir, et s'y instruise." [59]

III

It is fortunate that in considering the history of international law in Indonesia as "usable past" the scholar needs only to worry about whether that past is actually a useful scientific tool for understanding a future that begins only a fraction of a second before us. That it *is* usable to the student can be seen most recently in the fact that since 1955 such divergent figures as Mohammad Ali and Gouw Giok Siong, Korn and van der Kroef, Notohamidjojo and Soedjatmoko, Utrecht and Wertheim, have taken into account the findings of international legal history, while only Gouw Giok Siong and Utrecht have touched solely on its juridical-historical significance.[60] Its scientific usefulness for the very near future can, moreover, be seen from the fact that to my knowledge there are now seven Indonesian jurists, one Indonesian historian, and a Dutch Orientalist who are engaged in research which

[58] On the further significance of the dissertation by Noorduyn cited in note 10, see my essay named in note 5, pp. 442, 445, 448, 450–453.

[59] Van Vollenhoven, *Du droit de paix*, p. xi.

[60] See Gouw Giok Siong, *Segi² Hukum Peraturan Perkawinan Tjampuran* (dissertation, Jakarta, 1955; 2d ed., Jakarta, 1958), pp. 67, 68, and Utrecht, *Pengantar*, pp. 462–464, 535–536.

is wholly or very largely in this field.[61] This surprising usefulness of
the recent development of Indonesian international law was most
marked in the provinces of the general political, economic, and theoretical history of Indonesia.

For general political history it is naturally of importance that until
about 1910 Netherlands India was a state among other states in Indonesia and that enormous territories of the archipelago lay outside it
until 1907. Of no less significance is the manner in which the international feudal relationship between the VOC—later the Netherlands
Indies—on the one hand and the Indonesian states on the other appears
to have been compatible both with the independent existence of those
Indonesian states as subjects of international law and with their dependent existence as communities of law within the colony. This was
first brought to light by an eighteenth-century company report, which
was published in the nineteenth century and then neglected until 1940
by all writers on the feudal relationship, with the result that for decades (and more) the historical myth was preserved which claimed that
wherever a feudal relationship was introduced the Indonesian vassal
state promptly lost its independence and sovereignty.[62]

A third consequence of the rapid development of this branch of
history has been that it has given rise to attempts at completely different periodizations of Indonesia's history, of which that by Mohammad Ali, proposed at the Jogjakarta History Seminar of 1957, is
the most interesting in both content and methodology.[63] A fourth consequence, finally, of the discovery of what the *"state"* of the Company
and the state of the Netherlands Indies were *not* has been the discovery of what the Indonesian realms could have been—indeed must have
been—in international relations and international legal practice.
Through this it became clear how, even in Java, the relations of the
Princely Territories to the Government were loose and of a postinter-
national legal character, a feature which they maintained into the
present century and which makes it understandable that these lands
played such an extraordinary role in the nationalist movement.[64] This

[61] See *Berita M.I.P.I.*, II, no. 6 (Dec., 1958), 6, previously cited in note 5.
[62] For a more detailed discussion see my article "De rechts-historische ontwikkeling van het zelfbestuur op Madoera," *Indisch Tijdschrift van het Recht*, CXLIX
(1939), 732–775, and CL (1939), 1–21.
[63] See Mohammed Ali, "Sjarat² Mengarang Kitab Sedjarah Indonesia jang
bertjorak Nasional," report in the collection *Prasaran² dan kesimpulan² Seminar
Sedjarah 14–18 Desember 1957 di Djokjakarta*, pp. 1–11.
[64] See my paper *Java, 1900–1930*, written in 1958 for the Institute of Social
Studies in The Hague, no. SS/58–60/9a/i, pp. 20–23.

fact had its more-than-symbolic aftermath in the removal of the seat of government from Jakarta to Jogjakarta in 1945 and the actual transfer of sovereignty—alongside the formal transfer which took place in the Netherlands—of the last remnants of authority and power from the grip of the Dutch Representative of the Crown to the hands of the Sultan of Jogjakarta.

Van Leur's work on international trade in the archipelago is thrown into sharper relief against the background of seventeenth-century international legal relations,[65] for international commerce is the twin sister of the international contract. Moreover, the book by Burger and Prajudi on the social-economic history of Indonesia, published in 1958, notes more clearly than did the works of Wertheim and Gonggrijp the difference between the Netherlands Indies colony of Java and the outside world of Indonesian princedoms and states which existed until the twentieth century.

Seen in an economic-historical light, such important dates as the establishment of the KPM (Royal Dutch Packet Company) in 1888 and the Royal Dutch Shell in 1890, the first export of gasoline to the Netherlands in 1901, the introduction of the plantation cultivation of rubber in Sumatra in 1903 and in Java in 1906, the founding of the BPM (Batavian Petroleum Company) in 1907, and the beginning of the large-scale cultivation of oil palms in the now-familiar year 1910 are all more closely related to the years at the turn of the century, in which the Dutch abandoned their famous policy of noninterference in the islands outside Java, than with the year 1870, made "classical" by earlier economic-historical evaluations which linked the just-mentioned developments to the Agrarian Law, the direct application of which in the Agrarian Regulation was, however, limited to Java and Madura. In view of these generally known facts concerning the ships and the rubber and the oils on which the economy of the Netherlands Indies increasingly came to float, it is not surprising to see how Boeke's famous dissertation—dating again from 1910 and stating for the first time the problem of a tropical, colonial or dual, economy—relies in great part on facts which apply to the economic conditions on Java alone,[66] though that island's economy could not in any case have been drifting about on the well-known cork of its sugar industry.

[65] See my essay "Over ons gemeenschappelijk verleden in het recht van vrede," in *Gedenkboek rechtswetenschappelijk hoger onderwijs in Indonesië, 1924–1929* (Groningen and Jakarta, 1949), pp. 256–257.

[66] D. H. Burger and Prajudi Atmosudirdjo, *Sedjarah Ekonomis Sosiologis Indonesia*, I (Jakarta, 1957–1958), pp. 279 ff.

Completely in accord with all this is Cowan's demonstration, more recent than that made by Burger and Prajudi, that the image of one great Netherlands Indies has remained incomplete until this century in its economic aspect, as witness the fact that not until about 1920 were "sea-borne trade and communications of the archipelago centered on Java," while prior to that "the trade of most of the outer islands was channeled, not through Batavia, but through Singapore, and most of it was in non-Dutch hands." [67] Indeed, about 50 per cent of the "Eastern Archipelago" in the beginning of this century still lay outside the customs area of the Netherlands Indies. This situation only came to an end in 1913, with the exception of the Riau Archipelago. Parallel to the extension of the territory and the extension of the customs area of the Netherlands Indies in the first decade of this century runs the extension of the sphere of exclusive circulation of its currency. During that time in Sumatra (Acheh, Sumatra's eastern coast, Tapanuli, Jambi, Indragiri, Riau) and on the western coast of Borneo, several kinds of dollars were still circulating and the inroads made by the circulation of the so-called Straits dollar in Riau up till now are all too well known.[68] The tenacity with which the colony, even in its greatest expansion and deepest impact, preserved its "international character" in its juridical, economic, and international-political aspects was referred to more than once in the 1930's by an authority on international law of such stature and erudition as van Asbeck.[69]

We may note in passing that the consequences of our knowledge of international legal history shall only become clear for both the recent and the older history of Indonesian civilization when we cull from the treaties not merely more facts about juridical institutions and economic relations but also information concerning, for example, the spreading of Christianity by the VOC or the process of reverse acculturation that

[67] C. D. Cowan, "Indonesia and the Commonwealth in South-east Asia: A Reappraisal," *International Affairs*, XXXIV, no. 4 (Oct., 1958), 456–457.

[68] See the State Gazettes concerning the original circumference and the gradual extension of the Netherlands Indies custom areas, enumerated in F. C. Hekmeyer, *Alphabetisch register op de Staats en Bijbladen van Nederlandsch Indië* (Nijmegen, 1926), pp. 141–143; concerning the circulation of several kinds of foreign currency, see G. Vissering in ch. vi. "Muntwezen-Handel-Bankwezen" in pt. II of H. Colijn's *Neerlands Indië* (2d ed.; Amsterdam, 1913), pp. 244–247.

[69] In addition to F. M. Baron van Asbeck's articles listed under note 46 we may also mention his dissertation *Onderzoek naar den juridischen wereldbouw* (Leyden, 1916), his Dies Natalis speech *Samenhang van internationaal en koloniaal recht* (Batavia, 1931), and his inaugural address *Internationale invloed in koloniaal bewind* (Leyden, 1939). See also the literature listed on p. 463, note 4, of the book by Utrecht cited in note 52.

saw the Company take over the institution of *shahbandars* [70] and even respect ideas regarding mixed marriages, which judged the status of the married couple and their children according to the criteria of double-unilateral systems of relationship.[71]

The causes of the development and growth of the science of the history of international law in these last few years have brought us, finally, to the terrain of what Romein calls theoretical history—a subject which we can understand in Indonesia's case only if we recognize the fundamental cultural subjectivity of even this variety of history. If we have touched the edge of this field in dealing with new periodizations inspired by the history of international law, we move to the very heart of it when we ask ourselves why political history in general and the juridical sciences in particular were once able to overlook this reality and now suddenly are so concerned with it. The answer to this question shows not only how subjective historiography can be in what it sees but also how subjective it can be in what it does not see. And the penetrating question of how it happened that historians could be so blind to a history for which the published materials alone are overwhelming in quantity leads us to the myths or images of history which, as socialized historical tales, typify how a given culture is—or, more important, is not—willing or able to make history out of the past available to it.[72] It is the enormous imbalance between the large amount of material and the limited number of scholars working on it which threatens the historian of international law, here as elsewhere, with the danger of two sorts of overgreat subjectivity: first, that arising from the side of the subject matter itself, and, second, that coming from the side of the historian's subjective colleagues, who still have too much freedom of movement in their field to develop that balance weight of internal discipline so necessary to hold their scientific material and the scholarly opinions concerning it in that balanced subjectivity which we may call objective. In short, the history of Indonesian international law can serve as an illustration that will make understandable some problems with which theoretical history is now wrestling, a fact that is all the more important because theoretical history in and concerning Indonesia itself is still so young in years and poor in spirit.

The history of international law can be a liberating factor first of all

[70] See my article "Volkenrecht in vroeger Makassar," *Indonesië*, VI, no. 5 (1953), 400–403.
[71] See *Corpus Diplomaticum Neerlando Indicum*, pt. VI (1955), p. 14 (under XVIII), p. 416 (under XV), p. 446 (under 17), and p. 717 (under 18).
[72] See my article "Uit het stof van een beeldenstorm," pp. 445–446.

in the sense that it can free us from viewpoints too centered about the Netherlands and about Java and can show us methods of approach to Indonesia outside the history of the Javanese and Dutch on that island or elsewhere in the archipelago.[73] Other types of history, of course, can do this and thus contribute to a more Indonesia-centric and truly national historiography. However, the international character of the law of nations gives it the added advantage that it works not only in a liberating but also in a disciplining manner and can thus help prevent a nationalistic historiography which would cause us to repeat on a larger scale the same sort of Ptolemaic history writing that has entrapped the "provincial" historiographies—the Javanese, the Macassar Buginese, the Malay and the European colonial, of which the last was so closely bound to the culture of what du Perron called "the province of the province." [74]

The history of international law in Indonesia is becoming more and more closely involved with the history of global international law in both reality and theory. It is preeminently Copernican in attitude and aims and can thus be highly useful in freeing us from provincial-historical shortcomings and in protecting us from nationalistic-historical exaggerations, to the benefit of a truly national, self-created, and yet internationally acceptable Indonesian historiography. It can thus help to lead that historiography between its subject and its subjective writers at home and abroad toward that historical objectivity, which is a form of what Gabriel Marcel named "intersubjectivity." [75] But it can deserve that title only when it has come to recognize its fundamental subjectivity and by doing so distances itself from it.

[73] *Ibid.*   [74] E. du Perron, *Indies Memorandum* (Amsterdam, 1946), p. 17.
[75] Gabriel Marcel, *L'Homme problématique* (Paris, 1955), p. 70.

XX

The Significance of the Comparative Approach in Asian Historiography

BY J. M. ROMEIN

Late Professor of Theoretical History,
Municipal University of Amsterdam

THE NATIONAL AND SOCIAL REVOLUTION IN ASIA AND THE TIME FACTOR

The great English scholar Edward B. Tylor was perhaps the first to make extensive and intensive use of the comparative approach in one of the social sciences in preparing the material for his *Anthropology: An Introduction to the Study of Man and Civilization* that appeared in 1881. A couple of years later Emile Durkheim, the famous French sociologist, defended the same approach for his branch of study against the objections of Mill in his much-read *Règles de la méthode sociologique* from 1897. He even came to the conclusion that this was the only method fit for sociology, seeing in it an indispensable substitute for the experiment of the natural sciences. In the course of time other human sciences followed the lead of anthropology and sociology, e.g., the modern sciences of religion and literature.

But there was one exception: history seemed to fear the comparative approach. Although comparisons, e.g., between two rulers or two peoples, were not unknown in historiography, they were casual and in any case not accepted as a legal technique of research as was done by the other human sciences. Only some "revolutionary" historians like Karl Lamprecht and Kurt Breysig tried to apply this new method.

There was a reason for this lag. In the years around 1900 history, more than the other social sciences, rejected the lead of natural sciences. Therefore it stressed the uniqueness of all historical facts and situations, and of course to compare a phenomenon which *per definitionem* has no resemblance whatever to any other is futile. This was true as far as our knowledge goes, even into the twenties when the German historian Georg von Below persisted in rejecting the historical comparison as a useful instrument in understanding historical developments. He got his article, called "The Comparative Method," published in one of the leading historical periodicals in Germany. Thus it was some time before historians, too, began to understand that notwithstanding this uniqueness it could be fruitful to compare historical phenomena with one another, differences being eventually as instructive as resemblances—of course on condition that the historical or sociological categories used are applicable in both cases. They began to realize that uniqueness did not exclude common features. Is not every human individual unique? But do not all individuals nonetheless have certain fundamental characteristics in common? As evidence of this modern view the present writer may be allowed to quote one of his own writings. In a speech made and published shortly after World War II he distinguishes between "practical" and "historiological" subjects, defining the latter as subjects of a processual kind that are built up out of *comparisons* of historical phenomena in different times and in different places.

The comparative approach turned out to be very useful especially for broad subjects such as the study of civilizations or when one tries to find out, for example, what the common features are in situations leading to wars or to revolutions. Nowadays this technique can be said to be accepted among historians no less than in the other social sciences.

In the opinion of the present writer there is nevertheless one aspect of historical comparisons that seems to be neglected, the time factor. By time factor in this context is not meant that the phenomena to be compared happened in different times, for that goes without saying. What is meant is that the historian comparing two historical processes has to ask himself how much time the one took and how much the other and in what way and how much this difference in tempo may have influenced the final result. With the excuse that my subject may seem rather ambitious and refers only to Indonesia as part of a far bigger complex of countries—the present writer not being specialized in Indonesian history—I should like to apply this idea of the influence of the time factor on what is perhaps the main feature of contemporary history, i.e., the Asian revolution.

It will take generations of Asian historians to establish all the facts concerning this revolution from its hesitant beginnings to its final victory and from Turkey in Asia's Far West to Japan in the Far East. It will take more generations of them to solve the series of problems underlying these facts, from the preparatory role played willy-nilly by European imperialism and colonialism to the decisive role played by the countless nationalist movements in the revival or the awakening of the peoples concerned.

It is the purpose of the present paper to draw attention to one of the most difficult and at the same time one of the most urgent problems involved in the process. For the present writer is of the opinion that, although he as a contemporary and as a European knows less of what happened during this revolution, and even far less of what it exactly meant, than future Asian historians will know, there nevertheless is a possibility that he—and other European contemporaries—can help these colleagues by relating to them their own impressions of the period and by testing these impressions by some sociohistorical categories they (the Europeans) are accustomed to work with.

Take, for example, the writer's own case. He was a boy of about twelve years in 1905 but he nevertheless remembers quite well how deeply he was impressed by the defeats of the Russians and the victories of the Japanese in their war of 1904–1905. Being a contemporary, he does not need to learn from books about the primary importance of that phenomenon. It is clear to him without more ado that if he felt its impact at so tender an age and so great a distance, grown-up people in the more involved countries must have felt it far more deeply.

And as a European scholar he has the advantage of being able to compare some features of this Asian revolution with what happened in the European past. Up to a certain degree what happened in Asia in the course of this century can be seen as a repetition, on an immense scale and in another far bigger scene, of the revolutionary dramas played on a minor scale and a smaller stage in his own continent. For it is not true that history does not repeat itself, although it is true that it never repeats itself in quite the same way, surroundings and circumstances being always different. Take, for example, nationalism. No one can deny that the idea commonly called nationalism—with its historical, political, economic, social, cultural, and psychological elements and its international complications—originated in Europe and that it was unknown in the past to the Asian mind. In Asia the feeling of loyalty was directed either to the village and its nearby headman or to the far-off prince—exactly as was the case in Europe before the nation-state arose and drew loyalty toward itself. Therefore, knowing how complex a phenomenon nationalism is and how substantially it changed in the course of European history and again changed as it reached the minds of Asians and Africans in this century, the writer of this paper has no difficulty in imagining how difficult or even impossible it is likely to be for future Asian historians to grasp its essence and its influence, the more so because, however important it may have been as a stimulant to historical progress, it is now beginning to dwindle in a world that is bound to unite on penalty of complete destruction.

The last example brings us within the orbit of the problem we intend to deal with in these pages. For that reason we must say a few words more about the history of nationalism in the beginning of this century. At the same time as it began to trespass on the minds of those relatively few Asians educated in Europe or America or otherwise imbued with ideas from the West, it began to become a problem for some Europeans themselves—that is to say, not for the ruling class or its bourgeois followers and not for the laborers and peasants who, on the contrary, around the turn of the century began to feel themselves members of the nation-state in a measure they never had before, because of their rising standard of living. Both groups took nationalism for granted. But a problem it was for the opposition, the social democrats—and especially for its left wing, the true Marxists. Internationally minded as they were, nationalism was indeed one of their main points of attack against existing society. Was it not in its dividing force incompatible with the Marxian slogan, "Workers of the world, unite"?

It was, however, not as easy as that. Marx and Engels never formulated a distinct theory about nationalism and the part it played, according to them, in the development of world history. Moreover, things were not alike in this respect in Western and Eastern Europe. In the supranational empires of Russia, Austria-Hungary, and Turkey, dominated by a reactionary ruling class, and in the eastern parts of the German Empire, nationalism was a revolutionary force. Therefore not all Marxists held the same view on the problem of how to handle the nationalist trend among the minorities subject to these empires.

Roughly speaking, there seemed to be three solutions. One of them, advocated by Rosa Luxemburg, a Pole by birth, denied the future of

nationalities. Imperialism in her opinion would create bigger and bigger states and therefore the creation of many small nation-states could
only hamper the inevitable course of history. A second theory was defended by the Austrian Marxists Karl Renner and Otto Bauer. They
championed the policy of neutralizing the dangers of nationalism by
denying the national minorities all political rights but by granting
them a life of their own in all cultural fields. The third idea finally was
Lenin's—to unleash the forces of nationalism in order to further social
revolution.[1] In view of what has happened since World War I his idea
was the most revolutionary and at the same time the most realistic, or,
better perhaps, the most revolutionary while the most realistic. No one
will deny that the longing for a nationhood of their own fostered by
the subjected peoples was the main explosive force to split up the empire of Austria-Hungary and Turkey as well as the colonial empires of
Spain, Great Britain, France, the Netherlands, and Belgium; in the same
way it will cause in the end the fall of the only remaining colonial
"empire," that of Portugal. In the conference of Baku, held in the first
days of September, 1920, on Lenin's instigation, we see that idea of his,
so to speak, in action.[2]

However, the problem the present writer has in mind is not the
problem of nationalism as such; it is only connected with it, as has
already been said. The problem he has in mind is that of the *time
factor*, time playing quite a different part in the Asian revolution of
today from what it used to do in the European revolutions of the past.
Before, however, he can make clear what precisely is meant by this,
he has to expose another major problem of the Asian revolution, viz.,
that the national and political aspects of that revolution are intertwined inextricably with its social and economic aspects. This can be
seen quite clearly if we press somewhat further the above analysis of
the Marxian attitude toward nationalism.

The Second Congress of the Third International, the so-called Comintern, gathered at Moscow shortly before the Baku conference at the
end of July, 1920. It was attended by delegates not merely from the
non-Russian peoples of the former Czarist empire but from India, Persia, China, and Korea too. The newly founded Communist Party of

---

[1] I am indebted for this analysis to Mr. H. Daalder, who spoke about "Marxism
and the problem of nationalities" in a meeting of the Sociohistorical Circle, Nov.,
1958, Amsterdam.

[2] A French edition of the records of that conference is to be found in the International Institute of Social History at Amsterdam, *Le Premier Congrès des peuples
de l'Orient, Bakou 1920* (Editions de l'Internationale Communiste; Petrograd, 1921).

Indonesia was represented by Sneevliet under the name of Maring, and one of the main topics was "the national and colonial question." To consider this question and to draft a report on it a commission was appointed with Maring as its secretary.[3]

In the commission the discussion was mainly between two sets of theses presented respectively by Lenin and by Manabendra Nath Roy, the well-known Indian Communist from Bengal. Both knew of course quite well that the eventual proclamation of political independence of the former colonies was not alone enough to liberate the Oriental peasants from oppression, exploitation, and misery. The core of Lenin's thesis was to recommend that Communists in colonial countries give "active support" to the "bourgeois-democratic national liberation movements." Roy's thesis, however, not only sharply distinguished the purely nationalist movement from the "struggle of landless peasants against every form of exploitation" but also advanced the opinion that "these two distinct movements grew farther apart every day." According to him, therefore, the task of the Comintern was to resist all attempts to subordinate the second type of movement to the first, although he declared himself not against the cooperation of the two movements.[4]

Because both theses met with the same degree of sympathy in the commission, in the end a compromise was arrived at. Lenin's theses, somewhat amended, were approved and sent to the Congress, together with Roy's also suitably amended proposals as "supplementary theses."[5]

Thus it is clear that from the outset the intermingling of the contrasting bourgeois and proletarian aspects and of the political and social trends of the revolutionary movements in Asia proved to be a very intricate one.[6] It was not only the Marxian theorists and politicians who differentiated these two aspects of the Asian revolutionary movement. The same was the case with so intelligent and well informed a man as

[3] A German edition of its proceedings is *Der Zweite Kongress der Kommunistischen Internationale* (Hamburg, 1921). The appointment of the commission is to be found on p. 101. Cf. E. H. Carr, *The Bolshevik Revolution, 1917–1923* (London, 1953), III, 251.

[4] Carr, *Bolshevik Revolution*, p. 254.

[5] *Ibid.*, p. 255 and note 2 on that page.

[6] For a fuller discussion of the problem and the study of the documents involved the reader may consult Xenia Joukoff Eudin and Robert C. North, *Soviet Russia and the East, 1920–1927: A Documentary Study* (Stanford, Calif., 1957), pt. I, "The Nationality and Colonial Policies of the Russian Communists," pp. 15–44, with twenty-two selected documents on pp. 45–71. The texts of Lenin's and Roy's theses are to be found in documents 18 and 19, respectively on pp. 63 and 65.

the former American Secretary of State, Dean Acheson. In 1950, after there had been much criticism of the American Government for throwing away $6,000,000,000 on assistance to the side in China which had lost, he said on March 15:

Two facts are common to all Asian peoples: one is rebellion against the conception that poverty and misery are normal things of life, and the other is revolt against foreign domination. No matter whether this domination has the form of colonialism or whether it assumes the cloak of imperialism—it is finished for good. The Asian people have had enough of it, and they do not want it any more.[7]

However, the fact alone that those aspects and trends were intertwined in the Asian revolution does not mark it as a special case distinguishing this revolution from all former ones. All revolutions we know, beginning with that of the Netherlands in the sixteenth century to the general European revolution of the mid-nineteenth century, show a political as well as a social side. In all of them the form of government was changed more or less drastically and at the same time a new social class often took power either temporarily or permanently. The difference, the deciding difference, however, between these earlier revolutions and those of our century, the Russian, the Chinese, and the general-Asian revolution, is the following as far as I can see: whereas in the first category the leading revolutionary group was one, viz., the middle class, and its political and social demands therefore were coordinated, this is clearly no longer the case in the second category. Now, the social demands do not have their origin in the bourgeoisie alone, but peasants and laborers are making their own social demands which are very different from those of the middle class. It is true that something of this cleavage in the revolutionary front can be seen more or less clearly also in the earlier revolutions. The "image breakers" in the revolution of the Netherlands and the Levelers and Diggers in the English revolution are more radical than the Calvinist merchants and the lower nobility or than Cromwell and his followers in respect to social theory. As evidence of this cleavage there exists, for example, the report of a discussion that lasted for many hours between supporters of Cromwell on the one side and the leaders of the radical revolutionaries on the other side, in the course of which discussion the latter propagated among other things the demand of general franchise, un-

[7] See Vlada Teslić, "China's Foreign Policy," in *Review of International Affairs* (Belgrade), IX (Sept. 16, 1958), 6.

heard of at that time. And this cleavage becomes wider and wider as we approach our own times.

In the great French revolution the conspiracy of the secret society of the "Equals," as they called themselves (1796–1797), is a clear indication of the discrepancy between the main current and this undercurrent. And it is no wonder that this conflict ended with the execution of Babeuf, the leader of the "Equals." Even more clear is this lower-middle-class undercurrent in the revolution of February, 1848, in Paris, as is shown by the insurrection in June of the same year; whereas in the year 1871 the "Commune" of Paris was exclusively the affair of the radical lower and lowest middle classes. Hence it was only a question of about ten weeks before this uprising was smothered in blood.

The Russian revolution, however, is the first classic example of a revolution of the modern type. Already the frustrated attempt of the Russian middle class to seize power in 1905 was not the affair of that liberal class alone; peasants and laborers played a part in it, and not only as a blind tool for that matter. When that same liberal middle class repeated its endeavor twelve years later, in March, 1917, their effort turned out to be, it is true, a success; but half a year later, in November, it had become clear that its proletarian "allies" in the struggle against czarism were already so strong that they could seize power themselves under the guidance of the Communist Party. And the proletariat dismissed not only czardom but the middle class itself forever.

The Chinese revolution developed, it is true, at a slower pace but shows virtually the same picture. The struggle for power between the Chinese middle class and the old order lasted for about fifteen years, from 1911, when Sun Yat-sen succeeded in overthrowing the dynasty of the Manchus, till 1926—if we take the reunion of the empire under Chiang Kai-shek as the end of the first revolutionary stage. But this victory proved to be of relatively short standing. The same Chiang Kai-shek who carried the day in 1926 was forced to flee from the scene of his victory out of fear of his proletarian opposite number, Mao Tse-tung, within the span of twenty-five years.

A comparison between the revolutions before the twentieth century and those of our own lifetime leads us therefore to the conclusion that the difference in time is decisive. The middle-class revolutions of the past had the time for consolidation and development; those of the present are followed before long by a proletarian revolution—or at least there is this tendency to be seriously reckoned with. And the more so is this true because the Asian middle class generally is weak, as the Russian and Chinese middle classes were relatively weak. Above all, the Asian middle class is weak in numbers. Even in that part of the continent where it is strongest in this respect, viz., in India, it is small compared with the teeming population as a whole. Moreover, in every part of Asia the middle class is young. In this respect again a comparison with Europe shows that the middle class there had at its disposal, if one may say so, no less than 400 years—from about 1350 till 1750 —to prepare itself for the function of government; and after that again, about 200 years to exercise this function without being seriously disturbed either from "above" or from "below." For in this period the kings and their noblemen became weaker and weaker, and during the last part of that period, labor became stronger and stronger. But in doing so it became at the same time, to a certain degree, part of the middle class itself, as the American example shows best. That means, in short, that the Asian middle class had at best only as many decades to develop, to prepare itself for government, and to exercise power as the European middle class had centuries.

It is this difference in available time that causes a series of problems, each of which accentuates the already-marked weakness of the Asian middle class. Even as a ruling class they have not been able to gain, in the short time since they took over power from the colonial rulers, the social prestige that the European middle class had won long before it had to rule. Even now, to give only one example, money as such does not give direct social standing in Asia. This is the reason that middle-class people imitate and have to imitate the feudal classes, in the same way the European middle classes did over a long span of time. As a consequence they either invest the money they earn in landed property or spend it in "conspicuous waste." This means that the Asian middle class does not accumulate capital—or at least not enough of it—from the money earned in commerce or industry, and this in its turn means that there is a shortage of investment in modern industry and transport.

On the other hand, the need for industrialization in Asian countries is even greater than it was for those of Europe, as it seems to be the only way to raise the standard of living of the masses. And that again is an inescapable necessity, for two reasons. The first is that the rate of population growth in Asian countries is higher than anywhere else except in South America, which is in about the same condition. For it is a fact that the rate of mortality is already decreasing sharply, thanks to better hygiene and health practices, even if nutrition remains at the same insufficient level. (At mid-century the average death rate was 28 per thousand for the countries of South and Southeast Asia. The birth rate, however, did not go down markedly. In the same countries at the same time it was between 41 and 45 per thousand.) The second reason is that the masses of today are less and less willing to accept poverty and misery as nature's normal course or as God's inscrutable will. They too nowadays want to live better than their parents did and want to have their children live better still.

Of course this means progress. But progress has to be paid for by a higher rate of productivity. Again a comparison of the present industrial revolution in Asia with that of Europe in the first half of the nineteenth century is informative. If we reckon the industrial revolution in England to begin about 1750, British industry took 200 years to reach the point where it is now. It is true that for the other industrialized countries this period was shorter, but nevertheless it took the United States and France some 150 years, Germany about 100, and Russia and Japan still some 50 years. On the other side the question may be asked: is it possible to accelerate the rate of industrialization in Asia above the Japanese and Russian rate? But on the other hand one may ask: is half a century not too long a period for Asia? One has to ask whether in the meantime its standard of living is not bound to go down instead of rising. One thing only seems certain: peasants and laborers will formulate their demands more sharply and fight for them more desperately if their living conditions do not improve quickly enough. Again time is the decisive factor.

The time factor is the more decisive because it is not only the lack of capital of the Asian middle classes that hampers a thorough and rapid industrialization. Capital alone does not do the trick. It is, so to say, only the machine; it is not the oil that runs it. Let us suppose capital could be available in a short time and in sufficient quantity either by an intentional lowering of the standard of living for a period of transition (as was done in Russia and China, where people had to save willy-nilly) or by loans from abroad or in some other way. Then the fact remains that it takes time to familiarize people with regulated labor, which is inevitably connected with modern methods of production. Again we may learn from the European experience. It was not long ago that the European laborer protested against the monotonous, machinelike regularity of the process of labor. One cannot make out of an artisan who is used to mapping out his day as he likes, or out of a peasant who is used to going to his field only if need be, a factory hand who has to be punctual to the minute and has to work without interruption at the risk of being fired.

It is this problematic situation created by the time factor that may be found to be the deepest root of what I once called the " 'discordance' of the modern Asian middle class," in particular of the modern Asian intellectual. It is the intellectual with his subtle "feeling" for the slightest trembling of the soil beneath him who "registers" this situation most exactly, even though in all probability he is not aware of what makes him feel uncertain about himself. The fact is that his own social situation is "discordant"—and that in more than one respect. In the first place, he finds himself between past and present, a position, it is true, typical for every revolutionary situation but more marked in his case because his very modern present is very far away from his feudal past, much farther than the few years of transition may account for. In the second place—and that is more important—he avows himself to be a nationalist, but at the same time he knows, or at least he fears, that the idea of nationalism too is doomed in its orthodox form. He feels that nationalism was needed to make his nation independent, but at the very moment it reached that stage, he discovered that absolute independence is a thing of the past. It is not by chance that Nasser federated his Egyptian state with that of Syria and, by calling the federation the United Arab Republic, even gave up the age-old name of Egypt; nor that one of the first things Nkrumah did as the leader of the foreign policy of Ghana was to federate his state with newly independent French Guinea. And it is a token of the times to come that the French Africans founded a new political party called Party of African Federation with the outspoken view that the greatest problem of black Africa is the realization of African unity. These examples show that in modern times the negation of strict nationalism may even precede its full realization. In the third place—and that is most important—there is the fact that, as a consequence of the short span of time in which his national revolution was enacted and with the social revolution on the verge of being enacted, the position of his class *is* "discordant." For whereas the Asian middle class was more or less revolutionary as regards national independence to be gained, he is more or less inclined to the contrary as regards the social revolution that is on the order of the day. It is easy to grasp how this threefold "discordance" of the Asian intellectual is a function of the time factor.

With the foregoing in mind it is as easy to understand the peculiarly difficult position of the leaders of the political revolution in Asia. One would think of their problems as insoluble if one did not realize that history is averse to insoluble problems. What will be the way out of this "discordance" no one can tell. One can only pass on it a judgment of a very general nature. Nothing in history has ever been either purely an advantage or purely a disadvantage. History is not as simple as that. The main disadvantage of the time factor in the Asian revolution we hope is made clear in these pages—the intertwining of its political and social aspects, complicated by the fact that more than one class is trying to mold state and society according to its own interests. But the advantage may perhaps be as undeniable: the same time factor will shorten the tremendously difficult transitional period to a new and more stabilized state of affairs to come.

If these pages are of any use at all, they teach us the tremendous impact of the immensely accelerated pace in which the twentieth-century revolutions took and take place compared with those of the past. But what, in its turn, does this fact teach us? In the opinion of the present author three things can be deduced from it, the first two of a theoretical, the last one of a practical, nature.

In the first place, it shows the usefulness or, perhaps better, the inevitability of the sociological approach to history in a case like this, in which we are confronted with so complicated a historical phenomenon as a series of revolutions—all different, it is true, as regards their historical and actual surroundings, but nevertheless clearly all of the same stamp. In the second place, we see the inevitable necessity of the comparative method in history. In the third place emerges the urgent question: what attitude is to be adopted toward the ambiguous phenomenon of nationalism in its present phase?

As to the first point, the sociological approach, we do not have to go further into it because our highly esteemed colleague Wertheim treated it, in his contribution to this volume, in a way that the present author cannot surpass. Regarding the second point, the comparative method in history, we will have to say a few words more. The effectiveness of the comparative method, not only for purely scientific conclusions but for practical solutions as well, has already been proved in sciences other than history. In 1955, to give only one of many examples, the Indian medical profession undertook a systematic analysis of the medication prescribed by the Ayurvedic system in order to ascertain the chemical properties and method of action of the traditional remedies and to make possible the incorporation of this knowledge into general medical practice.[8] And of course the method of these scholars was to compare their findings with modern medicines and medical procedures.

This effectiveness does not mean, of course, that the comparative approach to history is without dangers. On the contrary. It does not make any sense to compare historical phenomena too different to be compared at all. Thus one who intends to use this method has first of all to be very careful in finding out which phenomena he will compare and in what respect; his second duty is to be fully aware of, and to take fully into account, the different surroundings and circumstances that always are present in more or less comparable historical situations. And finally he may never push the comparison too far, for if it is true that history repeats itself, it is no less true that it never repeats itself in the same way. Always the time factor is playing its elusive part and always the freedom—restricted, it is true, but freedom nevertheless —of human initiative makes every situation different from all others. This is the reason why it is impossible even for the most shrewd historian to forecast the future. He may discern specific trends in the present time that seem certain to assert themselves in the future—but even then they will do so only if no disturbing factors halt or delay them.

As the reader will have observed, our comparison of the revolutions of former centuries in Europe with those in Asia of the present time led us to the conclusion that a collision of the bourgeois and proletarian trends of the political and social aspects of these recent revolutions may be at hand in the not too distant future. But this is all the more reason why the present author is inclined to stress the theoretical possibility that this dreadful situation can be averted. It can be averted by human initiative, if in every Asian country sociologists and historians will analyze the situation of their own country in this respect, carefully and in detail, and if the leaders and governments of these countries are farsighted enough to see the signs of the times, to interpret them correctly and to act accordingly. In carrying out this policy sociologists and historians are of no use; they are even of no great value in shaping it; but in analyzing the situation and in formulating, according to their findings, the fundamentals of the best policy to meet the situation, they may be of the highest value to their country. This is especially so if they make a cautious use of the comparative method,

[8] Quoted from the manuscript of vol. VI (twentieth century) of UNESCO's *History of the Scientific and Cultural Development of Mankind,* of which the present author happens to be coauthor-editor.

comparing the present situation in their own country not only with comparable situations in their own past, not only with situations in other countries in the past, but comparing it, above all, with present comparable situations abroad. In the opinion of the present writer it is the main task they have to fulfill at the present moment, the most precarious one, perhaps, their nation has ever experienced.

We will conclude with a last word on nationalism and its impact on the human mind. A word of warning it will be, if that may be allowed to an outsider. Granted that nationalism was an indispensable instrument to liberate the Asian peoples from the yoke of imperialism, it has to be avowed now that it cannot be the last word in the present circumstances. "One world or none" is not an empty slogan; it is simply the truth which we have to realize in order not to perish. If we may define an intellectual as the man who by the torch of his reason has to enlighten the path of his fellow men into the dark future—dark because it is never known beforehand—the intellectual more than others has to be free of any prejudice and of the pressure of persons in power. Nationalism is one of those prejudices and one of those "persons" in power. *This* lesson at least the European can teach the other peoples without any fear of being rebuked as a man who thinks he knows all things better than others, because on this point he is speaking out of his own sad and humiliating experience. Therefore he is justified in saying to the Asians and Africans: "We know you needed the blow-torch of nationalism in order to sever the chains of your humiliation, but be aware that fire is a devastating element even if it is used for a good end. Your nationalism was useful; it is dangerous, and it will be fatal if you do not control it."

How can one achieve that detached attitude toward one's own nation without ceasing to love it as a good patriot must?

The old cultural philosopher Chaadajev, who lived in Russia in the first half of the nineteenth century in a situation not incomparable to the one the newly liberated countries of Asia experience now, said it better than we can. In 1837 he wrote some lines by which the present author was impressed forever as he read them for the first time now twenty-five years ago. These lines run as follows:

Undoubtedly there is impatience in my way of expressing myself, exaggeration in my fundamental thoughts. But that which inspires me is not hostility toward my nation; it is only that our weaknesses possess and obsess me. . . . I think one can serve one's country only if one sees it clearly. I believe the time of blind nationalism has passed; nowadays we owe our country, above all, the truth. . . . Even more, I am convinced that we are called upon to solve the most urgent social problems. . . . The past is in our power no more, but the future is.[9]

[9] From his essay "Apologie eines Irrsinnigen" in Peter Tschaadajew, *Schriften und Briefe* (Munich, 1921), p. 151.

XXI

Aspects of an Indonesian Economic Historiography

By F. J. E. TAN

Lecturer in History of Economic Institutions
in Indonesia, University of Indonesia, Jakarta

ISAIAH BERLIN has observed that the Greek poet's dictum "the fox knows many things, but the hedgehog knows one big thing" (Archilochus) could be used to illustrate or typify the frame of mind of many writers and thinkers, if not human beings in general.[1] For there is a deep gulf between those who tend to relate everything to a single vision or principle and those who pursue many unrelated ends, unconnected to a dominant inner vision—in short, whose thought is centrifugal rather than centripetal. Perhaps the community of historians could be divided along the same lines, since there are those like St. Augustine, Toynbee, Romein, F. J. Turner, or Spengler, who each in a sense were and are historians of the "hedgehog type," and those multitudes of monographical authors, who are historians of the "fox type," from Herodotus onward.

Indonesian economic history like Southeast Asian history generally shows one basic pattern, according to the hedgehogs [2] in the field of

---

[1] Isaiah Berlin, *The Hedgehog and the Fox* (New York, 1957), p. 7; an essay on Tolstoy's view of history.

[2] See G. Gonggrijp, *Schets ener economische geschiedenis van Nederlands-Indië* (Haarlem, 1949); D. H. Burger, *Sedjarah Ekonomis Sosiologis Indonesia*, vol. I, Indonesianized and adapted by Prajudi Atmosudirdjo (Jakarta, 1960); J. S. Furnivall, *Netherlands India: A Study of a Plural Economy* (Cambridge, 1944), and *Colonial Policy and Practice: A Comparative Study of Burma and Netherlands India* (Cambridge, 1948). While not precisely histories, there are J. H. Boeke, *Economics and Economic Policy of Dual Societies as Exemplified by Indonesia* (New York, 1953),

Indonesian historiography, since behind and below all economic change, especially that of the past, a basic element could be discerned as the village community. It is said that from the economic historian's point of view the village is the most important economic organization. It would seem, then, that only those facts which have changed or influenced the organization and life in the village would be crucial. The economic history of Indonesia would especially tell the story of how changes are effected in the economic structure of the village. If, so to speak, there were no change for very long periods in the ways in which the village community met its primary needs, then no economic history of that particular community would be possible. But economic history as an aspect of history is a combination of continuity and surprise.[3] The economic history of Indonesia and that of Southeast Asia in general centers, in modern times, on the economic development of these regions, which implies the process of change in the economic structure of the village. It tells the story of how this process of change opened the closed village economy and linked it to an international economy.

A man who thought himself a hedgehog, but who was by nature a fox, is J. C. van Leur, who shortly before World War II caused a revolution in Indonesian historiography.[4] His ideas may be summarized as follows. Indonesian economic history cannot be adequately approached along the lines of Western European historical categories. For a correct view of Indonesian history, a system of categories is needed which should be constructed from the wealth of factual historical materials. Systems of historical periodizations as borrowed from European historiography prove to have little value as effective heuristic aids. Categories such as village, town, bourgeoisie, handicrafts, nobility, and central authority must be given their appropriate definitions if they are

---

and J. van Gelderen, *Voorlezingen over tropisch-koloniale staathuishoudkunde* (Haarlem, 1927). In the above-mentioned works, stress is generally laid on the economic history of Java. While not written as an apology for Western enterprise (p. 7), G. C. Allen and A. G. Donnithorne's *Western Enterprise in Indonesia and Malaya: A Study in Economic Development* (New York, 1957) is seemingly an example again of that kind of writing about an aspect of Indonesia's history which J. C. van Leur once labeled as observing Indonesia's past "from the deck of the ship, the ramparts of the fortress, the high gallery of the trading house" (p. 261). The achievements of Western enterprise in Indonesia are eulogized somewhat, and not much is found of an Indonesia-centric viewpoint in economic development.

[3] See J. Romein, *Tussen vrees en vrijheid* (Amsterdam, 1950), p. 276.

[4] G. J. Resink, "Uit het stof van een beeldenstorm," *Indonesië*, IX (1956), 433; W. F. Wertheim, "Early Asian Trade: An Appreciation of J. C. van Leur," *Far Eastern Quarterly*, XIII (1953–1954), 167–173.

to be used.[5] Historical terminology, the determination of historical categories, should result from the autonomous evolutionary process of Indonesian economic history itself. The wealth in forms of Indonesian historical experience and the autonomous nature of its historical perspectives require their own historiographic treatment.

Moreover, Indonesian history as well as Indonesian economic history is an international history. For many outside forces have shaped the Indonesian historical scene, be they cultural, religious, economic, or political. A coordinated economic history is therefore needed—an Indonesian economic history written in the broader context of the economic history of Southeast Asia in general.[6]

This division or contrast between hedgehogs and foxes in economic historiography perhaps refers to the dilemma and antinomy of human idea or theory and the wealth in forms of historical experience. The deep-digging economic historian perpetually faces this antinomy as to how to harness together lively perception and theoretical reasoning.[7] Human thought and therefore historical thought are antinomical or polarical. Concepts generally go in couples and represent two contraries. There is hardly any concrete reality which cannot be observed from two opposing staindpoints, which cannot consequently be subsumed under two contradictory concepts.[8] This seems, then, to be a characteristic of human thinking in general. Human thought is apparently hung up between two opposites, which tend to exclude each other.[9] There is, however, an inner harmony of opposing things, a

[5] J. C. van Leur, "On the Study of Indonesian History," in his *Indonesian Trade and Society* (The Hague, 1955), p. 152.

[6] *Ibid.*, p. 155.

[7] W. Eucken, *Die Grundlagen der Nationalökonomie* (Godesberg, 1947), p. 37, mentions the existence of the same problem in economic theory. This fundamental difficulty underlies the dilemma in the modern theories of economic fluctuations and their conscious or unconscious quest for *the* theory of the business cycle and also the irrealism of even modern price theories when checked with real pricing policies of commercial corporations. Cf. J. H. Williams, *Economic Stability in a Changing World* (New York, 1953), pp. 14–15, and A. R. Oxenfeldt, *Industrial Pricing and Market Practices* (New York, 1951), p. 82. Recently, Clyde Kluckhohn stressed again that the "crucial problems of present science generally are those of organized complexity" (Clyde Kluckhohn, "Common Humanity and Diverse Cultures," in D. Lerner, ed., *The Human Meaning of the Social Sciences* [New York, 1959], p. 266).

[8] H. Bergson, *An Introduction to Metaphysics* (New York, 1955), p. 38; J. H. Thiel, "Oude geschiedenis en historische kritiek, voorheen en thans," *MKAWAL*, new ser., XV, no. 6 (1952), 4.

[9] J. Huizinga, *In de schaduwen van morgen,* quoted from F. Weinreb, "Het statistisch karakter van economische wetten," *Ekonomi dan Keuangan Indonesia,* VIII, no. 5–6 (May–June, 1955), 284.

duplicity in identity. The knowledge and recognition of this dilemma by the economic historian of Indonesia perhaps will enable him to avoid or mitigate to a great extent the pitfalls connected with being either a hedgehog or a fox in historiography.

Historians in general, and therefore also economic historians, are like painters. Like painting, historical writing is an art; and all art has in itself something of the subjective. History is an attitude, a manner in which a civilization accounts for its past.[10] This, then, is a characteristic of history; and it seems to be especially so in the economic historiography of Indonesia until that of very recent times. With the almost total lack of quantitative data and source materials (statistics), a view of ancient Indonesian economic history, at least to the sixteenth century, could, seemingly, be only a framework of intelligent conjectures—and it would perhaps be fun for any insider to make them misconjectures! In contrast it could be said that economic history's methodological distinctiveness hinges primarily upon its marked quantitative interest; for this reason, therefore, it should be the most exact branch of history.[11] The ideal economic historian, as Clapham said, should have to a considerable degree what might be called the statistical sense, the habit of asking in relation to any institution, policy, group, or movement these questions: how large, how long, how often, and how representative.[12]

The economic history of Indonesia, and of Southeast Asia in general, is still in its infancy. This is not strange, since even in Europe and the United States, where economic history originated as a definite branch of history, it has existed only for the last eighty to a hundred years. The separate discipline of economic history did not gain institutional recognition until the end of the nineteenth century, when in 1892 the first chair in economic history anywhere was founded at Harvard University and was occupied by the British economic historian W. J. Ashley.[13]

The sources for an economic history of Indonesia are as indeterminate as they are heterogeneous. The study of these sources by economic historians is in many ways in its initial phase, and aspects change time and again.[14]

---

[10] J. Huizinga, *Verzamelde werken* (9 vols.; Haarlem, 1948–1953), VII, 102.

[11] J. Clapham, "Economic History as a Discipline," in F. C. Lane and J. C. Riemersma, *Enterprise and Secular Change: Readings in Economic History* (Homewood, Ill., 1953), p. 415.

[12] *Ibid.*, pp. 416–417.

[13] F. Stern, *The Varieties of History, from Voltaire to the Present* (New York, 1956), p. 304.

[14] Van Leur, "On the Study of Indonesian History," p. 153.

Too much ardent debate about the scope and method of economic history could result in mere sterility. But there does not yet seem to be a clear concept of what the subject matter of this scholarly discipline is or will be among those who are students of it. Generally accepted is the opinion that it deals with all the economic factors in history or that it deals with those facts in history which are related to the successful or unsuccessful attempts of mankind to meet especially its primary needs, for food, housing, and apparel. A more dynamic opinion would be that economic history's subject matter is the progressive or retrogressive development of human material welfare. Does this therefore imply that all phenomena in the past resulting from the sequence of wants-efforts-satisfaction, from "prehistoric artifacts to moon rockets," should be the realm of study for economic history? What is the "economic" in history? What is the "economic" in Southeast Asian, in Indonesian, history?

Economic history studies all those factual materials in the past which have been the results of "economic" actions of individuals and societies. This discipline has as its subject matter the facts which refer to the application, consciously or unconsciously, directly or indirectly, by humanity of what is called the "economic" principle. This is the principle of rationality, of efficiency, perhaps innate in every human being, which urges him to achieve the most with the least. Human action and thought are one, but this [15] occurs in a special context, be it in a Western industrialized civilization or an Oriental peasant society. The driving principle is always human and therefore one, but the direction of "economic" action can be influenced by the special cultural context.[16]

Therefore "dualistic" economic theory and its interpretation of the contemporary economic history of underdeveloped areas with its concomitant stress on the bleak side of the prospect for economic growth in these areas are somewhat beside the point.[17] The Indonesian economic historian should have a deeper understanding of the past and present of Indonesia's economic and social development.

It seems to be a particularly hard and painstaking job to get at the "economic" in ancient Indonesian history. Perhaps a thorough perusal of the work done by the prehistorians and cultural anthropologists may shed some light on the wants-efforts-satisfaction sequence in ancient

[15] See Maurice Blondel, *L'Action* (Paris, 1893).

[16] See Raymond Firth, *Malay Fishermen: Their Peasant Economy* (London, 1946), pp. 311–312.

[17] See B. Higgins, "The 'Dualistic Theory' of Underdeveloped Areas," *Ekonomi dan Keuangan Indonesia*, VIII, no. 2 (1955), 58–78, and his *Economic Development: Problems, Principles and Policies* (New York, 1959), p. 277.

Indonesia: from the *Geographia* of the Alexandrian geographer Ptolemy to the accounts of Chinese pilgrims and seafarers, to Arabian mariners' itineraries, to the *Pararaton*, to the *Nāgarakĕrtāgama* and Borobudur reliefs.[18] The economic history of the Hindu period could possibly be somewhat aided by the work of the specialists, the archaeologists and the philologists chiefly. The Islamic period has been chiefly explored by the philologists alone.[19] For the colonial period and more recent times there do exist rich sources, which wait to be explored by the economic historians.[20] Therefore much of the relevant material has been worked upon by the prehistorians, the ethnologists, and the archaeologists as well as the philologists and colonial historians. But naturally the approach used has generally not been that of an economic historian. In this context an impediment looms: an economic historian who is not satisfied with secondary sources only must necessarily have the linguistic apparatus of the Oriental philologist. Without a working knowledge of Old Malay, Old Javanese, Old Balinese, Chinese, Sanskrit, etc., perhaps it would be impossible to write an adequate history of ancient Indonesian economic life critically.[21]

Moreover, no adequate economic history of Indonesia could limit itself to the study of the rich sources of the history of Java alone. The lack of "historical sensation" for the history of Indonesia outside Java, as noted by Resink,[22] has been a major pitfall, and the concomitant first Dutch-centric and then Java-centric viewpoints in Indonesian

[18] See J. C. van Eerde, *A Review of the Ethnological Investigations in the Dutch Indian Archipelago* (Amsterdam, 1923), p. 5. According to Professor G. J. Resink, van Leur once remarked to him how fervently he wished that a few *prasasti* (inscriptions) might be found which would shed a better light on the economic history of ancient Indonesia than the inscriptions found so far.

[19] See van Leur, "On the Study of Indonesian History," p. 152.

[20] Kristof Glamann, in his excellent book, *Dutch-Asiatic Trade, 1620–1740* (Copenhagen and The Hague, 1958), pp. v-vi, claims that the Dutch East India Company's allegedly held monopoly on many commodities never existed.

[21] These enormous requirements were also mentioned in a recent conference on Asian economic history ("Report on the Conference on Asian Economic History," *Journal of Asian Studies*, XIX [1960], 384).

[22] Resink, "Uit het stof van een beeldenstorm," p. 442. By making use of Joseph Conrad's novels as guides to Indonesia's social, economic, and political history of the late nineteenth and early twentieth centuries, recently Professor Resink clearly showed that a dualistic economy was apparently present only on the island of Java and perhaps at the periphery of the other islands. Seemingly not a dualistic economy (Boeke) but rather a "homogeneous" one was true for most of the Indonesian islands. Cf. G. J. Resink, "De Archipel voor Joseph Conrad," *BKI*, CXV (1959), 192–208, and his "Inlandsche staten in den oosterschen archipel (1873–1915)," *BKI*, CXVI (1960), 313–349; see also D. G. E. Hall, "Looking at Southeast Asian History," *Journal of Asian Studies*, XIX (1960), 253, and his *East Asian History Today* (Hong Kong, 1959), p. 6. The Western impact on Southeast Asian history,

historiography should be avoided. The future economic historian of Indonesia should devote his scholarly attention also to the regional economic history of Celebes, the other eastern Indonesian islands, Borneo, Sumatra, and so on.

The lack of "historical sensation" in economic history sometimes shows itself in a lack of appropriate questioning when facing the mass of historical facts. Without the aid of theoretical economics, the economic historian lacks the heuristic principle, *das heuristische Prinzip*.[23]

The economic historian of Indonesia must therefore be a kind of hybrid. He must be at the same time a good theoretical economist and a professional historian. He needs the problem approach to history. This approach could have two meanings.[24] It could mean that history is viewed in the light of contemporary problems of public policy, or it could mean that history is reexamined to throw light on an unresolved intellectual problem of contemporary interest. An example in the latter case is the verification of Schumpeter's theory of the "innovating entrepreneur" by means of biographical materials on great entrepreneurs in the past and present which are being collected in the United States.[25] The analysis of enterpreneurial history within the Indonesian economic context would perhaps throw some light on the actual problem of the prospects for a speedy economic growth.[26]

Another interesting problem that awaits verification bears on the issues of economic imperialism and colonialism. The sometimes vexing question of what is objective and what subjective in historical analysis seemingly never shines out more clearly than in the (historical) verification of the so-called drain or exploitation theories concerning the international economic relations of economically less developed countries.

---

however, cannot be totally disregarded. See J. Bastin, *The Western Element in Modern Southeast Asian History* (Kuala Lumpur, 1960).

[23] E. F. Heckscher, "A Plea for Theory in Economic History," in Lane and Riemersma, *Enterprise and Secular Change*, p. 429. Since economic history depends to a great extent on the heuristic value of economic theory, the present and future Indonesian economic historian should keep in touch with developments in economics. However, recent trends in economic theory, except as a priori model building, do not seem to have a high heuristic value and especially among Anglo-Saxon economists there is *too little* basic disagreement on fundamentals. Cf. P. A. Samuelson, "What Economists Know," in Lerner, ed., *The Human Meaning of the Social Sciences*, p. 193.

[24] W. W. Rostow, "The Interrelation of Theory and Economic History," *Journal of Economic History*, XVII (1957), 511.

[25] *Ibid.*, p. 511.

[26] The biographies of some successful Indonesian entrepreneurs and their enterprises such as Dasaad Musin, Rahman Tamin, etc., are well worth writing and analyzing.

The older literature on Indonesia, mostly of Dutch origin,[27] seems somewhat biased, and the case should be reappraised in the light of recent developments in the theory of international economic relations and empirical-statistical, historical research.[28]

It is, however, history viewed in the light of contemporary problems that offers the present and future economic historian of Indonesia his greatest challenge. And since one of the greatest problems facing Indonesia at present is its economic development, the question asked by the economic historian today is: what factors or variables were present in the past that were conducive to rapid economic growth? For example, if in a sense and to a certain extent the "Culture System" was a form of economic development, then what strategic variables, if applicable, are important for matters of public policy? The comparative study of Indonesian economic history with that of other countries, in particular those economically more advanced, would have fruitful implications.

In this context, it would seem that the sociological approach to Indonesian historiography is closely connected to the possibility of an adequate economic history of Indonesia.[29] An interesting research problem would be a socioeconomic investigation of the rice trade in Java and other islands before and after 1500. An important subquestion would perhaps be: who were the participants in this rice trade (sea or land)—Indonesians or foreign traders?

Concomitant with this interesting problem could be a historical analysis of prahu commerce on the seas of the Indonesian Archipelago and outside. Seemingly, sources for the historiography of the peoples of southern Sulawesi such as the Macassarese, the Buginese, and the Mandarese are quite plentiful.[30] Materials on early commercial voyages

---

[27] See Boeke, *Economics and Economic Policy*, pp. 216–230; van Gelderen, *Voorlezingen*, pp. 113–124; J. F. Haccoû, *De Indische exportproducten* (Leyden, 1947), pp. 72–84.

[28] See G. Myrdal, *An International Economy* (New York, 1956), chs. viii and xiii; H. W. Singer, "Distribution of Gains between Investing and Borrowing Countries," *American Economic Review: Papers and Proceedings*, XL (1950), 473–485; W. A. Lewis, *The Theory of Economic Growth* (London, 1955), pp. 176–189; H. Myint, "The Gains from International Trade and the Backward Countries," *Review of Economic Studies*, XXII (1954–1955), 129–142; and UN Economic Commission for Latin America, *The Economic Development of Latin America and Its Principal Problems* (New York, 1950).

[29] See W. F. Wertheim's article in this book.

[30] See C. C. F. M. Le Roux and A. A. Cense, "Boegineesche zeekaarten van den Indischen Archipel," *Tijdschrift van het Aardrijkskundig Genootschap*, LII (1935), 687–714, and A. A. Cense, "Enige aantekeningen over Makassaars-Boeginese geschiedschrijving," *BKI*, CVII (1951), 42–60.

of Macassarese-Buginese prahus have recently been published which could shed light on the ancient international economic relations of the Indonesians.[31]

Closely connected is the importance of a new branch in economic history, viz., business history, which has made great progress in the United States and Europe during the last two decades. These studies, which have a historical framework dealing with the promotion, organization, and administration of enterprise, either in general or in particular, if equally pursued for the genuinely Indonesian historical scene could bear important practical ramifications.[32]

Perhaps, for the time being, no adequate economic history of Indonesia is possible, except possibly for later periods, i.e., beginning with the sixteenth century onward, for which more material is available. In this, more preliminary work should be done, primarily the publication of source materials on the Indonesian past in general.

[31] A. A. Cense, "Makassaars-Boeginese prauwvaart op Noord-Australië in vroeger tijd," *BKI*, CVIII (1952), 248–264; W. Ph. Coolhaas, "Korte mededeeling," *BKI*, CXVI (1960), 480; and H. J. Heeren, "Indonesische cultuurinvloeden in Australië," *Indonesië*, VI (1952), 149–159. For the early voyages to Ceylon, Madagascar, etc., see C. Nooteboom, "Sumatra en de zeevaart op de Indische Oceaan," *Indonesië*, IV (1950), 119; B. Schrieke, *Indonesian Sociological Studies*, pt. I, *Selected Writings* (The Hague and Bandung, 1955), p. 19; and C. Nooteboom, "Galeien in Azië," *BKI*, CVIII (1952), 377.

[32] See J. B. G. Hutchins, "Recent Contributions to Business History: The United States," *Journal of Economic History*, XIX (1959), 103. There are, of course, many histories of Dutch enterprises formerly in Indonesia, like those of Mansvelt on the Netherlands Trading Society, or de Boer and Westermann on the KPM (Royal Dutch Packet Company), etc., but attention should be given also to the *windu* or other anniversary publications of many present Indonesian enterprises.

XXII

The Indonesian Historian
and His Time

BY SOEDJATMOKO

*Writer; formerly Visiting Lecturer in History,
Cornell University, Ithaca, New York*

AT this point an issue should be discussed which seems to underlie part
of the present controversies about Indonesian history and upon which
in large measure will depend what kind of historical studies will be
undertaken in the near future—i.e., the relationship of the modern
Indonesian historian to his time and his society. Two problems arise in
this connection. The first one is a question which every Indonesian
historian must inevitably face at some point in his search for a national,
Indonesia-centric viewpoint—the question of a nationalist historiography.

While it is his loving concern with the past in all its uniqueness and
his desire for concrete knowledge and understanding of historical
events, persons, and situations that generally motivate the historian, it
is for his contemporaries that he writes. Their interest in the past,
especially during periods of rapid and revolutionary change, constant
insecurity, and crisis, is bound up with and in proportion to their own
emotional involvement in the present and their quest for answers to
the problems that beset them. And especially when, as in Indonesia,
nationalism is the prevailing mood in the country, the search for these
answers will not take the form of contemplative introspection and
patient seeking for detailed knowledge and clarification. Rather it will
manifest itself in insistent demands for a nationalist historiography
and for national myths, from which new confidence can be gained and
sustenance drawn. Expression of this need can be found in the con-

tinued political use of myths already exploded by research, like the myth of Great Majapahit as the forerunner of Indonesian national unity and three hundred and fifty years of colonization over the whole archipelago as the basis for a common fate and common enmity, or even the attempt to establish a six-thousand-year history of the Indonesian flag. In historical research and education one can point to the reluctance to admit evidence that does not fit into the nationalist image and the insistence on patriotic and political qualifications for the historian and teacher of history. There is nothing particularly disturbing or frightening in this. Every nation has its normal share of myths. Myths are, to use C. C. Berg's phrase, socialized historical narratives. They are images of historical events or periods, partly derived from facts established by scholarly investigation, partly based on the provisional interpretation of their significance, but also partly a product of archetypal constructions fulfilling deeply and subconsciously felt individual and social needs. They are the aids of man in his orientation in the world, in relation to the past, present, and future of this life and in relation to life beyond this one. The passage from a scientifically justifiable historical interpretation into a historical myth signifies the social process through which society at large takes possession of this image, digesting it, grossly simplifying it and thereby suiting it to its own often subconscious purposes. In a period of the heightened self-assertion which nationalism constitutes, there is a great intensification and acceleration of this process of socialization of historical images and of this search for a new and significant relationship with the past and even for national self-justification through history. There is an acutely felt need to view history from the particular perspective which derives from an intensified expectation of the future. ("The future was present!" exclaims Michelet.) Few nations have been without a period of nationalist historiography. It took France a long while to outgrow Michelet's intensely nationalist conception. South African historiography has never really been emancipated from it. In a collection of essays dedicated to J. M. Romein, Ria Hugo writes: "History is by the South Africans still seen as a means for struggle, as exhortation or defense, and not as a science." [1] There is therefore little doubt that for quite some time the Indonesian historian will be confronted with demands for corroborative evidence for existing myths or for new myths, as well as for a historiography to justify them.

[1] Dr. Ria Hugo, "Die teoretiese geskiedenis en die Suid-Afrikaanse historiografie," in *Weerklank op het werk van Jan Romein* (Amsterdam, 1953), p. 65.

This obviously places the Indonesian historian in an awkward position. On the one hand, he is confronted with his society's demands for such a nationalist history. On the other hand, he realizes that a great deal more must be known before the structure of Indonesia's history can begin to take shape and before he is in a position to write any authoritative and responsible account of it. He also knows that the modern historian no longer enjoys the comparative isolation of his nationalist colleagues of earlier times in other countries and that his historical narratives should be able to stand up to other, non-Indonesian, accounts of what has taken place.[2] Moreover, even if a great deal more should be known about Indonesia's history, by the very nature of historical knowledge all the images he develops and all his interpretations and presentations will have only a provisional character, requiring constant reinterpretation. In fact, any discussion of the problems of historical interpretation and the synthesis of historical material into a coherent narrative in modern Indonesian historiography leads into questions regarding subjectivity and objectivity.

The great variety of documentary sources, records of the many ways their authors reacted to exposure to the unfolding of Indonesian history, each colored by the author's own values, his own cultural background, his individual training, his specific areas of interest, and the at least equally great variety in professional and general cultural background of those who have examined and synthesized this material into historical narratives are bound to make the modern Indonesian historian[3] aware of the polyinterpretability of historical reality and of the difference between *histoire-réalité*, the actual occurrence of events, and *histoire-récité*, the narration of those events—between objective and subjective history. This is further emphasized by the fact that he is faced simultaneously with several different types of historiography, among them the Malay, Macassarese-Buginese, Javanese, European, and modern Indonesian. He is also confronted with various systems of periodization dating from before independence, and with several systems proposed after. He is also aware that although not all Europeans concerned with Indonesian historiography in the past were Dutchmen —as a matter of fact many were not—they shared with their Dutch colleagues the same general cultural background, their values, their

---

[2] The work of non-Indonesians in the field of Indonesian history still continues, and with significant results.

[3] In the following discussion I have drawn heavily on G. J. Resink's reflections on this subject. An English translation of his articles is being prepared for publication as vol. VII of the series "Selected Studies on Indonesia" (The Hague), edited by W. F. Wertheim.

habits of thought, and their expectations of continued Dutch power. And even when scientific objectivity was striven for, it remained at best an objectivity within the cultural group subjectivity of the European historians and their public. All this inevitably leads the Indonesian historian to reflect upon the nature of history, its method, and the subjectivity of its results, both with regard to the establishment of so-called historical facts and to its general presentation. Through these reflections he must also become more aware of the relativist propensities of his own syncretistic culture, reinforced as these are by the ethnic heterogeneity of his present cultural situation. While in Western historiography the question of historical subjectivity and objectivity became an issue only at the end of a long period of development, modern Indonesian historiography, in its infancy still, is already possibly too familiar with the subjectivity of man's thought and vision. Such reflection will undoubtedly facilitate the Indonesian historian's search for an independent and new interpretation and presentation of his material. But the point is that he cannot escape confrontation with this problem. In order to write his Indonesian history he will have to reconcile or transcend the different regional historical traditions, and their conflicting versions of the same events, in a way that is acceptable not only to most modern Indonesians but also to those from the regions concerned. In many cases additional research that uncovers new data will enable him to do so. However, this "relational objectivity" [4] within the larger group subjectivity of the nation is not enough.

As has been stated earlier, the Indonesia-centric historical narrative will have to be able to stand up against other, non-Indonesian versions of historical events in Indonesia. Now our attempts to rewrite Indonesian history, or to write it anew, coincide with attempts elsewhere to write a universal history of mankind, or aspects of it. To mention two striking instances, there is, first, the more limited approach of an international commission under the auspices of UNESCO to prepare a *History of the Scientific and Cultural Development of Mankind*. Second, there is also the ambitious project decided upon by the Presidium of the USSR Academy of Sciences to prepare a ten-volume *World History* "based on Marxist-Leninist methodology, treating the main events in the history of mankind and portraying the world process of historical growth in all its unity and diversity." [5] It is much too early to

[4] Ernest Nagel, "The Logic of Historical Analysis," in *Readings in the Philosophy of Science*, ed. by Feigl and Brodbeck (New York, 1953), pp. 695–696.

[5] Y. M. Zhukov in *Voprosy istorii*, no. 5 (1954), pp. 175–178; translated in *The Current Digest of the Soviet Press*, vol. VI, no. 22 (1954), and reprinted in *Cahiers d'histoire mondiale*, II, no. 2, 489–493.

speculate on the effects both these endeavors will have on historical categories, periodization, and other tools for analysis or on criteria for organizing historical material, and nothing can as yet be said about the new historical images which will emerge from them. But it is clear that the Indonesian search for self-image and self-understanding through the study of Indonesian history is taking place in a period of rapid change and of shifting historical images the world over. It will be a difficult though not an impossible task to achieve that kind of presentation which can rightly claim at least "intersubjective value" [6] in this now much wider setting.

There is another difficulty for the Indonesian historian who wants to satisfy his society's demand for early production of a new nationalistic Indonesian history, or for simply a new Indonesia-centric history. This difficulty stems from the transitional character of the situation in which he and his society find themselves. [7] The patterns which we see in the unfolding of the historical process, or rather our choices from the possible patterns which we might discern, and the meaning which we see in history are intimately connected with our awareness of the present. This is influenced too by the conscious or subconscious expectations we have concerning the emerging future. As Karl Jaspers rightly says: "Without a perspective on the future, the historical vision of the past is final and completed, and therefore false." [8] And as that future materializes and this present changes, our awareness of this present changes also, including the viewpoint from which we regard the past and assess its significance. As a result of our changing perspective on the future, our system of periodization as the expression of a pattern of meaning which we discern has to change too. The two cannot be dissociated. The fact that at the Jogjakarta History Seminar at least five systems of periodization were presented, with no agreement reached on any one of them, reflects not only an insufficiency of data but also the present uncertainty of the historian's perspectives.

Thus we see the problem of the Indonesian historian: he cannot speak with the finality expected of him by his public. His professional training, so to say, has robbed him of the historical innocence which would enable him to write the kind of patriotic history many of his countrymen want. In that sense he is unable fully to meet the public's

[6] Maurice Merleau-Ponty, *Les Aventures de la dialectique* (Paris, 1955), p. 16.

[7] President Soekarno's favorite theme, "The Revolution is not yet over!" has some possibly unintended relevance here.

[8] Karl Jaspers, *Vom Ursprung und Ziel der Geschichte* (Zurich, 1949), p. 181.

need for certainty and emotional security. Nevertheless, he cannot withdraw into a splendid isolation from his society. Nor does he want to. On the contrary, he knows himself to be part of his society, caught in the same broad stream of historical events, moved by the same general impulses, committed to and fully engaged in the pursuit of the same goals. And while he might decide to postpone writing his definitive history and concentrate on his researches, he still has to play a major part in the writing of history textbooks for primary and secondary schools as his contribution to the building of his nation. This, however, he can do only with a great deal of inner reservation, realizing full well the very provisional nature of any historical narrative written now. Despite himself, he may often find that he is playing the role of the hewer of stones from which historical myths will eventually be built. But while playing this role, as a historian he is at the same time detached from it by his knowledge that through the study of history, in other words through his own work, the very same myths will in due course be destroyed and replaced by new images that reveal different, and, for another time, possibly more meaningful, aspects of historical reality.

All this is bound to create considerable tension between the historian and his society as well as within himself. The modern Indonesian historian's predicament is compounded by another aspect of his relationship to his society, and this is our second problem—i.e., that he is trying to establish the study of history as a scholarly discipline in what is, to a large extent, still an ahistorical culture. Man's attitude to history is an expression of the way in which he conceives time and his relationship with it. But one's concept of time is inextricably linked to one's view of the significance of life in this world and life's relationship to the universe. Therefore, when one speaks about history and one's attitude toward history, one speaks in the final analysis of the metaphysical presuppositions of his culture. The ahistorical outlook on life, closely connected with traditional agrarian society, perceives life and the flow of human events as a process beyond human control and therefore beyond human responsibility. The meaning of man's life is not in this world, but beyond it. Man has to live his life in harmony with the moral and esthetic order of the cosmos, the nature and meaning of which are to be known through symbols, myths, and analogies that reflect the relationships and correspondences of the cosmic order. In such a world, knowledge of the past is meaningful only to the extent that it provides the raw material for these myths, legends, and parables which remind man of how he is related to the cosmic order and provide clues to guide him as a human being who seeks security and strives for spiritual perfection.

The succession of events to which man is exposed in this world follows its own channel in recurring cycles of time. But especially in the face of great events and crises, man can sometimes orient himself through analogies with real or mythical events of the past, so that these crises lose much of their bewildering and terrifying aspect and become recognizable, though still awesome. History then becomes something that is humanly possible to endure and not entirely meaningless, because it is somehow related to events and conflicts at the cosmic level. Caught in the historical process, the question of man's ability and responsibility to influence the further course of events becomes irrelevant and unimportant. The only thing he can do is *derma-nglakoni*,[9] play out the part assigned to him in accord with that station in the order of things into which he is born and with the inner detachment [10] which is the precondition for his spiritual salvation. And thus, fearfully sometimes, but heroically, if he can generate that inner detachment, he seeks his acceptance of and adjustment to historical inevitability and to the not always intelligible succession of "situations." His knowledge of history then governs his inner attitude,[11] rather than his choice of action. His freedom, however, as well as his assessment of his own value as a human being, lies not in influencing or directing the predetermined course of events but in transcending it, by living in an eternal present, through self-knowledge and identification [12] with the essential unity of the permanent order beyond time and transient things.[13]

This sketch of the ahistorical view of life is couched in terms commonly used in the Javanese cultural tradition, where they are stated more explicitly than elsewhere in Indonesia. But there is little doubt that this type of outlook constitutes in large measure the cultural subsoil throughout Indonesia, which such later cultural influences as Islam,

[9] *derma* (Jav.) = *dharma* (Skt.). *nglakoni* (Jav.) = to fulfill, to implement.

[10] *Sepi ing pamrih, ramé ing gawé* (Jav.): inwardly quiet, outwardly active.

[11] *Mèsem sadjeroning wardojo* (Jav.): with an inner smile.

[12] *Nggolek banju pepikulan warih* (Jav.): to look for water with water, and *nggolek geni dedamaran* (Jav.): to look for fire with light. These are two favorite expressions in Javanese mysticism in connection with the concept of knowledge through self-identification.

[13] Or, less nobly, in trying to secure his personal safety, while the historical process takes its inexorable course, through magical manipulation of the cosmic relationships affecting his life (through fasting and meditation or, with the help of a *dukun*, through white or black magic).

Christianity, and modern secular education have not been able entirely to destroy or replace.[14] In short, the fact that the ahistorical view of life in Indonesia is nowhere systematically formulated, and has not yet been adequately described or studied, does not in any way diminish its reality and pervasiveness in Indonesian society today. Nor is it contradicted by the existence of indigenous historiographies. The papers on Malay and Javanese historiography in this book indicate their nonhistorical function. Neither is the undoubted interest of the Javanese *prijaji* or the Buginese-Macassarese noblemen in their own history proof of the "historical" nature of that interest as we now understand it.

It is almost impossible in our concern for the modern study of Indonesian history not to feel the impact of the ahistorical attitude of Indonesian traditional culture on its students, as well as on that part of the general public interested in history. This influence can be seen in the strong disposition to mythologize, the precipitous inclination to see relationships of a moral significance between events that are not necessarily related at all.[15] The popularity of pseudo-Marxist teleology may be indicative of a predisposition rooted in traditional Indonesian culture toward deterministic or eschatological forms of the historical process.[16] It is at this point that nationalism and the older layers of cultural tradition intersect. For although the nationalist movement in former colonies is in many ways a modern form of an old political struggle, once its main objective is achieved and unless it can outgrow its own limitations, it is increasingly compelled to turn in upon itself, to exalt the presumed uniqueness of the nation with a manifest destiny, and to elevate certain traits of its traditional agrarian culture into immutable virtues. Therefore, though certainly a modernizing force, nationalism by itself does not necessarily mean a break with the *Weltanschauung* of the closed agrarian society. On the contrary, it often tends to reinforce and revive elements of its traditional culture.

How, then, should the Indonesian historian cope with these pressures, which we have seen stem both from the nationalist upsurge and from the ahistorical outlook on life? How can he preserve the study of

[14] Probably in no culture, even in the most advanced industrial societies, has this type of outlook been supplanted completely.

[15] E.g., between the moral behavior of the Ruler and the condition of the Realm.

[16] The deterministic historical view apparently gives the same kind of comfort and emotional security which the closed cosmic order accords traditional ahistoric man. The "open" view of history, on the other hand, leaves man little comfort. It only makes "sense" in connection with man's freedom.

history as a scholarly discipline and ensure its healthy development? He can do so only through the strictest adherence to the disciplinary requirements of his branch of science: faithful observance of the critical method in dealing with his material, meticulous attention to detail, and the disciplining of his historical imagination. It will also be necessary for him to be constantly alert for the possible intrusion into his judgment and historical vision of elements which derive from the ahistorical attitude of his traditional culture, and for his unconscious adjustment or surrender to them. To this end, what is called for is a much fuller and more accurate description and clearer understanding than is yet available [17] of the Indonesian ahistorical *Weltanschauung* including its cyclical and eschatological elements. This investigation should also encompass the effect of Moslem and Christian influence on it, for to both of these, though in differing ways, history is religiously significant. At the same time, the clearer awareness which such a study will give him of the relativistic and syncretic propensity in his own cultural heritage should not lead the historian into a nihilistic paralysis of his yearning for historical knowledge and of his creative powers of interpretation and reconstruction. These problems force him, regardless of whether he wishes it, not to limit his reflection to the nature of historical knowledge and to the study of history as a specific search for truth alone, but to include also a consideration of the philosophical implications of his discipline and the question of the significance of what he is doing in relation to his own society and the situation in which he finds himself. He will then realize that the study of history can only be meaningful and is only possible if the historical process is seen as being essentially indeterminate and open to man's deliberate participation in it. History becomes important only when man realizes that he can make it. It is in his choice among the alternatives which he perceives, and which will affect the course of events, that his freedom and also his responsibility lie. In facing the choices he has to make, it is his vision of the meaning of history and his understanding of the historical process that guide him. At the same time, he cannot escape the realization of the inherent inadequacy of historical knowledge, its provisional character, and its subjectivity in relation to the multidimensionality of historical reality. He also becomes aware that with the emergence of historical consciousness in the life of a nation the comfort usually found in a final judgment on the meaning of life and history, as well as the

---

[17] For an Indonesian attempt in this direction, see Sartono Kartodirdjo, *Tjatatan entang Segi² Messianistis dalam Sedjarah Indonesia* (Universitas Gadjah Mada, 959).

security of the closed society, is forever denied to that nation. He must bear as the eternal burden of "historical man" the realization that he has constantly to work for a new, but still limited, understanding of his situation as it is brought about by the events of the past. In this historical vision of life, it is the task of the historian, with the fruits of his endless efforts, constantly to feed and refresh historical consciousness as a creative impulse in the life of his nation.

This is especially true for the Indonesian historian in the particular situation in which he finds himself. By strict adherence to his scholarly discipline he cannot avoid the tension between what he can do and what his society expects of him. Partly, this tension between the professional historian and his commitment to his time is rooted in the disjunction between knowledge and living, and to that extent he can only resign himself to it as part of the human condition. As Merleau-Ponty points out: "Le savoir et la pratique affrontent la même infinité du réel historique, mais ils répondent de deux façons opposées: le savoir en multipliant les vues, par des conclusions provisoires, ouvertes, motivées, c'est à dire conditionnelles, la pratique par des decisions absolues, partiales, injustifiables." [18] But in part this tension also stems from the condition that the historian's concerns as a historian are not unlike a contrapuntal accompaniment to the preoccupations of his society, different but always related. Following its own course, it sometimes trails, sometimes anticipates, but always enriches the main theme. In this realization he may find some degree of justification for his faithfulness to the rigid and critical requirements of his discipline. Moreover, even though he cannot satisfy all the needs of his contemporary society in this respect, the value of his function as a historian is determined not only by his writings and by the contribution he makes to the cycle of creation and demolition of historical myths. He is not simply the artisan constructing socially useful images. The significance of single-minded devotion to his discipline lies at a more fundamental level—in injecting into the life and thinking of his nation the element of historical consciousness. Put in Namier's words: "The aim [of the historical approach] is to comprehend situations, to study trends, to discover how things work; and the crowning attainment of historical study is a historical sense—an intuitive understanding of how things do not happen (how they did happen is a matter of specific knowledge)." [19] Historical sense therefore gives man a greater regard for the

[18] Merleau-Ponty, *Les Aventures de la dialectique*, p. 17.
[19] L. B. Namier, "History and Political Culture," in Fritz Stern, ed., *The Varieties of History* (New York, 1957), p. 375.

complexity of the gradual unfolding of human events in time and the relationship of human interaction with it.

It gives him a deeper respect for the uniqueness of each situation, even within the trend discerned, and it therefore helps him to guard against too simple reasoning, too superficial analogies, and too facile acceptance of patterns or laws governing the course of history. In this way man stands between the two extremes of historical determinism on the one hand and wishful thinking in choosing his course of action on the other. He becomes more aware of the distance and even disjunction between intention and realization in history.[20] Against the background of an ahistorical tradition, however, the concept of historical consciousness acquires a deeper meaning than Namier, speaking from a longer Western European historical tradition, probably had in mind. For historical consciousness relates man to the world differently from the way the ahistorical *Weltanschauung* does. It shows him that his situation is to a much larger, and indeed ever larger, extent open to his rational comprehension. It shows him that to the extent that he understands his situation as it has developed from past events, the scope of his freedom which enables him to act in a meaningful way in relation to the course of events and the scope of his personal responsibility to do so have widened. Historical consciousness therefore changes man's relationship to reality, changes and enlarges the area of meaningful interaction with the world, and to that extent increases the possibilities that he will master his destiny. It signifies man's freedom from historical inevitability and from the tyranny of conditions to which he is subjected, without recourse. It signifies his freedom to determine his own attitude toward and relationship with his situation. For though his freedom is limited because his situation is a historical datum, in the extreme he can still assert his freedom through his rational, moral, or, in a more relativistic setting, esthetic choice, to work within or without what seems at a particular time to be the mainstream of the historical process.

Historical consciousness, then, will bring a nation closer to understanding the realities of its historical situation. The modern historian's usefulness in this respect lies in widening the dimensions of his society's understanding of the present and of the possibilities for the future, thus opening the way to a positive and creative relationship to reality and therefore to history.

In conclusion, it may be said that only by his passionate but con-

[20] See Wilhelm Wundt, *System der Philosophie*, I (4th ed.; Leipzig, 1919), 326–327.

trolled dedication to the search for historical truth while knowing its ultimate elusiveness, by accepting the constant need for reinterpretation as part of the unending labor of the study of history, and finally by a constant awareness of his own cultural background will it be possible for the Indonesian historian to maintain and develop the study of history as a scholarly discipline in his country. The inner detachment which this ethos brings him in relation to his own total human situation, at a time when such fierce and exclusive loyalties are demanded, is bound to create many problems for him, leaving him, fully committed as he is, sometimes with a keen sense of inadequacy. Yet he may find sustenance in the awareness that he is leading a breakthrough to a new vision of life and society for his nation, based on man's willing assumption of his freedom and responsibility in relation to history. For it is only when man has accepted the possibility of at least helping to shape his future that he can assume his responsibility for it, as part of the assertion of his freedom. Then history ceases to be the mere fulfillment of man's curiosity, a mirror for his moral enlightenment or a fountain for narcissistic admiration, but becomes essential for man's orientation and meaningful participation in the modern world.

It is in this sense that the Indonesian historian will then become a small but important part of, to use Reinhold Niebuhr's words,[21] the emancipating force which is history.

[21] Reinhold Niebuhr, *Faith and History* (New York, 1949), p. 29.

INDEX

Names of people and places are included in this index only insofar as they are of historiographical interest.